AF476968

South African economy and policy, 1990–2000

Manchester University Press

South African economy and policy, 1990–2000

An economy in transition

Edited by
Stuart Jones and Robert W. Vivian

Manchester University Press
Manchester and New York
distributed in the United States exclusively
by Palgrave Macmillan

Published by Manchester University Press
Oxford Road, Manchester M13 9NR, UK
and Room 400, 175 Fifth Avenue, New York, NY 10010, USA
www.manchesteruniversitypress.co.uk

Distributed in the United States exclusively by
Palgrave Macmillan, 175 Fifth Avenue, New York,
NY 10010, USA

Distributed in Canada exclusively by
UBC Press, University of British Columbia, 2029 West Mall,
Vancouver, BC, Canada V6T 1Z2

British Library Cataloguing-in-Publication Data
A catalogue record for this book is available from the British Library

Library of Congress Cataloging-in-Publication Data applied for

ISBN 978 07190 8150 7 *hardback*

First published 2010

Typeset by R. J. Footring Ltd, Derby
Printed in Great Britain by TJ International Ltd, Padstow

Contents

Part IV: Conclusion

Figures

Tables

Contributors

Frans Barker is Senior Executive of the Chamber of Mines and Deputy President of Business Unity South Africa (BUSA). He represented business in the National Economic, Development and Labour Council (Nedlac) and the Commission for Employment Equity. He was Chairperson of the National Manpower Commission (NMC), which preceded Nedlac. He was President of the Industrial Relations Association of South Africa (IRasa) and Deputy President of the Economic Society of South Africa. He has authored numerous publications, including *The South African Labour Market* (5th edition, 2007).

Anthony Black is Professor in the School of Economics at the University of Cape Town. His fields of specialisation include industrial development, industrial policy, foreign direct investment and the automotive industry. Since 1995, he has also acted frequently as a policy adviser to government with regard to the automotive industry.

Philip Black is Extraordinary Professor in Economics at the University of Stellenbosch. He is the immediate past Managing Editor of the *South African Journal of Economics* and also past President of the Economic Society of South Africa. His research interests include micro-economics, behavioural economics, public economics and the philosophy of economic science.

Rulof Burger is Senior Lecturer in Economics at Stellenbosch University. He holds a masters degree in economics from Cambridge University, and is currently enrolled as a doctoral student at St Antony's College, Oxford University. His research areas include labour economics and econometrics.

Estian Calitz is Professor of Economics and a former Executive Director: Finance at the University of Stellenbosch. His main research interests are in macro-economic and fiscal policy and public finance. During South Africa's period of political transition he was the Director General of Finance of the National Government. He is a past President of the Economic Society of South Africa.

Anton Eberhard is a Professor at the University of Cape Town, where he directs the Management Programme in Infrastructure Reform and Regulation at the Graduate School of Business. His research and teaching focus on restructuring and regulation of the electricity and water sectors and linkages to sustainable development. He has worked in the energy sector for more than 25 years and was the founding Director of the Energy and Development Research Centre. He is also a former board member of the National Electricity Regulator of South Africa.

Roger Gidlow worked as an economist in the private sector before joining the Business Economics Department at the University of the Witwatersrand in 1975. He was an associate professor for five years before joining the South African Reserve Bank as an Economic Adviser in May 1985, and from 1994 he headed the Bank's Training Institute until his retirement in 2003.

Ruth Hall is a Senior Researcher at the Institute for Poverty, Land and Agrarian Studies (PLAAS) at the University of the Western Cape in South Africa. Her research interests include land and agrarian reforms in South and Southern Africa, farm worker rights, and the politics of rural development. Publications include an edited volume entitled *Another Countryside? Policy Options for Land and Agrarian Reform in South Africa* and, with Lungisile Ntsebeza, *The Land Question in South Africa: The Challenge of Transformation and Redistribution.*

Rachel Jafta is Associate Professor in Economics at Stellenbosch University. Her research interests include economics of innovation, competition policy, black economic empowerment and international trade. She is a director of companies and a trustee of various non-governmental organisations, several of which are in the field of education.

Stuart Jones was Acting Head of the Department of Economic History from 1978 to 1983 and Head of the Division of Economic History at the University of the Witwatersrand from 1987 to 1990. He was a professor at the University of South Africa from 1993 to 2004. He is the founder of the *South African Journal of Economic History* and editor of the journal.

Trevor Jones is Professor at and heads the School of Economics and Finance at the University of KwaZulu-Natal, and also serves as Director of the Unit for Maritime Studies within that same school. His research interests lie in the area of transport economics, particularly maritime transport economics. He served on the Maritime Transport Policy Working Group that advised the Minister of Transport in the mid-1990s.

Elsabé Loots is Professor in Economics and Dean of the Faculty of Economic and Management Sciences at North-West University (Potchefstroom Campus). She specialises in development economics and macro-economics. Her research focus is presently on matters relating to the New Partnership for Africa's Development (NEPAD) in general and African capital flow issues in particular. She is a past President of the Economic Society of South Africa..

The late **Anthony B. Lumby** was Professor and Head of the School of Economic and Business Sciences at the University of the Witwatersrand. He was the founder of the Economic History Society of South Africa.

Colin McCarthy retired as Professor of Economics at the University of Stellenbosch. He is an associate of the Trade Law Centre for Southern Africa, and earlier served as a member and chairman of the International Trade Administration Commission. He specialises in trade and industrial policy and in this has a special interest in regional economic integration.

Philip Mohr was Professor of Economics at the University of South Africa from 1984 to 2007. He has written a number of textbooks and books aimed at a wider audience, the latest being *Understanding the Economy (everything you always wanted to know about the economy but thought you would not understand)* (2010). His main research interests are macro-economic theory and policy.

Raymond Parsons is the Deputy Chief Executive Officer of Business Unity South Africa (BUSA) and teaches at the Department of Economic and Management Sciences at the University of Pretoria. From 1995 to 2010 he was the Overall Business Convenor at the National Economic Development and Labour Council (Nedlac). Professor Parsons is the immediate past President of the Economic Society of South Africa. He is an Honorary Professor in the Department of Economics and Economic History at the Nelson Mandela Metropolitan University (NMMU). His recent books include *Manuel, Markets and Money* (2004) and *Zumanomics – Which Way to Shared Prosperity in South Africa?* (2009).

Gillian Saunders is the Principal and Director of Grant Thornton Strategic Solutions and Head of Grant Thornton Specialist Advisory Services. She joined Grant Thornton in 1988 as a tourism and hospitality consultant and became manager of the tourism and hospitality consultancy subsidiary in 1997. As such she consulted extensively in all aspects of these industries for the public and private sector for more than 20 years. She is a guest lecturer at the University of Pretoria's Department of Tourism and at the University of Johannesburg's School of Tourism and Hospitality.

Krige Siebrits is Senior Lecturer in the Department of Economics at the University of Stellenbosch. He has also worked as a policy adviser in the National Treasury and a lecturer in the Department of Economics at the University of South Africa. His research interests include public economics, development economics and institutional economics.

Charles Simkins is the Helen Suzman Professor of Political Economy at the University of the Witwatersrand.

Grietjie Verhoef is Professor of Economic and Accounting History at the University of Johannesburg. Her specialisation is in banking and business history. She is President of the Economic History Society of Southern Africa and President elect of the International Economic History Association.

Nick Vink is Professor in Agricultural Economics at the University of Stellenbosch. He has been involved in a range of official government commissions and committees of investigation, *inter alia* into the deregulation of agricultural marketing, the provision of rural financial services and the implementation of a minimum wage in agriculture. He has published in the fields of agricultural and rural development policy, land reform and empowerment, agricultural marketing, tax and international trade issues.

Robert W. Vivian is the Professor of Finance and Insurance at the University of the Witwatersrand and former President of the Economic History Society of Southern Africa. He was the Head of the Department of Business Economics. He has authored numerous books, including on business history.

Acknowledgements

The editors gratefully acknowledge the willingness of the various authors who contributed to this book to meet tight deadlines and to accommodate the various editorial requests. It is self-evident that the various chapters reflect different points of view and the views of individual authors should not be attributed to other authors.

Special appreciation must be given to Frieda Garvie, for her assistance in typing and updating the text, to Frances Kuijpers, especially for her assistance with the index, to Anthony Mason of Manchester University Press, for his untiring encouragement and exhortation, without which this book would not have been completed, and to Ralph Footring, for his conscientious and meticulous copy-editing, design and page layout work.

Introduction

Stuart Jones

The 1990s were years of revolution in South Africa, with a political revolution capturing the headlines and completely overshadowing the economic revolution that followed on its heels. The political revolution was welcomed as a positive development that was expected to transform South Africa and produce a better life for all; the economic revolution was a negative one that began a long process of inflicting great damage upon the economy, even though it was not noticed at the time.[1] Instead, the economic policies were universally applauded[2] at the same time that they worked to undermine the proclaimed policies of the new government.

The political revolution dates from 1989, when F. W. De Klerk succeeded P. W. Botha as President and began the process that led to Nelson Mandela's release from prison in February the following year. It took four years from the time that De Klerk assumed office to reach the Kempton Park Agreement, which set the stage for an election with universal suffrage in April 1994, and during this time the African National Congress (ANC), organised by Thabo Mbeki and former exiles in London, ruthlessly took control of the party in the rural areas.[3] In many ways it was a coup by former communists that took place without the De Klerk government being aware of what was happening. The ANC alliance government comprised more than the traditional ANC party: it

1 R. W. Johnson, *South Africa's Brave New World – The Beloved Country since the End of Apartheid*, Allen Lane, 2009, p. 12.

2 For early endorsements of the economy after the advent of majority rule, see: Alan Hirsch, *Season of Hope: Economic Reform under Mandela and Mbeki*, University of KwaZulu-Natal Press, 2005; Cees Bruggermans, *Change of Pace: South Africa's Economic Revival*, Wits University Press, 2003; and the various contributors in Raymond Parsons (ed.), *Manuel, Markets and Money: Essays in Appraisal*, Double Storey, 2004.

3 See R. W. Johnson, *South Africa: The First Man, the Last Nation*, Jonathan Ball, 2005.

included the South African Communist Party (SACP), the Congress of South African Trade Unions (Cosatu) and others. This alliance enabled the SACP to exert influence far in excess of the actual support it enjoyed from the electorate. By the time of the election the result was not in doubt, save among the small group surrounding De Klerk, who fondly imagined that they were going to win. The election results showed clearly how out of touch the National Party was with the country at large and its subsequent meteoric collapse showed how intellectually bankrupt it had become. Fortunately, by 1994, Mandela had discarded the communist gestures and slogans that he had displayed on coming out of prison and on the surface he appeared to have been persuaded of the benefits of a market economy underpinned by private enterprise. It was a revolution because it represented the transfer of power from one ethnic group to another, although the new black rulers included more than a sprinkling of representatives from the Indian, white and coloured communities in the short-lived Government of National Unity. Perhaps even more important was the continuation in office of a white Minister of Finance, which gave confidence to the business sector and tended to cover up the extent to which fundamental changes were taking place. This was important, because in 1994 there was still a possibility of an army mutiny. General Constant Viljoen's support was critical during the first two years when Mandela was nominally in charge of the government. As a result, when Mandela was replaced by Mbeki on 16 June 1999, South Africa had passed peacefully through a far-reaching political revolution. For Africa, the peaceful handing over of power from one leader to another was itself a notable occurrence.

The economic revolution was a less happy affair. The impact of the economic changes made in the 1990s would become increasingly apparent in the next decade. The new government quickly replaced the system of public sector appointments (at all levels: national, provincial, local and parastatal) based on merit with one based on race (and gender) in particular and political affiliation in general. It was during the presidency of Mandela that the whole economy was, in the words of R. W. Johnson, bantustanised. In doing this, the new government was going down the well worn and unsuccessful route that other African states had taken on gaining independence. Unlike in the rest of Africa, this policy was also increasingly extended to the private sector, through the policy of black economic empowerment and transformation. A clear understanding of what was in fact happening was obscured by a policy of denial and a refusal both to debate issues and to appoint independent commissions to investigate and report on the issues as they appeared. The economic impact was compounded by a policy of centralism which inhibited solutions at the point of occurrence. It is our contention here that this led to the neglect and mismanagement of the country's infrastructure, which amounted to a negative economic revolution. This neglect became manifest in a number of ways: first, the refusal to invest in the infrastructure; second, the failure to maintain it; and third, the inability to operate complex systems such as electricity supply. The impact of these factors was brought out into the open in the next decade and revealed the true state of affairs.

What had happened can be illustrated by the electricity crisis that became manifest in the early 2000s. South Africa had a long history of inexpensive and reliable electricity. There were isolated occasions when problems were experienced, as in the 1970s, when areas in Natal suffered outages. The government of the day appointed a commission to investigate and report on the problems, which were then addressed successfully. In 2004 Johannesburg began to experience frequent and widespread outages. It became clear that these outages were here to stay. The decade of neglect led to two suburbs and the city's second hospital experiencing power outages for days. Subsequent inquiries then revealed that there had been no meaningful maintenance or expenditure on the infrastructure since 1994. At the local level, City Power of Johannesburg, which operated two large power stations, retired or retrenched its white electrical engineers. Power distribution at a municipal level was failing. The crisis progressed to the Cape region, which experienced widespread sustained outages, not at the municipal level but at the Eskom level. Eskom, South Africa's electricity public utility, experienced difficulties getting Koeberg, the nuclear power station, up and running, which resulted in the power outages. The relevant minister's explanation that the problems were caused by sabotage was implausible and quickly discredited. The breakdown of the Koeberg plant was the result of faulty maintenance; the government's response to the problems was denial and mendacity. The Cape crisis also highlighted another problem: additional power could not be supplied from the Transvaal, because there had been insufficient investment in Eskom's infrastructure – power stations and distribution network. The extent of the problems at Eskom quickly became clear. The country was, for the first time, subject to rolling blackouts. Eskom was forced to declare *force majeure* and to shut down the mining industry for a week to extract an undertaking from the mines that they would permanently reduce their demand by 10 per cent. The mining industry as a whole had not been shut down since the Boer War and the 1920 Rand unrest.

What was the cause of Eskom's problems? The South African Institute of Electrical Engineers called for an independent inquiry to investigate these problems. The response of President Thabo Mbeki was to declare that no crisis existed. There was no need for an inquiry and no one would be held accountable. The failure to appoint a commission was unfortunate, as members of the public were forced to draw their own conclusions from information leaked piecemeal.

The causes of the crisis were wide ranging. First, there was a failure of procurement. The power stations had been built next to coalmines, with the coal being fed via long conveyor belts. Eskom had set very exacting black economic empowerment (BEE) targets, including those for procurements, and proudly announced it had beaten these targets, with nearly 70 per cent of the procurement budget going to BEE suppliers. As a result, a significant quantity of coal was being supplied by hundreds of small suppliers via trucks and the roads were unable to cope with the traffic. The coal procurement system had failed. The coal was also purchased at high spot market prices. A significant portion of the 53 per cent increase in tariffs that Eskom sought was to pay for increased costs of coal and not for the funding of new power stations. Second, Eskom adopted an aggressive policy of transformation, replacing whites with blacks. It placed a ban on recruiting any white males. White males in particular understood that, in the long run, they had no future within Eskom. As a consequence, Eskom's skills base was depleted and areas such as technical maintenance suffered. Third, and this problem may become more apparent in the future, was the refusal of Mbeki to invest in new power stations, despite the official policy that aimed at a 6 per cent annual economic growth rate and despite the Department of Minerals and Energy arguing strongly for the need for new generating capacity from 1998 onwards. This refusal to face reality was compounded by the Communist Party's veto on any privatisation of electricity generation. As a result, Eskom was transformed from an efficient and reliable supplier of power to a shambolic repository of 'affirmative' employees. Skilled and experienced engineers and managers were replaced by affirmatives. Inefficiency and confusion followed as ANC policies began to destroy Africa's largest electricity undertaking. Both power stations and the network systems suffered in this respect.

The mismanagement of Africa's largest electrical undertaking was paralleled by the lack of maintenance of the country's roads. These, as Trevor Jones explains in Chapter 9, were already in a poor condition in 1990, as a result of the De Klerk government's abandonment of any serious efforts to maintain them. After 1994 this situation got worse, except for motorways, where the challenge of maintenance was solved by privatising them and allowing the concessionaires to place tolls on existing freeways. Rail transport experienced a similar lack of maintenance and capital investment. More serious was the refusal of the government to consider privatising the country's ports, where productivity at the container terminals was already well below that of the country's trading partners. Both ports and railways suffered from the fact that the railways owned loss-making South African Airways, a prestige company that the government wanted to keep going. It did this by appointing an American executive, Coleman Andrews, whose skill at creative accounting led the government to think that he had found a solution to the airline's financial problems and then to pay him an unprecedented multi-million rand severance package. In practice he had sold off the planes and then leased them back, thereby obtaining an apparently painless capital injection without putting pressure on the fiscus. Finally, the cooperative non-profit-making Rand Water Board was nationalised, with the now familiar consequence, the replacement of experienced and qualified white engineers with inexperienced and unqualified black ones. Maintenance ceased so that it became only a matter of time before a major crisis would occur. In Sandton, a virtual epidemic of office building took place at the intersection of two main roads, where the circulation of traffic was regularly impeded by the breakdown of the traffic lights. In the 1990s, little attention was paid to whether the existing roads could cope with the rapidly increasing flow of vehicles moving into the city's new financial centre, and even less to its effect upon the sewage disposal system and its ability to cope with the new high-rise office buildings.

This monumental neglect of the infrastructure deserves the name 'negative economic revolution'. An infrastructure that had led the League of Nations to place South Africa among the leading semi-industrialised nations as long ago as 1939 and which distinguished South Africa from all other states in Africa was systematically damaged in the 1990s. It was after 1994 that the crucial decisions were made that inflicted this disaster upon the country: the decision to place affirmative action above the importance of skills and experience; the decision to cease regular maintenance of existing plant; the decision to halt capital investment in the physical infrastructure; and the refusal even to consider privatisation and a market solution to the provision of a cost-efficient and reliable power and water supply and an efficient freight rail system. Not even the state's telephone monopoly was fully privatised. Patronage was more important than economic efficiency. The responsibility for all these disastrous decisions rests upon the shoulders of Mbeki, who was effectively in control of the government from 1994.

By the time the scale of the disaster had become clear, in the following decade, the backlog in capital investment and maintenance and the loss of the skilled personnel were so great that it was doubtful whether they could be reversed. In the 1990s this negative economic revolution formed the backdrop to an economy struggling to achieve positive real per capita growth. Only in 1999, after the South African Statistical

Services had creatively adjusted GDP figures upwards, did the country move into positive economic growth, and these figures are disputed. Indeed, confidence in the reliability of the Statistical Services steadily weakened, as the real effect of the negative economic revolution became manifest, with the cost of doing business in South Africa rising at a time when globalisation and the rules of the World Trade Organization were exposing the economy to the chill winds of real competition.

Even where money was poured into the infrastructure, into health and education, it did not yield many positive results. Affirmative heads of departments and apparatchik accountants were often casual in their use of state funds. As a result, educational standards in state schools continued to decline and infant mortality rates rose, leading to a decline in average life expectancy. Both schools and hospitals plumbed new depths with the demise of merit-based appointments. In the real world, outside the walls of hospitals and schools, police transformation was yielding similar results, corruption and incompetence. All these developments were brushed aside by much of the liberal press as the inevitable consequences of apartheid and relegated to the back pages, so that outside South Africa few persons were familiar with what was really happening to the economy. The De Klerk government must also share some of the blame, for in the 1993 Kempton Park Agreement De Klerk agreed to accept into the provincial governments all the corrupt and incompetent officials who had filled the bureaucracies of the former independent and semi-independent homelands. At a stroke of the pen, he made seven of the future nine provinces ungovernable. Gauteng and the Western Cape were the possible exceptions, because their borders did not incorporate any of the former homelands. The new incompetent provincial authorities were responsible for health, education and roads.

Although there can therefore be little doubt that endogenous factors contributed to setting South Africa on a downward economic path in the 1990s, outside events, both political and economic, also had influence. The most influential external event was the collapse of the Soviet Union and the ideology that had accompanied it. Had the Soviet Union continued to exist, it is unlikely that a South African government would have agreed to hand over power to the ANC. The end of Soviet communism not only removed the paymaster of black nationalist politicians and their paramilitary groups, but it also opened the way to globalisation, for after 1990 there was no real alternative to market economies and the 'Washington consensus'.

Exogenous forces therefore set the stage for the great transformation that was to take place in South Africa in the 1990s; but it was internal endogenous forces that determined how this occurred. It was domestic considerations that led to affirmative action, followed by racial charters and the subsequent assault upon the private sector, and it was domestic considerations that led the Mbeki government to begin its systematic destruction of the country's world-class infrastructure. Both revolutions, political and economic, were home grown.

The exogenous economic developments influencing South Africa were the revolution in communications and the price of commodities. The positive ones were the extraordinary developments in information technology associated with the appearance of personal computers, the internet and mobile phones. These occurred in the second half of the 1990s, when the internet was taking shape and when masts for mobile phones began to sprout in suburbs throughout the country. The Johannesburg Stock Exchange was quickly caught up in the mood of optimism sweeping the world and for five years, from about the middle of 1995 to February 2000, with the exception of a short-lived downturn at the end of August 1998, the market was dominated by the boom in information technology shares. The scale of this boom was sufficiently powerful to draw financial services into the maelstrom, with a rash of new banks and insurance companies appearing in the later 1990s. Other parts of the broader service sector were less buoyant.

The reason for this was the negative effect upon the South African economy of the fall in commodity prices, led by both gold and petroleum. Not even the end-of-the-decade platinum boom could make up for the catastrophic decline in the value of the country's gold output (Chapter 4). The writing had been on the wall for gold ever since US President Richard Nixon demonetised gold in the early 1970s; but this was compounded by geological conditions in the South African gold mines, where output had been declining since 1970. When the price of gold started to fall in the 1980s, it heralded the end of South Africa's importance to the international economy. This long secular decline in the price of gold lasted for over a quarter of a century and was particularly hard on the South African mines in 1990s. By the end of the decade over half the gold mines had become footnotes in economic history books. The decline in agriculture (Chapter 3) that accompanied the ending of protection and the threat to property rights was mild by comparison with what was happening to gold mining, but in an economy heavily dependent upon its primary sector these developments in both agriculture and gold reinforced the negative infrastructure policies. The value of the currency reflected these changes; it crashed. A rising gold price or gold output might have counteracted the negative forces, but the collapse of the main support to the value of the rand was accompanied by the arrival of a communist-dominated government and a return to trade deficits. The currency responded very quickly. In 1990, 1 rand was worth 40 US cents and 40 UK pence. Ten years later, it was worth only 13 US cents and 9 UK pence. Against the dollar the rand had depreciated by 10.5 per cent annually and against the pound by 8.7 per cent. Because the country was experiencing dollar deflation from 1995, Barings withdrew capital from South Africa. Not even the higher interest rates in South Africa[4] could make up for the risk of continued currency depreciation and potential capital loss. Other banks were less cautious; but little direct capital investment occurred. Some state assets were sold, but the country was increasingly relying on portfolio investments to balance its accounts.

The macro-economic background

These melancholy events form the backdrop to the chapters that follow. Part I sets the tone for the two substantive parts of the book, on the economy and on economic policy. First, Philip Mohr provides a stimulating and succinct summary of the major visible developments in the economy. Then, in Chapter 2, Charles Simkins adopts a statistical approach to the problems of demography, with a careful analysis of birth and death rates that shows how urbanisation was gradually leading to lower birth rates. This lowering of birth rates, however, needs to be seen in the context of a continent-wide population explosion, in which the danger of a Malthusian tragedy was becoming ever more likely. In South Africa the reduction in the birth rate was not sufficient to prevent the inexorable rise in unemployment, yet no South African political leader has advocated a population policy. Neither Mandela nor Mbeki addressed this crucial issue. In fact, no African politician from Cape to Cairo has had the courage to make population growth a political issue, despite the incontestable fact that it is population growth that is immiserating so much of the continent. In South Africa the small reduction in the birth rate was counterbalanced by other developments. These were, of course, the massive immigration from north of the Limpopo and the emigration of whites. Mandela invited all Africans to come to South Africa and the Nigerian mafia responded immediately. Others followed from the Congo, Uganda, Malawi, Zambia and Somalia, before the avalanche from Zimbabwe crossed the borders at the end of the 1990s. How the authorities thought this would fit into an environment of growing unemployment is not clear. Mandela was no economist and probably did not understand what he had done. By comparison with this huge demographic ethnic injection, the accelerating emigration of whites was

4 *Business Day*, 21 December 2001.

hardly noticed and was deliberately understated by the government. By 2000, though, possibly as many as 1.5 million whites had emigrated. Young adults did not appear in the official figures because they simply bought return tickets, which were cheaper than single tickets, and stayed overseas. Many older persons, too, simply relocated overseas without officially emigrating, so that their South African bank accounts would not be frozen. The brutal fact remains that an unquantifiable exodus of talent was replaced by a veritable avalanche of Third World immigrants, many of whom were barely able to read and write. At the same time that provincial governments were dismissing, or retiring, qualified and experienced white teachers, a huge and unexpected addition to the number of children of school age was taking place, extra burdens were being placed on the country's hospitals and clinics, the housing situation continued to deteriorate and the growing skills shortage, caused by the government's affirmative action policies, grew steadily worse. Demographic factors, both deliberate and unplanned, were seriously damaging the economy by the end of the 1990s.

Economic policy

In a market economy it might be thought that there is little need for policy, other than a responsible fiscal policy; but in practice, with the ending of the gold standard and of a circulating gold coinage, monetary policy became steadily more important in South Africa, leading to the post-war Keynesian policies that fuelled both inflation and the increase in the monetary supply. By 1990 South Africa was already committed to a 'Washington consensus' type of responsible fiscal and monetary policy. This is examined in Chapter 19, by Estian Calitz and Krige Siebrits, and Chapter 20, by Roger Gidlow. Outside of this macro-economic sphere, policy was less clear. South Africa may have operated in a free market before 1910 but this freedom was progressively limited from 1924 and after 1948 the government was in the hands of a party that placed great emphasis upon the role of the state. It operated a form of state capitalism, much like that which exists today in many of the Arab and South American states. Only at the end of the era of National Party rule did the government move in the direction of a free market economy and by then it was almost too late. The effective result was that a state-oriented white government handed over power to another state-oriented government. It was this contradiction – a government committed to free market policies at international conferences but in practice attached to a leading role for the state – that coloured economic policy. Monetary policy, for instance, could not make the leap to abolishing exchange control, though fiscal policy, aided by a reduction in military spending as the threat of civil war subsided, was able to move towards the balanced budgets that made it possible to bring inflation under control, with the accompanying benefit of lower interest rates, something that the previous government had not been able to achieve since the 1970s. This 'peace dividend' was the outstanding success in the area of economic policy. Tariff reform, for example, came to a halt in 1996, when Trevor Manuel was replaced by Alec Erwin, a hard-line communist, as Minister of Trade and Industry. As for competition policy (Chapter 26), in reality, it was almost the opposite of what it claimed to be, protecting producers rather than consumers, while mining policy (Chapter 23), which should have been at the forefront of the government's agenda for future economic development, was transformed into a sort of wish list of social improvements that could be derived from mining revenues. BEE in practice became a policy for creating a wealthy black elite, South Africa's own 'oligarchs', but the full assault on the private sector had only just begun by the end of the decade. Attention was paid in public to the environment (Chapter 24), but in practice this meant very little to the bulk of the population and there was no serious attempt to tackle the pollution caused by Eskom's power stations, by Sasol's plants for oil from coal or, in the Witbank region, by the local steel works. In South Africa, outside the area of labour, where both BEE and transformation simply meant replacing whites with blacks, continuity was the order of the day. Apart from fiscal policy with its peace dividend, economic policy, with one exception, seems to have had little effect upon the economy as a whole. Labour policy was the exception (Chapter 27). The new labour laws pushed through by Tito Mboweni, when he was Minister of Labour, damaged manufacturing by raising costs and making it more difficult to compete in global markets; but even this example of economic policy being put into practice was not fully thought through. Its effects upon manufacturing costs and the country's ability to compete overseas were not considered. It was the result of lobbying by a clique of Communist Party activists as a way of empowering black workers. Instead, it increased unemployment. First World legislation in a Third World country exacted its price.

The importance of economic policy grew steadily throughout the twentieth century in response to the increasing role of the state in everyday affairs. In South Africa it had taken a leap forward in 1948 with the election of the National Party government, driven by direct state involvement in the economy and the whole apparatus of apartheid labour legislation. In the 1980s both these aspects of state intervention in the economy were weakening and it seemed possible that South Africa might be moving closer to the old Commonwealth norms in managing economic development. This did not happen. The new regime that took over in 1994 brought with it an enormous amount of Marxist baggage. With a majority of cabinet members being active or former active members of the Communist Party, economic policy assumed a much greater role than before 1994. There was, however, a large gap between rhetoric and delivery and, in the 1990s, the effect of government intervention was mainly confined to fiscal policy and labour matters, either through BEE policies or via the new First World labour legislation. Monetary policy was left in the safer hands of the South African Reserve Bank. Yet the threat to property rights did not go away and, in the primary sector (in agriculture and mining), which formed the basis of the South African economy, capital investment was declining. This can be attributed to misguided policy pronouncements and the uncertainty they caused. With the exception of the peace dividend, which made a responsible fiscal policy possible, which in turn affected monetary policy, it is possible to argue that virtually all the policy initiatives were harmful to the economy and that the South African economy grew despite rather than because of its government, and that up to 1998 real per capita growth was probably declining. Part III of the book provides the details of how this occurred.

A statistical caution

Finally, a note upon the statistics and the decision in 1998 to adjust the figures upwards so that they revealed a positive growth rate from 1994. Adjusting the figures upwards or downwards was not unusual. What was unusual was that this took place after very considerable staff changes. In 1994 a professor of the University of the Witwatersrand was placed in charge of the Department of Statistics; but he did not stay there long and was replaced by an affirmative shortly before the figures were adjusted. These new figures, which appeared in the Reserve Bank's *Quarterly Bulletins,* went around the world. Their credibility may be tested in the following statistics.

In current prices, the economy was shown to be growing by 15.0 per cent between 1990 and 1994 and by 10.4 per cent between 1994 and 2000. Because inflation was still severe at the beginning of the decade, it is the figures in constant prices that are more revealing. These show a growth rate of 3.7 per cent per annum for the four years from 1990 to 1994, as opposed to 1.3 per cent from 1994 to 2000. That the economy was performing well, when interest rates were astronomical, commodity prices were falling, sanctions, especially financial sanctions, were being tightened and unrest was widespread, is simply not believable. These figures are the result of creative adjustments by the new affirmatives to show growth after the ANC came to power. Similarly, unbelievable statistics came out in the following decade purporting to show that the numbers of the white population had increased. By 2000 it is likely that the white population had probably shrunk to around 3.5 million; but this cannot be confirmed because the census data do not include racial categories. What seems clear is that figures on economic growth and for per capita GDP are not necessarily accurate reflections of what was happening in the economy. Economists may feel obliged to accept the validity of affirmative statistics, but economic historians with wider perspectives are in a better position to be critical and to reject their validity when they conflict with commonsense, as they do in connection with both economic growth and population growth in the 1990s.

Part I

Overview of the period

1

Overview of the South African economy and policy in the 1990s

Philip Mohr

Introduction

The last decade of the second millennium was an eventful, often dramatic period in South African history. President De Klerk's famous speech of 2 February 1990 signalled the beginning of major changes in the South African political landscape, which inevitably had significant implications for the performance of the South African economy. The immediate impact was great uncertainty about the economic policies to be adopted by the African National Congress (ANC) once it came to power, which seemed inevitable. At the same time, the collapse of Soviet communism and central planning, the communications revolution and the growing faith in markets worldwide significantly increased interdependence among nations. During the course of the decade, the South African economy was integrated into the increasingly globalised world economy on a scale that could hardly have been envisaged towards the end of the 1980s. This created many new opportunities for the South African business sector, but at the same time it also increased the vulnerability of the economy to international developments (e.g. international capital flows).

This chapter consists of three main sections. The first summarises the performance of the South African economy in the 1990s. The second section gives a summary of the broad debate on economic policy, starting with the initial uncertainty and the posturing of the various interest groups and culminating in the adoption of the neoliberal 'growth, employment and redistribution' (GEAR) strategy in 1996. The third section provides more information on the different types of economic policy adopted during the decade.

Overview of the performance of the economy

South Africa's growth performance during the 1990s is summarised in Table 1.1, which also places that performance in a historical context. As can be seen from the table, real GDP declined in 1990, 1991 and 1992; this was due mainly to the uncertainty about the future of the economy and the balance of payments constraint caused by the large deficits on the financial account of the balance of payments. Growth improved markedly after the 1994 elections, but for the decade as a whole the average annual growth rate was significantly lower than that for previous decades (even the 1980s). As a result, real GDP per capita was more than 7 per cent lower in 1999 than in 1989.

As far as sectoral economic growth is concerned, agricultural output was typically volatile. Sharp drought-related declines were recorded in 1992 and 1995, followed by recoveries. Over the decade as a whole, however, there was no growth in the value of the real output of agriculture, forestry and fishing. Likewise, the real output of the mining sector was also stagnant. Gold output fell from 605 tons in 1990 to 450 tons in 1999 but this decline was neutralised by a significant expansion of the platinum industry. By 1999 the total value of exports of the platinum group metals (platinum, palladium and rhodium) almost equalled the value of gold exports. The manufacturing sector declined significantly from 1990 to 1994 but subsequently recovered to its earlier levels, partly as a result of improved manufacturing exports. Over the decade as a whole, however, manufacturing recorded little or no real growth (like agriculture and mining). The only significant real growth during the decade was recorded in the tertiary sector, particularly the financial services sector, which grew by 40 per cent over the decade as a whole.

Table 1.1 also summarises South African inflation during the decade. The negative economic growth during the first few years was accompanied by double-digit inflation but, as in the case of growth, there was a significant improvement from 1993 onwards. The first single-digit annual inflation rate in 20 years was recorded in 1993 and the rate subsequently declined fairly consistently. By the end of the decade the inflation rate was lower than even the most optimistic observer could have deemed possible a decade earlier.

On the employment front, however, performance was much less satisfactory. In 2000 there were (according to the official statistics released at the time) 963,000 fewer people employed in the formal sector than in 1990. Both the public sector (159,000) and the private sector (804,000) contributed to this decline. The sectoral employment pattern largely mirrored the sectoral growth trends indicated above. Over the decade as a whole, the mining sector and the manufacturing sector each shed

Table 1.1 *Economic growth and inflation in South Africa*

Period	*Annual growth in real gross domestic product (%)*	*Annual increase in consumer price index (%)*
1990	–0.3	14.4
1991	–1.0	15.3
1992	–2.1	13.9
1993	1.2	9.7
1994	3.2	9.0
1995	3.1	8.7
1996	4.3	7.4
1997	2.6	8.6
1998	0.5	6.9
1999	2.4	5.2
1960–69	5.9	2.4
1970–79	3.3	9.7
1980–89	2.2	14.6
1990–99	1.4	9.8
1990–93	–0.6	13.3
1994–99	2.7	7.6

Sources: South African Reserve Bank, *Quarterly Bulletin*; International Monetary Fund, *International Financial Statistics*; Statistics South Africa.

more than 300,000 formal jobs (no comparable figures are available for the agricultural sector). Initially some jobs were created in the financial services sector but by the end of the decade most of the gains had been wiped out by restructuring, rationalisation and other cost-reducing efforts. In October 1999 the unemployment rate was estimated at 23.3 per cent according to a strict definition and 36.2 per cent according to a wider definition.

Large deficits were recorded on the financial account of the balance of payments from 1990 to 1993 (due to a combination of debt repayment and capital flight). These deficits, which amounted to about 1.6 per cent of GDP, had to be matched by surpluses on the current account. From 1994 onwards, however, the balance of payments position changed quite drastically. Significant (often huge) surpluses were recorded on the financial account (mainly as a result of strong inflows of portfolio capital) and the country could again afford to run significant current account deficits. As emphasised in Chapter 18, the changes in the balance of payments were significant determinants of the improved growth performance from 1994 onwards.

South Africa's personal income distribution is still among the most skewed of those that have been estimated in the world (bearing in mind that estimates for many developing countries are either unavailable or highly unreliable), with most estimates of the Gini coefficient at around 0.60. In the 1990s, however, some significant changes occurred. The gaps between the different race groups became smaller and the distribution within the black group became much more unequal. The latter trend can be ascribed to the increasing unemployment, the relatively fast rate of increase in the wages of blacks employed in the formal sector of the economy and increased poverty in the rural areas (due, *inter alia,* to severe droughts, floods and other natural disasters). Gini coefficients for the different population groups in 2000 were estimated at 0.57 (blacks), 0.51 (coloureds), 0.50 (Asians) and 0.45 (whites).[1]

Policy debate

In the 1980s the State President's Economic Advisory Council submitted a *Long-Term Economic Strategy* to the government but this document was released for comment only in 1991 and a *Revised Long-Term Economic Strategy* was published in 1992. Earlier, Dr Wim de Villiers, the Minister for Administration and Privatisation (and subsequently for Administration and Economic Coordination), had compiled an unedited confidential report on economic restructuring (entitled *Ekonomiese herstrukturering in Suid-Afrika*). This report was completed in February 1990 (i.e. at the time of President De Klerk's momentous speech). Both the Economic Advisory Council's document and the one prepared by de Villiers adopted a neoliberal, supply-side approach, emphasising a smaller role for the public sector, a greater reliance on market forces and greater scope for the private sector. This was, of course, directly the opposite of the policy of the African National Congress (ANC), which was (at that stage) still based largely on the Freedom Charter and which envisaged a greater role for the public sector (e.g. through nationalisation and punitive wealth taxes).

After February 1990 it was feared that an ANC-led government would apply an interventionist, populist approach to economic policy and the initial speeches by Nelson Mandela after his release served to confirm these fears. He stated, for example, that 'the nationalisation of the mines, banks and monopoly industry is the policy of the ANC and a change or modification of our views in this regard is inconceivable'.[2]

1 J. du Toit, *The Structure of the South African Economy*, SA Financial Sector Forum, 2002, p. 17.

2 H. Marais, *Limits to Change*, Zed Books/University of Cape Town Press, 2001, p. 122.

Internationally, however, a number of forces against populism emerged during this period, such as the demise of the Soviet Union, the rapid globalisation of the world economy and the growing pro-market orthodoxy (propagated, *inter alia*, by the International Monetary Fund and World Bank). At the World Economic Forum in Davos, Switzerland, in January 1992, Mandela, confronted by the disapproval of world economic leaders, discarded his prepared speech and adopted a much more moderate stance.[3]

The debate about the future of the South African economy that emerged during the early 1990s was significant in many respects. For the first time it focused on structural economic issues and the analyses conducted during this debate highlighted aspects of the economy (e.g. the extent of poverty, inequality and unemployment) which many South Africans (particularly whites) had been unaware of at that stage. At the same time the ANC leadership became aware of the need to formulate more coherent and feasible economic policies. This greater awareness of the features and problems of the economy and the challenges faced by policy makers was fostered by a number of scenario-building exercises, such as the Nedcor/Old Mutual 'change of gears' scenario and the Mont Fleur scenarios.

Various organisations and interest groups also formulated economic strategies. These included the ANC's *Growth Through Redistribution* and *Policy Guidelines*, Cosatu's proposals for economic reconstruction, the Development Bank of South Africa's macro-economic policy model for human development in South Africa, the Democratic Party's five-point economic rescue strategy (tax cuts, massive labour-intensive schemes, export processing zones, deregulation and privatisation), the *Economic Options for South Africa*, formulated by the South African Chamber of Business (Sacob) and *Making Democracy Work*, compiled by the Macro-economic Research Group (MERG).

In 1993 the government also published a new strategy, aimed largely at reducing uncertainty about economic policy. This document had a similar thrust to the earlier strategies formulated by the Economic Advisory Council and Wim de Villiers. By and large, the policy proposals in the *Normative Economic Model* (as it was called) contained all the basic elements of the structural adjustment programmes advocated and sponsored by the International Monetary Fund and the World Bank. At that time, however, the ANC/Cosatu/Communist Party alliance was

3 M. Kentridge, *Turning the Tanker: The Economic Debate in South Africa*, Research Report 32, Centre for Policy Studies, 1993, p. 5.

rigorously opposed to that particular type of economic strategy and the *Normative Economic Model* was never adopted officially. One of the problems was that this technocratic strategy was not sensitive enough to the political issues of the day and it was soon overtaken by the *Reconstruction and Development Programme* (RDP), which became the election manifesto of the ANC in the 1994 elections.

In the meantime, the President's Economic Advisory Council, which was dominated by the captains of industry, had been disbanded. It was replaced, in October 1992, by the National Economic Forum (NEF). This non-statutory consultative body, which consisted of representatives of labour, business and government, was initiated by Cosatu and organised business. Cosatu had long wanted to have a say in economic policy making and the NEF was seen as a means of blocking unilateral economic reform by the National Party government. The NEF and the National Manpower Commission were later replaced by a statutory body, the National Economic Development and Labour Council (Nedlac). This body, which was created by Act 35 of 1994 and which started functioning in February 1995, was originally a tripartite body, consisting of representatives from government, business and labour, but was later expanded to include representatives from civil society (the civics). Nedlac's aim was to seek agreement on policy matters and many of its initial efforts were directed towards establishing a new set of labour laws. Various other issues were also dealt with but towards the end of the decade its role in economic policy making had diminished greatly.

The Government of National Unity that was formed after the 1994 elections adopted a revised version of the RDP as its policy. The RDP had been an important political document, in that it provided a vision that the majority could relate to during the political transition. As an economic policy document, however, it was seriously flawed. By and large, it was too ambitious, too populist, too interventionist, too vague on constraints and implementation and tended to foster unrealistic expectations. Moreover, by the mid-1990s the underlying theme of growth through redistribution had become an anachronism.

Although Chris Stals, the Governor of the South African Reserve Bank (SARB), appeared to have a solid grip on monetary policy, there was still great uncertainty about the thrust of economic policy in general and fiscal policy in particular. Some clear direction was required and the International Monetary Fund and others urged the government to formulate a clear economic strategy and to commit itself to sound (conservative) stabilisation policies. In the absence of such a strategy, and to force the issue, both labour and business published strategy documents in early 1996. In February the South African Foundation released its *Growth for All* and the Cosatu-led South African labour movement responded with *Social Equity and Job Creation*. At the time, labour was still strongly opposed to privatisation, but in February 1996 an important agreement (the National Framework Agreement) was reached between government and labour regarding the restructuring of certain state assets (which was akin to privatisation).

Another key development was the appointment, in March 1996, of Trevor Manuel as the first ANC Minister of Finance. Manuel's interventionist approach as Minister of Trade and Industry, where he had mooted the idea of a developmental state, and his initial pronouncements about the 'amorphous' nature of international financial markets gave rise to negative sentiment in these markets and the rand depreciated sharply against the major international currencies. This exacerbated the need to establish confidence in macro-economic management in general and fiscal management in particular.

On 14 June 1996 the Department of Finance unveiled its new macroeconomic strategy, 'growth, employment and redistribution' (GEAR). GEAR took many observers by surprise, not least the ANC's political allies (Cosatu and the South African Communist Party) and the bulk of the ANC membership, none of whom had been consulted in the formulation of the strategy. GEAR entailed a switch to orthodox neoliberal or free-market conservatism and supply-side economics. Such an approach had been propagated by the previous government but had initially been resisted fiercely by the ANC and its allies.

With the adoption of GEAR, the emphasis suddenly switched from *growth through redistribution* to *redistribution through growth*, and from fundamental economic restructuring to a 'Washington consensus' type structural adjustment (as propagated by the international financial institutions and the US government). The key element in GEAR, however, was the emphasis on fiscal discipline and particularly on the reduction of the deficit before borrowing. Except for the fiscal elements, the strategy was fairly vague and amounted to a broad approach rather than a specific set of policies. Although it is often referred to in debates about policy, it is important to note that GEAR itself was never a policy. Instead it was, and still is, used as a term to indicate a commitment to an orthodox, neoliberal approach to economic policy. GEAR also contained a set of targets, which were clearly unattainable but were probably added in an attempt to gain political support for the strategy, which (in sharp contrast to the RDP) was formulated by technocrats without any consultation with other interested parties. Despite its fairly broad nature and despite the fact that few individuals or groups were familiar with its contents, GEAR became the cornerstone of economic debate in South Africa.

Economic policy

Fiscal policy

At the start of the 1990s South African fiscal policy was in a parlous state. Government spending, the budget deficit and the public debt were escalating and there were fears that South Africa was falling into a debt trap.[4] Government was under pressure to increase spending, particularly on social services, but negative economic growth and trade union pressure made it difficult to raise additional taxes. For example, in September 1991 sustained pressure by Cosatu and other trade union federations forced the government to implement the new value-added tax (to replace the existing general sales tax) at a rate of 10 per cent, instead of the 12 per cent that had been envisaged.

In the fiscal year immediately preceding the 1994 elections the budget deficit exceeded 9 per cent and there were fears that it would rise beyond control. The new government, however, raised taxes and after the resumption of economic growth and the adoption of the GEAR strategy the growth in government spending was arrested, with the result that the budget deficit declined as a percentage of GDP. By the end of the decade it was below 2.5 per cent of GDP, well within the target set in GEAR. During the mid-1990s, however, the public debt and the concomitant interest burden continued to escalate (partly as a result of the high prevailing interest rates). The government was still dissaving (i.e. current expenditure still exceeded current income) but the situation improved during the course of the decade and by the end of the period growth in public debt had halted. Although there were a number of important developments on the expenditure side (including significant changes in its composition, mainly a shift from military spending to social spending, and the adoption of the Medium-Term Expenditure Framework in the 1998/99 fiscal year), the reduction in the budget deficit can be ascribed largely to significant increases in tax revenue. The progressivity of personal income tax was reduced (by cutting the number of tax brackets from 15 to 6) but the top marginal rate was raised and tax collection was improved significantly, particularly towards the end of the decade. GEAR was aimed, first and foremost, at establishing fiscal discipline and in this key respect it was undoubtedly a resounding success. By the end of the decade the credibility of the fiscal authorities was firmly established and South African fiscal policy had become an example for other countries to follow.

4 See E. J. van der Merwe, 'Is South Africa in a debt trap?', Occasional Paper 16, South African Reserve Bank, May 1993.

Unfortunately, however, some of the fiscal discipline was achieved at the expense of essential investment in the maintenance and expansion of the country's infrastructure, for example with regard to electricity, road and rail transport and water supply. This resulted in serious bottlenecks, which affected the performance of the economy in the new millennium.

Monetary policy

Chris Stals, whose 10-year period as Governor of the SARB came to an end in August 1999, was firmly in charge of monetary policy in South Africa during most of the decade. After taking over the reins at the SARB, Stals immediately made it clear that he considered his main task to be to protect the domestic and international value of the rand. He soon showed that he would do everything in his power to achieve this goal. In particular, he was always prepared to use the country's foreign exchange reserves and interest rates to stabilise the international value of the currency. As a result, interest rates fluctuated quite significantly during the 1990s.

In sharp contrast to his predecessor, Gerhard de Kock, Stals was in the fortunate position of being able to conduct monetary policy without any undue political interference. President De Klerk never had any inclination to meddle with monetary policy and in 1996 the independence of the SARB was legally established in the new constitution, along with the commitment to price stability, as the overriding objective of monetary policy in South Africa.

During his tenure Stals had to deal with a number of financial crises, particularly the depreciation of the rand during the first half of 1996 and the impact of the Asian economic crisis two years later. Particularly during the latter, interest rates were raised sharply and large quantities of dollars were sold in an attempt to stabilise the external value of the rand. The impact of these policies, particularly the large sums spent in an attempt to stabilise the currency, was felt for a considerable period afterwards and caused his successor, Tito Mboweni, purposely to refrain from such measures, even when the rand collapsed towards the end of 2001.

During most of the decade, monetary targets or guidelines were announced by the SARB as part of its anti-inflation strategy. However, these targets or guidelines were seldom achieved and by the end of the decade preparations were being made to introduce inflation targeting as the framework for monetary policy in South Africa. This framework was adopted soon afterwards (in February 2000). As far as the implementation of monetary policy is concerned, the most important technical change was the introduction of the repurchase tender system (repo system) in March 1998. This system was immediately put to the test during the financial crisis of 1998. It weathered the storm but in November 1999 the repurchase (repo) rate, which had originally been a variable rate, became a fixed rate (similar to the Bank rate, the earlier name of the rate at which the SARB provided accommodation to the banking sector). Although Stals was subsequently criticised for some of the measures he took, particularly during the 1998 financial crisis, his resolute stance against inflation undoubtedly contributed to the decline in inflation during the decade (see Table 1.1).

Labour policy

One of the first priorities of the new ANC government in 1994 was to review South Africa's labour market policies. In May 1995 a Presidential Commission was appointed to investigate labour market policy in South Africa and the Commission's report was finalised a year later. In 1995 the government and the Commission also invited the International Labour Organization (ILO) to conduct a comprehensive assessment of the labour market in South Africa. The ILO report was published in 1996 and along with the Commission's report it served as an important input in the policy-making process. Work on the legislative programme proceeded rapidly and by 1998 a new set of four Acts were in place: the Labour Relations Act, the Basic Conditions of Employment Act, the Employment Equity Act and the Skills Development Act. The Labour Relations Act established a common industrial relations framework for all civilian employees, including public servants (who were previously covered by a different Act) and farm workers and domestic workers (who were denied bargaining rights under the previous Act). The Basic Conditions of Employment Act established a floor of basic rights for all workers and extended these rights by reducing the length of the working week, increasing annual and maternal leave periods and increasing overtime premiums. The Employment Equity Act was aimed at achieving equity in the workplace by promoting equal opportunity and fair treatment in employment through the elimination of unfair discrimination and by implementing affirmative action to redress the disparities in employment experienced by women, black males and people with disabilities. The Skills Development Act aimed to develop the skills of the labour force by increasing the investment in education and training in the labour market.

South African debates on labour market policy reflect strongly held views about the relative importance of labour market stability and flexibility. It is often argued that there is a simple choice between an investor-friendly flexible labour market (in which employers are able to adjust the size, remuneration and working conditions of their workforces speedily and at low cost) and a worker-friendly stable labour market (in which employees are protected against dismissal, reductions in earnings, discrimination and unhealthy or dangerous working conditions). Following the recommendations of the Presidential Commission and the ILO review, the South African government opted for an intermediate position, of regulated flexibility. Many observers, however, maintain that the new set of labour laws increased the direct and indirect costs of labour, thereby contributing onwards increased costs and/or increasing unemployment. They also emphasise that the labour laws were in conflict with the underlying theme of the GEAR strategy. Others, however, argue that the labour laws succeeded in establishing a more orderly and less conflict-ridden system of industrial relations.

Trade policy

One of the most significant policy developments in the 1990s was the liberalisation of South Africa's international trade. At the start of the decade the South African trade regime was a complex, highly discretionary one with a marked anti-export bias. To counter the latter, a significant set of export subsidies – the General Export Incentive Scheme (GEIS) – was introduced in April 1990. However, in April 1994 South Africa signed the Marrakesh Agreement on Agriculture and thereby agreed to liberalise international trade by lowering import tariffs, eliminating non-tariff barriers to trade and phasing out the GEIS. As a member of the World Trade Organization (WTO), which replaced the General Agreement on Tariffs and Trade (GATT) on 1 January 1995, South Africa significantly simplified its tariff structure and reduced import tariffs during the rest of the decade.

The liberalisation of international trade gave rise to an unprecedented increase in competition in the domestic market and played an important role in the reduction of inflation in South Africa during the second half of the 1990s.

Competition policy

Before 1994 the ANC had propagated a vigorous anti-monopoly policy. Barriers to entry were perceived to be at variance with the aspirations of previously disadvantaged groups and there was a strong belief that the economic power of the large conglomerates had to be curtailed to revitalise the economy and address the inequalities of income and wealth. It therefore came as no surprise that competition policy received renewed attention after 1994. Vigorous debate and negotiations between government, business and labour culminated in the promulgation of the Competition Act 89 of 1998, which provided for the establishment of a Competition Commission and a Competition Tribunal. Since then, particular attention has been directed to the evaluation of mergers and acquisitions, which have to be notified to the Competition Commission.

Conclusion

From this brief overview it should be obvious that a number of far-reaching policy measures were adopted in South Africa in the 1990s. In many instances, however, the capacity to execute the policies was lacking. Many government spending programmes, for example, were not executed, or executed inefficiently, due to a lack of experience and expertise, particularly at the middle-management level. The government became increasingly aware of the shortcomings in this regard and by the end of the century the need to increase the capacity to implement policies became a familiar theme in political speeches.

2

Demographic change

Charles Simkins

The statistical background

Population studies in South Africa entered the 1990s in a precarious state. Demographic analytical capacity was something of an Afrikaner preserve, concentrated in the Central Statistical Service, the Human Sciences Research Council, the University of Pretoria and Professor J. L. Sadie at Stellenbosch. Outsiders tended to regard the output of these enterprises with some reserve, especially when they dealt with fertility, contraception and population policy. Quite often, however, these studies dealt simply with population projections. Those made by Professor Sadie[1] were generally the best, but even these suffered from a serious undersupply of data.

The 1970 census was the last to enumerate the entire population of South Africa. Thereafter, territories granted 'independence' by Pretoria were dropped, and by the next census, in 1980, Transkei, Bophuthatswana and Venda had disappeared from the enumeration directed by Pretoria. By the 1985 census, Ciskei had disappeared as well. There were some attempts in these territories to conduct their own censuses or at least sample surveys, but these were not complete or reliable.[2]

1 See, for instance: J. L. Sadie, *A Reconstruction of Demographic Movements in the RSA and TBVC Countries*, Report 148, Bureau of Market Research, University of South Africa, 1988; J. L. Sadie, *A Projection of the South African Population 1991–2011*, Report 196, Bureau of Market Research, University of South Africa, 1988.

2 The 'independent state' reports published between 1980 and 1991 were: Bophuthatswana (South Africa), *1985 Population Census Report*, Department of Economics, Division of Statistics, 1985, and *1991 Population Census Report*, Statistics Branch, Department of Economics, Energy Affairs, Mines and Planning, n.d.; Ciskei (South Africa), *Ciskei Population: April 1985*, Office of the President, Directorate of Planning, 1985;

A population census, suitably worked over, provides a jump-off or check-point population for a demographic projection. Also necessary for such a projection is knowledge of fertility, mortality and international migration. The necessary vital statistics were differentiated by population group and were sometimes simply not collected. Black birth data, for instance, were simply not collected by government before 1991, although white, coloured and Asian births were recorded before this date. Black mortality data were collected in 34 urban magisterial districts between 1968 and 1977, but such mortality could not be regarded as representative of the whole black population. From 1978, mortality data were collected more widely, but by then the independent territories had started to be dropped from the South African statistics. And there are completeness issues with the data, especially in the early years. International migration was even harder to estimate. The Department of the Interior kept immigration and emigration statistics, but the immigration statistics captured only those who immigrated formally. In an era of tight foreign exchange controls, there was an advantage in declaring one's emigration formally because then one could take more money out of the country than otherwise. But those who had little to take, such as the young, often left without being counted as emigrants.

Some indication of the difficulties can be seen from the expedients used by Professor Sadie. He started his mortality projections from data in the 1960 population census and then adjusted his estimates downwards over time to allow for rising life expectancy. He worked with a racially differentiated fertility model, and assumed that black fertility would follow coloured fertility downwards with a lag of 30 years. On international migration, he used historic Department of the Interior statistics of white immigration and emigration and assumed that similar patterns would be followed in the future. He assumed net migration of coloureds and Asians and blacks born in South African was nil. Foreign-born blacks were identified in his analyses but no projections were made for them. The Human Sciences Research Council offered variations on these themes, and sometimes inserted fertility estimates from its survey research.

It became harder, too, to collect data. South Africa was in a state of almost continuous uproar in the last decade of apartheid. By the time of the 1991 census, it had become impossible for the Central Statistical

Transkei (South Africa), *Transkei 1980 Population Census: Summary Analysis*, Population Division, National Statistics Office, 1987, *Transkei 1985 Population Sample Census*, Population Division, National Statistics Office, 1987, and *The 1991 Population Census Report*, Central Statistics Office, 1994; Venda, *Population Census 1985*, Statistical Report No. 2 of 1987, Office of the State President, 1987.

Service to conduct the door-to-door enumeration in a large number of mainly black, mainly urban areas, and the Service had to estimate the population in these areas by dwelling counts from aerial photographs and sample-based estimates of dwelling occupancy. And, of course, Transkei, Bophuthatswana, Venda and Ciskei were still excluded. The enumeration was heavily adjusted to fit a population estimate by Professor Sadie.[3] At a time when all eyes were focused on the political transition, the defects of the 1991 census went unremarked. But when the new government took power, it found itself seriously short of the social statistics it needed to formulate the details of its policies. The new South African demography, bursting out of its old confines, would have to start with a new population census, scheduled for October 1996.

It follows that estimates of the population in the 1970s and 1980s are necessarily subject to large degrees of error. There are simply not enough data to anchor such estimates properly. The result is that we are uncertain about the onset and evolution of the black fertility transition, though it appears that this must have started in the 1970s or early 1980s and that it was quite rapid. Our account of international migration since the 1980s is completely inadequate. And it has taken quite some time to get to grips with the mortality experience of the population since the middle of the 1980s, when HIV/AIDS infection first reached South Africa. These sorts of uncertainties by no means disappeared from accounts of the South African population in the 1990s.

Moreover, post-apartheid analysts have not been inclined to dwell on conditions in the apartheid years. Statistics South Africa (the successor agency to the Central Statistical Service) developed a population projection model only in 2004 to support estimates of the population at mid-year,[4] and the model goes back only to 2001. The population projection model developed by the Actuarial Society of South Africa (ASSA), which models the spread of the HIV/AIDS epidemic in great detail, goes back further, to 1985, to pick up the first infections. This model has gone through several versions.[5] Successive versions have calibrated the results to data on HIV infection among pregnant mothers registered with government clinics, to survey data on HIV infection and to data

3 The adjustment procedure is set out in the document *1991 Population Census, Adjustments for Undercount 03-01-26*, Statistics South Africa, 1991.

4 For published information on this model, see 'Mid-year population estimates, 2005 and 2006', Statistical Release P0302, Statistics South Africa, 2006, available on the Statistics South Africa website, www.statssa.gov.za. Like the ASSA's model, the Statistics South Africa model has to contain an account of the HIV/AIDS epidemic. This it does by using a Spectrum/AIM projection package developed by the Research Triangle Institute in the USA.

5 This model can the downloaded from the ASSA website, www.actuarialsociety.org.za.

on deaths collected by Statistics South Africa. The earlier version of the ASSA model estimated heavier mortality than the more recent one. The range of options for projecting future mortality have become more complex as education campaigns have been augmented by a reduction of mother-to-child HIV transmission through the administration of drugs at birth and the greater use of anti-retroviral agents.

Census statistics

The first post-apartheid population census was carried out in October 1996. Developments in computer technology made possible new approaches to data capture, storage and use, although a relatively short preparation time and a degree of inexperience meant that these approaches were not always optimally used. Three innovations, in particular, are worth pointing out. The first was the use of a post-enumeration survey. In fact, the 1991 census had attempted a post-enumeration survey, but the results were so implausible that they were discarded. The results of the 1996 census post-enumeration survey were used to estimate that 10.7 per cent of the population had not been counted in the census.[6] A raw count of 36,246,591 was adjusted to a final estimate of 40,583,574. (The distribution of the population as adjusted by population group, gender and province is set out in Table 2.1.) The second innovation was the use of a geographical information system which identified enumerator areas, as far as was possible, on an electronic map of South Africa. Although not perfect, the geographical information system made it possible to represent data spatially as never before. The third, and related, innovation was to make census data available electronically in two formats: first, the data were organised into subsets, from which cross-tabulations as desired could be extracted; and second, a 10 per cent sample of person and household records containing all the available data was provided.

One surprising feature of the 1996 census results was the low estimate of the white population. The 1991 census raw count had been 4,521,873 and the adjusted count 5,068,300. By contrast, the 1996 adjusted count was 4,434,697, although some of the unspecified/other category could be added to it. Statistics South Africa estimated that the undercount was highest among Africans and coloureds (at about 11 per cent), lower among whites, at about 9 per cent, and lower still among Indians,

6 See *1996 Population Census: The Count and How It Was Done,* Statistics South Africa, 1996, table 13.

Table 2.1 *Population of South Africa, 1996 census*

Population group/region	*Census count (adjusted)*
African	31,127,631
Coloured	3,600,446
Asian	1,045,596
White	4,434,697
Unspecified/other	375,204
Male	19,520,889
Female	21,062,685
Eastern Cape	6,302,525
Free State	2,633,505
Gauteng	7,348,423
KwaZulu-Natal	8,417,021
Mpumalanga	2,800,711
Northern Cape	840,321
Northern Province [a]	4,929,368
North West	3,354,825
Western Cape	3,956,875

Note: [a] Now Limpopa Province.
Source: 1996 Census: Primary Tables, Statistics South Africa, 1996.

at 6 per cent.[7] A debate ensued about whether or not white under-enumeration had been accurately estimated. Certainly, there is evidence to suggest that, whereas blacks were the hard-to-enumerate population group under apartheid, whites have become harder to enumerate in the post-apartheid era. Statistics South Africa frequently refers to the difficulty of enumeration in the 'high-walled areas'. But it is also clear in retrospect that the adjustment in the 1991 census was too high. Even in the early 1990s, Sadie continued to project high white net immigration to South Africa, even as looming political change induced accelerated white emigration. It should also be remembered that fertility among whites has long been low and probably dropped to below replacement in the 1990s, so that even a modest rate of emigration would lead to a slow drop in the population.

The 1996 census anchored notions of population size and composition. The quality of that anchor can be checked against the results of the 2001 census, held exactly five years later. That census had an unadjusted

7 See *1996 Population Census: Calculating the Undercount in Census '96,* Statistics South Africa, 1996, chapter 4, figure 18.2.

count of 37,302,183. The 2001 post-enumeration survey found an undercount of 17.6 per cent and the adjusted count was 44,819,778.[8] The rate of growth of the population between the two censuses on the basis of the adjusted counts was 2.01 per cent per annum. This is too high an estimate in the light of estimates of vital statistics (see below), and so suggests that the undercount rate as estimated in the 1996 post-enumeration survey was too low.

There are also concerns about the reliability of the age and sex composition of the adjusted census counts. The Statistics Council carried out an evaluation of the 2001 census results and found that there was probably:

- an underestimate of the number of children below age five;
- an overestimate of the number of young people aged between 10 and 20 years;
- an underestimate of the number of men relative to the number of women;
- higher than expected numbers aged 80 or more in the African population;
- age misstatement in the age range 60–74.[9]

Non-census evidence

Apart from the 1996 census, the most important information source on fertility during the 1990s was the 1998 Demographic and Health Survey (DHS), believed to be much more reliable than its 2003 successor. Table 2.2 reports its main results. The 1998 DHS suggested that African fertility started to decline after 1960, slowly at first, but then more rapidly, dropping to about 4.5 in the mid-1980s and 4.0 in 1990.[10] In addition, Moultrie and Dorrington estimated fertility from the 2001 census data using careful and complex techniques to deal with the deficiencies.[11] They estimated the total fertility rate to have been 2.84, with the rates by population group being: African, 3.04; coloured, 2.41; Asian, 1.98; and white, 1.82.

8 See *Census 2001: How the Count Was Done*, Statistics South Africa, 2001, table 6.6.

9 *Census 2001: Primary Tables*, Statistics South Africa, 2001, p. 3, census '96 and 2001 compared.

10 The fertility rate represents the number children an average woman is likely to have during her childbearing years, conventionally taken to be 15–49. *The Economist*, 31 October 2009, p. 29.

11 Tom A. Moultrie and Rob Dorrington, *Estimation of Fertility from the 2001 South Africa Census Data*, Monograph 12, Centre for Actuarial Research, University of Cape Town, 2001.

Table 2.2 Fertility rates, 1995–98

Population subgroup	*Rate*
Total fertility rate	
Women 15–49	2.9
Urban women 15–49	2.25
Non-urban women 15–49	3.92
Africans	3.1
Coloureds	2.5
Whites	1.9
Age-specific fertility rates (per 1,000)	
15–19	76
20–24	139
25–29	143
30–34	109
35–39	74
40–44	29
45–49	9

Source: The 1998 Demographic and Health Survey, Department of Health, tables 3.1 and 3.2.

Arriving at mortality estimates is considerably harder. HIV prevalence as measured among ante-natal clinic attendees since 1990 is set out in Table 2.3. This shows HIV infection taking off in the mid-1990s and reaching high levels by the end of the decade. Using the Bongaarts rule of thumb, one would expect a take-off in mortality 10 years later.

Ante-natal clinic statistics display prevalence rates among a biased sample of women, so the results of a Human Sciences Research Council survey of HIV prevalence based on field testing for the virus conducted in 2002 are of interest. They are reported in Table 2.4, which indicates that male prevalence rates were below female rates. Female prevalence rates among the population 15–49 in general were considerably lower than the prevalence rates among pregnant women tested at ante-natal clinics. Rates were highest among Africans and lowest among Asians. They were higher in urban areas, especially urban informal areas, than in rural areas.

The third source of information is death registrations compiled by Statistics South Africa from data kept by the Department of Home Affairs in its population register. The 'Advance release of recorded deaths, 1997–2000'[12] is the most important document for the 1990s. It

12 'Advance release of recorded deaths 1997–2000', Statistical Release P0309.1, Statistics South Africa, 20 December 2001. There is also an advance release for 1996 in the same Statistical Release series.

Table 2.3 *National HIV prevalence, ante-natal clinics, 1990–2005*

Year	*Prevalence (%)*
1990	0.7
1991	1.7
1992	2.2
1993	4.0
1994	7.6
1995	10.4
1996	14.2
1997	17.0
1998	22.8
1999	22.4
2000	24.5
2001	24.8
2002	26.5
2003	27.9
2004	29.5
2005	30.2

Source: National HIV and Syphilis Ante-natal Sero-prevalence Survey in South Africa, Department of Health, 2005.

Table 2.4 *Overall HIV prevalence by sex and population group, 2002*

	HIV positive (%)	*95% confidence interval*
All	11.4	10.0–12.7
Male	9.5	8.0–11.1
Female	12.8	10.9–14.6
African	12.9	11.2–14.5
Coloured	6.1	4.5–7.8
Asian	1.6	0.0–3.4
White	6.2	3.1–9.2
Urban formal	12.1	10.3–14.0
Urban informal	21.3	16.2–26.5
Tribal	8.7	6.5–10.9
Farms	7.9	4.8–11.1
Children (2–14 years)	5.6	3.7–7.4
Youths (15–24 years)	9.3	7.3–11.2
Adults (25+ years)	15.5	13.5–17.5
Women 15–49	17.7	15.2–20.4

Source: Olive Shisana *et al., Nelson Mandela HSRC Study of HIV/AIDS,* HSRC, 2002, tables 12, 14, 15 and 22.

Table 2.5 *Numbers of registered deaths, 1997–2000*

Year	*Number of deaths registered*
1997	260,273
1998	299,077
1999	326,618
2000	362,450

Source: 'Advance release of recorded deaths 1997–2000', Statistical Release P0309.1, Statistics South Africa, 20 December 2001.

Table 2.6 *ASSA 2003 baseline estimates of mortality, 1990–2000*

	1990	*1992*	*1994*	*1996*	*1998*	*2000*
Non-AIDS deaths	296,961	314,308	334,159	354,119	381,410	377,113
AIDS deaths	545	2,650	10,152	30,857	75,371	147,525
Crude death rate (per 1,000)	8.1	8.3	8.5	9.1	10.4	11.6
${}_1q_0$ * 1,000	48	47	48	52	57	60
${}_{45}q_{15}$	0.290	0.293	0.300	0.318	0.369	0.41
e_0, male	58.6	58.5	58.1	57.0	54.8	53.2
e_0, female	66.5	66.6	66.2	65.0	62.2	59.3

Source: Actuarial Society of South Africa, ASSA 2003 model.

shows a rapid rise in the annual number of deaths between 1997 and 2000, reported in Table 2.5. For males and females the sharpest increases were in the 25–54 age range, as would be expected in a period of rising AIDS mortality.

Dorrington, Moultrie and Timaeus investigated the data on deaths in the 2001 census. They came to the conclusion that the data on child mortality were too poor to be used but that the information on adult mortality was reasonably coherent and consistent with other estimates.[13]

These sources of information on HIV infection and mortality have been used to calibrate the ASSA 2003 model (see above). That model divides the population into four HIV risk categories: not at risk, normal risk, sexually transmitted disease risk and commercial sex worker risk. It models the spread of the epidemic within and between these four categories. A large number of parameters have to be set within the model and the data impose limits on their combination. Table 2.6 sets out the

13 Rob Dorrington, Tom A. Moultrie and Ian M. Timaeus, *Estimation of Mortality Using South African Census 2001 Data*, Monograph 11, Centre for Actuarial Research, University of Cape Town, 2001.

ASSA 2003 baseline estimates of mortality variables in the 1990s, where ${}_nq_x$ refers to the probability of dying within *n* years of reaching exact age *x*; thus, ${}_1q_0$ * 1,000 is the infant mortality rate and e_0 is life expectancy at birth. If the ASSA 2003 estimates of mortality are correct, registered deaths were 65 per cent of total mortality in 1998 and 69 per cent of total mortality in 2000. Accumulated AIDS deaths to the middle of 2000 were estimated at 302,790. The ASSA 2003 finds that increases in infant mortality were proportionally lower than increases in adult mortality. There is just enough information to anchor approximate estimates of fertility and mortality. Estimation of international migration is more intractable.

Immigration and emigration

First, a distinction needs to be made between international migration flows and the stock of foreign-born people in South Africa. In 1995 Colonel van Niekerk, the national coordinator of border control and policing in the South African Police Service, said that there were some 5 million illegal immigrants from Africa, Asia and Europe in South Africa, an increase from 1.2 million in 1988.[14] In the same year, Thabo Mbeki (Deputy President) put the figure for illegal immigrants at 2–3 million.[15] The 1996 population census, however, found 958,186 people born outside South Africa (excluding those living in 'collective living quarters' other than hostels), made up as indicated in Table 2.7. Of whites, 9.5 per cent were foreign born, compared with 2.7 per cent of Asians, 1.6 per cent of Africans and 0.4 per cent of coloureds. The census did not ask about legality of residence, so the number of foreign-born people would include those legally present in the country, some of whom would have acquired citizenship. Statistics South Africa publishes data on self-declared emigrants (South African residents who, at the time of departing from South Africa, state their intention to leave the country and reside permanently elsewhere) and on documented immigrants (residents of other countries who have been accepted as permanent residents of South Africa, this status being awarded before or after arrival in South Africa). The statistics for the 1990s are reported in Table 2.8.

Statistics South Africa has compared South African emigration statistics with statistics of the stocks of South African citizens or residents abroad in the five leading overseas destination countries for South African emigrants: the USA, Australia, New Zealand, Canada and the UK. Flows are inferred from successive stock figures. Table 2.9 shows

14 *South African Survey 1995/96*, South African Institute of Race Relations, p. 30.
15 *Ibid.*

Table 2.7 *Numbers of foreign-born people living in South Africa, 1996*

Country of birth	*Number in South Africa*
Southern African Development Community	529,686
Rest of Africa	20,033
Europe	217,197
Asia	28,555
North America	5,683
Central and South America	8,689
Australia and New Zealand	3,887
Other	33,562
Not stated	110,894

Source: 2001 Census: Primary Tables 1996 and 2001, Statistics South Africa, 2001.

Table 2.8 *Numbers of documented immigrants and self-declared emigrants, 1990–2000*

Year	*Immigrants*	*Emigrants*
1990	14,499	4,722
1991	12,379	4,256
1992	8,686	4,289
1993	9,824	8,078
1994	6,398	10,235
1995	5,064	8,725
1996	5,407	9,708
1997	4,103	8,946
1998	4,371	9,031
1999	3,669	8,487
2000	3,053	10,262

Source: Documented Migration, 2003, Report 03-51-03, Statistics South Africa, 2003, table 1.

Table 2.9 *Comparison of South African emigration statistics and estimates of receiving country immigration, 1995*

Country	*Cumulated emigration*	*Immigrants*
USA	11,964	52,000
Australia	41,532	60,900
New Zealand	6,583	10,198
Canada	12,793	27,865
UK	91,300	84,020

Source: Documented Migration, 2003, Report 03-51-03, Statistics South Africa, 2003, table D.

the discrepancies between cumulated declared emigration (from 1970) and estimated numbers of immigrants from South Africa to each country in 1995. During the period from 1970 to 2001, South African emigration statistics record 205,022 as having left for the five main receiving countries, whereas the number of South African citizens or residents arriving in these countries is estimated at 322,499 over the same period. One of the remarkable features is the slowing of the rate of granting of permanent residence. At a historical peak of 50,464 in 1975, it slowed to 17,284 in 1985 and 3,053 in 2000, from which it picked up again, to 10,578 in 2003.

Un-enumerated international migration, then, is likely to be much higher than recorded international migration. Of course, it is possible to argue that illegal (or, to use the current United Nations term, 'irregular') immigrants would do everything in their power to avoid enumeration and, no doubt, a considerable number behave in that way. But there is a second process at work as well, which can be called 'self-naturalisation'. As elsewhere in Africa, the state boundaries which crystallised in the late nineteenth century cut across tribal boundaries. Lesotho, Swaziland, Botswana, Mozambique and Zimbabwe all share tribal populations with South Africa. Given South Africa's long northern border and its border with Lesotho, people have always found it possible to filter across the boundaries and to blend in with South African communities. The process is not confined to South Africa's rural areas or small towns; nor is it necessarily confined to tribal groups divided by state boundaries. In a study of social conditions in Johannesburg's inner city, which included the flatlands of Hillbrow, Joubert Park and Berea,[16] 40 per cent of the population returned itself as Zulu-speaking, much higher than any other linguistic group. Some of these people must have been foreigners in the process of constructing fictive South African origins – a process which starts with arrival, then assimilating the norms of a South African group and often ending up with a visit to a friendly Home Affairs official who will provide documents confirming the new identity. Such people then have little to fear from statistical enumeration, but at no time do they show up as international immigrants.

Two factors increasing movement across South Africa's borders were the war in Mozambique in the 1980s, when an estimated 350,000 refugees fled to South Africa,[17] and sharply deteriorating economic and

16 Charles Simkins, *Social Conditions in Johannesburg's Inner City at the Time of the 2001 Population Census*, report prepared for the Johannesburg City Council, 2004.

17 Jonathan Crush and Vincent Williams (eds), *Making Up the Numbers: Measuring 'Illegal Immigration' to South Africa*, Migration Policy Brief No. 3, Southern African Migration Project, 2001, p. 17.

Table 2.10 *Migrant population in South Africa*

Category	*Number*
Lawful entrants and stayers	
Skilled migrants on annually renewable visas and work permits	60,000
Contract mineworkers	190,000
Special zone agricultural workers (border areas)	20,000
Unlawful entrants and stayers	Unknown
Lawful entrants, unlawful stayers	
Contract workers who stay beyond the end of their jobs	
Entrants for purposes other than work who have jobs	
Entrants whose residence permits have expired	350,000
Unlawful entrants, lawful stayers	
Asylum seekers and refugees	250,000
Successful applicants for the immigration amnesty of 1996	
Undocumented migrants legalised for work purposes	11,000

Source: Making Up the Numbers: Measuring 'Illegal Immigration' to South Africa, Migration Policy Brief No. 3, Southern African Migration Project, 2001, p. 17.

political conditions in Zimbabwe after 2000. Neither of these is likely to have much influenced immigration in the 1990s; indeed, about 70,000 returned under a voluntary repatriation programme (run by the United Nations High Commissioner for Refugees) to Mozambique in the early 1990s.[18] Jonathan Crush breaks down the migrant population into constituent categories, based on legality of entry and legality of stay.[19] Table 2.10 sets out his findings.

Finally, Statistics South Africa's migration estimates for African immigration were 81,000 for the period 1991–95 and 145,000 for the period 1996–2000.[20] Population dynamics can be investigated only within the framework of a coherent demographic model. Table 2.11 sets out the principal results of the ASSA model, which has the following features:

- rapid population growth in the early 1990s, fuelled by the assumption of high immigration during that period (thereafter, population growth slows to just over 1.5 per cent in 2000);
- a decline in the total fertility rate from 3.76 in 1990 to 2.82 in 2000;
- a decline in life expectancy at birth from 62.5 years in 1990 to 56.2

18 *Ibid.*
19 *Ibid.*
20 'Mid-year population estimates, 2005 and 2006', Statistics South Africa, table 4.

Table 2.11 *Population summary statistics and trends, 1990–2000*

	1990	*1991*	*1992*	*1993*	*1994*	*1995*	*1996*	*1997*	*1998*	*1999*	*2000*
Population	36,129,744	36,987,349	38,015,542	39,031,589	40,026,130	40,985,799	41,886,566	42,700,054	43,471,883	44,196,808	44,871,939
Growth		2.37%	2.78%	2.67%	2.55%	2.40%	2.20%	1.94%	1.81%	1.67%	1.53%
Total fertility rate	3.76	3.67	3.57	3.47	3.37	3.26	3.17	3.08	2.99	2.91	2.82
Life expectancy at birth	62.5	62.5	62.5	62.4	62.1	61.7	61.0	59.8	58.4	57.1	56.2
Infant mortality rate (per 1,000)	48	48	47	47	48	50	52	55	57	59	60
Migration	74,864	239,074	221,128	198,053	167,683	118,738	42,565	38,709	34,891	31,109	27,360
Percentage less than 15	38.4%	38.0%	37.5%	37.0%	36.5%	35.9%	35.3%	34.9%	34.5%	34.0%	33.6%
Percentage 15–59	55.3%	55.6%	56.0%	56.5%	57.0%	57.6%	58.2%	58.5%	58.9%	59.3%	59.7%
Percentage 60+	6.3%	6.4%	6.4%	6.5%	6.5%	6.5%	6.5%	6.6%	6.7%	6.7%	6.8%

Source: Actuarial Society of South Africa, ASSA 2003 model.

years in 2000 and a rise in infant mortality from 48 per 1,000 in 1990 to 60 in 2000, both occasioned by AIDS;
- total net immigration of nearly 1.2 million during the decade;
- a drop in the proportion of the population aged under 15 from 38.4 per cent in 1990 to 33.6 per cent in 2000, accompanied by a rise in the population aged 15–59 from 55.3 per cent in 1990 to 59.7 per cent in 2000 and a rise in the population aged 60 or over from 6.3 per cent to 6.8 per cent.

The 1990s, therefore, were a transitional period in South African population history in at least three separate ways. First, there was a continuing fertility transition. By the end of the decade South Africa had reached the late stages of its fertility transition and, for that reason alone, population growth could be expected to slow further in the following decade. Second, there was the transition to high rates of HIV infection and AIDS mortality, with the scene set for a further drop in life expectancy in the following decade. Third, there was (probably) a transition to higher rates of African and irregular immigration.

There is a correlation between province of residence and first home language, as can be seen from Table 2.12. This is not surprising given that the new South African provinces are the outcome of historical patterns of settlement, already largely crystallised at the end of the nineteenth century. The correlation is clearest in the Eastern Cape, Free State, KwaZulu-Natal, Northern Cape and North West, where over 60 per cent of the population speaks predominantly a single language in each case, respectively IsiXhosa, Sesotho, IsiZulu, Afrikaans and Setswana. Limpopo is a variant, with 90 per cent speaking one of Sepedi, Tshivenda or Xitsonga. Mpumalanga is another: the preponderance of IsiNdebele and SiSwati speakers live alongside a considerable number of IsiZulu and Sepedi speakers. The Western Cape, like the Northern Cape, is dominantly Afrikaans speaking, though a dynamic aspect is the rapidly increasing number of IsiXhosa in the province. Gauteng, defined as an economic entity, is the exception to the rule: seven out of the 11 South African linguistic groups had more than half a million representatives there in 1996.

This picture can be complemented by an account of inter-provincial migration flows. The 2001 census enumeration of migration was probably more complete than that of the 1996 census. Table 2.13 presents the results. The two provinces which were greatest gainers of population through migration were the two richest – Gauteng and the Western Cape – and the two provinces which were the greatest losers were the two poorest – Eastern Cape and Limpopo. Gauteng gained more than 100,000 people over the five years from each of Limpopo, KwaZulu-Natal

Table 2.12 *First home language by province, 1996*

	Eastern Cape	*Free State*	*Gauteng*	*KwaZulu-Natal*	*Limpopo*	*Mpumalanga*	*Northern Cape*	*North West*	*Western Cape*	*Total*
Afrikaans	600,252	379,994	1,213,353	136,223	109,225	230,348	577,586	249,500	2,315,067	5,811,548
English	233,375	35,154	947,570	1,316,047	21,261	54,839	19,901	34,107	795,212	3,457,466
IsiNdebele	1,250	4,450	114,900	1,230	72,507	346,337	286	42,835	3,165	586,960
IsiXhosa	5,250,524	245,100	543,699	132,223	8,597	36,379	52,688	178,930	747,978	7,196,118
IsiZulu	25,322	125,079	1,559,520	6,658,439	36,252	706,817	2,304	82,070	4,344	9,200,147
Sepedi	2,570	4,708	688,607	1,776	2,572,492	291,923	261	132,376	1,135	3,695,848
Sesotho	139,671	1,625,954	953,239	45,677	56,001	90,011	7,420	171,549	14,677	3,104,199
Setswana	896	171,253	573,103	2,147	70,340	75,202	165,778	2,239,774	3,312	3,301,805
SiSwati	863	3,594	92,155	7,342	57,147	834,133	88	17,268	554	1,013,144
Tshivenda	514	1,713	99,838	595	757,682	3,346	87	12,211	433	876,419
Xitsonga	270	14,193	382,464	1,713	1,102,472	97,842	211	156,406	535	1,756,106
Other	12,007	7,456	96,940	38,634	13,226	10,607	6,450	18,086	24,867	228,273
Unspecified	35,012	14,851	83,037	74,977	52,162	22,928	7,264	19,712	45,592	355,535
Total	6,302,526	2,633,499	7,348,425	8,417,023	4,929,364	2,800,712	840,324	3,354,824	3,956,871	40,583,568

Source: Census: Primary Tables 1996 and 2001, Statistics South Africa, 2001.

Table 2.13 *Interprovincial migration, 1996–2001*

Province of previous residence	*Eastern Cape*	*Free State*	*Gauteng*	*KwaZulu-Natal*	*Limpopo*	*Mpumalanga*	*Northern Cape*	*North West*	*Western Cape*	*Undetermined*	*Out-migration*
Eastern Cape		16,686	89,487	59,114	6,358	9,983	4,113	21,093	141,386	1,590	349,810
Free State	8,679		59,588	8,479	4,396	6,936	6,335	19,986	12,942	722	128,063
Gauteng	28,743	24,840		43,928	38,747	34,151	6,742	52,854	57,540	2,756	290,301
KwaZulu-Natal	18,160	8,849	132,020		7,076	18,673	1,839	7,905	24,474	2,046	221,042
Limpopo	2,735	4,146	170,205	5,159		37,529	1,394	21,175	5,139	983	248,465
Mpumalanga	3,231	5,716	88,367	11,163	17,877		1,474	11,467	5,956	691	145,942
Northern Cape	2,948	7,581	11,033	1,856	1,716	1,421		7,428	21,140	308	55,431
North West	4,264	10,225	107,992	4,380	11,504	6,303	16,278		6,989	819	168,754
Western Cape	26,522	5,144	32,279	9,232	2,515	3,133	9,635	3,713		1,168	93,341
Undetermined	15,876	9,448	44,580	20,962	6,181	6,665	2,246	5,615	19,296		130,869
In-migration	111,158	92,635	735,551	164,273	96,370	124,794	50,056	151,236	294,862	11,083	
Net migration	–238,652	-35,428	445,250	–56,769	–152,095	–21,148	–5,375	–17,518	201,521	–119,786	

Source: 2001 Census, Supercross Tabulations (Migration), Statistics South Africa, 2001.

Table 2.14 *Marital status by population group and gender, 1996*

	Blacks		*Coloureds*		*Asian*		*White*		*Unspecified*	
	Male	*Female*	*Male*	*Female*	*Male*	*Female*	*Male*	*Female*	*Male*	*Female*
Never married	4,969,287	5,050,532	495,821	516,168	121,676	105,015	428,015	356,593	39,366	38,687
Married: civil/religious	1,702,204	1,887,071	454,272	471,688	196,505	197,274	986,713	986,779	28,425	30,152
Married: traditional	1,346,235	1,633,551	12,903	13,678	20,795	21,163	16,527	16,344	6,101	6,647
Living together	499,545	540,905	63,087	67,568	3,524	3,503	41,349	41,575	3,634	4,274
Widowed	122,887	766,417	24,542	96,914	6,563	40,393	33,725	180,177	1,758	8,547
Divorced/separated	133,472	285,482	27,256	55,490	7,022	14,487	74,883	116,409	2,741	4,921
Unspecified	100,505	99,442	7,092	7,463	1,999	2,045	7,094	7,734	13,815	15,917
Total	8,874,135	10,263,400	1,084,973	1,228,969	358,084	383,880	1,588,306	1,705,611	95,840	109,145
Proportion never married	56.0%	49.2%	45.7%	42.0%	34.0%	27.4%	26.9%	20.9%	41.1%	35.4%
Proportion never at 50	16.7%	19.5%	14.1%	15.3%	4.4%	7.6%	4.9%	4.2%		
Proportion divorced	1.50%	2.78%	2.51%	4.52%	1.96%	3.77%	4.71%	6.83%	2.86%	4.51%
Singulate mean age at marriage	31.1	28.5	28.1	27.1	26.7	23.5	26.7	24.4		

Source: 1996 Census: Supercross Tabulations, Statistics South Africa, 1996.

and North West, and Eastern Cape and Mpumalanga each supplied nearly that many. Western Cape immigration was more specific: 48 per cent came from the Eastern Cape. The provincial shares of population vary only slowly over the decades, with a secular increase in the share of Gauteng. And population profiles remained remarkably constant, with the exception of the Western Cape.

Table 2.14 sets out the population aged 15 years and older by marital status at the time of the 1996 census. The highest proportion never married is found among blacks (just over half the population over 15), followed by coloureds, then (at some distance) by Asians and whites. To some extent, this reflects the different age structures of the population, but the proportion never married at age 50 follows the same pattern, so age structure is not the whole story. Divorce and separation show almost the same pattern, with whites in the lead and blacks having the lowest rate. Coloured divorce and separation rates, however, are lower than the Asian rates. Among those who marry, blacks marry latest in life, followed by coloureds, then whites, with Asian mean age at marriage being the lowest. Male unemployment rates are one determinant of the extent of, and mean age at, marriage. Were they to drop among blacks, particularly, one could expect the mean age at marriage to come down from its present high level.

Mean household size dropped in the late 1990s (except among whites), as Table 2.15 indicates. In part, this was a result of dropping fertility. Cross-cutting this factor was the proportion of household heads who were female in 1996, itself a function of differential marriage rates. Forty-three per cent of black households were headed by a woman, compared with 29 per cent among coloureds, 22 per cent among whites and 19 per cent among Asians. Female-headed households tend to be smaller than male-headed ones, which helps explain why coloured households were, on average, slightly larger than black ones in both 1996 and 2001.

Table 2.15 *Mean household sizes, 1996 and 2001*

	1996	*2001*
Blacks	4.76	4.11
Coloureds	4.86	4.50
Asians	4.29	3.94
Whites	2.99	3.05

Source: 2001 Census: Primary Tables, Statistics South Africa, 2001.

Conclusion

The forces shaping the South African population in the 1990s were diverse. The single most important development was the continuing drop in fertility, representing a drive to sociological modernisation. It paves the way for higher levels of human capital. So far this has been realised in the form of more years spent in the educational system. Average quality of output has yet to rise significantly. Fertility rates dropping towards replacement levels normally indicate a shift from a wasteful to an efficient demographic regime. However, the rising mortality associated with HIV/AIDS is a tragic counter-trend, with about 300,000 people dying of the disease in the 1990s.

South Africa has to come to terms with migration from the rest of the continent, though most of the 1990s were wasted when it came to the development of a viable policy framework to deal with it.[21] The single exception was the 1997 amnesty. The early part of the twenty-first century will see the working out of these themes, with major effects on the economy and society.

21 On this, see Lyndith Waller, *Irregular Migration to South African During the First Ten Years of Democracy*, Migration Policy Brief No. 19, Southern African Migration Project, 2006.

Part II

Economy

3

Agriculture

Nick Vink

Introduction

This chapter is divided into two main sections. The first gives a sectoral overview of agriculture in the 1990s and the second looks at the impact of the policy shifts on the field crop, horticulture and livestock sub-sectors, respectively.

The changes in agricultural policy in South Africa are described in Chapter 22, but as this chapter inevitably discusses the impacts of some of these changes, it may be useful to summarise here briefly the agricultural policy reforms in South Africa in that decade. These included:

- a reduction in general support to agriculture in a process that started in the 1980s but continued through the 1990s;
- a reduction in commodity-specific subsidies, starting in the late 1970s and completed in the early 1990s;
- trade liberalisation as a result of the Agreement on Agriculture in 1994;
- deregulation of agricultural markets in a 'big bang' process during 1997.

These reforms were triggered by external macro-economic factors, when attempts to stabilise the economy, starting in the late 1970s, resulted in a rapid increase in interest rates to farmers, which had an immediate and strong impact on agriculture, triggering a long period of piecemeal deregulation in agricultural markets throughout the 1980s, followed by more concerted reforms during the 1990s. It is obviously difficult to ascribe a change in agriculture to the impact of a single policy change at a specific point in time; hence the discussion here focuses on the broader changes that took place within a policy environment that was relatively unstable over a period of up to two decades.

Sector-level changes

The impact of the policy shifts at sector level can be traced in the shifts in the contribution to GDP, in employment trends, in the extent of subsidisation to agriculture, in the trends in net farm income over time, in the changes to total factor productivity, in the competitiveness of the agricultural sector, in the composition of the export and import portfolios, in the distribution of farm sizes and in the composition of the country's agricultural output. Each of these changes is discussed in turn, before a brief comment is made on land reform over the decade.

Contribution to GDP

The structure of the South African economy differs somewhat from that of the other middle-income developing countries in the world. Table 3.1 shows these structural features for the middle-income countries as a whole and for South Africa. It is evident from these data that the agricultural sector is considerably smaller, relative to the rest of the economy, in South Africa, although the manufacturing sector is of the same order of magnitude as in other middle-income countries. However, this is largely because of the size of the mining sector in South Africa: when the primary sectors (agriculture, forestry, fishing, mining and quarrying) are added together, they contributed 14.4 per cent to GDP in 1990 and 10.1 per cent in 2004, which is in line with the contribution in middle-income countries. Table 3.1 also shows that the GDP contribution of the primary and secondary sectors is declining, as would be expected for a middle-income country.

Table 3.1 *Contribution to GDP of the agricultural and manufacturing sectors, 1990 and 2004 (%)*

	Agriculture		*Manufacturing*	
	1990	*2004*	*1990*	*2004*
Middle-income countries	16	10	25	18
South Africa: agriculture	5	3	24	20
South Africa: primary sectors	14.4	10.1		

Source: World Bank, *World Development Indicators*, International Bank for Reconstruction and Development, 2006.

Table 3.2 provides a general overview of the performance of the sector between 1993 and 2002 and indicates that the 1990s represented a period of prosperity for the sector. This was especially the case after

Table 3.2 *Principal statistics from the 2002 census of commercial agriculture*

	1993	*2002*	*Change (%)*
Number of farming units	57,980	45,818	–21%
Number of people in employment	1,161,912	986,842	–15.1%
Employees' cash remuneration (at constant 2002 prices) (R1,000s)	5,782,480	6,215,583	+7.5%
Gross farming income (at constant 2002 prices) (R1,000s)	38,813,291	52,971,214	+36.5%
Expenditure (at constant 2002 prices) (R1,000s)	33,984,385	45,038,908	+32.5%
Current	29,671,164	42,092,135	+41.8%
Capital	4,313,221	2,946,773	–31.7%
Market value of farming assets (at constant 2002 prices) (R1,000s)	138,836,539	98,428,254	–29.1%
Farming debt (at constant 2002 prices) (R1,000s)	31,738,817	30,857,891	–2.8%

Source: Census of Commercial Agriculture 2002: Financial and Production Statistics, Statistics South Africa, 2005.

the region-wide drought during the 1994/95 production season, which affected only the rate of growth in total agricultural production, as the declines in field crop production were more than compensated for by growth in the livestock and horticultural sectors. This increase in production resulted in a less than proportionate increase in recurrent and capital expenditure (33 per cent compared with 37 per cent), while at the same time the market value of farming assets (in real terms) declined by almost 30 per cent, largely as a result of the decline in the real value of farm land. Real current expenditure increased substantially over the period (by 42 per cent), while real capital expenditure declined by 32 per cent. Farming debt, however, declined only marginally in real terms, showing that borrowing was for recurrent expenditure rather than capital investment.

Employment trends

The 2002 census of commercial agriculture confirmed the continued exodus of commercial farmers from the sector, with the number of farmers declining by a fifth over the decade (Table 3.2). Employment declined by less: in this case by 15 per cent, to below 1 million in 2002. At the same time the real cash remuneration of employees increased by nearly 8 per cent, in a period before the introduction of the minimum wage. This conforms to the finding in the 'sector determination' for agriculture that real wages in the sector had increased at above the average rate for the country as a whole during the period 1970–98.[1] Despite this increase in the real wage, the unit cost of labour, measured as the ratio of the total cost of labour to the total value of output, remained relatively stable. In 1970, 16 cents was spent on labour for every R1 of output produced. This decreased to 13 cents in 1980, increased to 19 cents in 1994 and then decreased to 17 cents in 1998.

The 1996 agricultural survey[2] found that the average cash wage paid to regular and casual workers in agriculture was R419 per month or R544 per month at 2001 prices. At a provincial level there was considerable variation. Workers in Gauteng were paid an average of R790 per month, while those in the Free State and Northern Province received R407 and R416 per month, respectively. Aside from a cash wage, workers received additional income under the heading of 'other remuneration'. While cash wages varied across the provinces, the 'other remuneration' was fairly constant and averaged about 20 per cent of total remuneration. However, average wage data hide the distribution of wages. This is a particular problem in agriculture, where the distribution of wages consists of a clustering of workers at the lower levels and a distinct tailing off at the upper end of the distribution.

While agriculture has historically been a major employer, this role has diminished. Total employment on farms declined from 1,184,000 in 1990 to approximately 960,000 in 2001.[3] The introduction of labour regulation 'has been unable to stem the decline in employment' or the casualisation of the remaining labour force – both of which have undermined the social role played by agriculture.[4] A third of farm workers lost their jobs between 1985 and 1996.[5] Job losses among unskilled general workers continued thereafter, alongside an increase in the employment of skilled workers, while the overall number of people employed declined. In addition, the sector saw a shift to non-permanent or seasonal labour – the so-called casualisation of labour. Poor living and working conditions on many commercial farms meant that, by many socio-economic indicators, farm workers were the poorest South Africans and in some respects they were worse off than the

1 *Determination of Employment Conditions in South African Agriculture,* a report by the Department of Labour prepared together with the Centre for Rural Legal Studies and the National Institute of Economic Policy, Department of Labour, 2001.

2 *Agricultural Survey,* Statistics South Africa, 1996.

3 *Abstract of Agricultural Statistics,* National Department of Agriculture, 2006.

4 Nick Vink and Johann Kirsten, 'Agriculture in the national economy', in Lieb Niewoudt and Jan Groenewald (eds), *The Challenge of Change: Agriculture, Land and the South African Economy,* University of Natal Press, 2003, pp. 3–20.

5 *Determination of Employment Conditions in South African Agriculture,* p. 50.

unemployed.[6] Although real wages increased faster in agriculture than in other sectors during the 1990s, farm workers, together with domestic workers, remained the lowest-paid workers in formal employment.[7] By the end of the 1990s, labour accounted for a smaller proportion of input costs than it did in the previous decade, and in real terms the unit cost of labour had declined.[8]

In terms of the impact of state policy, 'the rural poor, including farm and other rural workers, and the rural unemployed have not (in aggregate) benefited, nor are they expected to benefit in the absence of state intervention'.[9] Although hard data do not exist, anecdotal evidence from all provinces suggests that evictions from farms substantially contributed to the growth of dense rural informal settlements, as well as to the growth of peri-urban informal settlements in both urban centres and in the *platteland*.[10] Farmers' interests in evicting those no longer employed were, according to AgriSA, compounded by the very legislation designed to stem evictions. However, the rise in the rate of farm evictions was also an indirect effect of long-term changes in the agricultural economy, as evictions usually followed job losses. Survey data now suggest that the loss of livelihoods resulting from disemployment and evictions from farms during the 1990s outweighed the creation of new livelihoods in agriculture through land reform.[11]

Level of subsidisation

South African agriculture has been subjected to analyses by the Food and Agriculture Organization of the United Nations,[12] the Organisation for Economic Co-operation and Development (OECD)[13] and the World

6 *Ibid.*, p. 70.

7 Vink and Kirsten, 'Agriculture in the national economy', p. 13.

8 *Ibid.*, p. 14.

9 *Ibid.*, p. 12.

10 C. Cross, S. Bekker, N. Mlambo, K. Kleinbooi, L. Saayman, H. Pretorius, T. Mngadi and T. Mbhele, *An Unstable Balance: Migration, Small Farming, Infrastructure, and Livelihoods in the Coastal Provinces*, unpublished report, Development Bank of Southern Africa, 1999; R. Hall, *Farm Tenure*, Evaluating Land and Agrarian Reform in South Africa No. 3, Programme for Land and Agrarian Studies, University of the Western Cape, 2003.

11 Marc Wegerif, Bev Russell and Irma Grundling, *Still Searching for Security: The Reality of Farm Worker Evictions in South Africa*, Nkuzi Development Association/Social Surveys, 2005.

12 Nick Vink, *Macroeconomic and Sector Policy Changes in South African Agriculture, 1996–2002*, FAO Project on the Roles of Agriculture in Developing Countries, Food and Agriculture Organization, 2003.

13 *Review of Agricultural Policies: South Africa*, Organisation for Economic Co-operation and Development, 2006.

Table 3.3 *Measures of support to South African agriculture, 1990–2000*

		1990	*1991*	*1992*	*1993*	*1994*	*1995*	*1996*	*1997*	*1998*	*1999*	*2000*
OECD	PSE					10	16	8	12	8	9	5
Kirsten *et al.*, 2000	PSE							1.78	10.89	4.18		
Helm and Van Zyl	PSE	11.56	13.69	16.74	31.04	14.50						
Kirsten *et al.*, 2006	TRA					5.36	7.06	–1.40	3.91	–8.28	–3.92	–3.85

Notes: PSE = producer support estimate (formerly producer subsidy equivalent); TRA = total rate of assistance. Both measure direct and indirect support to farmers, with the indirect support measured as the difference between world and domestic prices.
Sources: Review of Agricultural Policies: South Africa, Organisation for Economic Co-operation and Development, 2006; J. F. Kirsten, M. Gouse, N. Tregurtha N. Vink and J. Tswai, *Producer Subsidy Equivalents (PSE) for South African Agriculture for 1996, 1997, 1998,* report to the National Department of Agriculture, 6 March 2000; W. Helm and J. Van Zyl, 'Domestic agricultural support in South Africa from 1988/89 to 1993/94: a calculation', paper presented at the AEASA conference, Pretoria, 19–20 September 1994; Johann Kirsten, Lawrence Edwards and Nick Vink, 'Distortions to agricultural incentives in South Africa: 1995–2000', draft working paper, International Bank for Reconstruction and Development, 2006.

Bank.[14] These institutions have used a range of measures to describe the extent and the nature of state intervention in the agricultural sector. The results are summarised in Table 3.3. The high producer support estimate (PSE) in 1992/93 was the result of a huge one-off increase in direct income support to farmers, from R250 million the previous year to R2.6 billion.[15] This came in the form of a drought relief package, announced by the government in 1992, which consisted of R2.4 billion in debt relief. On average, these estimates of support to agriculture reflect the change in policy from protection in the 1970s and 1980s to a more liberal market in the 1990s. This is consistent with the abolition of the control boards and trade liberalisation under the Marrakesh Agreement on Agriculture.

Net farm income

Net farm income is a measure of the profitability of farming enterprises. It is calculated as gross farm income (turnover) minus depreciation, salaries and wages, interest and rent. Figure 3.1 shows the trends in real

14 Johann Kirsten, Lawrence Edwards and Nick Vink, 'Distortions to agricultural incentives in South Africa: 1955–2000', draft working paper, International Bank for Reconstruction and Development, 2006.

15 M. Rimmer, 'Debt relief and the South African drought relief programme: an overview', unpublished working paper, Land and Agricultural Policy Centre, 1993.

Figure 3.1 *Real gross and net farm income, and the cost of intermediate goods, 1989–2000*

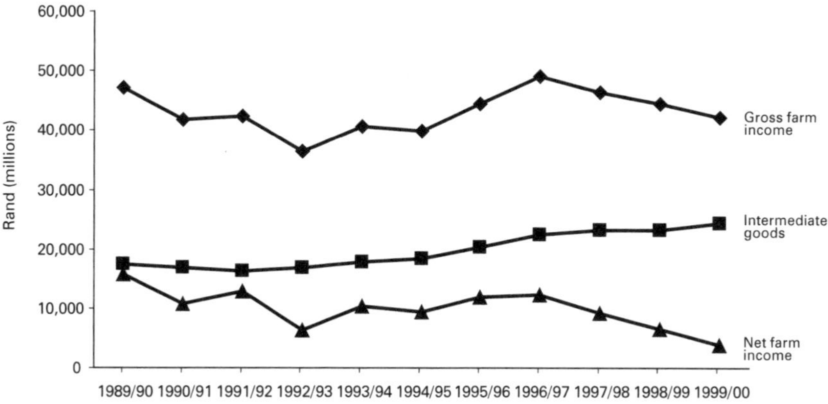

Source: Adapted from *Abstract of Agricultural Statistics*, National Department of Agriculture, 2006.

gross and net farm income and the cost of intermediate goods at prices in 2000. The trends in real gross and net farm income reflect the rapid increase in the producer price index for food products in the second half of the 1990s, which coincided with the economic downturn of 1997–99.

This decline in real net farm income should, however, be seen in perspective. Figure 3.2 shows that the value of capital assets in agriculture declined rapidly throughout the first half of the 1990s, then increased moderately in the second half of the decade. As a result, the amount

Figure 3.2 *Real value of capital assets on commercial farms, 1990–2000*

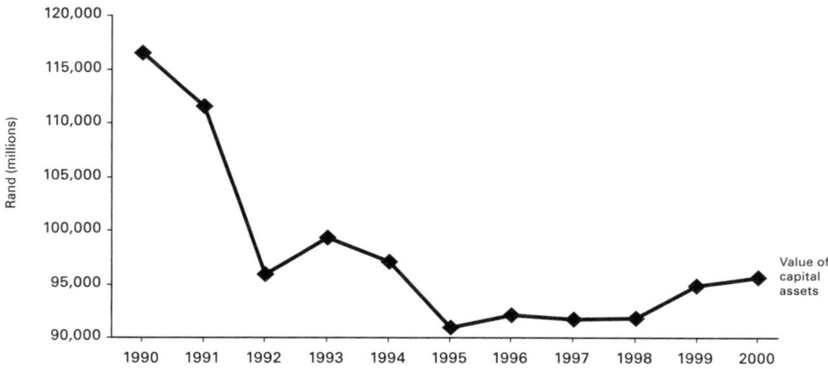

Source: Adapted from *Abstract of Agricultural Statistics*, National Department of Agriculture, 2006.

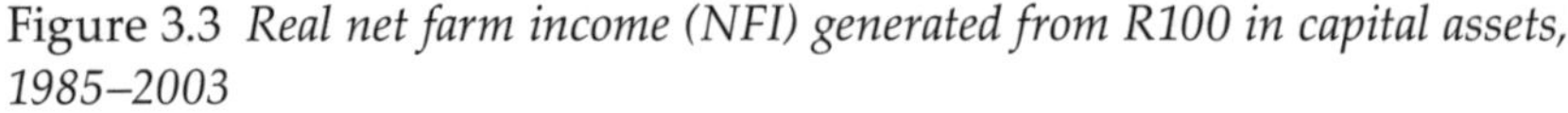

Figure 3.3 *Real net farm income (NFI) generated from R100 in capital assets, 1985–2003*

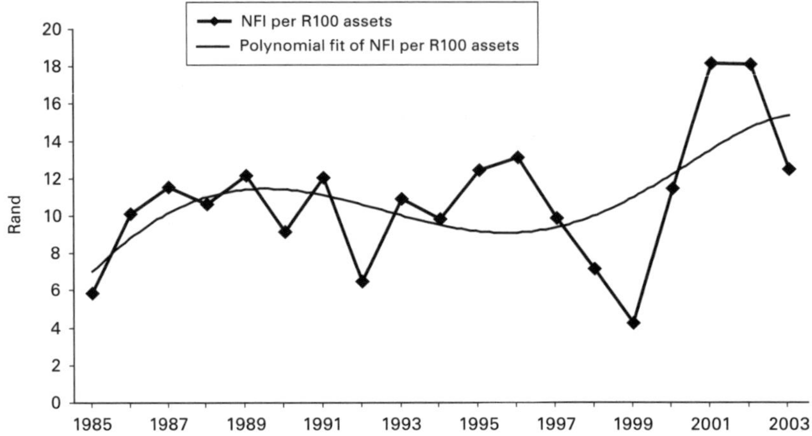

Source: Adapted from *Abstract of Agricultural Statistics,* National Department of Agriculture, 2006.

of real net farm income generated from each R100 in assets increased in the second half of the decade (Figure 3.3), evidence of improved efficiency in the use of capital.

Total factor productivity

The suggestion of improved efficiency in the use of capital is supported by the data on total factor productivity (TFP) (Figure 3.4). After remaining relatively constant through the first part of the decade, TFP, which measures physical output and the physical quantities of inputs used, declined with the drought in 1994/95, but then reversed in 1995/96.

Competitiveness of agriculture

Esterhuizen[16] used the Revealed Trade Advantage Index, an extension of the well known Revealed Comparative Advantage Index, to measure the extent of competitiveness of agribusiness supply chains in South Africa. His most important conclusions follow. First, South African agriculture as a whole was no more than marginally competitive in the global market. Second, South African agriculture was most competitive

16 Dirk Esterhuizen, *An Evaluation of the Competitiveness of the South African Agribusiness Sector,* unpublished PhD thesis, University of Pretoria, 2006.

Figure 3.4 *Output, input and total factor productivity (TFP) indices, 1985–2000*

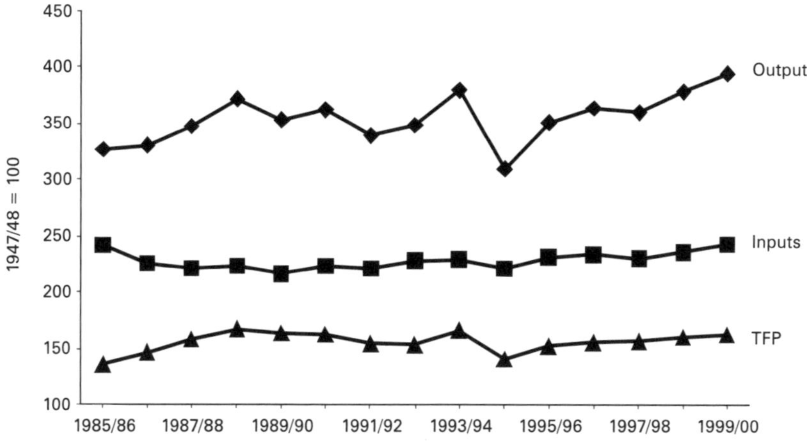

Source: Updated from C. Thirtle, H. J. Sartorius von Bach and J. van Zyl, 'Total factor productivity in South African agriculture, 1947–91', *Development Southern Africa*, 10(3) (August 1993), 310–318. Updated to 2000 by Thirtle. The raw data are available from the author.

in the mid-1970s and least competitive in 1985, with the degree of competitiveness increasing after 1993. Internationally, South Africa can be classified as a 'rising moderate performer', along with a number of EU member states such as Belgium, Germany, Italy and the UK, and Canada. This is in contrast to Argentina, Brazil, Chile, Australia and New Zealand, all strong competitors in export markets.

Table 3.4 *Competitiveness trends in agricultural supply chains, 1993–2002*

Competitiveness trend in the value chain	*Competitiveness of the primary product*		
	Competitive	*Marginal*	*Not competitive*
Increasing	Maize, apples, pineapples, grapefruit, mohair	Wheat, tobacco, chicken meat, pork	Cotton, barley
Decreasing	Sugar, groundnuts, oranges, grapes, wool, plums, hen eggs, hides and skins	Potatoes, sunflower, tomatoes, milk, soybeans, mushrooms, olives, beef	

Source: Dirk Esterhuizen, *An Evaluation of the Competitiveness of the South African Agribusiness Sector*, unpublished PhD thesis, University of Pretoria, 2006.

During the 1990s in South Africa, primary production was generally more competitive than the value-adding downstream industries, though the competitiveness of both was increasing over time. Subsectors that showed increasing competitiveness included maize, apples, pineapples, grapefruit and mohair (Table 3.4). No subsectors that were uncompetitive showed decreasing competitiveness.

Trade portfolio

Table 3.5 shows the trends in South Africa's agricultural trade during the 1990s. A number of important shifts can be identified. Agriculture's share of total exports increased during the 1990s to reach the levels achieved before the era of sanctions, so that during the 1990s agriculture played the role of a catalyst of export-led growth (Figure 3.5).

The effect of sanctions and the regulatory environment of the 1970s and 1980s led to exports reaching a low of less than 20 per cent of total output in the early 1990s (Figure 3.6). A recovery began in 1995–96, and by the end of the decade the proportion exported had regained the level of the early 1980s. During the 1990s the sector achieved little more than a re-entry into markets lost during the 1980s.

Table 3.5 *Trends in South Africa's agricultural trade, 1989–2001*

	1989–91	*1994–96*	*1999–2001*
Exports			
Total agricultural exports (R millions)	5,034	9,339	16,889
Agricultural exports as % of total exports	8.21	8.81	8.16
Agricultural exports as % of total agricultural output	23.49	29.61	35.32
Processed agricultural exports (R millions)	2,620	4,470	10,356
Unprocessed agricultural exports (R millions)	2,413	4,868	6,533
Processed agricultural exports as a % of total exports	52	48	61
Imports			
Total agricultural imports (R millions)	2,091	6,491	9,775
Agricultural imports as % of total imports	4.58	6.67	5.33
Agricultural imports as % of total agricultural output	9.76	20.58	20.44
Import cover (agricultural exports/ agricultural imports)	2.41	1.44	1.73
Exports + imports/total production (%)	33	50	56

Source: Adapted from *Abstract of Agricultural Statistics*, National Department of Agriculture, 2006.

Figure 3.5 *Agriculture's contribution to total exports, 1979–2000*

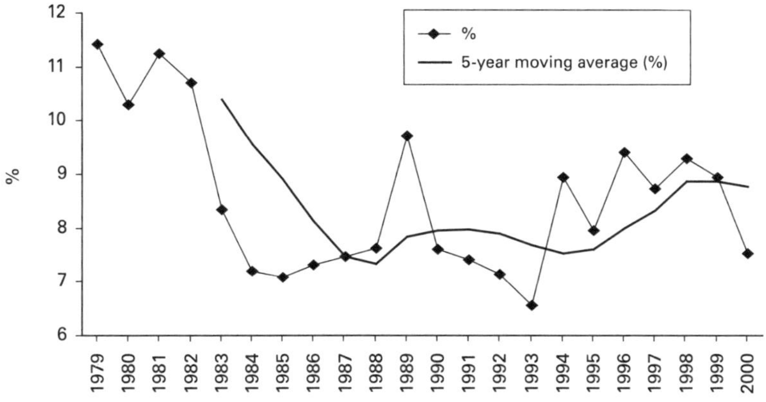

Source: Adapted from *Abstract of Agricultural Statistics,* National Department of Agriculture, 2006.

Figure 3.6 *Share of agricultural output exported, 1965–2000*

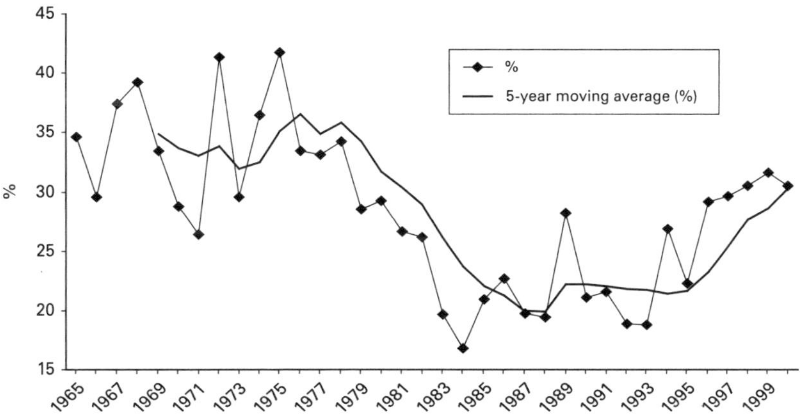

Source: Adapted from *Abstract of Agricultural Statistics,* National Department of Agriculture, 2006.

Over the 1990s, exports of processed agricultural products increased faster than exports of unprocessed agricultural products – increasing in proportion to around 60 per cent. Agricultural imports grew faster than agricultural exports, with agriculture's share of total imports increasing from 4.6 to 5.3 per cent. Imports increased from 9.8 per cent of total agricultural output to 20.4 per cent. As a result, import cover (the ratio of agricultural exports to agricultural imports, a measure of the ability of the agricultural sector to pay for its own imports) declined from 2.4–1 to 1.7–1. The increased 'openness' of the sector to trade may be seen in the ratio of exports and imports to total agricultural production.

There were three further shifts in the structure of South Africa's agricultural trade during the 1990s.[17] First, while the EU remained (and remains) the largest destination for agricultural exports, there was a rapid increase in exports to the rest of Africa. These made up 25 per cent of total agricultural exports by 2000. South Africa had a positive trade balance in agricultural and food products of around R2.5 billion with those member countries of the Southern African Development Community (SADC) that were not members of the Southern African Customs Union (SACU), but only three SADC countries featured in the top 25 import sources, namely Zimbabwe, Zambia and Malawi. Second, the 25 most important agricultural and food exports from South Africa were responsible for 92.2 per cent of total agricultural export earnings in 2000, with the horticultural industry responsible for 45.1 per cent and processed exports about half. Third, Argentina emerged as the main supplier of food and agricultural imports into South Africa (largely poultry feed). It was followed by the USA, the UK, Australia and Zimbabwe.

Distribution of farm sizes

Little is known about the distribution of farm sizes in South African agriculture. The census of 2002 provided data on the commercial farming sector (Table 3.6); according to the data, the 673 largest farming enterprises, representing 1.5 per cent of the commercial farmers, produced 33.5 per cent of gross farm income, using 16.5 per cent of the capital in agriculture. These farmers were responsible for 27.6 per cent of the capital expenditure in agriculture and paid cash wages that were some 66 per cent higher than the average cash wage in the sector. Farm enterprises having a turnover of more than R1 million per year dominated the picture, with these 23.1 per cent of farmers responsible for

17 Nick Vink, Norma Tregurtha and Johann Kirsten, *South Africa's Changing Agricultural, Food and Beverage Imports: Implications for SADC Suppliers. A Report to the World Bank*, unpublished mimeo, Department of Agricultural Economics, University of Stellenbosch, 2002.

Table 3.6 *Principal farming statistics by income group, 2002*

Income (R per year)	*No. of farms*	*Cumu-lative %*	*Wage per employee (R per year)*	*Gross farm income (R1,000 per year)*	*Cumu-lative %*	*Gross farm income per R1 of capital expenditure*	*Market value of assets (R1,000 per year)*	*Cumu-lative %*
Above 10,000,000	673	1.5	10,503	17,850,383	33.5	27.59	16,257,953	16.5
4,000,000–9,999,999	1,657	5.1	7,758	10,330,424	52.8	23.48	14,188,233	30.9
2,000,000–3,999,999	3,041	11.7	4,872	5,056,986	62.3	11.65	15,132,953	46.3
1,000,000–1,999,999	5,214	23.1	6,743	7,351,291	76.1	20.28	13,022,084	59.5
30,000–999,999	11,805	48.9	4,729	5,335,646	86.1	17.13	11,802,362	71.5
<300,000	2,3428	100	4,266	7 404 322	100	9.85	28,024 669	100
Total	45,818		6,298	53,329,052		18.1	98,428,255	

Source: Census of Commercial Agriculture 2002: Financial and Production Statistics, Statistics South Africa, 2005.

76.1 per cent of total output. This was typical of commercial agriculture globally. Conversely, the three-quarters of the farm enterprises with a turnover of less than R1 million per year were responsible for less than a quarter of gross farm income. These farmers paid less than the average cash wage and produced less than R10 for every R1 of capital expenditure, compared with the national average of R18 and almost R28 for the largest enterprises.

Composition of output

Given that most of South Africa is unsuited to cultivation, it is no surprise that the largest component of production comes from livestock, with field crop production substantially larger than horticulture in 1989/90 but less so in 1999/2000 (Figure 3.7). These data reflect the increasing importance of horticultural exports as a share of total agricultural output.

Figure 3.7 *Composition of farm output, 1989/90 and 1999/2000*

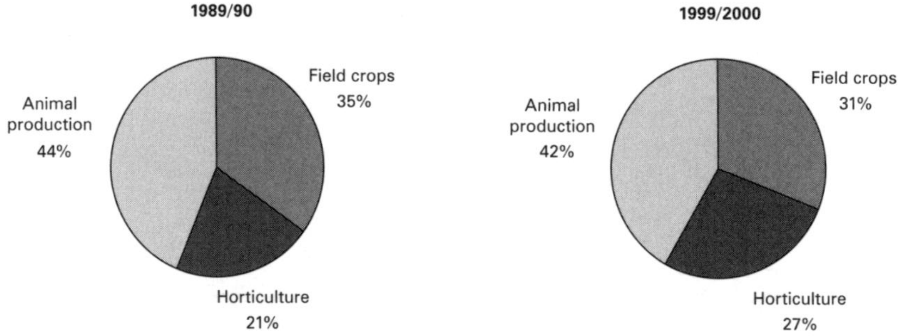

1989/90

Animal production 44%

Field crops 35%

Horticulture 21%

1999/2000

Animal production 42%

Field crops 31%

Horticulture 27%

Source: Adapted from *Abstract of Agricultural Statistics*, National Department of Agriculture, 2006.

Land reform

The 1990s saw little progress with the transfer of land ownership from commercial farmers to black farmers. Only some 1 million hectares of land, or less than 1 per cent, had been transferred by the end of 1999. This included 263,868 hectares through the restitution programme and 752,027 hectares through the redistribution and tenure reform programme.[18]

18 Commission on the Restitution of Land Rights (CRLR), *Honouring the Promise of Our Constitution: Strategic Plan 2003/04 to 2005/06*, unpublished document; Department of Land Affairs (DLA), internal electronic data supplied by the Department of Land Affairs Monitoring and Evaluation Directorate, February 2003.

Changes at the subsectoral level

Field crop production

The main changes in field crop production have been in the area planted and in average yields. Figure 3.8 shows the area planted with the principal field crops: maize, wheat, soya beans, sugar cane and cotton. The area planted with maize, which has traditionally fluctuated considerably because production is largely rain-fed, declined after the drought in the mid-1990s and had not recovered fully by the end of the decade. The area planted with wheat did not recover and had declined to below 1 million hectares by 1998/99. Sugar cane production moved in the opposite direction, its area under cultivation increasing throughout the decade. Despite the decline in the area planted with maize and wheat (and the other summer crops), output generally increased (Figure 3.9) as a result of rising yields (Figure 3.10).

With deregulation, the prices of field crops generally adjusted downwards to world market levels, and thereafter fluctuated with world market prices. As a result, commercial grain farmers shifted to minimum-tillage and low-tillage production systems. The result was a rapid decline in the use of fertilisers, insecticides and herbicides, tractors, combine harvesters and other implements, and fuel. These changes allowed farmers to maintain total output of the major field crops using fewer inputs, which also ensured more environmentally sustainable production. These new production practices have reduced the negative impact of agriculture on the environment.

Most of the major field crops had been sold under a 'single-channel fixed price' marketing regime, characterised by pan-territorial and pan-seasonal pricing. The main consequence of pan-territorial prices was that farmers closer to the market were effectively cross-subsidising those further away. With deregulation, prices started to become regionally differentiated, to reflect transport costs and regional variations in demand and supply. Another consequence of deregulation was that processors who had moved closer to the market (they paid the same price irrespective of the point of delivery) faced increased competition from small-scale processors, both on- and off-farm, who milled an increasing proportion of the maize crop. Industry estimates suggest this can be as high as 30 per cent of the crop. The main result of pan-seasonal pricing was that no grain was stored on-farm, as the entire crop was sold immediately after harvest. With deregulation, there has been an increase in on-farm storage.

As field crop prices adjusted downwards to world market levels there was also an on-farm shift in field crop production to better-quality soils

Figure 3.8 *Area planted with the principal field crops, 1989–2000*

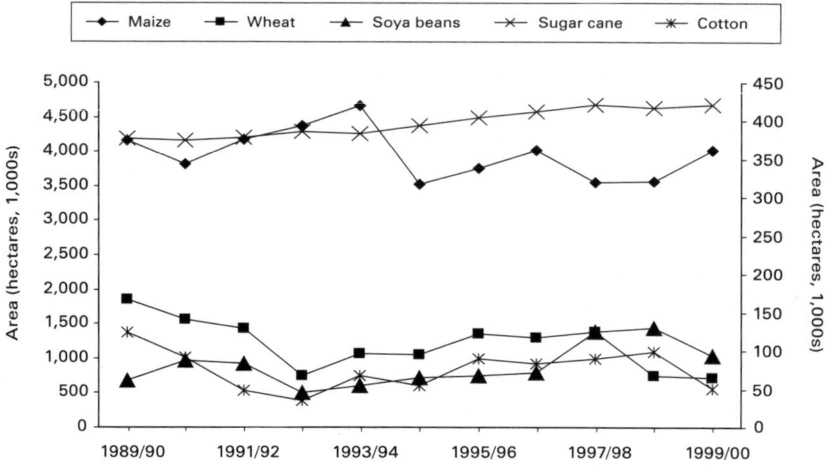

Note: Maize and wheat are measured on the left axis, and sugar cane, soya beans and cotton on the right.
Source: Adapted from *Abstract of Agricultural Statistics,* National Department of Agriculture, 2006.

Figure 3.9 *Total output of the principal field crops, 1989–2000*

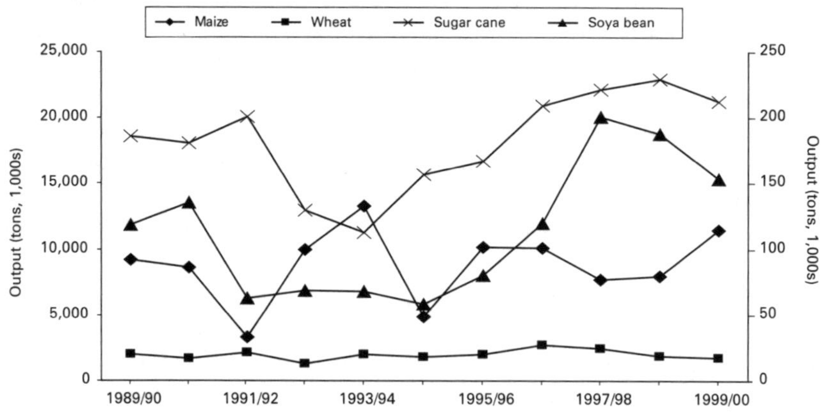

Note: Maize, wheat and sugar cane are measured on the left axis, soya beans on the right.
Source: Adapted from *Abstract of Agricultural Statistics,* National Department of Agriculture, 2006.

Figure 3.10 *Yields of the principal field crops, 1989–2000*

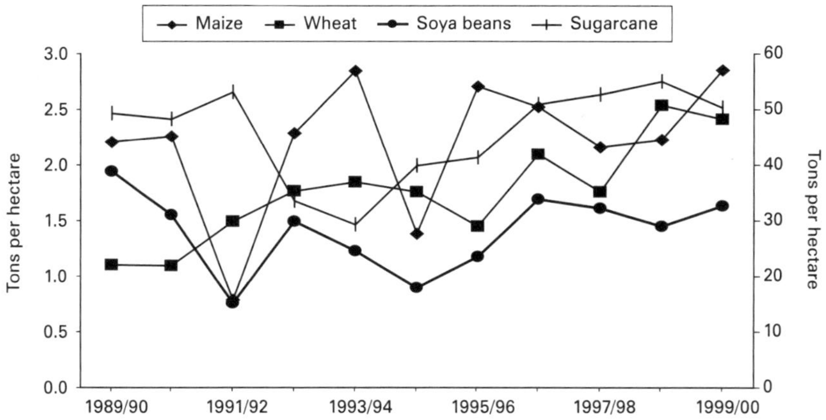

Note: Maize, wheat and soya beans are measured on the left axis, sugar cane on the right.
Source: Adapted from *Abstract of Agricultural Statistics*, National Department of Agriculture, 2006.

and a sectoral shift out of marginal areas such as the western parts of the North West and Free State (mainly maize) and the north-western and south-eastern parts of the Western Cape (wheat). Another feature of the regulated market had been that the price differentials between different grades and cultivars of grains did not reflect differential demand. A notable exception in the effects of trade reform on field crop production is the sugar industry, which still enjoys high tariff protection, partly because of the large investment in the processing of sugar, partly because the world market is heavily distorted by protectionism in the OECD countries, partly because of the large number of small-scale sugar producers, and partly because of the greater lobbying power of the industry.

Horticulture

Figure 3.11 shows the relative shift in horticultural output over the 1990s. Citrus was the only one of the major categories that increased its relative share, from 14 to 18 per cent. Vegetables and deciduous fruit lost ground relative to the total.

Citrus was the leading export, with an export proportion of 40 per cent in 1990/91 after a decade of decline (Figure 3.12). In the 1990s it recovered around 60 per cent of its losses in the 1980s. With deciduous fruit there was no overall increase over the decade. Subtropical fruit, where exports are dominated by avocados, experienced a very small increase.

Figure 3.11 *Composition of horticultural output, 1989/90 and 1999/2000*

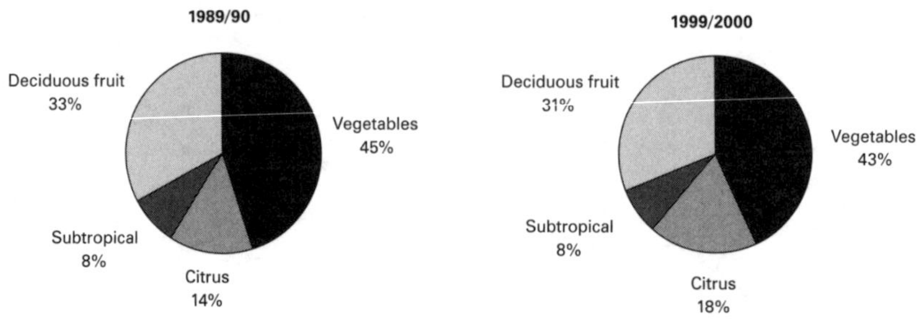

Source: Adapted from *Abstract of Agricultural Statistics*, National Department of Agriculture, 2006.

Tables 3.7, 3.8 and 3.9 provide more detail. Over the 1990s, in the case of deciduous fruit production, growth was strongest among 'other' types. Growth in the production of pears (47.2 per cent) and peaches (42.0 per cent) matched the rate of growth in the output of avocados (41.8 per cent) but they were all well below that for bananas, which expanded production by 67.0 per cent (Table 3.8). Yet the highest growth rates were recorded for citrus fruit (Table 3.9), led by naartjies (tangerines), whose output more than tripled, and grapefruit, whose output more than doubled. Almost all this growth occurred after 1993–94. The production of vegetables increased, but at a slower rate than for fruit.

Figure 3.12 *The share of fruit production exported, 1975–2000*

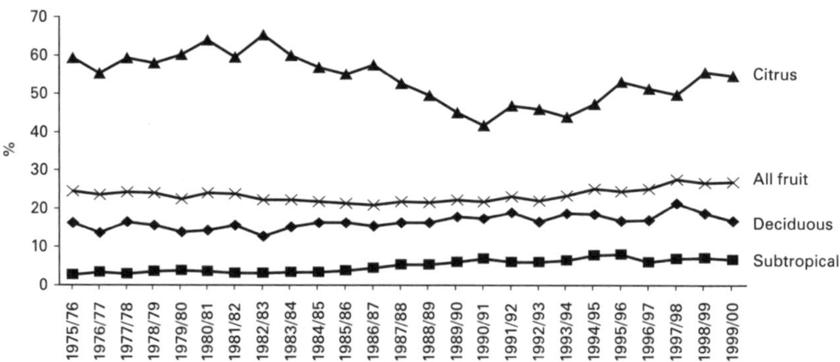

Source: Adapted from *Abstract of Agricultural Statistics*, National Department of Agriculture, 2006.

Table 3.7 *Growth in physical output of deciduous fruit in the 1990s (tons)*

	Apples	*Grapes*	*Pears*	*Peaches*	*Other deciduous*
1990/91	515,074	1,317,766	208,900	157,100	83,809
1991/92	518,492	1,407,157	212,901	169,792	88,500
1992/93	589,037	1,407,157	247,460	169,314	90,459
1993/94	563,473	1,292,201	222,589	151,530	93,114
1994/95	518,268	1,362,820	225,489	184,737	97,399
1995/96	608,408	1,411,310	228,705	182,801	110,113
1996/97	535,126	1,438,550	296,979	240,566	144,348
1997/98	586,346	1,333,481	264,842	214,040	111,526
1998/99	565,718	1,555,659	283,943	231,549	127,498
1999/00	573,966	1,454,729	307,516	223,069	99,097

Note: 'Other deciduous' includes apricots, plums, prunes, cherries, quinces and figs.
Source: Adapted from *Abstract of Agricultural Statistics*, National Department of Agriculture, 2006.

Table 3.8 *Growth in physical output of subtropical fruit in the 1990s (tons)*

	Avocados	*Bananas*	*Pineapples*	*Other subtropical*
1990/91	48,565	223,413	160,911	82,403
1991/92	45,710	243,075	164,002	88,186
1992/93	36,921	128,357	163,809	75,236
1993/94	41,072	126,445	120,118	96,423
1994/95	45,042	111,983	118,739	84,892
1995/96	50,580	158,853	124,058	84,407
1996/97	49,877	183,343	134,902	78,901
1997/98	57,053	215,655	146,539	99,998
1998/99	79,910	343,822	146,788	123,592
1999/00	68,876	373,177	160,216	117,252

Note: 'Other subtropical' includes granadillas, lychees, guavas, loquats, mangoes and pawpaws.
Source: Adapted from NDA, 2006. *Abstract of Agricultural Statistics*. Pretoria, National Department of Agriculture

The first effect of deregulation in the export of fruit was the entry of hundreds of new marketing enterprises. This led to a sharp decline in the price and quality delivered to the global market, characterised by a rising demand for new products and a stagnant demand for conventional cultivars. Nevertheless, total fruit exports increased in volume and value in the post-deregulation era. Under the new, deregulated trading regime, producers were exposed to the shifting demand for new fruit types and varieties. While this had a negative impact on sales in the short term, it also resulted in a new investment boom as farmers adapted to reflect this change in demand.

Table 3.9 *Growth in physical output of citrus in the 1990s (tons)*

	Oranges	*Lemons*	*Grapefruit*	*Naartjies*
1990/91	775,750	63,915	100,710	39,911
1991/92	711,897	66,934	112,539	37,878
1992/93	755,831	63,367	101,844	41,610
1993/94	782,429	61,360	89,367	44,212
1994/95	875,662	74,302	120,196	42,575
1995/96	745,051	73,006	128,046	55,793
1996/97	919,068	88,060	157,589	70,694
1997/98	978,416	88,901	155,477	76,015
1998/99	963,589	103,283	196,037	90,123
1999/00	1,156,359	101,669	212,181	136,901

Source: Adapted from *Abstract of Agricultural Statistics*, National Department of Agriculture, 2006.

The regions that benefited most from these changes in market conditions and the new opportunities that arose from them included the new table-grape production areas along the Orange River in the interior of the country and the wine-producing areas of the Western Cape. This expansion was driven largely by the early harvest (which created favourable market conditions), by production technologies such as precision irrigation and by infrastructural investments aimed at improving air and shipping transport.

The wine industry also underwent radical structural changes in the 1990s. Exports, for example, increased more than threefold, from less than 10 per cent of the total harvest to more than a third, driven by sustained investment. This led to a smaller total crop, as high-yielding grape varieties were replaced by low-yielding 'noble' cultivars. Because most of the investment was targeted at replanting, the area under vines grew slowly.

A further result of deregulation was that farmers were better able to withstand shocks in individual markets. While the bulk of exports of deciduous and citrus fruits were still destined for the UK market, the concentration of exports diminished considerably, with new markets opening in Eastern Europe, South and East Asia, the Middle East and Africa. The producers' ability to shift a wider variety of products to a wider range of markets also provided a measure of protection against competition from heavily subsidised producers in the northern hemisphere, for whom new technologies resulted in an extension of the production and marketing season, thereby closing the 'marketing windows' for counter-seasonal southern hemisphere countries. While this advantage was partially offset by new storage and shipping technologies for South African producers,

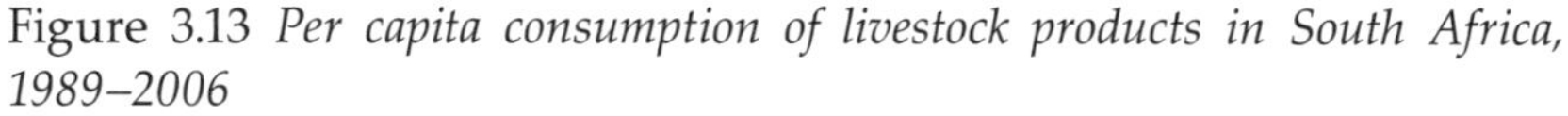

Figure 3.13 *Per capita consumption of livestock products in South Africa, 1989–2006*

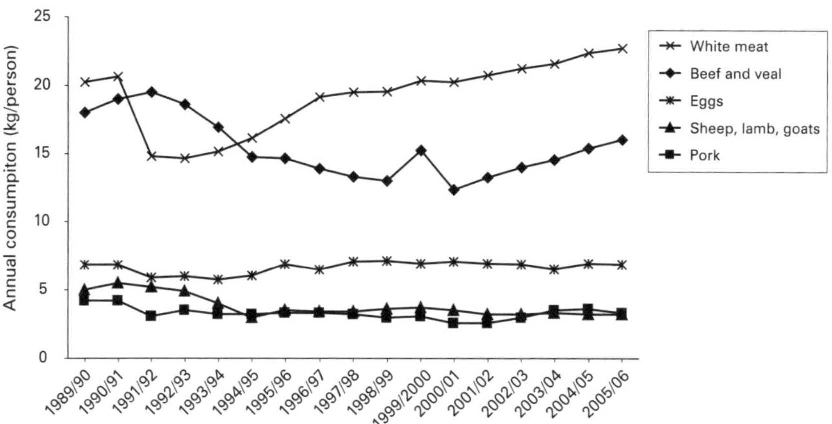

Source: Adapted from *Abstract of Agricultural Statistics*, National Department of Agriculture, 2006.

in the long run the reduction in state support for research and development posed a real threat to these industries.

Livestock

A relatively large proportion (up to 80 per cent of formal sector sales) of South Africa's red meat production comes off feedlots, mostly as a final finishing phase, ostensibly because of the lack of winter grazing in the summer rainfall areas. (It is not clear whether this practice increased in the post-deregulation era.) For this reason, prices of red meat remained particularly sensitive to changes in the cost of animal feeds. The decline in the real price of yellow maize, oil seeds and other components of animal feeds after deregulation therefore resulted in relatively low prices for red meat. As imports of animal feeds based on oil seeds increased, one of the possible locational effects was a shift in the dairy industry to the coastal regions with natural pasturage.

However, the biggest change with respect to livestock products was the shift in consumption away from red meat. The data are shown in Figure 3.13. Consumption data for red meat are notoriously inaccurate because of the prevalence of sales into the 'informal' market[19] and

19 See for example M. Karaan and A. S. Myburgh, 'Food distribution systems in the urban informal markets: the case of red meat markets in the Western Cape townships', *Agrekon*, 31(4) (1992), 289–293.

the movement of abattoirs back to the rural areas, and even back on to farms,[20] after deregulation. Nevertheless, the data clearly show the trend towards white (poultry) meat and away from beef and veal, sheep, lamb and goat meat, and pork in the 1990s.

Conclusion

When policy shifts disrupt markets, some people are better placed than others to exploit the changes. In the case of South African agriculture, these policy shifts, together with the rapid changes in the global political economy, created new opportunities.

While the growth in agricultural output was not spectacular in the 1990s, with its share of GDP declining, the sector did lead the country's export growth during the decade. This growth, moreover, was accomplished using less capital, with only a small increase in intermediate goods and a smaller total labour force. The greater employment of skilled workers led to an increase in total factor productivity.

The economy as a whole benefited, as agriculture became more export oriented and earned more foreign exchange, as agricultural growth created direct and indirect upstream and downstream multiplier effects throughout the rest of the economy, and as farmers directed income into related industries such as agro-tourism. In this regard, the rural areas also benefited, with the shift of some agro-processing activities (small-scale grain milling, abattoirs) back to the rural areas.

The products that benefited most from these changes were invariably those with an export orientation. Their number included some new, mostly niche products such as indigenous flowers. However, export growth during the decade was driven by the same commodities that South African farmers had been exporting for over a century: wine and fresh fruit. The export performance consequently took on the character of re-entering the markets that farmers had lost as a result of the country's isolation in earlier decades, rather than the growth of new markets.

For this reason, it is clear that commercial farmers generally benefited, and those best placed to exploit export markets benefited the most. The skewed distribution of production (and income) among commercial farmers led to a small proportion of commercial farmers reaping the most benefit. In this regard, South African agriculture has followed the worldwide trend to larger farms, especially in field crop and intensive livestock production.

20 C. Berning and P. J. Potgieter, 'Red meat processing in the Free State: problems encountered at farm level', *Agrekon*, 35(4) (1996), 271–275.

Those who were negatively affected by the changes included: the producers and sellers of fertiliser and tractors, as field crop producers shifted to minimum-intervention production practices after deregulation; farm workers who lost permanent employment opportunities; and farmers who, for various reasons, were not able to compete in the new, more market-led environment.

While changes such as those described in this chapter created opportunities for those already in the sector, the failure of South Africa's land reform programme limited the benefits to a broader group of farmers. Not only did the land reform programme fail to deliver land, but the withdrawal of state support to agriculture, first with the dismantling of the support systems that existed in the former homeland areas and then with the withdrawal of support to commercial farmers, meant that these support systems were not in place when land reform beneficiaries needed them most.

4

Mining

Stuart Jones

Introduction

Mining was transformed in the 1990s as the explosive growth of the platinum group of metals led to that industry's output surpassing that of gold in the last year of the twentieth century. In 1990 gold still dominated the scene, as it had done at the beginning of the century, despite the long-term decline in output that had been taking place since 1970 – a decline that had been reinforced by the slide in the gold price from its peak in 1980. Gold had fuelled the growth of the South African economy since the opening of the first Witwatersrand gold mines in the 1880s. It had enabled the country to play a larger role in the international economy than its size warranted.

All this changed in the 1990s. Gold ceased to be an engine of growth. Indeed, its declining output and declining real value led to its acting as a drag upon the economy, even though the gold industry remained the country's principal employer of labour and was crucial to the balance of payments. The decline in employment in the gold mines was not balanced by growth in other branches of the mining industry, which exerted a deleterious effect upon the economy of the whole of Southern Africa, but the decline in the value of the gold production was balanced by the growth in the value of the output of platinum group metals. In the year 2000 the value of exports of the platinum group of metals (including autocatalytic production) surpassed that of gold. Developments in 2000 consequently marked the end of an era for South Africa, the end of a century in which gold had dominated the economy and in which South Africa had dominated world gold production, and the end of a decade in which the value of gold production had been maintained only by the massive depreciation of the rand, by 67.5 per cent between February 1990 and December 2000.

Contribution to GDP

Mining's contribution to GDP was both direct, in its physical output, and indirect, as a result of its multiplier effects upon the economy. Together, in 2000, they contributed about 10 per cent of GDP.

Table 4.1 *Contribution of mining to GDP, 1990–2000*

Year	*Mining (R millions)*	*GDP (R millions)*	*Percentage*
1990	25,079	247,315	10.6
1995	34,330	500,354	7.0
2000	51,563	793,998	6.5

Source: Quarterly Bulletin, various issues, South African Reserve Bank.

The direct contribution can be measured. It grew absolutely in non-inflation-adjusted terms, but declined relatively (Table 4.1). In 1990 mining and quarrying contributed R25,079 million, which amounted to 10.6 per cent of GDP at factor cost. By 1999 this had fallen to 6.1 per cent. The rising platinum price then pulled it up to 6.5 per cent in 2000, with a total value of R51,563 million. Most of the decline occurred in the first half of the decade, when the economy was growing very slowly and the real value of mining and quarrying declined. In constant prices the value of mining and quarrying's contribution to GDP was lower in 2000 than it was in 1990. The annual decline was small but persistent, with the figure for 1995 smaller than that for 1990 and the figure for 2000 smaller than that for 1995. A decade of growth had been lost. The indirect contribution of mining and quarrying to GDP is around 50 per cent of that of its direct contribution, as a result of the multiplier effects of mining upon the economy. These multiplier effects have been outlined by Jones and Baxter.[1] They include:

- backward linkages (e.g. mechanical engineering products and electricity generation);
- forward linkages (e.g. 95 per cent of South African electricity generation used coal as a fuel);
- lateral linkages (e.g. banking, insurance and transport facilities);
- social multipliers (e.g. infrastructure and human resource development);
- the primary incomes multiplier (e.g. household expenditure derived from mining income);

1 Stuart Jones and Roger Baxter, 'Transformation in the 1990s', in Stuart Jones (ed.), *The Decline of the South African Economy*, Edward Elgar, 2002, ch. 5, part 2.

- the income terms-of-trade multiplier, resulting from the impact of mineral export earnings;
- the capital-formation multiplier, arising from mining's ability to draw in foreign capital, and its impact upon domestic capital formation.

Table 4.2 *Changes in the volume of mineral output, 1990–2000*[a]

Mineral	*Increase/decrease (%)*
Platinum group	45.7
Gold	–28.8
Coal	28.2
Diamonds	24.1
Iron ore	–11.1
Nickel	29.8
Copper	–27.1
Manganese	–17.4
Chrome ore	35.3
Aggregate and sand	68.8
Limestone and lime	–18.8
Granite	42.4
Natural gas[b]	13.2
Zinc	–22.8
Silver[b]	–3.4
Natural condensate	–15.8
Lead	–5.9

[a] All minerals with total sales of at least R100 million in 2000 listed in order of value.
[b] Figures from 1995.
Source: *Statistical Tables 1980–2000*, Minerals Bureau, 2000.

The year 2000 was a prosperous one for the mining industry, which saw the value of output increase by 29 per cent, despite the continued decline in the production of gold, because the non-gold mining sector increased the value of its output by 43 per cent. Platinum was the star performer, with the value of sales of the platinum group metals rising by 82 per cent and overtaking gold. Yet the output of nine of the 17 categories of minerals in 2000 was lower than at the beginning of the decade (Table 4.2). Platinum,[2] coal, diamonds, nickel, chrome ore, aggregate and sand, and granite all experienced significant increases in output and all, except coal, experienced a real growth in the value of their output. Although the output of coal had increased by 28.2 per cent,

2 *Statistical Tables 2000*, Chamber of Mines, 2000, p. 2.

Table 4.3 *Principal mineral sales, 1990–2000, in current prices and those of 2000 in constant 1990 prices*[a]

Mineral	*1990*	*1995*	*2000*	*2000 in 1990 prices*	*Percentage increase/ decrease*
Platinum group	5,164.2	6,572.5	27,094.6	10,709.3	107.4
Gold	18,994.0	23,465.0	25,272.0	9,988.3	–47.4
Coal	8,173.3	12,817.6	19,702.9	7,787.7	–4.7
Diamonds[b]	n.a.	n.a.	8891.1	3,514.3	n.a.
Iron ore	1084.5	1663.0	3064.8	1,211.4	11.7
Nickel	655.6	850.0	1994.3	788.3	20.2
Copper	1126.7	1701.8	1573.6	672.0	–44.8
Manganese	843.3	692.1	1232.1	487.0	–31.6
Chrome ore	485.9	608.1	1080.2	427.0	–12.1
Aggregate and sand	471.2	779.9	815.4	354.5	–24.8
Limestone and lime	435.6	707.8	792.4	319.2	–28.1
Granite	245.8	332.5	674.8	266.7	8.5
Natural gas	–	–	639.9	252.9	n.a.
Zinc	191.5	159.1	309.4	122.9	–35.8
Natural gas condensate	–	–	115.2	67.2	17.2
Lead	115.5	102.3	–	45.3	n.a.
Total	38,044.4	50,520.8	93,422.6	36,858.8	–12.2[c]

[a] All minerals with sales of at least R100 million in 2000.
[b] Diamond sales are included in 'Miscellaneous sales'.
[c] Excluding diamonds.
Source: *Statistical Tables 1980–2000,* Minerals Bureau, 2000.

export prices had fallen even faster, with the result that the value of coal produced over the decade declined by –4.7 per cent (Table 4.3). Iron ore went the opposite route. Its output fell by 11.1 per cent, while the value of sales rose by 11.7 per cent. Notwithstanding the phenomenal rise in the value of platinum production, there was no real growth in the value of mineral production over the decade. The massive fall in the value of gold output, together with the decline in the value of coal exports, counterbalanced the growth in the value of platinum production in the last years of the decade. If the growth in population is taken into account, then real per capita mineral output was considerably lower in 2000 than in 1990. For a country that had long depended upon its mineral production to sustain its economy, this was a disturbing development. It draws our attention, once again, to the decline taking place in the South African economy and the need to make prospecting economically viable.

Capital investment in the mining industry

Capital formation and investment in mining remained buoyant throughout the decade. In current prices it fluctuated from a low of R6,006 million in 1993 to a high of R11,231 million in 1998. The recession then sweeping across South East Asia led to capital investment dropping in the following two years. In constant prices the decline was most severe in the period 1990–93, when political developments within the country were threatening to overwhelm economic considerations. This was of particular importance to the mining industry, which had traditionally relied upon foreign investment for much of its capital needs. After 1994 capital investment rose markedly only over 1997–98. As a result, mining's proportion of fixed capital investment fell over the decade, from 13.3 per cent in 1990 to 8.0 per cent in 2000 (Table 4.4), before the government's mooted neo-kleptocratic policies towards 'transformation' and black economic empowerment further threatened to reduce the flow of direct investment.

Table 4.4 *Gross fixed capital investment in mining and its proportion of total fixed investment, 1990–2000*

Year	*Investment in mining (R millions)*	*Proportion of total investment (%)*
1990	7,176	13.3
1995	7,397	8.5
2000	7,949	8.0

Source: Quarterly Bulletin, various issues, South African Reserve Bank.

The nature of foreign investment changed. In the 1970s government and parastatal borrowing accounted for much of the investment from overseas. Then, in the next decade, there was some direct fixed investment, accompanied by much short-term borrowing. In the 1990s the early flurry of direct investment gave way to the much more volatile portfolio type of investment that was so much more sensitive to political developments and the perceived risks involved in placing money in South Africa. In the 10 years 1990–99 there were only two years when direct investment in the South African economy was positive. In eight years disinvestment took place, but portfolio investment was positive in nine of the 10 years. It was very short-term in outlook, the opposite of investment in mining, which requires a long period of gestation. The index of the value of mining shares on the Johannesburg Securities Exchange (JSE) reflected the decline in the value of gold shares and

Table 4.5 *Index of the value of leading mining shares, 1989, 1990 and 2000*

Mines	*December 1989*	*December 1990*	*December 2000*
All gold	2,220	1,129	768
Platinum	6,056	3,944	23,608
Mining finance	43,878	3,291	13,564
Metals and minerals	2,298	1,793	14

Source: Johannesburg Securities Exchange.

those of the mining finance houses, which in the year 2000 controlled not only the gold mines but also the bulk of the output from the platinum and coal mines, as well as that of other metals and minerals. This explains the dramatic fall in their weighting in the index. Moreover, the figure for December 1990 was very much lower than that for 1989. That of the gold mines had almost halved and platinum had fallen by a third in the course of 1990. Table 4.5 gives the details.

The picture presented is one of transformation, if by that is meant a massive relative decline in the weighting of gold and the rise of platinum group metals. This continued the trend that had begun in the 1980s and was reinforced by the end of the rapid expansion of coal mining that had also been feature of the 1980s.

Mining investment required political stability and the prospect of profits sufficiently large to provide a risk premium and the return of a portion of the original capital in what was clearly a wasting asset. In current prices this investment was very large. In June 2001 the market capitalisation of mining companies listed on the JSE was R471.8 billion; in fact, most of the trade in shares on the JSE was taking place in London, not Johannesburg. Unfavourable political developments within South Africa were likely to have an immediate impact upon capital flows that could threaten the long-term profitability of the industry. The experience of Zambia should serve as a warning of what not to do, for even the investment of close to R1 billion by Anglo American could not restore the run-down copper mines to profitability. The experience of the 1990s may consequently mark a turning point in the fortunes of the mining industry if direct investment becomes more difficult to obtain, for, as Frankel noted over 70 years ago, 'A serious decline in the annual increment of mining investment in the future would involve the Union [of South Africa] in a more than proportionate decline in the income and employment of the country as a whole'.[3] The truth of Frankel's

3 S. H. Frankel, *Capital Investment in Africa*, Oxford University Press, 1938, p. 105.

observation, however, is well known to the men who control the mining companies and at the end of the decade the industry was committed to capital investment of R78 billion.[4]

Labour in the mining industry

In the labour field, the outstanding feature of the 1990s was the fall in the number of people employed in mining. This occurred because employment in labour-intensive gold mining was falling faster than labour was being recruited in the more mechanised coal and platinum mining operations. Rising wages in the context of a stable or declining gold price spelled the doom of many marginal gold mines. Not surprisingly, the average number employed fell, from 489,541 in 1990 to 215,450 in 2000, a decline of 56.0 per cent.[5] The drastic decline in employment in the gold mines, which had traditionally relied upon foreign labour, led to an increasing reliance upon local labour and to a decrease in the importance of labour from other countries in Southern and Central Africa. To an extent this cushioned the South African labour market from the impact of the contraction in gold mining. Unionisation remained a noted feature of the mining industry but it was not always possible to devise a common policy for the mines, which often had little in common. Mechanised coal mines were more likely favour productivity agreements than less mechanised gold mines. Political posturing was common, but with the socialist miners' leader of the 1980s now a leading businessman and supporting privatisation, a time of growing unemployment did not lend itself to workers' solidarity. Action on the part of the unions seldom matched the rhetoric employed by union leaders.

Nevertheless, the changed political situation in the country led to significant changes in labour law and to work practices in the mines. At the top, management hierarchies were collapsed into narrower bands, a process made easier by the disappearance of the old mining finance holding companies. At the bottom, the mining companies mapped out career paths that their workers could follow, while training programmes were introduced to equip workers with the skills needed for progress. At an elementary level, an agreement was reached between the Chamber of Mines and the unions to provide basic adult education. This new approach may have been forced on the mines by the government, but it should not be seen as an act of charity. It represented a prudent investment in human capital that paid off in the form of rising productivity.

4 *Annual Report*, Chamber of Mines, 2000/01 p. 7.
5 *Statistical Tables*, Minerals Bureau, 1980–2000.

Table 4.6 *Total numbers of accidents, fatalities and injuries in South African mines, 1991–2000*

Year	*Gold*	*Platinum*	*Coal*	*All minerals*
Accidents				
1991	7,587	340	388	9,183
1994	6,941	435	267	8,036
1997	5,713	789	302	7,195
2000	3,597	668	231	4,851
Fatalities				
1991	461	37	43	602
1994	371	24	54	482
1997	277	53	40	415
2000	175	45	30	285
Injuries				
1991	7,531	313	370	9,058
1994	6,888	415	240	7,934
1997	5,707	755	270	7,095
2000	3,546	638	213	4,728

Source: Statistical Tables, Chamber of Mines, 2000, pp. 5–6.

Associated with these changes in work practice was a new concern for safety, initiated by new legislation, the Mines Health and Safety Act 29 of 1996. The number of reportable accidents decreased by almost 50 per cent, fatalities by over 50 per cent and serious injuries by almost 50 per cent over the course of the 1990s (Table 4.6). The greatest reduction in the number of accidents and fatalities occurred in the last three years of the century, after the introduction of the new legislation.

However, it would not be correct to attribute the gains to the new political climate. Many of the accidents occurred in the deep gold mines, as opposed to the open-cast operations. Among the gold mines registered with the Chamber of Mines the number of accidents fell by 52.6 per cent and fatalities by 62.0 per cent, at a time when the number of mine workers fell by 54.0 per cent. In other words, there was no reduction in the number of accidents in proportion to the labour employed. The gold mines had not become safer. The fatality rate had fallen from 1 per 932 mine workers in 1991 to 1 per 1,129 mine workers in 2000, but the accident and injury rates remained the same.

Labour costs as a proportion of total sales remained fairly constant in gold, coal and iron ore mining, but dropped sharply in the platinum group of minerals, when the price rocketed (Table 4.7). It is noticeable, too, that in the newer mineral developments, in platinum and iron ore and coal, labour costs were markedly lower than in the older gold mines.

Table 4.7 *Labour costs as a proportion (%) of sales in platinum, gold, coal and iron ore mining, 1990–2000*

Year	*Platinum*	*Gold*	*Coal*	*Iron ore*
1990	29.0	35.4	26.0	11.5
1995	38.4	35.3	18.5	14.1
2000	16.1	38.7	21.6	11.3

Source: Statistical Tables, Minerals Bureau, 1980–2000.

In fact, labour costs appear to have diminished proportionately with each new mining development. Within individual mining industries, labour costs were relatively steady as a proportion of total earnings, rising in the second half of the decade in the older, more aggressively unionised gold and coal mining sectors. By contrast, capital earned a rising return in the newer, more costly developments associated with platinum and iron ore mining. Since the prices of all these minerals were determined outside South Africa, in the long run the rise in the proportion of wealth going to labour was determined by balancing price changes with productivity gains, which increased the importance of good management, labour relations and skills training.

Mining's contribution to exports

Mineral exports continued to dominate exports in the 1990s despite the decline in the gold mining industry. However, as the importance of gold declined, so too did South Africa's importance to the international economy. Yet in the 1990s mining generated 41 per cent of total exports[6] and in 2000 mining's contribution to exports increased for the first time since 1993. The rise in the platinum group of metal exports was the reason for this development. In 2000 platinum group exports reached R24.6 billion, only some R400 million less than gold exports (Table 4.8).

If beneficiated minerals are added to the total, the contribution of the mining industry to exports comes to almost 60 per cent of merchandise exports. At the end of the decade of 'transformation', the South African economy was still very dependent upon the mining industry and its external markets. Five of the main mineral commodities exported depended on external markets to take over 90 per cent of their output and another two to take over 70 per cent of output!

6 *Annual Report,* Chamber of Mines of South Africa, 1999–2000.

Table 4.8 *Exports of selected minerals by value and their growth rate, 1990–2000* [a]

Mineral	*1990 (R millions)*	*1995 (R millions)*	*2000 (R millions)*	*Growth rate (%)*
Platinum group	5,164.2	6,572.5	24,645.0	16.9
Gold	18,994.0	232,110.0	25,054.6	2.8
Silver	50.8	61.0	155.5	11.8
Chrome ore	220.5	247.0	360.8	5.0
Copper	662.8	813.5	598.5	5.0
Iron ore	782.9	1,052.9	2,469.1	12.2
Lead concentrate	115.1	98.8	89.0	–2.5
Manganese ore	610.4	452.2	863.5	3.5
Nickel	452.5	470.3	805.8	5.9
Asbestos	189.7	116.1	30.6	–16.7
Coal	4,026.9	6,478.8	10,925.9	10.5
Granite	241.2	302.7	627.3	10.0
Total	32,975.0	43,356.0	76,245.0	8.7
Miscellaneous [b]	1,261.5	3,566.5	5,487.3	15.8

[a] Only minerals with exports worth more than R100 million in 1990 or 2000.
[b] The miscellaneous total includes diamonds, the exports of which were growing almost as fast as those of platinum group metals.
Source: Statistical Tables 1980–2000, Minerals Bureau, 2000, save for the 'Miscellaneous' figures, which are taken from *Statistical Tables*, Chamber of Mines, 2000.

Table 4.9 *Exports of selected minerals by volume and their growth rate, 1990–2000*

Mineral	*1990 (kg, 1,000s)*	*1995 (kg, 1,000s)*	*2000 (kg, 1,000s)*	*Growth rate (%)*
Platinum group	135.6	175.2	198.9	3.9
Gold	595.8	518.2	403.9	–3.8
Silver	135.6	175.2	198.9	3.9
Diamonds [a]	8,708.0	9,684.0	10,805.0	2.2
Copper	121.0	81.0	49.0	–8.6
Lead	82.5	86.1	74.2	–1.1
Manganese ore	2,160.0	1,589.0	1,845.0	–1.6
Nickel	21.2	16.7	14.6	–3.7
Asbestos	178.8	88.0	16.6	–21.2
Coal	49,625.0	59,676.0	68,281.0	3.2
Granite	241,194.0	302,713.0	627,291.0	10.0

[a] Diamond figures are carats and are of total production, the bulk of which was exported.
Source: Statistical Tables 1980–2000, Minerals Bureau, 2000.

Over the decade mineral exports benefited considerably from the depreciation of the rand. The ending of selective sanctions benefited the coal industry and also had an impact upon gold exports, as a result of the growth of private gold sales to India. In 1996 the authorities in Pretoria decided to treat gold as an ordinary commodity and exports of that commodity are now placed in the category 'Precious stones and precious metals' in the trade statistics published by the Commissioner for the South African Revenue Service. In 2000 the five largest mineral exports were platinum, gold, coal, diamonds and iron ore, all of which had exports worth at least R1 billion. Five minerals had export growth rates in double digits: platinum group metals, diamonds, iron ore, silver, coal and granite. Only manganese and copper had larger domestic sales than exports.

South Africa's dependence upon the global economy is highlighted by the pattern of mineral exports. Because the current value of mineral exports was heavily influenced by the fall in the value of the rand, a more realistic view of what was happening to mineral exports may be obtained from the volume exported, accepting that these figures, too, will be subject to price fluctuations according to the ratio of demand to supply. Table 4.9 provides details of the leading mineral exports by volume in 1990s.

Platinum group metals

Output

The year 2000 was a watershed, in that it was when the value of sales of platinum group metals overtook that of gold. This change occurred suddenly in the last years of the decade and could not have been foreseen in 1990. It was driven by the rising demand for platinum group metals in the jewellery, automobile and electronics industries. The rising employment in the platinum group minerals industry, however, could not compensate for the loss of jobs in gold mining. There was also greater price volatility among the platinum group metals, which are more vulnerable to changes in the international economy. Nevertheless, when the relative failure of manufacturing is taken into account,[7] the 1990s deserve to be known as the 'platinum decade'. From an economic point of view, it was not political developments that were determining

7 Trevor Bell and Nkosi Madula, 'The manufacturing industry', in Stuart Jones (ed.), *The Decline of the South African Economy*, Edward Elgar, 2002, ch. 6.

Table 4.10 *Total sales of platinum group metals and gold, 1990–2000*

Year	*Platinum group (R millions)*	*Gold (R millions)*
1990	5,164.2	18,994
1991	5,692.1	19,296
1992	4,677.8	19,513
1993	5,188.8	23,239
1994	5,809.6	24,953
1995	6,572.5	23,465
1996	7,486.2	26,468
1997	8,509.7	24,905
1998	11,929.7	24,295
1999	14,887.5	24,990
2000	27,094.6	25,272

Source: *Statistical Tables 1980–2000*, Minerals Bureau, 2000.

Table 4.11 *Rate of growth of sales (%) of platinum group metals and gold, 1990–2000*

	Platinum group	*Gold*
1990–95	4.9	4.3
1995–2000	32.7	1.5
1990–2000	18.0	2.9

Source: *Statistical Tables 1980–2000*, Minerals Bureau, 2000.

the future wellbeing of the country, but the rise of a major new industry based upon the platinum group metals.

The growth in the value of sales of platinum group metals accelerated until the year 2000 (Tables 4.10 and 4.11), when output fell as a result of labour unrest and flooding in the mines of Anglo Platinum and Impala Platinum. This surge in the value of the platinum group metals was to a great extent market driven, though the seemingly inexorable decline in the value of the rand was also an important factor. This contrasted with the condition of gold mining, the rising value of which was made possible only by the massive depreciation of the rand. The fading fortunes of the gold mining industry help to explain why the Oppenheimers decided to loosen their hold on Anglo American and concentrate on diamonds.

By volume, growth was still impressive (Table 4.12). Over the decade output grew at the rate of 3.9 per cent for platinum and 3.8 per cent for platinum group metals as a whole (Table 4.13). In the first half of the decade all platinum group metals expanded faster than platinum, 5.2

Table 4.12 *Platinum and platinum group metals output by volume (metric tons), 1990–2000*

Year	*Platinum*	*Platinum group*	*Group output per employee*
1990	78.2	141.9	1,453.3
1991	78.5	142.9	1,372.1
1992	78.0	152.9	1,472.0
1993	95.3	176.2	1,726.7
1994	89.6	183.9	1,883.3
1995	95.5	183.1	2,000.4
1996	96.1	188.6	2,021.3
1997	104.9	196.6	2,162.3
1998	104.3	200.0	2,224.5
1999	110.6	216.5	2,368.1
2000	114.5	206.8	2,149.0

Source: Statistical Tables 1980–2000, Chamber of Mines, 2000.

Table 4.13 *Annual growth rates in the production of platinum and platinum group metals, 1990–2000*

	1990–95	*1995–2000*	*1990–2000*
Platinum	4.1	3.7	3.9
Platinum group metals	6.6	1.0	3.8

Source: Statistical Tables 1980–2000, Chamber of Mines, 2000.

per cent versus 4.1 per cent, but in the second half of the decade this was reversed and platinum output rose by 3.7 per cent a year against 2.5 per cent for platinum group metals. The reason for this was that the greater stability in the platinum price compared with that for palladium led some buyers to switch orders back to platinum.

Productivity was also growing, particularly in the first half of the decade. This, together with the increase in price, enabled average earnings per employee to treble over the decade. Sales per employee rose very much faster, from R23,933 in 1990 to R71,808 in 1995 and R281,702 in 2000 (a 12-fold increase). This was made possible by a 46 per cent increase in output and a marginal reduction in the labour force.

Sales of platinum group metals were driven by both export demand and local demand. In 1990 domestic sales were negligible, but five years later had risen to R2.5 billion.[8] The reasons for this were twofold. First,

8 *Annual Report,* Chamber of Mines, 2001, pp. 15–17.

the Motor Industry Development Programme supported the export of car components, including catalytic converters, which use platinum group metals. Sales of these rose from R388 million in 1995 to R4.2 billion in 2001. Second, the demand emanating from the domestic jewellery industry was expanding rapidly, reaching around 200 kg in 2000.

In 2000 the total world demand for platinum increased only marginally, as a result of the falling demand for jewellery fabrication in Japan. Growth elsewhere did not make up for the decline in Japan. Counterbalancing this decline from the jewellery industry was renewed growth in demand from the motor industry, mainly as a response to emission control legislation in North America, Europe and Japan. Elsewhere, demand continued to grow, for example in the electrical application sectors for products such as hard disks, thermocouples in the steel industry, semiconductors and specialty glass plants. Demand from the chemical and petroleum industries declined, with some disinvestment taking place in response to the rising price in 2000. Platinum began the year with a price of $442 per ounce and ended the year at $625, with considerable fluctuations en route, which were much influenced by the resumption of Russian shipments. Over the decade as a whole, platinum output had increased by 46.4 per cent and platinum group metals by 45.7 per cent, with growth more vigorous in the first half of the decade (see Table 4.12).

Capital investment

Capital invested in the platinum mines rose rapidly from the middle of the decade (Table 4.14), as a result of rising demand. By then, too, the industry had digested the flurry of new companies listed on the JSE.

Table 4.14 *Market capitalisation of platinum and gold mining companies, 1992–2000*

Year	*Platinum companies (R millions)*	*Gold companies (R millions)*
1992	14,239.0	18,192.4
1993	15,020.8	18,192.4
1994	26,905.2	17,761.7
1995	16,362.0	11,105.2
1996	15,368.6	12,412.8
1997	17,322.6	7,617.2
1998	23,487.5	22,817.7
1999	59,588.3	54,227.3
2000	138,709.0	43,584.2

Source: Johannesburg Securities Exchange.

At the beginning of our period, in 1990, there were seven platinum companies listed, but only four were paying dividends[9] and total market capitalisation was less than R10 billion. Ten years later this figure stood at R138.7 billion[10] and there were 10 firms listed on the JSE, though this figure included two mining houses, Gencor and Longfin, and East Daggafontein, a gold producer. Only five were registered with the Chamber of Mines, namely: Anglo Platinum, Barplats Mines, Impala Platinum, Longfin Platinum and Northam Platinum.

Labour

The number of workers employed in the mines extracting platinum group metals did not increase over the period, despite the very considerable increase in output. The platinum mines were not deep level like the gold mines and mechanisation could be more easily introduced. While, therefore, platinum was able to replace gold in relation to the balance of payments, it could not replace gold in the labour market. Table 4.15 gives the details of labour employed in the gold and platinum mines and reflects how the new government in 1994 encouraged employers to replace labour with capital and how the expansion of platinum mining did not compensate for the loss of jobs in the gold mining industry.

Table 4.15 *Labour employed (numbers of workers) in gold mines and platinum group metals mines, 1990–2000*

Year	*Gold mines*	*Platinum group metals*
1990	489,541	97,019
1991	438,822	104,152
1992	411,686	103,871
1993	394,508	102,043
1994	392,327	97,643
1995	379,423	91,528
1996	350,050	93,304
1997	338,658	90,918
1998	258,821	89,905
1999	234,206	91,420
2000	215,450	96,183

Source: *Statistical Tables 1980–2000*, Minerals Bureau, 2000.

9 *Financial Mail*, 21 December 1990.
10 Figures provided by the Johannesburg Securities Exchange.

Table 4.16 *The productivity of labour in the platinum group metals industry, 1990–2000*

Year	*Output per employee (metric tons)*	*Earnings per employee (R)*	*Sales per employee (R)*
1990	0.0015	15,462	23,933
1995	0.0020	27,555	71,808
2000	0.0021	45,409	281,702

Source: Statistical Tables 1980–2000, Minerals Bureau, 2000.

This capital investment led to significant gains in productivity (Table 4.16), which were reflected in output per employee, earnings per employee and sales per employee. Only towards the end of the decade was it followed by a rise in prices. Most of the increase in output per employee occurred in the first half of the decade.

Gold

Output

The gold mining industry in the 1990s was assaulted on two fronts: by the declining output from the country's ageing mines and by the declining dollar price of the metal. Then, on top of this, there was the matter of transformation and the government's policy of forcing companies to develop programmes for the promotion and skill acquisition of the hitherto disadvantaged population groups. Rising labour costs exacerbated the difficulties confronting the mining companies, which were themselves in a state of flux as a result of the break-up of the old mining finance houses. In this situation, the fact that South Africa was able to produce 17 per cent of the world gold output in the year 2000 was something of an achievement, even though it was made possible only by the massive depreciation of the rand.

In that decade, gold was effectively commoditised in South Africa. Central banks began to sell some of their reserves of gold, while the demand from the jewellery and electronics industries continued to grow. According to the Chamber of Mines, over the decade as a whole, new gold output averaged only 27 per cent of total demand. The balance was made up by sales from central banks, scrap, net producer hedging and disinvestment.[11] In 2000 world gold demand was 3,739 metric tons,

11 *Statistical Tables 1980–2000,* Chamber of Mines, 2000, pp. 3–4, 12.

Table 4.17 *South African gold output, 1990–2000*[a]

Year	*Metric tons treated*	*Fine gold (kg)*	*Value (R millions)*
1990	129,410	602,999	19,239.3
1991	125,879	599,195	19,224.5
1992	124,414	611,149	19,468.3
1993	119,959	617,505	23,182.6
1994	100,893	583,893	25,081.3
1995	101,473	522,377	23,218.6
1996	95,000	494,618	26,373.4
1997	91,253	492,534	24,222.2
1998	84,772	464,391	24,353.2
1999	89,360	449,472	24,679.0
2000	90,230	427,981	26,506.7

[a] Mines affiliated to the Chamber of Mines.
Source: Statistical Tables 1980–2000, Chamber of Mines, 2000.

of which 3,175 tons came from the jewellery industry and 283 tons from the electronics industry. The balance came from hoarders or central banks.[12]

As Table 4.17 indicates, the monetary value of gold sales rose from R19,239 million in 1990 to R23,219 million in 1995 and R26,507 million in 2000, with the growth rate in the second half of the decade slower than in the first half, notwithstanding the greater fall in the value of the rand in this period.

The physical volume of output presents a more meaningful picture of what was happening in the gold mining industry. Output fell by 29 per cent, from 602,999 kilograms in 1990 to 427,981 kilograms in 2000, as the mines with the poorer grades of ore closed. The decline, moreover, was accelerating. Between 1990 and 1995 output of fine gold was declining by 2.8 per cent a year, between 1995 and 2000 by 3.9 per cent a year. Ore treated fell at a marginally greater rate than the output of fine gold. And the Chamber of Mines' grip on the gold mining industry was weakening. In 1990 members of the Chamber of Mines were responsible for 93.8 per cent of output, in 2000 for 88.3 per cent

The value of output rose in rand terms over the decade (Table 4.17), from R19,239.3 million in 1990 to R26,506.7 million in 2000. When converted into dollars, the results are very much lower. In 1990 the approximate dollar valuation was $7,597 million; in 2000 this had fallen to $3,305 million. The dollar value of South African gold production was declining at the rate of 8 per cent a year. Moreover, this decline was

12 *Annual Report,* Chamber of Mines, 2000, p. 9.

Table 4.18 *Annual average working revenue, costs and profits of Chamber of Mines gold mines, 1990–2000* [a]

Year	*Working revenue per metric ton of ore*	*Working costs per metric ton of ore*	*Working costs per kg of gold*	*Working profit per metric ton of ore*
1990	163.50	130.34	25,733	33.16
1991	171.14	136.05	26,136	35.09
1992	175.62	141.82	26,373	33.80
1993	206.45	153.26	27,547	53.19
1994	233.83	172.86	31,973	60.97
1995	219.00	185.15	39,040	33.85
1996	260.75	206.75	42,111	54.00
1997	259.07	228.01	46,100	31.06
1998	296.13	236.00	46,444	60.13
1999	272.20	229.63	49,751	42.57
2000	284.25	219.54	48,752	64.71

[a] Mines affiliated to the Chamber of Mines.
Source: Statistical Tables 1980–2000, Chamber of Mines, 2000.

accelerating. Over 1990–94 the dollar value of the gold output fell at an annual rate of 3.2 per cent and after 1994 by 11 per cent a year.

The rise in the average rand price of gold per fine ounce was impressive. In 1970 the rand price of gold was 53.8 per cent higher than in 1940; in 2000 it was 7,355 per cent higher than in 1970. In the course of the 1990s it rose by 94 per cent. Yet in the 1990s working profits did not rise significantly. They fluctuated sharply, from a low of R31.06 per metric ton in 1997 to a high of R60.97 in 1994. Working costs had, however, been rising apparently inexorably since 1936, with the exception of one year, 1959. Working revenue was also rising, though not so consistently as working costs. In the 1990s working costs rose at the rate of 5.4 per cent a year, working revenue per metric ton at the rate of 5.7 per cent (Table 4.18). Had the year 1998 been the final year, then the average annual working revenue would have risen by 7.7 per cent, the same as costs. The decline in working costs in the last two years of the decade, which led to the rise in working profits, was the result not of a higher gold price but of better labour management and the more efficient use of labour. In the last year of the century, both working costs per metric ton of ore milled and working costs per kilogramme of fine gold produced fell. The mining companies were very responsive to movements in the gold price and switched to less rich ores when the price rose. In this way, for example, in 1999 the volume of ore milled rose but the production of fine gold fell. Over the decade as a whole, working costs per metric ton treated rose at the rate of 5.4 per cent a year while working revenue per metric ton rose at the rate of 5.7 per cent a year and working profit per metric ton by 6.9 per cent a year. The depreciation of the rand, together with the closing down of some of the older and less rich mines, made this possible.

Capital investment

At a time of falling output and market capitalisation of the gold mines (see Table 4.14), the opportunities for capital investment were limited. It was in the second half of the decade that the current monetary value of gold shares listed on the JSE began to fall steadily. In real terms, of course, investors lost even more and foreigners holding gold mining shares incurred very considerable losses. The question mark over the security of property rights and mining rights in particular also discouraged investment in gold mining. This unfavourable economic and political environment inevitably influenced capital investment. In 1990 capital expenditure by the gold mining companies affiliated to the Chamber of Mines amounted to R2,475.1 million. Ten years later, at R2,450.7 million, it was still below this level in current prices. In real terms this amounted to a significant decline in the level of capital expenditure.

Over the course of the decade the structure of the mining companies was transformed as the six traditional mining houses of 1990 gave way to two major groups, Anglo Gold and Goldfields. Rand Mines had faded from the scene, Johannesburg Consolidated Investment Company (JCI) had hived off its main investment into Anglo Platinum, Gencor's gold interests were united with those of Goldfields in the new Goldfields, and Anglo Vaal had unbundled its mining interests from its industrial ones. Meanwhile, Anglo American had shed some of the gold mines controlled by Anglo Gold and a new dynamic entrant in the form of Harmony had appeared and demonstrated an ability to turn loss-making mines into profitable ones. What these developments revealed was the inefficiency locked into the old system of control by the traditional mining finance houses. When individual mining companies took control of all aspects of management and introduced new labour practices into the industry, productivity rose markedly.

Some idea of the changes that took place may be gained from listings on the JSE. In 1990 there were 14 counters listed under the heading 'Mining financial', 21 under the heading 'Mining holding' and 56 individual mining companies, with two listed as curtailed operations. Ten years later the number of gold counters had fallen to 13 and the 35 listed under the categories 'Mining financial' and 'Mining holding' in 1990 had been reduced to 14 listed under 'Mining holding and houses'. The

Table 4.19 *Labour productivity in the gold mining industry, 1990–2000*[a]

Year	*Metric tonnes of ore milled per employee*	*Kilograms of gold produced per employee*
1990	0.23	1.19
1991	0.25	1.32
1992	0.26	1.41
1993	0.27	1.49
1994	0.25	1.37
1995	0.26	1.28
1996	0.27	1.34
1997	0.29	1.65
1998	0.32	1.65
1999	0.39	1.80
2000	0.42	1.91

[a] Mines affiliated to the Chamber of Mines.
Source: *Statistical Tables 1980–2000*, Chamber of Mines, 2000.

JSE accurately mirrored the changes taking place in the fortunes of the gold mining industry.[13]

Labour

What distinguishes the 1990s from other decades is the sharp fall in gold mining employment accompanied by a marked rise in productivity and the introduction of staff training schemes across the whole range of mining activities. Mines that were, or would have become, unprofitable under the old system of control by mining finance houses were able to return to, or maintain, profitability as a result of the new approach to labour management induced by the changed political environment. Such gains, though, may prove to be one-off gains that cannot be repeated, as the mines get deeper and the richer grades are worked out. Productivity rose slowly in the early 1990s and then fell in the year of the election (1994) and again in 1995, when measured by the amount of gold produced per employee (Table 4.19).

Sustained growth in productivity dates from 1994. Over the decade the tons of ore milled per worker rose at the rate of 6.2 per cent per year, while gold produced rose at the rate of 4.8 per cent, reflecting the lower grades being mined. These lower grades declined from 5.05 grams per metric ton in 1990 to 4.5 in 2000.

The improvement in productivity was the direct result of the increased attention being paid to human capital. Career paths were

13 *Financial Mail*, various issues.

defined and training programmes introduced and the Chamber of Mines signed an agreement with the unions to introduce adult basic education. The government further stimulated change with the passage of a new mines Health and Safety Act. Also the collapsing of managerial hierarchies into narrower bands spurred management into making greater efforts to raise productivity and incentivise workers.[14] Significant steps, therefore, were being made to rectify the legacy of apartheid, which had retarded the development of an educated workforce and the acquisition of skills that would have accompanied it.

Coal

Output

Coal was the star performer of the 1980s and, like platinum, benefited from breakthroughs in technology. In the case of platinum it was the development of autocatalysts to reduce the carbon emissions from cars and the growth of the electronics industry; in the case of coal it was the revolution in the economies of long-distance transport with the introduction of the bulk carrier that made it possible to move coal thousands of miles economically. When this was accompanied by far-reaching fuel economies in the iron and steel industry, the world's heavy industry began to move to coastal areas suitable for importing both coal and iron ore. Until the last third of the twentieth century, the world's iron and steel industry had been tied to coalfields, for the simple reason that more coal was consumed than iron ore in the production of iron and steel. It made economic sense. In the last third of the century this changed and Europe and East Asia began to import coal for their industries. Australia was the principal beneficiary at first, followed by Canada and South Africa for the Asian market, but for the European market South Africa was more favourably situated. Coal from the Eastern Transvaal was closer to European markets than coal from Australia or western Canada. Export demand, therefore, was the driving force behind the expansion of coal mining in South Africa.

This growth of a major new mineral export in the 1980s coincided with the end of the inefficient and harmful system of government-regulated prices that had held back investment in the industry. It coincided, too, with the disappearance of coal-burning locomotives from the railways and the coming on stream of the large new power stations that had been planned and built in the 1970s. As a result, both

14 Jones and Baxter, 'Transformation in the 1990s', pp. 91–93.

Table 4.20 *Growth of coal sales and production, 1990–2000*

Year	*Domestic sales*		*Export sales*	
	By value (R millions)	*By weight (1,000s tons)*	*By value (R millions)*	*By weight (1,000s tons)*
1990	4,146.4	135,795	4,026.9	49,625
1991	4,505.9	132,604	4,279.4	49,265
1992	5,066.7	129,580	4,357.1	49,638
1993	5,193.1	131,812	4,520.9	52,189
1994	5,520.3	138,824	4,832.3	54,838
1995	6,338.8	146,030	7,478.8	59,676
1996	6,786.6	146,048	8,104.4	60,169
1997	7,799.6	159,454	8,468.5	57,637
1998	8,217.9	156,814	9,699.1	66,134
1999	8,305.6	155,307	9,181.8	64,907
2000	8,774.0	154,674	10,925.9	68,281

Source: Statistical Tables 1980–2000, Minerals Bureau, 2000.

external and internal conditions favoured the expansion of coal mining in the 1980s.

In the 1990s the economic environment was less favourable. The South African economy itself was sluggish, beset by political unrest at the beginning of the decade and then strangled by the labour legislation imposed by the new government. For most of the decade there was excess capacity in the electricity supply industry. This dampening down in the domestic demand for coal coincided, in the early years of the decade, with intensified trade sanctions (France reduced its imports of South African coal) and was then followed by the ending of rapid growth in East Asian and South East Asian countries, which reduced their demand for coal imports. By the end of the decade there was global excess capacity in the iron and steel industry and the price of coal, which had remained buoyant in the 1980s, began to slide.

In this harsher climate the South African coal industry performed satisfactorily. By 2000 South Africa had become the world's fourth largest producer of coal and the second largest exporter,[15] a role not so very different from that of Britain a century earlier. By value, in 2000, 55.3 per cent of coal sold was exported (Table 4.20). In the 1990s exports grew at the rate of 3.9 per cent a year, dominated by steam coal, with Europe the most important market. To achieve this, the Richards Bay Coal Terminal underwent a series upgrades and in the year 2000 plans were underway to expand its capacity to 84 million tons by 2004.

15 *Statistical Tables 1980–2000,* Minerals Bureau, 2000.

Inflation was distorting the figures, but it was slowing down. In the 1980s the price of domestic coal trebled; in the 1990s it almost doubled. Coal for the export market experienced almost a quadrupling of prices in the 1980s, which declined to a doubling in the 1990s. In monetary terms the total value of sales in 2000 was impressive. They had reached R19,699.9 million, with the value of exports growing at the rate of 10.5 per cent a year and total sales by 9.2 per cent. Actual tonnage moved grew at a slower rate, with exports increasing at the rate of 3.2 per cent and domestic sales at the rate of 1.3 per cent. Exports by volume had increased from 26.8 per cent of total production to 30.6 per cent of total production. The value was much higher. The 30.6 per cent of production exported earned 55.3 per cent of sales. Exporting was very profitable and, once sanctions ended, market forces ensured rapid growth, almost all of which took place after 1994. In 1995 the value of exports overtook those of domestic sales and exports regained the position they had occupied in 1986.

Capital and labour in coal mining

Information on capital invested in coal mining is no longer published, because the larger mines passed into the total ownership of holding companies that delisted them from the JSE. In 1990 nine coal mining companies were listed but in 2000 only two, of which one was in Zimbabwe. The local South African company, Century, had a market capitalisation of less than R12 million. The Swiss commodity group

Table 4.21 *Employment, per capita output and per capita earnings in coal mining, 1990–2000*

Year	*Total number of workers employed*	*Per capita output (tons)*	*Per capita earnings (R)*
1990	103,531	1,690.1	20,526
1991	96,197	1,855.2	25,364
1992	75,858	2,338.2	27,426
1993	61,163	3,007.7	30,710
1994	60,187	3,264.1	33,572
1995	62,012	3,316.1	38,212
1996	62,656	3,271.8	44,135
1997	61,607	3,559.2	52,087
1998	60,310	3,710.6	58,411
1999	55,048	4,037.8	69,284
2000	51,235	4,378.7	83,122

Source: *Statistical Tables 1980–2000*, Minerals Bureau, 2000.

Glencore bought control of Duiker from the London Finance and Investment Group and established itself as the world's largest coal exporter, a position held until 2000 by Billiton with its Ingwe Coal Mining Company, which was also delisted. Competition intensified towards the end of the decade, with prices falling sharply.[16] This was the driving force behind the rationalisation of the coal business that led to the disappearance of Trans-Natal, Ingwe, Duiker and Goldfields Coal, all large and well established companies. It may be interpreted as a response to the reintegration of the South African economy into the international economy after the 1994 election.

Labour conditions in the coal mines were dominated by rising output, rising productivity and rising earnings (Table 4.21). Employment in the coal mines, which had peaked in 1981 with a total of 136,187, had fallen to 103,531 in 1990. Ten years later it had halved, to 51,235, and per capita earnings had risen to R83,122, more than four times average earnings in 1990. Mechanisation had made this possible, as per capita output rose during the decade at a rate of 10 per cent a year. Per capita earnings rose at the rate of 15 per cent, well above the inflation rate. Coal mining typified the ANC's economic policy, with unemployment accompanying a significant rise in real earnings for the employed. John L. Lewis, the coal mine trade union leader, had adopted a similar policy in the USA in the third quarter of the century.

Diamonds

Diamonds contributed the fourth highest mineral earnings, if the bulk of the 'Miscellaneous' figures published by the Chamber of Mines was made up by diamonds. Production was relatively stable, fluctuating from a high of 10,854 carats in 1994 to a low of 8,431 carats in 1991. It was rising slowly. In the 1980s there were four years when production rose above 10,000 carats; in the 1990s there were seven years above 10,000 carats (Table 4.22). In 2000 this amounted to less than 10 per cent of global output, and was valued at 11 per cent of global production. As the world diamond jewellery market in 2000 was valued at $56 billion, South Africa's 11 per cent of it was worth $6.16 billion, though foreign exchange earnings from diamonds amounted to $5.2 billion. The difference, if the estimates are accurate, would have been consumed by the domestic market.[17]

16 *Financial Mail, Top Companies Millennium Edition*, 2000, p. 214.
17 *Statistical Tables 1980–2000*, Minerals Bureau, 2000, p. 3.

Table 4.22 *Output, employment and earnings in diamond mining, 1990–2000*

Year	*Output (carats)*	*Employment*	*Earnings per capita (R)*
1990	8,708	22,982	21,539
1991	8,431	21,516	26,812
1992	10,177	19,654	31,755
1993	10,324	14,880	36,133
1994	10,854	15,828	35,754
1995	9,684	15,547	37,494
1996	9,956	15,518	45,484
1997	10,086	15,935	51,902
1998	10,751	14,781	61,183
1999	10,024	15,367	64,993
2000	10,805	15,007	71,432

Source: *Statistical Tables 1980–2000,* Minerals Bureau, 2000.

South Africa's interest in diamond sales was not confined to its production of rough stones, because of the importance of De Beers' control over global sales. In calendar year 1999 these amounted to $5.2 billion at a time when the Central Selling Organisation's share of world trade in rough diamonds had fallen from 80 per cent to somewhere between 60 and 70 per cent.[18] In 1999 its cash flow surged to $1.9 billion, allowing the size of the stockpile to be reduced by $859 million. However, this still left a stockpile valued at $3.96 billion, more than double the record cash flow of that year. Indeed, before the stockpile was reduced, De Beers had close to R40 billion locked up in it, striking evidence of the amount of capital required by the cartel to maintain diamond prices at acceptable levels.

The main media interest in diamonds at the end of the decade lay in struggles for control of Ocean Diamond Mining, in which Anton Rupert, the tobacco and luxury goods magnate, was defeated by Christo Wiese and his allies in the Namibian Minerals Corporation. Trans Hex then merged with a black economic empowerment firm, Gem Diamond Mining, controlled by an ANC politician and Benguela Concessions Ltd. This left three main marine diamond players: De Beers Marine, Trans Hex and the Namibian Minerals Corporation.[19]

The ongoing controversy over diamonds originating in war zones, such as Angola, Congo or Sierra Leone, led to the formation of the World Diamond Council in 2000 and its attempt to certify the origin of rough diamonds. However, with the move of De Beers to London and its delisting, the importance of South Africa to diamond mining is

18 *Financial Mail, Top Companies Millennium Edition,* p. 211.
19 *Ibid.*, pp. 212–213.

much diminished and disputes over 'blood diamonds' are less likely to involve South Africa directly.

Australia remained the world's largest producer of diamonds, followed by Botswana. Both produced more than double the output of South Africa. They were followed by Russia and the Congo, with South Africa in fifth place. As with almost all South African mineral production, the demand was coming from overseas. America was the main market, taking about half the global output. Europe, Asia–Pacific, India and the Arab region accounted for the most of the rest. Though the industrial demand for diamonds was growing, jewellery took the bulk of sales and that market was particularly buoyant in the 1990s, reflecting the long stock market boom in the USA.

Capital and labour

In March 2000 the market capitalisation of De Beers was about $10 billion and diamonds accounted for $3 billion of this according to N. Oppenheimer.[20] He also argued that the market seriously undervalued the De Beers diamond business. In current prices this would place the capitalisation of that business somewhere between R25 billion and R40 billion, a far cry from the figure in the late 1980s, when, for a moment, the market capitalisation of De Beers overtook that of Anglo American.

Ferrous minerals: iron ore, chrome and manganese ore

The rapid growth of ferrous mineral production reflected both the expansion of the domestic iron and steel industry and overseas demand, which developed as a consequence of the transport revolution initiated by bulk ore carriers. The opening up of the Sishen iron ore deposits in the Northern Cape in the 1970s was made possible by this development and led to South Africa entering upon the world stage as a major iron ore exporter (Table 4.23).

According to the 2000 *Annual Report* of the Department of Minerals and Energy, in the 15 years from 1986 to 2000 the dollar earnings of ferrous minerals outpaced those of all other primary minerals, growing at the rate of 3.5 per cent a year.[21] South Africa has become the world's leading supplier of chromium, manganese and vanadium and a significant provider of iron ore and silicon. Together, they accounted for an eighth of total mineral sales and an eighth of total mineral exports.

20 *Ibid.*
21 *Annual Report*, Department of Minerals and Energy, 2000, p. 102.

Table 4.23 *Production and sales of ferrous minerals, 1990–2000*

Year	*Iron ore*		*Manganese ore*		*Chrome ore*	
	Output (tons, 1,000s)	*Sales (R millions)*	*Output (tons, 1,000s)*	*Sales (R millions)*	*Output (tons, 1,000s)*	*Sales (R millions)*
1990	30,347	1,085	4,402	848	4,618	486
1991	27,037	1,164	3,146	767	5,100	485
1992	25,171	1,133	2,464	600	3,363	388
1993	27,169	1,281	2,507	549	2,838	356
1994	30,488	1,405	2,851	645	3,642	400
1995	31,944	1,663	3,199	692	5,086	608
1996	30,828	1,699	3,240	784	5,078	835
1997	33,224	2,099	3,121	887	6,162	1,000
1998	32,964	2,504	3,044	955	6,480	912
1999	29,507	2,229	3,122	934	6,817	1,005
2000	33,707	3,065	3,635	1,232	6,898	1,080

Source: *Statistical Tables 1980–2000,* Minerals Bureau, 2000.

Other minerals

Nickel and copper were the only two other minerals that achieved sales of over R1 billion in 2000. The former, which had not increased its output in the 1980s, began to expand before the impact of a buoyant domestic market. In the 1990s domestic consumption expanded by 8.9 per cent a year, at a time when exports were falling by 3.7 per cent a year. In monetary terms, of course, both exports and home sales increased. Copper, by contrast, experienced a continuous decline in output of –3.1 per cent a year, caused by the loss of export markets, which contracted at the rate of –7.3 per cent a year, while domestic consumption increased by only 1.3 per cent a year. In this respect the fortunes of copper mining paralleled those of manganese. In both, the illusion of monetary expansion was the result of currency depreciation. Building materials for the domestic market propelled the continued expansion of aggregates, sand, limestone and lime minerals, but zinc followed the pattern of copper, with total output over the decade declining by –1.7 per cent a year. Granite quarrying was also expanding, though at a slower rate than in the 1980s, and once again most of the demand was coming from overseas markets. Two new minerals appear in the statistics in the 1990s: natural gas and natural gas condensate. These were the result of developments around Mossel Bay and were relatively small scale. Other minerals produced by South Africa were specialty minerals such as cobalt, asbestos, uranium, vanadium, titanium, zirconium and vermiculite. In many of these South Africa was the world's leading producer, but their economic impact was small. South Africa's importance to the global economy rested on the 'big five': platinum, gold, coal, diamonds and iron ore. It was these that underpinned the economy.

Changed environment of the 1990s

By the changed environment of the 1990s is usually meant the changed political situation, with a communist-dominated ANC government. This new government, with its emphasis upon transformation and black economic empowerment, according to R. W. Johnson, produced a *de facto* minority government of fat cats. Their policies led to a steady job loss of 100,000 a year and a continued decline in real per capita income. In practice, political correctness was the outstanding feature of the business environment, in which the political imperative of producing black business leaders outweighed economic reality. This is why Johnson could argue that government policies were inimical to South Africa's real interests and why criticism of them is routinely dismissed as racist.[22]

Not only has the structure of the mining industry changed, with the breaking up of most of the old mining finance houses (Anglo American is the exception), but the Chamber of Mines itself has been transformed. From being a body that provided a whole range of services to the mining industry, it has been converted into a department of public relations that acts as a lobbyist for the industry, by maintaining close relations with government departments, the media and the various mining companies. Its annual reports reflect the changing priorities. They are now more thorough pieces of work, with 14 pages devoted to a detailed economic review, but with 48 pages devoted policy, education and labour issues.

New labour laws and the prospect of a new minerals policy coloured thinking and policy in the 1990s, particularly after the failure of the first implementation of black economic empowerment project with some of the mines that had belonged to JCI. At the same time, the mining industry found itself behind its global competitors in terms of best practice.[23] Archaic work practices needed to be reformed, but the popularly held notion that the industry suffered from lack of access to global finance, before 1994, is true only insofar as it applies to attempts to develop worldwide mining activities from a South African base. Within South Africa there was no shortage of finance. Rather the opposite

22 *Business Day*, 9 October 2002.
23 Jones and Baxter, 'Transformation in the 1990s', p. 90.

prevailed, with the large mining finance houses, led by Anglo American, increasing their grip on the JSE, because of the lack of sufficient suitable opportunities for investment in mining within the country.

A paradox developed, in that the declining gold price and the need to manage the mines more efficiently was taking place in a new labour law environment that made it difficult to deploy labour more efficiently. Outside the gold mining industry it led to a renewed emphasis upon capital replacing labour. Mechanisation was not a practical alternative in the gold mining industry, but it was possible to use the existing workforce more efficiently, though at the risk of a confrontation with the unions.

A potential threat to property rights existed. This did not deter continued investment in the industry, though it undoubtedly increased the perception of the risk involved. Over time this led to high interest rates and to a discount on the value of investments in the country, which was not helped by the experience of mining investments in Zambia and Zimbabwe.

It is easy to demand transformation in the mining industry, but if this means replacing white ownership with black ownership, it is not clear how this can be achieved by ordinary market forces, when the market capitalisation of the mining companies on the JSE at the end of December 2000 amounted to R493 billion.[24] If the state printed money to buy them, it would be devastatingly inflationary and even R. W. Johnson's fat cats could not mobilise more than a fraction of this amount. As a result, government-imposed quotas of minimum black ownership have added to the uncertainty prevailing. It would, therefore, seem reasonable to describe the mining sector in the 1990s as being in a state of partial transformation, in which the process of change has begun, but in which the end result is not clear. Meanwhile, the experience of Zambia serves as a warning against state control, while the employment equity legislation may be interpreted as a form of legalised theft from pension funds.

Conclusion

Mining in the 1990s was coloured by three main developments: the coming to power of a communist-dominated government; the rise of the platinum group metals to premier position; and the massive decline in the volume and real value of gold output. The first of these was not directly the result of market forces, though apartheid policies had become too costly to maintain, but the second was a dramatic example

24 *Statistics 2000*, Chamber of Mines, p. 2.

of the impact of the market in creating economic growth and wealth. Concurrently, too, market forces were propelling the continued expansion of coal mining, diamond mining and iron ore mining and, less propitiously, contributing to the decline in gold production.

By the end of the decade the direct contribution of mining to GDP had shrunk to 6.5 per cent and the indirect contribution to around 10 per cent. From an international point of view, mining remained very important, because it underpinned the balance of payments, providing, in 2000, 41 per cent of exports. Excluding gold, the mining sector had out-performed the rest of the economy, growing at the rate of 2.6 per cent during the decade as against 1.6 per cent. However, if one includes gold, the value of mineral output production had been declining in real terms at the rate of –0.7 per cent a year. Taking into account the increase in the size of the population, per capita mineral sales had experienced a marked decline. Nevertheless, in 2000, mining remained of vital importance both to the labour market and to the fiscus. To the latter it contributed R2.5 billion directly and perhaps the same again indirectly. With over three-quarters of output exported, the mining industry had benefited from the long boom that was driving the American economy and much of the international economy in the 1990s, though these exogenous forces were not strong enough to pull the whole mining sector into real growth at a time of rapid decline in gold mining.

5

Manufacturing: facing up to trade liberalisation

Colin McCarthy

Introduction

The periodisation of economic history is always problematical. The identification of turning points and the events that brought them about is often difficult and at times arbitrary. To review developments during specific periods such as successive decades is not periodisation but it does shed light on events that, in time, would seem to have been the dominant feature during a particular decade.

In considering the development of manufacturing during the last decade of the twentieth century, the experience of the 1980s provides appropriate perspective. The story to be told about the manufacturing sector during the 1980s is a dismal one, of virtually no growth in output and employment.[1] In a review of that decade, it was concluded that if the experience of the 1980s was repeated in the 1990s there would be reason to face the future with trepidation.[2] As it turned out, manufacturing performance during the 1990s remained poor, with manufacturing value added in 2000 in real terms only 8.6 per cent higher than in 1990, but even more disconcerting was that there were 18 per cent fewer factory jobs in 2000 than in 1990.[3] This chapter reviews this poor performance but also focuses on some other important developments, the outcome of which is still uncertain. The main concern underlying the chapter

The author benefited from assistance by Theo-Chris Groenewald on the statistical information used and from valuable comments by Stuart Jones and Pieter Laubscher on an earlier draft of the chapter.

1 Colin McCarthy, 'The 1980s – a lost decade for the South African manufacturing sector?', *South African Journal of Economic History*, 9(2) (1994), 66–83.
2 *Ibid.*, p. 82.
3 Derived from South African Reserve Bank, *Quarterly Bulletin*, June 1998 and June 2002.

can best be summarised in the words with which Bell and Madula concluded their review of South African manufacturing industry:

> Manufacturing … matters a good deal. Given trends in other sectors of the economy, it is hard to see how growth rates of the sort needed not only for economic, but also for political reasons, can be achieved without a substantial acceleration of the growth of manufacturing industry.[4]

Changing policy environment

The 1990s was an eventful decade, characterised by fairly radical changes in the policy and market environment of manufacturing industry. To an important extent the changes can be linked to the major political event of the decade, namely the transition from apartheid to an inclusive democracy in 1994 and with this a change of government, and to the process of trade liberalisation, which drastically lowered the protective shield of manufacturing.

The Government of National Unity (GNU) led by the African National Congress (ANC) adopted two economic strategies that had implications for manufacturing development, with a commitment by the new government 'to avoid deindustrialisation, and to accelerate the growth of the manufacturing sector in South Africa as a key driver for growth and development'.[5] In May 1994 the GNU adopted the *Reconstruction and Development Programme* (RDP), a comprehensive plan aimed at a reduction of poverty and inequality but also emphasising economic growth and improved social service delivery. Although RDP goals remained an essential feature of government policy, the focus in June 1996 shifted to the 'growth, employment and redistribution' (GEAR) macro-economic policy framework. GEAR built on the vision contained in the RDP but was more committed to securing macro-economic stability and high job-creating economic growth; it accepted as a point of departure that 'sustained growth on a higher plane requires a transformation towards a competitive outward-oriented economy'.[6] GEAR provided for an integrated development strategy built on fiscal discipline, trade liberalisation, wage discipline and a host of supply-side measures, which, as a strategy, was expected to encourage rapid

4 Trevor Bell and Nkosi Madula, 'The manufacturing industry, 1970–2000', in Stuart Jones (ed.), *The Decline of the South African Economy*, Edward Elgar, 2002, p. 126.

5 *Accelerating Growth and Development – The Contribution of the Integrated Manufacturing Strategy*, Department of Trade and Industry, 2002, p. 10.

6 *Growth, Employment and Redistribution – A Macro-Economic Strategy*, Department of Finance, 1996, p. 1.

investment growth, real private investment in particular, and high real non-gold exports. The projected outcome for 2000 was a GDP growth rate of 6.1 per cent, 409,000 new jobs in that year and manufactured exports growing at 12.8 per cent in real terms.[7] Compared with these expectations, the real outcome was depressing.

For manufacturing, the most important development of the decade was the acceleration of trade liberalisation. Before 1990 the encouragement of export-led growth had been heralded by the 1972 report of the Reynders Commission of Inquiry into South Africa's export trade, but the introduction of the General Export Incentive Scheme (GEIS) in April 1990 signalled an intensification of this approach.

To appreciate the rationale of the measures implemented, it is useful to employ a framework that defines trade strategies with reference to the concept of trade neutrality and differences between the effective exchange rates, adjusted to include price incentives, that apply for the production of respectively import-competing and export goods.[8] The trade regime is neutral if the effective exchange rate (EER) for a country's export production more or less equals the rate that applies for import-competing industries. Should tariff and non-tariff protection produce an EER for import-competing goods that exceeds the rate for exports, a bias exists in favour of the production of import-competing goods. If price incentives produce an EER for export goods that exceeds the rate for import-competing goods, the bias is in favour of export production.

Within this framework it is clear that a country going through a process of inward-looking development, with protection and import substitution, will have price incentives that reflect EER levels that are biased against export production. This bias will need to be removed if export-oriented development becomes the chosen strategy. This can be achieved in a number of ways, of which comprehensive trade liberalisation, that is, the removal of all forms of protection against imports, is at one extreme. Such a strategy is likely to have high transitional costs, since the resources released from inefficient import-competing industries are not rapidly and smoothly re-employed in the more efficient industries that can compete in world markets. Hence, the preference often is to lower protection only gradually and to supplement this with measures that will neutralise the cost-increasing impact of protection for export producers. These measures can include subsidies and the rebate or drawback of import duties levied on goods used in the production

7 *Ibid.*, p. 7.

8 See Jagdish Bhagwati, 'Outward orientation: trade issues', in Vittorio Corbo, Morris Goldstein and Mohsin Khan (eds), *Growth-Oriented Adjustment Programs*, International Monetary Fund and the World Bank, 1987, pp. 258–259.

of export goods.[9] Conceptually, we distinguish trade liberalisation, defined as a lowering or removal of the trade barriers that may exist either for the encouragement of export production or for the protection of import-competing industries, from measures such as direct and indirect export subsidies, which seek to achieve a level playing field for export- and import-competing producers.

The measures introduced during the 1970s and 1980s were mostly aimed at reducing the cost disadvantage facing South African export producers and included export subsidies, tax concessions on export turnover and profits, rail freight concessions, assistance with meeting the cost of export marketing and the rebate and drawback of import duties on imported inputs.[10] On the import side, developments saw the change in 1985 of import control from a positive to a negative list of products subject to import control by permit, a hardening in the stance by the Board on Tariffs and Trade to requests by the private sector for tariff protection and the replacement of quantitative import restrictions with tariffs at lower levels than those implicit in the quantitative restrictions.

Direct and indirect subsidies that encourage export production operate on the demand side of the export equation by effectively lowering the price of exports. Subsidies provided in an economy that does not protect its domestic industry represent protection against competition of domestic industries in foreign markets. In economies that protect their domestic industries, protection in foreign markets would also be the outcome but the principal intention would then be to neutralise the cost disadvantage facing an exporter whose costs are higher because of the protected economy. For South African exporters that had to contend with the constraint of sanctions, export subsidies could also be regarded as partial compensation for the costs of sanctions and trade boycotts.

9 The extreme variant of this would be to establish an industrial estate that operates as an enclave within the national customs area, usually near an international port or airport. Such an estate, referred to as an export processing zone (EPZ), will be properly controlled to provide for the duty-free importation of goods for use in export production. This duty-free access to imported inputs is the defining characteristic of an EPZ. The number of EPZs has grown very rapidly in the developing world, with this concept proving a popular means of encouraging export-oriented development in economies that wish to maintain protection of domestic industries. Often the zones operate with dedicated infrastructure that is superior to that available in the domestic economy. Other cost benefits, such as low-rent factory suites and exclusion from domestic labour legislation with respect to wage determination, are also available, as is the absence of foreign exchange control.

10 For a brief overview of the successive phases of trade liberalisation in South Africa up to and including the 1990s, see Rashad Cassim, Donald Onyango and Dirk Ernst van Seventer, *The State of Trade Policy in South Africa,* Trade and Industrial Policy Strategies (TIPS) Forum, December 2002, pp. 8–11.

The introduction of the GEIS represented a forceful effort by the government to encourage export production by offsetting the price disadvantages South African exporters faced in export markets. The scheme was very liberal and provided cash subsidies to export producers in four categories, defined by value added and local content. In the first category, exporters qualified for a tax-free grant amounting to 2 per cent of export value; this increased up to the fourth category, which presented the exporter with a nominal subsidy of 19.5 per cent of export turnover.

During decades of import-substituting industrialisation, the South African government encouraged industrial growth on a highly selective basis. This contributed to the complexity of the tariff structure, an issue that is discussed below. The shift in emphasis towards export production was accompanied by something similar. An indirect export subsidy was applied for a relatively brief period to encourage mineral beneficiation through tax concessions that were provided under section 37E of the Income Tax Act. This incentive was terminated in September 1993.

An important selective strategy was implemented to develop the motor vehicle industry. The auto assembly industry was established in the early 1920s behind high tariff walls. In 1961 a series of programmes commenced to increase local content. In 1989 the policy shifted from import substitution to export promotion. A scheme of reciprocity was introduced that provided for the duty-free import of components or complete vehicles in return for the export of a part of their production. The Motor Industry Development Programme (MIDP) was initiated in 1995, providing for: a phase-down of import tariffs; a removal of requirements for local content; duty-free imports of components up to 27 per cent of the wholesale value of a vehicle; and duty rebate credits (import credit certificates) to be earned on exports.[11]

The textile and clothing industry also benefited from selective intervention through a scheme of trade reciprocity. The Duty Credit Certificate Scheme (DCCS) was introduced in the mid-1990s to coincide with the lowering of import duties on textiles and clothing. The DCCS is an export incentive that allowed firms to claim a remission of duty, that is, a duty credit that covers the duties payable on clothing and textile imports, for proven exports.[12] Similar to the GEIS, the level of the

11 David Kaplan, *Manufacturing Performance and Policy in South Africa: A Review*, Trade and Industrial Policy Strategies (TIPS) Forum, 2003, p. 15.

12 The DCCS provides the textile and clothing exporter with an *alternative* to customs rebate provision number 470.03, which is available for use by all exporters who use imported inputs in the production of export goods. Clothing firms make extensive use of the 470.03 facility, but those who do cannot also avail themselves of the DCCS.

incentive increases as the relevant product proceeds further down the textile pipeline (or moving up the textile value chain, as it is also called), with clothing receiving the highest support, followed by fabric and then yarn. To further encourage export orientation, a threshold was built into the scheme, such that firms were given greater support if they exported more than 15 per cent of their turnover.

The measures discussed so far aimed to neutralise the higher costs facing export producers in a protected domestic market. Earlier strategies of import-substituting industrialisation, the development of so-called strategic industries and efforts to add value to minerals through beneficiation resulted in a trade regime described in a World Bank study[13] as 'complex, highly discretionary … with a significant anti-export bias', a situation that was largely unaffected by efforts to liberalise trade and to offset the anti-export bias. The characteristics of the trade regime included the following: extensive quantitative restrictions; an exceptionably large number of tariff lines (12,500 in 1990); wide dispersion in tariff levels (with a coefficient of variation of 159.8); and various forms of protection, including formula, specific and *ad valorem* import duties.[14] An import surcharge added to the complication of the system of protection. A surcharge of 10 per cent on import values was introduced in 1985 to counter the large and sustained balance of payments deficit that was part of the fall-out of the 1985 debt crisis. The surcharge had a dramatic effect on the level of effective protection. The weighted average effective rate of protection, estimated for 1987, increased from 30 per cent to 70 per cent.[15]

The signing by South Africa of the Marrakesh Agreement in April 1994 brought about a major shift in trade and industrial policy. South Africa's final offer in the Uruguay Round of trade negotiations (submitted after extensive discussions of the draft offer in the National Economic Forum between government, the recently unbanned opposition parties, labour unions and business) included significant steps in liberalising the country's trade regime. The considerations in compiling this offer included: the potential for import-substituting growth behind a protective tariff wall had been depleted; further industrialisation and job creation required an export orientation; there was a need to simplify the complex protective system, which had become cumbersome to administer; the high tariffs required to counter short-term disruptive

13 Jeffrey D. Lewis, *Reform and Opportunity: The Changing Role and Patterns of Trade in South Africa and SADC*, World Bank Africa Region Working Paper Series Number 14, World Bank, March 2001, p. 2.

14 *Ibid.*, pp. 2–3.

15 Cassim *et al.*, *The State of Trade Policy*, p. 10.

imports had become an unfair burden on the consumer over the long run; there was a need to introduce supply-side measures to improve the competitiveness of the South African economy; and full participation in the Uruguay Round was wanted to ensure better access for South African exports to the markets of other member countries.[16]

The new tariff regime for industrial goods (chapters 25 to 99 of the 'Harmonised System') and the commitments contained in the offer, which officially took effect in January 1995, included the following:

- a phased reduction in tariff levels by one-third on simple average over five years (average weighted import duties to be reduced from 34 per cent to 17 per cent for consumption goods, 8 per cent to 4 per cent for intermediate goods and 11 per cent to 5 per cent for capital goods), excluding textiles and clothing and the automotive sectors, as sensitive industries, which were given eight years to reach the offer levels;
- the replacement of all the remaining quantitative import restrictions and the formula duties with *ad valorem* import duties;
- a drastic simplification and standardisation of the tariff structure, reducing the number of tariff rates from more than 80 to six ceiling rates (0, 5, 10, 15, 20 and 30 per cent), applied to a sharply reduced number of tariff lines;
- in support of export-oriented industrial development and employment creation, a cascading tariff structure with tariff rates of 0–10 per cent applied to primary products and capital goods, 10–15 per cent to components and 15–30 per cent to consumer goods;
- increasing the proportion of bound tariffs from 55 per cent to 98 per cent of all tariffs.

Furthermore, the GEIS was to be phased out by the end of 1997. The GEIS was a clear contravention both of article XVI (on subsidies) of the General Agreement on Tariffs and Trade (GATT) and of article 3.1(a) of the Agreement on Subsidies and Countervailing Measures, which describes prohibited subsidies as 'subsidies contingent, in law or in fact … upon export performance'.[17]

The progress made in the transformation of the tariff regime was substantial. Between 1990 and 1999, as far as all rates (including zero-rated items) are concerned, the number of tariff lines was reduced by 38 per cent, from 12,500 to 7,743, the number of different tariff rates (bands) by 76 per cent, from 200 to 47, and the unweighted mean

16 P. E. Kotzé, *Reform of the Protective System*, Information Series (IS 1/94), Industrial Development Corporation, 1994, pp. 1–2.

17 World Trade Organization, *The Legal Texts – The Results of the Uruguay Round of Multilateral Trade Negotiations*, Cambridge University Press, 1999, p. 233.

rate by 74 per cent, from 27.5 per cent to 7.1 per cent (7.5 per cent for manufacturing).[18] However, the major part of liberalisation took place in the early years of the decade; after 1996 the pace declined significantly.[19] This can hardly be regarded as surprising, since it was to be expected that tariff management bodies would find it more difficult to simplify the system as they moved from the easier and less sensitive to more complicated and sensitive products. Nevertheless, a comparison of average import-weighted tariffs shows that, for industrial products, the applied rate declined from 11.4 per cent in 1996 to 8.6 per cent in 2000, which indicates that some progress was made in the latter half of the decade.[20] The World Trade Organization (WTO) reported a decline in the simple average applied rate for non-agricultural products from 15.4 per cent in 1997 to 12.9 per cent in 2000 and 11.4 per cent in 2002.[21]

Compared with tariff reductions, less progress was made in reducing the range and number of tariffs in South Africa. Early in the next decade there were still nearly 50 tariff bands, as opposed to the six bands envisaged in the offer.[22]

All things considered, however, the overall situation with respect to trade liberalisation may be less than clear when the effective level of protection and the existence of the anti-export bias are considered.

- The relatively large number of zero rates means that, in comparison with other countries, the average South African tariff is lower than what the average of positive rates would reveal, namely an average in 1999 of around 17 per cent for positive rates only, compared with 7 per cent for all rates.[23]

18 Lewis, *Reform and Opportunity*, pp. 3, 5.

19 *Ibid.*, p. 3.

20 Cassim *et al.*, *The State of Trade Policy*, p. 15.

21 *Trade Policy Review: Southern African Customs Union*, WT/TPR/S/114, World Trade Organization, March 2003, p. 19.

22 Cassim *et al.*, *The State of Trade Policy*, p. 15.

23 Lewis, *Reform and Opportunity*, p. 4. Lewis further argues that many middle-income countries have well developed duty drawback or rebate systems that allow export producers to obtain imported inputs at world prices, thus avoiding the impact of higher average tariffs, something that South Africa apparently, according to Lewis, does not have. Elsewhere, Lewis argued that 'South Africa has had little experience with efforts to encourage non-mineral export activities through export processing zones or duty drawback and rebate schemes' (Jeffrey D. Lewis, *Policies to Promote Growth and Employment in South Africa*, World Bank Southern Africa Department Discussion Paper Number 16, July 2001, p. 24). This is true with respect to EPZs, an instrument considered but rejected in South Africa, but the statement on drawbacks and rebates is simply not true. South African export producers make extensive use of customs provision number 521.0, which allows drawback of duties, and number 470.03, a rebate provision that allows access to duty-free imported inputs.

- There is evidence that, because of the tariff cascade, with tariff levels increasing from capital to intermediate and then consumer goods, trade liberalisation has not extended to effective protection. Drawing on work by Fedderke and Vaze, Lewis concludes that, although tariffs have fallen, they have tended to fall more on inputs than on output, leading to increases in effective protection.[24]
- The lowering of tariff levels has been accompanied by intensive use of contingent protection in the form of anti-dumping action. Worldwide, the lowering of tariffs has been accompanied by an increase in the use of non-tariff barriers, of which anti-dumping action within the framework of the WTO agreements has proven to be popular. During the period 1995–2001, South Africa initiated 156 dumping investigations, which are fewer than the 255 initiations of the USA, the 248 of India and the 246 of the EU, but if calculated on an import-weighted basis, South Africa lies far above these countries.[25]

The policy changes discussed so far cover trade liberalisation within the multilateral framework of the WTO. For the tariff, the target was to lower and simplify the 'most favoured nation' or general tariff. However, the three-column tariff structure that developed during the 1990s – the EU and Southern African Development Community (SADC) columns, added to the general tariff column – testified to trade liberalisation, which was also actively pursued through preferential trading arrangements. In 1996 a SADC Trade Protocol was signed to begin the progressive creation of a SADC free trade area. The Protocol was implemented in September 2000, after it had been ratified by 11 SADC member states. Three categories of goods were identified. Category A goods, mostly capital goods, were liberalised to zero rates in the first year. Category B goods, mostly those that generate significant revenue, were to be liberalised by 2008 (although to date, 2010, no clarity exists on the progress that has been made in this regard). Category C goods are regarded as sensitive by the respective countries but limited to a maximum of 15 per cent of each member's merchandise trade. These goods were to be liberalised between 2005 and 2012. A limited number of goods are excluded from preferential treatment under general and

24 Lewis, *Reform and Opportunity*, p. 5.

25 These are the number of dumping initiations as reported to and published by the WTO on its website (www.wto.org). Using imports in 2000 as weight and using the number of initiations by the USA as base (i.e. USA = 100), the comparative index value for the EU is 55, for India it is 2490 and for South Africa 2,625. On this import-weighted basis, South Africa appears as the second most prolific user of anti-dumping action, second only to Argentina, with its index value of 3,275.

security exceptions. It is envisaged that by 2012 about 98 per cent of intra-SADC trade will be zero rated.

Although the development of a SADC free trade area cannot be regarded as insignificant, the fact is that, on the basis of existing trade flows, Europe has long been South Africa's major trading partner. Hence, the conclusion in October 1999 and the coming into force on 1 January 2000 of the Trade, Development and Cooperation Agreement (TDCA) between South Africa and the EU will prove to be a much more important event in terms of its impact on South African industry. The TDCA provides for the development, in an asymmetrical fashion, of free trade between South Africa and the EU by 2012. During this transitional period the EU will phase down its tariffs faster than South Africa, whose sensitive products (which comprise about 16 per cent of its imports from the EU) will be fully liberalised only at the end of the period. The existence of significant tariff protection, albeit lower than before, and the phasing out of export subsidies imply that an anti-export bias remains in place. Since the total removal of tariffs is not on the cards, the only solution to this problem in a way that is acceptable within the WTO is to change the focus from trade policy to industrial policy, with an emphasis on supply-side measures, that is, measures that will increase efficiency by improving the conditions under which goods are produced. In the reference above to GEAR, the implementation of a whole package of supply-side measure was alluded to.

The logic of the use of supply-side measures to encourage export-oriented, labour-absorbing growth, led by the manufacturing sector, was based on the role of fixed investment in driving economic growth and employment creation (labour and capital being complements and not substitutes in the growth process). Hence, the emphasis fell on two fiscal incentives aimed at the encouragement of new investment. The first was a scheme that provided for accelerated depreciation allowances, available for a three-year period (1 July 1996 to 31 September 1999). Only existing firms could qualify on the basis of new investment in manufacturing plant and equipment. The second fiscal incentive was a tax holiday, available to new firms active in completely new pre-approved projects that met certain qualifying conditions, such as a sufficient level of domestic value added and evidence of a commitment to important economic goals, including human resource development, foreign exchange conservation and environmental responsibility. New firms could qualify for a tax holiday of six years' duration, two years each for the three criteria of labour absorption, regional location and industrial priority. Presumably, to avoid falling foul of the WTO Agreement on Subsidies and Countervailing Measures, which includes in its definition of subsidies in article 1.1 'government revenue that is otherwise due is foregone or not collected',[26] export-orientation was not listed as a condition or criterion. However, the Minister of Trade and Industry could define priority industries in a number of categories, one of which could be seen as a somewhat veiled reference to export orientation, namely 'future industries defined in terms of their potential to secure a larger share of global consumer expenditure'.[27]

In addition to the tax incentives, a number of other supply-side measures were also implemented. These included the enhancement of the industrial innovation support programmes and measures aimed at improving productivity, competition and the promotion of small, medium and micro-enterprises. Like elsewhere in the world, a focus on industrial clusters also became a fashionable idea in South Africa, with studies undertaken to identify mechanisms to make selected clusters more competitive. The clusters could qualify for the tax holiday, with specific interventions considered where necessary.

Manufacturing performance

The poor performance of manufacturing growth during the 1990s, and specifically the fact that the sector experienced no growth in employment during this decade, has already been alluded to. During 1990–2000, manufacturing value added in real terms increased at an annual average of only 0.8 per cent. The growth in the physical volume of manufacturing output is shown in the trend line of Figure 5.1. The cycle during the 1990s, with an upward movement during the first half of the decade followed by a decline in average growth rates, is clear,[28] but the growth pattern stayed near the zero line and movements around a rising long-term trend did not materialise. The picture that emerges is one of improvement on the experience of the 1980s but still far below the expectation for a sector that should remain a force of growth in a developing economy. Furthermore, the growth that took place did not add to manufacturing employment; Figure 5.2 shows that manufacturing employment tended to fall over the decade, in a process of jobless growth.

26 World Trade Organization, *The Legal Texts*, p. 231.

27 *Growth, Employment and Redistribution – A Macro-Economic Strategy (Appendices)*, Department of Finance, appendix 11, p. 26.

28 An upward phase of the business cycle lasted from June 1993 until November 1996 with the downward phase running from December 1996 until August 1999. See South African Reserve Bank, *Quarterly Bulletin*, June 2002, p. S-147. It should be noted that the production volumes of Figure 5.1 include intermediate goods and will therefore be different from manufacturing value added (manufacturing GDP), valued at constant prices.

Figure 5.1 *Physical volume of manufacturing output: seasonally adjusted, actual values, monthly year-on-year percentage change, 1991–2000*

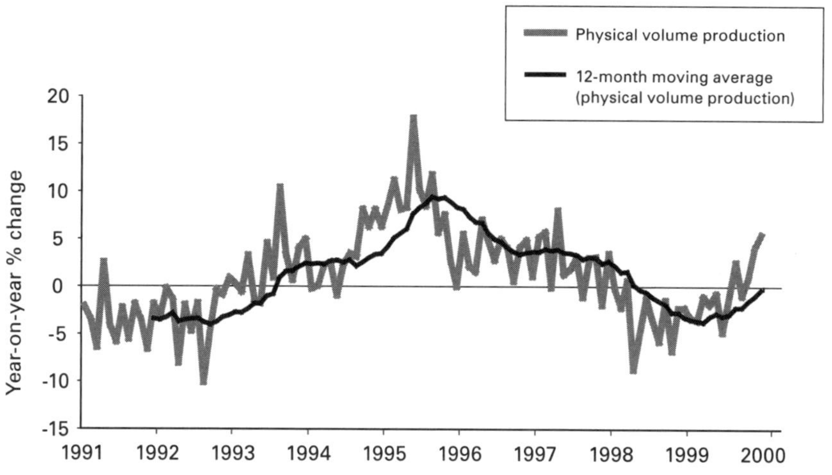

Source: P3041.2, Statistics South Africa, 2003.

Figure 5.2 *Total employment in the manufacturing sector, 1980–2000*

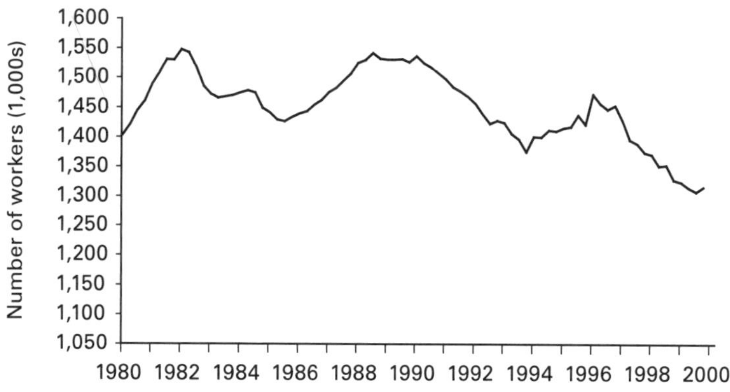

Source: P0271, Statistics South Africa, 2003.

Figure 5.3 *Manufacturing as percentage of GDP, 1990–2000*

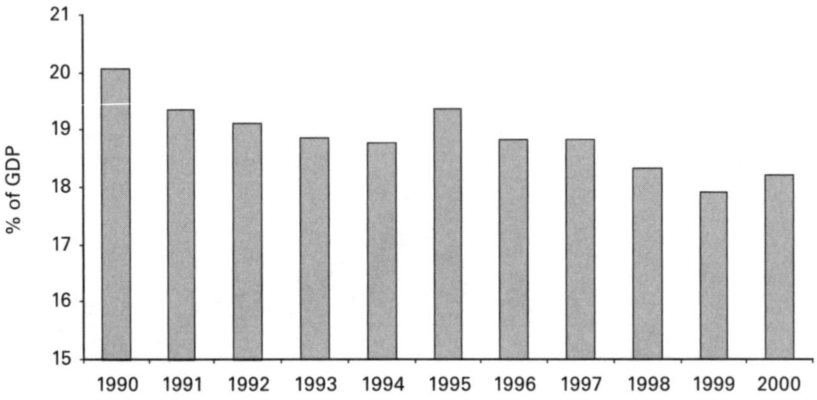

% of GDP
21
20
19
18
17
16
15
1990 1991 1992 1993 1994 1995 1996 1997 1998 1999 2000

Source: S-107, South African Reserve Bank, 2003.

A disturbing feature of manufacturing growth during the 1990s was the tendency for the sector to do worse than the economy as a whole, which meant that the share of manufacturing in GDP declined during the 1990s (Figure 5.3). It is not unknown for developing countries with a sizeable manufacturing sector to experience a decline in the relative contribution of manufacturing to GDP in the process of trade liberalisation. In fact, this is what theory would predict, with resources shifting from the less efficient use in protected industries to more productive use in sectors that have a comparative advantage. This was the experience when, for example, Chile during its trade liberalisation of the 1970s experienced an initial increase in the share of its competitive agricultural sector commensurate with a decline in the share of manufacturing.

However, in South Africa an explanation for the change in the relative contributions of sectors should rather be sought in the growth of services, driven especially by the information technology and telecommunications sectors. Bell and Madula refer to the fact that during the 1990s the finance, insurance, real estate and business services sector, together with transport, storage and communications, which includes the cellular phone industry (all being part of the 'new economy'), were the fastest-growing contributors to value added in the economy. They link this to a sanguine view that apparently regards the stagnation of manufacturing as a 'natural and beneficial transition from the old to the new economy'.[29]

29 Bell and Madula, 'The manufacturing industry, 1970–2000', p. 125.

Real growth in output, albeit mediocre, and growth in the stock of fixed capital, read together with the decline in the number of manufacturing jobs, brought about an increase in the capital–labour ratio and an increase in labour productivity, simplistically defined as net output (value added) per worker. Labour productivity in manufacturing increased by 6 per cent from 1990 to 1995 but then in the downward phase of the business cycle accelerated to make output per worker in 2000 no less than 32 per cent larger than in 1990. Capital intensity in production increased rapidly, with the capital–labour ratio 23 per cent higher in 1995 than in 1990 and in 2000 no less than 63 per cent higher than in 1990. The larger increase in the amount of fixed capital per worker than in output per worker portrays a fall in the productivity of capital, as revealed by the increase in the capital–output ratio by 16 per cent between 1990 and 1995 and by 23 per cent between 1990 and 2000.[30]

The reasons for the increase in capital intensity can, in an accounting sense, be twofold. The first is that capital has been substituted for labour in production, essentially because of changes in the relative prices of labour and capital in favour of the latter. To identify the extent to which this had been a cause requires production function studies for the different industries that make up the manufacturing sector, an approach that falls outside the scope of this chapter. However, it is often argued, as will be referred to below, that labour legislation and the cost of labour in South Africa are constraints on employment growth. Hence, it could be suggested on *a priori* grounds that this might have contributed to mechanisation in production activities, where this is technically feasible and economically viable, because of changes in relative factor prices.

A second cause of increasing capital intensity would take cognisance of the different factor intensities of the branches of manufacturing, that is, distinguishing between those that are relatively capital intensive and those that are labour intensive, and subsequently focus on the different rates of growth of these industries. In this respect Table 5.1 shows that, during the 1990s, the more labour-intensive branches of manufacturing (like food processing and textiles, clothing and footwear) grew more slowly, with their contribution to manufacturing GDP declining during the decade. The shares of capital-intensive sectors (like chemicals and basic metals) in manufacturing GDP, in contrast, increased significantly.

A closer look at the growth performance of selected manufacturing subsectors (Table 5.2) further reveals the differences in growth patterns and the impact that the policy environment could have had on this. In the iron and steel pipeline, the much faster growth upstream of

30 Calculated from data published in South African Reserve Bank, *Quarterly Bulletin*, June 1998 and June 2002.

Table 5.1 *Structure of manufacturing value added (%), 1990 and 2000*

	1990	*2000*
Food, beverages and tobacco	14.5	12.8
Textiles, clothing, leather and footwear	8.4	7.1
Wood products (including furniture)	3.4	3.9
Paper, printing and publishing	8.5	8.3
Chemicals, petroleum, rubber and plastic	19.9	20.8
Non-metallic mineral products	4.9	3.7
Basic metals	12.9	16.0
Metal products (including machinery)	25.7	26.0
Other manufacturing	1.9	1.5

Source: David Kaplan, *Manufacturing Performance and Policy in South Africa – A Review*, Trade and Industrial Policy Strategies (TIPS) Forum, 2003, p. 9.

Table 5.2 *Growth in the physical volume of production for selected manufacturing sectors, 1995 and 2000 (constant 2000 prices, converted to 1990 = 100)*

	1995	*2000*
Food	107.2	106.3
Textiles	91.2	92.8
Clothing	116.3	101.7
Leather and products	132.5	165.8
Footwear	95.0	62.2
Wood and products	129.1	154.1
Furniture	101.0	99.8
Publishing/printing	105.3	92.5
Basic chemicals	100.0	131.9
Rubber products	92.5	91.3
Plastics	145.0	130.0
Basic iron and steel	104.8	121.8
Fabricated metal products	102.1	105.6
Machinery and equipment	94.9	94.5
Motor vehicles	127.9	147.1
Total manufacturing	107.4	113.9

Source: P3041.2, Statistics South Africa, 2003.

the capital-intensive basic iron and steel industry compared with the slower growth of downstream industries in fabricated metal products and in machinery and equipment is conspicuous. The large investment in projects such as Saldanha Steel and the Columbus stainless steel project, both assisted by the Industrial Development Corporation and benefiting from the section 37E tax incentive, referred to above, as well as South Africa's low energy costs, contributed greatly to the growth of the upstream industries.

The continued importance of what has been termed the 'minerals–energy complex'[31] is clearly revealed in the growth performances summarised in Table 5.1 and especially of the iron and steel and chemicals subsectors. To this must be added the growth of indirect platinum exports contained in the production, primarily for export, of catalytic converters. Like leather products, the latter can also be attributed to the MIDP.

Table 5.2 also reveals the impact of the MIDP. The production of motor vehicles increased by 27.9 per cent during the first half of the 1990s and by 47.1 per cent over the decade as a whole. This is an impressive performance but one which has been questioned with respect to economic benefit.[32] But perhaps the most interesting impact of the MIDP can be read in the comparative growth performances of the footwear and leather and leather product industries. It is difficult to envisage that the comparative advantages of the labour-intensive leather product and footwear industries could be significantly different. Nevertheless, the sharp fall in the physical output of footwear contrasts with the rapid growth of leather products. The latter's growth was the result of the production, mostly for export, of leather seats for motor vehicles as a major earner of import credit certificates in terms of the MIDP. A superficial comparison shows that the textile and clothing industries did not benefit to a similar extent from sectoral development programmes. Textile production declined and remained stagnant during the 1990s, while clothing increased significantly during the first half of the decade but then fell back sharply during the second half.[33]

Subsectoral differences apart, the overall picture of manufacturing during the 1990s that emerges is one of mediocre aggregate growth characterised by significant variations in the growth of different industries, no net job creation and increasing capital intensity. In one respect, however, the sector did behave as one would expect with greater

31 Ben Fine and Zavareh Rustomjee, *The Political Economy of South Africa: From Minerals–Energy Complex to Industrialisation,* Witwatersrand University Press, 1996. This is not the place to review this book, but it should be noted that the authors' differentiation of import substitution and the development of the minerals–energy complex as driving forces of industrial development is contentious. At the very least it seems to ignore the fact that growth in the energy complex was directly linked to efforts by a beleaguered economy to substitute petrol from coal and gas for imported fuel.

32 See Kaplan, *Manufacturing Performance and Policy,* pp. 15–25.

33 During the first years of the new decade, clothing production increased, mostly because of higher exports associated with improved market access to the USA under the African Growth and Opportunity Act (AGOA). At the time of writing, however, the industry was reporting large output losses because of the appreciation of the rand and increased competition from cheaper imported clothing, especially from China.

outward orientation: manufactured exports grew significantly, with the volume of manufactured exports overtaking the amount of non-gold primary exports in 1996. During 1990–95, manufactured exports in real terms increased by 5.4 per cent per annum and then accelerated to a growth rate of 11.6 per cent per annum during the second half of the decade, thus increasing the contribution of the manufacturing sector to total exports (including services) from 39.5 per cent in 1990 to 41.3 per cent in 1995 and 56.2 per cent in 2000.[34]

The only major change in the product composition of exports associated with this growth was a significant increase in the share of transport equipment (from 3.5 per cent of total exports in 1995 to 6.8 per cent in 2000) and machinery (from 5.4 per cent in 1995 to 7.3 per cent in 2000). The shares of the other two dominant export product categories, namely base metals and chemicals, declined marginally over this period, base metals from 14.6 per cent to 14.1 per cent and chemicals from 6.1 per cent to 5.8 per cent.[35] What is interesting, and disturbing in view of South Africa's factor endowments and development needs, is that the factor intensity of manufactured exports increased considerably in favour of human capital intensity, from an estimated 49.5 per cent of manufactured exports in 1992 to 58.5 per cent in 1999. In contrast, the share of unskilled-labour-intensive manufactured exports decreased from an already low 8.9 per cent in 1992 to 6.8 per cent in 1999. The share of natural-resource-intensive exports during this period decreased from 24.0 per cent to 19.6 per cent and that of technology-intensive manufactured exports from 17.5 per cent to 15.1 per cent.[36]

As might be expected of an economy that had shaken off its pariah status in Africa, the growth of exports to the continent increased substantially, especially in the first years after 1993. This is illustrated in Figure 5.4. After the initial increase, the share of exports to Africa levelled off. Africa could be regarded as South Africa's natural market and provides significant opportunities for export growth, but African countries in general are poor and the effective market remains small considering the size of the continent's population. Nevertheless, two African countries outside the SACU, Zimbabwe and Mozambique, made it onto the list of South Africa's top 10 export destinations in the course of the 1990s. However, in 1999 the combined value of South African exports to Zimbabwe and Mozambique, which came to R9,199 million,

34 Derived from Quantec Research for Trade and Industrial Policy Strategies (TIPS) Industrial Databank.

35 Bureau for Economic Research, University of Stellenbosch, *Trends*, third quarter 2002, pp. 16, 19.

36 Lewis, *Reform and Opportunity*, p. 13.

Figure 5.4 *South Africa's exports to Africa: percentage share of total exports, 1992–2000*

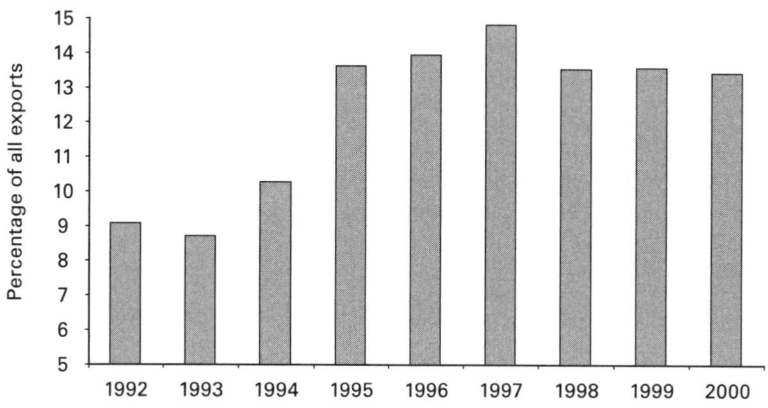

Source: Trade Statistics, South African Reserve Bank Series, 2003.

was less than South Africa's exports to each of the top three destinations, namely the USA, the UK and Germany.[37] This indicates that South Africa's traditional markets in the industrialised world remained the most important destination for export-oriented growth.

Perceptions of industrial performance and the road ahead

The chosen development path for manufacturing growth was that of export orientation and the means to achieve this was through major adjustments in trade and industrial policy. Trade policy reform consisted of substantial trade liberalisation, which was set to increase in intensity during the first decade of the new century as the SADC and especially the EU–South Africa free trade agreements proceeded towards full implementation, new bilateral free trade agreements were negotiated and the WTO multilateral negotiations of the Doha Work Programme were revived and successfully completed. These changes exposed manufacturing industry in the import-competing sector to strong competition and required export producers to be competitive in foreign markets. To

37 Stuart Jones, 'External trade, 1970–2000', Stuart Jones (ed.), *The Decline of the South African Economy*, Edward Elgar, 2002, p. 205.

assist industry in this regard an active industrial policy consisting of WTO-acceptable supply-side measures was designed.

Trade policy reform changed the external environment of the manufacturing sector fairly dramatically in the course of the 1990s. The South African economy has always been quite open, as indicated by the ratio of exports plus imports to GDP, and while this ratio had increased from 46 per cent during 1990–91 to 52 per cent during 1999–2000,[38] this does not fully reveal the impact on economic activity at the level of the firm and industry. For import-competing industries, the cosy protective barrier of relatively high tariff levels and trade sanctions is something of the past. Import penetration ratios have grown for virtually all manufactured products,[39] and for domestic industries it is no longer a question of only export producers being exposed to foreign competition: with freer trade, import-competing industries in the domestic market are equally exposed to the cold winds of foreign competition.

The decline in manufacturing employment has been emphasised. It is tempting to link this causally to trade liberalisation and an increase in import penetration of the South African market not compensated by growth in export production. Trade liberalisation is usually justified by efficiency considerations and the anticipated welfare benefits to be derived when resources are relocated from less efficient to more efficient use. However, there is a large difference between the model and the real world, especially with regard to the speed and cost of adjustment. A number of rigidities, including those related to the availability of skills and geographical mobility, will make high transitional costs inevitable as capital and workers are released faster and in larger numbers in less efficient industries than they are absorbed in more efficient industries. Using data for the manufacturing sector, Bhorat has found evidence that from 1993 to 1997, a critical time in the process of trade liberalisation, trade led to a decline in labour employment.[40] However, it is not unambiguously clear whether employment has been influenced by trade directly, such as increased import penetration, or by technological changes in production, which may also be trade-related, with export producers down-sizing and changing production processes to be able to compete in foreign markets.[41]

38 South African Reserve Bank, *Quarterly Bulletin*, March 1994, p. S-89, and June 2002, p. S-109.

39 See Cassim *et al.*, *The State of Trade Policy*, p. 83.

40 Quoted in *ibid.*, p. 88.

41 For a brief review of the employment implications of trade policy during the 1990s, see *ibid.*, pp. 84–91.

In considering the overall reaction of manufacturing to the new policy environment, it appears that the response of industry was mediocre. Sectoral growth during the 1990s also shows that the old pattern of faster growth in the upstream, capital-intensive industries was maintained. The number of manufacturing jobs declined, while the volume of production showed no clear signs of developing a new upward-sloping trend, such as the one that characterised industrial development from 1933 until the mid-1970s. Manufactured exports, however, responded quite sharply to the new trading environment. Had it not been for this growth, the performance of manufacturing and the decline in this sector's contribution to GDP would have been worse. But even this export growth performance was, on a comparative basis, not good enough to elevate South Africa to the category of export winners identified by the United Nations Conference on Trade and Development (UNCTAD) on the basis of gains in export market share, hence the observation that 'Sub-Saharan Africa is conspicuous by its absence, with even South Africa failing to appear among the top 20'.[42]

In evaluating this relatively poor outcome, a number of factors need to be considered. The first is the obvious point alluded to earlier, namely that the reaction time of different industries will vary. In general, the impact on import-competing industries and their reaction to increasing competition could be hypothesised to be more immediate, with these industries' first reaction being to down-size and cut costs. Firms with surplus production capacity that were in the export market would have been in a better position to expand exports as an immediate reaction to improved market access, especially when sanctions and consumer boycotts disappeared from the scheme. Such quick responses could not be expected of firms that required new business strategies and investment, both in capital equipment and in the development of export logistical systems, to expand export production. It would therefore not be surprising if a considerable lag exists in the response of export-oriented production to trade liberalisation.[43] In this respect, shifting the 10-year period forward to 1993–2003, the average growth of manufacturing production volume of 2.7 per cent per annum could have been a signal of better things to come. Unfortunately, the sharp appreciation of the rand in the course of 2003 presented a stumbling block in the way of

42 United Nations Conference on Trade and Development, *World Investment Report 2002*, United Nations, 2002, p. 150.

43 It is in this respect that a subsequent sharp appreciation in the rand in 2003 had a highly detrimental impact on the development of export capacity in the manufacturing sector. The earlier depreciation, which started in final quarter of 2001, had prompted many firms to develop export markets, a capacity than could be destroyed by the expensive rand and the instability of the currency.

export-oriented industrial growth, and is an important explanation for the fall in annual average growth in production volume to 1.9 per cent during 1995–2005.

The second point to consider is trade and industrial policy and the view that changes in trade policy have dominated the policy equation. It has been observed that 'it proved to be far easier to remove demand side measures than to put in place effective supply side measures'.[44] Many observers of the South African industrial policy scene will point to the disjuncture between the existence of impressive lists of incentives and a lack of use made of these measures, with blame allocated to both government as the incentive provider and business as the target group that should have responded to the offer of incentives. However, according to Kaplinsky and Morris: 'The result is that firms have tended to feel the icy, chilling winds of trade liberalisation much more than the warm, smoothing breath of supportive supply side measures'.[45]

But perhaps the most important point to consider in evaluating the response of manufacturing firms to the new trade and production environment is the multi-determinant nature of the applicable investment function. Growth in investment is an important prerequisite for rapid, job-creating growth on the basis of export production[46] and in this regard little purpose is served by presenting firms with an impressive list of incentives, including a favourable tax regime, if there are other constraints on investment that firms regard as more important. Exchange rate instability has been mentioned above. Other factors that feature prominently when the lack of sufficient investment is considered are the deterrent presented by the high crime rate and labour legislation and labour cost. In 1999 a survey by the Greater Johannesburg Metropolitan Council and the World Bank of chief executives of large manufacturing firms unambiguously revealed crime to be the leading constraint to investment, followed by labour regulations, exchange rate instability and the cost of capital and credit, all of these in

44 Raphael Kaplinsky and Mike Morris, 'How do South African firms respond to trade policy reform?', in Hossien Jalilian, Michael Tribe and John Weiss (eds), *Industrial Development and Policy in Africa: Issues of De-industrialisation and Development Strategy*, Edward Elgar, 2000, p. 126.

45 *Ibid.*, pp. 126–127.

46 In a study on the growth of South Korea and Taiwan, Rodrik identified the rapid growth in private investment as the force that drove their economic take-offs during the 1960s. He found the growth in exports to have been the outcome of an investment boom that followed policy initiatives by the Korean and Taiwanese governments, which engineered a significant increase in the private return to capital. See Dani Rodrik, 'Getting interventions right: how South Korea and Taiwan grew rich', *Economic Policy*, 20 (April 1995), 55–107.

turn quite far ahead of tax regulations as a constraint.[47] As far as labour cost is concerned, research has shown that South Africa's unit labour cost compares favourably with those of the developed countries but, with respect to 'other developing country exporters of manufactures … South Africa appears to have a serious labour cost problem'.[48]

Conclusion

The jury is still out on the impact of the major changes in the policy environment within which manufacturing industry has to operate. It would be less than wise to blame the lack of output and employment growth on the lowering of protection. For one thing, the ubiquitous problem that economists face, namely the counterfactual, complicates firm conclusions: how would manufacturing have performed had trade liberalisation not taken place? But most importantly, it seems reasonable to argue that the impact of the policy changes still has to work through industry, also bearing in mind that market access (both the domestic and foreign markets) and the supply-side incentives on offer may not adequately cover the most important determinants of investment in production capacity. Manufacturing has been protected for many decades and there can be little doubt that this protection, as in all economies with sizeable manufacturing capacity (bar Hong Kong as an exceptional case), contributed to the development of Africa's most formidable industrial capacity. But most economists would also agree that the South African market is too small to maintain a sustainable inward-looking growth path. The need to establish an outward-looking economy is inevitable. How to go about this most effectively in the international environment of globalisation is open to some debate. What would be difficult to comprehend is a belief that the necessary changes could, on balance, have had an immediate positive impact or that the required changes could take place without pain.

Considering the prospects for manufacturing growth during the early decades of the twenty-first century, the exchange rate will continue to remain an important factor. As far as policy is concerned there are important developments that could have a meaningful impact on manufacturing growth, notably the expected adoption and implementation of a national trade and industrial policy in the spirit

47 See Vandra Chandra, 'Constraints to growth in South Africa's manufactured exports sector', *Trade and Industry Monitor*, 21 (March 2002), p. 3.

48 Stephen Golub, 'South Africa's international competitiveness: the role of labour costs', *Trade and Industry Monitor*, 16 (December 2000), p. 16.

of the developmental state which the government of President Jacob Zuma propagates. The implementation, eventually, of article 38 of the Southern African Customs Union (SACU) agreement of 2002, which requires the members of the customs union – South Africa, Botswana, Lesotho, Namibia and Swaziland – to develop common industrial policies, could also turn out to be an important factor. Having common industrial policies will be of particular importance for the management of the import tariff and in the development of a common SACU position in the negotiation of international trade agreements. In a regional context the development of South Africa's position on an Economic Partnership Agreement (EPA) between the SADC group – consisting of Botswana, Lesotho, Namibia, South Africa and Swaziland (all SACU members), Angola and Mozambique – and the EU could also have a significant impact on trade relations, with spin-offs for industrial development.

6

The automotive industry: seeking a new road

Anthony Black

Introduction

The automotive industry is a key industrial sector not only because of its sheer size but also because it incorporates a wide range of manufacturing processes. In many developing countries it has been seen as emblematic of industrialisation and as a result the sector has frequently been subject to concerted government efforts to promote its development. This is certainly the case in South Africa.

Tariff protection and a growing economy ensured rapid growth for the South African automotive industry until the early 1980s, but the growing political crisis and difficult market conditions of the mid-1980s exposed the fundamental weaknesses in the industry, which had developed under high levels of protection. The industry was high cost and inefficient. It exported little and imports were kept in check only by high tariffs on built-up vehicles and by local content requirements.

In a process that began haltingly in 1989 and accelerated in 1995, the automotive industry became increasingly exposed to international competition as protection was reduced. The key features of the 1990s were policy shifts which partially liberalised the industry and led to major structural changes. This chapter, therefore, focuses on the interplay between policy and structural change during this period.

Early developments

The South African automotive industry has a history dating back to the 1920s, when Ford and General Motors established a production

Figure 6.1 *Vehicle sales, 1950–2000*

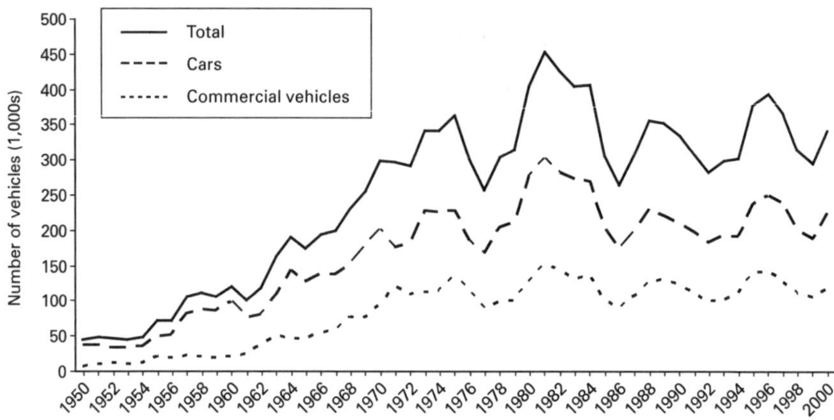

Sources: Annual Reports, National Association of Automobile Manufacturers of South Africa, 1994, 1997, 2000.

presence.[1] High tariffs were placed on built-up vehicles, which, when combined with a rapidly growing market, acted as a magnet to a large number of (initially foreign) companies, which established assembly plants in the country. These operations, although in many cases highly profitable, were very small by international standards, with correspondingly high unit costs. Production was aimed solely at the domestic market and South African assembly plants were kept isolated from the global production networks of the parent companies, except as markets for components. Domestic production expanded rapidly but the level of local content at this stage was low, prompting the introduction of the first phase of a Local Content Programme in 1961. Later phases of the programme increased local content requirements to 66 per cent for all light vehicles.[2]

The South African vehicle market grew very rapidly from 1950 to the early 1980s (Figure 6.1). After the peak in 1982, sales went through a period of 'volatile stagnation' as the economy entered a phase of very slow expansion. At the beginning of the 1990s there were seven major

1 For detail on the history of automotive development policy, see: A. Black, *An Industrial Strategy for the Motor Vehicle and Component Sector,* University of Cape Town Press, 1994; and D. Duncan, *We Are Motor Men,* Whittles Publishing, 1997.

2 This requirement was introduced under phase III of the Local Content Programme in 1971 and was extended to light commercial vehicles in phase V, introduced in 1980.

light-vehicle plants, which were located outside Pretoria, in Durban and in the Eastern Cape. A number of these firms, such as Automakers (producing Nissan and Fiat brands), Samcor (Ford), Delta (General Motors) and Toyota, were locally owned and operated under licence agreements with foreign multinationals. The German-based firms (BMW, Mercedes Benz and Volkswagen) were foreign controlled. In addition, there were a number of low-volume medium- and heavy-vehicle producers.

Domestic ownership was also high in the component sector, which numbered some 350 firms and produced a wide range of components for the domestic and export market. During the 1990s and particularly after 1994, with the ending of sanctions, foreign ownership started to increase in both the assembly and the component sectors as many locally owned firms, producing under licence, were bought out by foreign multinationals or entered into joint ventures.

The policy environment: phase VI and the Motor Industry Development Programme

Phase VI of the Local Content Programme, 1989–95

The effects of high protection had become increasingly apparent by the late 1980s. South Africa's automotive industry was inefficient and highly inward oriented. A key objective of the Local Content Programme had been to save foreign exchange but the fact that local content was measured by mass meant that new, lightweight, high-cost electronic components were still being imported and the sector remained import intensive.

The international context was strongly supportive of trade liberalisation and even apartheid South Africa was not immune to this trend. Phase VI of the Local Content Programme, introduced in 1989, marked the beginning of the liberalisation of the industry. It was the first attempt to address the problems of an inwardly oriented industry characterised by low volume output and high unit costs. Importantly, local content was to be measured not just by the value of domestically produced components fitted to locally assembled vehicles but also on a net foreign exchange usage basis. In other words, exports by an assembler counted as local content and enabled it to reduce actual local content (to a minimum of 50 per cent) in domestically produced vehicles. Tariffs on built-up vehicles remained at prohibitive levels.[3] Phase VI was intended to encourage both local content and specialisation. However, it was introduced rapidly and

3 Tariffs on passenger cars were 105 per cent and in addition there was a 10 per cent import surcharge.

with insufficient consideration of its likely impact. There were a number of unintended outcomes and the programme came in for fierce criticism from large sections of the component industry.

The Motor Industry Development Programme (MIDP), 1995–2000

In 1992, the Minister of Trade and Industry appointed the Motor Industry Task Group, comprising all stakeholders, to advise on a new policy for the automotive industry. The eventual outcome was the Motor Industry Development Programme (MIDP), introduced in 1995. It continued the direction taken by phase VI and entrenched the principle of import–export complementation. However, it went a step further by introducing a tariff phase-down at a steeper rate than required by the terms of South Africa's World Trade Organization (WTO) obligations. Tariffs were scheduled to phase down to 47 per cent for light vehicles and 35 per cent for components by 2000, with gradual tariff reductions continuing until 2002.[4] Minimum local content requirements were also abolished and manufacturers of light vehicles were entitled to a duty-free allowance equal to 27 per cent of the wholesale value of the vehicle for the importation of original equipment components.

Importantly, however, import duties on components and vehicles could be offset by import rebate credits derived from the export of vehicles and components. So while nominal duties on imported vehicles remained fairly high, the ability to rebate import duties by exporting enabled importers to bring in vehicles at lower effective rates of duty. Import–export complementation also enabled assemblers to use import credits to source components at close to international prices, so that declining nominal protection on vehicles was to some extent offset by reduced protection for components. This meant that there was still a significant incentive to assemble locally.

The orthodox rationale for tariff reductions is to realign relative prices, reduce input costs and correct anti-export bias. While these objectives were important in the automotive industry phase-down, policy makers also sought to rationalise the industry, which in effect meant encouraging a greater degree of specialisation, in order to achieve economies of scale. This could best be achieved through greater levels of international integration. The impact of the changes was awaited with a degree of trepidation by policy makers, the industry and trade unions. Key indicators would be not only the level of penetration by imports but also the supply response in terms of investment and export expansion.

4 Further tariff reductions to 2007 and then to 2012 were scheduled at later policy reviews.

Liberalisation and structural change in the 1990s

Markets and production

As indicated in Figure 6.1, the 1990s was a period of stagnant sales, although there were substantial cyclical fluctuations. Sales recovered from the 1992 low of 284,000 units to reach 393,000 in 1996 but fell sharply following the drastic increases in interest rates which followed the fallout from the Asian economic crisis. Production closely tracked sales, although by the end of the decade both vehicle imports and exports were growing in significance. During this period there were few dramatic changes in the market share of the leading firms. Toyota remained dominant in both passenger cars and light commercial vehicles. In 1990 its share of the passenger car market was 23 per cent, followed by Volkswagen at 20 per cent and Ford at 15 per cent, while Delta and Nissan both had strong positions in the market for light commercial vehicles. BMW and DaimlerChrysler battled for market share in the premium segments of the passenger car market. By 2000, firms with no domestic production were also making inroads into the market.

Imports

Reducing protection in a highly protected economy could be expected to lead to increased levels of imports. The correction of anti-export bias,

Figure 6.2 *Automotive trade balance, 1990–2000 (R billions)*

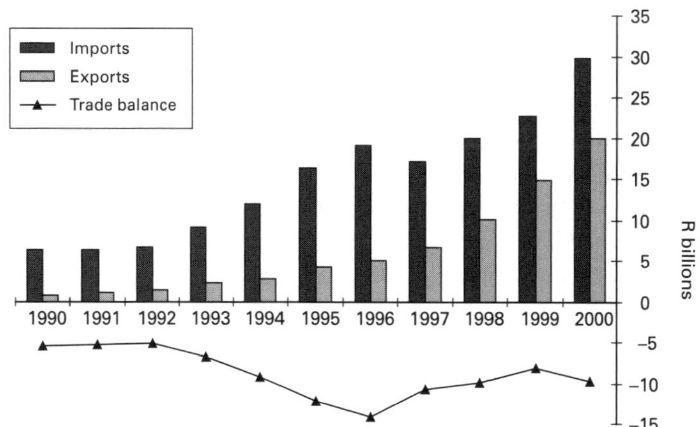

Sources: Current Developments in the Automotive Industry, Department of Trade and Industry, 1997 and 2001 editions.

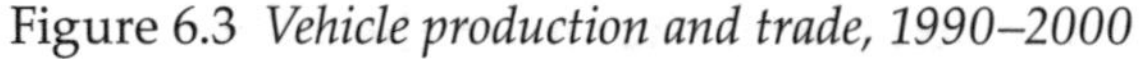
Figure 6.3 *Vehicle production and trade, 1990–2000*

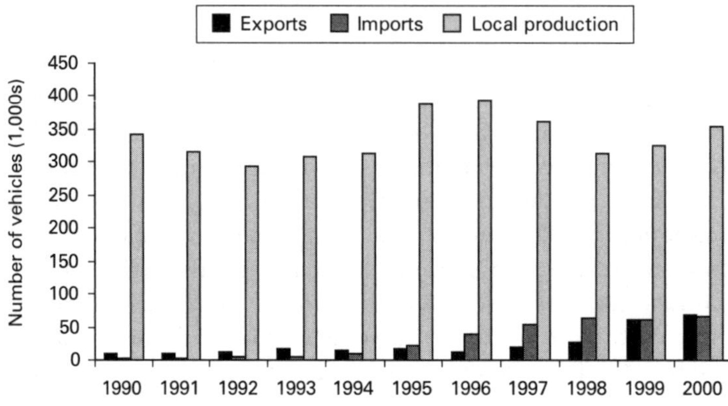

Sources: Annual Reports, National Association of Automobile Manufacturers of South Africa, 1997, 2001; *Current Developments in the Automotive Industry,* Department of Trade and Industry, 1997 and 2001 editions.

on the other hand, may encourage exports. The overall trade balance in the 1990s for South Africa's automotive sector is presented in Figure 6.2. Import expansion was strongly related to domestic demand – hence the fall in 1997 – and in spite of gradual liberalisation, in real terms, imports grew at only a moderate pace over the decade as a whole. With the rapid increase in exports, especially from the mid-1990s, the overall automotive industry trade deficit actually declined sharply, from R14.1 billion in 1996 to R9.7 billion in 2000. In real terms the trade deficit in 2000 was lower than in 1990.

Until the early 1990s, prohibitive tariff levels resulted in negligible imports of vehicles into South Africa. The opening up of the economy and the lowering of tariffs led to a growing level of imports of light vehicles, which increased from under 2 per cent of the market in 1990 to 13.9 per cent in 1997 and 19.3 per cent in 2000. These increases were roughly in line with the expectations of policy makers and, as indicated in Figure 6.3, vehicle exports were approximately equal to imports over the period 1999–2000. Korean vehicles, mainly Hyundai,[5] were the

5 A plant producing Hyundai vehicles was opened in Botswana in 1998 but shut down a few years later. Up until this point Hyundai vehicles had been imported into South Africa via Botswana under a special concession. See A. Black and S. Muradzikwa, 'The limits to regionalism: the automotive industry in the Southern African Development Community', in Y. Lung, J. Carrillo and R. van Tulder (eds), *Cars, Carriers of Regionalism?,* Palgrave Macmillan, 2004, pp. 173–188.

largest import brands but the domestic vehicle producers themselves accounted for significant imports. Growing exports enabled them to offset duties on imported vehicles.

With the introduction of phase VI and later the MIDP, the component sector came under increasing pressure from imports. The short-term impact of phase VI was felt in three main areas. First, the switch from mass to value had a highly differentiated effect on the component sector. Vehicle producers began looking at ways to increase local content by value rather than by mass. Heavy components such as body pressings were no longer required and came under increasing pressure. Secondly, components which formed part of sub-assemblies also came under threat because it became cheaper to import these in a semi-assembled form, thus simplifying assembly and limiting the problems of local re-engineering, quality and supply complexities. The third group of firms which was vulnerable comprised those with high tooling costs in relation to the cost of the component, for example plastic moulded components. Again, low volume production for the domestic market made these uneconomic.

However, for models introduced under phase V, manufacturers tended to maintain sourcing arrangements, as they had already invested in tooling. Also, it took time to build up large export volumes. Thus the increased flexibility to source additional components abroad was most apparent with new model introductions and started to have a significant impact from 1992. Increased foreign sourcing was not the expected result of the programme. The National Association of Automotive Component and Allied Manufacturers (NAACAM) initially welcomed phase VI, expecting a substantial increase in local content. The Board of Trade also anticipated rapid growth in the component sector.[6]

After lengthy negotiations, the MIDP was introduced in 1995. Component producers continued to come under severe pressure, with annual price increases significantly below inflation levels. One major concern in the late 1990s was that new models were being introduced with very low levels of local content in some cases.[7] The measurement of local content is complicated, however. The most widely used 'official' measure included assembly costs, with the result that an increase in assembler margins translated into higher local content. According to this measure (value of production less foreign exchange used), the level

6 *Investigation into a Structural Adjustment Programme for the Industries Manufacturing Motor Vehicles and Automotive Components: Phase VI of the Local Content Programme*, Report No. 2767, Board of Trade and Industry, 1989.

7 A. Black, 'Globalization and restructuring in the South African automotive industry', *Journal of International Development*, 13(6) (2001), 779–796.

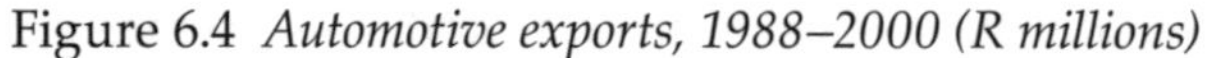

Figure 6.4 *Automotive exports, 1988–2000 (R millions)*

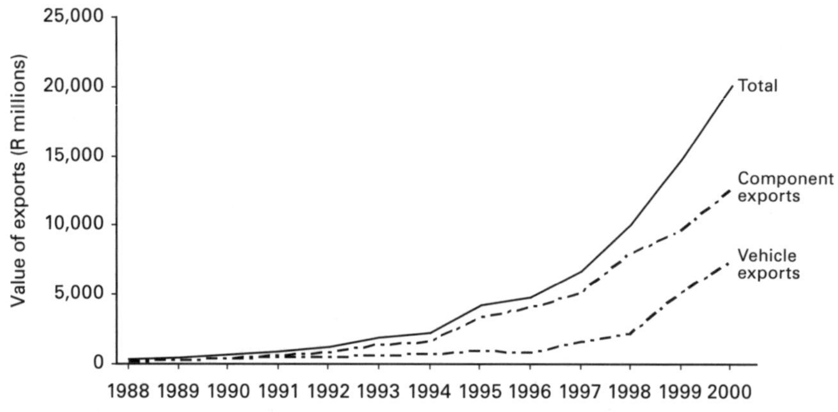

Sources: Current Developments in the Automotive Industry, Department of Trade and Industry, 2000 and 2001 editions.

of local content was 51 per cent in 2000 but if the measure is restricted to component purchases only, local content was only 32 per cent in that year. Levels of local content have tended to fluctuate depending not just on actual local components fitted but also on variables such as the exchange rate.

Exports

The reduction of anti-export bias, and consequent export expansion, was the major objective of South Africa's programme of trade liberalisation. Automotive industry exports grew rapidly after 1990 (Figure 6.4). A number of factors accounted for this but the import–export complementation arrangements of phase VI and the MIDP were crucial. In addition, falling protection and limited possibilities for growth in the domestic market forced firms into the export market.[8] The international political acceptance that came with the advent of democracy was also a critical factor.

Under phase VI, exports rose from a tiny base of only R443 million in 1989 to R2,245 million in 1994. Under this scheme, all exports, including components produced by independent suppliers, were channelled

8 Black, 'Globalization and restructuring in the South African automotive industry'.

through the assemblers. Many components suppliers and all the assemblers instituted significant export drives. Assemblers developed international marketing channels, frequently via their overseas principals, and identified the types of components where local producers had a competitive advantage. The position of assemblers in the automotive industry's producer-driven value chain proved critical and helps to explain the strong supply response to the changes to incentives.

In developing international networks and markets, the German-based vehicle manufacturers were in an advantageous position because their parent companies were keen to incorporate their South African subsidiaries into their respective global production systems. For firms which were locally owned at the time, such as Toyota and Automakers (Nissan), this course of action was more problematic. There was much less incentive for the Japanese parent companies, which had no equity stake in the South African firms, to source supplies from South Africa.

Many domestically owned component firms were dependent on licence agreements with foreign principals, and these frequently placed restrictions on exports. Foreign ownership or a joint venture arrangement with a foreign firm therefore conferred significant advantages under this new scenario and foreign-owned firms were, in many cases, quickly incorporated into the worldwide sourcing arrangements of the parent company.

Component exports expanded dramatically during the decade. The prime objective of the export complementation scheme was to assist component suppliers to generate high volumes, which would make them more efficient and able to compete in the domestic market against imports. While this objective was to some extent achieved (Table 6.1), the bulk of export expansion was not by 'traditional' component suppliers but by a rapidly emerging new group of mainly foreign-owned firms, frequently with links to vehicle manufacturers.[9]

Relatively light investments with a low level of integration into the domestic industry either in terms of supply to domestic vehicles or in terms of the use of subcomponents was one outcome. While a wide range of components were exported, much of the expansion in exports was in a small range of products, some of which could be described as

9 Similar trends have been observed in other countries experiencing rapid international integration and export expansion, such as Brazil and Argentina, on which see, respectively, A. Posthuma, *Restructuring and Changing Market Conditions in the Brazilian Auto Components Industry*, Economic Commission for Latin America and the Caribbean, ECLAC/UNIDO Industrial and Technological Development Unit, 1995; M. Miozzo, 'Transnational corporations, industrial policy and the "War of Incentives": the case of the Argentine automobile industry', *Development and Change*, 31 (2000), 651–680.

Table 6.1 *Exports of motor vehicle components, 1995–2000 (R millions)*

	1995	*1996*	*1997*	*1998*	*1999*	*2000*	*Percentage of 2000 total*
Catalytic converters	388	485	835	1,520	2,569	4,683	37.0
Stitched leather covers	1,019	1,259	1,408	1,854	1,888	1,926	15.3
Tyres	219	296	342	498	639	682	5.4
Road wheels/parts	175	227	325	446	518	551	4.4
Engine parts	112	137	285	390	383	409	3.2
Silencers/exhaust pipes	76	170	151	493	598	377	3.0
Automotive tooling	259	279	309	256	264	362	2.9
Wiring harnesses	41	92	136	207	304	319	2.5
Glass	49	71	105	112	147	171	1.4
Ignition/starting equipment	4	16	30	47	94	128	1.0
Transmission shafts, cranks	29	38	7	62	85	127	1.0
Filters	13	42	55	72	85	118	0.9
Batteries	53	60	88	79	68	100	0.8
Brake parts	23	29	39	76	79	95	0.8
Car radios	7	4	29	47	73	89	0.7
Body parts and panels	18	39	39	30	75	84	0.7
Shock absorbers	38	53	56	63	77	81	0.6
Engines	10	86	111	334	54	76	0.6
Radiators	77	107	93	108	111	72	0.6
Gauges/instruments/ parts	18	28	29	30	59	64	0.5
Other components	690	533	643	1,171	1,504	2,126	16.7
Total	3,318	4,051	5,115	7,895	9,674	12,640	100.0

Sources: Current Developments in the Automotive Industry, Department of Trade and Industry, 1997 and 2001 editions.

peripheral[10] (Table 6.1). By the mid-1990s, the labour-intensive industry supplying leather seat covers supplied the bulk of BMW's global requirements and was an important supplier to a number of other foreign vehicle manufacturers. The catalytic converter industry is more capital intensive and by 2000 supplied approximately 14 per cent of total world supply and was set for further expansion. These two products accounted for over 50 per cent of total component exports in 2000, though there was also expansion in a wide range of other components.

10 The visiting chief executive of a major carmaker referred to them as 'salami'.

Exports of light vehicles increased from under 10,000 units in 1990 to 67,352 units in 2000.[11] The main destination for vehicle exports was initially the rest of Africa. However, by the end of the decade the main markets were Germany, Australia, Japan, the UK and the US. This expansion in vehicle exports also led to a certain amount of investment in the supply base.

While the trade balance in the automotive industry showed substantial improvement during the 1990s, from the perspective of the national automotive strategy, the nature of export expansion is extremely important. Given that exports were assisted by (declining) complementation arrangements, there were concerns regarding the sustainability of export expansion and also the degree to which it improved overall competitiveness by increasing the level of industry integration. The concern was that vehicle manufacturers were embarking on strategies to generate import credits by exporting components, especially products, which required only light investments. This would allow them to continue to introduce new, low-volume models into the domestic market utilising imported components. To some extent this strategy was adopted as an 'easy' route to achieve duty neutrality, certainly much easier than increasing local content in low-volume, locally assembled vehicles. It therefore caused concern among some traditional original equipment component suppliers to the domestic market, which found assemblers adopting much more aggressive pricing requirements. By failing to increase vehicle volumes through exporting, unit production costs were likely to remain high and vehicle manufacturers would be left vulnerable to tariff reductions. In the mid-1990s these concerns appeared to be borne out by the relatively slow growth of vehicle exports. However, vehicle exports started to grow rapidly from 1997 (see Figure 6.4) and by 2000 three manufacturers had established significant, long-term vehicle export programmes.

Investment

A key indicator of the impact of liberalisation of the trade regime is the level of capital investment. It is likely, for example, that profit margins will fall in the short term and this would impact negatively on both the motivation and capacity to invest in the sector. However, the investment behaviour of the assemblers was influenced by a number of industry-specific factors. The importance of economies of scale meant that the increased competition placed pressure on firms to increase production

11 *Annual Report*, National Association of Automobile Manufacturers of South Africa, 2005.

as a way of reducing unit costs. This in turn required the parent company to create export opportunities for the South African subsidiary and invest accordingly. Investments had to be enlarged or firms faced the prospect of losing market position and eventually becoming unviable.[12] Given that the key investment decisions were made outside South Africa, by the global parent, short-term profitability in a relatively small South African subsidiary was likely to be a lesser consideration than medium-term market prospects and strategic concerns related to market share and the requirements of global production networks.

Net profits before tax of the seven manufacturers of light vehicles increased from a low base of R328 million in 1992 to a record level of R2,032 million in 1995 on the back of booming sales.[13] Profits then dipped precipitously and the industry incurred a large aggregate loss in 1997 as the entry of imported vehicles in significant volumes led to much greater price competition and lower margins, which added to the pressures of stagnating sales volumes. Profits recovered to R1,285 million in 2000, marking the beginning of a boom in the domestic market. Data for the component sector are sketchier but profitability appears to have followed a similar trend. During this phase, there was a clear division in the fortunes of component suppliers: exporters did well, while those restricted to the domestic market for reasons of size, licensing restrictions or the lack of a link to a foreign company came under growing pressure.

Fixed investment in the assembly sector amounted to R660 million in 1990 and declined sharply in 1993–94 (Figure 6.5), reflecting uncertainty both in the general political situation and in the automotive policy environment. Investment then increased steadily to R1,561.5 million by 2000, with firms such as BMW and DaimlerChrysler announcing major expansion plans.[14] While inflows of foreign direct investment into the South African economy were no more than moderate in the period following the 1994 elections, the automotive sector was the fourth largest recipient (after telecommunications, energy, and food and beverages). This is particularly significant given adverse domestic market conditions and the fact that the industry was facing declining protection. Much of this inward investment took the form of the purchase of majority or minority stakes by Ford (in Samcor), Toyota

12 Black, 'Globalization and restructuring in the South African automotive industry'.

13 *Current Developments in the Automotive Industry*, Department of Trade and Industry, 2000 edition.

14 See, for instance, 'South Africa becomes global "hub" of DaimlerChrysler', *Automobil*, October 2000; *Annual Report*, National Association of Automobile Manufacturers of South Africa, 2000.

Figure 6.5 *Capital expenditure in the vehicle assembly industry, 1990–2000*

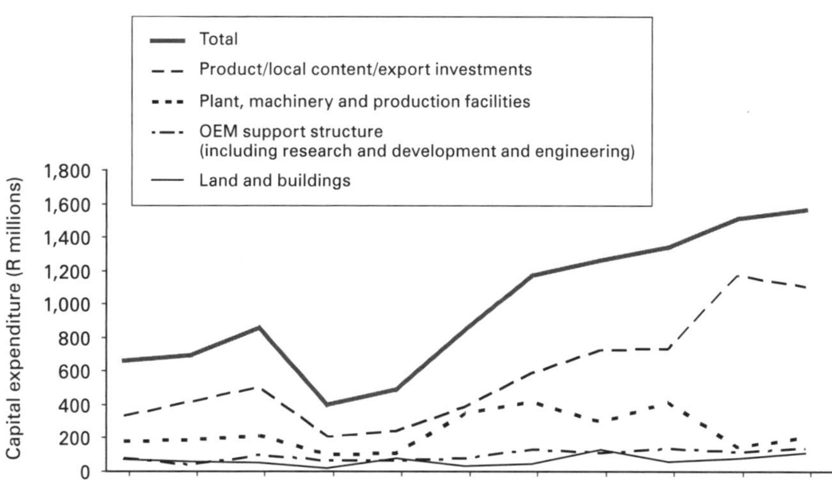

Sources: Annual Reports, National Association of Automobile Manufacturers of South Africa, 1994, 1997, 2000.

Motor Corp. (in Toyota SA), Nissan Motor Corp. (in Nissan SA) and General Motors (in Delta) rather than investment in new production facilities. Moreover, the fixed investments made in plants lagged well behind the level of the massive investments that were being made in emerging markets such as Brazil, Thailand and Eastern Europe during this period. Neither, with a few exceptions, were major investments being attracted into first-tier components.

The impact on vehicle prices

In the early 1990s South African car prices were well above international prices. Differentials varied and were generally higher at the luxury end of the market. Furthermore, prices had been rising at a higher rate than the consumer price index until 1993. Phase VI was widely blamed in the media and by industry analysts as a contributing factor.

The growth in exports greatly increased the flexibility of component sourcing, which allowed assemblers to take advantage of cheaper foreign components. This led to a substantial reduction in costs, especially for new models. Component suppliers, who were used to prices being determined on a 'cost plus' basis, faced ultimatums to reduce prices in real terms, which forced them to become more efficient and to reduce their margins.

The gradual reduction in tariffs under the MIDP led to a decline in prices in real terms but with substantial fluctuations as a result of currency volatility. For the period 1995–2000, the average annual increase in vehicle prices was lower than that in consumer prices, 5.6 per cent as against 6.9 per cent, and marked a sharp break with the experience of the previous quarter of a century. There was also a huge increase in the choice of vehicles available on the domestic market, while the entry of new independent importers, such as Renault, on a significant scale further increased competition.

Productivity and employment

Automotive industry productivity has historically been low in South Africa but this improved rapidly during the 1990s. Data collected by the International Motor Vehicle Program, based at the Massachusetts Institute of Technology (MIT), drawing on assembly plant surveys conducted in 1994 and 1996, showed that the average South African assembly plant compared poorly with assembly plants in other countries. The main reasons for this can be ascribed to the relatively low levels of automation and the complexity of most assembly plants, which produced a wide range of models in relatively low volumes. However, the rate of improvement was rapid. For instance, between 1994 and 1996, direct labour hours per vehicle were reduced by 32 per cent. Rapid improvements were also achieved in the component sector. Over the period 1994–97, the benchmarking of component firms in KwaZulu-Natal showed significant improvements in inventory levels, quality and indicators of external and internal flexibility.[15] Productivity growth in the automotive industry also outstripped that of manufacturing as a whole after 1995.

The automotive industry is exceptionally cyclical and this showed up in employment levels. Disaggregating the effect of trade liberalisation from the impact of market conditions is complicated by the impact on market growth of the reduced price of vehicles in real terms, which in turn was partly the result of liberalisation. By the late 1990s the export sector had also become a major source of employment. Total employment in the vehicle manufacturing industry increased from 73,800 in 1994 to 82,100 in the boom year of 1996, before declining to 70,800 in

15 J. Barnes and R. Kaplinsky, 'Globalisation and trade policy reform: whither the automobile component sector in South Africa?', *Competition and Change*, 4 (2000), 211–243.

2000. Because this was a period of significant decline in manufacturing employment in South Africa, the share of the automotive industry in total manufacturing employment actually increased.

Rationalisation and the strategies of vehicle manufacturers

The scale of production was one of the central policy issues facing the South African automotive industry. South Africa's eight light vehicle plants[16] produced an average of only 40,000 vehicles in 1999, with 36 different basic models. The resulting average volumes per model were way below the world norm and significantly lower even than in relatively low-volume producers such as Brazil and Australia. The cost premiums incurred by assemblers and especially by component makers for producing a wide range of products at low volume were considerable.

Phase VI was intended to encourage both local content and specialisation, but it did not address the major factor influencing the scale of production in the component sector – the proliferation of makes and models in the domestic market. In fact, its impact was rather the reverse. By increasing the flexibility of component sourcing (and hence reducing protection on components) but at the same time maintaining high nominal protection levels on built-up vehicles, the effective rate of protection on vehicle assembly increased sharply under phase VI. This led to an increase in the variety of models and makes being assembled locally in a stagnant market. Part of the rationale of the MIDP was to encourage firms to specialise by means of exporting. This policy was aimed at encouraging a phased transition from CKD assembly[17] to full manufacturing, with the attendant benefits of higher volumes and increasing localisation of components. It had not succeeded by 2000.

There was no significant improvement in model volumes during the 1990s, in spite of the new competitive pressures introduced by the MIDP (Table 6.2) and the number of passenger car models being produced at volumes of under 10,000 units per annum actually increased. While component producers were able to attain high volumes through exports, in the assembly industry low-volume production continued in spite of growing price pressures on vehicle manufacturers. This occurred because the effective rate of protection on assembly remained relatively high, because of the ability to reduce component prices and because of the abolition of local content requirements.

16 This includes the niche market producer Land Rover.

17 Completely knocked down (CKD) assembly refers to the simple process of assembly, common in the early stages of industry development, when kits of parts (CKD packs) are imported and assembled.

Table 6.2 *Volume performance by passenger motor vehicle model line, 1992–2000*

Production volumes	*1992*	*1993*	*1994*	*1995*	*1996*	*1997*	*1998*	*1999*	*2000*
0–9,999	10	8	8	10	9	12	12	13	12
10,000–19,999	9	8	8	7	8	7	6	6	4
20,000–29,999	0	0	1	3	3	2	3	2	3
30,000+	1	1	1	1	1	1	1	–	3
Total	20	17	18	21	21	22	22	21	22

Source: Current Developments in the Automotive Industry, Department of Trade and Industry, 1997, 1999 and 2001 editions.

Vehicle exports took longer to materialise, although by 2000 some vehicle manufacturers were increasing vehicle exports, allowing them to import significant volumes of both vehicles and components duty free. This created an opportunity to rationalise their operations to achieve the higher model volumes that would place them in a stronger position to encourage investments by their first-tier suppliers. Other vehicle manufacturers continued to pursue multi-model strategies (in some cases with low local content levels) and used component exports to offset duties on CKD component imports. This option was unlikely to be sustainable in the medium to long term.

The strategies of the Japanese-based assemblers during the 1990s were determined by the relatively low level of direct investment in their South African operations. After 1994 this policy changed and by 2000 both Nissan and Toyota had acquired equity stakes in the South African operations. To some extent this led to an increased level of integration with the South African plants, which were now able to export to most African countries. These, however, were very small markets. Toyota remained in a relatively strong position because of its large domestic market share. Nissan, by contrast, had a less secure position in the domestic market.

The US-based firms, Ford and General Motors, both disinvested in the 1980s, as a result of political pressures.[18] After 1994 both firms reinvested in South Africa and established closer links with the South African operations, but were initially reluctant to source vehicles from South Africa on a significant scale. This was partly the result of having surplus

18 There was substantial disinvestment by international firms during the 1980s as a result of the international campaign against apartheid. US firms took the lead in this process.

capacity worldwide, as well as already having assembly plants in all significant markets. Both companies exported a wide range of components.

By 2000 the strategies of German-based firms (BMW, VW and DaimlerChrysler) were far more advanced in terms of global integration. All the plants were wholly owned by the parent company and increasingly integrated into global networks for both vehicles and components. All three had developed significant export strategies. They had been assisted in this process by the fact that none of the German companies had a wide geographical distribution of plants – the South African plants were, therefore, benefiting from the globalisation of German vehicle manufacturers looking to expand capacity, increase their share of output outside high-cost Germany and retain their strategic foothold in the southern African market.

So, although little rationalisation took place during the 1990s, by the end of the decade there were encouraging signs that firms were developing significant export programmes. This in turn required substantial investments and was accompanied by a rationalisation of the product line and efforts by the car companies to increase local content by encouraging foreign first-tier suppliers to locate production in South Africa.

Conclusion

The 1990s was a period of rapid change for South Africa's automotive industry. Two policy changes had a major impact. Phase VI of the Local Content Programme affected mainly the component sector; the MIDP liberalised the entire industry. This occurred during a period of low growth and, until 1994, of significant political uncertainty. Total production changed little over the decade but this conceals the wrenching changes that occurred. The industry became much more internationally integrated. Both imports and exports grew rapidly, foreign ownership expanded and competitive pressures together with the requirements of exporting led to the rapid introduction of new technology and new methods of production organisation.

Some important problems remained. Arguably, too much pressure had been placed on component suppliers relative to the assemblers. Suppliers had to meet increasingly stringent pricing demands in spite of the fact that domestic volumes remained low. The result was to some extent the emergence of dualism in the sector – the growth of a large export sector, which was not very closely integrated with the remaining low volume, low local content industry assembling vehicles for the domestic market. Parts of the 'traditional' component industry were not able to adjust and contracted. While the rationalisation process was slow, three vehicle manufacturers made considerable progress towards rationalising their operations and there were clear signs that others would follow suit. Exporting also enabled many component firms to achieve reasonable economies of scale.

By the end of the decade important progress had been made in dismantling the prohibitive levels of protection that prevailed in 1990. In real terms, vehicle prices declined during the 1990s and, with the growth in imports, buyers could choose from a far wider variety of products. Most importantly, the industry, while far from being competitive, was moving towards a more efficient structure and was in a much sounder position to take advantage of the favourable domestic market conditions of the early twenty-first century.

7

The chemical industry

Grietjie Verhoef

Introduction

This chapter considers developments in the manufacturing sector in South Africa during the 1990s, with special emphasis on the chemical industry and its major components, Sasol, AECI and Sentrachem. The manufacturing industry in general in South Africa was profoundly affected by globalisation. Firms operating in the chemical industry responded positively to these global developments, enhanced by the concurrent political changes in the country. The overall performance of the manufacturing sector in South Africa had been relatively impressive in the 1960s, as a result of the government's systematic protection policy, and an advanced and diversified manufacturing sector had come into existence. Thereafter, a steady decline occurred in the relative contribution of manufacturing to the South Africa economy. This became most noticeable in the 1990s. While manufacturing in general stagnated in the 1990s, investment in chemicals and petroleum-related activities increased markedly. This reflected an imbalance in the allocation of investment within the manufacturing industry and, despite an overall increase in gross domestic fixed investment, value added by the manufacturing industry declined significantly after the 1970s.

The most remarkable shift in the direction of the manufacturing industry in the 1990s was an abrupt involuntary redirection of production away from import substitution and towards export-orientated production. This was caused by the 1993 agreement with the World Trade Organization, which brought about tariff reductions.[1]

1 P. H. Lindert and T. A. Pugel, *International Economics* (10th edition), Irwin, 1996, pp. 134–135.

The chemical industry as part of the manufacturing sector

The South African economy entered a phase of gradual recovery during the 1990s and, except for the impact of the Asian crisis during the late 1990s, an annual growth rate of over 3 per cent was recorded from 1994 to 1997 and again in 2000 (Table 7.1). Table 7.1 also shows the relative contribution of the manufacturing sector to GDP. This remained virtually static, declining slightly from 18.86 per cent in 1990 to 18.19 per cent in 2000, after reaching a peak at 19.37 per cent in 1995.

Table 7.2 shows the indices of manufacturing production between 1990 and 2000, which reflect this slow progress. Over the decade as a whole the physical volume increased by 13.9 per cent, after declines

Table 7.1 *Contribution of the manufacturing sector to GDP, 1993–2000, at 1995 constant prices*

Year	*GDP*		*Manufacturing production*		*Manufacturing as % of GDP*
	R millions	*% change*	*R millions*	*% change*	
1993	514,886		97,114		18.86
1994	531,537	3.13	99,706	2.59	18.75
1995	548,098	3.02	106,180	6.09	19.37
1996	571,706	4.12	107,648	1.36	18.82
1997	586,838	2.57	110,562	2.63	18.84
1998	591,265	0.74	108,419	–1.97	18.33
1999	603,290	1.99	108,085	–0.30	17.91
2000	624,378	3.37	113,596	4.85	18.19

Source: Gross Domestic Product, P0441, Statistics South Africa, May 2003, Table 1, pp. 15–16.

Table 7.2 *Indices of the physical volume of manufacturing production, 1990–2000 (2000 = 100)*

Year	*Indices*
1990	87.8
1991	84.8
1992	82.2
1993	84.1
1994	87.2
1995	94.3
1996	97.7
1997	100.3
1998	96.9
1999	96.4
2000	100.0

Source: P3031.3, Statistics South Africa, 10 February 2003, p. 5.

Table 7.3 *Indices of physical volume of selected chemical and petroleum production, 1990–2000 (2000 = 100)*

Year	*Coke and refined petroleum products*	*Basic chemicals*	*Other chemical products and man-made fibres*	*Plastic products*
1990	89.2	75.8	86.0	76.9
1991	88.9	70.9	86.0	78.0
1992	95.0	61.6	86.9	83.1
1993	103.8	61.4	88.7	87.3
1994	96.9	67.8	91.7	102.3
1995	95.7	75.8	98.2	111.5
1996	91.0	81.9	100.9	110.3
1997	95.3	86.1	104.1	103.7
1998	95.9	88.7	101.2	101.3
1999	101.7	96.1	101.4	96.5
2000	100.0	100.0	100.0	100.0

Source: Manufacturing Statistics: Indices of the Physical Volume of Manufacturing Production. Base: 2000 = 100, P3041.3, Statistics South Africa, 10 February 2003, pp. 27–31.

in 1991 and 1992, years of political uncertainty. Growth began again in 1993 and lasted for five years until the impact of the Asian financial crisis brought it to a halt.

In the 1990s value added in manufacturing in general was low. In 2000 the real value added by manufacturing industry was only 5.1 per cent, compared with 7.6 per cent in agriculture, forestry and fishing and 7 per cent in transport.[2] Nominal value added was 19 per cent, with the chemical industry's contribution being 4.6 per cent.[3] Capital expenditure in the manufacturing industry rose marginally from R14.8 million in 1993 to R23.5 million in 1997, but then entered a period of steady decline until 2000. The annual percentage increase in capital expenditure in manufacturing also declined, from 18.4 per cent in 1996 to –3.8 per cent in 2000.[4] Manufacturing industry was not operating at full capacity and there was virtually no improvement in the decade, which ended with capacity utilisation at only 79.5 per cent.[5] Within manufacturing the most impressive performance occurred in chemical and petroleum

2 *Gross Domestic Product,* P0441, Statistics South Africa, 2003, p. 1.

3 *Gross Domestic Product,* P0441, Statistics South Africa, 2006, p. 55.

4 *Manufacturing: Capital Expenditure on New Assets,* P3042.3, Statistics South Africa, 2001, pp. 2, 6.

5 *Manufacturing Utilisation of Production Capacity by Large Enterprises (Preliminary),* P3043, Statistics South Africa, August 2001, p. 4.

production. These benefited from the strong focus on global markets via joint ventures with international partners, the acquisition of overseas companies and export-driven production.

The indices of physical volume of manufacturing production (Table 7.3) indicate a stronger performance by the chemical sector than the manufacturing index, but basic chemicals remained well below it. The category of basic chemicals, which includes fertilisers and nitrogen compounds, plastics in primary form and rubber, expanded by 62.9 per cent between 1993 and 2000, after declining in the three preceding years. The next category, 'other chemicals', which included pesticides, paints, pharmaceuticals, soaps and other cleaning compounds, toiletries and cosmetics, also grew in the middle years of the decade. Over the decade as a whole the strongest growth occurred in basic chemicals, at 31.9 per cent, just ahead of plastic products at 30.0 per cent.

The three major chemical corporations

The contribution of the chemical industry to manufacturing in South Africa during the 1990s may be gauged from a more detailed investigation into the activities of the three major chemical corporations in South Africa, Sasol, AECI, and Sentrachem.

Sasol was established in 1950 at Sasolburg in the Free State to manufacture oil from coal, but in the 1970s, in response to the dramatic rise in oil prices in 1973 and 1979, Sasol embarked upon an ambitious expansion programme into synthetic fuels. The company invested R245 million in the construction in Secunda in the Eastern Transvaal of Sasol 2 in 1980 and then Sasol 3 in 1982, to increase its production of oil from coal. Sasol 1, based in Sasolburg, diversified into related chemicals production in the 1990s and attempted a takeover bid of AECI in 1998, but was prevented from doing so by the Competition Commission. Joint ventures between Sasol and AECI followed.[6]

AECI was formed in 1923 by the merger of a number of chemical operations in Natal, the Cape and Modderfontein in the Transvaal. It focused primarily on the production of explosives and inorganic chemicals and became the major chemical company in South Africa during the 1980s, as a result of acquiring Chemical Services and diversifying into speciality chemicals. AECI entered into a joint-venture soda-ash project in Botswana in 1991 and in 1993 AECI Bioproducts and AECI

6 G. Verhoef, 'Innovation for globalisation or globalisation of innovation: Sasol in the chemical industry during the 1990s', *South African Journal of Economic History*, 18(2) (September 2003), 188–201.

Aroma and Fine Chemicals were formed to manufacture speciality chemicals in Umbogintwini and Richards Bay.

The third prominent group in the chemical industry was Sentrachem, formed in 1967 through the merger of a number of organic chemical fertiliser and pesticides manufacturers. Sentrachem produced a wide variety of organic compounds, including ethyl and n-butyl alcohols, ethyl, butyl and amyl acetates, acetone and phthalic anhydride. Fermentation of molasses also produced carbon dioxide and a solid residue. Another area where Sentrachem became a major force was in the manufacture of agriculture and veterinary chemicals. In 1944 National Chemical Products (NCP) was established in Germiston to produce ethanol, methylated spirits and a variety of other organic solvents from maize fermentation. NCP joined forces with Sentrachem in the late 1960s to produce synthetic rubber and other mining and industrial chemicals.[7]

Gent has argued that the chemical industry entered one of its very long cyclical phases of revival–prosperity–recession in the 1990s. This cycle is similar to the business cycles identified by Kondratieff, which last for 50 years, but represents fluctuations only in an individual industry. According to Gent, the last Kondratieff cycle for the chemical industry began in 1950 with a period of prosperity, which was followed by decline towards the middle of the 1970s. The revival began only at the end of the century. The most prosperous period was between 1954 and 1965, after which investment in research and development declined. The depression phase between 1979 and 1994 was characterised by the closure of chemical companies, mergers and down-sizing operations. It was only in the mid-1990s that 'companies began to feel enough pain to take the risk of innovation again'.[8] This major drive towards innovation which characterised the 1990s was most apparent in the South African chemical industry, led by Sasol.

Innovation at Sasol

At the beginning of the 1990s the dominant exposure of Sasol was to the domestic market, with the emphasis on synthetic fuel production, which produced 37 per cent of operating profits. Sasol Mining (coal) contributed 15 per cent, Sasol Oil (oil refining and gas marketing) 28 per cent and Sasol Chemicals 20 per cent. In 1993 Sasol management

7 G. S. Harrison and G. C. Gerrans, 'The South African chemical industry 1896–1996', *Spectrum*, 36(4) (1998), 8–11.

8 C. Gent, 'Changes in the chemical industry: the perspective of a catalyst supplier', *Chemical Communications*, 24 (December 2002), 2926–2928, at p. 2927.

restructured the operations of the group to shift the focus away from synthetic fuel production by applying the advanced technologies developed for Sasol 2 and Sasol 3 to global chemical production. All fuel production was moved to the two Secunda plants, with Sasol 1 restructured to concentrate on chemical production.[9] The old ammonium plant in Sasol 1 was closed down and the production of liquid fuel was terminated in June 1993, when the R820 million renovation project to transform Sasol 1 from a synfuel and basic chemicals producer into a producer of specialised chemicals was completed.[10] Sasol's strategy shifted towards speciality chemicals with the emphasis on added-value products. The Sasol restructuring in 1993 entailed the reorganisation of operations into the following companies:

- Sasol Chemical Industries (Pty) Ltd housed the divisions engaged in the production of chemical products;
- Sasol Synthetic Fuels (Pty) Ltd was the vehicle for producing synthetic fuels;
- Sasol Mining (Pty) Ltd coordinated all the group's mining activities;
- Sasol Oil (Pty) Ltd was the new company responsible for oil refining and fuel marketing.

This functional restructuring contributed to the more effective use of the technological resources within the group. The challenge for Sasol lay in translating the technological advantage it had acquired into increased profitability, for, in the mid-1990s, the company was achieving only modest growth and was dependent on the domestic market in South Africa. Between 1989 and 1994 Sasol's capital expenditure exceeded R6 billion and the company planned to spend another R1.6 billion in 1994 on synthetic fuel production, as Sasol synfuels and synchemicals were proving to be the best way to add value to low-grade coal that could not be exported.[11] Government subsidisation of Sasol eroded significantly during the 1990s as a result of the dramatic rise in international oil prices. Tariff protection was also becoming less important, though Sasol was restricted in the domestic supply of fuel by its so-called 'blue pump' agreement. This agreement restricted the retail sale of Sasol products. Synthetic fuel could be sold only at roster sites (numbering just 194 in South Africa) and from blue pumps at the service stations of other oil companies, and Sasol's market share was not to exceed 9.23 per cent of the total domestic market.[12] The 1998 energy White Paper announced the

9 *Chemsa*, July 1991, p. 151,
10 *Annual Report*, Sasol, 1991, pp. 11–12; *Review*, Sasol, 1998, p. 11.
11 *Chemical Processing South Africa*, 1(1) (February 1994), p. 2.
12 Verhoef, 'Innovation for globalisation or globalisation of innovation'.

government's intention to deregulate the petroleum industry and to terminate the subsidies to the synthetic fuels industry within three years, in order 'to promote a level playing field between the crude oil refining industry and the synthetic fuels industry'.[13] Sasol welcomed the government's policy on the liquid fuels industry, as it would afford participants in the industry the opportunity to grow and become more competitive. Sasol decided to terminate the blue pump agreement and to utilise its advanced Sasol Advanced Synthol (SAS) technology developed for Sasol 2 and Sasol 3 in the domestic market as well as globally. The SAS technology utilised fixed fluidised beds to produce gas from coal instead of the conventional circulating bed reactors. It was less capital intensive, reduced operating costs and improved the process of conversion.

The shift towards chemical production that exposed Sasol to the fluctuations of the chemical cycle was enhanced in 1994 when Sasol and AECI merged sections of their petrochemical, plastics and chemical interests to form Polifin Ltd. The joint venture produced and marketed monomers and polymers.[14] Four years later Sasol acquired the full shareholding of Polifin, which then became a subsidiary of Sasol Chemical Industries (SCI). SCI followed this by merging its wax production with Schümann Waxes in Hamburg to establish Schümann Sasol AG, which expanded its operations into the USA and Africa. SCI increased its exports of fertilisers, cresol, ammonia, phenolicsanode coal and alpha-olefins to the USA, northern Europe, Japan, India, Pakistan, Turkey, the Middle East, Australia and China. The global penetration was effected through two distribution companies: SCI Europe in alliance with Petrochem UK and Sasol Chemicals Pacific, operating from Hong Kong.[15]

Chemical beneficiation increasingly fed the global expansion of SCI. In 1997 Merichem-Sasol was formed as a 50–50 joint venture between the Merichen Company of Houston to supply phenolics and cresylics to the international market. Sasol Mining Explosives (SMX) developed and patented the new EXPAN explosives-grade ammonium nitrate products in demand by DHB Holdings in Minnesota and increased its investment in DHB to 60 per cent before expanding operations in Wyoming and Canada. This investment was not a success and declining profitability led to disinvestment in 2002.

Sasol Techologies' research and development in Sasolburg developed linear alpha-olefins and purified 1-octene from the Secunda olefin

13 *Star Business Report*, 18 November 1998; N. Lambrechts, *South African Liquid Fuels Industry*, ABN-AMRO Bank, 1998, pp. 67, 96–99.

14 *Chemical Processing South Africa*, 1(1) (February 1994), p. 10; *Annual Report*, AECI, 1995, p. 24.

15 *Annual Report*, Sasol, 1995, pp. 23–29; *Annual Report*, Sasol, 1998, p. 6.

pool for use in the international polymer industry; the operation was described as 'a unique and successful process by world-best chemical-processing standards'.[16] Dow Chemicals in the USA signed a supply-agreement with Sasol, recognising the extensive chemical beneficiation process undertaken by Sasol Technologies.

This innovation enabled Sasol to obtain a controlling interest in Condea, the world's largest producer of raw materials and an intermediary for the detergent industry. Its acquisition in 2000 increased the non-African revenue of the Sasol group of companies from 21 per cent in 2000 to 47 per cent the following year. It also offered the synergies needed to increase the production and distribution of chemical products for the East Asian markets developed by SCI from the late 1990s.[17] The Condea acquisition transformed Sasol from a South African-based group to a global player in the chemicals industry. It accelerated the entry of SCI into the surfactants markets by four to six years. Condea focused on applied research and development in the surfactants markets and SCI on basic applied research for the development of new products and markets. The Condea takeover created the opportunity to merge the olefins-based SCI products with the customer-driven surfactants production of Condea. Synergies existed in almost every aspect of SCI–Condea operations: in base products such as alpha-olefins, fatty alcohols and inorganic speciality chemicals and also in intermediaries, such as surfactants, solvents and fine chemicals and performance chemicals. In reality it may have been a move in the wrong direction, for two years later Sasol announced that it intended to sell Condea.

In the 1990s Sasol Polymers expanded production to new plants in Malaysia and China, which led to a 50 per cent increase in its annual polymer production at the Sasolburg plant to approximately 200,000 metric tons per annum. Sasol Polymers invested about R1.2 billion into three Asian joint ventures, with Optimal Olefins (Malaysia), Sdn Bhd, Petlin (Malaysia) and Wesco China Ltd. Optimal Olefins was a joint venture between Petronas Berhad of Malaysia (64 per cent), Dow Chemicals of the USA (24 per cent) and Sasol Polymers (12 per cent). Production commenced in November 2001. The Petlin plant at Kertih was a joint venture between Sasol Polymers (40 per cent), Petronas (40 per cent) and DSM, a Dutch polymer producer (20 per cent), and was expected to produce 255,000 metric tons of polymers per annum, making it one of the largest of its kind in the world. The last venture of 2000 was the acquisition by Sasol Polymers of a 10 per cent stake in

16 'Everything you wanted to know about South Africa's energy policy, but were afraid to ask Minister Maduna', *Engineering News*, 19–25 June 1998.

17 *Review*, Sasol, 2001, p. 33.

Wesco, a distributor of polymers in southern China. Wesco had been distributing Sasol Polymers' polypropylene in China since 1990 and absorbed about 80 per cent of the Malaysian polymer production. The remainder was sold in Africa and Australia.[18]

By early 1999 Sasol Synfuels had commissioned the last of its eight new-generation SAS reactors at Secunda. A ninth reactor was commissioned in 2001. The 1-octene plant also at Secunda was commissioned in 1999 and commenced supply of alpha-olefins to Dow Chemical polyethylene plants in May 1999.

While technological innovation in SCI transformed the chemical operations of Sasol into a global enterprise, it did not result in technological stagnation in the synthetic fuels operations. Sasol Petroleum International (SPI) was established in 1995 to undertake oil and gas exploration and production in selected high-potential areas in West and Southern Africa. The successful fuel production operations at Sasol 2 and 3 stimulated further research. The unique Sasol slurry-phase distillate technology, developed at Sasol Technologies, was ready for commercial application by 1997. This process offered an efficient and cost-effective method of converting natural gas into high-quality new-generation diesel, which was environmentally friendly. At the Middle East petroleum and gas conference in Abu Dhabi in 1997 Sasol announced the new GTL technology to convert gas into liquid fuel. The existing technology for that procedure was extremely expensive. The Sasol slurry-phase distillation process, developed on a modular basis, required limited initial investment and GTL plants would be profitable even if the oil price dropped to $10 per barrel.[19] The new technology also offered impressive environmental benefits: it was free of sulphur and low in aromatic compounds, while its use led to reduced exhaust emissions.[20] The high-value hydrocarbons (olefins and alcohol etc.) were removed, leaving synthetic oil. Although a synthetic refinery is similar to a conventional crude refinery, synthetic oil differs from crude oil. In the normal crude oil refinery, the petrol–diesel–kerosene ratio is approximately 3–3–1. In the Sasol synthetic process the ratio is 12–4–1, that is, with significantly more petrol.[21]

The GTL technology was immediately implemented via joint ventures. In 1998 Sasol Synfuel International (SSI) and Qatar General Petroleum Corporation and Phillips Petroleum of the USA established a company to build a GTL plant in Ras Laffan in Qatar. A joint venture

18 *Review*, Sasol, 2001, pp. 21–24.
19 *Survey*, Sasol, 1998, pp. 56–58.
20 *Survey*, Sasol, 1999, pp. 22–23.
21 Lambrechts, *South African Liquid Fuels Industry*, p. 57.

Table 7.4 *Divisional contribution to turnover of the Sasol group of companies, 1990–2000*

Year	*Sasol Oil*		*SCI*		*SSF*		*Sasol Mines*		*Other*		*Total*
	R (millions)	*%*	*R (millions)*	*%*	*R (millions)*	*%*	*R (millions)*	*%*	*R (millions)*	*%*	
1990	491	28.00	349	20.00	657	37.00	262	15.00	–	–	
1995	2,465	14.70	5,535	33.02	6,510	38.83	2,072	12.36	182	1.09	16,764
1998	3,542	16.76	7,655	36.22	6,877	32.54	2,768	13.09	794	1.39	21,136
2000	4,635	17.00	12,409	48.00	10,915	42.00	3,343	12.00	462	0.10	25,762 [a]

[a] *Annual Report*, Sasol 2001, p. 113; an amount of R6,002 million was entered as 'elimination'.
Sources: Annual Report, Sasol, 1990, p. 9; *Annual Report*, Sasol, 1996, p. 9; *Annual Report*, Sasol, 1999, p. 21; *Annual Report*, Sasol, 2001, p. 113.

was also signed with the US oil company Chevron in Nigeria to conduct extensive feasibility studies for GTL application in Nigeria and with the Norwegian Statoil to conduct feasibility studies on the conversion of offshore Norwegian plants to GTL technology. Sasol and Chevron then entered into an agreement to develop GTL technology globally. This alliance combined 'Sasol's slurry-phase distillation process with Chevron's hydrocracking technology – called isocracking – in pursuit of GTL projects with outside partners'.[22]

The key to the successful implementation of GTL technology was access to sufficient gas deposits. Sasol therefore invested, between 1997 and the end of 2000, approximately US$175 million in exploration. Towards the end of 2000 SPI (the vehicle for oil and gas exploration) reported an increase of 250 per cent in its gas deposits, which could be converted into 260 million barrels of oil.[23] SPI was active in Gabon, Equatorial Guinea, Nigeria and Mozambique, but the bulk of its deposits were in Mozambique, where the World Bank approved a US$30 million credit towards the Pande natural gas project in 1994.[24]

The diversification of Sasol's operations away from only synthetic fuel production in the 1950s to the end of the 1990s is illustrated in Table 7.4. Sasol had increased its operations in the global chemical industries from 20 per cent of total turnover in 1990 to 48 per cent in 2000; in a similar fashion fuel production had risen from 37 per cent of turnover to 42 per cent. The decline in oil and refinery production (which is domestic production) provides striking evidence of the globalisation of Sasol's chemical operations and of its GTL technology in synfuels production.

AECI

The second most important chemical company in South Africa was AECI, which was controlled by Anglo American until it bought back 40 per cent of its shares from that corporation in 1998. In 1995 AECI's turnover was 40 per cent of that of the Sasol group, but by 2000 this had declined to 23.3 per cent. AECI had consolidated its position as the major chemical company in South Africa during the early 1980s after acquiring Chemical Services in 1980. After 1985, when the production of explosives was phased out at the Somerset West plant, AECI moved into speciality chemicals with the formation in 1991 of AECI Bioproducts and AECI Aroma and Fine Chemicals with plants in Umbogintwini and Richards Bay. By 1990 AECI Chlor-Alkali and Plastics Ltd contributed

22 'Sasol, Chevron form global GTL partnership', *Oil and Gas Journal*, 14 June 1999.

23 *Annual Report*, Sasol, 1999, p. 15; *Annual Report*, Sasol, 2000, p. 55.

24 *Chemical Processing South Africa*, 1(4) (May 1994), p. 4.

28 per cent to the AECI group's turnover. Explosives, chemicals and agricultural products contributed 34 per cent to turnover, polymer derivatives 20 per cent and other trading activities 17 per cent.[25] The limitation of the domestic market was recognised as a serious constraint by AECI management in the early 1990s. The chief executive commented in 1990 that the group would have to 'get their skates on' if they were to achieve any significance in world terms.[26] The bulk of AECI production went into commodity chemicals destined for the domestic market, which exposed the group to the cyclical fluctuations of the mining and agricultural sectors and to conditions in the domestic economy. At the beginning of the 1990s AECI's turnover exceed R5 billion for the first time, but group profits had declined by 25 per cent and profitability remained under pressure until the mid-1990s.

AECI invested in long-term research to improve the competitiveness of the group. In 1990 AECI and C. G. Smith opened the first dimethylether (DME) plant in Durban to manufacture ozone-friendly alternatives to chlorofluorocarbons. This was the first plant of its kind in Africa and the third in the world.[27] As South Africa was a signatory to the Montreal Protocol on environmental protection, AECI investigated every opportunity to develop environmentally friendly production. In 1990, in another joint venture with C. G. Smith, the construction of a hydrogen peroxide plant was undertaken as an alternative to the fast aggressive oxidisers, such as chlorine-based chemicals, which were harmful to the environment.[28] The focus of operations remained on explosives, paints, fertilisers and pharmaceuticals, with the export of fertilisers into Africa as its most impressive achievement. After 1994, when Imperial Chemical Industries (ICI) sold its shareholding in AECI,[29] AECI responded by investigating export opportunities for Kynoch Ltd, its fertiliser producer and by 1996 that company contributed 28 per cent to the AECI group's turnover. In 1996 AECI Explosives bought Ashanti Goldfields' 49 per cent stake in ICI Explosives (Ghana) and via this wholly owned subsidiary gained access to West Africa's expanding mining operations.[30]

Yet in 2000 AECI remained an embattled chemicals group. Turnover was falling and had declined to below the level of 1995. Between 1990 and 2000 it had risen by only 1.99 per cent annually and the group's net trading income had declined by 0.5 per cent, while net income after tax

25 *Annual Report*, AECI, 1990, p. 9.
26 *Chemsa*, November 1991, p. 239.
27 *Chemsa*, July 1990, p. 166.
28 *Annual Report*, AECI, 1990, p. 11; *Chemsa*, November 1990, p. 245.
29 *Annual Report*, AECI, 1994, p. 6.
30 *Annual Report*, AECI, 1996, pp. 20, 25.

rose by a mere 5.57 per cent. Return on assets declined from 13.1 per cent in 1990 to 9.0 per cent in 2000. Return on shareholders' funds also declined, from 17.9 per cent to 9.4 per cent in 2000. This weak performance of AECI at the end of the Kondratieff cycle led to a takeover bid in 1998 by Sasol, but the Competition Commission aborted the project. AECI then embarked on a fundamental restructuring of its operations and by 2000 the group consisted of three focused chemical concerns. The transformation strategy was announced in October 1998 and concluded in 2000. The three core clusters were mining solutions (explosives under the name African Explosives Limited – AEL), speciality chemicals, repositioned in the Chemical Services group, and speciality fibres (SANS Fibres).[31] From this repositioning AECI started global expansion, with moves into West Africa, when a manufacturing facility was established in Mali, and an investment of R80 million in the USA.

Sentrachem

Sentrachem was the smallest of the more prominent local chemical concerns in the 1990s. Because Sentrachem was not performing well, in the mid-1980s Sanlam, the majority shareholder in FVB (Federale Volksbeleggings), instructed its investment company, Sankorp, to take action to restore it to profitability. Major restructuring followed. In part it resulted in the sale of Sentrachem's fertiliser concern, Fedmis, to AECI, Sasol and Omnia. In 1990 a loss-making afprene plant in Newcastle was closed down.[32] Sentrachem then consolidated its production of generic agricultural chemicals in Sanachem, which was exporting 60 per cent of production by 1994.[33] Sentrachem also controlled Mega Plastics, the largest diversified plastics manufacturer in Southern Africa in 1994.[34] Although the cyclical nature of the chemicals industry remained a risk, management was spending money in the right places and one analyst believed that the group would outperform AECI in the next upswing in the cycle.[35]

The Sentrachem of 1994 was a very different group from the one in which Sankorp had obtained an interest in 1985. In the 1990s the group had altered its strategy to develop a more balanced portfolio in petrochemicals, general industrial chemicals, high-technology plastics processing and in the manufacture of value-added chemicals. The

31 *Annual Report*, AECI, 2000, pp. 10–23.
32 Sankorp board minutes, 14 March 1990 (Sankorp archives).
33 Sankorp executive management minutes, 3 August 1994 (Sankorp archives).
34 Sankorp board minutes, 10 February 1993, 30 November 1994 (Sankorp archives).
35 *Sentrachem Investment Report*, Martin & Co., 31 December 1990.

strong cyclical nature of chemical commodities led Sentrachem to make a gradual, but decisive, shift away from commodity-type chemicals towards value-added chemicals after Sankorp's research had indicated that the industry index (the commodity cycle together with the GDP) illustrated a clear correlation between Sentrachem's results and the chemical commodity cycle. Up to 1991 a sharp decline in GDP was accompanied by a decline in Sentrachem's operating profit before interest and after tax. After 1991 Sentrachem's results maintained a stable trend, despite a further decline in GDP. This counter-cyclical trend was ascribed to the stronger concentration on the manufacturing and export of value-added fine chemicals and to the further rationalisation of non-performing assets in Sentrachem and NCP. By 1994 Sentrachem exported 60 per cent of its production through Sanachem. Sentrachem was able to compete internationally with its fine chemicals, because transport costs (volumes were much lower than with commodity chemicals) and economies of scale were less important. Furthermore, the technology for the manufacture of fine chemicals was not widely available. Sentrachem had invested substantially in research and the development of fine chemicals via Delta G Scientific, which it had bought in August 1993. In 1994 Sentrachem also acquired Farm-AG for R238 million, making the company a full subsidiary of Sentrachem.[36] Although Sentrachem's return on investment (ROI) stood only at 15.9 per cent in 1994, compared with 18.9 per cent in 1989, Sankorp was satisfied that Sentrachem was well positioned for growth and expansion. The reduction in import tariffs and requirements under the General Agreement on Tariffs and Trade (GATT) further convinced Sankorp of the importance of strengthening its focus on value-added fine chemicals and export markets. To achieve its goal of raising fine chemical exports to 25 per cent of group turnover, Sentrachem International Holdings opened a head office in Jersey, and other offices in London, Houston and Hong Kong. In 1994 Kooltherm in the UK, a company manufacturing fenolic foam under patent, was acquired. This led in 1994 to foreign exchange consumption in Sentrachem breaking even for the first time since its devastating foreign exchange losses in the mid-1980s.[37] Strong local and international demand for chemicals continued during the first six months of 1995 and resulted in a growth in turnover of 27 per cent.[38] Between 1991 and 1995 Sentrachem's market capitalisation had increased fivefold, but exports had risen even faster, from $30 million in 1991 to $200 million in 1995.

36 *Chemical Processing South Africa*, 1(7) (August 1994), p. 2.

37 Sankorp board minutes, 30 November 1994 (Sankorp archives).

38 Sankorp executive management minutes, 7 June 1995 (Sankorp archives).

Sankorp had achieved its goal with Sentrachem by the end of 1995, when the emphasis on the manufacturing of value-added fine chemicals was further enhanced by the acquisition of the Hampshire Chemical Corporation. Through international equity placing by means of global depository receipts, $60 million was raised to finance the transaction. With this acquisition Sentrachem succeeded in raising exports to 20 per cent of turnover, close to its target earnings distribution ratio of 50–25–25 for local, export and foreign in earnings.[39] Earnings from the local subsidiaries had also improved dramatically, with NCP's profit before tax rising by 100 per cent by August 1995 and Safripol's by 80 per cent by year end. Sentrachem was then poised for further cooperation in the domestic market and negotiations with both AECI and Sasol were in progress on building a world-scale methanol plant for Mossgas. Sentrachem was also looking into the conversion of the distillation train into a condensate refinery to produce fuel and into the potential development of a naphtha cracker.[40]

Unfortunately, in 1995 and 1996 poor financial management led to Sentrachem experiencing three crises that seriously weakened the company. In July 1995 an unauthorised loan from Sentrachem's surplus funds was made to a Greek shipping magnate just as Sentrachem bought Hampshire Chemical Corporation; the second crisis occurred when the Greek shipping magnate went insolvent and Sentrachem had to write off the loan as a bad debt. The third crisis struck in October 1996, when Sanachem found itself with a vast open position in foreign exchange just as the value of the rand started declining. Millions of rands again had to be written off during the first six months of 1997, leading to severe cash flow constraints, a ruined balance sheet and plummeting profits.

Under these circumstances the US chemicals company Dow put in an offer for Sentrachem. To obtain full control of Sentrachem, Dow needed the agreement of 90 per cent of the shareholders and to make an offer to minority shareholders. Sankorp, with 38.7 per cent of the shares, was satisfied with the offer, given the premium on the share price, the difficulties Sentrachem was experiencing and the desire on the part of its management to move out of a non-core non-strategic investment, but the Sentrachem board declined the Dow offer as too low. However, they decided to send a delegation to the USA to discuss the offer with Dow at a time, in the fourth quarter of 1997, when the South African currency was once more weakening. Meanwhile, in the USA, the American Competition Authority demanded on the strength of the Hart/Scott/Redino clause that Sentrachem should sell its holding in Hampshire Chemical

39 Sankorp board minutes, 29 November 1995 (Sankorp archives).

40 Sankorp board minutes, 8 August 1995 (Sankorp archives).

Corporation (acquired in 1995) if the transaction were to be authorised. Dow then agreed to increase its offer and in early December 1997 the Sentrachem board accepted it. Dow immediately purchased Hoechst South Africa's interest in Safripol and restructured Agrihold into Dow Agrosciences. Finally, towards the end of the 1990s, Dow Sentrachem was further restructured to focus on agricultural operations and plastics.

Conclusion

The chemical industry displayed a gradual shift in its focus of production in the 1990s from commodity chemicals to speciality chemicals and value-added production in the downstream chemical production of fibres, plastics and agricultural chemicals. The inward-looking production for the protected South African market was slowly changing towards the end of the decade, as the reduction in tariff protection pushed the industry to invest more in research, technological innovation and cost-effective production. Strategic alliances were concluded with international chemical concerns, beginning with Sasol and Schümann and then Sentrachem and Dow Chemicals. Sasol was the most successful and was transformed into a global chemical company by the end of the decade, though its most important competitive advantage lay in extracting synthetic gas from coal and converting it into hydrocarbons. Significant moves overseas had also started to evolve in both AECI and Dow Sentrachem. All three were responding to the increased competition and the small size of the South African market.

In 2000 the chemical industry remained the dominant sector in manufacturing, with 21.3 per cent of total sales.[41] The largest contributor to capital investment in the chemical industry in the 1990s was Sasol. Capital investment depended on the competitiveness of the domestic manufacturing sector, which was determined to a great extent by the cost of labour, both skilled and unskilled. The challenge to all manufacturing, and to the chemicals industry in particular, was to penetrate international markets through the application of technology with more skills-intensive, higher-value-added manufacturing products. The chemical industry embarked on such course of action in the 1990s through the restructuring of the major chemical conglomerates into more focused production entities. This work was completed only by the end of the decade. Sasol remained the dominant player in the industry.

41 *Manufacturing: Production and Sales*, P3041.2, Statistics South Africa, 2001.

8

Electricity supply

Anton Eberhard

Introduction

As South Africa approached its first democratic elections in the early 1990s, its electricity supply industry reflected the dichotomies that were starkly evident in the broader society and economy: almost all of the white population had access to electricity, including households, commercial enterprises, industry, mining and even remote white-owned farms. Few black households had access to electricity. Ironically, there was no shortage of electricity. Eskom, the dominant, state-owned electricity corporation, had surplus generation capacity as a result of heavy investment in the 1970s and 1980s. The problem was at the distribution end of the network, where the supply of electricity was compromised by a highly fragmented and racially based system of local government with inadequate resources for service delivery.

The first challenge for the new government in 1994 was to facilitate access to electricity. The initial focus was on rationalising and reforming the electricity distribution industry. A national electricity regulator was established to control and harmonise tariffs. Eventually, attention also turned to restructuring Eskom as part of a broader drive to increase efficiencies in state-owned enterprises. In line with international trends, the 1990s also saw the introduction of new thinking on the reform of electricity markets, including the unbundling of vertically integrated state-owned utilities, the introduction of competition and private sector participation. However, as electricity demand grew and excess supply capacity eroded, the brief experiment in designing a competitive market was quickly abandoned and Eskom once again assumed primary responsibility for new generation investments, with private independent power producers permitted to operate only at the margin. However, delays in deciding on new investment during this period of reform later came to haunt the industry and South Africa would run out of power before new power stations could be commissioned.

In this chapter, the key features of the power sector in South Africa are described; this is followed by a discussion of power sector reforms during the 1990s. The discussion is broken down into broadly chronological episodes where the rationale for reform, the interests of the different stakeholders, the reform models and the outcomes of reform are analysed. The concluding section reflects on the nature and direction of the reforms and some of the reasons why the state is once again playing a lead role in the power sector.

Overview of the electricity industry

The South African electricity supply industry (ESI) remains dominated by the state-owned and vertically integrated utility, Eskom, which ranks ninth in the world in terms of electricity sales.[1] With capacity of 40 GW out of a total system capacity of 43 GW, Eskom generates about 96 per cent of South Africa's electricity requirements, which amounts to more than half the electricity generated on the African continent. Private generators contribute about 3 per cent of national output (mostly for their own use) and municipalities contribute an additional 1 per cent. South Africa's electricity infrastructure is heavily dependent on coal (93 per cent), with nuclear, bagasse, hydro and emergency gas turbines accounting for the balance.

South Africa is largely self-sufficient in electricity production. While Eskom imports some power from the Democratic Republic of Congo and from Zambia, mainly for peak load management, and is contractually bound to take electricity from a hydro plant in Mozambique, it also sells electricity to neighbouring countries: Botswana, Lesotho, Mozambique, Namibia, Swaziland, Zambia and Zimbabwe. This amounts to less than 5 per cent of total net energy produced.

Eskom also owns and controls the high-voltage transmission grid and supplies about half of the electricity produced direct to customers (Figure 8.1). The other half is distributed by local authorities. They buy bulk supplies of electricity from Eskom, and some also generate small amounts for sale in their own areas of jurisdiction.

Eskom's average tariffs cover its average costs. However, tariffs for rural and low-income residential customers are cross-subsidised from industrial tariffs and surpluses earned on sales to municipalities. The

1 *Annual Report*, Eskom, 2003.

Figure 8.1 *Structure of the electricity supply industry in South Africa*

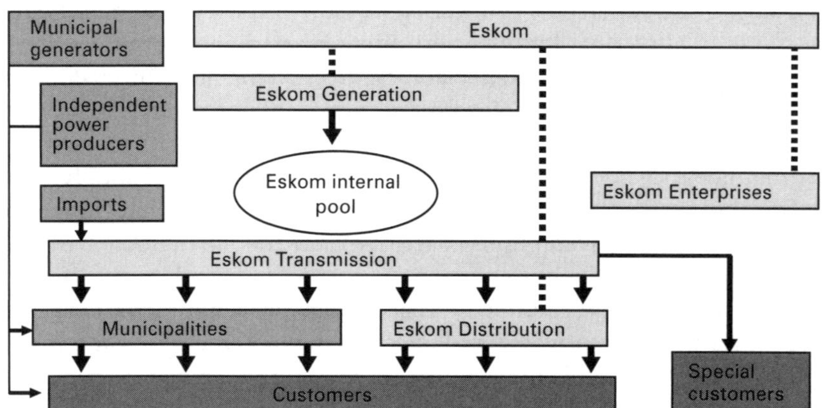

large municipalities, in turn, make an additional profit from reselling Eskom electricity, which enables them to subsidise property rates and to finance other municipal services. Municipalities' dependence on this profit has been an obstacle to distribution reform. In the 1990s this benefit was limited by the non-payment of tariffs by some low-income consumers, by inefficient operations and by a lack of technical and managerial capacity.

Eskom led an impressive national electrification drive. The proportion of households with access to electricity rose from about one-third in 1990 to about two-thirds a decade later. About two-thirds of these connections were accomplished by Eskom and the remainder by local authorities. The electrification programme resulted in significant increases in peak demand in the morning and early evenings, with profound implications for future generation plant mix. The need for demand-side management programmes became more apparent.

Reform of the electricity distribution industry: meeting the needs of consumers

At the beginning of the 1990s the two overriding political concerns were the financial problems of the municipal distributors of electricity and the low levels of access to electricity. Small, poorly run municipal distributors were a legacy of the apartheid era and the creation of separate local black municipalities. These municipalities struggled with lack of technical capacity, a paucity of income-generating industrial customers and a huge backlog in new connections for low-income consumers. Some of these smaller distributors were amalgamated into larger entities, but most of them still lacked viability. Non-payment from customers compounded the problem of accumulating debts owed to Eskom (the supplier of bulk power). Many distributors also curtailed spending on the maintenance needed to assure security and reliability of supply.

For the same customer categories, tariffs varied widely between distributors, as it proved impossible to regulate the 188 municipal distribution entities effectively. Reporting was inadequate and it was difficult to obtain accurate information on costs. It also proved difficult to attract and retain skilled, motivated and adequately paid employees and managers in the industry. Political attention to the problems of distributors grew because distributors in the poorest areas were unable to finance new connections and subsidise services to poor customers. Reform of the electricity distribution industry (EDI) was intended to address these related challenges of jump-starting rural electrification, restructuring distributors and creating a new electricity regulatory agency which would protect electricity consumers.

An accelerated national electrification programme

With the exception of some studies in the 1980s that highlighted the inequity of electricity provision, little data existed on demand from unserved households.[2] Some researchers began to map out what a national electrification programme might look like and argued that it would be important to restructure the inefficient EDI.[3] The changes in the political landscape in South Africa, after 1990, lent some urgency to these calls for action.

The African National Congress's 1994 election platform, the *Reconstruction and Development Programme*, set out the goal of electrifying 2.5 million new homes between 1994 and 1999, a goal that was exceeded by the new government (Figure 8.2).[4]

2 A. Eberhard, *Energy and Poverty in Urban and Peri-urban Areas Around Cape Town*, Second Carnegie Inquiry into Poverty and Development in Southern Africa, Conference Paper No. 155, University of Cape Town, 1984.

3 C. Dingley, *Electricity for All: The Needs and the Means*, monograph, Department of Electrical Engineering, University of Cape Town, 1990; P. Theron, A. Eberhard and C. Dingley, 'Electricity provision in the urban areas of South Africa: towards a new framework', *Urban Forum*, 2(2) (1992), 1–24.

4 African National Congress, *Reconstruction and Development Programme*, Umanyano Publications, 1994.

Figure 8.2 *Cumulative electricity connections, 1991–2001*

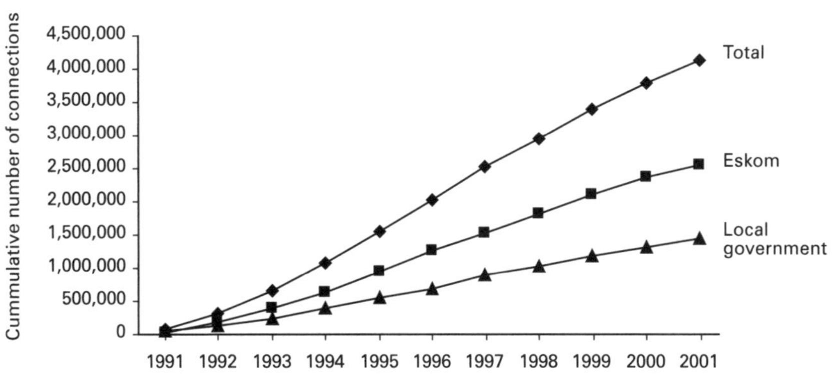

Source: Electrification Statistics, National Electricity Regulator, 2001.

Until 2000, the entire electrification programme was funded by Eskom, either through internal subsidies (garnered mainly from higher-than-cost electricity charges to large industrial and mining customers) or through transfers to an electrification fund that the National Electricity Regulator allocated to municipalities.

From the mid-1990s it was national policy for a portion of the capital cost of connections to be subsidised.[5] In practice, the subsidy extended to the entire cost of connection as well as a portion of the operating costs because actual consumption of electricity in low-income homes was much lower than forecast, and revenues from electrification also fell short of expectations. At the beginning of the programme it was estimated that the average monthly consumption of newly connected, low-income households would be 350 kWh per month (compared with an average of 750 kWh per month for a middle-income family in South Africa). However, actual average monthly consumption was less than a third of these estimates. Government responded by granting 50 kWh per month free to poor consumers.

Nearly all of these new connections used pre-payment technology, whereby customers buy tokens or top-up electronic cards to activate their electricity dispenser. The costs of the electricity supply and use

5 *White Paper on Energy Policy for the Republic of South Africa,* Department of Minerals and Energy, 1998, p. 37.

were to be recovered through a flat energy unit charge. Many connections involved informal houses (shacks) and used pre-wired 'ready boards' with a few light and plug points.

As the government began to reform the power sector, it moved to secure the national electrification programme through establishing a separate National Electrification Fund in the Department of Minerals and Energy funded by the National Treasury. Eskom was required to pay taxes and ceased to subsidise the electrification programme from its internal income. This experience was important by demonstrating that the meeting of social goals and public benefits was independent of the industry structure.

The electrification programme in South Africa was remarkable in a number of respects. Doubling the access to electricity from one-third to two-thirds of the population in less than a decade was probably without precedent. The programme was clearly driven by the unique challenges that South Africa faced in overcoming the legacy of apartheid inequity. Yet there are lessons from this programme that have a more universal relevance. The South African experience demonstrates that it is possible to make substantial progress in widening access to electricity services for the poor, even as the electricity industry is restructured. Although Eskom was not unbundled or privatised, it did face pressure to operate on a sound commercial basis and discontinued internal subsidies for new electricity connections. The electrification programme was driven by a political commitment to provide services for the poor. It was made possible by an electricity industry that was technically competent and financially strong. The lesson from South Africa appears to be that the most important variable for the success of public benefit programmes is not the form of the industry structure or ownership but rather the existence of explicit public policies, regulatory instruments, a dedicated implementation agency and funding to achieve the desired social goals.

Restructuring the electricity distributors

Critical to the task of accelerating the electrification programme was restructuring the electricity distributors. Attention to distributors was not always welcomed by the large metropolitan governments which had gained surplus income from the sale of electricity and feared the loss of that revenue. The South African Local Government Association (SALGA) and the Association of Municipal Electrical Undertakings (AMEU) were consequently ambivalent in their support for rationalisation. Eskom was an early supporter of EDI restructuring in principle, although in practice it often resisted reforms that would strip it of its distribution services.[6] The unions, on the other hand, strongly advocated distribution reforms that would create one single, publicly owned national distributor.

After a protracted period, involving a number of studies, a stakeholder forum, government committees and negotiations, the cabinet agreed in June 1999 that the large number of municipal distributors and Eskom's distribution business should be merged into six regional electricity distribution companies (REDs). REDs would be defined so as to ensure the financial viability of each, but the central problem was drawing the boundaries. To be financially viable, each RED would require the right balance of below-cost (low-income residential) and above-cost (commercial and industrial) users. In early 2000 the government appointed a consortium, led by consultants PricewaterhouseCoopers (PwC), to examine and provide recommendations on the REDs' boundaries, ownership, asset valuation, regulation and human resources. The government's Electricity Distribution Industry Restructuring Committee – comprising relevant government departments, Eskom, local government and the National Electricity Regulator – oversaw the process and produced its own 'Blueprint for EDI Reform'.[7] The cabinet's review led to a decision – in January 2001 and reconfirmed in May – to adopt the Committee's blueprint and rationalise distribution into six REDs, with an EDI holdings company to manage the transition.

Elements of local government remained ambivalent or hostile to the proposal and threatened to challenge the plan in the Constitutional Court. The ruling African National Congress (ANC) was split on the matter. The ANC's leadership asserted the importance of a national solution to the problems of electricity distribution, but those involved at local government feared losing their influence.

While conflicting interests slowed the reform process, it is also probably true to say that one of the original reasons for reform, the need to strengthen the capability of distributors to extend access to electricity to the majority of the population, was obviated by Eskom simply getting on with the job. However, the other reasons for distribution reform were beginning to receive more public attention: local government finances were in a parlous state and industry was greatly concerned at the lack of investment and the deterioration in the reliability of the system. These concerns about the quality and reliability of supply re-ignited moves to restructure the industry. EDI reform was still a work

6 Eskom, 'Proposals for the restructuring of the electricity supply industry in South Africa and implications for Eskom', confidential internal document, 16 July 1990.

7 *Electricity Distribution Industry Restructuring Blueprint Report*, Department of Minerals and Energy, 2001.

in progress in 2000. Major differences between the various stakeholders remained unresolved and government seemed unwilling to face the reality that the creation of the REDs would almost certainly require an amendment to the constitution, which limited the role of local government in electricity distribution.

The new electricity regulator

Accompanying these moves to restructure the electricity distribution sector, the government decided to clarify its multiple governance roles in the sector. The government owned much of the ESI and had expectations of adequate financial performance and returns. It also had a responsibility to protect consumers and ensure that electricity services were provided at as low a cost as possible. Following a global trend, it created an independent regulator to take on responsibility for the latter functions. The National Electricity Regulator (NER) was established in 1995 with a legal mandate to license all electricity suppliers, to approve their tariffs, to monitor the quality of supply and to settle disputes.

Many of the initial staff in the NER were ex-Eskom employees. Over time, the NER built up its own staff and emerged as one of the more capable independent regulatory institutions on the African continent and its mandate was extended to include gas and petroleum pipelines. The NER developed professional capacity in rate-of-return regulation, which formed the basis for moving subsequently to a multi-year price-cap regulatory regime. Its tariff determinations were consistently below those applied for by Eskom and the municipalities, though the tariffs still allowed these utilities an economic rate of return. Nevertheless, the NER (later renamed NERSA) faced huge challenges in terms of building sufficient capacity to ensure further improvements in efficiency by Eskom and the many municipal distributors. Indeed, the creation of new, stable and competent institutions in developing countries is a formidable task, particularly when there is little tradition or experience of independent regulation.

Reforming the governance, structure and competitiveness of the ESI

Accompanying the EDI reforms was a demand for a more fundamental restructuring of the ESI, and Eskom in particular. These pressures took three forms. First, South Africa in the 1990s underwent a process of macro- and micro-economic reform, which included moves to improve governance in large state-owned enterprises such as Eskom, in part through corporatisation. Second, a closer scrutiny of Eskom's own performance suggested that some degree of restructuring would lead to performance improvements, particularly in its investment decisions. Third, the idea of private participation in the ESI and a shift towards competition gradually gained currency.

State-owned enterprise restructuring and the corporatisation of Eskom

South Africa has not been subject to any direct World Bank or International Monetary Fund structural adjustment programmes. Nevertheless, in the mid-1990s the government adopted a process of 'self-imposed structural adjustment'. Following a period of attention to macro-economic reforms, the emphasis moved to micro-economic reforms, including a new focus on improved efficiencies and governance in government-owned entities. In August 2000 the Department of Public Enterprises (DPE) published *A Policy Framework: An Accelerated Agenda Towards the Restructuring of State Owned Enterprises*. Because of union pressure and concerns in its own political constituency, the government described its restructuring agenda very broadly as follows:

> Government's policy with regard to State Owned Enterprises is more properly referred to as a *restructuring* programme, and not in the more simplistic terms of privatization. The programme was … designed to ensure the maximization of shareholder interests defined in economic, social and development terms. Thus restructuring refers to the matrix of options that include the redesign of business management principles within enterprises, the attraction of strategic equity partnerships, the divestment of equity either in whole or in part where appropriate, and the employment of various immediate, turnaround initiatives.

The government decided to focus its restructuring efforts on the four largest state-owned enterprises, one of which was Eskom.[8] Although created through statute, Eskom's ownership status had never been formally defined. It paid no taxes and there was no formally expressed set of performance expectations or obligations. The government wished to clarify its relationship with the utility and to formalise a performance contract. In the words of the Department of Public Enterprises' *Policy Framework*:

> Eskom will be corporatized, with transmission, distribution and generation each forming a separate corporate entity. Different generating companies will be formed to promote internal competition prior to the

8 Media release by the Minister of Public Enterprises, 2000.

introduction of private sector participation in generation, in conjunction with new power requirements.

The Department understood the importance of not simply privatising a monopoly, but of creating a competitive industry structure before privatisation. The *Policy Framework* also suggested that transmission should probably remain in the hands of the state and that it was likely to take the form of a separate independent company.

The Eskom Conversion Act of 2001 replaced the old Eskom Act of 1987 and subsequent amendments. There was strong opposition to this bill from organised labour, which argued that the government had not followed the procedures agreed to the National Framework Agreement, whereby representatives of the government and unions would negotiate the restructuring of individual state-owned enterprises. In May and June 2001, the Congress of South African Trade Unions (Cosatu) made a submission on the Eskom Conversion Bill to the Public Enterprise Parliamentary Portfolio Committee. Its opposition centred on three main concerns: the bill would pave the way for the privatisation of Eskom; the taxation of Eskom would impinge on its developmental role; and the taxation would result in upward pressure on electricity prices. An agreement was reached in principle that new clauses would be included in the bill regarding the developmental role of Eskom and the protection of employees, but not about Eskom paying taxes and dividends.[9]

Investment in the ESI: a re-evaluation of Eskom's performance

Within South Africa and internationally, Eskom was widely perceived to be a well managed public utility. However, there was considerable scope for improvement, particularly in Eskom's investment decisions.

At first glance, Eskom appears to have performed well during the 1990s. It supplied electricity at among the lowest prices in the world. The average cost of electricity generated was around 1.5 US cent/kWh. It consistently made a positive return on assets. The reliability and quality of supply were good. Average energy availability[10] from its power stations increased from 76 per cent in 1991 to 92 per cent in 2000.

9 Labour became increasingly alienated from government from the late 1990s onwards. Gwede Mantashe, the General Secretary of the National Union of Mineworkers, warned at a rally in Johannesburg that the ANC should not take the support of workers for granted. 'It must listen to the working class and get their support, or it should listen to big capital and lose their support.' Cosatu embarked on a political strike on 30 and 31 August 2001 and marched to Parliament in protest against the government's plans to privatise state assets.

10 Defined as capacity hours available × 100 / total capacity hours in a year.

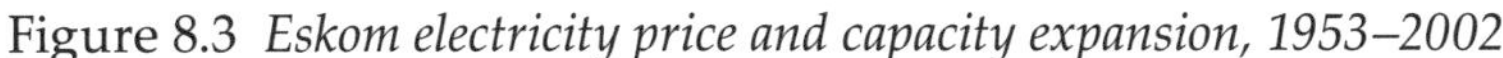
Figure 8.3 *Eskom electricity price and capacity expansion, 1953–2002*

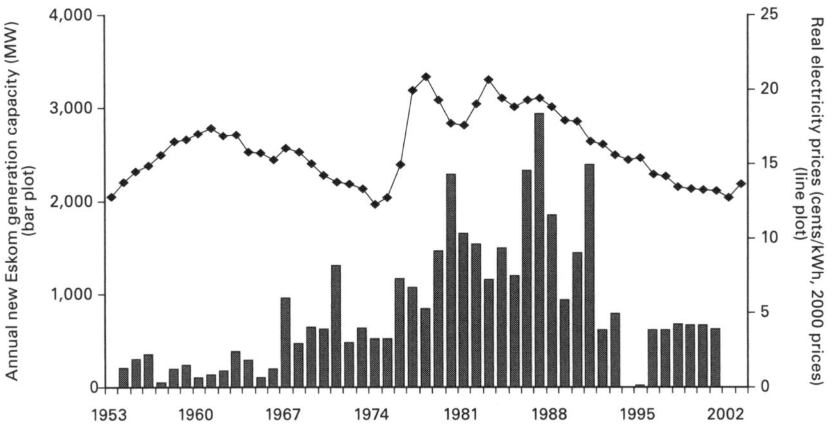

Sources: Annual Reports, Eskom, 1980–2002; *Statistical Yearbooks*, Eskom, 1985–1996.

Labour productivity increased and employee numbers dropped from over 66,000 in 1985, to 46,600 in 1991 and to 32,800 in 2000. The national electricity utility was commercially run with no recourse to the national fiscus. It raised finance through commercial debt, mostly through issuing bonds, which were well supported by local and international capital markets. The government no longer provided guarantees for Eskom's debt.[11]

Eskom's low prices and exemplary electrification performance left the impression that it was highly efficient and that there was no need for reform. Many would simply equate low prices with efficiency. However, this was not necessarily the case.[12] A close examination of the South African ESI shows that low prices and the ability to fund electrification emanated, in part, from very low coal prices (by international standards) and exemption from taxation and dividends.[13] Moreover, if

11 *Annual Reports*, Eskom.

12 G. Steyn, *Governance, Finance and Investment: Decision Making and Risk in the Electric Power Sector*, DPhil, University of Sussex, 2001; M. Davis and G. Steyn, *Electricity in South Africa*, Financial Times Business Limited, 1998; A. Eberhard and M. Mtepa, 'Rationale for restructuring and regulation of a "low priced" public utility: a case study of Eskom in South Africa', *International Journal of Regulation and Governance*, 3(2) (2003), 77–102.

13 G. Steyn, 'A competitive electricity market for South Africa: the need for change and a strategy for restructuring South Africa's electricity supply industry', paper prepared for the Department of Minerals and Energy, February 2000.

Figure 8.4 *Historical growth in maximum demand and capacity at Eskom, 1954–2001*

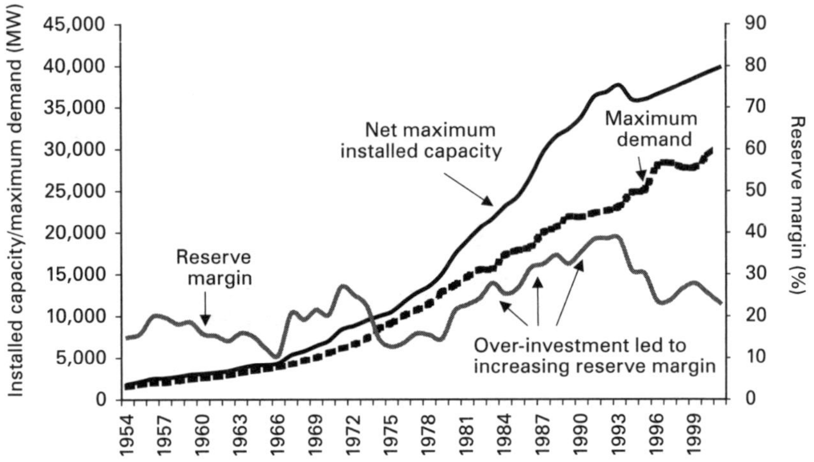

Sources: Annual Reports, Eskom, 1980–2002; *Statistical Yearbooks*, Eskom, 1985–1996.

long-term price trends are examined, in real terms prices in the 1990s were no lower than in the early 1950s or 1970s. This would seem to indicate that Eskom had not significantly improved its performance.

Prices in the late 1970s and early 1980s rose steeply because Eskom invested massively in new generation capacity. However, its investment decisions were poor, resulting in expensive excess capacity, as shown in Figures 8.3 and 8.4.

This pattern of over-investment and subsequent contraction was not dissimilar to that experienced by many vertically integrated power company monopolies during the 1970s and 1980s. When economic growth was forecast to be rapid and shortages in power supply seemed imminent, new expansion projects were undertaken, mostly within a context of investors or managers of state-owned enterprises assuming little risk. The costs were then passed through to electricity consumers and the debt was guaranteed by the state, but the investments were lumpy and had long lead times. Expected growth rates were often not realised and the inevitable consequence was wasteful overcapacity. Planning new plants and further investment then stopped until a new crisis in meeting future demand arose.

Figure 8.5 *Eskom capital expenditure and price trends, 1980–2001*

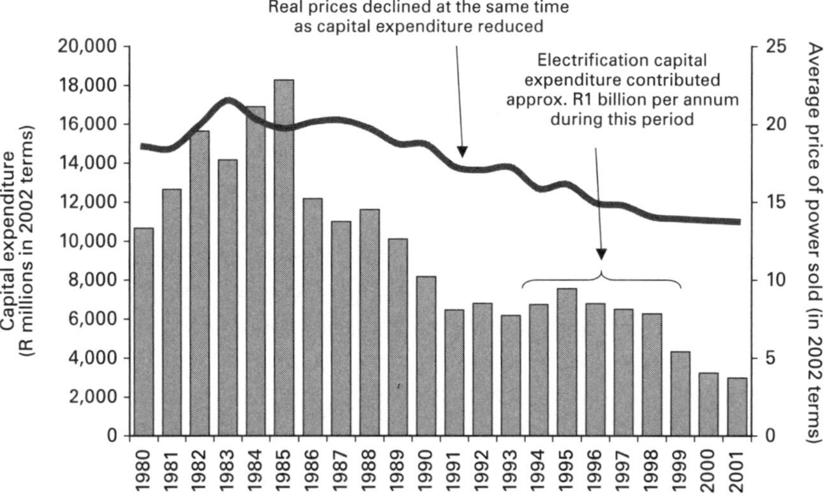

Source: Econ, *Electricity Price Scenarios for South Africa,* report to the Department of Minerals and Energy, 2002.

Low Eskom prices in the 1990s (Figure 8.5) stemmed primarily from the fact that consumers had largely amortised the debt which funded the large investment programme of the 1980s that provided the power. Eskom had not had to invest significantly in new generation capacity for many years, with the result that the largest contribution to lower overall costs (and prices) was lower debt and financing costs. Eskom's debt–equity ratio fell from 2.93 in 1986 to 0.63 in 2000.[14]

This analysis of Eskom's investment record was not widely shared in South Africa. Most people equated low prices with efficient performance. Few recalled the debacle of Eskom in the late 1970s and early 1980s, the high price hikes, and the criticisms of Eskom's government and management. Few understood the consequences of the massive over-investment. Tariff reductions in the 1990s erased memories[15] and the

14 *Annual Reports,* Eskom.

15 Through a series of pricing compacts with the government, Eskom committed itself to a price decrease of 20 per cent between 1992 and 1996, and a 15 per cent reduction between 1994 and 2000. Actual price reductions were a little less than this.

overall standing and image of Eskom in the 1990s was much improved. Few stakeholders understood that prices were economically unsustainable and would later lead to under-investment and power outages.[16]

A paradigm shift: towards competition in electricity and energy policy

In the mid and late 1990s, two further developments had an impact on power sector reform. One was the articulation of a new energy policy – including electricity policy – and the other was the 'black economic empowerment' movement (see Chapter 25), which aimed to privatise into the hands of black business leaders a portion of state-owned enterprises, of which Eskom was the crown jewel.

A new energy policy emerged from the process, culminating in a cabinet-approved White Paper on energy policy released in December 1998. This new policy framework was consistent with the government's macro-economic policy in that it emphasised the need to attract private investment into the energy sector and to promote efficiency through competition. It marked a sharp break from the earlier apartheid-era energy policy, which was guided by two main threads: the provision of low-cost energy supplies to mining and primary industry, and energy security for the state. The policy processes during this period were characterised by excessive secrecy, which made rational and public debate on energy policy impossible. The needs of those who most lacked adequate energy supplies were ignored. The shift to a new energy policy was supported by three developments: first, the intellectual development (mainly through an ANC-sympathetic research group) of a new paradigm with emphasis on the 'three Es' (economic efficiency, social equity and environmental sustainability); second, the political process of legitimising the new paradigm (through public consultation and publication of a White Paper); and third, its structural realisation in the economy and society – such as the shift in funding to the national electrification programme.[17]

While not all aspects of the 1998 White Paper were implemented, it became the reference point for policy in the sector. The overall policy

16 Econ, *Electricity Price Scenarios for South Africa*, report to the Department of Minerals and Energy, 2002.

17 A. Marquard and A. Eberhard, 'Towards energy equity, efficiency and environmental sustainability in South Africa: policy challenges', *Energy for Sustainable Development*, 4(4) (2000), 3–7; A. Eberhard and C. van Horen, *Poverty and Power: Energy and the South African State*, Pluto Press, 1995.

objectives were seen to be improvements in social equity, economic competitiveness and environmental sustainability, as well as in energy sector governance and energy security. Remarkably, it emphasised the importance of: giving customers the right to choose their electricity supplier; introducing competition into the industry, especially in the generation sector; permitting open, non-discriminatory access to the transmission system; and encouraging private sector participation in the industry.[18]

These bold statements originated not from any commissioned studies; neither did they emerge from a formal consultative process with industry members. Reform was not driven by the usual concerns of poor technical and financial performance, or the need to attract investment. Rather, it was the result of the convictions of a small group of analysts and government officials who were observing international trends in power sector reform and were beginning to be concerned at the potential problems of monopoly power.

In echoes of the standard international model for power sector reform, the White Paper stated that government believed that Eskom would have to be restructured into separate generation and transmission companies and that the government intended to separate power stations into a number of companies. The White Paper also affirmed the importance of independent regulation.

The main supporters of the White Paper were industrial electricity users, who wished to contain future rises in electricity prices. Initially, Eskom also supported the White Paper process, despite its traditional uneasiness in engaging with policy processes in the public eye. Eskom supported competition in principle, but in practice resisted the proposal that it should divest more than 30 per cent of its generation stations. At times it also suggested the introduction of a private strategic equity partner in the Eskom holding company, which would have had the effect of slowing down, or making more difficult, a subsequent unbundling of Eskom. It also attempted to delay the separation of transmission services from Eskom's other lines of business. At times, it argued that placing transmission into a subsidiary company within the Eskom group would yield sufficient unbundling. It also presented alternative models for distribution that would preserve a more prominent role for the firm as a vertically integrated monopoly.

Major opposition to the proposals in the White Paper were presented to Parliament by Cosatu. In essence, it opposed privatisation and argued that Eskom should remain a vertically integrated, publicly

18 *White Paper on Energy Policy.*

owned utility and should be used as an agent of government to provide low-cost electricity services to all, especially the poor.[19]

The 1998 energy policy White Paper created the foundations for a restructured electricity supply industry in South Africa, though much work was still required to define what a competitive industry would look like and when and how private sector involvement would be introduced. It was followed by one of the rare occasions of World Bank involvement in South Africa, when it sponsored the Ministerial Workshop on Electricity Supply Industry Reform, 3–5 April 2000, in Midrand. At the workshop, the Minister of Minerals and Energy stated that the government's main objectives of reform were, first, to increase economic efficiency in investment decisions and operation so that costs and prices would be as low as possible and, second, to maximise financial and economic returns to government from the ESI. The third and fourth objectives were to increase the opportunity for black economic empowerment and to protect public benefits such as widened access to the poor, energy efficiency, research and development and environmental sustainability.[20] The ministerial workshop brought to South Africa a number of experts with detailed knowledge of reforms in their own countries. There was no single ideologically inspired message or proposed model. Yet all advocated the merits of competition, but warned of the importance of careful design of the electricity market. At the end of the workshop senior government officials, including representatives from Eskom and the NER, agreed to a draft policy paper on restructuring the ESI.[21]

Eskom's top leadership, in the meantime, was alarmed at the extent of the reform proposals, particularly the recommendation to reduce Eskom's market share of generation to 35 per cent. It lobbied at the very highest levels in government, drawing on its reputation for delivering low prices and for supporting the government's *Reconstruction and Development Programme* goals and its growing vision of an African renaissance, embodied in early versions of the New Partnership for African Development (NEPAD). Despite serious consideration being given to separating Eskom generation, transmission and distribution into different companies, to selling off a portion of Eskom's generation

19 E. Tinto, *Restructuring South Africa's Electricity Supply Industry*, MPhil thesis, University of Cape Town, 2002.

20 P. Mlambo-Ncguka, 'Electricity supply industry (ESI): vision and objective', paper presented at the Ministerial Workshop on Electricity Supply Industry Reform, 3–5 April 2000, Midrand.

21 'Draft policy and strategy for electricity supply industry reform for the Republic of South Africa', internal government paper, version 5, Department of Minerals and Energy, April 2000.

assets and to introducing competition, none of these reforms was implemented and Eskom retained a dominant market position and the inefficiency that went with it.

Conclusion

There are elements of power sector reform in South Africa which are peculiar to its recent history, namely its transformation into a democratic state after the long, dark years of apartheid repression. Within this context, it was inevitable that energy policy would be transformed from a defensive obsession with security to a new focus on promoting social equity and improving economic competitiveness as South Africa reintegrated with the global economy. The energy policy White Paper gave expression to this policy shift, but it was already evident in the launch of an impressive electrification programme that sought to tackle the huge backlog of the previously disenfranchised's demand for affordable access to electricity. There was also the intent to consolidate and reform the highly fragmented and inefficient electricity distribution sector that originated in the separate development policies of the previous government. The urgency of promoting social equity and extending improved infrastructural services to the majority forced Eskom and the large municipalities to respond to the challenge of electrification, while the reform of the overall ESI lagged behind. Surplus and cheap electricity was available as a result of over-investment in the previous decades, and a strong, large industrial consumer base enabled the ESI to cross-subsidise the electrification programme without the need to impose unaffordable price hikes.

The process of reform of the distribution sector was slow and was frustrated by the complex web of political interests at local government level and the fear of loss of control of an important infrastructure service and large income streams.

The emphasis on corporatisation reflected a general commitment to reassess government's role in the economy, particularly the state-owned enterprises in the infrastructure sector. Government began to examine the administration and performance of these enterprises. As a consequence, Eskom became a state-owned public corporation subject to the Companies Act. It lost its currency guarantees and other implicit subsidies and its operations were placed on a more commercial footing. Eskom, along with other state-owned enterprises, had to pay taxes and dividends and was subject to a shareholder performance contract. At the same time, the relationship of the state to the sector was clarified through the creation of an independent electricity regulator.

The government continued to have doubts about unbundling, competition and privatisation. Eskom was seen as an important instrument of government policy, an apparently well performing infrastructure industry that supported the government's economic and social programme. However, low prices created a false complacency. Deeper reform measures were not implemented and in the subsequent decade serious problems would emerge within Eskom, with significant costs to the country in terms of power failures and steep increases in costs and prices.

9

The freight transport sector: a stumbling giant

Trevor Jones

Introduction

The transformation of the South African political economy in the 1990s posed many challenges for the transport sector. Domestically, the sector would be required to service the needs of the full population, not merely those of a privileged minority, while internationally the economy was pitchforked from the periphery to the centre of an increasingly globalised and borderless trading community. Many of these challenges should not have been beyond the compass of a transport sector that had undergone substantial positive change in the quarter century prior to 1994. In the 1970s the freight transport sector had moved irreversibly into the era of high-mass transportation, with bulk commodities moving through the newly constructed ports and land-side infrastructure associated with Richards Bay and Saldanha. General cargo handling by rail, road and sea was overtaken by the container revolution and these flows passed, for the most part, through facilities that were up to the task, although the domestic transport market retained significant imperfections that limited the participation of private commercial road hauliers in long-distance intercity freight movements. The decade of the 1980s witnessed a deepening and consolidation of these facilities and activities, together with significant deregulation of domestic land transport, through the final abandonment of the road permit system that had all but eliminated private road transport in the long-haul domestic market.

Consequently, by 1990 the South African transport sector possessed many apparent strengths. World-class bulk ports and rail systems transferred substantial volumes of low-value primary exports to world markets at low cost; fairly static volumes of general cargo flowed through a physically extensive rail infrastructure and increasingly by road between domestic centres and ports that were reasonably adequately equipped;

world-class national roads linked cities, some of whose residents enjoyed high levels of private car ownership; and commercial agriculture was reasonably well integrated into the broader transport infrastructure.

Other segments of the economy were significantly less well served. Many rural communities were excluded from the transport network, large numbers of black commuters were forced to shuttle daily over long distances between dormitory suburbs and urban industries, and other peri-urban residents distant from commuter rail services were left to the mercies of chaotically organised taxi and bus services. This split personality on the part of the transport sector may not have been an intractable problem for a political economy that sought to serve the interests only of a minority of the overall population, but in many respects the sector was poorly prepared for the needs of a more inclusive structure, and a more outward-looking trading economy, to a point where the Department of Transport's influential *Moving South Africa* study identified 'a transport system and infrastructure … in fundamental misalignment to the new national objectives'.[1]

This chapter seeks to explore certain dimensions of that misalignment. Areas of technical and policy interest emerge in the spheres of both freight and passenger transport, but coverage here is limited to the carriage of goods rather than people, and by the three principal surface modes of sea, rail and road transport.

Ports and maritime transport

After substantial capital-widening investment in the 1970s and consolidation in the 1980s, the South African ports sector entered the 1990s with assets that were massive by the standards of the African continent and of economies elsewhere in the southern hemisphere, but also with a configuration that was heavily skewed towards bulk-related sea-borne commerce. Thereafter, port expansion slowed significantly. A growing realisation dawned that world-beating bulk ports and mediocre general cargo facilities were seriously at odds with the development orientation of a 'new' South African economy predicated upon export promotion, based principally not upon primary products exported in bulk, but rather, as acknowledged by the State President, upon 'the expansion and modernisation of the manufacturing sector of the economy and the shifting of our export mix in favour of manufactured goods'.[2] For the

1 *Moving South Africa*, Department of Transport, 1998, p. 5.

2 Keynote address of President Thabo Mbeki to the National General Council of the African National Congress, Port Elizabeth, 12 July 2000.

most part, however, this realisation has largely failed to translate into new marine facilities or cargo-handling systems.[3] The limited investment that took place between 1990 and 2000 served largely to increase the degree of asymmetry in the ports: some extensions to bulk and neo-bulk cargo[4] facilities in Richards Bay were completed, and some downstream steel activities were incorporated into the port infrastructure in Saldanha. By contrast, no significant new marine infrastructure for general cargo activity was created, despite tortuous attempts to identify sites for additional cargo-handling capacity in Durban,[5] while long-term plans for a new industrial bulk port and proposed container 'hub' at the virgin site of Nqura in Algoa Bay were viewed with scepticism by many sections of the commercial fraternity, and would in any event influence port capacity only in the latter part of the first decade of the twenty-first century, as would more ambitious plans to remodel Durban's general cargo infrastructure. Improvements in the general cargo-handling arena were consequently limited to extensions to landside back-of-port facilities, principally associated with the Durban container terminal, and more substantial capital deepening of existing facilities, via investment in further cargo-handling superstructure.

This evolution from expansion through consolidation to slow-down is mirrored by the traffic performance of the South African ports. After doubling from 40 million tons in 1969/70 to 80 million tons by 1977/78, total cargo handled by the six major ports in the Saldanha–Richards Bay range increased by a further 70 per cent, to reach 136 million tons by 1989. In the 1990s, as shown by Table 9.1, traffic growth was more muted, with overall volumes rising a little over 40 per cent from their 1989 level, to stand at some 193 million tons by 2000.

The traffic growth that was recorded over the decade can be attributed principally to additional port activity in Richards Bay, through

3 *Moving South Africa*; and Derek Lawrance, 'Ports and transport logistics in Southern Africa: performance and prospects', in *Maritime Africa 2000 Conference Proceedings*, Butterworths, 2000.

4 Sea-borne traffic is most broadly disaggregated into homogeneous bulk cargo, such as coal, grain or sugar, where individual units of cargo cannot be identified on the basis of individual mark or number; and heterogeneous general cargo, with individual marks or numbers. Neo-bulks are cargoes that have some characteristics of bulk cargo but are partially differentiable. Examples would include steel rolls, coils and I-beams, reels of paper or various grades of fruit shipped as refrigerated cargo in 'reefer' vessels.

5 The most protracted of the planning processes was a broad integrated environmental management exercise managed by the municipal authorities in the city of Durban in 1995–96, which weighed up several potential sites for augmented container handling, before the port authorities pre-empted the process by tabling their own plans, which conformed to none of the earlier planning options. In the event, no new marine infrastructure emerged.

Table 9.1 *Cargo handled at South African ports, 1989–2000, selected years (all cargoes, including petroleum products,[a] in millions of metric tons)*

Year	*Richards Bay*	*Durban*	*East London*	*Port Elizabeth*	*Cape Town*	*Saldanha*	*Total traffic*[b]
1989	55.8	43.8	3.8	6.2	6.1	20.4	136.1
1990	52.6	38.4	2.5	5.3	7.1	25.0	130.9
1991	56.7	39.6	1.6	4.7	7.0	19.7	129.3
1993	60.6	46.6	1.6	4.7	7.3	24.4	150.7
1994	69.0	41.4	3.2	4.9	9.8	23.3	151.6
1997	81.4	52.7	1.8	6.7	9.8	24.9	177.3
1998	86.4	52.4	1.6	6.7	8.5	26.6	182.2
1999	86.4	51.8	1.3	6.7	8.3	24.6	179.1
2000	91.8	55.0	1.5	8.1	10.1	26.4	192.9

[a] Estimates of oil and petroleum movements from 1989 to 1994 are based on Charlier's work and may be conservative. 1997–2000 data in respect of these products are more accurate.

[b] Total traffic excludes the activities of Mossel Bay, where volumes were tiny before the Mossgas project came on stream from 1992. By the late 1990s, about 1.7 million tons of traffic, almost all of it petroleum products, were handled annually.

Sources: Jacques Charlier, *Le système portuaire sud-africain á l'aube du 21eme siècle*, Académie Royale de Marine de Belgique, 1996; Port of Durban annual statistical summaries, 1997–2000 (Portnet, Johannesburg); Keren Giladi, *The South African Oil Industry and Its Relationship with the Ports*, MBA dissertation, University of Natal, 2003 (oil and petroleum product volumes 1997–2000).

increased coal exports and further diversification into various mineral products and neo-bulk cargoes such as steel and forest products. These pushed the annual traffic base of the port up from 56 million tons in 1989 to over 90 million by 2000, a level unmatched by any comparable port in the southern hemisphere.[6] The second source of national traffic growth is less easy to pin down, but emanated largely from the port of Durban, where increased containerised sea trade and expanded capacity in the local oil-refining industries raised port activity quite substantially over the full decade, though with considerable year-to-year variability, except over 1997–2000, when annual volumes fluctuated in a relatively narrow band above 50 million tons. In the remaining ports, no monotonic growth trend is discernible in the 1990s.

Despite its slowing growth over the decade, overall South African port activity remained enormous by regional standards. This is revealed by Table 9.2, which sets out the performance of a representative selection of leading African and southern hemisphere ports in terms of

6 Institut für Schiffahrtswirtschaft und Logistik (ISL), *Shipping Statistics Yearbook – 2002*, ISL, 2002.

Table 9.2 *African and southern hemisphere port traffic, selected ports,*[a] *2000*

Port	*Total port traffic*		*Container traffic*	
	Millions of tons	*Rank*	*TEUs (1,000s)*[b]	*Rank*
Richards Bay	91.8	1	5	15
Newcastle	73.9	2	9	14
Durban	55.0	3	1,291	2
Santos	43.1	4	945	4
Sydney	24.6	5	999	3
Melbourne	22.3	6	1,322	1
Casablanca	19.8	7	311	9
Abidjan	14.6	8	434	7
Auckland	13.3	9	561	6
Cape Town	11.8	10	395	8
Lagos	9.1	11	178[c]	11
Mombasa	8.9	12	219	10
Buenos Aires	7.8	13	716	5
Dakar	7.2	14	149	13
Port Louis	4.7	15	161	12

[a] Most prominent multi-purpose ports are included. What are not are one-commodity 'industrial' ports, such as pure oil terminals, and single-commodity bulk export terminals.
[b] TEU = twenty-foot equivalent units (see note 11).
[c] 1997 magnitude.
Source: ISL, Bremen, 2001; this study (South African ports data).

total traffic handled and in terms of container volumes. A consideration of the latter is vital, as different types of traffic have obviously different economic impacts.[7] In terms of economic linkages and value adding, handling a ton of crude oil is not the same as handling a ton of refined sugar, while both of these differ markedly from the handling of a ton of containerised machinery parts. It is the broad category of general cargoes, now almost universally moved in standard freight containers, which confer the richest economic linkages on the local economies of the ports where they are worked, and on the wider national economies where they originate or are absorbed.[8] Of the principal components of global sea trade – wet bulk, dry bulk and heterogeneous general cargo – containerised general cargo exhibited the greatest sustained

7 Jacques Charlier, *Le système portuaire sud-africain á l'aube du 21eme siècle,* Académie Royale de Marine de Belgique, 1996.

8 Containerised import–export traffic per capita is used as one of many indicators of economic development. On this basis, South Africa still lags behind the performance of other comparable middle-level developing economies, suggesting that container traffic growth may well continue to outpace overall GDP growth.

growth throughout the last quarter of the twentieth century, with little indication that this growth would abate in the foreseeable future.[9]

In terms of indicators of both total port traffic and container traffic, the South African ports emerge as colossal by African standards and as dominant within the broad trading community of the southern hemisphere. Richards Bay topped the league table in terms of total port traffic (followed by the rather similar coal-oriented Australian port of Newcastle), while Durban occupied the third spot on the basis of total traffic and was second only to Melbourne in respect of container activity, but well ahead of Sydney and Santos. Durban does, however, command a substantially more diverse traffic base than of either of the major Australian general cargo ports. South Africa (and indeed the province of KwaZulu-Natal) thus possesses both the leading multi-purpose general cargo port and the most active diversified bulk port on the continent of Africa and in the southern hemisphere.

The heavyweight relative status of the country's ports should come as no surprise, since South Africa had become a major sea-trading nation in the late twentieth century. The 193 million tons of traffic handled in 2000 represented approximately 3.6 per cent of world sea trade in tonnage terms. In terms of 'real' sea transport activity, traffic passing through local ports generated some 12,300 million ton-miles of maritime freight activity, or over 6 per cent of global activity – a performance that placed South Africa within the top 12 nations on the international maritime trading league table.[10] The country's share of global maritime activity consequently exceeded its share of global GDP by more than 20 to 1.

All of this appears to signify a vibrant, growing and sophisticated ports sector, appropriate for the needs of a middle-income developing economy. Appearance and reality may well not coincide in this regard, however: in the 1990s a growing realisation dawned that the facilities and services provided by the ports were seriously out of line with the development needs of the economy. For the 'old' South Africa, growth through penetration of relatively anonymous bulk markets made considerable sense, as did the creation of world-class bulk transport facilities. The growth of manufacturing output and expansion of

9 ISL, *Shipping Statistics Yearbook – 2002*, tables 2.1.1.1 and 2.1.1.2.

10 These estimates are the author's own, and are based upon South African port data, disaggregated across broad geographical regions, and then associated with the steaming distance to a median major port in each region. It is the combination of relatively high traffic volumes and the substantial lengths of haul that separate South Africa from its major international markets and suppliers that drives up 'real' sea-borne activity in ton-miles. Similar estimates, also based on this author's work, can be found in the 2005 *Maritime Yearbook* of the national Department of Transport and in the September 2006 White Paper *National Maritime Transport Policy*.

manufactured exports required general cargo-handling facilities of the requisite quantity and the highest quality in the nation's ports, at the lowest price. Sadly, in terms of all three of these desiderata, the performance record of the South African ports was well below the world-class benchmarks achieved in the bulk arena.

Because the transport and handling of general cargoes is now dominated to an overwhelming degree by containerisation and unitisation, the efficiency of general cargo-handling facilities is essentially determined by the existence and maintenance of suitable container terminals and distribution systems. When South African maritime transport joined the 'container revolution' in 1977, port capacity well beyond the traffic parameters of the time was provided for. This installed capacity (in terms both of the basic marine infrastructure of the various port terminals and of the equipment and logistical networks required to move boxes between the terminals and their hinterlands) remained reasonably adequate until the early 1990s, when national traffic levels were approaching the 1 million TEU level;[11] thereafter the container-handling problems of the South African ports escalated.

This problem had several dimensions, affecting both the demand and the supply sides of the transport market mechanism. On the demand side, the re-entry of the economy into the mainstream of the international trading community from the early 1990s precipitated a surge in sea-borne container volumes as the leading liner carriers returned to (or joined) the South African trades, and as container penetration rates rose from levels that had been low by international standards. Container sea-trade growth traditionally outruns GDP growth in all significant trading economies, with trade elasticity coefficients of some 1.8 reported from middle-level economies.[12] That would suggest that a rate of growth in GDP of, say, 5 per cent per annum would be associated with growth of 8 per cent in containerised sea-trade volumes. In South Africa's case, however, a protracted period of 'catch up' resulted in coefficients of more than 2, indicating that container traffic growth from the early 1990s outpaced GDP growth by more than 100 per cent, catching port planners, terminal operators and the carrying lines alike by surprise.

In Durban, the leading container port, container traffic rose by 23 per cent in 1993–94, by 14 per cent in 1994–95 and by a further 10 per cent

11 Container traffic levels are conventionally measured in terms of twenty-foot equivalent units, or TEUs. One TEU represents a standard 20-foot (6-metre) freight container. Since 40-foot boxes are increasingly supplanting 20-foot containers, the number of physical box moves through a port is lower than the number of TEUs.

12 Bureau for Transport and Regional Economics, *Australia's Seaborne Containerised Freight – Forecasts to 2010–11*, Working Paper No. 50, Commonwealth of Australia, 2002.

in 1995–96. These booming volumes threatened to overwhelm terminal capacity, with the inevitable concomitants of berth delays, cargo distribution hold-ups and vessel queues outside the port. Though the pace of demand growth slowed somewhat in the late 1990s, by 2000 the South African ports handled a total of 1.8 million TEUs (Durban alone 1.3 million), with the same basic container quays that had been constructed in 1977, albeit supported by an enhanced cargo-handling superstructure. These enhancements, however, had not raised cargo-handling productivity to acceptable international levels, nor had they alleviated the congestion, which remained a semi-permanent feature of the general cargo-handling scene to the end of the decade.

At the same time as these demand-supply pressures were emerging, a series of exogenous supply-side changes were unfolding in the international liner shipping industry. When container operations first superseded conventional break-bulk shipping services, the routes over which vessels operated changed relatively little; many liner vessels continued to ply north–south, region-to-region routes. After 1990 this pattern changed significantly, with most high-density liner companies organising their operations around skeins of round-the-world or long-swing pendulum services. In this way, container vessels moved from the east coast of the USA, across the Atlantic to a single port of call in north-west Europe, through the Mediterranean and the Suez Canal to a single port such as Singapore in South East Asia and thence to a single Japanese port, before finally reaching a single port on the west coast of North America. These long-distance routes were serviced by collaborative consortia of shipping lines, connecting at a limited number of 'hub' ports, from which 'spoke' services radiated to feed cargoes to secondary ports. Two powerful concomitants of these arrangements were the deployment of larger, deeper-drafted container vessels and a reduction in the number of port calls in a particular geographical region. These arrangements first took root on the highest-density northern hemisphere trade routes, but many southern hemisphere services followed suit, albeit with smaller vessels more suited to lower levels of demand. The consequences for ports were substantial, as the container 'majors' attempted to concentrate their activities at a single regional 'hub' that acted as both a sink for national cargoes and as a distribution centre for trans-shipment traffic. Because successful 'hub' ports needed to provide capacity in excess of national demand, attainment of 'hub' port status was inordinately difficult in a capacity-constrained situation. That was exactly the situation in which the South African ports in general, and the dominant port of Durban in particular, found themselves after the early 1990s. Durban was the only South African port with any pretensions to 'hub' status, and it became the principal South African port of call on a sustained basis for many liner operators.[13] Preference for Durban was a consequence of its proximity to the economic powerhouse of Gauteng, ample spare capacity on inland rail and road arteries,[14] and an excellent network of port ancillary industries serving the needs of vessels and cargoes.[15]

From the 1990s, these strengths were threatened by capacity constraints, which were exacerbated by a reluctance on the part of shipowners to shift to less-preferred ports, such as Port Elizabeth, despite the blandishments of (uneconomic) rail-rate equalisation to bring rail costs on the longer Cape–Gauteng routes in line with the shorter route from Durban and the virtual absence of competing port facilities within Southern Africa, but outside the range of ports administered by Transnet, the state-owned and economy-wide public sector of transport services and infrastructure. The overall picture to emerge from this account is of container facilities that lurched from capacity crisis to capacity crisis after 1993, with investment spending well below long-term capital requirements.[16] The response of the port authorities, which were still also the terminal operators at that time, was muted to a point of virtual suspended animation. In Durban, a reconfiguration of the port to permit container expansion into a port segment hitherto dedicated to neo-bulk activities was planned to create a capacity growth window of five to seven years. However, if container sea trade were to continue to grow at the annual average 7 per cent rate recorded from 1992 to 2000, major new infrastructure would need to be created, preferably on the eastern seaboard. This had not been done by 2000.

The final dimension of the South African ports sector causing concern was the cost of port functions to users. The *Moving South Africa* study demonstrated that waterfront charges in the country's ports were high when measured against those of comparable ports in both developed and developing countries.[17] Since the most basic economic function of seaports is to lower the generalised cost of through-transport, ports with artificially high costs should be seen as failing to fulfil their essential economic purpose.

High South African port costs arose principally because charges for port infrastructure, rather than terminal-handling or marine

13 *Lloyd's Africa Weekly*, 1999, published liner sailing schedules in various issues.

14 On the Durban–Johannesburg rail line, the highest utilisation rates (of approximately 50 per cent) was experienced on the Durban–Pietermaritzburg segment and in the environs of Johannesburg. Elsewhere, utilisation levels of 28–30 per cent were typical in the mid-1990s.

15 Trevor Jones, *The Port of Durban and the Durban Metropolitan Economy*, Economic Research Unit, University of Natal, 1997.

16 *Moving South Africa*, p. 50.

17 *Ibid.*, p. 46.

charges, were high, especially the unduly high costs incurred by cargo owners for the use of the ports' cargo-working infrastructure. These charges, which historically were raised on an *ad valorem* basis, and which consequently lacked any association with pricing efficiency, were levied differentially on imports and exports, and most notably affected high-value cargoes – the very cargoes that headed the state's manufacturing-led development strategy. To its credit, the port management within Transnet did attempt to mitigate the price–cost distortions associated with various port functions during the 1990s and signalled its intention to phase out the *ad valorem* basis of wharfage charges, as part of a planned and very welcome move to separate the landlord functions of the South African port authorities (as managers of port infrastructure) from the essentially operating functions of port terminals. This reform had, however, not yet been implemented by 2000 and the ports sector ended the decade with a tariff structure that was still seriously at odds with cost-based economic efficiency and that was at times actively injurious to trade promotion.

In overall terms, in 2000 the South African ports sector retained a distinct schizophrenia: a top-quality bulk infrastructure offered first-world services to bulk exporters and importers at competitive prices, while container and general cargo terminals, operating at their elastic limits, supplied poor services at high cost. The relative neglect of general cargo-handling facilities was notably at odds with the development needs of the transport sector and the wider economy.

Rail transport

By 1990, rail transport[18] was in incipient eclipse. An exuberant phase of expansion in the 1970s, driven by burgeoning bulk export traffic, had been followed by something very close to a static state during the 1980s. The 1990s were to witness a decline in the substance, if not necessarily in the full arithmetic, of rail performance. Total route kilometres of track under the control of Spoornet, the rail division of Transnet, fell marginally as certain low-density branch lines were closed. Total freight conveyed fluctuated in a broad band between 168 and 186 million tons (below the peak reached in 1981); but below the surface of this aggregated tonnage, serious inroads into the carriage of higher-rated general cargo were made by privately owned commercial road

18 Coverage of rail transport is limited to the network and activities of Spoornet, the rail division of Transnet Ltd. The few privatised lines, as well as rail transport effected 'in house' by various mining and industrial organisations, are ignored.

Table 9.3 *Rail transport size and scale indicators, for selected African and southern hemisphere countries, mid-1990s* [a]

Country	*Total length of network (km)*	*Number of staff*	*Number of locomotives*	*Number of freight wagons*	*Freight (millions of tons)*	*Freight ton-km × 10^6*
Argentina	34,059 [b]	67,000	992	32,823	no data	7,860
Brazil	26,648	61,645	1,805	52,039	105.03	45,664
Chile	2,472	2,237	132	347	4.53	967
South Africa	20,441 [c]	47,140	3,547	133,645	180.13	95,591
Nigeria	3,054	11,346	200	no data	0.16	no data
Egypt	4,810	91,065	835	3,102	52.41	no data
Algeria	4,290	15,847	231	572	1.80	no data
Australia [d]	16,492	28,765	2,007	12,807	76.10	40,000

[a] Years of enumeration vary across countries, but are generally drawn from the 1990–95 period. The South African staff level is based on 1998 data.
[b] Over 10,000 kilometres of Argentina's rail infrastructure comprise narrow-gauge lines.
[c] Excluding private lines operated by various mines and industries; 1998 data.
[d] The Australian information represents an amalgam of the activities of the Australian National Railways (ANR) and state operations in South Australia and New South Wales. Ton-kilometre calculations were furnished only by the ANR, but have been aggregated heroically for the whole country.
Source: Business Rail Report, Railway Gazette International, 1998, international databases; RailRoad Association of South Africa website, www.rra.co.za.

carriers freed from the shackles of the restrictive road permit system. By the end of the decade rail had developed the same chronic bipolar disorder as the ports, with a world-class bulk export infrastructure co-existing with a general cargo-handling network of increasing fragility and a traffic base heavily skewed towards low-value bulk staples. Once again, the overarching development imperatives of the South African economy would have been better served by greater relative strength in general freight networks.

South Africa's public rail network, rolling stock and output levels compared very favourably with those of other major economies in Africa and in the southern hemisphere (Table 9.3). The country's basic rail backbone, measured in route-kilometres, was well below that of Argentina and somewhat below that of Brazil, but exceeded those of other South American, other African and Australasian countries. In terms of locomotives, freight wagons, freight tons carried and freight ton-kilometres of 'real' activity, South Africa eclipsed all other countries enumerated, in most cases by a wide margin. By contrast, staff numbers employed by the national rail carrier, Spoornet, were well below railway employee levels in Argentina, Brazil and Egypt, despite the generally lower levels of output generated in all three of these countries. This broadly favourable comparative international performance of South African rail largely mirrored the dominance of the ports sector, and suggests that the country was generally well equipped, if measured alongside other middle-income developing economies, in terms of hard-core transport infrastructure.

The data in Table 9.3 can also be used to generate various measures of rail productivity. In terms of freight ton-kilometres per employee, South African rail outperformed Australia by 70 per cent, Brazil by a factor of three and the others by larger margins. In terms of freight ton-kilometres per wagon, the country's rail productivity was 54 per cent of the level produced by Australian National Railways (an Australia-wide calculation cannot be made) and a little over 80 per cent of the Brazilian level.

Other useful performance indicators may be constructed, for example measures of the cost of rail services to users. On the basis of 1998 traffic levels, price per ton-kilometre weighted across the aggregate South African rail traffic base was R0.22. This compared unfavourably with the USA (R0.11 per ton-kilometre) and Sweden (R0.13), but favourably with developed economies such as France (R0.37), the UK (R0.48) and New Zealand (R0.51).[19] Comparative data for other middle-level developing economies are not available. In user cost terms, South African rail services were moderately priced by international norms across the full gamut of traffic, while the specialist Coallink 'produce[d] the lowest-cost inland coal transport in the world at a high level of efficiency'.[20]

The above account generates a picture of South African rail that is substantially positive: the country possessed a larger and more productive rail network and offered its services to users at costs in line with, or below, those of many other comparable nations. These broad indicators may, however, convey a distorted image of a mode of transport that was far from healthy, and far from fulfilling the role it should have played in the South African economy.

The overall fortunes of rail may perhaps more accurately be represented by the changing composition of its traffic base, rather than by the performance of nominal or real output. Figure 9.1 depicts the evolving size and shape of total rail freight traffic from 1976, the year when high-mass bulk cargo begun to flow to Richards Bay and later to Saldanha, to 1999. In terms of crude tonnages of freight conveyed, freight activity increased from 141 million tons in 1976 to a peak of 188 million tons in 1981, as coal and then iron ore exports made their presence felt, but by 1990 this had fallen back to 176 million tons. During the 1990s, no simple growth trend emerged, with volumes fluctuating between a low

19 *Business Rail Report*, Railway Gazette International, 1998; and Spoornet data.
20 *Moving South Africa*, p. 36.

Figure 9.1 *Evolution of rail freight traffic, 1976–1999 (metric tons per annum)*

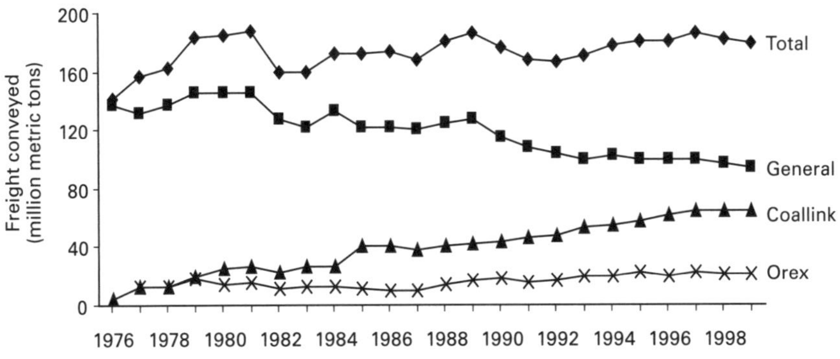

of 167 million tons in 1992 and a high of 186 million tons in 1998. In real terms, this latter represents approximately 99,000 million ton-kilometres of transport activity.

Traffic growth was driven by two dominant and relatively limited activities – the transport of iron ore from the Sishen area in the Northern Province to Saldanha on the Orex line and the carriage of coal from mines in Mpumulanga to Richards Bay. These two niche activities were of world class, both technically and in user-cost terms. What was less than world class was virtually everything else in the rail arena. The category of general freight (a congealed aggregate of activities on routes other than the Coallink and Orex operations) fell from over 130 million tons in 1976 to some 120 million tons in 1990, and then more steadily to 95 million tons in 1999. This represents a 21 per cent decline over the 1990s. Although the broad category of general freight includes a number of low-value primary products, its secular decline was part of a longer-term phenomenon whereby rail lost command over higher-valued, and consequently higher-rated, goods.[21] This had some serious implications for pricing and sustainability.

In terms of legislation,[22] public rail has historically been recognised as the national domestic carrier and, as such, has been required to act as a common carrier and to operate several uneconomic freight (and, in the past, passenger) services. Moreover, the same legislation required the

21 G. D. Van der Veer, 'The role of rail transport in the total transport scene: freight transport', in *Annual Transportation Conference Proceedings*, Council for Scientific and Industrial Research, 1982, p. 6.

22 Republic of South Africa Constitution Act (Act 32 of 1961), section 103(1).

national transport services to operate in terms of business principles and to balance their books. The latter was always interpreted very broadly and was applied to the broad gamut of transport activities falling under the umbrella of Transnet and its predecessors, rather than to individual modes, and certainly not to discrete services within modes. The result was a complex web of cross-subsidisation, with generally profitable ports and pipelines subsidising loss-making rail activities.

Within rail, the tariff philosophy adopted was that followed by most common carriers (in all transport modes) that faced a diverse traffic base covering a broad spectrum of commodity types and values. That standard practice was to raise rates on higher-value cargo, in respect of which demand was relatively price inelastic, in the process charging 'what the market would bear', while low-value cargo, for which demand was conventionally believed to be more price elastic, attracted lower rates.[23] This type of Ramsey pricing had been a permanent feature of South African railway rating, but in the last quarter of the twentieth century, and particularly in the 1990s, it became increasingly difficult to implement, for four principal reasons. The first was the increase in low-rated bulk traffic associated with the new bulk-export ports. The second was the increased dominance of containerised general cargo traffic, for which unitary tariff rates became the only sensible pricing mechanism. The third emanated from the recommendations of a series of public Commissions of Inquiry and multidisciplinary studies that were tasked to investigate domestic transport policy.[24] Common to all of these was the advocacy of a more competitive domestic transport market, characterised by freer competition between road and rail, with both modes charging the 'right' (cost-related) prices for their services, but with rail relieved of the financial burden of providing uneconomic services, most notably the transport of commuters from distant black dormitory suburbs to industrial areas. The fourth and most powerful reason was the emergence of a largely unregulated road freight transport industry based on prices that were emphatically 'wrong', insofar as heavy freight vehicles systematically underpaid for the use of the road infrastructure. The result of these influences was a set of rail prices that more closely approximated underlying cost, albeit based on capital cost levels that were below long-term capital replacement needs, but which

23 In the case of high-value goods, freight charges represented a small fraction of total distribution costs, hence cargo owners were relatively unresponsive to tariff changes and were consequently vulnerable to price mark-ups. For low-value staples, the opposite argument applied.

24 The most influential included the Schumann (1964), Marais (1969) and Van Breda (1973) Commissions, and the broadly directed National Transport Policy Study (NTPS) group, orchestrated by the Department of Transport in the mid-1980s.

nonetheless failed to undercut road rates,[25] and which therefore also failed to stem the migration of general cargoes from rail to road.

These institutional factors were aided and abetted by rank bad service to general users and, towards the end of the 1990s, also to some bulk-cargo clients. The *Moving South Africa* study reported widespread dissatisfaction with general freight services and unreliability in the case of break-bulk freight.[26] These views were also strongly reinforced by a study of the perceptions of cargo owners and port ancillary operators in the port of Durban, who indicated substantial unhappiness with operating performance measured by such indicators as rail wagon availability and the supply of locomotives at the times when they were required. These trenchant criticisms were not limited to the general cargo arena but extended across a broad gamut of neo-bulk and low-value bulk commodities, to a point where the viability of some export shipments was jeopardised.[27]

The combination of indifferent service quality and the inability to set prices at levels that were both competitive and sufficient to cover long-term capital replacement needs boded ill for the sustainability of general freight services by rail in South Africa. Public utterances by senior officials and the recommendations of transport economists argued that rail should have been fulfilling a larger role in the long-distance carriage of commodities other than bulk mineral exports. Without a fundamental revision of modal costs and the general quality of service delivery, these fine sentiments could not be transformed into changed behaviour on the part of transport users and rail transport providers.

Road transport and intermodal competition

The dominant symbol of change in South African transport markets during the decade of the 1990s was the absolute and relative growth of road transport, to a point where it became the largest single domestic mode of freight transport. This transformation was effected from a narrow base, for prior to the 1980s commercial road haulage operators were regulated virtually out of existence by a permit system that favoured rail on long-haul inter-city routes. In 1980 public carriers

25 *Moving South Africa*, p. 51.
26 *Ibid.*, p. 46.
27 Durban Metropolitan Local Economic Development Study, *Report 5: The Port of Durban – Characteristics, User Perceptions and Growth Constraints*, Ethekwini Municipality, 2003 (unpublished).

were responsible for only a minuscule share of the market.[28] Twenty years later, the road had entrenched itself as the dominant land mode in terms both of nominal tonnage and of 'real' transport activity. The regulatory and policy framework within which road transport functions had lurched from draconian dirigisme to virtually untrammelled laissez faire in the 1990s. There is very little positive that can be said about either arrangement. The history of South African road freight transport is consequently largely a story of regulation, its relaxation and its mismanagement. The road hauliers themselves were almost incidental actors in the drama.

Until well into the 1980s the commercial road freight industry remained a stunted creature, denied natural growth by the legacy of the 1929 Road Motor Competition Commission, whose recommendations to control road transport in order to eliminate 'wasteful and destructive competition' were embodied in the 1930 Motor Carrier Transportation Act.[29] This piece of legislation provided the blueprint for the controversial permit system that effectively shut commercial public carriers out of the long-distance land transport market.

Some relaxation of these restrictive practices followed from the provisions of the 1977 Road Transport Act and its subsequent regulations. These extended the gamut of permit-exempt goods, increased the radius of unrestricted carriage and lifted permit restrictions in certain areas. This did not signal the end of the road permit system, and it did not immediately fashion a competitive land transport market in South Africa, but it did usher in a period of somewhat greater competition between road and rail. Formal deregulation of road transport was to come only in 1989 with the abandonment of the permit system, but thereafter liberalisation of the environment in which road freight transport operated proceeded at breakneck pace.

A number of significant changes were introduced between 1987 and 1996. In 1987, a government White Paper stipulated that a comprehensive road transport quality system (RTQS) should be in place before transport deregulation took place. Maximum permissible vehicle lengths were increased to 20 metres, and gross combination mass (GCM) was increased to 47 tons and the maximum payload to 33 tons. Then in 1989 the road permit system was abandoned, signalling de facto deregulation of road transport, but without the RTQS being implemented. One year later, the maximum permissible vehicle length was increased to

28 Van der Veer, 'The role of rail transport'.

29 Peter Freeman, *The Recovery of Cost from Road Users in South Africa – Part 1: Background and Theory*, National Institute for Transport and Road Research, 1982, p. 27.

22 metres and interlink multi-trailer combinations came into regular use for long-haul freight traffic. This was followed in 1991 by GCM being increased to 56 tons, permitting a maximum (legal) payload of 37 tons, and in 1994 an overloading tolerance of 5 per cent was allowed on GCM to increase effective payloads to 39 tons for lightweight trailer combinations. Finally, in 1996, axle load limits of 8.2 tons, for which most South African bridges and roads were designed, were replaced by a limit of 9 tons, with a 5 per cent tolerance. This made it possible for legal payloads of up to 45 tons to be achieved.[30]

From the end of the permit system in 1989, in the space of a single decade, the South African road freight transport industry moved from the periphery of the market to a central position, from which it now operates with some of the largest heavy vehicles in the world that are not restricted to designated routes.[31] Under these circumstances, it is not surprising that road's freight market share rose markedly, largely at the expense of rail, but also to some extent at the expense of coastal sea transport. Precise estimation of modal shares is bedevilled by a paucity of accurate data relating to road freight activity, most notably the activities of private carriers transporting their own products. Unlike the port and rail sectors, no continuous time series of performance exists, so more fragmentary sources must be relied upon. One such source is the work of van der Veer, whose data show private 'in-house' carriers controlling some 35 per cent of total land transport tonnages in 1980/81, while the share of public carriers stood at some 12 per cent in a still heavily regulated environment.[32] This contrasts strongly with 1999 estimates produced by Spoornet and the Railroad Association, which put total land-based transport volumes at some 820 million tons, of which rail controlled 180 million tons (or 22 per cent of the total) and commercial hauliers 140 million tons (17 per cent), leaving 500 million tons (or 61 per cent) in the hands of private carriers of their own products. All of these exercises suffered from the common weakness of a nominal tonnage rather than a real ton-kilometre basis. This has had the effect of overstating road's share in general and the share

30 Willem Kempen, 'The road to ruin', *Financial Mail*, 19 January 2001; Railroad Association of South Africa website, www.rra.co.za.

31 The maximum permissible GCM per vehicle in South Africa of 56 tons (or 58.8 tons with the 5 per cent overload tolerance) exceeds that in all other countries within the Southern African Development Community except Zambia and stands well above levels in developed economies. In the USA, for example, the federal limit is 36.7 tons, although higher loads are permitted in some states; in most European countries it is 40 tons; and in Japan and the UK 38 tons.

32 Van der Veer, 'The role of rail transport'.

of generally short-haul private road in particular.[33] By the late 1990s, rail transport generated some 99,000 million ton-kilometres of 'true' transport activity, while a very rough and ready estimate puts road's output at approximately 113,000 million ton-kilometres.[34] The road had established itself as the senior partner in the South African land transport market by the end of the decade, with a modal share of about 55 per cent of aggregate transport activity, while rail commanded the remaining 45 per cent, albeit with a traffic base heavily skewed towards basic bulk commodities. This represented a startling transformation in the fortunes of road transport, and one that would have been both welcome and unremarkable had it come about as a consequence of freer-working and more efficient transport markets, driven by the right price signals. Sadly, the overwhelming weight of evidence points to a market mechanism so distorted by externalities that the resultant patterns of resource allocation threaten the sustainability of both the road infrastructure and the rail system.

South Africa's road infrastructure is substantial – comprising a little under 60,000 kilometres of paved roads – but by no means all of this is in good condition. The 1998 *Moving South Africa* study reported that only 18 per cent of national roads were in 'very good condition'.[35] Intercity trunk roads were generally in the best condition, and long-distance secondary and rural roads in the worst. The biggest problem was the long-term financial sustainability of the road network, with a backlog of R40–57 billion estimated in *Moving South Africa* 'just to maintain the current-sized network – already deteriorated – in a steady state'.[36] At the heart of this problem was the absence of clear user charges for the country's roads: users pay through the fuel levy, through licence fees and through charges on toll roads, but with the exception of the last there is no direct link to specific road expenditure. In many areas, but particularly in the case of heavy road freight, the wrong prices have been put in place, thereby 'distorting the true economies of road freight with effects on modal choice and the balance of modal competition'.[37] Many studies have explored the extent to which various users pay for the damage they have inflicted on the road infrastructure, and although the precise results generated are open to interpretation, most reveal a strongly positive correlation between vehicle mass and the extent of

33 Average rail haul is approximately 550 kilometres, perhaps comparable to long-haul road. Private road movements are much shorter, generally of the order of 100 kilometres or less.

34 Based on 1999 Spoornet data.

35 *Moving South Africa*, p. 79.

36 *Ibid.*, p. 80.

37 *Ibid.*, p. 49.

underpayment. A study commissioned by the Automobile Association in the mid-1990s indicated that light vehicles overpaid by some 7 cents per vehicle-kilometre, or by R3.02 billion annually (in 1994 prices) in aggregate terms. All categories of heavy vehicles underpaid, with the extent of under-recovery of pavement damage rising from 15 cents per vehicle-kilometre in the case of two-axle heavy vehicles, to R1.49 for six-axle heavies, and to a peak of R2.04 per vehicle-kilometre in respect of the heaviest seven-axle rigs. Total under-recovery from the heavy road freight industry was estimated at R3.87 billion in 1994.[38] These estimates were based on legal maximum payloads and do not take into account overloading. The obvious conclusion to be drawn from these exercises is that the licence fees and road levies faced by light road users were too high and that this overpayment was more than offset by an array of 'prices' for heavy road users that were (and still are) manifestly too low. These wrong prices were passed on to cargo owners in the form of freight rates that did not capture full economic costs and consequently distorted patterns of demand.

Developments that took place principally during the 1990s resulted in a situation in which too much freight transport activity in South Africa was conducted by road, in vehicles that were too heavy and which inflicted significant net damage costs on the roadway. The heavy road hauliers were not villains (other than those that systematically overloaded), but both operators and users alike were confronted with the wrong price signals. The task of road freight policy makers to get prices right had not been achieved by the end of the decade.

Conclusion

The overall picture of the South African freight transport sector in the 1990s is that of a system that was large and sophisticated by regional standards, but one that was coping increasingly poorly with the fundamental requirements of the economy. This applied to all sectors – road, rail and sea transport.

The South African ports were the maritime giants of the southern hemisphere and produced certain products – notably bulk services – to the highest world standards. Bulk-handling strength is an undoubted attribute for a trading economy, but even more important is enhanced capacity and lowered user cost in respect of general cargoes, yet it was precisely these port functions that largely were denied investment in the

38 *Heavy Vehicle Overloading in South Africa*, Automobile Association of South Africa, 1995.

1990s. A realignment of port priorities did not take place. There were, however, some improvements. The separation of landlord and operator functions within port management that was planned by Transnet in the late 1990s and implemented early in the first decade of the new century moved the ports sector closer to international best practice and eliminated some pricing anomalies. Profitable ports are also good candidates for long-term privatisation, but this option had not appeared on transport planning agendas in the 1990s. Nevertheless, South African ports were served by most of the leading global carrying lines in what had become an increasingly competitive sea transport industry, while planned improvements in the marine infrastructure should permit these operators to deploy larger and more efficient general cargo vessels in the South African trades.

By 2000, the outlook for rail and road–rail competition was more complex and less sanguine. To an increasing extent during the 1990s, rail developed the same split personality as the ports, with strength in bulk operations and weakness in general freight. There was spare capacity on arterial routes, often negated by poor operating performance. Rail capillaries serving lower-density areas faced a cloudier future, as these were poor candidates for privatisation, while retaining responsibility for maintaining the rail infrastructure. More ambitious models of infrastructure/operating separation, along the lines already initiated by the ports, had not been considered seriously. A rail renaissance could not realistically be fashioned without a simultaneous reconsideration of the entire regulatory and pricing environment within which land transport functioned. The *Moving South Africa* report called for a 'restoration of value-based competition between rail and road', with a larger stake for rail in the long-haul transport of a wide array of products,[39] but this would have required a firm commitment on the part of policy makers to re-establish the right price signals in these transport markets. This had not happened by 2000. The misalignment between transport performance and national objectives had deepened during the decade of the 1990s.

39 *Moving South Africa*, p. 112.

10

The banking sector

Stuart Jones

Background to the financial sector

In the last decade of the twentieth century the financial sector underwent considerable structural change, affecting banking, insurance and the stock exchange. Market forces were the driving force behind the introduction of the changes, for what was happening in South Africa was already in progress outside the country. The unusual South African condition that influenced these developments was the installation of a communist-dominated government committed to transformation, which, in practice, meant replacing whites with blacks in as many sectors as possible. A new black elite quickly emerged in both the public and the private sectors, including a few black-owned banks and insurance companies. It was also a factor in the rush by the country's largest corporations to transfer their main listing from the Johannesburg Stock Exchange to that of London. If the market had had as much confidence in the South African political dispensation as it had in that of Australia or Canada, it is highly unlikely that Anglo American, Billiton, Old Mutual or South African Breweries would have so hastened to transfer their base of operations out of the country. It was the combination of a left-wing government and the retention of exchange controls that made transfer desirable in the eyes of business. The new political dispensation made it a practical possibility. Confidence in the management of the economy and the currency was weakening, highlighted by the relative failure to attract significant foreign direct investment, the continued flight of professionals out of the country and the acceleration in the decline of the rand. Above all, the continued enforcement of exchange controls was a vote of no confidence in the management of the economy by the government in charge of it.

Outside South Africa, globalisation was the force most affecting the financial sector. With hindsight we can now see that the global economy was reacting to the unparalleled boom in the USA that characterised the decade after the collapse of the Soviet system. The triumph of free market capitalism over Soviet communism gave a tremendous boost to market forces throughout the world. The power of the International Monetary Fund was immeasurably increased. For developing nations there was now no alternative. Globalisation in the 1990s was accompanied not merely by structural adjustment programmes imposed upon failed socialist regimes but also by worldwide privatisation campaigns, most conspicuously in Eastern Europe, although also in Third World countries. South Africa, alas, did not respond with vigour to the new opportunities. Talk of privatisation and a belief in free markets were not accompanied by much positive action. Bureaucratic structures, often filled with apparatchiks, still controlled transport, the postal and terrestrial telephone services and, most disastrously, electricity production.

Patronage frequently determined the handing out of government contracts, while affirmative action policies led to persons being appointed to positions for which they were not qualified. In the financial sector this is widely believed to have contributed to an increase in theft and a decrease in efficiency. The banks do not reveal their losses through internal theft, but the external losses through armed attacks on banks and cash in transit received much publicity. As a result, the full benefits of globalisation were not realised and South Africa became steadily poorer throughout the 1990s. This was very apparent in the financial sector once the stock market boom faltered at the end of August 1998, two years ahead of a second and greater collapse in April 2000.

Financial institutions prospered in the new global conditions. Outside South Africa, bigger banks and insurance companies emerged, led by the free play of market forces in the USA and the repeal of the New Deal legislation that had so restricted the growth of powerful world-class banks across that country. New stock exchanges emerged focusing on 'new economy' companies and there were attempts to amalgamate a number of the European exchanges. The notion of bank assurance gained ground, with some banks proclaiming the virtues of such initiatives and others announcing their intention of staying with the business they knew.

At the beginning of the 1990s Afrikaner interests in Volkskas and Trust Bank were the driving force behind the formation of Amalgamated Banks of South Africa, which eventually embraced Volkskas, Trust Bank, the United Building Society and the Allied Building Society. Both the building societies had become banks and the new mega-bank was able to boast of its leading position as a deposit taker and as a lender. Then, in 1997, the Rand Merchant Bank took the lead by forming First Rand, a company that joined together First National

Bank, the Rand Merchant Bank, Momentum Insurance and Southern Insurance. Finally, at the end of the decade Nedcor attempted to take over the Standard Bank, an initiative that was widely believed to be orchestrated by Old Mutual, anxious to conform to the policies of the London Stock Exchange by reducing its holding in Nedcor. All these initiatives took place in an optimistic global environment, characterised by massive wealth creation, which was very different from the South African situation, in which real per capita GDP was falling.

The success, or failure, of bank assurance is not yet clear. Some of the largest banks in Europe promote it; in the UK, Lloyds Bank bought control of Scottish Widows, but the other three of the UK's 'big four' confined themselves to buying up, or amalgamating with, other banks. In South Africa, Old Mutual did not take the lead in promoting bank assurance, despite its control of Nedcor. Instead, it expanded into asset management, a seemingly rational development at a time of rising stock market prices. Sanlam, by contrast, eschewed bank assurance and placed its emphasis upon its traditional insurance business and at one stage even planned to reabsorb Metropolitan Life, an empowerment company that was formerly part of Sanlam. The top management of Rand Merchant Bank proclaimed their faith in bank assurance, as did three-quarters of South African banks,[1] but the expected increase in earnings proclaimed by the creators of First Rand had not materialised by the end of the year 2000, and it has been suggested that the management of Rand Merchant Bank underestimated the difficulties of integrating the business of the Cape-based Southern Life with the Johannesburg-based Momentum.[2] Nor did Sanlam's control over Absa yield noticeable results in the field of bank assurance. In fact, in the 1980s, the big four banks in South Africa had all been controlled by insurance companies, before the idea of bank assurance became fashionable, not as a result of a deliberate policy of seeking the benefits of tying large insurance companies to large banks, but as a result of peculiar South African conditions that were favourable to life insurance companies. In practice in the 1990s, Liberty Life seems to have put pressure on Standard Bank to allow its sales staff to have access to customers' accounts. The withdrawal of Donald Gordon, the founder and chairman of Liberty Life, from South Africa and from his company led to an end to this practice. The global downturn in the world's stock markets in 2000 weakened life insurance companies and reduced the enthusiasm for bank assurance.

1 *Strategic and Emerging Issues in South African Banking*, PricewaterhouseCoopers, 2000, p. 9.

2 'Top companies 2000', *Financial Mail*, 30 June 2000, p. 316.

Bank assurance was expected to lead to a growth in business, but this did not apply to demutualisation, the other financial trend sweeping the world. Demutualisation was expected to lead to a reduction in costs. South Africa was leading a trend that had begun in 1985 when Southern Life demutualised and converted itself into a public company in the belief that this would stimulate an enterprise culture within the company. It failed and Southern Life was absorbed into First Rand in 1998. To be fair, this may not have been the result of demutualisation, but the result of passing into the control of Anglo American, a corporation whose expertise in mining was unsurpassed but whose influence upon financial institutions (First National Bank and Southern Life) was anything but dynamic.

Demutualisation was not only expected to infuse new energy into sleepy mutual insurance companies and building societies, it was also expected to enable them to raise capital more efficiently. At the same time, though, it made it possible for them to be taken over by larger and hungrier financial institutions. While both policy holders with mutual insurance companies and depositors of building societies gained from allotments of free shares in the new companies, it is arguable that the chief beneficiaries were the top executives, who gained access to stock options. Nevertheless, at the beginning of the 1990s the building societies took the lead in demutualising, led by the United and Allied and then followed towards the end of the decade by the Natal Building Society, the Eastern Province and Saambou. They all converted themselves into banks and were almost immediately taken over by larger banks, with the result that, by the end of the decade, competition for retail deposits had virtually disappeared and bank charges had risen sharply. At the end of the decade, too, the country's largest life insurers decided to demutualise. Sanlam took the lead, closely followed by Old Mutual. The former chose to remain firmly based within South Africa, but Old Mutual was lured by the idea of becoming an exchange-control-free global financial institution based in London. Within a year the remuneration of its top executive had risen to over R100 million.

The second half of the decade saw a worldwide boom in asset management and all the banks hastened to take part in this business by establishing and managing unit trusts. As a result, the 31 unit trusts with assets of R6.6 billion in 1990 had grown to 260 unit trusts with assets of R112 billion in 2000 and pension fund socialism had given way to unit trust capitalism. The brokerage houses that controlled the Johannesburg Stock Exchange and acted as agents for the unit trusts were, like the building societies, also transformed out of existence. They were incorporated and almost immediately taken over by banks or insurance companies. The local banks were joined by overseas banks in acquiring brokerages with seats on the Johannesburg Stock Exchange, as, almost immediately after the 1994 general election, HSBC, Société Genérale, Deutsche Bank and National Westminster led the way in entering the South African market, though the last mentioned stayed only a short time before withdrawing.

Though the increase in the number of financial institutions operating in South Africa seemed to create a climate of dynamism, these developments need to be placed in their international context. The globalisation of banking was accompanied by a decline in the importance of interest earnings and an increase in the importance of fee earnings. At the same time the banks began to trade more and more on their own account. This increased the risks very considerably and draws attention to Walter Wriston's observation of some half a century ago that 'banking is not about money, it is about information'. By the 1990s this information included detailed analyses of risks and the use of the latest mathematical techniques to measure and assess risk. The increasingly technical nature of banking did not automatically lead to a significant reduction in the risks, as the collapse of Barings in London and the Bank of Commerce and Credit International in New York made plain. Nor did the new mathematical techniques provide a solution to the woeful state of banking in Japan, nor prevent the banking collapse in South East Asia.

Peter Drucker warned of these dangers in an article in *The Economist* in 1999. He argued that the financial services industry was in trouble because there had been no major innovation for over 30 years.[3] The Eurobond, the Eurodollar, the first modern pension fund by General Electric in 1950, the first modern institutional investor, Donaldson, Lufkin & Jenrette, the new role for the private investor as initiator of mergers and acquisitions by Felix Rohatyn, and the invention of the credit card, all occurred before 1970.[4] These developments entered South Africa later than Europe or America and were restricted by both exchange controls and sanctions before 1994 and by exchange controls after 1994, thereby insulating the country, to some extent, against the full effects of a major financial crisis. Nevertheless, the commoditisation of financial services was making traditional banking services less profitable at a time of increasing risk, as the downward movement of a Schumterian cycle took hold in the absence of innovation. South Africa could not remain immune to these developments and at the time of economic stagnation in Japan and the collapse of the information

3 Major innovations were being made in the 1990s that were implemented in the following decade with disastrous result for both the financial sector and the global economy.

4 Peter Drucker, *The Economist*, 25 September 1999, p. 31.

technology boom, few foresaw the coming transformation in global banking functions in the next decade.

Despite the growing risks of operating in a global environment, in which universal banks were increasing their influence, and the continued decline in real per capita GDP in South Africa, the financial sector continued to increase its weighting in the economy. From accounting for 14.4 per cent of GDP in 1990 it rose to 20.3 per cent in 2000, an increase of 41 per cent. In current prices the value of the sector rose from R34,192 billion to R160,954 billion, growing at the rate of 16.8 per cent a year, while its weighting in total GDP was growing at the rate of 3.5 per cent a year. This was quite an achievement. It reflected the relaxed approach to credit creation and monetary expansion on the part of the Reserve Bank, which allowed credit to expand at the rate of 13.5 per cent and the monetary supply (M1) by 17.5 per cent a year.

On the one hand, the expansion of the financial sector might have been considered a dynamic force for growth in a sluggish economy; on the other, it could be seen as a response to the liberal monetary and credit policy of the authorities in Pretoria, which was at variance with the needs of a developing economy experiencing a massive relative decline in its secondary sector from 33.3 per cent of GDP in 1990 to 24.4 per cent in 2000.

The currency base of the country experienced both expansion and significant structural changes in the 1990s. The number of cheque transactions fell from 335 million in 1990 to 270 million in 2000 and their value fell correspondingly from R797 million to R562 million. To an extent, the decline in cheque usage was made up for by an increase in credit card transactions (Table 10.1). The value of these quintupled, from R9,259 million to R46,944 million. Political pressure to grant credit to lower-income groups may have contributed to the growth in the credit card business. However, the major change in the 1990s was the explosive growth of electronic money transfers. These increased by 2,363 per cent over the period, rising from R119,218 million in 1990 to R2,936,100 million in 2000, or at a compound annual rate of 37.8 per cent. The banks favoured

Table 10.1 Annual compound rate of growth of currency transactions, 1990–2000

Instrument	%
Cheques	2.2
Credit cards	17.6
Electronic transfers	37.8

Source: Quarterly Bulletin, various issues, South African Reserve Bank.

electronic transfer of money, because it helped to reduce their costs, and customers welcomed it because of the increased risk of theft and mistakes in the banks' ordinary operations. By 2000 it was only a matter of time before electronic monetary transfers overtook those by the traditional cheque, which had transformed payments two centuries earlier.

Commercial banks

General

The 1990s saw the continued erosion of the dominant position once occupied by Standard and First National, the two former imperial banks. At the same time the threat of passing into the control of life insurance companies diminished. More importantly, the notion of what were the proper functions of banks was changing. While this was part of a worldwide trend, in South Africa it was reinforced by political pressure to provide banking services to the previously disadvantaged section of the community. The question of whether it was the function of the commercial banks to act as money lenders of last resort, as was common in India, was ignored in statements emanating from bank executives, the media and politicians. Only when micro-lending had brought losses to all the major banks, brought down Saambou and helped to bring down BOE did the issue of micro-lending receive the critical attention it merited, but by then the 1990s had given way to the new millennium.

Easy credit in the 1990s also led to the failure of a number of retail firms, the most notorious of which, the collapse of the McCarthy Group in 1998, was triggered by losses in its vehicle financing division and then by further losses in its furniture division. In 2002 this led to First National Bank owning 79 per cent of the equity in exchange for loans that could not be repaid.[5] The political transition, therefore, was accompanied by a relaxation in the strict credit controls of the commercial banks and a sense of a lack of direction in the country's leading financial institutions.

The Standard Bank also incurred large losses in the late 1990s, in connection with Soda Ash and New Age Beverages, which provoked a research report by HSBC Simpson McKie entitled *Stanbic: A Bridge Too Far*, which stated: 'The track record of Stanbic's management has been tarnished in recent years by large individual debt write offs'.[6] Somewhat illogically, the report then went on to argue that the Standard Bank should change its management culture from risk averse to calculated

5 *Financial Mail*, 28 June 2002.

6 'Top companies', *Financial Mail*, 25 June 1999, p. 378.

risk taking and from status-conscious managers to performance-conscious managers. It was this change in management thinking that led to the losses incurred by the commercial banks in the 1990s.

In the 1990s Nedbank, which had almost gone under in the 1980s, experienced a renaissance and established itself as the most efficient bank in South Africa. With its absorption of the former Permanent Building Society in 1989 its name was changed to Nedcor and it was positioned to challenge the dominant business-oriented banks, Standard and First National. This renaissance of Nedcor led to an attempted takeover of the Standard Bank in 2000/01, which was blocked, not by the market, but by political intervention. The Standard Bank, with its government accounts, had better lines of communication to the authorities in Pretoria than did Nedcor, but whether this was in the long-term interests of South Africa is not clear, as the media campaign by the two banks provided no overwhelming arguments for or against the takeover.

What did become clear, though, was the greater efficiency of Nedcor when measured by its cost–income ratio. The figures are available for the second half of the decade and show how Nedcor maintained its lead over the other banks, despite a slippage in 1997 and 1998. Its chief executive was credited with running a tight ship, though its bank charges for ordinary customers were widely considered to be higher than those of the Standard and First National. Without significant government business, it is possible that Nedcor had been more entrepreneurial than its competitors. The figures for First National are not available for the middle years of the decade, when Rand Merchant Bank was forming First Rand by tying together First National Bank, Rand Merchant Bank, Southern Life and Momentum. Absa was the least efficient of the big four banks, a reputation it had long held, partly as a result of its former cosy political relationship with the ruling party and partly as a consequence of the long stream of bad debts emanating from the Trust Bank. Possibly, because the bad debts were working their way through the system and because of efficiencies resulting from the amalgamation of the two former building societies, the United and Allied, Absa was reducing its cost–income ratio faster than its competitors in the last four years of the century. In the last two years, 1998–2000, when comparisons can be made with First Rand, Nedcor reasserted its lead and ended the century with its cost–income ratio very much lower than that of the other banks (Table 10.2). Since all the banks were improving their cost–income ratios in this period, it seems likely that there was a general cause operating that affected all the banks. This general cause was the investment in information technology at the time of the 'reintegration' of South Africa into the world economy and the increased competition that came with it. Both the cosy cartel established in the pre-First World

Table 10.2 *Cost–income ratios of the four leading commercial banks, 1996–2000*

Year	*Absa*	*Standard*	*First Rand*	*Nedcor*
1996	68.4	62.3	–	51.4
1997	67.2	63.4	–	58.4
1998	65.4	62.3	62.4	56.8
1990	63.3	61.9	61.1	51.7
2000	63.6	58.9	60.2	50.0

Source: 'Top companies', *Financial Mail*, 2001.

War era and the protection afforded by semi-isolation in the sanctions era were now things of the past and the invigorating winds of competition were sweeping through the financial sector.

Assets of commercial banks

The current value of the assets of the leading banks grew rapidly over the decade as a whole. The Standard Bank maintained its leading position, but Nedcor, which was second in 1990, had fallen to fourth by 2000, and Absa had moved up to second position as a result of its amalgamation. Only the results of the Standard Bank and Nedbank are comparable, because their growth in this decade was internal.

Table 10.3 *Assets of the four leading commercial banks, 1990–2000*[a]

Year	*Absa*	*Standard*	*First National/ First Rand*	*Nedcor*
1990	15,844	45,511	30,278	35,080
1991	82,512	50,397	36,597	41,605
1992	80,305	52,647	42,693	34,972
1993	81,745	56,800	51,830	39,821
1994	89,612	86,855	61,809	53,577
1995	105,326	100,441	77,270	67,997
1996	124,044	127,063	89,715	79,680
1997	134,470	139,859	103,233	95,644
1998	152,821	160,384	138,573	117,527
1999	168,737	184,308	149,129	129,844
2000	177,461	208,277	159,205	158,259
Growth rate 1990–2000 (%)				
Current prices	10.4	16.4	18.1	16.3
Constant prices	1.4	6.1	7.6	6.0

[a] Figures for the end of bank's financial year: Absa 30 June; Standard 31 December, First National/First Rand 30 September; Nedcor 31 December.
Source: 'Top companies', *Financial Mail*, 1991–2000.

Table 10.3 provides the details of the annual growth of their deposits, together with their growth rate over the decade in both current and constant prices. Both the Standard Bank and Nedcor managed to achieve real growth rates of 6.0 per cent in their total assets, without major acquisitions. In real terms the value of Absa's assets increased by 1.4 per cent a year, while the figure for First Rand is inflated by the amalgamation of 1998. Given the economy's failure to achieve real per capital growth in this period, the banks' performance may be seen as creditable. Most of the growth occurred after the 1994 election, for, in real terms, the assets of all the banks, except First National, declined in the first three years of the decade.

A breakdown of the assets of all the banks in December 2000 provides us with a picture of what they were doing. Private sector overdrafts formed the principal portion of bank assets, as they always had done. These still outweighed the credit extended on instalment sales, leases and credit cards. The big four dominated the picture, but in 2000 two of the 10 largest banks were overseas banks that had re-entered the country, namely Citibank and Credit Agricole. Public sector overdrafts remained the domain of the big four, with Absa and First Rand the banks with the closest relationships with government bodies.

Table 10.4 *Distribution of bank assets in 2000*

Bank	*Instalment sales*	*Leases*	*Credit cards*	*Private sector overdrafts*	*Public sector overdrafts*	*Investments*
Standard	11,679.9	5,819.4	2,687.3	41,175.9	1,458.3	12,949.9
Absa	14,634.9	4,891.8	2,493.7	38,673.5	4,086.9	11,855.2
Nedcor	6,533.1	2,153.0	3,868.1	35,705.0	447.0	16,821.1
First Rand	16,099.3	7,333.3	2,558.6	37,907.6	3,462.5	25,589.0
BOE	2,354.7	204.7	199.5	9,391.5	8.3	5,234.6
Investec	963.7	413.5	113.4	10,631.3	–	13,370.5
Saambou	555.1	611.3	–	4,110.1	0.5	15.1
Citibank	–	1,146.2	–	2,199.5	–	90.3
Credit Agricole	–	–	–	145.4	–	907.0
Gensec	–	–	–	1,963.6	–	3,251.5
Total of all 57 banks	57,094.0	24,185.9	12,163.7	208,999.0	9,785.7	98,318.7
Proportion of top 4 (%)	85.7	83.5	95.4	73.4	96.6	68.4
Proportion of top 10 (%)	91.0	93.3	98.0	87.0	96.7	91.6

Source: 'Top companies', *Financial Mail*, 2001.

Absa through its Volkskas component had been closely involved with government bodies in the apartheid era and First Rand had obtained the accounts of most of the new provincial governments. Table 10.4 provides the details.

Despite the poor economic performance of the economy as a whole in the 1990s, the big four banks were very profitable. In fact they increased their profitability over the decade, with the exception of Absa, which experienced both a decline in its return on assets from 1998 and a decline in its return on equity, at a time when the other three were increasing their return on equity. Clearly, Absa was experiencing difficulty in operating the four banks/building societies that it comprised.

A strict comparison of the four large groups is not very meaningful, given the amalgamations that occurred. Also, after the 1994 election, the South African banks were able to expand northwards into Africa as well as in London. By 2000, for example, the Standard Bank was claiming that 25 per cent of its revenue was coming from outside South Africa. Bank profitability consequently reflected the size of the groups and not just their economic well-being within South Africa. The latter is reflected in their return on equity and their return on assets, though according to PricewaterhouseCoopers' 2001 study of banking in South Africa, the banks rated their return on capital as most important and placed return on equity as tenth out of 15 criteria; earnings per share came eleventh and share price thirteenth.[7] The interests of shareholders and pension funds do not appear to have greatly troubled the professional managers of South Africa's banks, in marked contrast to their growing appetite for stock options in the 1990s.

An indication of the dynamism in the growth of profitability in the leading banks may be seen in the profits of the Standard Bank and Nedcor. Despite its close relations with the new government, the Standard Bank's profitability declined after the 1994 election, from 25.6 per cent annually in the first four years of the decade to 20.8 per cent in the next six years. Nedcor, by contrast, without significant government accounts, increased the growth of its profits from 20.4 per cent to 30.9 per cent in the same period. It was this reversal of the historic situation that enabled Nedcor to make its bid for the Standard Bank in the following year. It suggests, too, that the existing corporate structure of the Standard Bank, which had merged its large retail bank with its merchant bank, may have been an impediment to the growth of profits, despite the fact that the bank executives identified investment and merchant banking as one of the two most profitable segments in

7 *Strategic and Emerging Issues in South African Banking*, PricewaterhouseCoopers, 2001, p. 25.

Table 10.5 *Profitability of the four leading banking groups: return on profits, assets and equity, 1990–2000*

Year	*Absa*			*Standard*			*First National/First Rand*			*Nedcor*		
	Profits (R millions)	*Assets (%)*	*Equity (%)*	*Profits (R millions)*	*Assets (%)*	*Equity (%)*	*Profits (R millions)*	*Assets (%)*	*Equity (%)*	*Profits (R millions)*	*Assets (%)*	*Equity (%)*
1990	197	1.4	14.3	413	0.9	19.0	330	1.1	23.1	287	0.9	20.0
1991	321	1.0	15.4	511	1.0	19.4	385	1.1	22.8	344	0.9	20.0
1992	–	–	–	623	1.0	12.9	479	1.2	19.1	408	0.9	12.1
1993	695	–	–	822	1.2	14.2	691	1.3	22.0	486	1.0	12.4
1994	699	0.9	12.3	1,027	1.3	21.3	751	1.3	21.8	603	1.2	21.8
1995	854	0.8	15.0	1,268	1.4	20.7	874	1.3	21.7	782	1.3	20.8
1996	1,210	0.9	12.3	1,552	1.4	18.9	1,010	1.2	21.3	1,082	1.4	21.9
1997	1,298	1.1	17.7	2,006	1.5	20.7	217	1.1	17.7	1,492	1.6	23.1
1998	1,674	1.2	18.9	2,060	1.7	18.0	688	1.1	18.0	1,900	1.7	23.3
1999	1,968	1.2	18.5	2,420	1.4	20.6	1,898	1.3	22.5	2,406	1.9	25.3
2000	1,988	1.2	17.1	3,197	1.4	21.9	2,190	1.5	24.2	3,027	2.1	24.0

Source: 'Top companies', *Financial Mail*, 1991–2000.

Table 10.6 *Analysis of the profitability of the different segments of banking in South Africa in 2000*

Segment	*Proportion of capital employed in segment*				
	Loss–0%	*0–10%*	*10–20%*	*20–30%*	*30%+*
Retail banking	*	**	*	**	*
Corporate banking	*	******	********	*****	**
Investment and merchant banking		***	*****	********	****
Private banking	*	***	***	***	*
Treasury	*	***	****	***	********
Internet banking	*****	***	*		
Credit cards	**	**	**		
Asset management and unit trusts	**	******	**	*	*
Life insurance		**	***	**	
Brokerage	**	***	********	*	**

* represents an individual bank, from a total of 27.
Source: Strategic and Emerging Issues in South African Banking, PricewaterhouseCoopers, 2001, p. 26.

banking.[8] It suggests, too, that the election of 1994 was not the main determinant of the growth in profits. This, rather, was the effectiveness of management in controlling costs and raising income.

The return on equity was impressive. By the end of the decade both First Rand and Nedcor were earning almost 25 per cent on their equity (Table 10.5). The former had been the most profitable bank in 1990 and it regained this position in 2000. Its earnings, too, were more stable than those of the other banks, dipping significantly only at the time of the great amalgamation. Nedcor, by contrast, experienced sharp declines in its return on equity in 1992 and 1993, as did the Standard Bank. Only in 1997 did the return on assets begun to move significantly upwards, pushing Nedcor into first place by the end of our period. Traditionally Nedcor had relied on wholesale deposits more than the Standard and First Rand and this had encouraged the bank's managers to push for a greater return on investments and to accept greater risks.

The PricewaterhouseCoopers 2001 survey of banking in South Africa provides us with an analysis of the profitability of the different banking segments in the last year of the century.[9] The two most profitable sectors were 'treasury' and 'investment and merchant banking' (Table 10.6).

8 *Ibid.*, p. 27.
9 *Ibid.*, p. 26.

In treasury eight banks reported earning more than 30 per cent (after deducting costs on capital employed in the various segments) and in investment and merchant banking four banks earned more than 30 per cent and another eight between 20 and 30 per cent. Only one bank found retail banking very profitable, while one made a loss in this sector of the business. Five of the reporting banks made losses on internet banking. None made large profits in this sector. In seven of the 10 sectors analysed very large profits, profits of more than 30 per cent, were made by at least one bank. Life insurance, credit cards and internet banking were the exceptions. This suggests once again that it was management and not the type of activity that made the difference. Indirect evidence in support of this comes from the survey's findings that the major issue confronting the banks in 2001 was the recruitment of good personnel.[10]

The impact of globalisation together with the ending of sanctions led to a host of foreign banks moving into South Africa. By the end of 2000 two of the 10 largest banks (measured by assets) were foreign based, namely Citibank and Credit Agricole–Indo Suez, and of the next 10 largest banks six were from overseas (Table 10.7). The most striking difference between local domestic banks and the foreign-controlled ones was in the size of their capital. The overseas banks were able to draw in local funds with only a fraction of the capital employed by the South African banks. Their international reputations enabled them to attract deposits without worrying about their local capital–asset ratios. This gave them a considerable competitive advantage in the quest for deposits. Genbel Securities, for instance, with a similar asset base to that of Credit Agricole–Indo Suez, had to produce earnings for a capital base more than four times larger than that of the French bank. Similarly, Barclays, with assets of just under one-twelfth those of Investec, was operating on a capital base of one-sixty-fifth of that of the local bank. This success of the stronger foreign banks in attracting local funds into their coffers aroused the ire of Joseph Stiglitz – he considered it unfair, unequal competition[11] – but it is part of the natural working of the market mechanism. The corner grocer is at a disadvantage against the supermarket, but preventing larger institutions from providing effective competition merely keeps prices higher than they would otherwise be. In practice, the arrival of foreign banks in South Africa on a large scale had the effect of stimulating the somewhat sleepy cartel that had dominated the South African banking scene for so long. Their arrival in the 1990s may be compared to that of the imperial banks in the 1860s; and in both cases the country benefited. The main difference was the

10 *Ibid.*, p. 20.

11 Joseph E. Stiglitz, *Globalization and Its Discontents*, Norton, 2002, p. 69.

Table 10.7 *Total assets and capital (R millions) of the 20 leading banks in South Africa on 31 December 2000*

Bank	*Assets*	*Capital and reserve*
Absa	169,960.9	12,321.8
Standard	150,983.7	14,556.5
Nedcor	145,825.1	11,442.7
First National	141,828.1	8,179.2
BOE	54,600.3	5,465.0
Investec	50,627.4	3,817.8
Saambou	15,261.6	1,063.1
Citibank	9,599.0	522.3
Credit Agricole–Indo Suez	6,716.1	186.7
Genbel Securities	6,270.2	816.7
African Bank	5,779.2	792.3
Morgan Guaranty	4,524.4	465.0
Rand Merchant Bank	4,274.4	938.8
Unibank	4,203.6	695.6
Imperial Bank	4,165.7	521.5
Mercantile Lisbon	4,094.0	526.2
Barclays	4,016.0	58.4
ABN Amro	3,851.3	219.6
MLS Bank	3,346.5	277.8
Commerzbank	3,310.5	274.0

Source: 'Top companies', *Financial Mail*, 2001, p. 246.

change in ownership. As recently as the third quarter of the twentieth century British banks had dominated the banking scene. In 2000 they were conspicuous by their absence. Only Barclays had returned to South Africa and its business was confined to trade finance and the requirements of its multinational customers.

Judged by the growth in the assets of the four leading banks, the 1990s were a period of bank expansion. The two former British-owned banks grew internally, having eschewed growth by amalgamation since the second decade of the twentieth century, with the exception of First National's attempt to take over the Allied in 1992. The growth in their assets was therefore more remarkable than that of Absa or Nedcor, for the former had absorbed the first and third largest of the former building societies, and the latter had absorbed the second largest. Two years into the new century Nedcor would absorb BOE and with it the fourth largest of the former building societies. Its assets accordingly contained a large proportion of residential property. The assets of Absa had declined in real terms, but those of the other three had grown at over 6 per cent a year. Only one or two of the foreign banks, starting from small bases, had grown at faster rates. In absolute terms the growth in the resources controlled by the banks was enormous. Between 1990 and 2000 the Standard, First Rand and Nedcor had experienced an increase in their assets of over R400 billion. If Absa is included after 1991 the increase in total assets amounted to over R500 billion.

Despite this apparent success there were grounds for concern. Bad and doubtful debt provision had been increasing at twice the rate of the growth in advances, giving the impression that there had been a long-term erosion in the quality of advances. The ratio of net interest earnings to total assets, which had been rising in the first half of the decade, peaked in 1996 at 4.2 per cent. By 2000 it was down to 3.2 per cent.[12] It was the deteriorating interest margins that were driving down the price–earnings ratios, though, as the *Financial Mail* noted, this was not discussed in the banks' annual reports. It led the banks to place greater importance upon non-interest income, but here too the ratio was declining. The net income to total assets ratio peaked in 1993 at 6.9 per cent, three years before the interest–income ratio peaked. In the 1990s, therefore, there was a weakening both in the banks' intermediary role between lenders and borrowers and in their dominance of fee-based services.

Liabilities of commercial banks

The strength of the four leading commercial banks lay in their large deposit bases and especially in the credit balances of ordinary customers. Increased competition forced the banks to pay interest on these and computerisation made it possible to do this on a daily basis. In current prices the deposits grew substantially and at a slightly faster rate than total assets, emphasising once again the buoyancy of the financial sector in the 1990s. Not surprisingly the market capitalisation of the banks reflected these developments. The Standard Bank maintained its leading position throughout the decade, but the greatest change was the emergence of Absa as the leading deposit taker. Table 10.8 provides the details together with rates of growth over the decade.

The banking sector in the 1990s reflected the prevailing mood of expansion within and without South Africa. The background to growth of bank assets and liabilities was sustained inflation, in which the monetary base of the country (M1) was expanding at an annual rate of 17.5 per cent and credit by 13.5 per cent.[13] The growth of bank capital

12 'Top companies', *Financial Mail*, 2001, p. 250.
13 *Quarterly Bulletin*, South African Reserve Bank, March 2001.

Table 10.8 *Deposits (R millions) of the four leading banks and their rate of growth, 1990–2000*

Year	*Absa*	*Standard*	*First National/ Rand*	*Nedcor*
1990	13,467	38,182	26,599	28,869
1991	45,180	43,509	32,160	35,449
1992	70,795	57,968	35,717	40,622
1993	72,467	62,630	47,350	45,403
1994	79,932	72,607	54,782	48,842
1995	94,738	84,267	68,019	62,920
1996	110,328	102,989	79,787	73,504
1997	124,283	128,476	94,431	87,271
1998	139,989	147,162	126,863	106,900
1999	153,938	172,659	129,190	118,225
2000	161,919	189,598	151,835	140,689
Deposit growth rate (%) 1990–2000	10.9 [a]	17.4	19.0	17.1
Assets growth rate (%) 1990–2000	10.4 [a]	16.4	18.1	16.3

[a] 1992–2000.
Source: 'Top companies', *Financial Mail*, 1991–2001.

Table 10.9 *Market capitalisation (R millions) of the leading South African banks, 1991–2000*

Banks arranged in order of size in 1991	*3 January 1991*	*3 January 1992*	*28 June 1994*	*4 June 1996*	*23 June 1998*	*22 August 2000*
Standard	3,197	5,707	13,496	19,168	33,168	39,884
Nedcor	1,952	3,161	6,417	13,139	29,507	37,103
First National/ Rand	1,747	3,965	9,403	12,755	47,864	41,602
United	1,904	–	–	–	–	–
Volkskas	666	–	–	–	–	–
Allied	562	–	–	–	–	–
NBS	439	753	2,832	5,520	11,366	
Bankorp	326	1,175	–	–	–	–
Investec	252	420	2,142	5,180	18,640	19,486
BOE	97	166	313	963	7,237	23,743 [a]
Boland	74	147	165	546	–	–
Saambou	–	–	232	644	1,698	1,572
Absa	–	4,953	4,727	13,341	20,143	18,743

[a] includes NBS.
Source: Financial Mail, various issues.

and reserves was also expanding dramatically and this was reflected in the market capitalisation of bank shares.

Table 10.9 shows how the market judged the banking sector. From the beginning of 1991 to August 2000 the market's valuation of the Standard Bank had risen more than 12-fold, without any significant acquisitions within South Africa. Nedcor had increased its market value even more rapidly. Comparison with Absa and First Rand is not appropriate, because they each represent the amalgamation of four separate institutions. Significantly, the value of these two groups fell substantially after the end of the banking boom in 1998, confirming the modern view that shareholders of firms taking over other firms seldom benefit from the process. The banks, along with information technology and media companies, were in the forefront of wealth creation in the 1990s and their market values ran far ahead of the capital employed in them. There were two periods of very rapid growth, the first in 1991 and 1992, and the second in 1997 and the first half of 1998.

The capital employed in the banks kept pace with market capitalisation, evidence of the efficiency of the market in valuing the banks and of the banks in employing their capital efficiently. In both the Standard Bank and First National, capital employed grew faster in the first two years of the decade than over the decade as a whole, which casts some doubt on the efficacy of financial sanctions in affecting economic growth. Nedcor admittedly grew its capital faster after 1992, but this may be

Table 10.10 *Growth of capital (R millions) employed in the leading South African banks, 1990–2000*

Banks arranged in order of size in 1990	*Capital at year end 1990*	*Capital at year end 2000*	*Rate of growth 1990–2000 (%)*
Standard	2,202	14,557	20.8
Nedcor	1,583	8,802	18.7
United	1,454	–	–
First National/Rand	1,430	8,179	19.1
Bankorp	1,260	–	–
Volkskas	888	–	–
NBS	309	–	–
Allied	295	–	–
Saambou	201	1,063	18.1
Investec	83	3,818	46.7
BOE	68	5,465	55.0
Boland	–	–	–
Absa	–	12,322	12.2

Sources: 'Top companies', *Financial Mail*, 1991; *Strategic and Emerging Issues in South African Banking*, Pricewaterhouse Coopers, 2001, p. 72.

attributed to its more aggressive management style than to the ending of sanctions. Bank dividends generally kept pace with the growth of capital employed and hindsight now tells us that the 1990s were years of unparalleled expansion in banking, a boom that lasted until 1998. Table 10.10 provides details of the growth of capital employed.

The unusually high growth rate of both Investec and BOE was the result of a series of amalgamations and acquisitions. Investec's growth was by acquisitions mainly outside South Africa, with the exception of its stake in Fedsure, whose growth in the 1990s was paralleling that of Investec. BOE's was the result of its acquisition of NBS and Boland Bank and the various deals of the controlling consortium with Christo Wiese's Pepcor. Standard, First Rand and Nedcor grew their capital bases at roughly similar rates. Absa lagged behind at 12.2 per cent, because of the continuing difficulties experienced with Trust Bank's losses and its relative weakness in servicing the country's major corporations.

Merchant banks

In 1990 merchant banks still formed a distinctive group in the financial sector. There were eight of them – Finans Bank, First Corporation, Investec, Rand Merchant Bank, Senbank, Standard Merchant Bank, UAL and Volkskas Merchant Bank – but six of them were already part of larger banking groups. Only Investec and Rand Merchant Bank were truly independent. BOE had not yet made its move into merchant banking. In 1990 the most profitable merchant bank was Standard Merchant Bank, with an after-tax income of R30.2 million, though Rand Merchant Bank was more efficient and achieved earnings per employee of R127 as opposed to Standard's R120. First Corporation, the merchant banking arm of First National Bank, led the group with the highest return on equity, of 33.1 per cent. It also achieved the highest return on assets. By the last decade of the twentieth century South Africa was well provided with merchant banks.

Ten years later this situation had changed radically. Of the eight major merchant banks in 1990, only Investec remained as an independent entity. Rand Merchant Bank had been subsumed into the greater First Rand Group. Finans Bank and Senbank were tucked into Absa and Standard Merchant Bank had been merged into the ordinary commercial bank. BOE was the outstanding new entrant into merchant banking, having made its ill-fated decision to compete with the larger banking groups in the middle of the decade, a decision that led to its ill-considered move into money lending in the guise of micro-lending, which led to the end of its independence two years later.

The experience of Investec, the remaining significant independent player, provides us with an example of dynamic growth in the closing years of the century. Its growth was acquisition driven. Founded as a leasing company in 1974, Investec secured a banking licence in 1980 and then merged with the asset management company Metboard in 1986. The Investec Group was listed on the Johannesburg Stock Exchange in 1988.

Digesting the company's new dual structure took over two years. Then, in 1990–91, Investec took over I. Kuper, a property company, Corporate Merchant Bank (formerly Hill Samuel) and Reichmann, a trade finance company, and forged its link with Fedsure by means of an exchange of shares. The stage was now set for international expansion. The decision to expand overseas was taken in 1992, when international hostility towards South Africa was easing but when the domestic situation was still fraught with danger. Beginning in that year, a series of overseas acquisitions propelled Investec into the first rank of South African banks. There were two types of acquisition: mass-enhancing ones to expand existing operations, and platform ones, to facilitate entry into new markets.

Expansion proceeded at a breakneck pace. Between 1992 and 2000, 15 foreign operations were acquired and representative offices were opened in the Channel Isles, Australia, Hong Kong, Botswana and Namibia. Overseas expansion continued at a brisk pace until the global boom came to an abrupt halt in 2000. It was accompanied, too, by brisk expansion at home. Eleven local firms, or portions of firms, were acquired, four in 1995, culminating in the takeover of the venerable broking house of Fergusson Brothers in 1996 and the private client business of HSBC Simpson McKie in 1999. By the end of the century Investec had established itself in the UK, Israel, the USA and Australia and over half its income was derived offshore. It was strongest in the UK, where the business of the Allied Trust Bank, the first overseas acquisition, had been bolstered by: the business of the Clive Discount House, the money broking business of Cazenove; the private portfolio business of Carr Shepherd and Guinness Macon; the asset management business of Guiness Flight, Hambros and Henderson Crosthwaite; and the private banking business of Kleinwort Benson, one of the most distinguished names in the City of London. In the course of this expansion Investec's strategy became clear. It was a niche bank, specialising in asset management, private client activities, investment banking and treasury activities.[14] The impact of this growth upon the accounts was

14 *Strategic and Emerging Issues*, PricewaterhouseCoopers, p. 68.

Table 10.11 *Growth of Investec, 1990–2001*

Year end (31 March)	*Total assets*	*Total capital employed (R millions)*	*Headline earnings*	*Headline earnings per share (R)*	*Return on equity (%)*	*Return on assets (%)*	*Net tangible asset value per share (R)*
1990	1,263	83	17.5	0.9	23.5	1.6	4.1
1991	2,882	131	24.0	1.2	22.4	1.5	6.8
1992	3,867	378	52.0	1.5	17.8	1.4	11.5
1993	5,619	497	57.0	1.8	17.9	1.8	11.8
1994	10,971	909	88.0	2.2	17.2	2.0	15.5
1995	15,265	1,829	181.0	3.1	15.0	2.3	25.1
1996	48,127	2,289	265.0	4.2	15.5	2.5	27.8
1997	63,269	3,500	419.0	5.2	16.0	2.5	36.0
1998	86,000	5,919	562.0	6.7	15.2	2.5	51.2
1999	118,000	7,667	1,016.0	9.9	19.0	2.5	53.6
2000	174,000	7,895	1,553.0	13.0	24.3	2.8	55.7
2001	195,000	10,884	1,825.0	16.3	28.6	3.0	60.7

Source: Annual Reports, Investec, 1997, 2001.

dramatic (Table 10.11): over the decade, assets increased by 15,439 per cent, total capital employed by 13,113 per cent, headline earnings by 10,428 per cent, headline earnings per share by 1,811 per cent and net tangible asset value per share by 1,480 per cent. Assets, capital employed and headline earnings continued to growth until March 2001, but the growth in headline earnings per share peaked in 1999.

Investec's dash for growth had occurred at the price of reduced efficiency. The bank had been able to follow this course while the boom lasted. Already in 1995, when the big expansion was just beginning, the *Financial Mail*'s 'top company' writers had noted that Investec came fourth out of the top six in return on assets and fifth in return on equity. Return on equity rose markedly in 1999, 2000 and 2001 and return on assets followed a similar pattern (Table 10.11). They had remained fairly stable from 1995 to 1999, but moved upwards in the financial year ending 31 March 2000 and repeated this improvement in the following year. These figures suggest that the bank had developed a tighter and more focused grip on its business in the new and harsher business climate after August 1998. Headline earnings per share rose from 1998 and by 2001 had almost trebled. Losses, however, continued to be incurred in its US operations. This is perhaps understandable, as Investec had grown up in the less competitive South African market. Adjusting to conditions in the world's most competitive financial market was bound to be difficult.

The success of Investec may be gauged by the bank's standing among its peers. Brian Metcalfe interviewed 27 bankers for his 2001 analysis of the strategic and emerging issues in South African banking.[15] His peer review asked bankers to rank banks by their position in 15 different classes of banking business. These were: corporate banking; listings, mergers and acquisitions; foreign exchange trading; capital markets bonds and derivatives; money markets; structured finance institutional brokerage; retail brokerage; institutional asset management; retail asset management unit trusts; retail lending and deposits; retail mortgages; vehicle financing; internet banking; private banking; and private equity investments. Investec was ranked first in private banking and institutional asset management, second in retail asset management unit trusts, third in structured finance and fourth in institutional brokerage and corporate banking. Investec achieved high ratings in almost half the categories defined by Metcalfe, with its core competence in private banking, brokerage and asset management clearly recognised by its peers. This was a considerable achievement for a company that had acquired its banking licence only in 1980 and moved into portfolio and unit trust management only in 1986.

New institutions

The ending of sanctions, together with the prospect of good profits to be made in the relatively uncompetitive South African market, led to a flurry of new bank formations inside South Africa and the arrival of a host of foreign banks anxious to share in the expected bonanza. Black empowerment pressure from the government contributed further to the formation of new banks. Consequently South Africa in the 1990s experienced the paradox of a banking boom occurring in the midst of a declining economy. The formation of the new banks also occurred at the same time that the big four banks were themselves pushing energetically into merchant banking and industrial banking. Standard Bank, for example, disbanded Standard Merchant Bank and combined its merchant banking business with its traditional retail business. Meanwhile, not only was Investec expanding rapidly, but Rand Merchant Bank was making the dash for growth that eventually led to its takeover of First National Bank, and BOE was making the sustained move into merchant banking that eventually led to its collapse. Until 1998, all three were in the van of wealth creation on an unparalleled scale.

15 *Ibid.*

The new banks included: PSG Investment Bank, Corpcapital Bank, Brait, FBC Bank, Decillion, the Business Bank, Real Africa Durolink, Regal Bank and Peregrine. There was never sufficient business for them all and the real question is why they managed to fool the market for so long. They were fair-weather banks that could keep going only so long as the financial boom continued and with it the illusion of wealth creation. Imaginative accounting also helped a number of them to ride the crest of the wave, until the market crashed at the end of August 1998. When the deals stopped and asset values fell, many of them were exposed for what they were: bubble banks without solid foundations. Many, of course, enabled their founders to make large sums of money. In fact, one suspects that was why some of them were promoted. Leading bankers in Johannesburg jumped onto the bandwagon. A former managing director of Nedbank took the lead in establishing the Business Bank and used his contacts to draw deposits into it. When it failed, it was revealed that over 10 per cent of the bank's assets had been placed in one risky venture. Meanwhile, the failures, beginning in 1998, continued to work their way through the economy and by the beginning of the new millennium it was doubtful whether the rash of new bank formations had added value to the South African economy.

The collapse of so many of the new banks was exacerbated by government pressure on the banks to lend to small businesses and to provide banking services to the disadvantaged. It was the same sort of thinking that forced Telkom to provide telephone services and Eskom to provide electricity to customers in remote rural areas who did not have the means to pay for them. Politicians were demanding the banks provide loans to people who could not afford them. Spin doctors in the banks went along with this while the boom lasted, even though it was in direct conflict with historic bank practice. In effect, the government was pushing the banks to take on the function of the moneylender and to lend money to persons without collateral and without business experience. This works in India, where the moneylender charges interest of 100 per cent or more, but banks cannot do this. Commenting upon the fact that the Standard Bank was adding 2,500 new low-income customers a month to its client base, I forecast in 2000 that such political imperatives might well alter the face of banking in South Africa.[16] My prophecy proved to be correct. Imprudent lending on the part of Saambou brought that bank down in 2002 and the panic it generated then led to a run on BOE, which had also been engaging in non-traditional banking activities, and brought about that bank's collapse.

16 Stuart Jones, 'The financial sector, 1970–2000', in Stuart Jones, ed., *The Decline of the South African Economy*, Edward Elgar, 2002, p. 189.

With the disappearance of the country's sixth and seventh largest banks, the face of banking in South Africa was indeed altered. The meteoric rise and fall of BOE provides us with an excellent illustration of how a long-established traditional trust company and private bank was seduced by the opportunities presented by the ending of South Africa's pariah status. Unfortunately for shareholders, the controlling consortium of BOE, led by its executive chairman Bill McAdam, sought to engage in a dash for growth and wealth without giving up control of the company. Members of the consortium feathered their nests very nicely. In 1994 partners in the controlling consortium paid R36.7 million for their shares, which at the height of the boom in 1998 rose to almost R900 million. Fifteen managers, led by the chairman, paid R23.7 million for shares that rose to almost R600 million. In the process they established a most convoluted system of control by a series of holding companies, namely, Orion Holdings, Orien, BOE Holding and BOE. All these drained wealth from the company, but enabled the consortium to do its deals with the Pepkor chairman, Christo Wiese, and take control of Boland Bank and NBS without weakening their own control of BOE. Pride comes before a fall and BOE, like so many of the new formations, was riding the crest of wave that was driving the expansion the financial sector. This helps to explain why the consortium could get away with buying 20 per cent of a grocery chain that included the country's biggest retail disaster, OK Bazaars. When asset management went into a nosedive after the collapse of the 'new economy' in March 2000 and this was followed by losses in micro-lending and a reduction in merchant banking opportunities, BOE was in trouble. Now, instead of riding the crest of the wave, it was engulfed by it. Shareholders and management learned from the experience the hard way by losing their money and their jobs. However, it is not clear that politicians learned from it. Banking, as BOE learned to its cost, depends upon the confidence of the market and, if the managers of banks indulge themselves in political wooing and engage in non-traditional banking practices, they can expect to lose the confidence of the market.

This did not apply to the foreign banks that moved into South Africa in the aftermath of the 1994 election. Their reputations had been solidly established elsewhere. By early 1996, when Brian Metcalfe conducted his first study for PricewaterhouseCoopers,[17] there were over 60 foreign banks with a presence in the South African market and almost all of them had arrived after the May 1994 election. Metcalfe, already in February 1996, expected that many of them would withdraw from the

17 Brian Metcalfe, *Foreign Banking in South Africa: Survey*, PricewaterhouseCoopers, 1996.

country when they found that profits did not come up to their expectations. This had been the experience in both Australia and Canada and, of course, it has been the experience in South Africa since 1998. Nevertheless, the 15 foreign banks interviewed by Metcalfe confirmed the local banks' belief that the foreign banks were targeting the top 100 companies for international banking services, corporate advisory services and treasury activities. In 1996 their greatest success had been achieved in foreign exchange, the money market, corporate treasury and major corporate lending. They had been unsuccessful in the middle market and individual market and, already in February 1996, 70 per cent of the banks interviewed reported that profits had been less than expected. Their loans portfolios were strongest in three sectors: manufacturing, finance and mining. Not surprisingly, they considered that their entry into the South African market was viewed favourably by both the government and corporate South Africa and unfavourably by the local banks. Citibank was considered the top corporate bank and the top treasury bank. Almost all the foreign banks were naively expecting the abolition of exchange controls and stating that finding good personnel was their most difficult task in doing business in South Africa.

They stated this early in 1996, before government passed its affirmative action labour laws that forced companies to employ blacks and women in senior positions. By 2000 the staff situation had deteriorated and was becoming a major problem. Expertise was crucial, for the larger foreign banks derived most of their income from fees rather than interest. What is clear from the PricewaterhouseCoopers study is that the foreign banks had injected a new element of competition into the South African market. This was most conspicuous at the top of the market in the quest to provide financial services to the country's largest corporations.

Conclusion

Despite the restrictions of exchange controls and government interference in whom the banks could employ and how they conducted their business, private enterprise found a number of ways to drive the growth of the economy and, in the process, increased the contribution of the financial sector to GDP. Moreover, entrepreneurs in the banking sector managed to achieve this in an economy experiencing a decline in real per capita GDP. Market forces led to the amalgamations that produced Absa and First Rand, to the arrival of a veritable avalanche of overseas banks and to the formation of a host of new banks, whose entrepreneurial founders sought to take advantage of the new opportunities opening up before them. At the same time, the old distinction between commercial banking and merchant banking finally disappeared before the much more radical innovation of bank assurance. The Standard Bank managed to escape the embrace of Liberty Life; two of the big three banks, Absa and Nedcor, ended the decade, as they had begun it, controlled by insurance companies; and First Rand was controlled by the people who founded Momentum Life Insurance Company. In none of these had bank assurance yet yielded significant returns. The global threat to banking posed by the absence of innovation in the last third of the twentieth century did not represent a serious threat to South African banking, which was operating on the fringe of the international economy. (The GDP of the whole of sub-Saharan Africa was not much more than half that of Belgium.) More serious for South African banks was the fact that the rate of return on assets was not increasing as rapidly as the growth of their assets. This was the result of the increased competition that followed from the globalisation of banking in the wake of the Soviet Union's collapse. Globalisation is the great enemy of state-created and state-supported monopolies everywhere.

In the 1990s private enterprise in the financial sector displayed considerable skill in meeting the challenges presented by the last years of sanctions, by a global boom, by increased competition at home and by the African National Congress/Communist Party government that appointed active communist politicians without any banking or business experience as governor and deputy governor of the Reserve Bank.

Banking functions were adapted and broadened, new financial enterprises established and the established banks restructured. The old building societies disappeared from the scene, followed by almost all the separate merchant banks. Private enterprise in the financial sector stands out as the dynamic element in a sluggish economy. Not only did the sector adapt to increasing political interference in the form of unbridled affirmative action and threatened equity legislation to force financial institutions to hand over 25 per cent of their shares to black economic empowerment groups, but it managed to grow at a much faster rate than the economy as a whole. Indeed, throughout the decade, the financial sector was increasing its contribution to GDP by 3.4 per cent a year. Banking was the driving force behind this achievement.

11

The retirement funding and insurance industries

Robert W. Vivian

The retirement funding market

The key to understanding South Africa's financial markets is the system of retirement funding.[1] Employed persons generally save for retirement via occupational retirement schemes. Self-employed persons can save via endowment and retirement annuity policies. The R694 billion aggregate of retirement funds in 2000 indicated in Table 11.1 was the largest single South African financial asset. This was in excess of 75 per cent of GDP and, in those terms, was one of the largest in the world. The reason for the high level of contractual savings is the absence of a Bismarckian type of state pay-roll social pension system. The operations of retirement funds are defined largely by law; the most important pieces of legislation are the Pension Funds Act 24 of 1956 and the Income Tax Act 58 of 1962. The definitions of the different types of retirement schemes (i.e. pension fund, provident fund, retirement annuities) appear in the Income Tax Act, not the Pension Funds Act. Occupational retirement plans are voluntary, but can be imposed by employers as a condition of employment. Employers may define different classes of employees for purposes of retirement funding but, having done so, it becomes compulsory for all employees of that class to join the fund. Savings (contributions) are, in the case of occupational retirement plans, deducted from employees'

1 For further discussions of South African financial markets consult: B. C. Benfield and R. W. Vivian, 'Insurance in the 1990s A: the long-term insurance market 1990–2000', *South African Journal of Economic History*, 18 (2003), 275–288; B. C. Benfield and R. W. Vivian, 'Insurance in the 1990s B: the short-term insurance market 1990–2000', *South African Journal of Economic History*, 18 (2003), 289–309; and R. W. Vivian, 'South African insurance markets', in J. David Cummins and Bertrand Venard (eds), *Handbook of International Insurance*, Springer, 2007, pp. 679–741.

Table 11.1 *Aggregate net assets (R millions) of all pension funds, GDP and inflation, 1994–2003*

Fund type	*1994*	*1995*	*1996*	*1997*	*1998*	*1999*	*2000*	*2001*	*2002*	*2003*
Self-administered funds	170,741	203,706	249,604	266,450	277,750	302,080	329,119	369,996	351,760	367,751
Exempt funds	84,644	93,954	102,362	117,716	132,431	142,810	115,068	188,581	196,077	213,073
Official funds	77,266	87,061	97,620	124,131	152,502	161,859	206,733	238,745	277,452	291,644
Transnet fund	17,266	19,773	28,465	30,057	33,195	30,859	36,965	32,874	34,076	30,209
Telkom fund	3,366	4,108	261	1,436	479	527	499	185	190	144
Post Office fund	1,423	269	1,927	2,409	7,801	3,520	4,084	4,580	5,914	4,890
Bargaining council funds (industrial council funds)	885	2,556	2,876	365	680	2,667	1,589	613	1,927	1,388
Total	356,019	411,427	483,115	542,564	604,838	644,322	694,057	835,574	867,396	909,099
GDP (R millions) (at market prices)	482,120	548,100	617,954	685,730	743,424	813,683	922,148	1,020,007	1,164,945	1,251,468
Funds/GDP	0.74	0.75	0.78	0.79	0.81	0.79	0.75	0.82	0.74	0.73
Inflation (CPI) (%)	8.90	8.70	7.40	8.60	6.90	5.20	5.40	5.70	9.20	5.80
Growth (year-on-year) (%)		13.7	12.7	11.0	8.4	9.5	13.3	10.6	14.2	7.4

Sources: Annual Reports, Registrar of Pension Funds, 1994–2000; GDP and inflation figures are from the *Quarterly Bulletin,* South African Reserve Bank.

salaries and paid over to the retirement fund. Employers and employees contribute to the fund. Larger employers establish their own retirement funds. Smaller firms can establish funds via insurance companies. The funds are usually separate juristic bodies, controlled by a part-time management board (usually incorrectly but universally referred to as 'trustees', a term which does not appear in the Pension Funds Act). Trustees are appointed by the employer as well as elected by members of the fund, in equal proportions. Professional administrators are often appointed, as are professional fund managers, to manage the assets of the fund. There is a tendency for a number of smaller funds to be managed by a single management board established by a third-party service provider. These are the so-called umbrella funds.

After collection, the savings are distributed via the funds themselves (in the case of large employers), insurance companies or fund managers across different asset classes such as equity markets, bond markets, offshore investments and so on. In attempting to get a clear picture of contractual savings in South Africa, the problem of double counting must be borne in mind. Savings are owned by retirement funds, but much of the money is paid over to insurance companies and asset managers to invest. Thus, the assets of an insurance company may well primarily be the assets of retirement funds. Insurance companies also invest the assets of pension funds they manage, and investments for retirement, in the equity market. The market capitalisation of the equity market largely reflects the assets of institutions such as pension funds and insurance companies. This chapter does not attempt to desegregate these assets. The largest single fund is the pension fund of the employees of the government.

The operation of each fund is defined by the rules of that fund. These have to be approved by the Financial Services Board (FSB), the regulator, and the South African Revenue Service (SARS). The approved rules are registered with the FSB. Individual funds have a great deal of discretion in defining the operation of the fund and thus wide variations in the details of the rules of the funds exist. However, in general terms the following can be noted. The assets of a fund belong to the fund itself, not the employer, nor the employee. Since membership of a fund is a condition of employment, employees cannot make any withdrawals from the fund, unless they resign. It is possible for a fund to grant a member a loan that relates to property (real estate), usually the purchase of a house for the member to live in. The modern tendency is not to do this, but for the fund to assist the member to get a loan from a bank, secured by a guarantee from the fund against the member's accumulated assets in the fund. The employer has very limited rights of recourse to members' assets held in the fund. The right of recourse is restricted to offsetting any outstanding property loans (including securities) and losses suffered by the employer as a result of the admitted dishonesty of an employee or on conviction by a court of law with respect to this dishonesty. Employees may withdraw their savings if they resign or transfer the savings to another fund or retain the savings in a preservation fund. If they withdraw savings, the withdrawal can become subject to taxation. It is possible, and this was common, on withdrawal, for rules to disallow the employee from receiving the employer's contributions, but pension funds adjudicators voiced unhappiness with this and the more recent tendency is for the employee to be entitled to the employer's and the employee's own contributions together with the investment gains. A fund may not invest in the business of the employer without agreement of the members and the permission of the Minister of Finance. Notwithstanding this, there is a case on record where the entire fund, consisting of R80 million, was invested in the business of the employer, which later became insolvent and the subsequent criminal prosecution against the employer did not succeed.

Individual employees seldom had any direct control over their savings or choice of investment, but rather elected trustees and received regular feedback concerning matters of the fund. This, too, was changing and evolving to a system of greater individual investment choice. Retirement funds constituted 'the major provider of capital for the equity listed on the JSE'.[2] Savings, apart from those in retirement funds, in South Africa diminished substantially. Discretionary savings were negative during the period. Thus, the main source of savings available for investments was retirement funds.

Exchange controls trapped the bulk of South African savings within South Africa. The government did not fulfil its earlier undertaking to abolish exchange controls (it maintained that its policy was gradually to abolish them). The South African Reserve Bank (SARB) is responsible for administering the exchange controls. It, in turn, has appointed the major banks as its authorised agents (or authorised dealers). Any South African resident wishing to invest outside South Africa must apply to a bank as the SARB's agent for permission to take funds out of the country. The SARB communicates the exchange control rules to its authorised dealers in terms of exchange control circulars. The contents

2 Committee of Inquiry into a Comprehensive System of Social Security for South Africa, *Transforming the Present, Protecting the Future* (Taylor report), Government Printer, 2002, at para. 9.1.1. Note that the name of the JSE changed during the period. It started off as the Johannesburg Stock Exchange, commonly referred to as the JSE, a mutual society, and became the JSE Securities Exchange of South Africa. When it demutualised in July 2005 it became the JSE Ltd.

of the circulars (started in 1961 with the introduction of exchange controls) were not available to the public but, in any event, they would not be of much use to the average individual because of their complexity. A detailed summary of the exchange control requirements is now set out in an exchange control manual available on the SARB's website.[3] The SARB works closely with the South African Revenue Service.

Persons who emigrated were not allowed to take more than a prescribed maximum out of South Africa. What was left was kept in 'blocked rand accounts', maintained and under the strict control of a local bank. Once so deposited, funds therein could be used only for purposes specified in the exchange control circulars. The total amounts kept in blocked rand accounts were not disclosed, but were believed to be substantial. The Minister of Finance in his 2003 budget speech announced that amounts kept in these accounts could be taken out of the country, subject to a forfeit penalty, and that those South Africans who had taken money out of the country in violation of the exchange control regulations could apply for an amnesty and then regularise their affairs.

In contrast to South African residents, non-residents were free to invest and disinvest at will, subject to prescribed procedures. After 1994 there were substantial inflows of foreign capital into South Africa in the form of portfolio flows, or carry trade. Increasingly, South African equities were bought by foreign investors and major South African companies disinvested from South Africa and listed on other stock exchanges, usually maintaining a dual listing. Thus Sasol, South Africa's coal-to-oil company, and Sappi, a paper manufacturer, have secondary listings on the New York Stock Exchange. Anglo American, the mining company, and the Old Mutual, South Africa's largest life insurer, and SABMiller have their main listing on the London Stock Exchange.

The older schemes (private and public sector) were almost exclusively defined benefit pension schemes, but there has been a marked movement in South Africa's private sector towards defined contribution schemes since the late 1980s. The public sector, however, continues to have largely defined benefit schemes.[4]

Employers are allowed to claim a tax deduction for contributions up to 10 per cent of the employee's remuneration and employees can claim an additional 7.5 per cent under paragraphs 11(l) and 11(k) of the Income Tax Act 58 of 1962. In terms of the specific wording of the section, SARS has the discretion to allow a greater percentage and it is accepted that 22.5 per cent of the employee's remuneration will be allowed. Anecdotal

3 See www.reservebank.co.za. The manual can be downloaded in pdf format or as a zip file.

4 'Retirement fund reform – a discussion paper', National Treasury, 2004, p. 10.

evidence, however, indicates that very few companies make the full use of the 22.5 per cent deductions and surveys indicate that the contribution rates are 16.5 per cent. Administration and other costs amount to 5.7 per cent, giving a net contribution rate of 10.8 per cent, which is at the lower level recommended by the World Bank. The costs are, however, among the highest in the world. Most pension funds also provide risk coverage such as life insurance and these pension contributions may include life coverage.[5]

The single largest pension fund is the government employee pension fund, which, because of its size, has considerable influence on the JSE. Being a defined benefit fund, it is in the interest of government employees (and Members of Parliament), who have considerable influence over Parliament, to pay as little as possible into the fund and to get as large a benefit as possible. If the fund is in deficit, this is not a concern for the member of the defined benefit scheme. It is the concern of the government, which has to fund the deficit. Andries Wassenaar found that parliamentarians, government and local government employees had indeed exploited the system for their own benefit.[6]

It is not clear whether private sector defined benefit schemes were correctly managed or whether managers of large companies were able to manipulate these schemes for their own benefit. This could be done, for example, by ensuring that when employees left the company they were refunded only their own contribution (with some interest on it), but not the employer's contribution. This would result in the remaining long-serving members benefiting from the forfeited contributions and investment gains. This was the norm until 1996, when pension funds adjudicators were appointed and indicated displeasure with this arrangement.

Conversions from defined benefit to defined contribution produced a substantial surplus which remaining members were distributing to themselves until it was realised what was happening. In one case, it was discovered that the remaining members (directors) would be entitled to a payout of R23 million from the surplus left in the fund.[7] The realisation that surpluses existed in pension funds resulted in an analysis of all South African pension funds. It was estimated that an aggregate of R80 billion existed as a surplus in retirement funds. Very complicated legislation was then passed in 2001 to deal with this surplus. Attempts were made to find all former members of funds who would be entitled to portions of the surplus. It is not clear whether this elaborate and

5 *Ibid.*, p. 13.

6 Andries Wassenaar, *Squandered Assets*, Tafelberg, 1989.

7 'Pepkor in a pickle over landmark pension fund ruling', *Sunday Times – Business Times*, December 2001, p. 23.

expensive exercise was a success. Legislation has been proposed to transfer the surplus, including any unclaimed benefits, past and future, to a fund under the control of the government or its appointees. SARS has also seen an opportunity to obtain a share in the unclaimed benefits. It issued a directive (GN 35) to the effect that unclaimed benefits are deemed to have passed from the fund to the member and as such are treated as a withdrawal. In terms of the directive, all funds must deduct taxes on the unclaimed portion and forward the deduction to SARS. In some cases it was discovered that substantial surplus funds were transferred to individuals, and there followed criminal proceedings against these individuals. The state has generally been shown to be incapable of prosecuting these cases, which have dragged on for years.

All the increased legislation (relating to fund administration, surplus, taxation) has imposed additional burdens on employers. These additional burdens may contribute to the apparent declining interest of employers to provide or to be involved in occupational retirement funds.

Pension funds and black economic empowerment (BEE)

Since pension funds own a significant portion of equities on the JSE and if, as stipulated by one of various charters, 25 per cent of this equity should find its way, largely uncompensated, to blacks in terms of the BEE programme, then a great portion of this cost ultimately must be borne by future pensioners. The mechanism of transferring pension fund savings to individuals is of course well known, having existed for some time via the operation of share options schemes to managers, which became more sophisticated with the introduction of share buy-backs by companies. The dilution of equity in BEE schemes will ultimately be manifested as lower pensions for future pensioners. It is not clear that future pensioners can afford the generosity of giving away substantial portions of retirement fund assets. To understand the impact of giving away pension fund assets, the question which should have been answered was whether the current system provided adequate pensions.

Providing an adequate pension

The question of considerable importance is, did the South African defined contribution system provide adequate pensions? An answer to this question was not forthcoming, which was surprising considering that South Africa had a multimillion rand industry tasked to provide pensions. One would expect the answer to the question to be readily available. The evidence suggested that the South African defined contribution system failed the vast majority of members. The author often made that point, including on national television and national conventions of retirement funds.[8] The evidence suggested that the vast majority of persons who go on pension would end their lives facing financial depravation unless they had family members to support them.

For example, in 1995 the Smith report attempted to determine the level of pensions paid by occupational schemes.[9] It stated: 'the fact that 40 per cent of pensions paid are less than R410, i.e. the current old age grant, is a matter of concern'. Despite this acknowledgement, nothing was done to remedy the problem.

In another example the author calculated that the pension available to a university professor after in excess of 30 years' service would start at one-third of his or her final salary. This was the maximum this university employee would receive without any adjustment thereafter for inflation. In addition, as discussed below, retired members increasingly had to fund their own post-retirement medical expenses. The best option for employed persons is to work for as long as possible and not rely on savings until forced to do so.

A third example is that virtually all South African pension fund administrators publicly admit that in 96 per cent of the cases where a person retires in South Africa on a defined contribution system, that person will not be financially independent, because the occupational pension will be inadequate. Finally, representatives of old age organisations admit that the vast majority of their members do not earn an income sufficient to warrant filing tax returns.

Action taken by the government after 1994 exacerbated the position of future pensioners. As the result of recommendations of the Katz Commission on taxation, a tax was imposed on the interest income of pension funds. This resulted in lower future pensions and forced pension funds to invest in more risky assets, such as equity. It should be clear that pensioners could not afford to give away substantial portions of their assets via BEE programmes.

Conclusion

Excluding contractual savings, the national savings rate was very low in the 1990s. In short, most of the nation's savings were entrusted to the retirement industry and its alter ego, the long-term insurance market,

8 Robert W. Vivian, 'Taxation of retirement funding – a time to revolt?', paper presented at the Institute of Retirement Funds Conference, 13 September 2004, and abridged version published in *FA News*, October 2004.

9 *Report of the Committee on Strategy and Policy Review of Retirement Provision in South Africa* (Smith report), Department of Finance, 1995, p. 18.

discussed in the next section. Economic theory recognises the great importance of savings being converted into productive assets to produce growth. The contractual savings of retirement funds were increasingly diverted to non-productive purposes. A large portion was diverted to fund share options for managers and, by extension, using a similar approach to fund BEE transactions. Increasingly savings, which are supposed to be capital, were also diverted to the Receiver of Revenue. What was unknown was the benefit members would receive for their lifetime of contributions. The evidence suggested they would receive very little. Should it become increasingly clear that contractual savings do not produce meaningful returns, the public is likely to lose confidence in this institution.

The insurance market

From 1943 onwards, the legislation governing insurance markets was the Insurance Act 27 of 1943, a single Act covering both the long- and the short-term markets, the focus of which was the stability of the industry, not consumer protection.[10] This Act was replaced on 1 January 1999 by two insurance Acts, the Long-Term Insurance Act 52 of 1998 and the Short-Term Insurance Act 53 of 1998. In terms of the new legislation, the registration of composite primary insurers (i.e. insurers that underwrote both long- and short-term insurance) was prohibited. It is possible, though, to have a holding company holding both long- and short-term companies.

The authorities clearly did not want, in the case of insolvency, that both the long- and the short-term companies be liquidated. There is reluctance on the part of the authorities to prejudice policyholders who have invested their savings in a life company to lose these if the short-term business gets into trouble. After the promulgation of the two Acts, the remaining composite primary insurers, as required, separated their operations. Thus, South Africa no longer has or permits composite primary insurers. Composite reinsurers continue to exist.

The insurance market, especially the short-term market, is based largely on British insurance practice. A reason why British insurance practices have been important is that the Roman Dutch law, the 'common law' of South Africa, did not recognise the specific contract of insurance, especially the life contract. It is thus not surprising that South African courts turned to English law to resolve insurance matters. The Cape

10 For a history of South African insurance legislation see B. C. Benfield, 'South African life assurance legislation', *South African Journal of Economics*, 65 (1997), 568–594.

Table 11.2 *Numbers of registered insurers, 2001*

	Number registered
Long-term insurers	
Primary insurers	
Typical	40
Health insurers	2
Cell captive insurers	2
Assistance insurers	6
Link investment only	12
Subtotal	62
Reinsurers	
Long-term only	3
Subtotal	3
Subtotal, long-term primary insurers and reinsurers	65
Short-term insurers	
Primary insurers	
Typical insurers	29
Specialist	40
Captive insurers	17
Subtotal	86
Reinsurers	
Short term only	4
Long and short term	3
Subtotal	7
Subtotal, short-term primary insurers and reinsurers	93

Source: Annual Report, Financial Services Board, 2004.

Parliament in 1879 promulgated an Act recognising the law of Britain as the law applicable to insurance contracts[11] and English law of insurance was applied to the whole of South Africa. It was only in 1977 that the statutes applying English insurance law were repealed. Since then on only a few issues have South African courts deviated from British law.[12]

The long-term (life) insurance market

Table 11.2 indicates that in 2001 there were 62 primary long-term insurers, 3 long-term reinsurers, 86 primary short-term insurers, 4 short-term reinsurers, and 3 composite long- and short-term reinsurers operating

11 General Law Amendment Act 8 of 1879.

12 Probably the most well known case is that of *Mutual & Federal Insurance Co. Ltd* v. *Oudtshoorn Municipality* 1985 1 SA 419 A.

Table 11.3 *Income and expenditure (R billions) of long-term insurers, 1990–2000*

	1990	*1991*	*1992*	*1993*	*1994*	*1995*	*1996*	*1997*	*1998*	*1999*	*2000*
Primary insurers											
Income	40.141	43.724	52.228	54.204	64.448	86.97	96.011	114.614	153.401	149.551	191.967
Net premiums	21.807	24.523	31.217	38.378	46.079	61.772	68.402	82.474	114.517	115.539	147.747
Investment income	10.584	12.029	13.844	15.445	17.727	23.174	25.841	28.994	36.01	31.963	36.506
Other income	7.75	7.172	7.167	0.381	0.642	2.024	1.768	3.146	2.874	2.049	7.714
Expenditure	16.629	18.778	26.173	32.93	41.808	53.695	64.096	80.736	108.425	118.906	140.675
Benefits	12.215	13.81	20.111	25.85	34.736	44.61	53.776	69.347	92.47	104.787	118.233
Management expenses	1.967	2.375	2.951	3.266	3.65	4.489	5.089	5.952	9.504	8.521	9.006
Commissions	1.792	2.033	2.427	2.948	3.422	4.52	4.79	4.903	5.621	5.358	6.061
Other expenditure	0.655	0.56	0.684	0.866	0	0.076	0.441	0.534	0.83	0.24	7.375
Ratio, income–expenditure	2.41	2.33	2.00	1.65	1.54	1.62	1.50	1.42	1.41	1.26	1.36
Percentage year-on-year increase in income		12.45	27.30	22.94	20.07	34.06	10.73	20.57	38.85	0.89	27.88
Rate of increase in benefits paid		13.06	45.63	28.54	34.38	28.43	20.55	28.96	33.34	13.32	12.83
Reinsurers											
Income	0.401	0.532	0.656	0.856	0.786	1.041	1.37	1.348	1.565	1.707	2.171
Net premiums	0.293	0.387	0.5	0.571	0.589	0.724	0.841	1.002	1.199	1.245	1.473
Investment income	0.102	0.133	0.15	0.271	0.192	0.241	0.306	0.327	0.354	0.378	0.409
Other income	0.006	0.012	0.006	0.014	0.005	0.076	0.223	0.019	0.012	0.084	0.289
Expenditure	0.251	0.319	0.428	0.459	0.507	0.593	0.734	1.066	1.242	1.378	1.717
Benefits	0.159	0.212	0.283	0.318	0.368	0.438	0.541	0.707	0.987	1.013	1.057
Management expenses	0.034	0.039	0.045	0.053	0.057	0.068	0.078	0.102	0.108	0.196	0.161
Commissions	0.058	0.068	0.1	0.088	0.082	0.087	0.115	0.173	0.124	0.166	0.258
Other expenditure	0.002	0	0.004	0	0	0	0	0.084	0.023	0.003	0.241
Ratio, income to expenditure	1.17	1.21	1.17	1.24	1.16	1.22	1.15	0.94	0.97	0.90	0.86
Percentage year-on-year increase in net income		32.08	29.20	14.20	3.15	22.92	16.16	19.14	19.66	3.84	18.31

Source: Annual Reports, Registrars of Insurance and Long-Term Insurance, 1990–2003.

Table 11.4 *Assets and liabilities (R billions) of long-term insurers, 1990–2000*

	1990	*1991*	*1992*	*1993*	*1994*	*1995*	*1996*	*1997*	*1998*	*1999*	*2000*
Direct insurers											
Assets	141.541	176.956	204.438	243.491	317.341	369.754	443.234	497.976	515.811	645.11	709.382
Liabilities	104.676	150.831	177.815	211.581	259.623	305.362	354.832	402.214	432.704	525.731	601.326
Ratio, assets–liabilities	1.35	1.17	1.15	1.15	1.22	1.21	1.25	1.24	1.19	1.23	1.18
Reinsurers											
Assets	1.12	1.43	1.60	2.03	2.43	2.81	3.18	3.55	3.62	4.59	4.67
Liabilities	0.70	1.88	1.51	1.58	1.67	2.22	2.52	2.92	3.01	3.73	3.71
Ratio, assets–liabilities	1.59	0.76	1.06	1.29	1.45	1.27	1.26	1.22	1.20	1.23	1.26

Source: Annual Reports, Registrars of Insurance and Long-Term Insurance, 1990–2000.

in South Africa. Table 11.3 shows the income and expenditure of the life industry throughout the 1990s. The net premium inflows increased from R21.81 billion in 1990 to R147.75 billion in 2000, an average year-on-year increase of 21 per cent. This is well in excess of both the annual GDP growth and inflation (Table 11.1). Thus the net premium growth was more than satisfactory, indicating at least that the long-term industry had a stable and growing income stream and/or its marketing campaign was successful. On the other hand, the average year-on-year rate of increase in benefits paid (withdrawals) was 25.9 per cent. Funds flowed out of the industry at a much faster rate than they flowed in. It is not clear what caused the outflow. An explanation could be the expected and actual retrenchments of whites resulted in them cashing in their savings, especially government employees. In 1992, benefit withdrawals increased by 46 per cent, and in 1998 by 33 per cent. Another explanation could be that the public started to lose faith in insurers' ability to produce meaningful investment returns, caused partly by the low investment returns of capital markets during the period. The JSE All Share Index had the same value in September 1998 as in February 1994. The problem with this explanation is that one would expect to see the lack of confidence reflected in diminished flows into the industry, which did not happen until after 2000.

The high rate of withdrawals in relation to inflows was also reflected by the deteriorating ratio of income to expenditure. This declined from 2.41 in 1990 to 1.36 in 2000 and continued to decline thereafter. Clearly, the industry was in trouble. This took time to be acknowledged. As inflows deteriorated to the level of outflows, a corresponding deterioration in the ratio of assets to liabilities occurred. In an era of defined contribution retirement funds and linked investment products, insurers promise very little, resulting in low contractual obligations, and they may remain solvent even with high rates of outflows. Table 11.4 shows the reduction in the ratio of assets to liabilities. In 1990, the ratio stood at 1.35 but by 2000 it had declined to 1.18 and continued to decline thereafter. The decline was a matter of concern, but did not attract any comment from the regulator other than to attribute it to the strengthening of the rand.

Table 11.5 indicates the product segmentation. The single largest line of business was the pension fund and group life business. The vast bulk of the 'life' business was pensions and not life insurance, illustrating the point that the so-called 'insurance' market was mainly an asset management market. Pension fund business represented 35.2 per cent of the market's activities in 1990 and 49.6 per cent in 2000, underlining the importance of corporate business. As indicated above, most firms had a pension fund which they either managed themselves or entered into a contract with an insurer to take over the responsibility. Table 11.1

Table 11.5 *Product segmentation of the long-term insurance market, 1990–2000 (R billions)*

	1990	*1991*	*1992*	*1993*	*1994*	*1995*	*1996*	*1997*	*1998*	*1999*	*2000*
Pension fund and group life benefits											
Premiums	7.72	8.554	11.477	13.506	15.581	20.975	22.367	29.995	48.721	49.989	66.918
Percentage	35.2	34.8	36.5	35.0	33.9	34.2	33.1	37.4	43.0	45.4	49.6
Retirement annuity fund business											
Premiums	2.632	2.429	2.779	3.112	3.591	4.491	4.775	5.64	10.051	7.953	10.388
Percentage	12.0	9.9	8.8	8.1	7.8	7.3	7.1	7.0	8.9	7.2	7.7
Immediate annuity business											
Premiums	3.834	4.463	5.6	7.156	7.488	10.039	9.931	10.621	12.445	13.384	12.007
Percentage	17.5	18.2	17.8	18.6	16.3	16.4	14.7	13.3	11.0	12.2	8.9
Disability and health insurance											
Premiums	0.187	0.277	0.573	0.747	1.054	1.412	1.63	2.035	2.469	3.182	2.787
Percentage	0.9	1.1	1.8	1.9	2.3	2.3	2.4	2.5	2.2	2.9	2.1
Single premium											
Premiums	0.271	0.236	0.56	1.638	3.653	5.42	8.225	8.881	10.897	10.664	17.847
Percentage	1.2	1.0	1.8	4.2	7.9	8.8	12.2	11.1	9.6	9.7	13.2
Periodic premiums											
Premiums	7.28	8.608	10.481	12.397	14.625	18.986	20.69	22.96	28.788	24.827	24.895
Percentage	33.2	35.0	33.3	32.2	31.8	31.0	30.6	28.7	25.4	22.6	18.5
Premium totals	21.924	24.567	31.47	38.556	45.992	61.323	67.618	80.132	113.371	109.999	134.842

Source: Annual Reports, Registrars of Insurance and Long-Term Insurance, 1990–2000.

indicates the assets of pension funds. In 2000, the assets under management of exempt funds (or insured funds) totalled R115 billion. It is this line of business in particular which is managed to a large extent by insurance companies. By handing over these assets to insurance companies, pension funds were exempt from certain of the detailed statutory provisions. Table 11.5 indicates that this line of pension fund business formed a substantial part of life insurers' business. Approximately half of the long-term market's net premium income came from managing firms' pension funds and group life benefits, and not from the more traditional life insurance sold directly to the public. In addition to providing pensions, many firms provided their employees with an extensive range of other group benefits, such as group life insurance, group personal accident cover and so on. In fact, as a general rule, anyone employed by a large South African firm had little need for life or personal accident insurance.

Retirement annuity fund business constituted 12.0 per cent of the market activities in 1990 but this had declined to 7.7 per cent in 2000. This line of business, also related to pension fund business, is usually bought by persons employed in smaller companies which do not have pension fund facilities as well as by individuals, especially self-employed persons. It is not clear why this line declined in importance. The relative decline may indicate a decreasing ability of self-employed persons, or persons employed by smaller corporations which do not provide occupational pensions, to provide for retirement, or a loss of confidence in insurers' ability to do so.

Immediate annuity business also declined in importance. In 1990 it represented 17.5 per cent of the market; by 2000 it had declined to 8.9 per cent. During the period, there was a swing from defined benefit pension schemes to defined contribution schemes, particularly in the private sector. Usually, upon reaching retirement age, it is possible to commute a portion of the pension into a lump sum. In terms of the definition of a pension fund in the Income Tax Act 58 of 1962, not more than one-third of the capitalised value of an annuity can be commuted into a lump sum. In the case of a provident fund, a lump sum becomes available which can be used to purchase an annuity. With the defined contribution pension fund, the member may also receive a lump sum on reaching retirement age and use the balance to purchase an annuity.[13] It is rational to expect that the immediate annuity business would have increased with the change to defined contribution schemes. However,

13 The complex rules governing the taxation of lump sums are set out in the second schedule to the Income Tax Act 58 of 1962.

this did not happen. An explanation may be that persons did not want an immediate annuity but rather a delayed one, resulting in the increase in the single-premium business.

Disability and health insurance increased in importance during the decade, from 0.9 per cent in 1990 to 2.1 per cent in 2000. The net premium income increased from R0.187 billion to R2.787 billion, an increase of 14.90 times its initial value. This increase was brought about by the expansion of the long-term market into the medical insurance arena. Traditionally, as discussed below, medical expenses were provided by the medical aid industry, but in the early 1990s insurers began to offer medical insurance products. The development resulted in an unseemly demarcation argument between regulators of the respective industries, which continued well into the next decade.

Single-premium business represented 1.2 per cent of the market's business in 1990, increasing to 13.2 per cent in 2000. This line of business showed the greatest increase in premium flows, from R0.271 billion in 1990 to R17.847 billion in 2000, an increase of 65.9 times its initial value. This could be ascribed to two issues: the increasing withdrawals from life companies and the change from defined benefit to defined contribution pension schemes. When an employee resigns or is laid off, the employee has a capital sum to invest. This capital can be invested with an insurer as a single-premium investment. Second, with the change from defined benefit to defined contribution, members who leave employment (e.g. through retirement) often receive a lump sum, but may not perceive a need to purchase an immediate annuity. A single-premium policy could be purchased with a maturity date in the future. This might be preferable to purchasing an annuity.

Periodic or recurring premium business represents the more historical line of business of life insurers, which is to accept periodic premiums and to pay lump sums upon defined events. The market share of this class of business declined from 33.2 per cent in 1990 to 18.5 per cent in 2000. The FSB's extensive legislative programme, especially the passing of the Financial Advisory and Intermediary Services Act 37 of 2002, added considerable costs to the provision of insurance. At the lower end of the market in particular, insurance business became less economically viable. This was unfortunate, since it was the lower-income group that was in most need of life insurance. It was this group that was most affected when the financial markets were compelled by BEE considerations to design products for the lower end of the market.

From the above analysis it can be seen that approximately 80 per cent of the life business is, in one way or another, related to the retirement or savings business, hence the above observation that the key to understanding South Africa's life market is to understand the country's retirement funding industry.

In 1990, three insurers dominated the life market: the Old Mutual (established in 1845), Sanlam (established in 1917) and Liberty Life (established in 1958).[14] These three accounted for 76 per cent of the market, measured by premium income, in 1990; this declined to 43 per cent in 2000 and continued to decline thereafter. The Old Mutual lost 41 per cent of its market share and Sanlam lost 54 per cent, while Liberty Life remained constant at approximately 8 per cent. Sanlam demutualised in 1998 and listed on the JSE. Its loss of market share may have been brought about by its loss of business from government employees, which had a large Afrikaans complement, committed to saving via Afrikaans institutions, the premier of which was Sanlam. The Minister of Finance announced on 1 September 2000 that all salary debits on Persal, the automatic debit order system, which allowed the collection and payment of premiums to insurers directly from the government payroll, would cease.[15]

Tables 11.5 clearly indicates that the main function of the life market is to manage the savings of policyholders. This begs the question of whether life insurers provide any meaningful returns to the insured. As in the case of pension funds, there is no clear answer to this important question, nor is there any easy way of arriving at that answer. One of South Africa's senior financial investigative reporters, Dion Basson, examined his policies and calculated the returns. The first policy, with Liberty Life, ran for 13 years and grew by 27.7 per cent over this period (an average of 2.1 per cent per annum). The second policy, again with Liberty Life, ran for 10 years and grew by 6.6 per cent (an average of 0.7 per cent per annum). The third policy was with Sanlam. This had declined by 36.4 per cent over a 16-year period. Old Mutual was unable to provide sufficient information for him to carry out the calculations. He then advised the public to surrender their policies.[16]

Conclusions regarding the long-term insurance market

The decade under review was probably the most traumatic in the 180-year history of South Africa's life market. The nature of the long-term industry changed to be that of a wholesale supplier and not a retail

14 A history of Liberty Life and its founder, Donald Gordon, is provided by Ken Romain, *Larger Than Life*, Jonathan Ball, 1989.

15 The official notice appeared in the government gazette of 9 April 2001, and the measure became effective on 1 July 2001.

16 Dion Basson, 'Surrender – why you should get rid of your policies', *Finance Week*, 29 November 2004.

supplier. It is largely the alter ego of the retirement fund industry. Sales to individuals declined in importance, while sales to corporations for the benefit of employees increased. The well-being of the industry was intimately tied to the country's retirement system and the industry faced declining public confidence in its ability to provide meaningful returns on retirement savings. The problems facing the industry were, oddly, hardly noted by the media, industry or regulator. The two leading insurers experienced massive outflows and loss of market share.

Short-term insurance market

Table 11.2 indicates there were 86 primary (direct) short-term insurers registered in South Africa in 2001. These were conventional direct or primary insurers, reinsurers, captive insurers and bank insurers. Although captive insurers are indicated in Table 11.2, technically there were no specific legislative provisions recognising captive insurers. Starting in the mid-1970s, major industrial companies began to establish their own insurance companies to insure risks faced by the parent companies. These insurers are called captive insurers. In the mid-1980s, one of South Africa's largest motor insurers, the AA Mutual, failed and the government appointed a judicial commission of inquiry, the Melamet Commission (1986), to investigate the failure. It discovered, unrelated to the failure, the existence of captive insurers and recommended that these be investigated. A second commission of inquiry was duly appointed, with the same chairman, Mr Justice David Melamet, as a result of which the operation of captive insurers in South Africa became much better understood. It also gave rise to the cell captive industry, with the leading cell captive insurer being Guardrisk.[17]

The large life insurers had substantial shareholdings in the banks and in short-term insurers. In some cases there were cross-holdings, that is, insurers also holding shares in banks. Thus, Sanlam had holdings in Absa (which were sold to Barclays Bank); and Old Mutual, the life insurer, had holdings in the Permanent Bank and Nedcor. Old Mutual was the dominant owner of the Mutual and Federal Insurance Company, South Africa's second largest short-term company.

Initially, banks placed their clients' insurance business with their shareholders' short-term insurer. Thus, the Permanent Bank placed its business with the Mutual and Federal, the Old Mutual's short-term

17 The position of captive insurers in South Africa is extensively covered by Paul A. Bawcutt, *Captive Insurance Companies: Establishment, Operation, and Management* (4th edition), Witherby, 1997.

insurer. The Standard Bank had a controlling relationship with Liberty, which had a relationship with Guardian National, so the Standard Bank placed its business with the Guardian National (subsequently taken over by Santam).

The 1990s saw the establishment of bank insurers (i.e. the banks establishing their own insurers). These insurers were positioned to pick up insurance business from the bank's clients. Thus, where a client secured a mortgage bond with the bank, the bank also offered insurance covering the buildings and credit life covering the outstanding mortgage, should the borrower die. The bank could also offer to insure the household contents and motor vehicles and so on. It is illegal for the bank to make it a condition of any loan that the insurance be purchased from the bank. The consumer has the free choice of insurer and the bank must advise the client accordingly (under section 43 of the Short-Term Insurance Act).

Bank insurers generally will also, of course, offer to insure members of the public other than the bank's own clients, and would like to increase market share. Some bank insurers such as the First National Bank's Outsurance publicise themselves widely, as direct insurers, in an attempt to attract insureds directly from the public. Table 11.6 indicates the gross short-term premium income for the South African short-term insurance market over the period 1992–2000. In 2000, it was R24.67 billion. Since a single power station costs R30 billion to replace, it should be clear that South Africa's short-term insurance market is not large enough to cover all South Africa's risks. The international market and reinsurance into the international market are essential. It is thus not surprising that, until the 1990s, major short-term insurers (an exception being Santam) had a foreign shareholder. The short-term market maintained close links with international insurers, especially reinsurers. This situation prevailed for centuries. Both large European reinsurers, Munich-Re and Swiss-Re, have subsidiary reinsurance companies in South Africa. Swiss-Re made clear its unhappiness with the idea that it should dilute its ownership through BEE, and threatened to withdraw from South Africa.[18]

The ratio of net income to expenditure averaged 1.06 over the decade. The market was generally regarded as well capitalised, with Mutual and Federal declaring a R1 billion special dividend refunding unrequired capital back to the shareholders. In this case, that may well have been the wrong decision, since shortly thereafter Guardian National, a large insurer, came on the market and was acquired by Santam, which

18 Swiss-Re effectively did withdraw from South Africa in 2009.

Table 11.6 *Income and expenditure (R billions) of the short-term insurance industry, 1992–2000*

	1992	*1993*	*1994*	*1995*	*1996*	*1997*	*1998*	*1999*	*2000*
Primary insurers									
Income	8.678	9.943	11.196	13.333	15.961	18.25	19.671	20.836	21.204
Gross premiums income	9.552	11.133	12.581	15.055	18.065	20.737	22.697	21.25	24.67
Net premiums	7.578	8.714	9.927	11.844	14.077	16.044	17.116	16.205	16.345
Investment income	1.100	1.229	1.269	1.489	1.884	2.206	2.555	4.631	4.859
Expenditure	6.783	9.39	9.017	10.624	12.359	14.811	16.764	15.001	16.45
Claims paid	4.963	6.76	6.78	7.871	8.976	10.503	11.975	10.889	11.812
Management expenses	0.948	1.119	1.146	1.468	1.74	2.265	2.657	2.314	3.002
Commissions	0.872	1.511	1.091	1.285	1.643	2.043	2.132	1.798	1.636
Underwriting profit	0.541	0.448	(0.210)	0.412	0.679	0.497	(0.086)	(0.004)	(0.337)
Underwriting profit + investment income	1.641	1.677	1.059	1.901	2.563	2.703	2.469	4.627	4.522
Ratio, net income–expenditure	1.12	0.93	1.10	1.11	1.14	1.08	1.02	1.08	0.99
Reinsurers									
Income	0.644	0.825	0.826	1.031	1.328	1.488	2.011	2.428	2.537
Gross premiums income	1.098	1.388	1.448	1.735	2.341	2.709	3.236	3.179	3.689
Net premiums	0.539	0.678	0.679	0.859	1.12	1.261	1.753	1.895	2.14
Investment income	0.105	0.147	0.147	0.172	0.208	0.227	0.258	0.533	0.397
Expenditure	0.493	0.621	0.687	0.749	0.958	1.211	1.333	1.862	2.212
Claims paid	0.315	0.406	0.456	0.441	0.577	0.763	0.883	1.219	1.526
Management expenses	0.055	0.058	0.062	0.069	0.086	0.096	0.113	0.152	0.153
Commissions	0.123	0.157	0.169	0.239	0.295	0.352	0.337	0.491	0.533
Underwriting profit	(0.056)	(0.065)	(0.123)	(0.005)	(0.095)	(0.092)	(0.185)	(0.356)	(0.138)
Underwriting profit + investment income	0.049	0.082	0.024	0.167	0.113	0.135	0.073	0.177	0.259
Ratio, net income–expenditure	1.09	1.09	0.99	1.15	1.17	1.04	1.32	1.02	0.97

Source: Annual Reports, Registrars of Insurance and Short-Term Insurance, 1992–2000.

Table 11.7 *Assets and liabilities (R billions) of short-term insurers, 1990–2000*

	1990	*1991*	*1992*	*1993*	*1994*	*1995*	*1996*	*1997*	*1998*	*1999*	*2000*
Primary insurers											
Assets	10.870	13.329	15.493	19.205	22.451	26.774	31.977	36.634	35.621	39.122	37.729
Liabilities	5.340	5.501	6.040	7.542	8.311	9.643	11.436	13.420	15.237	19.778	17.935
Ratio, assets–liabilities	2.036	2.423	2.565	2.546	2.701	2.777	2.796	2.730	2.338	1.978	2.104
Reinsurers											
Assets	1.07	1.259	1.485	1.978	1.952	2.425	2.948	3.325	3.834	4.975	5.599
Liabilities	0.732	0.828	0.974	1.408	1.616	1.634	2.139	2.407	3.090	3.885	4.518
Ratio, assets–liabilities	1.462	1.521	1.525	1.405	1.208	1.484	1.378	1.381	1.241	1.281	1.239

Source: Annual Reports, Registrars of Insurance and Short-Term Insurance, 1990–2000.

Table 11.8 *Product segmentation of the short-term insurance market, 1990–2000 (R billions)*

	1990	*1991*	*1992*	*1993*	*1994*	*1995*	*1996*	*1997*	*1998*	*1999*	*2000*
Property (fire) business											
Premiums written	1.129	1.351	1.465	1.803	2.115	2.399	2.672	3.004	3.125	5.150	5.594
Percentage	18	18	18	19	20	19	18	17	17	28	30
Transportation (marine) business											
Premiums written	0.137	0.151	0.164	0.196	0.232	0.325	0.364	0.409	0.466	0.535	0.496
Percentage	2	2	2	2	2	3	2	2	2	3	3
Motor											
Premiums written	2.424	3.056	3.282	3.799	4.220	5.114	6.163	6.960	7.332	6.682	6.942
Percentage	40	41	40	40	40	40	41	40	39	37	38
(Personal) accident and health											
Premiums written	0.274	0.210	0.180	0.261	0.397	0.413	0.484	0.488	0.671	0.566	0.876
Percentage	4	3	2	3	4	3	3	3	4	3	5
Guarantee business											
Premiums written	0.091	0.108	0.134	0.151	0.171	0.188	0.276	0.319	0.384	0.379	0.439
Percentage	1	1	2	2	2	1	2	2	2	2	2
Liability business											
Premiums written	–	–	–	–	–	–	–	–	–	1.513	0.482
Percentage	–	–	–	–	–	–	–	–	–	8	3
Engineering business											
Premiums written	–	–	–	–	–	–	–	–	–	0.324	0.385
Percentage	–	–	–	–	–	–	–	–	–	2	2
Miscellaneous business											
Premiums written	2.068	2.577	2.893	3.171	3.470	4.264	5.240	6.124	6.891	2.952	3.288
Percentage	34	35	36	34	33	34	34	35	37	16	18
Totals											
Premiums written	6.123	7.453	8.118	9.381	10.605	12.703	15.199	17.304	18.869	18.101	18.502

Source: Annual Reports, Registrars of Insurance and Short-Term Insurance, 1990–2000.

resulted in Santam becoming South Africa's largest insurer. An interesting feature of the market is that it returned an underwriting profit over the period of nearly R2 billion. In some countries a market underwriting profit is unusual.

The assets and liabilities of the short-term market are shown in Table 11.7, from which it can be seen that the ratio of assets to liabilities was fairly stable over the 1990s, slightly declining, following the underwriting cycle. In the early part of the decade, the market was probably over-capitalised. In 1996, the assets covered the liabilities by a ratio of 2.8. The larger insurers in particular were over-capitalised and thus were well placed to take over foreign insurers (discussed below) or to return excess capital to shareholders.

Table 11.8 indicates the product segmentation of the short-term market. Traditionally, six insurance classes were reported to the regulator. The 1998 Short-Term Insurance Act redefined the classes and two classes were added: liability business and engineering business. Engineering business includes, for example, machinery breakdown insurance and construction insurance of large projects. Performance in the eight classes is indicated in Table 11.8, from which it can be seen that property (i.e. fire) (30 per cent), motor (38 per cent) and miscellaneous insurance (18 per cent) were the three largest classes of business in 2000.

Liability risks are, in many parts of the world, a matter of concern. There was, for example, the asbestos crisis, which it is estimated cost American companies in excess of $200 billion and has caused the insolvency of a large number of industrial and insurance companies. The separate reporting of this class of business will enable the regulators to monitor the position in South Africa more closely. Not all liability risks are reported separately or covered in the insurance market. Motor passenger liability is covered as a section of the motor policy and appears in the transportation category. Motor third-party bodily injury claims are covered by the government's insolvent Road Accident Fund (RAF), discussed below, as is workers' compensation, also discussed below. Some liability risks are not covered in the market at all.

In 2000, Santam, with 17 per cent of the market, and Mutual and Federal, with 11 per cent, were South Africa's largest short-term insurers. The 1990s were characterised by a contraction in the market and the departure of virtually all foreign shareholders of short-term companies in South Africa. SA Eagle was the remaining large, long-established insurer with a foreign shareholding, being part of the Zurich Financial Services Group.

The following companies closed down or disinvested: IGI, Aegis, Commercial Union (later CGU), General Accident (GA), Guardian National, StanGen, the St Paul, Allianz (although Allianz has kept a small office going) and Gerling General SA (although it subsequently returned). The Royal and SunAlliance, a major shareholder of the Mutual and Federal since the early 1800s and for a long time South Africa's largest short-term insurer, sold its shareholding to the Old Mutual in a controversial disinvestment exercise. It had offered the minority shareholders an amount less than the quoted price of the shares. There is no single reason for these departures and most had nothing to do with South Africa. It seems most decisions to depart had more to do with the state of the world market at the time and decisions by the foreign companies to concentrate on their core activities. Though the South African operations may have been regarded as profitable – maybe even the most profitable in the various companies – in absolute terms the contribution to group profits was probably not material.

Santam had 19 per cent of the market in 1998; it then acquired the Guardian National, which had 14 per cent the market, to become South Africa's largest short-term insurer, over its long-time rival the Mutual and Federal, until then South Africa's largest insurer. The broker community was of the opinion that the market was too concentrated, with insufficient competition. The arrival in 1995 of AIG, a US insurer, was regarded by the brokers as most welcome and timely. AIG more than doubled its market share over a few years and surpassed Lloyd's, which had had agents in South Africa since the early 1800s.

The South African short-term market is traditionally considered to be a broker-dominated market, that is, most of the business is placed via independent insurance brokers. The broker market included Alexander Forbes, GlenRand MIB, Aon and Marsh. In the 1990s a new short-term insurance distribution channel began to develop, the independent underwriting manager (IUM). The IUM accepts business on the basis of an insurer's licence, pays claims and shares the profits with the insurers. In some cases the insurer may have equity in the IUM. The insurer essentially authorises the IUM to accept risks, settle claims and possibly even design new products without any reference to itself. The insurer hands over, so to speak, its underwriting pen to a third party. The exact relationship between the insurer and IUM may differ from manager to manager and may not be clearly defined, in fact or law. It is estimated that there were about 250 IUMs by the end of the decade. The reason for their formation is not clear but may be related to the closing down of a number of long-established insurers, which resulted in the laying-off of staff, who could not find employment in the remaining companies. A consequence was that many experienced insurance persons were unemployed and it would make sense for them to come up with a scheme to continue to provide a service within the insurance industry with which they were familiar. A further contributing factor was fixed regulated commissions, the abolition of which had been under consideration and agreed to for a number of years, but the implementation of which was continually delayed. The IUM makes a profit, rather than a commission, which is shared with the insurer and this may well be more attractive than working for a commission.

The forms of policies generally follow British wording, which has had considerable influence on the market. Each insurer is free to adopt any wording it chooses. The wording is not subject to approval by the FSB. The standard practice in the personal lines market is to put all policies together in one booklet (as in the case of Santam's Multiplex policies) and for the insured to select which coverage he or she desires (motor, public liability, house owners, etc.). Most premiums are paid monthly, by way of a debit order. However, insureds can select to pay premiums annually, in which event they will get a discount. Santam claimed credit for introducing this system.[19] A similar system, the origins of which are not related to the personal lines policies, is used for small to medium enterprises (SMEs). In this case, the MultiMark policies are used. The wording of these was agreed to by brokers and insurers, to avoid the necessity of time-consuming independent negotiations between brokers and companies. The negotiations on the MultiMark wording took several years to complete and has undergone several revisions. The responsibility for the project was transferred to the South African Insurance Association (SAIA).

Conclusion regarding the short-term market

The general consensus is that the short-term market ended the decade in a healthy state but, as happens, experiencing negative underwriting profits (Figure 11.1). The overall profits came from investment income. The negative underwriting profit part of the cycle can be severe, threatening the solvency of some companies. The point is reached when the negative profits can no longer be sustained and premiums rise. Sometimes the rise is brought about by an event, such as the failure of an insurance company, as happened with the collapse of the AA Mutual in the mid-1980s. The negative cycle at the end of the 1990s was broken by the events in the USA of 11 September 2001, thereafter ushering in one of the longest positive cycles.

19 R. W. Vivian, *Morgan's History of the Insurance Institute Movement in South Africa, 1898–1999*, Francolin, 2002, p. 120.

Figure 11.1 *Short-term underwriting cycle, 1992–2000: underwriting profit*

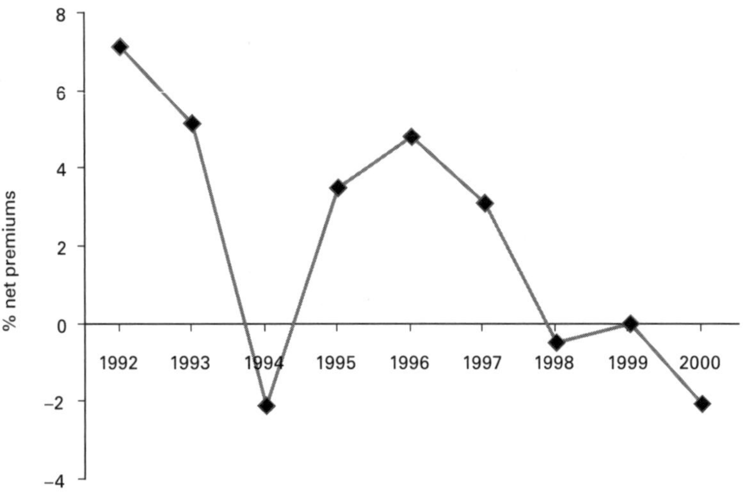

Medical health funding

The funding of medical expenses is another aspect of insurance originally tied to employment. Most large employers offer medical aid to their employees but there is no legal obligation to do so. The employer establishes a medical aid scheme, which, because membership is confined to employees, is referred to as a closed or restricted scheme. In terms of these schemes, employees receive medical treatment in the private sector from doctors and suppliers usually of their own choice. Certainly up to 1994, South Africa's private medical sector was regarded as being in line with the best in the world. There is virtually no delay in obtaining medical treatment for those on medical aid schemes. Medical bills are forwarded to the employer's medical aid department to settle. The cost of medical aid is funded by contributions from the employer and employee (member). Medical aid is not regarded as insurance and schemes do not fall under the insurance legislation for supervisory purposes, nor are they supervised by the FSB. Historically, medical aid continued after retirement, initially at little or no cost to the former employee, now pensioner. This is fast disappearing, leaving pensioners with the additional problem of funding post-retirement medical costs. In some cases, employee organisations have taken employers to court to force them to continue to provide medical aid after employment. Post-retirement funding of medical expenses is a matter of increasing concern, for which no clear answer is forthcoming.

Medical aid schemes are regulated by the Medical Schemes Act 138 of 1998. Briefly, every medical aid scheme must be registered with the Registrar of Medical Schemes and operate in terms of rules adopted by the scheme and approved by the Registrar. The Act lays down a number of provisions which the rules may and may not contain. The Registrar reports to the Minister of Health and not the Minister of Finance. The Act requires, for example, that no scheme can be a profit-making entity or have shareholders, and that minimum benefits are to be provided. Medical aid schemes are thus mutual associations. A new requirement of the legislation is the so-called community rating system, which is applied to determine the levy. The idea of community ratings is that the community stands together, negating the idea of a risk-rated premium. Schemes may not differentiate on the basis of age, gender or health conditions. They may differentiate on the basis of income and number of dependants. There is thus a considerable degree of forced cross-subsidisation. Members and their dependants can be covered by the scheme. With the passing of time, specialist medical aid administration companies have developed. These include very large administrators, such as Discovery Health and Medschemes. The system has expanded to include open schemes, that is, schemes not tied to employment. More members now belong to open schemes than restricted schemes. Since medical schemes cannot risk rate, this could result in the levy of some funds being much greater than that of others where the proportion of high-risk individuals is greater. The government proposed a risk equalisation fund to cater for this possibility. The representatives of medical aid schemes meet with representatives of the medical profession to establish a tariff of fees for services. Individual doctors are not always satisfied with the tariff rates and can contract out of the tariff rates, in which event the member is liable for the difference.

The Council for Medical Schemes issues a detailed annual report. During the 1990s there were about 7 million beneficiaries of medical schemes, 5 million in open schemes and 2 million in closed or restricted schemes. This figure remained virtually constant during the decade, with a slight increase in membership and a corresponding decrease in dependants. The contributions to medical schemes exceed those made to short-term insurers. Since medical schemes by law are mutual insurers, they cannot distribute profits to shareholders. Profits (if any) are made by scheme administrators with respect to fees charged. The Registrar noticed that some of the schemes had incurred what he considered disproportionate reinsurance charges. He also noted that this happened when the administrator purchased reinsurance from an insurer within the same group of companies as the administrator. To put it succinctly, administrators were thought to be gaining additional income via incorrectly priced reinsurance premiums – a transfer pricing problem. This led to a very public confrontation between the Registrar and some administrators and the monitoring of reinsurance contracts. As a result of the monitoring, the net reinsurance costs (premiums less claims) decreased by 58.5 per cent and declined to 1.9 per cent of gross contributions, compared with the previous figure of 5.1 per cent. The Registrar further decided that all schemes would have to increase their solvency so as to reduce their reliance on reinsurance contracts for solvency purposes, and this led to yet another public confrontation. As a consequence of these steps, medical schemes became more solvent, with the aim that medical schemes would achieve 25 per cent free reserves as a percentage of gross contributions by 2004.[20]

South Africa does not have a national health insurance scheme but it does have a public health system, including hospitals funded out of current taxes. The public health system is regarded as inadequate and as having deteriorated since the advent of the African National Congress (ANC) alliance government.[21] Those who are not on medical aid (the majority) and cannot afford medical treatment have access to public hospitals. It is of course in the interest of the government to shift, as far as possible, the burden of the provision of medical health to the medical aid system. A number of new proposals were published for comment. By the end of the decade, none had been adopted. One proposal was that all medical aid members should pay 4.5 per cent of their income to the medical aid industry and that be used to expand the medical aid system to those who were not on the system. This essentially would have increased income taxes by 4.5 per cent. To put it another way, the government would have liked to transfer its health funding obligations to the medical aid industry.

In the 1980s the insurance industry decided to enter the health market and offer medical insurance, cover additional to medical aid. This caused the then Registrar of Medical Schemes some considerable unhappiness and attempts were made to prevent insurers from entering the field. The entry of insurance into the medical field resulted in tension between the two industries and regulators. At one time, the Registrar of Medical Schemes threatened to prosecute insurance companies, but this did not happen. It took some 15 years to come to a very

20 For an overview of some of the health economic issues, consult W. Duncan Reekie, 'The economics of health and the health of economics', *South African Journal of Economics*, 65 (1997), 283–313.

21 An anecdotal example may illustrate the point. An elderly lady developed gangrene and as a consequence had a limb amputated. The next day she was sent home and the family was told they were responsible for nursing her. They of course knew nothing about nursing – she died a few days later.

complex agreement on the demarcation between medical aid and health insurance. As can be seen from Tables 11.5 and 11.8, medical insurance is offered by both long- and short-term insurers but it did not constitute a major component of the insurance industry's business.

State insurance schemes

Five state insurance schemes are of importance: Compensation of Occupational Injuries and Diseases (COID, which is workers' compensation) (under Act 130 of 1993); the Compensation for Occupational Diseases in Mines and Works Fund (under Act 78 of 1973); the Road Accident Fund (RAF) (under Act 56 of 1996); the Unemployment Insurance Fund (UIF) (under Act 63 of 2001); and the South African Special Risks Insurance Association (SASRIA), an insurer established to pay for damages caused by politically motivated persons (i.e. terrorism insurance) and nationalised by the government in terms of the conversion of SASRIA Act 134 of 1998.

Workers' compensation

South Africa has a compulsory workers' compensation scheme, which, since 1993, covers all employed persons.[22] When mining started to develop, the mine owners decided in 1894 to establish a mutual insurance scheme to provide compensation for workers injured at work. This became the Rand Mutual Assurance Company, which is still in existence, covering mines affiliated to the Chamber of Mines. Workers' compensation was thereafter introduced to cover all employees and extended to cover occupational diseases. Two categories of occupational diseases are considered: first, diseases with a known link to specific types of work (set out in the third schedule to COID); and second, diseases for which there is no such link. For the first category, it is presumed that the disease arose from the occupation; for the second, the employee must prove the connection. For example, if an employee works with lead and gets a disease associated with lead, the presumption is that the work caused the disease. If the employee is afflicted with a lead-related disease but does not work with lead, the employee must prove causation.

22 For a history of workers' compensation in South Africa, consult Debbie Budlender, 'Workmen's compensation', *South African Labour Bulletin*, 9 (1984), 22–40. For a short overview of workers' compensation in South Africa, consult A. C. Valsamakis, R. W. Vivian and G. S. Du Toit, *Risk Management* (4th edition), Heinemann, 2010, pp. 158–162, and the sources quoted therein.

A second (much smaller) mutual insurance company was founded much later to cover employees in the building industry.

By law, only a mutual insurer can offer workers' compensation and to do so requires the approval of the Compensation Commissioner. Workers' compensation initially applied only to employees earning amounts below a prescribed figure, until Act 130 of 1993 extended coverage to virtually all employees. Persons excluded from workers' compensation include domestic servants, who are excluded because of the difficulties in collecting the levy.

The levy is based on the employee's salary, is risk rated and is paid exclusively by the employer. Compensation is on a no-fault basis. It resembles personal accident insurance and not liability insurance. Industries with better than average claims experience pay less than industries with higher claims experience. Individual companies qualify for a rebate if their safety record is better than the norm for their industry. The employer is relieved of all common-law liability. However, if an employee is injured as a result of the negligence of a limited number of persons (the so-called vice employers) or a patent defect, then the employee can apply to the Commissioner for additional compensation.

Workers' compensation operated successfully for well in excess of a century. Very few, if any, risk managers included workers' compensation costs as part of their risk costs. After the ANC alliance government took over, the existing senior experienced staff were replaced with inexperienced staff and reports began to surface of administrative failures, with lawyers having to sue the fund to get it to process certain classes of claims.[23] The number of reportable accidents was stable at about 260,000 per annum in the mid-1990s, reflecting the country's static employment figures, and the fund was solvent.

Occupational Diseases in Mines and Works Fund

The Occupational Diseases in Mines and Works Fund was established by the Occupational Diseases in Mines and Works Fund Act 78 of 1973 and is not a well publicised fund. As the name implies, its purpose is to provide compensation for occupational diseases in mines and the works associated with the mines. It has its origin in the phthisis crisis of the 1900s. It has been renamed several times. Occupational diseases in

23 'Workers' compensation system of compensation mired in incompetence', *Business Report*, 7 July 2003; 'Time to scrap workers' compensation', *Business Report*, 31 October 2003; 'The ills surround workers' compensation', *Business Report*, 26 July 2004. Eventually the head of the fund was suspended.

mines and works have been subject to a large number of commissions of inquiry over the years, and their reports can be consulted for a clear picture of occupational diseases in mines in South Africa. This fund, unlike the workers' compensation fund, ended up being actuarially insolvent and received qualified audits. It also failed to carry out some of its functions. When the fund was first established, it paid some of the most generous benefits in the world (for which it was criticised). One of the failings of the fund was that the benefits were not sufficiently revised to make the compensation realistic.

Road Accident Fund

A road accident scheme has been on the books in South Africa since 1942 (under the Motor Vehicle Insurance Act 29 of that year). Because of the Second World War, it became operational only in 1946. Since its inception, the system has had a variety of names, the current being the Road Accident Fund. The operation of the system has also changed over the years. Initially, drivers were simply required to purchase third-party liability insurance from an insurer prepared to underwrite the coverage at its own rates. In 1964 the legislation was amended to allow the Minister to set the premiums. Thereafter, insurers had to approach the Minister to increase the premiums and, when insurers approached the Minister for a 20 per cent increase, he refused and some insurers withdrew from the market. In response, in 1966 the State President restricted involvement in third-party insurance to a consortium of 16 insurers and set up a fund called the Motor Vehicle Assurance Fund to reinsure the risk. In 1969 the Act was amended to allow the state to take control of the Motor Vehicle Assurance Fund, but the consortium still consisted of the insurers and dealt with the claims. Insurance was sold annually (all on the same day) and motorists were issued with a token which they had to display on their cars as proof of insurance (this is no longer the case though). The government decided on the recommendation of a minority report to the Grosskopf Commission (1981) to fund the scheme via a levy on fuel, which came into operation in May 1986. The consortium nevertheless continued to handle claims as the agent of the fund. Claims were allocated to a consortium member according to the day of the week on which the accident occurred.

It was clear for a long time that the fund was heading for financial disaster,[24] as it had become insolvent. The government appointed the

24 Robert W. Vivian, 'Identifying the source of the MVA rate crisis', paper presented to the Noschon Conference, Sun City, 8 May 1984.

Satchwell Commission in June 1999 to investigate the fund, which had been riddled with corruption for a long time. The corruption was identified by the Melamet Commission (1992) and investigated by the Heath Commission, a standing commission specifically set up to investigate corruption, but this investigation was stopped by the constitutional court. Lawyers have a vested interest in the continuation of the status quo and receive by far the largest portion of the fund's income. The chairman and chief executive of the fund were suspended in June 2004, followed by the suspension of the board in June 2005. The chairman was reinstated and then dismissed. The government seemed incapable of resolving the problems of this fund.

An unusual feature is that the fund is financed out of a levy imposed on fuel. There is thus no separate premium paid by drivers or owners of vehicles. According to a survey conducted by Swiss-Re, South Africa was the only country which adopted this scheme of funding. In essence, the scheme is now a pay-as-you-go scheme and the multi-billion deficit is largely the cost of outstanding claims.

Unemployment Insurance Fund (UIF)

The UIF is another government-administered fund which was at one time in financial difficulties. This was, however, solved by extending the operation of the fund to cover high-salary earners (as they are unlikely ever to claim) and by capping the amount that may be claimed. This levy is simply a payroll tax on high-earning persons. As a result, there has been a turnabout in the fortunes of the fund. The UIF, unlike workers' compensation, was extended to domestic workers. The fund faced further allegations of maladministration. However, the claims did not involve material amounts and did not affect the solvency of the fund.

South African Special Risks Insurance Association (SASRIA)

SASRIA is the insurer formed to deal with claims caused by persons who are politically motivated. Its long-standing chief executive was Mike Strydom. SASRIA was established after the 1976 Soweto riots, in the face of insurers having difficulties in settling resulting claims. It was possible before the establishment of SASRIA to get a measure of coverage for damage caused intentionally in terms of the riot, strike, and malicious damage (RSMD) extension to property policies, but the Soweto riots showed the inadequacy of this method. Because of these difficulties the insurance industry decided to establish a 'section 21' (non-profit) company named SASRIA to underwrite risks emanating from damage to property, including consequential losses (business interruption). SASRIA was structured on the basis of a risk pool. Each participating company committed a fixed sum of capital and the liabilities of the companies were limited to their capital commitments. If possible, reinsurance was to be arranged and the government approached firstly to grant tax exemption to SASRIA (which was not unreasonable since SASRIA was a non-profit-making company, with surpluses being retained to build up reserves) and secondly to act as the insurer of last resort. The government agreed to both requests. To further limit SASRIA's liability, a maximum limit for any one party insured was specified (which was a source of contention). It did not insure loss of profits, the government being of the opinion it could not underwrite private sector profits. Loss of profits was insurable in the London market.

Since SASRIA was in a sense a collective company of the industry, the industry did not want to establish an expensive administration system for it, so it was decided that most of the administration would be carried out by the existing conventional property insurance companies. The main policies, the conventional policies, would be the existing property policies. SASRIA, as an insurer, unlike other insurers, cannot cancel nor refuse cover.

The premium was excessive over the entire history of SASRIA, quickly outpacing the claims, resulting in a substantial surplus. The premium was not risk rated. The same premium applied throughout South Africa, irrespective of conditions prevailing at the risk location. The market referred to this as a flat-rated premium. This created the problem of adverse selection. The public would purchase political unrest cover from the London market when the risk was low. If unrest broke out, the overseas insurers would cancel cover; the public would then purchase cover from SASRIA, which it could not refuse. To overcome this problem, the Reinsurance of Damage and Losses Act 56 of 1989 was passed, which made it a criminal offence to purchase political damage cover except from SASRIA. There is no obligation to purchase political damage cover, but if it is purchased it must be purchased from SASRIA. South Africa is one of the few countries where the mere purchase of insurance can constitute a criminal offence. The system, however, worked exceptionally well, generating profits for SASRIA.

The South African government was never called upon as a reinsurer. It never paid a single claim. After the ANC alliance took over in 1994, it became clear that the funds being held by SASRIA would not be used. By this time, it had accumulated several billions as a reserve. The government nationalised SASRIA under the Conversion of SASRIA Act 134 of 1998 and, once nationalised, it paid itself a multibillion-rand dividend. Stripped of its assets, the government tried to sell it back to the industry, but there was not much enthusiasm for the purchase. The government, failing to find a buyer, announced it would continue operating the scheme for a few years and then reconsider the matter.[25]

Conclusion

The South African economy was the most successful economy on the African continent. The pensions and life markets played an important role in this achievement, by channelling the nation's savings to productive assets. This resulted in life insurers moving away from their traditional insurance role and to become largely asset managers. The bulk of South African savings are contractual savings; there is a very low level of non-contractual savings. As the 1990s progressed, the data revealed a loss of confidence in the life market as withdrawals increased and premium inflows declined. Considerable portions of the institutional savings were diverted to the government's BEE policy, and this will affect future pensions. The short-term market continued largely as before, with a feature of the decade being disinvestment by foreign companies.

25 'Sasria shelves its privatization plans for 5 years', *Business Report*, 3 October 2001.

12

The Johannesburg Stock Exchange and capital markets

Stuart Jones

Continuity and change

In the last decade of the twentieth century the Johannesburg Stock Exchange (JSE) was superficially transformed while remaining essentially unchanged. It remained essentially unchanged because its principal functions remained in place. These were:[1]

> The provision of a market where securities could be freely traded. The provision of investment liquidity. The evaluation of securities and management. The channelling of savings into investments.

It appeared to be transformed because ownership changed from individuals to companies and because the volume of business flowing through the exchange rose dramatically. In 1990, too, the economy was entering upon its third decade of little or no growth. This had reduced any sustained demand for change in the JSE's essential functions. Moreover, exchange controls remained in force and continued to exert a deleterious impact upon both the JSE and the economy. Indeed, while privatisation became the order of the day in much of the global economy in the wake of the collapse of Soviet communism, in South Africa it was only halfheartedly introduced. In South Africa under the African National Congress (ANC), weak politicians shied away from any sudden removal of exchange controls, thereby emphasising yet again continuity with the past.

1 Stuart Jones, 'The financial sector, 1970–2000', in Stuart Jones (ed.), *The Decline of the South African Economy*, Edward Elgar, 2002, p. 179.

Economic growth and the JSE

Ultimately, the performance of the JSE depended upon the performance of the South African economy, which, in the 1990s, was not keeping pace with population growth. The earnings of the JSE, in real terms, in 2002 were below the level of the early 1980s and early 1990s. The main driving force behind this was the decline in the price of resources.[2] This in turn was reinforced by the collapse of personal savings to less than 0.3 per cent of GDP in 2000.[3] The macro-economic environment was not favourable to significant domestic investment by individuals. With government borrowing growing (negative government saving) the capital market depended upon corporate savings at a time when resource-based companies, which were experiencing falling prices in their basic commodities, accounted for around half the market capitalisation of the JSE.

Although 'the bond market sets the benchmark for expected returns in all markets and so determines the cost of capital, or the required returns, in all markets for all classes of investment',[4] the return upon equities in the 1990s was very much less than that on bonds. In real terms it was 3.2 per cent on equities, compared with 5.3 per cent on bonds in the period 1990–96. Then, at the time of the technology bubble, the real return on equities fell to 2.0 per cent, while that on bonds rose to 12.2 per cent.[5] Evidently the bond benchmark was not very effective in these years in guiding investment decisions. This suggests that there was a surplus of capital chasing relatively few investment opportunities on the JSE, at a time when inflationary expectations were driving investors away from the bond market. What is clear, though, is that currency and inflation volatility increased after 1996 and that the yield on bonds reacted slowly to the decline in the rate of inflation.[6] Inflation began to decline in 1993, the yield on bonds only in 1999. One could therefore argue that declining mineral prices, on which much of the economy rested, accompanied by irrational exuberance in the technology and media sectors, determined the rate of return on equities in the 1990s.

The government did little to encourage saving in these years. Its policy of forcing the telephone company to install phones in uneconomic areas and pressuring the banks to allow persons of little substance to open accounts tended to encourage spending, though in

2 Brian Kantor, 'Trevor Manuel and the markets', in Raymond Parsons (ed.), *Manuel, Markets and Money*, Double Storey, 2004, p. 151.

3 *Quarterly Bulletin*, South African Reserve Bank, March 2003.

4 Kantor, 'Trevor Manuel and the markets', p. 140.

5 *Ibid.*, pp. 131, 134.

6 *Ibid.*, pp. 134, 135.

2000 the capital gains tax and the disastrous tax on pension funds had not yet been introduced.

This somewhat unfavourable domestic background to the capital market in the 1990s was overshadowed in the second half of the decade by the great boom in telecommunications and information technology that began in the USA and swept over the whole world. With Vodacom effectively controlled by Vodafone in England and Telkom, the main opportunity for South African investors resided in MTN, which was slow to get off the ground, leaving the field free for information technology companies to bring real growth to the market, until the crash at the end of the first quarter of 2000 signalled the end of the boom in information technology. Realism replaced public relations propaganda and the share prices of information technology companies collapsed, with those of the leading companies, such as Dimension Data and Datatec, eventually falling by over 95 per cent. Persetel-Comparex, once the market leader, went out of existence. Ephemeral though many of the information technology companies were, their meteoric rise dazzled the financial community for three or four years. The accompanying boom in media companies and new financial institutions was completely overshadowed by the growth in both the size and the number of information technology companies. The JSE provided a good barometer of the impact of the new globalisation upon South Africa with the increase both in the volume of business flowing through the Exchange and in its market capitalisation.

South Africa's full reintegration into the international economy occurred at a time of extraordinary growth and speculation in world stock markets. This caught the imagination of the South African financial community to such an extent that one major development took place almost unnoticed. The JSE was being marginalised. The communist-dominated ANC government may not have copied the example of Samora Machel in Mozambique by overthrowing capitalism and destroying the economy, but the risk of doing business in South Africa was perceived to have increased. Anglo American had tried to operate a multinational business from its Minorco base in Luxembourg with only moderate success. The combination of perceived political risks and domestic exchange controls had made it difficult to operate a multinational organisation from within South Africa. This did not change in 1994. As a result, some of the leading JSE-based companies transferred their headquarters to London, led by Billiton, Anglo American, South African Breweries and Old Mutual. For a brief moment Dimension Data joined their ranks, when its London listing in 2000 gave it a market capitalisation that placed it among the top 100 companies listed there. Richemont, based in Switzerland, had already taken over the non-South

African interests of the Rembrandt group and placed them outside the control of the South African authorities. By the end of the decade, therefore, the two largest mining houses, the largest life insurance company, the largest information technology firm, the largest tobacco firm and breweries had 'internationalised' themselves and abandoned their South African base for the greener pastures of London and Switzerland. Investec and Datatec were pressing on their heels, but in 2000 they had not yet managed to move out of South Africa. Even so, by the end of 2000 the JSE's position in the international economy was much diminished.

The decline in the importance of the JSE was accompanied by a decline in the influence of Anglo American and the Oppenheimer family. In the 1980s it was reputed that Anglo American and the Oppenheimers controlled between 65 and 80 per cent of the market capitalisation of the JSE,[7] at a time when the Oppenheimers owned a mere 8 per cent of Anglo American. Financial sanctions, together with a perceived increase in the risk of doing business in South Africa, had resulted in the largest of the mining finance houses becoming an enormous unwieldy conglomerate. It was not a healthy development, as it restricted competition and gave one company too much control over large sections of the economy. It was the result of the combination of exchange controls and the peculiarly complicated structure of the Oppenheimers' investments, which were based on using the two dominant companies in the group to control them. The Oppenheimers had used the resources of Anglo American to control De Beers and then used De Beers to control Anglo American. In this way, shareholders' money was used to maintain control firmly in the hands of the Oppenheimer family. This symbiotic relationship ended when the Oppenheimers decided to convert De Beers into a private company. This required them to increase their holding in De Beers to 47.5 per cent and to reduce their holding in Anglo American to a mere 2 per cent. Both companies moved their administrative headquarters to London, where the former dominant JSE company itself became a takeover target. Ironically, therefore, while the reduction in the influence of the Oppenheimer family and Anglo American might be seen as a move to a more democratic structure within South Africa, it has also been accompanied by increasing dependence upon overseas investors, whose interest in short-term profits might conflict with the long-term investment needs of the country. Before 1994 the main focus of the mining finance houses, Old Mutual and South African Breweries was on South Africa. By 2000 this was not the case.

7 Jones, 'The financial sector', p. 178.

Growth of business on the JSE

Growth occurred across a broad front in the 1990s, though this was most striking in the market capitalisation and volume of business passing through the Exchange. Political uncertainties were holding back growth at the beginning of the decade. It took off as the Kempton Park discussions between the government and the ANC got underway. Then, in one year, from December 1992 to December 1993, the market capitalisation of the JSE almost doubled. In no other year did such growth occur, though at the height of the technology bubble in 1999 it reached 61 per cent. Table 12.1 provides the details.

Table 12.1 *Market capitalisation of the JSE, 1990–2000*

Year (December)	*Capitalisation (R millions)*
1990	304,789
1991	340,079
1992	336,643
1993	646,946
1994	815,997
1995	893,092
1996	1,129,949
1997	1,129,362
1998	1,001,343
1999	1,616,207
2000	1,551,489

Source: Dr Auret and I-Net Bridge.

However, when current prices are adjusted to take into account inflation, the figures of growth are not so dramatic. Instead of increasing fivefold over the 1990s, the market capitalisation of the JSE only doubled. Declines occurred in six of the 10 years. Venture capital raised in the market achieved the greatest growth, rising by 11,551 per cent to reach R4,046 million in 1998. Industrials, by comparison, rose by a mere 160 per cent, above that of the JSE as a whole but well below that of the financial sector, which had risen by 673 per cent by the end of 1998. With resources struggling in the 1990s, a time of falling prices, the gold mining sector of the JSE achieved a growth in current prices of only 5.5 per cent, which of course represented a considerable fall in real terms. Diamonds paralleled gold, growing by 13 per cent and experiencing much greater volatility in price than the gold mining sector. The diamond sector, dominated by De Beers, had a greater value than the gold mines sector in five of the nine years from 1990 to 1998, which helps to explain the Oppenheimers' decision to move out of gold and focus on diamonds.

With low mineral prices and the technology bubble the determining influences on the JSE once the fear of civil war had receded, the boom in information technology, telecommunications and media shares captured the newspaper headlines. A few individuals became very wealthy and many people lost a lot of money. Dimension Data became an international company with its headquarters in London, as realism gave way to irrational exuberance and price earnings multiples rose to stratospheric levels. By 15 February 2000, 11 information technology companies had market values of over R1 billion, with astronomical price–earnings ratios.[8] Dimension Data was valued at R35,199 million, with a price–earnings ratio of 60.0. That of Idion, a darling of the media, rose to 119.7 and that of another favourite, I-Exchange, to 99.0. These were unsustainable and by the end of the year many of the new firms had left the scene. Large though the valuation of the information technology firms was, in February 2000 it accounted for only around 5 per cent of the market capitalisation of the JSE. It had, however, together with that of the financial sector, tended to cover up the diminished international importance of Johannesburg, before the impact of a declining gold price, a declining gold output and firms moving to London.

Another factor that influenced the market capitalisation of the JSE was the growth of the financial sector. This was partly in line with international developments overseas, but was also boosted in South Africa by the demutualisation of life assurance companies. Old Mutual and Sanlam, with valuations of R59,936 million and R21,104 million respectively in August 2000, made a considerable impact upon the financial sector.[9]

Yet, in December 1998, before the two life insurance companies were listed on the Exchange, the financial sector had risen in value by 672.7 per cent, from R40,096.8 million in 1990 to R309,809.0 million in 1998,[10] with a value 70 per cent greater than that of diamonds, gold mines and mining financials added together. The growth of the big five commercial banks and the focused merchant banks, such as Investec, Rand Merchant Bank and BOE, were the main driving force behind this development. They were assisted by the appearance of a number of new financial intermediaries and the demutualisation of some of the smaller life assurance companies.[11]

8 *Financial Mail*, 18 February 2000.
9 *Financial Mail*, 25 August 2000.
10 *Annual Reports*, JSE, 1990, 1998.
11 See Chapter 11.

Growth in the JSE was most dramatically revealed in the growth of the business flowing through the market. Turnover rose by 2,268 per cent, from R23,677 million in 1990 to R536,877 million in 2000 (Table 12.2). As with capitalisation, turnover began to increase in 1993, with the largest increase occurring in the following year, when it rose by 83.3 per cent. The second most rapid increase occurred in 1996, the year when interest in information technology shares began to quicken and when Manuel became Minister of Finance and put aside the communist rhetoric that had accompanied his rise in the ANC before 1994. Even in real terms, the increase in turnover was massive, 796 per cent. Most of the increase occurred in the second half the decade: between 1990 and 1995 the increase was 167 per cent, compared with 749 per cent between 1995 and 2000. The driving force behind this expansion was exogenous. It was the global economy, which is why the bulk of the business flowing through the JSE, by the end of the decade, originated in London. The movement of some of the country's largest companies to London consequently had the effect of reinforcing an existing trend: the emergence of a handful of capital mega-markets. The globalisation of capital markets was in turn boosted by the boom in technology shares that coloured the second half of the decade.

Table 12.2 *Turnover of the JSE, 1990–2000*[a]

Year	*Turnover (R millions)*
1990	23,677
1991	22,231
1992	21,740
1993	34,127
1994	62,542
1995	63,247
1996	117,099
1997	206,542
1998	319,334
1999	448,381
2000	536,877

[a] Excluding arbitrage business.
Source: Dr Auret and I-Net Bridge and JSE.

The full extent of South Africa's reintegration into the world markets is revealed in the figures of foreign purchases and sales of JSE-listed companies. From 1993, purchases exceeded sales and by 2000 they were 62 times larger than in 1991. Sales followed a similar pattern, rising to almost 22 times their level of 1991. Volatility was increasing. In 1994, the year of the election, sales were more than double those of 1993 and purchases were almost double those of 1993. In 1991 total foreign purchases and sales had amounted to 40.7 per cent of turnover, so that even in the sanctions era the impact of sanctions was limited. By 2000 the foreign proportion had risen to 55.5 per cent. A mere 36 per cent increase in the foreign business of the JSE at the time of the technology bubble may perhaps give us a rough idea of the limited effect of sanctions at the beginning of the decade.

It is not the change in the foreign proportion that is important, it is the volume (Table 12.3). Not only had turnover increased substantially but, by the end of the 1990s, the bulk of the business of the JSE had ceased to originate in South Africa. It was foreign based and South African capital markets were more vulnerable than ever to movements and trends in overseas capital markets.

Table 12.3 *Foreign purchases and sales on the JSE, 1991–2000*

Year	*Purchases (R millions)*	*Sales (R millions)*
1991	2,544	6,496
1992	4,865	5,345
1993	11,664	8,855
1994	22,427	22,242
1995	25,148	19,336
1996	41,524	36,270
1997	79,515	53,314
1998	112,071	69,785
1999	143,964	103,306
2000	157,797	104,375

Source: N. C. Cooper, Director, Kagiso Securities Ltd, and *Annual Report*, JSE, 1991.

The increasing importance of foreign purchases and sales of JSE-listed securities did not make the JSE one the world's major exchanges. Indeed, by world standards the JSE was a relatively small market. In August 1999 its turnover was less than a third that of Greece, a twelfth that of South Korea and a thirteenth that of Taiwan.[12] It was even lower than the turnover of Brazil's stock exchange. Increased foreign interest in the JSE did not transform it into one of the world's major markets.

Nor was growth in the volume of business accompanied by growth in the number of securities traded. These, in 1991, numbered 740 and in 2000, 616. The number fell steadily in the first half of the decade and rose

12 Jones, 'The financial sector', p. 191.

only briefly at the height of technology bubble in 1997 and 1998. This further increased the weighting of the handful of large multinational conglomerates that dominated the market.

Table 12.4 *Capital raised from new issues on the JSE, 1990–2000*

Year	*Capital raised (R millions)*
1990	8,060
1991	9,637
1992	12,304
1993	13,558
1994	9,988
1995	19,495
1996	28,399
1997	49,862
1998	66,749
1999	39,109
2000	71,498

Source: N. C. Cooper, Director, Kagiso Securities Ltd, and *Annual Report*, JSE, 1991.

New issues and new capital raised (Table 12.4) also grew substantially, though proportionately not as rapidly as turnover, rising by less than a factor of 7.5, from R9,637 million in 1991 to R71,498 million in 2000. The latter sum suggests that the local capital market was able to provide a substantial proportion of the economy's needs for development purposes, even those of the electricity sector if the government had allowed it. Both Vodacom and MTN raised large amounts of capital for their telecommunication networks and showed how much more efficient private enterprise was than public enterprise in meeting market demands.

Like other world stock exchanges, the JSE in 1990 was a private association of individual members. Companies could not become members and partnerships could not incorporate themselves. It was the same with the bar and the legal profession in much of the English-speaking world. This changed in the 1990s. In 1996 the JSE allowed corporations to become members and by the end of the decade only one of the former stockbroking firms remained. Banks and financial institutions of all kinds were admitted, so that by 2000 the 392 members of 1991 had been replaced by 79 firms. The JSE had been partially transformed. Tax considerations and a desire to take one's capital out of the exchange for investment elsewhere rather than a growth in business were the driving forces behind this development. Full transformation was to come in the next decade with the dematerialisation of share certificates and the incorporation of the JSE itself on the Exchange.

Conclusion

The ending of the political campaigns against South Africa in 1993–94 led to the international economy exerting a greater impact upon the country. In practice this meant that South African companies could move overseas more easily and foreign companies could move into South Africa. Foreign-generated business on the JSE accordingly expanded significantly and more than made up for the falling domestic savings rate and the rise in government borrowing that was taking money out of the capital market. Indeed, foreign purchases and sales of JSE-listed equities counterbalanced the dismal performance of the domestic economy in this decade and provided the backdrop for the technology bubble that engulfed the Exchange during the last third of the decade, when asset price inflation began to replace monetary inflation as the dominant market characteristic. Considerable amounts of new capital were raised, but much of this was for the purchase of existing assets rather than for new development. The combination of foreign interest and the technology bubble also tended to direct attention away from the massive decline that occurred in the 1990s in the gold mining sector – the sector that had enabled South Africa to play above its weight in world markets for almost a century.

In the last decade of the twentieth century private enterprise responded in a myriad of ways to the market opportunities presented by the collapse of Soviet communism and the new political dispensation in South Africa. In the process, local firms moved their head offices out of South Africa and established branches overseas, while a bevy of dynamic local entrepreneurs hastened to join in the great technology boom that was sweeping across the globe. As a result, competition increased, with its rewards of greater efficiency both to the economy in general and to the JSE in particular. The efficiency gains in the capital market, however, could not make up for the decline taking place in agriculture, in mining struggling under the impact of falling mineral prices, and in manufacturing before the impact of globalisation, less protection and the labour legislation introduced by Tito Mboweni as Minister of Labour in Mandela's government. Such an environment did not encourage large-scale local saving. It does, though, help to explain why the turnover of the JSE was increasingly generated overseas; but nothing could make up for the declining output of the gold mines, which, in the 1990s, was heralding the end of a century of world importance for both South Africa and the JSE.

13

The information technology sector: riding the roller coaster

Stuart Jones

Introduction

The boom in information technology (IT) was late in coming to South Africa and lasted barely five years, from the last quarter of 1995 to the year 2000. Even in this brief period there was one sharp correction, at the end of August 1998, when many of the newer and smaller IT firms went out of business, along with a number of the newer financial institutions. The warning administered by this first crash went unheeded by the market and the pundits of the 'new economy'. When growth reasserted itself a few months later, it was forgotten and South Africa along with the rest of the world rode the boom into its final hectic last 12 months. Even then the end was not universally recognised and both economists and journalists were hoping for a recovery early in 2001. In the event, the full effect of the collapse in market demand in 2000 was not felt until the following year, when the fall in turnover and profits was revealed. With the collapse of the technology bubble went all talk of a new economy, escaping from the confines of the business cycle and a US move to a long-term higher growth rate.

South Africa's fate was to be embraced by the international economy in its new aggressively expanding stance just after the 1994 election, which replaced the former white government with an African National Congress (ANC)/Communist one. This embrace occurred on the eve of the IT boom and provided South Africa with a veritable baptism of fire that may be compared to the great gold mining mania of 1895, or that of Wall Street in 1929. In both 1929 and 2000, warnings were ignored: in the case of the former, the market slippage of 1928; in the case of South Africa, the UK and the USA, the price collapse of 1998. This confirms the view that, when a speculative boom is approaching its climax, rational thought is overwhelmed by what US Treasury Secretary Alan Greenspan termed irrational exuberance.

Yet there are major differences between the crashes of 1929 and 2000. After 1929 US policy played the major role in driving the global economy into recession. After 2000 US policy played the major role in preventing the global economy from sliding into recession. As a result, the world economy continued growing and globalisation is more pervasive today than ever before. It is this period of steady growth after 2000 (Japan and Germany excepted) that provides us with the perspective to see both the real economic growth and the extent of the bubble in the last five years of the twentieth century.

The IT boom of the 1990s was an example of extraordinary economic growth driven by unparalleled innovation in the North American market.[1] Efficient economic organisation in an environment that guarantees property rights leads to economic growth, which, in the 1990s, was associated with rapid technological change and innovation. Technological progress is not something that occurs accidentally; it is the result of prior investment in technological know-how, manufacturing experience and market research. In a suitable economic environment this will lead to innovation, which is widely believed to account for over half of all economic growth – hence the emphasis, in recent years, on the importance of entrepreneurs, the men and women who put into practice the breakthroughs in technology and organisation. This has led some economists to float the idea that innovation is a fourth factor of production.

What is clear is that the production of entrepreneurs is not spread evenly around the globe: some societies are more likely to produce them than others. Such societies are likely to be those that foster competition, have invested heavily in education and have secure property rights. At the level of individual enterprises, those that encourage innovation systematically and support individuals who are internally driven (by a desire for power, money or simply to prove themselves) are likely to produce entrepreneurs and reap the benefits of innovation.

South Africa, with its long statist history of government intervention in the economy, was less favourably situated for the production of entrepreneurs than North America and other more market-friendly countries, but it was very much more favourably placed than any other African country or, indeed, any Latin American or Arab country. Since the discovery of diamonds, South Africa has been a country that has rewarded its successful entrepreneurs handsomely. Admittedly, a communist-dominated government was a cause of concern after 1994; but in the 1990s the financial sector was strong, property rights (with

1 For example, one firm, American Telephone and Telegraph, at the Bell Laboratories in New Jersey was responsible for developing: the transistor, the laser, fibre optics, the solar cell, the communications satellite and digital transmission.

a few exceptions) were still secure and the educational system was producing a flow of well qualified graduates. Excessive affirmative action and the legal compulsion to hand over a fixed proportion of one's property to black-owned firms lay in the future in 1990, and even in 2000 it was still not much more than a dark cloud on the horizon. Once the fear of revolution had receded after the 1994 election, the stage was set for exogenous forces to trigger the IT boom that brought the global economy well and truly to South Africa.

The early 1990s

In 1990 the South African market did not make a clear distinction between IT firms and general electronic businesses, many of which owned IT subsidiaries. Moreover, in 1990 the electronics sector was in the midst of a five-year slump that lasted from 1987 to 1992, after the ending of the mini-boom associated with computers that had been one of the few growth sectors in the 1980s. The recovery that began in the last quarter of 1992 was led by electronic firms generally rather than by IT firms and it stalled in 1993, along with the rest of the economy.

In 1990, manufacturing operations along the lines of the big US companies, such as IBM, Microsoft, Oracle, Dell or Hewlett Packard, were not possible in South Africa. The market was too small and the pool of talent too limited. Nor was the environment conducive to enterprise. For far too long the South African market had been dominated by uncompetitive practices and large conglomerates that tended to discourage innovation and competition at a time when the new technology-based industries were thriving on competition. Excessive regulation, overlarge conglomerates and exchange controls would have impeded the growth of the 'new economy' in South Africa even if the market had been large enough to support a technology manufacturing base.

As a result, in the years when the internet was taking shape, the IT industry in South Africa was dynamic only in parts. In June 1993 the 'Top companies' supplement of the *Financial Mail* listed nine IT firms. Of these, four were to be delisted in 1993–95: Persetech, SPL, Datakor and Elcentre. The remaining five, in order of market capitalisation, were: ISG, Siltek, Dimension Data, Fintech and Q Data. One major new firm, Persetel, had appeared by December 1993. Persetel was founded out of the delisted Persetech, which was sponsored by Barlow Rand (South Africa's biggest manufacturing company), one of its two major shareholders. It had been closely involved with the electronics side of the armaments industry. It was growing rapidly, too, with contracts from the national telephone monopoly. By the end of December 1993 its market capitalisation had overtaken that of Q Data and it was on course to become, for a short while, the country's leading wealth creator. In 1993 and 1994, though, the rapid growth of Persetel and Dimension Data was the exception. In the period 1990–94, Dimension Data's operating profit rose by 29.3 per cent annually, but operating profit per employee declined by 2.6 per cent annually, as the number of employees increased from 184 to 574.

It was in this period too that the IT section of the electronics sector began to separate itself from the rest of the sector, namely telecommunications (MTN and Vodacom opened for business in 1994), defence work, consumer electronics, commercial electronics and electrification. Many firms, such as Barlows and Altron, engaged in a number of these activities and were adapting to the new conditions by creating separate IT subsidiaries.

There are hints of future growth in what was happening in the first four years of the decade. The independent IT firms, such as Dimension Data as well as the recent arrivals Persetel and Q Data, were growing rapidly. Others grew more slowly, such as Fintech, controlled by William Venter's Altron Group, Grintek by Anglovaal, Datakorp by Sankorp and ISG and Persetech, both controlled by Barlow Rand. Their background was not particularly conducive to the production of dynamic entrepreneurs, which is one of the reasons why so many of the IT firms had difficulty when they moved overseas into more competitive environments.

Nevertheless, in the early 1990s internal competition was increasing as the big electronic groups sought to expand their IT operations. Barlow Rand's Persetech derived most of its income from selling and servicing Hitachi mainframe computers, but its growth occurred at the expense of the subsidiary ISG, which sold IBM products. These moves into the market for software and services pointed the way to future growth. Already, networking was attracting the attention of some of the IT companies. Datatec Networking and Communications was established in 1987 when Jens Montanana (its founder) returned to South Africa with qualifications in electronic engineering; but at this juncture he did not stay, preferring to return overseas until after the 1994 election. Significantly, the infant Datatec incorporated UUNet Africa, which had grown out of the acquisition of Internet Africa and Datatec's joint venture with Unipalm-Pipex of the UK. The timing was propitious. In 1993 the IT market was forecast to grow at between 14 and 15 per cent annually.[2]

At the time of the 1994 general election it was estimated that the electronics sector was an R15 billion a year industry and that the IT section

2 'Top companies', *Financial Mail*, 25 June 1993.

accounted for a little under half of it. Dimension Data and Q Data had established solid track records and Persetel was growing rapidly; but some of the older companies, which had adapted too late to the new environment, fell by the way.

With the ending of sanctions and new international respectability after the election, two developments took place in the South African IT sector: local firms were listed on the Johannesburg Stock Exchange (JSE); and foreign firms moved into South Africa. Montanana returned to the country and Datatec was listed on the JSE in December 1994, while Digital Equipment, Sun Microsystems, Apple, Microsoft, IBM and Lotus all opened offices for business in South Africa. Many of them followed the example of IBM and linked up with local firms. As a result the middle years of the decade witnessed a significant increase in competition that, according to Venter, required local firms 'to improve their management and operational efficiencies and develop new domestic and international markets if they were to remain competitive'.[3]

The golden age of information technology in South Africa, 1994–98

The changed political environment in South Africa was a necessary precondition for the rapid expansion of the IT sector, but it was not a sufficient condition. The driving force behind the extraordinary expansion of the IT industry was exogenous to South Africa: the coming of the boom depended upon events unfolding in the USA, at a time when the global economy was adjusting to both the collapse of the Soviet Union and the abandonment of economic communism by China. By the last quarter of 1995 the internet had assumed its modern shape and Microsoft was on the way to becoming a household name, as its software began to dominate the market.

The imminent arrival of the boom in South Africa was not foreseen by leading IT entrepreneurs in South Africa. The *Financial Mail* was arguing in June 1995 that the IT market had marked a turning point in the last six months of 1994, while Jeremy Ord, the founder of Dimension Data, was saying that the IT industry appeared to have moved into a more mature phase in 1995, after a high-growth phase in the 1980s.[4] Yet by the end of 1995 the market in LANs (local area networks) was growing at 80 per cent a year and that in WANs (wide area networks) at 30 per cent a year! In this rapidly changing environment, Persetel,

3 'Top companies', *Financial Mail*, 24 June 1994, p. 135.
4 *Ibid.*, p. 158.

Dimension Data, Datatec and Q Data were the leaders; but in June 1996 the 'Top companies' supplement of the *Financial Mail* was still reflecting earlier views and informing its readers that the electronics and electrical sector of the JSE had not yet regained the status it held in 1995.[5] This comment occurred after the share price of Persetel had rocketed from below R10 at the beginning of April to R16 two weeks later! The purchase of a 40 per cent holding in Cornparex in Germany was the cause of this development. The boom was in fact already gathering pace. Networking was forecast to grow at 25 per cent a year until the end of the decade[6] and IT expenditure was forecast to rise from R11 billion in 1994 to R20 billion in 1998.[7]

The high-growth areas of the IT market were: networking, outsourcing, services and software. The provision of services in practice meant the distribution and installation of software and hardware. Persetel, for example, distributed Hitachi mainframes in South Africa and continued to function in this manner when it bought into Comparex in Germany. All the leading IT firms sought to move up-market, from merely selling products to providing higher-value services. This, however, was easier said than done and for most of the 1990s the leading IT firms continued to draw the major portion of their revenues from marketing the products of international technology.

Major changes occurred in the IT sector in 1996. In that year there was a sustained effort by the leading firms to move into value-added activities as opposed to merely selling software, as increasing competition steadily forced down margins. Persetel, for example, pulled out of distribution and Dimension Data took over the information systems of Automakers, the Nissan holding company. Subcontracting, outsourcing in IT speak, expanded rapidly; it was estimated to be worth R500 million a year in 1996 and by 2000 was forecast to reach R4 billion, a 700 per cent increase in four years!

Also in 1996 the more enterprising of the IT firms sought to expand overseas. The publicly stated reason was the small size of the South African market and the opportunities overseas for dynamic entrepreneurs. The unstated reason was the desire to spread one's risks out of Africa, given the record of mismanagement by the countries north of the Limpopo and the constraints of exchange control. Persetel led the way with its acquisition of 40 per cent of Comparax in Germany in April. Dimension Data followed in August with the acquisition of 45 per cent of Com Tech Communications in Australia, and Datatec in May 1997 with

5 'Top companies', *Financial Mail*, 28 June 1996, p. 161.
6 Citing Da Silva of Smith, Borkum Hare.
7 Citing BMI Technology.

the acquisition of Logical Networks in the UK. Within the space of two years all three had transformed themselves into international companies that derived the bulk of their revenues from outside South Africa.

The answer to the question 'What made this possible?' seems to lie in what was happening both outside South Africa, in the global economy, and inside the country. Outside South Africa the pace of technological change in the USA was transforming international communications. Microsoft became a household name and the internet an established fact. In 1994, when South Africa was still suffering from embargoes and international sanctions, the domestic IT industry lagged behind developments in Europe and America. Nevertheless, the business and educational background in South Africa was sufficiently in tune with modern economic developments for it to produce home-grown entrepreneurs. These were the people who spotted the market opportunities and had the drive and business ability to establish companies. Montanana of Datatec additionally possessed technical ability as a trained electronics engineer. These conditions also applied to the UK and Australia, which, relatively, did not produce so many dynamic entrepreneurs in the 1990s. The explosive entry of South African IT companies into the global economy may perhaps be explained by the release of energies that had been bottled up in the country for so long. International respectability was a new phenomenon, which allowed this energy to be channelled into global expansion. The big mining houses, Old Mutual and South African Breweries followed the IT companies out of South Africa, but theirs were not new growth industries. They were very large, capital-rich corporations that needed to be based in a financial centre free from exchange controls.

Eventually Dimension Data felt obliged to follow this route; but in the period 1996–98 this was not yet an option and all the South African IT firms had to struggle to raise capital overseas. The Manuel mantra that exchange controls had virtually gone is not true. South African corporations could not purchase foreign corporations with their shares. They had to use cash, which they could not take out of South Africa. This forced them to borrow in the host country at relatively high rates of interest. While this might have acted as a permanent spur to efficiency, it also placed South African companies at the mercy of interest rate changes, as SAPPI found out to its cost. Conversely, foreign companies could not buy up South African companies with their shares. They, too, had to pay cash. It is, therefore, all the more remarkable that so many South African IT firms were able to expand overseas in the closing years of the century.

Notwithstanding the exchange difficulties, expansion overseas continued to gather pace throughout 1996 and 1997 and the leading IT companies managed to combine the attractions of a rand hedge

Table 13.1 *Market capitalisation of leading IT companies on the JSE, 1993–98*

Company (in order of listing)	*1993, 20 December*	*1994, 19 December*	*1995, 27 December*	*1996, 30 December*	*1997, 30 December*	*1998, 14 December*
Siltek	452.2	778.0	1,355.2	1,616.7	316.2	359.1
ISG	490.0	803.0				
Datakor	294.7					
Elcentre	272.3					
SPL	121.3	95.3				
Fintech	365.0	582.4	899.9	826.9	1,078.5	566.9
Q Data	211.8	453.4	739.9	2,770.2		
Dimension Data	422.1	586.6	1,936.5	6,135.9	11,895.3	13,823.1
Spescom			116.2	207.1	245.9	517.6
Persetel/ Comparex	363.4	695.9	1,202.1	6,974.5	8,610.0	14,703.2
Datatec		69.0	165.0	516.8	2,020.0	5,865.1
MGX			116.2	375.6	718.5	959.4
Mustek					763.8	789.2
Softline					537.2	1,927.4
Ixchange						1,370.2
CC Holdings					337.4	1,786.8
Connections					162.0	291.5
Datacentrix	2,720.5	40,640.0	6,531.0	19,423.7	26,684.8	129.7
Total						43,089.2

Source: Financial Mail, various issues.

investment with that of a high-growth industry. Overseas expansion of a truly entrepreneurial kind not only enabled some of the IT firms to experience very rapid growth, it also altered their relative position in the domestic pecking order. When Datatec was listed on the JSE in December 1994, its market capitalisation was a mere R69 million. At that time nine other companies had larger capitals, led by ISG with R803 million and Siltek with R778 million. Siltek had fallen behind and ISG had been delisted by 1996, when the expansion overseas began that transformed first Persetel, then Dimension Data and finally Datatec. Table 13.1 shows how this occurred.

The moves overseas coincided with continued rapid growth at home (Table 13.2). Persetel was still heavily committed to selling mainframes in Germany and South Africa and heavily dependent upon contracts with the Post Office in South Africa and the Bundespost in Germany. Dimension Data had been organised into three divisions: communications, value-added services and software. The first of these led to the acquisition of ComTech and Datecraft Australia, the second to the

Table 13.2 *Growth rates (%) in market capitalisation of leading IT companies, 1993–98*

	Persetel/ Comparex	*Dimension Data*	*Datatec*	*All companies*
1993–94	91.5	39.0	–	49.4
1994–95	72.9	230.0	139.1	60.7
1995–96	479.7	216.9	304.1	197.4
1996–97	23.4	93.7	291.0	37.2
1997–98	70.8	24.7	190.3	65.2
1993–98	109.6	103.8	203.6	74.6

formation of EDS–Africa, a joint venture between Dimension Data and EDS of Dallas (the firm founded by Ross Perot) and the third to the acquisition of SPL in 1996. Q Data, a firm put together in 1992 by Roux Marnitz, out of seven companies specialising in payroll systems, was also growing very rapidly in 1996–97.

With public confidence in the new economy rising and the JSE reflecting this confidence, Datatec's share price rose from R28 at the end of October 1997 to R76 at the end of March 1998 and to R126 at the end of August 1998. It had replaced Persetel/Comparex as the market leader. Yet at the World Electronic Forum held in Tel Aviv in June 1998, South Africa was singled out as having the 'worst possible profile for investment in the electronics industry', because of a shortage of both skilled personnel and venture capital.[8] Intel's vice-president also noted that South Africa was not very competitive, ranked 44 out of 55 countries. South Africa lagged behind in the adoption of e-mail and the use of the worldwide web. In 1998 South African per capita spending on IT was only one-fifth of that of Europe and a mere 9 per cent that of the USA, but this is understandable given the large semi-subsistence agricultural sector.

In the developed sector, the country compared favourably with Europe. On the eve of the first IT market crash, at the end of August 1998, the two-year lag in adopting new technology of 1990 had fallen to a few weeks. In a couple of years, 1996–98, South Africa had caught up with Europe[9] and by 1998 South Africa was estimated to be spending R57 billion a year on IT, compared with R18.6 billion in 1992. As a proportion of GDP, in 1998 South Africa may have been investing half as much again as Europe. It rose from 2.9 per cent in 1997 to 6.9 per

8 'Top companies', *Financial Mail*, 26 June 1998, p. 198.
9 *Ibid.*

cent in 1998.[10] Though large by South African standards, it formed only a tiny proportion of total global spending on IT, in dollar terms less than $10 billion out of a total of $1.8 trillion. The new political dispensation undoubtedly played a major role in bringing about the growing investment in IT in South Africa in the later 1990s, assisted of course by the country's notorious labour laws, which encouraged employers to replace labour with capital.

Total IT spending in South Africa did not necessarily benefit South African IT companies. The bulk of the spending, including that of the government, went to multinational corporations. There is, therefore, some truth in the oft-repeated assertion that it was the small size of the market that drove South African companies to move out of the country. These were the dynamic companies that focused on software and its applications. The strengths of software development in South Africa were summarised by Rainer Zinow, the vice-president of SAP, in 1999 as follows:[11]

- good skills available;
- high-quality universities;
- a low rand and a competitive currency;
- the use of English;
- the time zone.

It was these strengths that compensated to some extent for the small size of the market and allowed the emergence of a handful of enterprising firms that had developed their skills in South Africa and then felt strong enough to take on the world.

The opinion of the vice-president of SAP also contradicts the earlier view expressed at the Tel Aviv Forum that South Africa was suffering from a skills shortage. Evidently this no longer existed by the end of 1998, in a way that marked South Africa out as being noticeably different from other developed economies, where rising executives boosted their careers by 'company hopping' up the promotion ladder. The market in South Africa had responded energetically to the demands being placed upon it. In fact, the years between 1996 and 1998 might be considered the golden age of IT in South Africa. It was a period of rising expectations and growing confidence that a real new economy was being born, even though 80 per cent of the new strategic applications used in the country still ran on old mainframe platforms linked to up-to-date software.[12]

10 'Top companies', *Financial Mail*, 22 June 1990, p. 207.
11 'Top companies', *Financial Mail*, 25 June 1999, p. 211.
12 *Ibid.*

Some IT companies

From a possible skills shortage to skills available supported by high-quality universities, the picture of the IT market in South Africa had changed considerably in the two years from 1996 to 1998. Evidence of how this came about may be glimpsed in the experience of one or two of the leading companies. Few of the older firms that existed at the beginning of the decade were able to adapt to the more competitive and rapidly changing environment of the later 1990s. Siltek and Fintech, both controlled by Grinaker Holdings, struggled. The former was reorganised in 1997 and fell out of the mainstream of IT companies. Fintech did better, though its share price halved after the market collapse at the end of August 1998. Of the IT companies founded and listed in the 1980s, only Q Data, Dimension Data and Spescom prospered in the 1990s. Dimension Data made huge fortunes for its shareholders, as its share price rose almost 10-fold between 1990 and 1998 (Table 13.3). Persetel/Comparex made less money for its shareholders, its share price rising 11-fold in four years. Datatec, by comparison, showed very rapid growth in 1995 before its expansion overseas began and then again in the first half of 1998, when its share price more than trebled, to a peak of R126 in September.

Such massive growth in the value of IT companies listed on the JSE reflected both entrepreneurial vigour overseas and in the domestic industry. At a time of rapid inflation, currency depreciation and lingering concern over the future under a communist-dominated government, one of the key selling points for some IT shares was their rand hedge

Table 13.3 *Share prices (R) of selected IT companies, 1990–98*

Company	*1990*	*1993*	*1994*	*1995*	*1996*	*1997*	*1998*
Siltek	8.30	9.00	16.00	27.00	30.00	5.90	6.70
Fintech	4.25	30.00	47.00	70.00	69.00	87.00	4.55[a]
Qdata	2.15	13.00	27.00	39.00	11.80[a]	–	–
Dimension Data	2.40	15.50	27.00	47.50	14.00[a]	20.75	22.70
Spescom	0.26	0.90	2.70	3.85	6.45	6.40	10.75
Persetel/ Comparex	–	–	4.00	7.75	36.00	26.25	44.40
Datatec	–	–	2.35	8.00	16.10	40.00	65.30
MGX	–	–	–	4.40	13.00	20.40	23.25
Mustek	–	–	–	–	–	–	–
Softline	–	–	–	–	–	1.85	6.17
Ixchange	–	–	–	–	–	–	11.95

[a] Share split 10 for 1.
Source: Financial Mail, various issues.

status, which was superimposed upon their value as representatives of the new economy. This helps to explain the phenomenal increase in their market capitalisation. In the five years from December 1993 to 1998, over R41 billion was added to the value of IT companies listed on the JSE. The whole sector had grown at a rate of almost 75 per cent a year; but the companies that expanded overseas grew at a much faster rate, with Datatec leading the pack. Its market capitalisation grew on average by 203.6 per cent per annum (Table 13.3). While this did not equate with growth in South Africa, it did encourage trade in the company's shares on the JSE, which added to the profits of the banks and brokers providing the services.

Dimension Data, Persetel/Comparex and Datatec

A more accurate idea of the wealth created may be obtained from the performance and prices of some individual companies. Operating profit, referred to in some of the annual reports as trading profit or operating income, rose rapidly (Table 13.4), though not quite as rapidly as turnover (Table 13.5). Persetel/Comparex was unusual. It managed to increase operating profit at a faster rate than turnover: 49.7 per cent annually, as opposed to 49.4 per cent. Datatec, though, in its rapid pursuit of growth, saw operating profit growing more slowly than revenue: 138.7 per cent against 232.7 per cent. Profit may have been sacrificed to growth, but with an annual growth in operating profits of 138.7 per cent margins were not yet being squeezed. Admittedly, too, this growth came off a small base, an operating profit of R5.4 million in 1995. This then fell slightly in the year to 31 March 1996, before rising rapidly in the next two years to R73.4 million in the year ending 31 March 1998. By 31 March 1999 operating profit had reached R405.8 million and Datatec could boast of operating profit growing at an annual rate of 194.4 per cent! Headline earnings per share followed a similarly dramatic path (Table 13.6). Those of Dimension Data rose from 7 cents in 1993 to 52 cents in the year ending 30 September 1998; those of Persetel/Comparex from 0.24 cents to R1.05; and those of Datatec from 12 cents in 1996 to 0.87 cents in 1998 and 267 cents in 1999. The three companies had annual growth rates in earnings per share of 49.3 per cent, 34.3 per cent and 82.6 per cent respectively.

Wealth creation of this magnitude was not only unparalleled, but appeared to be based on the solid foundations of real earnings growth. The balance sheets of Dimension Data, Persetel/Comparex and Datatec provide evidence of this. Revenue grew very rapidly, with a marked acceleration about the time of the 1994 election. Dimension Data, for example, had a revenue of R218.4 million in the year ending

Table 13.4 *Operating profits and growth rates of Dimension Data, Persetel/Comparex and Datatec, 1993–2001*

Year ending	*Dimension Data*	*Persetel/Comparex*	*Datatec*
Operating profit (R)			
1993	24.2	43.5	–
1994	35.5	48.0	–
1995	82.7	64.9	5.4
1996	126.8	87.7	5.3
1997	226.5	146.3	19.1
1998	482.0	326.8	73.4
1999	764.2	431.5	405.8
2000	212.4	212.4	553.0
2001	180.9	254.0	889.0
Compound interest growth rates (%)			
1993–98	81.9	49.7	138.7[a]
1998–2001	34.0	–8.1	129.7
1993–2001	n.a.	24.7	134.1[b]

[a] 1995–98.
[b] 1995–2001.
Source: Company annual reports.

Table 13.5 *Revenue of Dimension Data, Persetel/Comparex and Datatec, 1993–2001*

Year ending	*Dimension Data, 30 September*	*Persetel/Comparex, 31 May*	*Datatec, 31 March*
Revenue (R millions)			
1993	147.7	571.3	–
1994	218.4	617.2	–
1995	719.8	775.8	37.3
1996	1,019.0	1,079.4	64.4
1997	1,670.3	1,666.3	463.9
1998	4,711.5	4,251.9	1,373.6
1999	6,697.1	7,681.3	6,640.8
2000	$1,976.5[a]	7,274.0	11,524.0
2001	2,460.3	5,389.8	20,158.0
Compound interest growth rates (%)			
1993–98	99.9	49.4	232.7
1998–2001	26.8	8.2	144.8
1993–2001	n.a.	32.4	185.4

[a] Dimension Data ceased presenting annual results in rands in 2000. With the rand depreciating rapidly against the dollar converting the year-end figure into rands is not very meaningful.
Source: Company annual reports.

Table 13.6 *Headline earnings (R) per share of Dimension Data, Persetel/Comparex and Datatec, 1993–2001*

Year ending	*Dimension Data, 30 September*	*Persetel/Comparex, 31 May*	*Datatec, 31 March*
1993	0.07	0.24	–
1994	0.09	0.25	0 [a]
1995	0.13	0.34	
1996	0.21	0.46	0.12
1997	0.32	0.65	0.39
1998	0.52	1.05	0.87
1999	0.82	–	2.67
2000	0.16	–	3.25
2001	0.13	–	3.76

[a] In 2001 all the earlier figures were adjusted downwards back to 1996. These are the 2001 figures.
[b] These figures are taken from the 1999 annual report.

30 September 1994 (Table 13.5). The following year, before the move overseas, this had exploded to R719.8 million and four years later in 1994 it rose to R6,697.1 million. By September 2000, when figures were presented in US dollars, revenue had expanded by a further 63.7 per cent. Persetel/Comparex followed a similar path, with growth accelerating in the second half of 1995 to reach its peak in the year 1 June 1997 to 31 May 1998. Datatec was a late starter, but already in the calendar year 1996 it too had experienced a massive growth in turnover, of 620 per cent in one year. Two years later, in 1998, Datatec again experienced a huge growth in revenue. Between 1993 and 1998 the revenues of Dimension Data and Persetel/Comparex grew at the rate of 99.9 per cent and 49.9 per cent, respectively, while Datatec's expanded by 232.7 per cent between 1995 and 1998! There was growth across a broad front in the new economy.

Growth of this magnitude inevitably resulted in bureaucratisation (Table 13.7). Dimension Data moved furthest along this route, with its number of employees rising from 391 in 1993 to 5,382 in 1998. Between 1994 and 1995 the number more than trebled and between 1996 and 1997 it doubled. Persetel/Comparex followed on Dimension Data's heels, with its largest increase occurring in the year ending 31 May 1998, when the number of staff more than quadrupled and revenue per employee declined by over a third. By the end of 1998 both Dimension Data and Persetel/Comparex had developed large and somewhat unwieldy bureaucracies, which should have raised some questions about the ability of founding entrepreneurs to manage large multinational organisations. In the event, Persetel/Comparex did not long survive its

Table 13.7 *Number of employees and revenue per employee of Dimension Data, Persetel/Comparex and Datatec, 1993–2001*

Year ending	*Dimension Data, 30 September*		*Persetel/Comparex, 31 May*		*Datatec, 31 March*	
	No. of employees	*Earnings (R)*	*No. of employees*	*Earnings (R)*	*No. of employees*	*Earnings (R)*
1993	391	378	n.a.	n.a.	n.a.	
1994	574	380	n.a.	n.a.	n.a.	n.a.
1995	1,894	380	n.a.	n.a.	57	655
1996	2,033	501	1,450	744	104	620
1997	4,122	405	1,676	994	507	915
1998	5,382	875	6,781	627	1,200	1,145
1999	7,767	862	8,692	884	2,913	2,280
2000	10,273	$192.4	7,423	980	4,135	2,787
2001	12,623	20	6,344	850	3,830	5,263
Growth rates (%) in revenue per employee						
1993–98		18.3		–8.2[a]		20.5[b]
1998–2001				10.7		66.3

[a] 1996–98.
[b] 1995–98.

reckless dash for growth and even Dimension Data found it advisable to replace Jeremy Ord, its founding entrepreneur, as chief executive. But in 1998 these developments still lay in the future. Rapid growth in revenue and operating profit enabled many mistakes to be covered up while the good times lasted. Datatec, a much smaller company, experienced a much higher rate of growth in the number of staff employed than its larger competitors. Its workforce mushroomed from 57 in 1995 to 1,2000 in 1998, with the most rapid growth occurring in 1996. Datatec experienced a fall in revenue per employee in the year ending 31 March 1996, though not nearly as great as that experienced by Persetel/Comparex in the year ending 31 May 1998, after its hasty expansion into Continental Europe. Dimension Data's progress was more erratic, with falls in revenue per employee occurring in 1992, 1993 and 1997 and virtually no growth in 1994 and 1995. As a result, between 1990 and 1998 turnover per employee was rising at an annual rate of 12 per cent a year, compared with a workforce growth of 52.5 per cent a year. Other figures also suggest that the seeds of future difficulties were being sown in these years. Andy Andrews and Ted Black made use of the return on assets managed (ROAM) to show that the decline started in 1996. ROAM fell from 20 per cent in 1996 to 5 per cent in 2000. This was the result of a decline in ATO (the ratio of sales divided by assets). Had the ROAM and ATO models been widely used in 1996, shareholders and asset managers might not have experienced the losses they did.[13] What is clear, though, is that all the IT companies found trading conditions outside South Africa more taxing than conditions within the country and that rapid expansion frequently had a negative impact upon profitability.

Datatec

The experience of Datatec shows us how a small company developed its business in the boom years 1996–98. Though founded back in 1988, Datatec became a holding company when it acquired UUNet Africa in 1994. Three small acquisitions followed in 1995 that positioned the company firmly in the networking and services market in preparation for the great expansion of 1996–98, which culminated in the purchase of Logical Networks in the UK for a price of £12 million cash plus a further £20 million. By the last quarter of 1997 Datatech was operating 11 subsidiary companies. Its major acquisition, Westcon in the USA, occurred in April 1998. This established Datatec as a major supplier of Cisco Systems equipment. By that date Datatec had 22 subsidiary companies and the company's focus was clear: it lay in distributing products from the world's leading vendors of networking equipment, such as Cisco Systems and Nortel Networks, in providing internet services and in moving into software development, training and integrations skills. To achieve this the company had created four divisions: products and distribution; software and services; internet and telecommunications; and international (divided into two sections, distribution and services). The first two of these divisions were the most important and were replicated in the international division. In South Africa, Datatec's Workgroup Distribution Unit claimed to have 60 per cent of the software distribution market. The Channel Retail Works Unit packaged products for the retail computer market; the US Robotics Division had the exclusive right to market Robotics computer modems; the Postec Unit focused on digital cameras, laser communications scanning for bar coding and wireless technology; and the fourth area of specialisation, the Datetec Distribution Network Division, comprised Data Connect and Netcorp. These combined, according to the 1997 annual report, 'the franchises of 3Com, Bay Networks and Motorola and other specialist remote-access and internet-working product lines into a single complete LAN/WAN networking operation'.

13 Andy Andrews and Ted Black, *Who Moved My Share Price? All Roads Lead to Roam or Ruin*, Jonathan Ball, 2002.

The software and services division was made up of: Datasoft; the Workgroup Institute; and Systems Education and Logical Network Services. The first of these provided integrated business solutions through a suite of software modules, the second provided technical training, and the third combined the business of Workgroup Technology with CCEB Integrated Solutions.

This divisional system worked well in 1996 and 1997, but needed to be changed in 1998 with the acquisition of Westcon, which was so much larger than all the other operating units. The company was now reorganised into two main operating divisions, Westcon and Logical, supported by an e-business solutions division. By the end of 1998 Datatec had assumed its modern shape and was well positioned to take advantage of the last 18 months of the 'new economy boom'. It was operating in 14 countries and generating 85 per cent of its revenue outside South Africa. Not surprisingly, most head office functions had been moved to London. Unlike Dimension Data, which developed a huge bureaucratic complex in Johannesburg, Datatec maintained a small head office in Johannesburg, where its annual general meetings were held in an extraordinarily informal manner.

The culmination of irrational exuberance, 1999–2000

By the end of 1998 the IT industry had come of age. The internet was an established fact, Windows was a household product, and software was widespread in the management of salaries, stock control, purchasing supplies, the control of sales and the storage of information. Both the typewriter and the card index were well on their way to obsolescence. South Africa had caught up with the rest of the developed world in its investment in the new technology and brought forth a number of internationally active companies. At the same time, wealth had been created on the JSE in ways not seen since the formation of the first gold mining companies a century earlier.

In the last two years of irrational exuberance, South Africa, like Europe and America, witnessed a flurry of new listings and market capitalisation rising to spectacular heights, along with a veritable avalanche of stock options for senior executives in the IT industry. The market crash at the end of August 1998 was soon forgotten and by early 1999 the new economy was bowling along in high gear. There were one or two warning signals. The financial sector had not recovered from the crash at the end of August 1998; nor had many of the smaller IT companies.

With the growth in IT spending in 1999 still rising and the companies reporting ever larger profits, market capitalisation raced to new heights.

Table 13.8 provides the details. Already Comparex, the leader of a year or two earlier, was falling out of the race. At the height of the boom 12 companies had market capitalisations of over R1 billion and Dimension Data was poised to list in London and become a member of the select group of 'blue chip' companies. Others had a very short life span. In December 1999, 47 companies were listed; one year later 49 companies were listed, evidence that new companies were being promoted right up to the moment of collapse. Aplitec, for instance, appeared in 2000 and had a market capitalisation of R576.8 million in December, only to be delisted a few years later. The figures of total market capitalisation showed no decline between December 1999 and December 2000, for one reason: Dimension Data. In that 12-month period Dimension Data had listed in London and raised additional capital there. As a result, its market capitalisation added over R41 billion at a time when many of its peers were collapsing, with the result that the total value of IT shares listed on the JSE rose from R85,817.5 million to R89,337.9 million. This state of affairs could not last, yet throughout 2000 many analysts continued to predict an upturn in the market in 2001. The severity of the collapse in confidence was underestimated. The capital destruction that followed was enormous. In the tax year March 2000–01, the value of IT companies fell by 55 per cent, that of Datatec by 85 per cent and that of Dimension Data by 25 per cent. When the bottom was eventually reached, the shares of both companies had fallen by 96 per cent!

Datatec's fell first. Its business was closely tied to that of Cisco Systems, whose sales collapsed in America. Cisco's chief executive commented that his group had experienced 'what may be the fastest deceleration any company has ever experienced'.[14] Technology company investors shared in this decline. In the 12 months following the crash, in March 2000, R25 billion was lost by Datatec, Softline, Idion, Ixchange, MB Technologies, Prism, MGX and Mustek. Dimension Data lost a further R40 billion in the six months after September 2000. Large though these losses were, they pale into insignificance when compared with the losses in the USA, of R4,000 billion. Astronomical price–earnings ratios fell proportionately from an average of 134 for the 12 largest companies in March 2000 to 14.5 in March 2001. With the collapse of IT share prices in the USA (Cisco, Qualcom, Sun and Oracle all fell by 90 per cent) the 'new economy' disappeared from the radar screens of financial journalists. Yet progress had been made in both 1999 and 2000. Business efficiency had increased in tandem with competition and the IT companies had led the moves into globalisation. According to Duncan

14 'Top companies', *Financial Mail*, June 2001, p. 141.

Table 13.8 *Market capitalisation of IT companies on the JSE, 1999 and 2000*

Company	*Capitalisation at 28 December 1999*	*Capitalisation at 12 December 2000*
Aplitec	–	576.8
Asas	28.5	–
Astgroup	1,057.6	1,654.1
Brainware	85.0	11.6
Bynx	785.0	85.0
CCH	2,396.4	327.3
Comparex	14,504.5	2,732.0
Compclear	95.8	71.8
Connections	62.9	60.9
Crux	196.7	54.4
CS Holdings	145.5	155.5
CTech	41.7	5.0
Datacentrix	523.6	199.1
Datatec	12,822.3	5,207.1
Dimension Data	28,941.7	70,300.2
Elexir	17.5	18.2
EOH	129.5	63.8
Faritec	420.9	35.0
Glotec	379.6	328.7
Hi Corp	44.9	18.0
Idion	1,064.2	973.9
I-Fusion	105.0	134.5
Infii/Jiti	14.6	14.6
Intervid	–	518.9
I Tech	19.4	9.3
ITI Tech	265.2	10.8
Ixchange	3,957.6	770.5
KTL	164.3	–
Maxtech	120.6	34.4
MB Tech	1,562.2	482.2
MGX	1,418.4	534.8
MMWTech	13.0	10.6
Mustek	770.6	90.2
OAI	646.0	148.8
OSI	28.5	10.3
Paracon	488.4	547.2
Pinnacle	26.3	10.4
Prism	953.8	1,064.7
PTH	28.1	12.1
Rectron	90.0	78.0
Siltek	427.1	71.7
Softline	3,420.4	690.3
Spescom	553.4	71.7
Spicer	86.3	36.4
SQ One	–	48.2
Top Tech	131.4	137.2
UCS	818.1	231.8
Unihold	–	141.9
USKO	272.9	426.0
Vesta	144.0	118.4
YTHRK	17.1	5.2
Total	85,817.5	89,337.9

Table 13.9 *Growth of Datatec, 1995–2000*

	%
Operating earnings	165.2
Headline earnings per share	65.9
Tangible net asset value per share	74.3
Shareholders' funds	135.7
Reserves	267.7
Number of employees	135.6
Revenue per employee	35.2

Source: Annual Report, Datatec, 2000.

Todd of Prism, early in 2000, before the crash, IT spending was constantly changing as the market developed. In the 1980s it had focused on improving the quality of internal business operations; in the 1990s it moved upwards into enterprise resource planning and supply chain efficiency. In the first decade of the new century he was expecting it to be externally focused on managing customer relations in areas such as e-commerce, networking, data storage, internet applications and secure electronic transactions.

These moves outside the firm also coincided with moves out of South Africa. By 1999, 90 per cent of Datatec's revenue was earned outside South Africa and 74 per cent of Dimension Data's revenue came from overseas in the six months September 1999 to March 2000. Both companies had correctly identified the dynamics at work in the global economy. Dimension Data had focused on networking, with operations in 36 countries. To its original overseas operations in Australia and South East Asia it had added companies in Japan and the UK, culminating in the acquisition of Comparex's European operations for R7 billion in 2000.[15]

Datatec's expansion overseas was more spectacular, with revenue rising from R64 million in 1996 to R12 billion in 2000, when Westcon in the USA was the largest contributor. Datatec was slowly moving into higher value-added services from distributing and selling equipment bought from Cisco, Nortel Networks and Lucent. Unfortunately, in 2000 the company still remained heavily dependent on wholesaling and an expanding market. This, however, was not apparent at the beginning of the year, when its annual report was being prepared. At that time the company was still exuding optimism and boasting of its annual growth in profits of over 50 per cent. The company's achievements, as indicated in Table 13.9, were indeed impressive, with growth across a broad front.

15 Dimension Data Holdings Ltd, circular to shareholders, 3 February 2000.

All the divisions were performing well. Westcon, producing two-thirds of the company's profits, had developed strategic relationships with Cisco, Nortel and Lucent and was planning to list in New York and free the company from the restrictions associated with exchange control. Logical, based in the UK, was earning over 90 per cent of its revenue outside South Africa, 30 per cent of which was coming from higher-value services; and it was planning a listing in London. Mason, the telecommunications consultancy, also based in the UK, was paralleling Logical geographically and UU Net Africa had revenue growth of 113 per cent annually over five years. On the eve of the market crash, Datatec appeared to be a perfect model of a 'new economy' company, distinguished by its entrepreneurial drive and technical brilliance. Dimension Data and Datatec provided value-added services and dominated that section of the market in South Africa. Others sought to expand by developing proprietary software. Ixchange and Idion adopted this approach. Ixchange developed software that targeted customer relations management and infrastructure resource management. At the same time the company expanded overseas by acquisition, and growth was so rapid that the company, founded in 1997, was deriving 85 per cent of its revenue from overseas by early in 2000 and its market capitalisation had risen to over R4 billion. Idion followed a similar path, buying Silverlake in the USA and then developing its own proprietary software that was designed to work with IBM 400 computers at a cost saving for customers of between 30 and 50 per cent. Founded in 1994, after the election, and listed in 1998, Idion's rise was spectacular. Within two years of listing, Nicholas Vlok, the company's chief executive, was talking of Idion moving into data storage, systems management and computer clustering software areas.[16] Support from IBM boosted Idion's reputation; but, as with all software developers, the company needed to maintain sales and to keep on bringing out new products.

Other companies developed niche markets. N1BT, for example, focused on the automation of internet service providers and of application service providers. Spescom, a relatively old IT company, developed its own proprietary software and stayed in South Africa. Research and development absorbed 7 per cent of its turnover and occupied 20 per cent of staff. Earnings per share rose over a five-year period at 45 per cent a year and the company was appointed a Cisco 'advanced technology' partner. Sadly this sterling performance was rewarded with a below-average rating in South Africa. Spescom had not sought the glamour of an overseas listing and its growth in earnings did not compare with

16 'Top companies', *Financial Mail*, 30 June 2000, p. 162.

that of the market leaders. Prism, another favourite of the analysts, developed its own technology and entered into partnerships with international companies such as Microsoft and De Ie Rue. Prism developed South Africa's first electronic banking payments system, Saswitch, as well as the Pick'n'Pay payments system. The company moved into the USA in the second half of 2000 and invested R175 million there. Of this, R131 million was for goodwill, which shortly afterwards had to be written off. Offshore sales rose to 50 per cent of turnover, before the company collapsed. Over-hasty expansion, when the market was falling, suggests management failure was widespread in the company. Softline, another stellar IT company, which had developed Pastel, its own accounting software, expanded rapidly and then almost destroyed itself by moving into the USA at the peak of the boom. Having niche products and technical competence was not sufficient to ensure survival, if the timing was not right and the expansion was too rapid. Yet, even if the timing was against a company, prudent management with niche products could prosper. This was the experience of Aplitec and Intervid in 2000–01. The former developed smart card technologies and the latter specialised in visual information systems.[17]

Conclusion

Private enterprise, responding to market forces, was the driving force behind the growth of the IT sector in the 1990s. Policy played no role in determining the course of events. So powerful were the market forces that, at the height of the boom in 1998 and 1999, investment in IT was accounting for 8 per cent of South Africa's GDP.

These were the years when the personal computer and Windows captured the imagination of the public and provided access to information on a global scale. Music and photographs could be downloaded from anywhere in the world. Indeed, by the beginning of the new century some of the world's greatest libraries were preparing to make the contents of their eighteenth- and nineteenth-century books available via the internet. Admittedly, the high cost of telephone services in South Africa retarded the growth of internet usage; but the backwardness in adopting the new technology, which was marked in 1990, had virtually disappeared by 2000.

Glamorous though the internet was, it was in the more bread-and-butter areas of processing information that the greatest cost savings

17 'Top companies', *Financial Mail*, June 2001.

occurred. These included point-of-sale outlets in retail establishments, processing salaries and keeping track of supplies, suppliers and customers. Electronic banking developed and, in business, personal secretaries gave way to personal computers.

The IT boom hit South Africa when the country was becoming internationally respectable. This had the effect of compressing into a few years what had been developing in a somewhat longer time frame overseas. However, this should not be exaggerated. Technological progress was rapid worldwide, in a way that tended to level the playing field for new entrants; and in South Africa, both the educational system and the business environment were favourable to the production of entrepreneurs. These were forthcoming, led at first by Jeremy Ord of Dimension Data and Jens Montanana of Datatec, and culminating in Kreunen of Ixchange, Vlok of Idion and Mark Shuttleworth of Thort (the last named perfected a security system for computers and sold it to a US firm for $350 million cash at the height of the boom). Large fortunes were made; but so too were large losses. Over the years of the boom there were few gains in long-term wealth creation. In December 1994 the market capitalisation of all the IT firms was R9,335.3 million, in December 1999 R69,817 million, and in December 2000 R9,653 million. Over R60 billion had been made and lost!

These effects were dramatic. Less obvious, but in the long run more important, were the gains in efficiency that resulted from this massive investment, the full benefits of which had not yet been realised in 2000. These lay in the future, as more and more hum-drum tasks were automated and time horizons were shortened, raising the productivity of both capital and labour, as more and more institutions and individuals were connected to the internet with access to information on a global scale, and as e-mail became a normal means of communication.

In a little over five years private enterprise, responding to market forces, had found ways to create what was virtually a whole new infrastructure. As a result, the dynamic forces of market capitalism were able to reduce dependence upon the inefficient state postal service, in which theft was widespread, and to provide a much-need jolt to the high-cost, state-controlled terrestrial telephone service.

14

The retail sector: steady as she goes

Stuart Jones

Introduction

The market rather than policy determined how the retail sector developed in the 1990s and the market was not favourable to sustained expansion. The long decline that had been affecting the South African economy since the middle of the 1970s continued through the 1990s. In an environment where per capita GDP was falling and poverty increasing, there was little room for innovation or major new developments. Moreover, the expectations of a large dynamic black middle-class market emerging and expanding rapidly had not taken place even by the end of the decade. Any significant expansion of the black middle class appears to have been balanced by white emigration and by growing unemployment. What happened in retailing therefore reflected what was happening in the broader economy.

Geographical distribution of sales

National retail sales

In current prices, the total value of retail sales rose considerably, from R71,012.4 million in 1990 to R173,324.4 million in 2000 (Table 14.1). In constant prices, however, total sales declined, notwithstanding the growth in the population, clear evidence that the 1994 election had not been followed by an increase in consumer spending. In fact, retail sales declined faster after 1994 than the rate at which they had declined in the first four years of the decade. This would help to explain the presence of so many empty shops in the northern suburbs of Johannesburg and the frequency with which small business were opening and closing.

Table 14.1 *Growth of retail sales, 1990–2000*

Year	*Total sales (R millions)*
1990	71,012.4
1991	79,691.4
1992	87,597.5
1993	94,938.1
1994	104,049.2
1995	122,579.0
1996	132,613.1
1997	144,692.9
1998	152,446.1
1999	160,074.0
2000	173,324.4

Source: Bulletin of Statistics, various issues, South African Government Publications.

Table 14.2 *Growth rate (%) of total retail sales in current and constant prices and of per capita retail sales in constant prices, 1990–2000*

	Current prices	*Constant prices*	*Per capita sales (constant prices)*
1990–94	10.5	–0.1	–2.2
1994–2000	8.4	–0.5	–7.3

Source: Bulletin of Statistics, various issues, South African Government Publications; *Quarterly Bulletin*, various issues, South African Reserve Bank; and *Annual Surveys*, South African Institute of Race Relations, 1990–2000.

A reduction in credit sales was responsible for this decline. Non-hire purchase credit sales, which had been declining at a rate of 0.5 per cent a year in the first four years of the decade, were falling by 5 per cent a year after 1994 in constant prices and their decline counterbalanced the 8.14 per cent increase in hire purchase sales financed by retailers. Cash sales also declined, though at a slower rate than before the election, falling by 0.3 per cent as opposed to 1.3 per cent in the earlier period. These disappointing figures of retail sales take no account of population movements. On a per capita basis the decline is more pronounced.

In constant prices, the rate of decline of total retail sales quintupled after 1994, a faster rate of decline than that of per capita sales. The latter, however, experienced a much greater absolute decline of 7.3 per cent a year from 1994 to 2000 (Table 14.2). Given the doubts about the population figures, these rates of decline need to be treated with caution. Nevertheless, they do not support the contention that the South African economy was experiencing positive economic growth in the last years of the century and once again raise questions about the adjustment of figures of GDP in 1999 that reversed the decline and purported to show significant real per capita growth after 1994.

Regional retail sales by province

The Transvaal dominated retail sales in 1990 and this was still the case in 2000. The reasons were simple. The Transvaal included the business heart of the country, Johannesburg, and political administrative centre, Pretoria. Almost half the country's retail sales occurred within the boundaries of the old Transvaal. The creation of new provinces, though, led to the creation of new centres of patronage and spending. As a result, after 1994, retail sales in Gauteng, in current prices, grew less rapidly than in the old Transvaal and in constant prices declined more rapidly than in the North West Province or Mpumalanga. Limpopo, as shown in Table 14.3, was the exception. In Limpopo, the province in which the African National Congress (ANC) had achieved its largest share of the vote in the 1994 general election, real retail sales rose 0.06 per cent in the period 1995–99. Since this province is reputedly the one with the greatest poverty, it would appear to have been greatest beneficiary of the 1994 election, with the former Southern Transvaal as the greatest loser.

The two smaller provinces, KwaZulu-Natal and the Free State, fared less well than the Transvaal in the first period; but the Free State experienced a small relative improvement after 1994, when retail sales declined by only 0.17 per cent. KwaZulu-Natal, by contrast, experienced a quadrupling in the rate of decline. By 2000 KwaZulu-Natal accounted for a mere 16.3 per cent of total national sales, compared with 18.0 per cent in 1994 and 17.7 per cent in 1990. The Free State followed a similar pattern of decline, being responsible for 6.1 per cent of sales in 1990, 5.4 per cent in 1994 and 4.8 per cent in 2000. Its economy was suffering from a double blow: declining gold production and the closure of gold mines, together with a reduction in military spending on the bases in the province. KwaZulu-Natal was experiencing a population explosion

Table 14.3 *Pattern of retail sales in the Transvaal, in constant prices, 1990–2000*

	Transvaal	*North West*	*Gauteng*	*Mpumalanga*	*Limpopo*
1990–94	–0.05	–	–	–	–
1995–2000	–1.26	–0.26	–1.8	–0.45	1.56

Source: South African Government Publications, *Bulletin of Statistics*, various issues; South African Reserve Bank, *Quarterly Bulletin*, various issues; and *Annual Surveys*, South African Institute of Race Relations, 1990–2000.

Table 14.4 *Average annual rates of growth (%) of retail sales in the Cape Province, in constant prices, 1990–2000*

	Western Cape	*Eastern Cape*	*Northern Cape*	*Cape Province 1990 boundaries*
1990–94	–	–	–	0.78
1994–2000	–	–	–	0.19
1995–2000	0.94	0.56	3.85	–

Source: South African Government Publications, *Bulletin of Statistics*, various issues; South African Reserve Bank, *Quarterly Bulletin*, various issues; and *Annual Surveys*, South African Institute of Race Relations, 1990–2000.

that was not balanced by provincial service delivery or by the presence of a dynamic metropolitan hub.

The Cape Province was the exception in retail spending. Before 1995 it achieved positive sales growth in real terms of 0.78 per cent a year. This then declined to 0.19 per cent a year from 1995 to 2000. Evidently neither the popularity of Cape Town as a tourist destination, nor the ANC's concern for the Xhosa homeland, could maintain growth in total sales. Most surprising, perhaps, was the growth in sales in the Northern Cape once it became a separate province possessing a bureaucratic capital in Kimberley. As Table 14.4 shows, growth of sales in the Northern Cape, at 3.85 per cent a year, was considerably better than the 0.94 per cent of the Western Cape or the 0.56 of the Eastern Cape.

At the provincial level, the pattern of retail sales does not provide evidence of an expanding economy. It does, however, suggest that the growth of the bureaucracy was beginning to affect sales in the poorer parts of the country, such as the Northern Cape, the Eastern Cape and Limpopo, all of which achieved positive sales growth in the last five years of the decade.

Retail sales in metropolitan centres

Metropolitan spending provides us with another perspective on how the former centres of economic dynamism were faring. The principal metropolitan centres in South Africa in the 1990s were generally the ones that had dominated the economy a century earlier: Greater Johannesburg, Durban–Pinetown, Greater Cape Town, Port Elizabeth–Uitenhage and Greater Pretoria. The last, as a major centre of consumption, was a product of the second half of the twentieth century.

These five metropolitan regions mirrored conditions in the retail market, which in turn reflected the decline in the South African

Table 14.5 *Average annual rates of growth (%) of retail sales in the larger metropolitan regions, in constant prices, 1990–99*

	1990–94	*1994–99*
Greater Johannesburg	–0.4	–1.6
Greater Cape Town	0.7	0.7
Greater Durban	–1.0	–4.4
Greater Pretoria	–0.8	–1.3
Greater Port Elizabeth	0.6	–2.6

Regions are listed in order of overall size of sales in 1990–94.
Source: South African Government Publications, *Bulletin of Statistics*, various issues; South African Reserve Bank, *Quarterly Bulletin*, various issues; and *Annual Surveys*, South African Institute of Race Relations, 1990–2000.

economy. Only one of the metropolitan regions, Greater Cape Town, experienced positive sales growth in the years 1994–99 and only two of them, Greater Cape Town and Port Elizabeth–Uitenhage, did so in the first four years of the decade (Table 14.5).

In the first four years of the decade, retail sales were positive only in Greater Cape Town and Port Elizabeth. In Johannesburg the relatively small decline of 0.4 per cent in the first years of the decade accelerated to 1.6 per cent in the period 1994–99 as the emigration of skilled workers was counterbalanced by an influx of impoverished refugees and increasing unemployment. Taking into account the growth in population of Greater Johannesburg, retail sales figures paint a gloomy picture of an economy in which real per capita incomes were falling and unemployment was increasing. Indeed, there were only two years when sales grew, 1991 and 1995, and there was a particularly sharp decline in 2000, when sales fell by 3.2 per cent.[1]

Greater Durban experienced a much greater decline in sales than any other metropolitan centre. In the first four years the decline was 1.0 per cent, which accelerated to 4.4 per cent between 1994 and 1999. The birth rate in KwaZulu-Natal was probably responsible for most of the increase in poverty in the province, but it was not helped by Tito Mboweni's First World labour legislation and the vulnerability of the province's textile industry to foreign competition once South Africa had become a member of the World Trade Organization. For total sales to collapse by 25.4 per cent in five years at a time of sustained population growth was not something that people expected to occur in the 'New South Africa'.

1 See Stuart Jones (ed.), *The Decline of the South African Economy*, Edward Elgar, 2002.

Table 14.6 *Retail sales (R millions) in the major metropolitan centres, 1990–99*

	Greater Johannesburg	*Greater Durban*	*Greater Pretoria*	*Cape Peninsula*	*Port Elizabeth–Uitenhage*
1990	8,819.4	5,565.6	6,182.4	7,819.1	2,366.0
1991	10,181.8	6,047.5	6,656.4	9,300.1	2,793.2
1992	10,983.8	6,491.5	7,003.6	10,373.7	3,034.8
1993				10,984.5	3,246.7
1994	13,149.5[a]	7,847.7	8,912.7	12,170.7	3,669.7
1995	15,117.8	9,825.9	9,955.7[b]		
1996	16,301.0	10,612.8	10,671.3		
1997	17,349.7	11,315.5	11,370.6	16,128.0	4,228.3
1998	18,371.6	11,832.1	11,804.0	18,127.9	4,682.8
1999	19,185.6	12,644.0	11,887.9	19,608.7	5,017.0

[a] Excludes Midrand.
[b] Includes Midrand.
Source: Bulletin of Statistics, various issues, South African Government Publications.

Both metropolitan regions in the Cape experienced positive sales growth in the last years of white rule. Cape Town combined the advantages of a major financial and commercial centre with those of a tourist destination and a place of political importance, home to both the national parliament and a provincial government. Certainly after 1994 its importance as an international tourist centre increased and tourist spending must have played a part in maintaining turnover. Yet even the Greater Cape Town region experienced a decline in per capita spending. Sales in Greater Port Elizabeth, the home province of the ANC leaders, grew until the change of government, and then declined. Again, one suspects that growth in unemployment was mainly responsible. This in turn was the result of population growth and a lack of investment in employment-creating enterprises.

With a communist-dominated government in power one might expected that sales in Pretoria, the bureaucratic capital, would experience considerable expansion. They did not. They declined at the rate of 0.8 per cent a year from 1990 to 1994, which accelerated to 1.3 per cent a year after 1994 in constant prices. In current prices, of course they almost doubled, to R11.89 billion, making Pretoria the country's fourth largest market, after Johannesburg, Cape Town and Durban (Table 14.6). With the exception of Greater Cape Town, all the major metropolitan regions in South Africa experienced not only declining real sales in absolute terms, but also a very considerable decline in per capita sales.

Table 14.7 *Growth or decline (%) of retail sales by type of merchandise, in constant prices, 1990–2000*[a]

	1990–94	*1994–2000*
Food and meat	–0.2	–0.8
Non-edible groceries	–9.0	–0.8
Women's, girls' and babies' clothing	4.5	–0.8
Pharmaceuticals	–0.4	2.8
Men's and boys' clothing	2.9	0.3
Drinks and beverages	–1.8	–1.8
Furniture	–2.3	4.2
Footware	5.8	–0.6
Sports and entertainment goods	3.9	–1.7
Hardware and building materials	6.4	–1.8
Domestic appliances	–0.6	–0.4
Glass, crockery and kitchenware	2.0	–2.1
Books and magazines	–3.5	–0.8
Audio products	–8.1	–5.2
Cigarettes and tobacco	4.0	–
Television sets	–2.6	–5.0

[a] All types of merchandise with sales of R1 billion or more, in 1990 in order of size.
Source: As Table 14.2.

Retail sales by type of merchandise

Sixteen categories of merchandise achieved sales of R1 billion or more in 1990. Foodstuffs headed the list by a wide margin. At R21.7 billion they were almost three and a half times greater than the next largest type of merchandise, non-edible groceries. Women's, girls' and babies' clothing came third, at R5.8 billion, well ahead of men's and boys' clothing, at R3.5 billion. The depreciation of the rand revealed itself in the rapidly growing value of pharmaceutical sales, which were just below R5 billion in 1990, well ahead of men's and boys' clothing, beverages and furniture. No other type of merchandise achieved sales of R3 billion in 1990. Four categories achieved sales of over R2 billion: footwear; sports and entertainment goods; hardware and building materials; and domestic appliances. The remaining five categories with sales of over R1 billion rands were: glassware, crockery and kitchenware; books and magazines; audio equipment; cigarettes and tobacco; and television sets. The position occupied by food and groceries is evidence of the underdeveloped state of much of the country and of the low per capita incomes associated with it. Food and clothing were the crucial items in the budgets of a large proportion of the population.

Table 14.8 *Growth or decline (%) of per capita retail sales by type of merchandise, in constant prices, 1990–2000*

Merchandise	*1990–94*	*1994–2000*
Food and meat	–2.4	–3.0
Non-edible groceries	–11.0	–3.0
Women's, girls' and babies' clothing	2.3	–3.0
Pharmaceuticals	–2.5	0.5
Men's and boys' clothing	0.7	–1.9
Drinks and beverages	–3.8	–2.9
Footware	3.6	–2.9
Furniture	–2.3	- 1.9
Sports and entertainment goods	0.4	–2.9
Hardware and building materials	2.7	–4.0
Domestic appliances	–2.7	–2.6
Glassware, crockery and kitchenware	10.7	4.3
Books and magazines	–5.5	–3.0
Audio products	–10.2	–7.1
Cigarettes and tobacco	–1.1	–
Television sets	–4.7	–7.1

Source: As Table 14.2.

With a new government in 1994 committed to uplifting the incomes of the very poor and to an extensive programme of electrification in rural areas this pattern was expected to change. This had not occurred by 2000. As a proportion of total sales, spending on food in 2000 was back to the level of 1990, having risen from 30.6 per cent in 1990 to 31.3 per cent in 1994, before falling to 29.9 per cent in 2000. A fall in the proportion of total sales going to food products would normally be a sign of a developing country beginning to benefit from sustained economic growth; but in South Africa it is harder to interpret, because of the luxury spending of the new black beneficiaries of affirmative action and the racial quotas in employment and because many of the unemployed returned to rural areas that were still locked into a semi-subsistence economy that did not buy food in the market. What is clear is that, in constant prices, the decline of food and meat sales after 1994 continued at an even faster pace than before 1994 (Table 14.8).

Six of the 16 types of merchandise achieved positive growth in sales in the first four years of the decade: women's, girls' and babies' clothing; men's and boys' clothing; footwear; sports and entertainment goods; hardware and building materials; and glass, crockery and kitchenware. Only the last mentioned achieved positive growth in the period 1994–2000. Relative luxuries expanded in the last six years of the century:

pharmaceuticals, furniture and glassware. A further seven declined less rapidly: non-edible groceries, drinks and beverages, footwear, furniture, domestic appliances, books and magazines and audio products.

The per capita decline in the retail sale of basic commodities such as food, clothing and non-edible groceries provides evidence of the widening gap between per capita incomes in the 'New South Africa', a characteristic, one might note, of so many of the countries to the north of the Limpopo. The decline in the sale of building materials and hardware also suggests that this is what was happening. At the luxury end of the market, the continued decline in the sale of audio products, television sets and sports and entertainment goods again suggests that the emergent black middle-class spending was not yet making up for the emigration of so many young white professionals. The pattern of retail sales in the last decade of the century was, therefore, a continuation of that of the previous decade, when real per capita economic growth was negative and the market environment singularly undynamic. While this may have been expected, what was not expected was that the condition of the majority of the population would continue to deteriorate and that, in some cases, notably food and clothing, this deterioration would accelerate.

Leading retailers in South Africa

In a declining market environment there was less room for rapid growth than in a more dynamic arena. Yet the very undynamic nature of the shrinking market tended to intensify the competition for sales. As a result, there were significant changes in the country's shopping centres as old and familiar names disappeared and others, already well known, became steadily more conspicuous. Shopping centres were filled with the same collection of stores and originality inevitably suffered.

Since the beginnings of South Africa's modern economic growth in the nineteenth century, distance and isolation had made the South African market a less competitive place than markets in Europe and America. Monopolies talked of favouring competition but did not always practise it. Retail price maintenance was ever present, while the pyramiding so beloved of the Johannesburg Stock Exchange allowed entrepreneurs with only a minority of the shares in issue to control large corporations. In this regard it is noticeable that retail enterprises controlled by the Anglo American Corporation performed relatively poorly. OK Bazaars had virtually disappeared from the metropolitan scene by 1990. Edgars in clothing suffered a similar fate and the furniture and special stores controlled by that corporation all under-performed. Other large corporations were more successful, which suggests that it was not size that hindered profitable growth, but focus, or, to be precise, the lack of it. The JD Group, for instance, comprised many different furniture chains, but kept its main focus on its customers and what the market wanted and, as a result, did well in the decade.

Good management was more likely to be rewarded in the 1990s, because its value was increasing in the more competitive environment. Accession to the World Trade Organization and the impact of globalisation were beginning to bring benefits to the South African consumer. Supermarkets, for example, were now able to import more recognised international brands as import controls fell away. European cheeses and Danish butter showed local producers how far they needed to improve quality if they were going to be able to compete. In clothing and footwear, foreign brands flooded the market, provoking a barrage of complaints from the local producers, whose unit labour costs were high and quality control often poor. Technology played a role in strengthening the hand of the good manager as computerisation and bar-coding made it so much easier to keep track of stock control. Supermarkets, for example, were following in the steps of the Japanese automobile factories that operated with minimum supplies of goods in storage, because of their efficient system of control over inflows of raw materials and their close monitoring as they proceeded along the route to final assembly. Clothing manufacturers could see which fashion products were selling and instantly order more. Technological progress placed a premium not only on good management but also on size. Stores were getting bigger in order to provide a wider range of goods (an aspect of globalisation) and in order to keep unit costs down. Just as the first chain stores in the 1870s undercut the traditional grocer, and the supermarket undercut the older chain stores in the 1950s and 1960s, so too did the new hypermarkets and out-of-town shopping centres in the 1990s undercut the older supermarkets. Competition was not perfect, as exchange controls effectively kept out foreign retailers and delayed the implementation of best business practice, which helps to explain why South African retailers, such as Woolworths, Truworths and the Lewis Group, experienced difficulties with their overseas subsidiaries. The parent companies were not accustomed to the intensity of competition overseas. Imperfect competition helps to explain, too, why these retailers were more successful in African ventures north of the Limpopo. There, the market was even less competitive than in South Africa.

The leading retailers of 1990 were household names in South Africa and most of them were still there in 2000 (Table 14.9). The exceptions among the larger groups were CNA Gallo, which had got into difficulties and been taken over by Woolworths, and the Anglo

Table 14.9 *Market capitalisation (R millions) of leading retailers, 1990, 1994 and 2000*

Company	*1990*	*Company*	*1994*	*Company*	*2000*
Edgars	2,795.0	Edgars	7,324.4	Pick n Pay	6,115.5
Wooltru	2,371.0	Foschini	4,751.6	JD Group	4,131.1
Pick n Pay	1,741.3	Pepkor	4,306.6	Shoprite	3,778.6
Foschini	1,663.9	Wooltru	3,259.7	New Clicks	2,941.7
Pepkor	1,580.9	Metro Cash	1,892.4	Metro Cash	1,712.8
CNA Gallo	853.9	Pick n Pay	1,549.6	Massmore	2,010.8
Waltons	334.4	CNA Gallo	1,435.0	Woolworths	2,700.2
Ellerines	317.4	Shoprite	1,383.7	Truworths	1,846.2
		JD Group	1,034.6	Foschini	1,669.2
Metro Cash	279.7	Waltons	489.4	Edgars	1,436.1
Score Clicks	229.0	Score Clicks	464.8	Ellerines	1,258.4
OK Bazaars	172.9 [a]	Protea Furniture	143.5	Pepkor	716.9
Shoprite	162.5				
JD Group	142.5				

[a] March 1990.
Source: Financial Mail, various issues.

American-controlled Store Clicks, which had changed ownership and re-emerged as New Clicks. In the last years of National Party rule, the lack of competition combined with the lack of investment opportunities in an exchange control environment had led to Anglo American taking effective control of companies that together possessed around three-quarters of the market capitalisation of the Johannesburg Stock Exchange. In a similar line of development in the 1990s, it led to Woolworths, the clothing and food store modelled on Marks and Spencer in England, converting itself into a less efficiently managed conglomerate, owning Woolworths, Truworths, Makro, Dions, Topics and CNA. Not surprisingly, all the individual branches suffered from this development; but unbundling had to wait until the new century dawned.

Of the 13 largest store groups by market capitalisation in 1990 (Table 14.9), four were clothing retailers (Edgars, Wooltru, Foschini and Pepkor); three were food retailers (Pick n Pay, Metro Cash and Carry, and Shoprite, or three and a half if Woolworths is included as a food store); two were furniture retailers (Ellerines and the JD Group); and three were speciality shops – Waltons for stationery, CNA Gallo for magazines and music, and Store Clicks for toiletries and music. OK Bazaars remained as an all-purpose popular department store that had grown out of a dime store. Ten years later the picture was very different. Food chains had established their pre-eminence, furniture stores had strengthened their position and clothing stores (led by Edgars) had weakened. Even Woolworths was relying more on its food sales in the new food halls.

In the first four years of the decade, business continued much as it always had done, with the larger groups getting larger, both by internal growth and by acquisition. Clothing stores were the best performers. Edgars retained its top position by market capitalisation, followed by Foschini, Pepkor and Wooltru. Edgars had begun its long march to the top position in the 1970s, with its decision to move up-market, and control by Anglo American had not arrested this process. Indeed, in the early 1990s Edgars and the other clothing stores were outperforming the market and, as Table 14.9 shows, achieving positive economic growth. Why clothing sales expanded when grocery sales were falling is not clear. Edgars, Foschini and Wooltru were urban, First World-situated stores, catering to the middle class, and they benefited from the growth in disposable income and of the new black middle class. All three were well managed groups and all three invested heavily in advertising. All three also relied heavily on credit sales. It was these that probably made the difference. It was in the years after 1994 that the clothing stores pushed their own credit cards and extended credit somewhat liberally. It is possible that the clothing stores were better at appealing to the expanding black market in the major urban areas at a time when emigration and uncertainty may have been eating at the traditional market of the major food retailers.

In the second half of the decade, when the squeeze on disposable incomes was tightening, clothing sales began to slip and by 2000 the new leaders in terms of market capitalisation were the two big supermarket chains and the JD furniture group. The rise of Shoprite, the group that had taken over the failing Checkers supermarkets, was most marked. Conversely, Edgars had slipped badly. In six years its market capitalisation had fallen by 80.4 per cent in current prices, in constant prices by around 87 per cent.

Unbundling and the shrinking of Anglo American were features of the later 1990s. South African Breweries, the immediate controller of Edgars in 1994, was unbundled from Anglo American and moved its base to London, a development that enabled Edgars to break free and become an independent company under the new name of Edgars Consolidated Stores. This move transformed the group from being a clothing merchandiser into one controlling clothing stores, stationery and household goods, with well known names such as Edgars, Boardmans, CNA, Cuthberts, Jet, Legit, Prato, Red Square, Sales House and Super Mart. Ellerines was unbundled from Malbak, which in turn broke free from Sankor, the industrial holding company of the giant life insurer Sanlam; and New Clicks escaped from the clutches of Anglo

American. The Pep Group, led by Christo Wiese, both expanded and unbundled. The group took over the failing Checkers grocery chain and merged it with its own Shoprite chain, which in turn was freed from control by Pepkor and Tradehold, with the former much diminished and the latter transformed into a holding company for retail interests in Europe. The JD Group, previously controlled by Absa and Old Mutual, also regained its independence and this sparked a burst of energy that took the company almost to the top of the retail sector. The unhappy amalgamation of Woolworths with Truworths was undone in 1997, with the two firms being listed separately. Thus, despite a hostile economic environment for retailing in the 1990s, much movement and reorganisation took place and efficiency improved. The sector was far from static.

The reasons why greater changes occurred in the 1990s than in probably any other decade was the impact of market forces and competition. In the apartheid era, monopolies had flourished and been protected by a battery of government controls, of which import controls and exchange controls were the most damaging. The long-term effect of government intervention was to make companies become slothful and less competitive. The situation shared some of the characteristics experienced by the City of London before the Second World War. Johannesburg did not operate like a gentleman's club, but the pre-eminence of a relatively small number of monopoly holding groups and shared directors meant that a small number of persons controlled the fortunes of much of the economy. This feature of the economy had got much worse during the last 20 years of National Party rule. When an anti-capitalist government took office in 1994 the need for change increased considerably. Managers and entrepreneurs were pushed to increase competition, a development reinforced by entry into the World Trade Organization in 1996. With Anglo American, South African Breweries and Old Mutual based outside the country by 2000, there was less need to fear being swallowed up by giant capital-rich corporations in an exchange control environment. The Rupert group of companies had also moved its main activities out of the country, into Richmont (Switzerland), and reduced its influence over banking and insurance, while Sanlam, by concentrating on its core insurance business, no longer threatened to become an unwieldy conglomerate. Taken together, all these developments were pushing South Africa in the direction of becoming a more efficient market and one in which the more efficient marketers could reasonably hope to flourish.

The end result of these changes was that, in the later years of the decade, free market capitalism probably exerted a greater impact upon the retail sector than it had been able to do for a very long time, while the better-managed groups were able to bring considerable benefits to the South African consumer. Others, such as Woolworths, which had

Table 14.10 *Turnover and net profits of the leading retail enterprises in South Africa, 1990, 1994 and 2000*

Turnover		*Net profit*		
Company	*R millions*	*Company*	*R millions*	*Year end*
1990				
Tradehold	7,232.7			8.90
Pick n Pay	5,189.2	Wooltru	153.4	6.91
Metro Cash & Carry	4,064.3	Edgars	136.6	3.91
OK Bazaars	3,844.4	Pep	87.4	2.91
Wooltru	3,303.2	Pick n Pay	86.6	3.91
Edgars	2,475.8	Foschini	61.6	2.91
Pep	1,957.4	Ellerines	59.9	8.90
		CNA Gallo	52.8	3.91
Score Clicks	1,904.2	Waltons	37	2.91
Foschini	822.0	OK Bazaars	28.5	3.90
		Score Clicks	24	2.91
CNA Gallo	798.4	Shoprite	11.7	12.90
Shoprite	732.1	Tradehold	0.3	6.91
Waltons	685.3	JD Group*	–51.4	12.90
JD Group	645.7	Metro Cash & Carry[a]	–53.8	6.91
Ellerines	489.2			
1994				
Pep	9,684.6	Wooltru	321.8	6.95
Wooltru	8,108.0	Pep	207.4	2.95
McCarthy Retail	8,003.0	Foschini	188.4	3.95
Pick n Pay	7,919.5	Edgars	175.5	3.95
Metro Cash & Carry	6,681.3	McCarthy Retail	148.0	3.95
Shoprite	6,363.6	Shoprite	99.6	2.95
Edgars	4,265.2	Metro Cash & Carry	87.6	4.95
JD Group	1,884.3	Ellerines	78.8	8.94
Foschini	1,442.4	JD Group	63.6	6.95
CNA Gallo	1,273.3	Waltons	62.0	2.95
Waltons	1,021.8	Pick 'n Pay	60.6	2.95
Ellerines	839.4	CNA Gallo	56.6	3.95
2000				
Metro Cash & Carry	35,625.9	Protea Furnishers	636.8	12.00
Shoprite	19,472.5	Pick n Pay	478.4	2.01
Pick n Pay	15,126.1	Shoprite	375.0	2.01
Mass Mart	11,568.4	JD Group	351.4	8.00
Woolworths	7,026.6	Metro Cash & Carry	275.7	8.00
Edgars Consolidated	6,844.8	Woolworths	265.3	6.01
Pep	4,762.0	Mass Mart	251.8	6.01
Protea Furnishers	4,215.7	Ellerines	218.5	8.00
Nu Clicks	3,997.5	Edgars Consolidated	196.2	3.01
JD Group	3,366.9	Truworths	189.8	6.01
Foschini	2,980.2	Nu Clicks	173.6	8.00
Truworths	1,676.4	Pep	152.9	6.01
		Foschini	23.0	3.01

[a] Enterprises undergoing restructuring
Source: 'Top companies', *Financial Mail*, 26 July 1991, 27 July 1997, 28 June 2002.

Table 14.11 *Return on equity and return on assets (%) of the leading retail enterprises in South Africa, 1994 and 2000*

Company	*Return on equity*		*Return on assets*		*Year end*
	1994	*2000*	*1994*	*2000*	
Wooltru	27.7	–	17.6	–	6.01
Pep [a]	17.3	–7.4	11.2	2.7	6.01
Foschini	24.7	1.2	22.1	2.3	3.01
Edgars	28.6	7.9	17.6	6.9	3.01
McCarthy Retail	54.6	–	18.3	–26.7	6.01
Shoprite	26.8	16.7	6.4	4.4	6.01
Metro Cash & Carry	19.1	–58.5	8.5	0.3	8.00
Ellerines	21.5	17.5	15.3	14.5	8.00
JD Group		17.3		12.3	8.00
Waltons [b]	19.5	–	11.1	–	2.01
Pick n Pay	17.9	28.2	8.3	9.2	2.01
CNA Gallo [c]	25.6	–	13.8	–	3.01
Woolworths	–	11.2	–	8.4	6.01
Truworths	–	20.5	–	15.7	6.01
Mass Mart [d]	–	43.3	–	6.6	6.01
Clicks [e]	6.4	21.1	8.3	11.1	8.00

[a] Pep Ltd the grocery chain was merged into the holding company Pepkor in 1999 and Pep Ltd was delisted from the Johannesburg Stock Exchange.
[b] Waltons was renamed Impotek Group Holdings in 1997 and Waltons Stationery delisted in 1998.
[c] Controlled by Woolworths Truworths Holdings
[d] Controlled by Woolworths Truworths Holdings until Massmart required Game in 1998.
[e] Score Clicks delisted in 1996 and New Clicks was established, when Anglo American and the Premier Group unbundled.
Source: 'Top companies', *Financial Mail*, 27 July 1997, 28 June 2002.

lost focus, struggled to adapt, and yet others, such as Foschini, steadily lost market share, while its controlling shareholder, the Lewis family, refused to implement the necessary changes. As a result, the improved standing of the retail enterprises in the country's top industrial companies, which had risen markedly in the early years of the decade, stalled. There were three among the top 50 by market capitalisation in 1990 and six in 1994, but thereafter the number ceased growing.

Net profitability and turnover show how the major firms fared in the 1990s (Tables 14.10 and 14.11). In 1990, the leading company by profitability was Wooltru, at R153.4 million, followed by Edgars, at R136.6 million. In turnover, Ellerines came bottom of the list; high mark-ups were a feature of its business. The reverse also occurred. Tradehold, owner of the failing Checkers grocery chain, had the largest turnover and the smallest net profit. However, once Christo Wiese took control and amalgamated the supermarket chain with Shoprite, controls were tightened and the turnaround began. In the process Tradehold had Shoprite delisted in 1997 and the Stuttafords department stores were unbundled and sold to Cashbuild in 2000.

In 1994 the largest retailer by turnover was Pep Ltd, with its chain of shops across the country catering to the lower end of the market. Wooltru and McCarthy Retail followed closely behind, ahead of Metro Cash and Carry, Pick n Pay and Shoprite. McCarthy Retail was the outstanding profit earner, with a return on equity of 54.6 per cent. McCarthy Retail grew as a motor vehicle retailer that branched out into the Game discount stores that were one of the more striking features of the retail scene in the 1990s. Top in the return upon assets was Foschini, with a return of 22.1 per cent. By the end of the century changes in the pattern had begun to appear. McCarthy Retail had over-extended itself in the motor trade and been forced to sell its profitable Game discount stores to Makro. Shoprite had strengthened its position and CNA and Waltons had dropped out of the list. Metro Cash and Carry now boasted the largest turnover, over R35 billion, well ahead of its nearest rival, Shoprite. Shoprite, though, was the third most profitable retailer measured by size. At the head of the table was Protea Furnishers, the dynamic newcomer that was in the process of pushing credit sales at the expense of its own internal controls. Its fall from grace was as rapid as its ascent. In 2000 furniture retailers were two of the top four profit earners, but Mass Mart had the highest return on equity, followed by Pick n Pay, Profurn, New Clicks and Truworths (Table 14.11). Two firms had a negative return on equity, Metcash and Pepkor. Both of these were in the process of being reorganised and unbundled.

Towards the end of the decade the furniture sector displayed new life. According to the *Financial Mail*, pressure on less efficient operations, like Beares, OK Bazaars and Amrel, from focused, aggressive companies like Ellerines and the JD Group, as well as from newcomers like Protea Furnishers, became more intense in 1997 and 1998. Amrel, for example, was hit by bad debts and its own inefficiencies, with each chain operating its own administrative and credit departments, which resulted in high gearing on low operating margins.[2] Finance was important, not just in the extension of credit, but in insuring the risks. In 1997 Ellerines made as much from insurance as it did from trading. Inflation was still a problem and when interest rates rose at the end of the decade the furniture and white goods boomlet faded away. Ellerines and the JD Group were badly hit. Stores relying predominantly on cash sales were better

2 'Top companies', *Financial Mail*, 26 June 1998, p. 211.

Table 14.12 *Turnover, net profit, return on assets and return on equity of South Africa's leading retail enterprises, 2000*

Enterprise	*Turnover (R millions)*	*Net profit (R millions)*	*Return on assets (%)*	*Return on equity (%)*	*Year end*
Pick n Pay	15,126.1	478.4	9.2	28.2	2.01
JD Group	3,366.9	351.4	12.3	17.3	8.00
Shoprite	19,472.5	375.0	4.4	16.7	6.01
New Clicks	3,997.5	173.6	11.1	21.1	8.00
Woolworths	7,026.6	265.3	8.4	11.2	6.01
Mass Mart	11,568.4	251.8	6.6	43.3	6.01
Truworths	1,676.4	189.8	15.7	20.5	6.01
Metro Cash & Carry	35,625.9	275.7	0.3	–58.5	6.01
Foschini	2,980.5	23.0	2.3	1.2	3.01
Edgars	6,844.8	196.2	6.9	7.9	3.01
Ellerines	1,571.0	218.5	14.5	17.5	8.00

Holding companies, whose subsidiaries are also listed, such as Wooltru and Pepkor, have been excluded.
Source: 'Top companies', *Financial Mail*, 2002; *Financial Mail*, 15 December 2000.

placed to withstand the pressure of rising interest rates. This benefited Pick n Pay and Metro Cash and Carry, and chains whose management was alert early on to the deteriorating economic conditions, such as Mr Price, New Clicks and Queenspark. The successful stores were the ones that had invested heavily in information technology for point-of-sales stock control, accounting and electronic procurement.

Finally, one might note that the direction of expansion outside the country changed in the course of the 1990s. In the early years Woolworths and Truworths were attempting to break into the Australian market with Country Road and Sports Girl, but the Australian fashion market was tough and neither company was very successful with its Australian operations. With the opening of the African market north of the Limpopo, their focus changed. Protea Furnishers led the rush northwards, followed by Shoprite, as supermarkets, clothing stores, fast-food chains, cinemas and hotel groups all sought to take advantage of the opportunities in the Southern African Development Community and of the partial relaxation of exchange controls for companies investing in Africa. Just as established First World retailers had advantages over the newcomers in Australia, South African retailers that had done their market research thoroughly found that they, too, had a competitive advantage in neighbouring markets in Southern and Central Africa. Retail business at the end of the twentieth century was following in the footsteps of the railways and banks at the end of the nineteenth century.

Geography and market forces were reasserting their importance in the process of economic development and, to a small extent, in overcoming the barriers imposed by distance and erected by politicians.

Conclusion

Conditions in the retail sector provided an accurate mirror of conditions in the economy at large, where a prosperous First World sector coexisted with an increasingly impoverished Third World sector. Economic policy affected this development indirectly in the case of the government's more responsible fiscal policy and better monetary policy; but those gains were offset by market-hostile labour policies, by affirmative action policies, by exchange controls and by the growing fear of an attack on property rights, which lie at the heart of modem economic development. The main driving force was private enterprise in a framework of market capitalism. This was evident both in the changes taking place within South Africa and in the growing importance of geographical and transport realities throughout the larger Southern African regions.

The economic conditions facing the retail sector at the end of the decade were summarised in the 2001 edition of the *Financial Mail*'s 'Top companies'.[3] To these I have added the persistent decade-long factors that, taken together, were holding back sales:

- a poor economy with rising unemployment;
- ever-rising prices;
- affirmative action;
- high taxation (for a developing economy);
- skilled white emigration;
- little foreign direct investment;
- exchange controls;
- high unit labour costs;
- backward-looking, ideologically motivated trade unions;
- cell phone spending;
- gambling amid a forest of new casinos;
- rising fuel costs;
- rising health care costs;
- rising electricity costs;
- cost of the new technology;
- rising interest rates.

3 'Top companies', *Financial Mail*, June 2001.

The paradox of retailing in the 1990s was that the very harshness of the prevailing economic conditions created Schumpeterian opportunities for renewed growth, partly through the technological impact of computerisation in raising productivity and a widening of the productivity gap between the more and the less efficient firms, and partly through the increasing intensity of competition among efficient firms. However, counterbalancing these moves towards greater efficiency was the effect of legislated affirmative action, which frequently led to less well trained, less efficient and less well motivated black staff replacing, or being promoted over, experienced and skilled white staff. This was most conspicuous in some of the supermarket chains.

15

The tourism industry

Gillian Saunders

Introduction

By 1990 tourism was one of the world's largest industries, having quadrupled in size between 1965 and 1990, growing at an average annual rate of more than 6 per cent between 1960 and 1990. There were 457.6 million international arrivals worldwide in 1990 and by 2000 this had grown to 686 million, with a slightly lower average growth rate of 4.1 per cent per annum. South Africa, by contrast, experienced an acceleration in the growth of its tourism industry to an average of 19.0 per cent per annum.

Tourism is defined differently by the World Tourism Organization (WTO), an intergovernmental organisation affiliated to the United Nations, and the World Travel and Tourism Council (WTCC), an international private sector tourism association. The WTO definition is:

> Tourism comprises the activities of persons travelling to and staying [overnight] in places outside their usual environment for not more than one consecutive year for leisure, business and other purposes.[1]

The WTTC definition is:

> The travel and tourism industry is defined by the economic activities (personal, investment, government, business and net exports) associated with travel as measured by the wide variety of current and capital expenditures made by or for the benefit of a traveller, before, during and after a trip.[2]

The WTTC definition does not state that trips include 'staying' and therefore includes day-visitor travel. It also indicates the expanded

1 *World Tourism Organization Technical Manual: Concepts, Definitions and Classifications for Tourism Statistics*, WTO, 1995.

2 *Travel and Tourism: A New Economic Perspective* (research edition), WTTC, 1995.

view taken of tourism's economic activity, which includes, for instance, a portion of private vehicle usage for holidays, purchase of holiday personal goods (guide books, sun tan lotion, clothing, camping equipment etc.) and capital and government expenditure. The WTTC avoids in its definition 'outside their usual environment'. Many countries in collecting tourism information have developed distance definitions for 'outside their usual environment' (SA Tourism introduced a 40 km limit in 2005, which effectively excluded much 'tourism' from current tourism statistics). The WTTC uses specific statistical analyses for each situation to define when a trip is tourism.

Tourism, the activity of travelling and staying away from home for any motivation or purpose, has been with us for centuries, but it has been recognised as an industry only since the early 1900s. International tourism became a significant activity in the 1950s and 1960s, when the people of developed nations at middle and lower socio-economic levels began to take regular holidays outside their own country and wide-bodied aircraft opened up international air travel for business and pleasure travel. In 1990 South Africa, as a dichotomous nation, with both a developed and developing profile, positioned far from major international tourism-generating countries, and just beginning to shed its apartheid mantel, but still a pariah on its own continent, had not yet entered the era of international tourism.

Tourism is an industry influenced by domestic factors in generating countries as well as the situation at the destination. Economic downturns in generator countries reduce outbound tourism flows. Wars, disease and terrorism reduce travel globally. At the destination, levels of safety and security are of critical importance in attracting tourists.

Tourism is multifaceted, comprising many elements of sectors considered to be other industries. Much of the transport industry, for example, is tourism, but much is not. Similarly, large portions of the sports industry are tourism, but much is not. Some activity within the hotel industry is not tourism (having a meal or a coffee at the restaurant in a local hotel is not tourism), although most people would describe hotels as being part of the tourism industry. Tourist spending, which comprises the entire spend of a person travelling, includes spending in the retail industry, at petrol stations, in theatres and cinemas, so that parts of the performing arts, entertainment and retail industries may be considered part of the tourism industry. As a result, the tourism industry is hard to measure and this is compounded by the fact that there is no legislation that requires registration of supply within the industry, nor any that requires the recording of domestic activity within the industry.

Statistics are drawn from border control and sample surveys. In 1990 the industry was relatively unsophisticated and unrecognised in South

Figure 15.1 *Number of international arrivals in South Africa, 1990–2000*

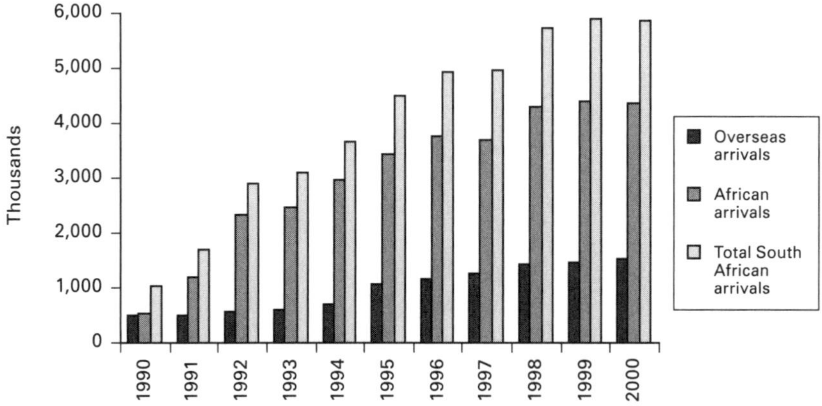

Source: Statistics South Africa.

Africa, and data collection was minimal and fragmented. While the situation had improved significantly by 2000, data collection remains inconsistent and is still fragmented, so that quantifying the industry in its various dimensions is still problematical. The data provided here relate mainly to overnight tourism, and all overnight tourism is included.

Foreign tourism in South Africa

The first year in which foreign tourist arrivals to South Africa topped 1 million was in 1990, when 1,029,000 foreign tourists visited the country. Ten years later this had risen to 5,872,250.[3] Of the 1990 arrivals, 493,000 were overseas visitors and 536,000 were from Africa, roughly a similar number from each. However, the counting methods for African arrivals varied over the period 1984 to 1992. Prior to 1984 no African arrivals were counted, from 1984 to 1990 only arrivals from Botswana, Zimbabwe and Lesotho, and after 1990 from Namibia. It was only in 1992 that visitors entering South Africa included all African arrivals.

The 493,000 overseas arrivals in 1990 was the fourth consecutive year of good growth, at an average of 13.8 per cent per annum, from a low of only 293,000 overseas arrivals in 1986, after P. W. Botha's Rubicon speech. In 2000 South Africa hosted 1,518,000 overseas arrivals and the average annual growth rate for the decade had risen to 11.9 per cent,

3 Statistics South Africa.

Figure 15.2 *Growth in international arrivals, 1991–2000*

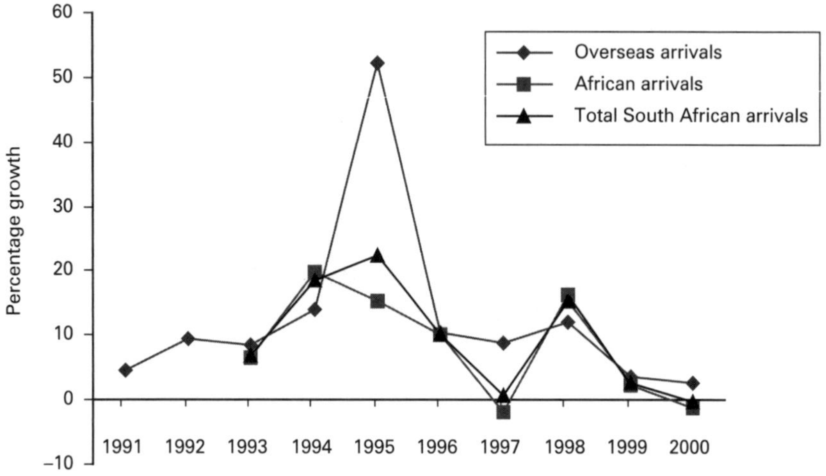

Source: Statistics South Africa and GT Analysis.

far outpacing the international average of 4.1 per cent for the decade (Figure 15.1). Under the revised counting base for African arrivals, the first comparable base year is 1992, when 2,328,000 African arrivals were recorded. This had grown to 4,354,500 by 2000, representing an average annual growth of 8.1 per cent over the eight years, almost twice that of the international average (Figure 15.2).

The first post-election year, 1995, saw a huge increase in overseas arrivals, with a growth of 52.3 per cent over the number in 1994 (see Figure 15.2), as holiday tourists and business people flocked to the 'new' South Africa (Table 15.1). This level of annual growth is unheard of in worldwide terms and has not since been repeated in South Africa. It was boosted a little by the Rugby World Cup in 1995, which was reported to have attracted about 27,000 foreign visitors, but this amounted to only 2.5 per cent of total overseas arrivals. The growth in African arrivals, by contrast, saw no such quantum leaps, but progressed steadily until the last few years of the decade, when small declines occurred in 1997 and 2000. The large base number of African arrivals had the effect of retarding the growth of total arrivals.

In 1990, 79.8 per cent of arrivals were for holiday purposes and 18.6 per cent for business purposes.[4] Since few African arrivals were recorded in

4 Statistics South Africa.

Table 15.1 *Selected overseas arrivals in South Africa and annual growth rates, 1990–2000*

	Number in 1990 (1,000s)	*Number in 1993 (1,000s)*	*Average annual growth, 1990–93 (%)*	*Number in 1995 (1,000s)*	*Average annual growth, 1993–95 (%)*	*Number in 1998 (1,000s)*	*Average annual growth, 1995–98 (%)*	*Number in 2000 (1,000s)*	*Average annual growth 1998–2000*	*Average annual growth, 1990–2000*
UK	135	154	4.5	244	25.9	244	0.0	350	19.8	10.0
Germany	84	108	8.7	168	24.7	195	5.1	210	3.8	9.6
Netherlands	17	20	5.6	27	16.2	59	29.8	91	24.2	18.3
France	20	27	10.5	54	41.4	63	5.3	90	19.5	16.2
Italy	16	18	4.0	47	61.6	29	–14.9	38	14.5	9.0
Switzerland	20	20	0.0	30	22.5	33	3.2	33	0.0	5.1
Australia	19	25	8.8	47	38.5	56	6.0	57	0.9	11.6
USA	47	66	12.0	103	24.9	133	8.9	175	14.7	14.0

Source: SA Tourism.

Figure 15.3 *Foreign air arrivals in 2000 and the main purpose of visit*

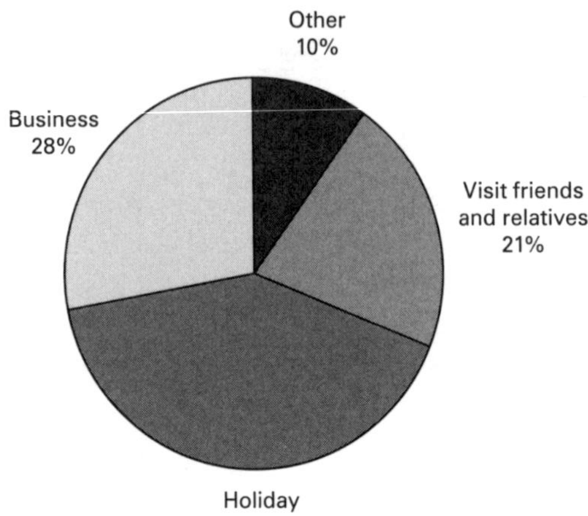

Source: SA Tourism.

1990, these figures represent mainly arrivals from overseas. Because of the lack of survey data on cross-border arrivals until the early 2000s and because foreign tourism surveys covered only air arrivals, the following purpose-of-visit information relates to air arrivals only. These were the 'real' or 'true' tourists. Most cross-border African tourists tended to be shoppers, traders or job seekers.

In 2000, 41 per cent of air travellers visited South Africa for holiday purposes. This equates to some 742,000 holiday air arrivals in 2000. A further 28 per cent visited the country for business purposes and 21 per cent travelled to South Africa mainly to visit friends and relatives ('VFR'). The remaining 10 per cent of foreign air arrivals visited South Africa for other purposes (Figure 15.3).

If we assume the VFR arrivals in 1990 were recorded as holiday arrivals, then the 80 per cent of the total 'holiday' arrivals in that year compares with 62 per cent in 2000 (see Figure 15.3). This decline in the proportion was probably due to growth in international trade and other links with both Africa and the rest of the world, resulting in more business travellers entering the country.

In 2000 the average foreign travel tourist arriving by air in South Africa spent R14,801 on accommodation, food, drink, shopping, transport and recreation (including pre-paid expenses) during their stay in the country. This was a small increase on 1999 (R14,636). Including airfare, the average tourist's expenditure was R24,500 in 2000. Business travellers had the highest daily expenditure (R1,277), followed by holiday travellers (R1,185 per day). Tourists staying with friends and relatives spent, on average, only R550 per day in 2000.[5]

Domestic tourism

Domestic tourism is unregulated and therefore not counted. However, various *ad hoc* surveys by SATOUR (the forerunner of SA Tourism; the statutory body responsible for promoting tourism) and other organisations gave an indication of this sector of the industry. A domestic tourism study by the Board of Trade and Industry[6] indicated that, in 1989, 10 million South Africans took an overnight leisure holiday, with a total estimated spend of R2.8 billion. Reserve Bank figures on domestic holiday spending indicated that this had risen to R3.3 billion in 1990. Estimates[7] put business travel and tourism spending at R2.5 billion, resulting in a domestic tourism industry worth some R5.8 billion in 1990.

The first comprehensive survey of domestic tourism, in 1993,[8] concentrating on holiday travel found that 69 per cent of whites, 42 per cent of Asians, 28 per cent of coloureds and 26 per cent of blacks went on holiday in 1992. KwaZulu-Natal attracted the largest proportion of trips (24.6 per cent), followed by the PWV (Pretoria, Witwatersrand Vaal – effectively Gauteng) (18.6 per cent), the Eastern Cape (15.5 per cent) and the Western Cape (13.5 per cent). The average length of stay was 8 nights (down from 12 nights in a 1988 survey). Of these holidaymakers, 57.4 per cent stayed with family or friends, 12.4 per cent stayed in self-catering accommodation and 9.2 per cent went camping or caravanning. Only 8.3 per cent stayed in hotels. A 1995 survey (of 2000 households)[9] indicated similar destination patterns, with an average spend per trip of R1,020 for all people travelling, and an average duration of 7 days. The shorter duration of holiday was a response to increasing costs.

In 1996 the first study to quantify all leisure (broader than holiday but excluding business travel and tourism) domestic tourism[10] (9,527 respondents) found that 16 million adult domestic tourists (63.2 per cent of the adult population) took 30.4 million domestic tourism trips that year. Of all these trips, 53 per cent were to VFR and most were

5 *Foreign Tourism Surveys*, SA Tourism, summer and winter 2000.
6 *Investigation into the Tourism Industry*, Board of Trade and Industry, 1990.
7 *Tourism Talk*, Kessel Feinstein Consulting (now Grant Thornton), 1994.
8 *Domestic Tourism Survey*, Satour, 1993.
9 *Domestic Tourism Survey*, Satour, 1995.
10 *Domestic Tourism Survey*, SA Tourism, 1996.

Figure 15.4 *Province of origin of domestic tourists, 2000/01*

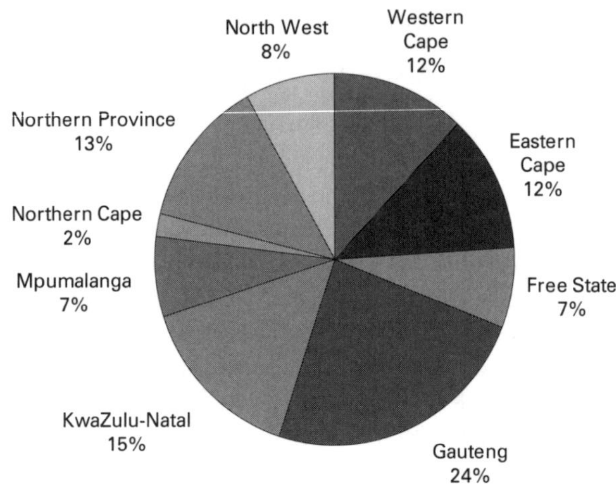

Source: Domestic Tourism Survey, SA Tourism, 2001.

to KwaZulu-Natal (26 per cent), followed by the Western Cape (22 per cent), the Eastern Cape (13 per cent) and then Gauteng (12 per cent). The average spend per person per trip was R281 and the average duration of a trip was 6.2 nights. Of these tourists, 44 per cent stayed with family and friends, 26 per cent stayed in self-catering accommodation and 10 per cent stayed in hotels.

SA Tourism conducted its sixth domestic tourism study in 2001, based on the travel activities of 9,527 respondents over the period May 2000 to April 2001. This was the first comprehensive survey covering all types of domestic tourism. The study indicated that 33.5 million overnight trips were made by domestic tourists travelling and staying overnight for holiday, business, VFR and other purposes. Gauteng was the main generator of domestic tourists, followed by KwaZulu-Natal, Northern Province (now Limpopo) and the Western and Eastern Capes (see Figure 15.4).

Figure 15.5 shows that the same provinces dominated as domestic tourism destinations as generators, with Gauteng just surpassing KwaZulu-Natal, followed by the Northern Province, the Eastern Cape and then the Western Cape. Over the decade the destination preferences remained much the same. It was probably the incorporation of business travel into the 2001 survey that pushed Gauteng up to the level of KwaZulu-Natal. Most domestic tourist travel was for VFR purposes (59 per cent), followed by holiday (21 per cent) and religious purposes (14 per cent) (see Figure 15.6).

Figure 15.5 *Destination provinces for domestic trips, 2000/01*

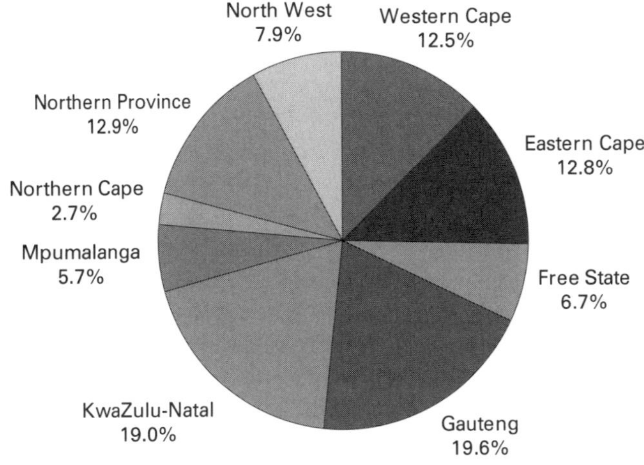

Source: Domestic Tourism Survey, SA Tourism, 2001.

Figure 15.6 *Purpose of visit of domestic tourists, 2000/01*

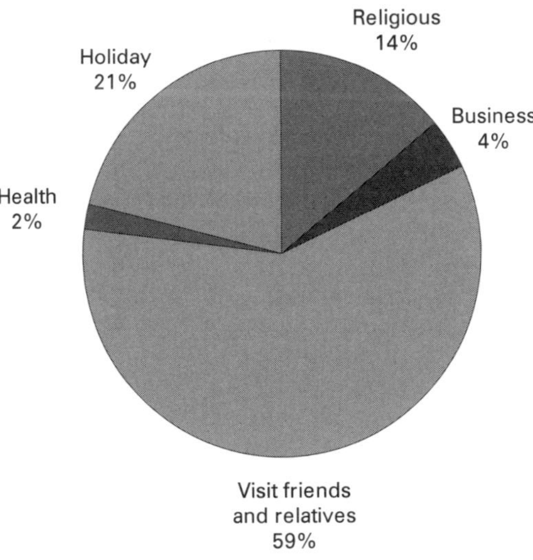

Source: Domestic Tourism Survey, SA Tourism, 2001.

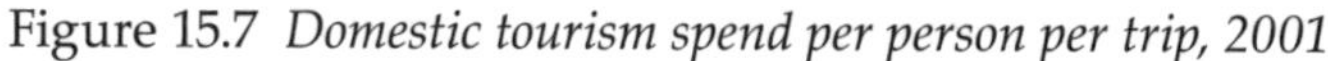

Figure 15.7 *Domestic tourism spend per person per trip, 2001*

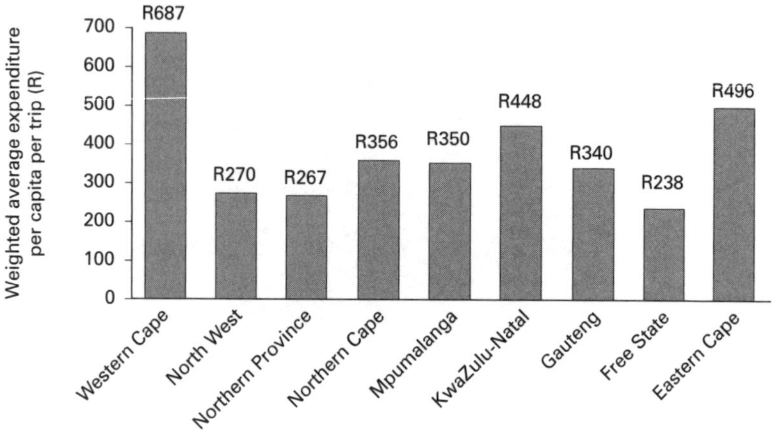

Source: Domestic Tourism Survey, SA Tourism, 2001.

The overall South African per capita average spend on a trip was R437, of which a large proportion, R182 (42 per cent), was spent on transport, R97 (22 per cent) on accommodation, R105 (24 per cent) on food, R34 (8 per cent) on entertainment and R20 (5 per cent) on gifts. The highest-spending domestic tourists visited the Western Cape (Figure 15.7).

It is likely that the decade saw a strong increase in domestic tourism, but there are few statistics to corroborate this. The estimated growth in non-hotel tourist accommodation room supply in the country over the decade (6.4 per cent per annum over 1993–2001) and the fact that this accommodation was largely used by domestic tourists (see 'Other accommodation sectors', below) suggest that the decade did see good growth in domestic tourism.

In spite of this increase, many in the industry believed that the full potential of domestic tourism among all population groups had not been reached. While in the developed world 'blue collar' workers are significant holiday takers, for instance sustaining mass charter tourism, in South Africa the working class still predominantly visit friends and relatives. However, through church groups religious travel began in the 1990s to take such people away from home, but holiday taking is not a social or cultural norm for most black working-class people.

Hotels and accommodation

Different grading systems and the exclusion of hotel rooms in the 'homeland' states of Bophuthatswana, Transkei, Venda and Ciskei before 1994 have made the tracking of the hotel and accommodation industries difficult, from both a supply and a performance perspective. In 1990 there were, under the old compulsory hotel grading system, around 1,300 hotels, which offered a total of 46,000 rooms, down from 1,400 hotels and some 48,000 rooms in 1982. This decline continued to 1993, when there were 1,200 hotels. The grading system then changed to a new voluntary system. Under the new system, in 1995, 440 graded hotels offered 26,000 rooms.

The main part of the decline in the number of hotels in the 1980s and early 1990s involved one-star hotels, which numbered 1,070 in 1981 but fewer than 800 in 1991. Under the new 1995 system only some 31 one-star hotels were graded. A previous liquor dispensation, whereby a hotel licence was required for a liquor licence, had led to an excess of one-star properties which operated primarily as pubs and bars. The 440 graded hotels in 1995 represented 84 per cent of SATOUR's estimated 520 true hotels in South Africa.

By 2000 the grading system was again undergoing change, forced by the withdrawal of the large groups from the grading scheme. They opposed having to pay a hotel development levy when they had been graded. As a result, a new voluntary grading system for all types of accommodation establishments was introduced in 2001, under which the number of hotels in South Africa was estimated at 1,032, with 60,000 rooms. The number of hotel rooms had doubled since 1995, with an exceptionally high average growth of around 38 per cent per annum over the six years.

Grant Thornton has been tracking the formal hotel stock in major centres, including limited-service hotels, since 1993. In Johannesburg 27 hotels were identified in 1993, with 4,711 rooms. This had grown to 93 hotels with 13,002 rooms in 2000, a total growth in room supply of 176 per cent over the period. High growth came in 1995 (26 per cent) and 1996 (42 per cent), but there was some growth every year, though by 2000 it had fallen to 3 per cent. In Cape Town the 32 formal hotels, supplying 1,840 rooms in 1993, had grown to 73 hotels with 11,077 rooms in 2000, a growth of 502 per cent. The highest annual growth, of 222 per cent, occurred in 1996, followed by 22 per cent growth in 1997. Thereafter growth tailed down to 1 per cent and 5 per cent in 1999 and 2000 respectively. In both Cape Town and Johannesburg there was an increase in both business and leisure tourism from 1994 onwards, which led, between two and five years later, to the increase in accommodation.

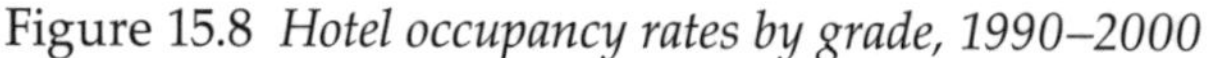
Figure 15.8 *Hotel occupancy rates by grade, 1990–2000*

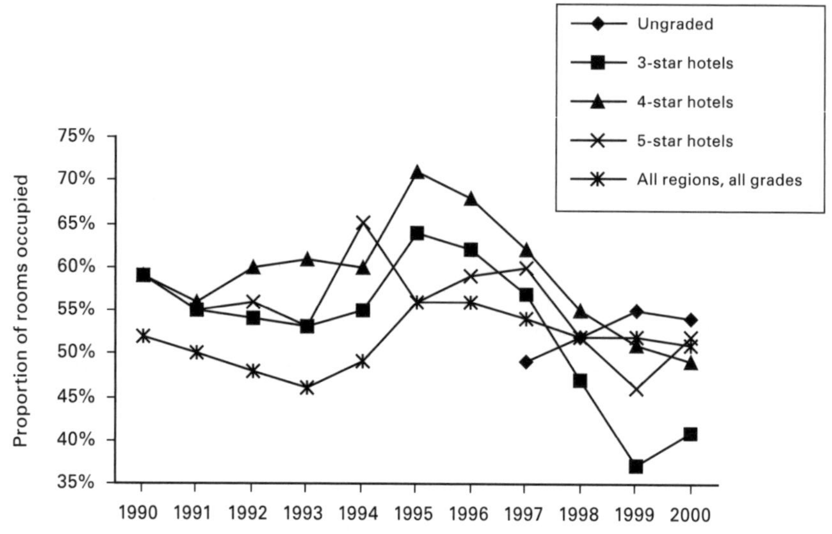

Source: Statistics South Africa and GT Analysis.

Durban had the largest number of rooms available. There were 32 hotels in Durban in 1993, offering 6,837 rooms. They had benefited from the existence of domestic and international leisure, sport and conference tourism in the late 1970s and 1980s, when the Southern Sun company developed the Maharani, Elangeni, Malibu and Holiday Inn hotels along the beach front. By 2000 Durban's hotel stock had grown to 42 hotels with 7,767 rooms, a growth in room supply of only 13.6 per cent over the seven years. Durban was falling behind Cape Town as a holiday destination.

Hotel performance over the decade fluctuated. Occupancy of all graded hotels was 52 per cent in 1990 and 51 per cent in 2000. The decade had ended with similar industry performance levels that it had started with.[11] In between it peaked at 56 per cent in 1995 and bottomed at 46 per cent in 1993 (Figure 15.8). The poor level of national confidence caused the industry's poor performance in 1993. The improvement started in 1994 (observer missions and other international interest contributed to this) and the incredible growth of occupancies in 1995 followed from the 52 per cent growth in overseas arrivals that year.

11 Statistics South Africa.

Figure 15.9 *Hotel occupancy rates by main centres, 1990–2000*

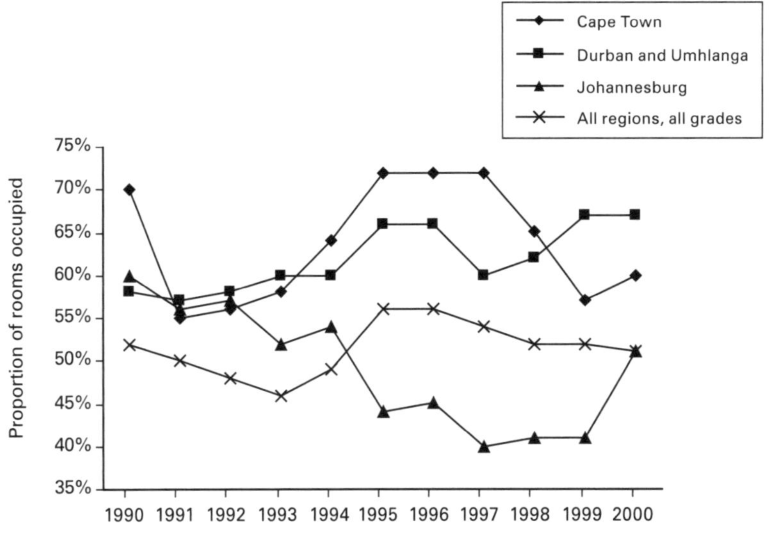

Source: Statistics South Africa and GT Analysis.

After 1995 occupancy rates reflected normal market conditions. They declined, particularly sharply in 1997, largely as a result of major increases in hotel supply and the limited growth in tourist arrivals. Three-star hotels and five-star hotels fared worst in occupancy rates; four-star hotels achieved better rates. Ungraded hotels outperformed the graded hotels (see Figure 15.8). Many of these were newer, good hotels, often branded, that opted not to be graded.

Figure 15.9 shows the hotel occupancies by main centre. Cape Town saw the longest sustained higher occupancy rates, helped by buoyant overseas holiday arrivals. Supply growth then drove average occupancies down. Johannesburg, which had experienced earlier high levels of supply growth, saw occupancies drop drastically from 1990, improving only at the very end of the decade. Durban, with limited supply growth, maintained the highest occupancy rate over the decade.

Occupancy is only one side of the equation in hotel performance. Hotel revenue is maximised only when both occupancies and achieved room rates are optimum. Average room rate is the industry measure of net accommodation income per room-night sold, and is averaged over single- or double-room occupancy and, after discounting, deduction of allocations for meals and other inclusive elements and net of VAT. Average rates are often significantly below the quoted tariffs (or 'rack

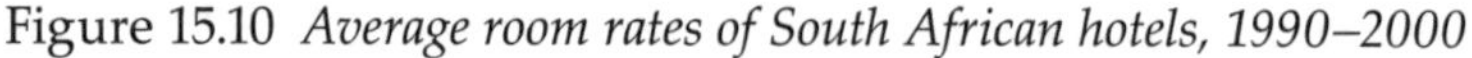

Figure 15.10 *Average room rates of South African hotels, 1990–2000*

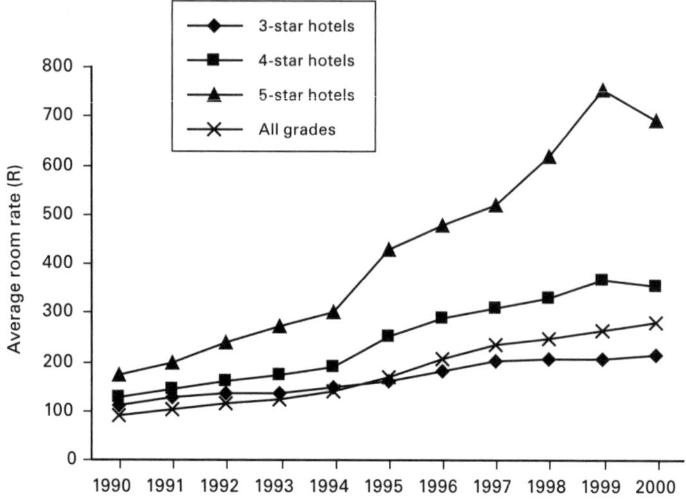

Source: Statistics South Africa and GT Analysis.

rates'). Figure 15.10 shows the nominal average room rates of South African hotels for the decade and Figure 15.11 the real average room rates. Five-star rates showed significant growth, while three-star rates barely increased. In constant 1990 prices three-star rates declined from R110 to R88 over the period, while four-star rates increased from R127 to R145. In constant 1990 prices five-star average rates grew by 60 per cent, from R174 to R283 in 2000 (after a peak at R324 in 1999). Other grades of hotel saw very little real growth in room rates. In 1993, when the average rate for all grades was at its lowest, at R84, *Tourism Talk* commented that:

> Generally, the accommodation industry once again fared poorly in 1993, with average room occupancies of registered hotels falling marginally to 46 per cent, two per cent points lower than 1992…. The 1993 average room rate of R124 was almost exactly what we predicted and reflects growth slightly below the inflation rate.[12]

At the same time, Kessel Feinstein noted that the stock market was demonstrating some bullishness on the outlook for hotels, as, after consistently trailing industrial prices on the Johannesburg Stock Exchange

12 *Tourism Talk,* Kessel Feinstein Consulting, 1993.

Figure 15.11 *Real average room rates of South African hotels, 1990–2000*

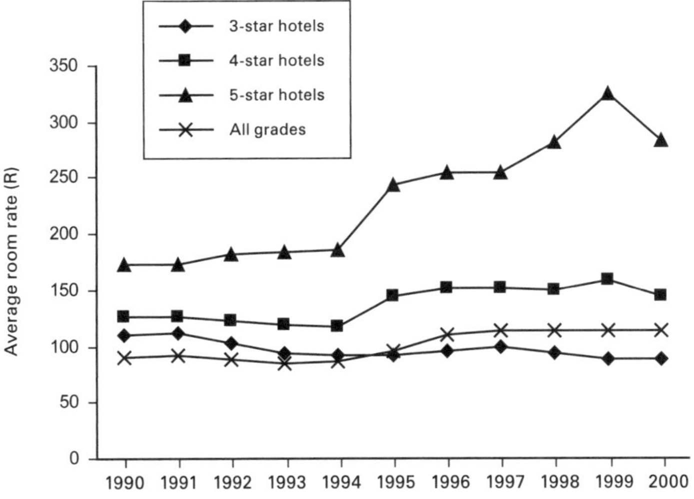

Source: Statistics South Africa and GT Analysis.

since early 1992, the beverages, hotels and leisure sector outperformed industrials from 1993.

The bullishness was probably well placed in terms of prospects for demand growth, but no one expected the excessive supply growth that materialised after 1995. This resulted in better, but not substantially good, hotel performance at the end of the decade. The huge supply growth was, however, an indicator of general confidence in tourism to and within South Africa on the part of both local and foreign investors and hotel operators; many investors, especially where Cape Town, an iconic city, is concerned, simply wanted to ensure a presence in the city/country and were willing to take a very long-term view.

Other accommodation sectors

Total size of the sector

If tracking the hotel industry is problematic, following the remaining sectors in tourism accommodation supply is very difficult. The first attempt to quantify the supply of resorts, self-catering flats, time-share, guest-houses, bed and breakfasts, game lodges and park board

Figure 15.12 *Breakdown of non-hotel accommodation, 1993*

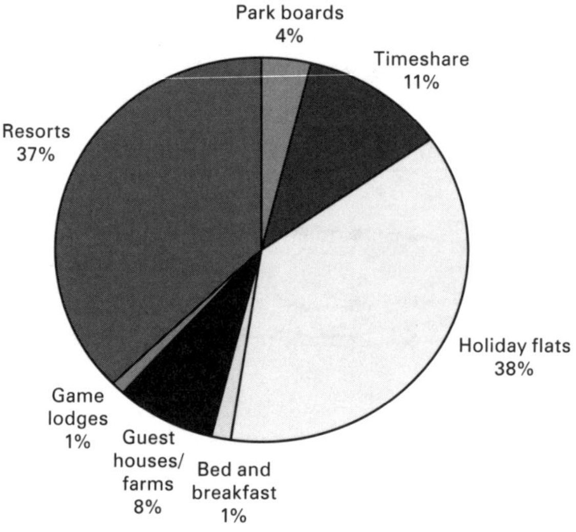

Source: Tourism Talk, Kessel Feinstein Consulting, 1993.

Table 15.2 *Estimated supply of tourist accommodation, 2001*

	Number of establish-ments	*Number of units or rooms (1,000s)*	*Number of beds (1,000s)*	*% beds*	*% rooms*
Hotels	1,000	60.0	120.0	26.5%	35.6%
National and provincial parks	95	2.9	9.5	2.1%	1.7%
Timeshare	167	6.1	24.4	5.4%	3.6%
Resorts and self-catering	1,950	48.5	194.0	42.9%	28.7%
Youth hostel	70	0.5	2.4	0.5%	0.3%
Executive apartments	34	2.0	5.0	1.1%	1.2%
Game and hunting lodges	745	12.6	25.2	5.6%	7.5%
Bed and breakfast	3,700	13.0	26.0	5.7%	7.7%
Guest-houses and farms	3,300	23.1	46.2	10.2%	13.7%
Totals	11,061	168.7	452.7		

Source: GT Analysis, *Tourism Grading Council Masterplan,* Tourism Grading Council, 2002.

accommodation in 1993 (Figure 15.12) estimated that there were 202,000 beds available across these establishments, in some 80,000 rooms and units.[13] Figure 15.2 indicates the breakdown of this accommodation by type. Three years later the figure had grown to 249,000 beds.[14]

Table 15.2 shows the estimated tourist accommodation supply in South Africa developed by Grant Thornton Kessel Feinstein for the new Tourism Grading Council.[15] In 2001 non-hotel beds were estimated at 332,700, indicating that between 1993 and 2001 they had grown by 65 per cent, as the market responded to the new opportunities that were emerging. There are no data collated on occupancies for the non-hotel accommodation sectors, so it is difficult to determine whether demand lagged or outstripped bed supply, but the extent of supply growth indicates a reasonable growth in demand over the period, probably at least equalling economic growth, if not surpassing it. It is likely that the non-hotel bed supply followed a similar pattern to that of hotels, with supply outpacing demand in the second half of the decade.

National and provincial parks

The national and provincial parks remained a significant player, providing, in 2001, 9,500 beds in 95 establishments.[16] National and KwaZulu-Natal parks provided 7,800 beds in 1992 and 8,100 beds in 2001, indicating a modest growth in supply of 3.8 per cent for the period. It is unlikely that the other provincial parks experienced a different pattern of supply growth.

The government parks continually experienced good to excellent occupancy rates, with the national parks reporting 75 per cent unit occupancy and 60 per cent bed occupancy in 1992, and Natal Parks 40 per cent bed occupancy that year.[17] In 1999 the Kruger National Park was running at 85 per cent unit occupancy and 75 per cent bed occupancy, with the rest of the South African national parks achieving 72 per cent unit occupancy and 52 per cent bed occupancies. KwaZulu-Natal Parks achieved a 61 per cent unit occupancy in 1999.[18] While there are indications that occupancies in the parks peaked in 1997/98, the strong occupancy improvement over most of the decade indicates strong growth in demand for the parks' products. However, this was probably

13 *Tourism Talk*, Kessel Feinstein Consulting, 1993.
14 *Tourism Talk*, Kessel Feinstein Consulting, 1996.
15 GT Analysis, *Tourism Grading Council Masterplan*, Tourism Grading Council, 2002.
16 *Study on Tourism Promotion and Development Plan in South Africa*, JICA, 2002.
17 *Tourism Talk*, Kessel Feinstein Consulting, 1993.
18 *Study on Tourism Promotion and Development Plan in South Africa*.

restrained by the limited growth in supply and the government probably missed out on opportunities to expand the accommodation during the decade. The general lack of government priority with respect to tourism (see below) and parks was responsible for this.

Self-catering and timeshare

The self-catering sector at the beginning of the decade was characterised by resorts (an estimated 700 around the country) comprised of self-catering chalets, often municipal or government owned, and self-catering holiday flats. These always provided the lion's share of accommodation supply. Holiday flats were popular in seaside resorts such as Durban, Umhlanga, East London, Port Elizabeth and Cape Town.

While this core of the self-catering industry remained, new products arrived during the 1990s, including serviced suite hotels with self-catering facilities, which often targeted the longer-stay market, such as the Villa Via, Courtyard and Don groups, and the second-home estates. The number of such estates was not tracked in the 1990s, but there is no doubt that, while few in number at the beginning of the period (Sanlameer was the forerunner of these estates), there were many by the end of the decade. These properties provided self-catering holiday accommodation for the owner while on holiday and were frequently rented for the same purpose to the general public at other times, thereby adding to the self-catering stock in the country. Many other phenomena are associated with these estates, such as co-ownership and consortium ownership and fractional title (where ownership is of four to six weeks in an exclusive property, usually on a second-home estate, though the last-mentioned was only just beginning to be developed in 2000).

The era of strong timeshare growth in the 1980s came to an end in the 1990s, by which time there were an estimated 200,000 unit weeks of timeshare owned in South Africa, in about 150 resorts. The 200,000 unit weeks of 1991 had grown to 215,000 owners (many owning multiple weeks) in 170 resorts by 1997; but little growth occurred after that date. Indeed, the 2001 estimates indicate a small decline to 167 resorts from 170 resorts. Timeshare had grown rapidly in the 1980s and, while many schemes were sound and well managed, a number of fly-by-night developers had brought a bad reputation to the industry. In 1992 the industry attempted to improve its image with Timeshare 2000. This introduced a five-day post-purchase cooling-off period and a timeshare ombudsman to handle disputes. The Timeshare Institute of South Africa later introduced a code of conduct for members. Despite these changes, the timeshare industry's growth remained low during the 1990s, with few new developments.

Bed and breakfasts and guest-houses

Only a few guest-houses existed in 1990, and bed and breakfasts were almost nonexistent. The decade, however, saw a huge growth in supply in this sector. Portfolio of Country Places launched its first bed and breakfast guide in 1993/94, in which 75 bed and breakfasts were listed. This had doubled to 142 in its second edition in 1994/95 and its 1999/2000 edition had 515 entries. Portfolio's Town and Country Retreats, which mainly offer 2–16 bedrooms and can be said to cover the main guest-house sector (the super-luxury guest-houses are listed elsewhere), had 49 properties listed in 1991/92 and this number had grown to 234 by 1999/2000. While not a statistical survey, representation in this type of guide is a good indicator of growth in the industry, which amounted to a 22 per cent increase in the number of guest-houses over eight years, and a 38 per cent increase in the number of bed and breakfast establishments over six years.

Bed and breakfasts and guest-houses have long been commonplace in the UK and much of Europe and are more and more favoured by foreign holiday and domestic business and holiday tourists; this trend manifested in South Africa in the 1990s. The high rate of growth in this sector led some in the hotel sector to bemoan loss of market share to the bed and breakfasts and guest-houses, which had about 20 per cent of bed supply by the end of the decade. Coupled with the high growth in hotel bed supply, this probably did dent some hotels' business. By the end of the 1990s this sector of the industry had probably reached its equilibrium point *vis-à-vis* the supply of hotels in the tourism accommodation sector. It is unlikely that bed and breakfasts and guest-houses will ever provide 50 per cent of accommodation; around 20 per cent is probably the level at which the demand for this type of accommodation is in balance with supply.

Game lodges

Game lodges were a well known product at the start of the 1990s, but few in number and limited mainly to either super-luxury lodges (Mala Mala, Londolozi and Sabi Sabi being the pioneers) and hunting lodges. The first edition of Kessel Feinstein Consulting's *Tourism Talk,* from 1992, did not cover game lodges separately; the 1993 edition estimated they provided some 2,400 beds. This had grown to an estimated 25,200 beds in 2001 in some 745 hunting and lodge establishments, indicating a growth of around 30 per cent per annum in supply. Game lodges range from upper-middle market to super-luxury, with the high-end lodges targeting only foreign tourists at exceptionally high tariffs. The lure of

Figure 15.13 *Breakdown of South African conference venues by size, 1994*

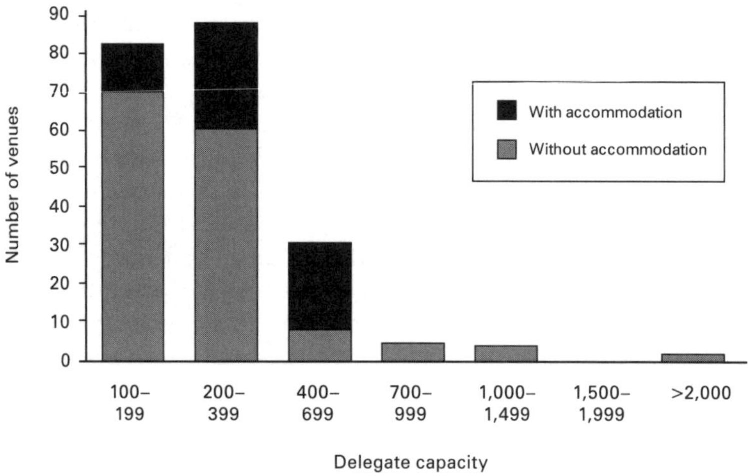

Source: Tourism Talk, Kessel Feinstein Consulting, 1994.

these tariffs and the growth in overseas tourism to South Africa during the mid-1990s induced many game-farm owners to develop luxury lodges; the industry became oversupplied towards the end of the decade and competition became fierce. Average bed occupancies across the industry were estimated to be as low as 45 per cent in the early 2000s.

Other tourism industry sectors

Conference industry

In 1991 there were only 12 conference venues in the country that could accommodate more than 1,000 delegates and 10 of these were simple multi-purpose halls. Nationwide there were an estimated 1,250 conference venues, but two-thirds could accommodate fewer than 100 delegates.[19] Figure 15.13 shows the numbers of venues by size in 1994 and Figure 15.14 the proportions of venues by size in 2001.

Kessel Feinstein Consulting estimated the size of the industry in 1992 at 81,600 events, of which 1,600 were international, worth some 10 million delegate-days.[20] By the end of the decade the size of

19 *Tourism Talk,* Kessel Feinstein Consulting, 1992.
20 *Tourism Talk,* Kessel Feinstein Consulting, 1993.

Figure 15.14 *Breakdown of South African conference venues by size, 2001*

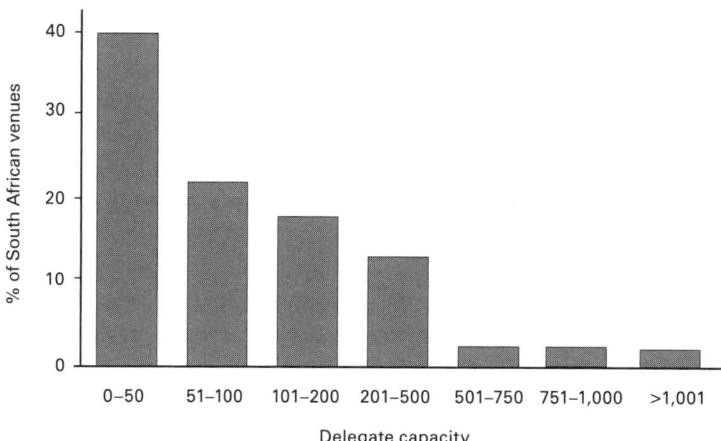

Source: Study on the Development and Promotion of Tourism in South Africa, JICA, 2001.

the industry was estimated at around 101,300 events and 14.7 million delegate-days – a growth rate of 5 per cent per annum in delegate-days and 3 per cent per annum in number of events.[21]

Conferencing was already seen as a growing industry, worth R400 million, and the three main South Africa cities were all considering developing major conference facilities. Large modern convention facilities are usually financed by the public sector because they do not provide a return on investment, but do generate significant tourism and related economic benefits. Durban, a cash-rich municipality, invested in its own International Convention Centre (ICC), which opened in 1997 with a plenary seating capacity of 5,000 at a cost of R260 million. Sandton followed suite in 2000 with the R350 million Sandton ICC, part of Tsogo Sun's bid for the Monti Casino licence in Johannesburg's northern suburbs, which was effectively cross-subsidised by the casino. Cape Town had to wait till after 2000 (2003) to get its ICC, partly funded by monies provided by Sun International for its successful Cape Town Casino bid and by the City and the Province. These venues have all been successful and helped South Africa become a convention destination on the international stage.

21 *SA Tourism Conference Study*, Grant Thornton Kessel Feinstein Consulting, 2000.

Gaming industry

The gaming industry in South Africa is one which underwent significant change in the 1990s under a radically re-engineered gambling dispensation. The decade started with no casinos in 'South Africa', as they were illegal, but 17 casinos did operate in homelands and 'homeland states'. Speculation was rife at the beginning of the decade that a new South African government would change the casino regulatory environment, and indeed the old government began the process with the Howard Commission in 1993, which concluded that there should be 10 licences for large casinos awarded in the country, none of which could be less than one hour's drive from metropolitan centres. The government passed the Lotteries and Gambling Board Act at the end of 1993, which remained broad and side-stepped all contentious issues. In late 1994 the Wiehahn Commission's *Main Report on Gambling in the Republic of South Africa* was released, which recommended that a further 23 casinos be allowed, bringing the total in the country to 40 – with no restrictions as to location. The National Gambling Bill released in September 1995 indicated how the 40 licences might be provincially distributed. Table 15.3 shows the allocation of licences. Both the Eastern Cape and North West Province had a reduction in the number of their licences.

The awarding of casino licences was a provincial responsibility and by the end of the decade the provinces had awarded 26 of the 40 licences to six major and five minor players in the casino industry (Table 15.4). With this, South Africa saw the advent of mega-city casino complexes in most primary and secondary cities. An original contention of the Howard Commission, and espoused by most provinces, was that casino developments should contribute to tourism infrastructure. While fantastic conference facilities, entertainment, museum and recreation facilities

Table 15.3 *Allocation of casino licences, by province, 1995*

	Existing licences	*Numbers proposed in National Gambling Bill (1995)*
Eastern Cape	7	5
Free State	2	4
Gauteng	–	6
KwaZulu-Natal	–	5
Mpumalanga	–	4
Northern Cape	–	3
Northern Province	1	3
North West Province	7	5
Western Cape	–	5

Source: Tourism Talk, Kessel Feinstein Consulting, 1996.

Table 15.4 *Numbers of casino licences and operating casinos, by province, 2001*

Province	*Entitle-ment*	*Issued/held*	*Consortium*	*Location*
Eastern Cape	5	3	Sun International	Wild Coast Sun
			Sun International	Port Elizabeth
			Tsogo Sun	Outside East London
Free State	4	2	Sun International	Naledi Sun
			Sun International	Thaba 'Nchu Sun
Gauteng	6	5	Afrisun	Carnival City, Brakpan
			Global Resorts	Caesars, Kempton Park
			Gold Reef Casinos	Gold Reef City, Johannesburg
			London Clubs International	Emerald Casino, Vanderbijlpark
			Tsogo Sun	Fourways
		On appeal	Ramada Rhino	Kromdraai
KwaZulu-Natal	5	5	Balele Leisure	Monte Vista, Newcastle
			Gold Reef Casinos	Msunduzi, Pietermaritzburg
			Tusk Casino Group	Umfolozi Casino, Richards Bay
			Afrisun	Sibaya Resort, Umdloti
		Under contention	Tsogo Sun	Village Green, Durban
Mpumalanga	4	3	Tsogo Sun	Emnotweni, Nelspruit
			Tsogo Sun	Champions, Witbank
			Global Resorts	Graceland, Secunda
North West	5	5	Sun International	Sun City
			Sun International	Morula Sun
			Sun International	Carousel
			Tusk Casino Group	Taung Sun
			Tusk Casino Group	Mmabatho
Northern Cape	3	3	Desert Palace Hotel Resorts	Upington
			Magic Mountain Casino	Colesberg
			Sun International	Flamingo Resort, Kimberley
Northern Province	3	2	Sun International	Venda Sun
			Meropa Leisure and Entertainment	Pietersburg
Western Cape	5	4	Tusk Casino Group	Pinnacle Point, Mossel Bay
			Sun International	Grandwest Casino, Cape Town
			Gold Reef Casinos	Mykonos, Langebaan
			Century Casinos	Caledon

Source: GT Analysis.

have been built as part of these developments, in many places the largest bid appears to have been successful and some casinos are patently not providing tourism facilities except in the case of basic hotel accommodation and gambling entertainment for tourists. The casino landscape changed enormously in the latter part of the decade as the new mega-casinos established themselves. In 2000, 10 per cent of foreign tourists departing by air indicated that they had visited a casino complex, evidence of their value as tourism attractions.

Transport industry

Coaches

The coach industry, like much of tourism, was not a popular topic, nor well documented, at the start of the decade. By 1992, concerns were being expressed about the size and standard of South Africa's coach fleet and whether it would be able to cope with an increase in tourism. High import duties were said to be further compounding the problem of modernising the coach fleet.

In 1995 the Coach Operators Association of South Africa (COASA) was inaugurated and there were said to be an estimated 640 luxury coaches in the country, of which 300 were operating on inter-city routes. Operators estimated that, in season, October to March, these coaches were operating at maximum capacity. The government responded and import duties on new and second-hand coaches were reduced from 100 per cent to 20 per cent in December 1995. By 2001 COASA estimated the number of tour coaches at 400, an annual growth rate of 3 per cent. Inter-city coach capacity remained at 300, still serving mainly the less-affluent sections of society, but charter/tour coach capacity had increased, serving the growth in international tourism.

Car hire

The car hire fleet in South Africa was estimated at 13,500 in 1990 and at 25,000 in 1995. The growth then slowed down and by the end of the decade it was 27,000. Local business travellers dominated the sector, accounting for 80 per cent of rentals, with international customers accounting for a mere 10 per cent.[22]

Airlines

In 1991 only 21 international airlines flew into South Africa. By 1995 this number had tripled, to reach 63 airlines. The number remained above

22 *Tourism Talk*, Kessel Feinstein Consulting, 1996; *Study on Development and Promotion of Tourism in South Africa*, JICA, 2002.

60 until 1998, when some airlines began to cut services to South Africa and by 2001 the number of international airlines flying in had dropped to around 40. Some decline was due to the demise of carriers from both Africa and further afield, and the rest simply to oversupply developed during the heady days of growth in the mid-1990s.

In the early 1990s flight capacity to South Africa to support international tourism was not a problem, but in 1995 lack of airline capacity started to raise its head as an issue and by 1998 tour operators, hoteliers and other industry players were citing the lack of seats, particularly on the European routes, as a constraint on the growth of tourism. South Africa operates bilateral air agreements with other countries. The contention was that the government, in negotiating flight frequencies with other countries, was acting to protect South African Airways (SAA) and therefore not increasing frequencies. The excess frequencies, it was feared, would be taken up by foreign airlines, as SAA had neither the aircraft nor the resources to take up its full share of excess frequencies and would be squeezed out of the market.

The decade saw a chequered air industry performance in South Africa. SAA was loss making when it was unbundled from Transnet to be commercialised. A foreign expert, Coleman Andrews, was recruited to take over the helm in 1998, to improve its financial situation, which he seemingly achieved. However, after his sudden resignation in 2001, it was discovered that the airline has been making losses throughout his tenure as chief executive.

Many new airlines started up during the mid-1990s, when growth was strong, and many withdrew equally fast. Flitestar and Luxavia closed down in 1994, and USA Africa, launched in 1994, closed in 1995. Avia airlines lasted only three months, from May 1995 to August 1995, while Phoenix Airways closed in October 1995. Some new entrants survived such as SA Express, which started in 1994, and some endured, taking on growth and new mantles. Comair, which started in 1946, the longest surviving private airline, was listed in July 1998; it had taken on the local British Airways franchise in 1996 to have a global branding to attract customers locally in South Africa. By 2000 there were seven domestic airlines, of which SAA was by far the strongest. With its code-sharing and cross-shareholding with SA Airlink and SA Express respectively, it handled 85 per cent of the 4.5 million domestic passengers. Low-cost airlines had not yet made their debut in South Africa in 2000.

Tour operators and travel agents

In 1998 there were an estimated 400 inbound tour operators to South Africa and this number had grown to 460 by 2001. Earlier estimates had indicated only around 135 operators in the first half of the decade.

About 15 of these were major operators, carrying from 4,000 to 50,000 tourists a year, while the rest were often small, handling from a few hundred to a few thousand tourists. The proportion of overseas tourists to South Africa on tours increased during the first half of the decade, reaching 17 per cent in 1995 and 27 per cent in 1998. Subsequently the data are no longer available for overseas tourists only and are diluted by African visitors, who do not usually use tour operators.

In the early 1990s the travel agency industry was deregulated and entry became open to anyone. By 1996 there were in South Africa 600 travel agents registered with the International Air Transport Association (IATA), a number that had grown to 820 by 1998. It then declined to 800 in 2001. The worldwide trend to net fares or zero commission had not reached South Africa in 2000. The industry was competitive and low margin, and somewhat overtraded, but it continued to thrive, despite the threat from technology and the internet providing an alternative travel marketing mechanism.

Attractions

In 2000, eight of South Africa's top 10 attractions visited by foreign air tourists (Figure 15.15) were located in the Western Cape, which

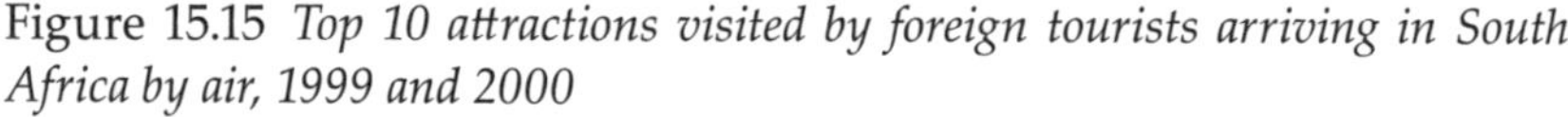

Figure 15.15 *Top 10 attractions visited by foreign tourists arriving in South Africa by air, 1999 and 2000*

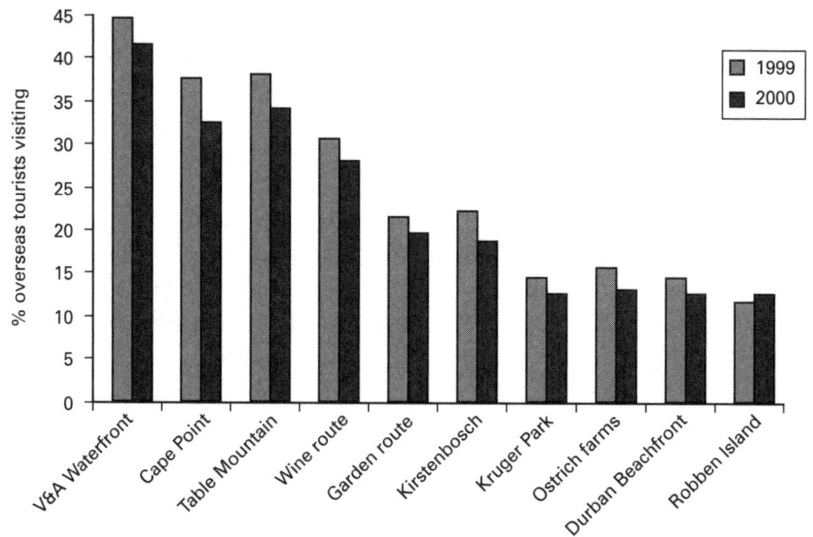

Source: SA Tourism.

dominated the leisure tourism industry. The most popular tourist attraction was the V&A Waterfront in Cape Town. In 2000 around 42 per cent of all foreign air tourists to South Africa visited the V&A Waterfront, equivalent to some 760,000 visitors, down slightly from 45 per cent in 1999. Table Mountain attracted 34 per cent of foreign air tourists in 2000 and Cape Point around 33 per cent. Outside the Western Cape, the Kruger National Park attracted 13 per cent of foreign air tourists (235,300 visitors). Robben Island was the only top 10 attraction that experienced an increasing proportion of foreign visitors in 2000, from 12 per cent in 1999 to 13 per cent in 2000.

Table 15.5 *Economic contribution (R billions) of the tourism industry and economy in South Africa, 1990–2000*

	1990	*1993*	*1995*	*1998*	*2000*
Personal travel and tourism	8.99	13.86	17.22	23.96	30.59
Business travel and tourism	1.73	2.59	5.64	10.07	15.59
Government expenditure, individual	0.08	0.11	0.12	0.22	0.27
Visitor exports	3.68	5.37	9.63	18.91	23.19
Government expenditure, collective	0.15	0.22	0.28	0.51	0.61
Capital investment	4.61	7.63	10.37	17.16	19.69
Exports, non-visitor	0.65	1.94	2.53	5.80	8.04
Total travel and tourism demand	19.88	31.72	45.79	76.63	97.98
Travel and tourism industry					
Travel and tourism employment	251,820	253,570	288,060	393,520	342,270
Percentage of GDP	1.83%	1.74%	2.19%	2.78%	2.80%
Percentage of employment	2.28%	2.12%	2.29%	3.30%	2.78%
Travel and tourism economy [a]					
Percentage of GDP	4.45%	4.61%	5.44%	7.08%	6.97%
Percentage of employment	4.77%	4.43%	5.07%	7.28%	6.17%
Travel and tourism employment	526,790	529,440	636,680	868,340	758,900

[a] *Note:* The WTTC calculates the travel and tourism 'industry' and travel and tourism 'economy' contributions. The travel and tourism industry relates to all direct tourism expenditure and the indirect and induced spending generated by this. The direct expenditure includes spending on personal consumption related to tourism. The tourism economy includes capital expenditure as well as direct tourism expenditure and the indirect and induced economic contribution from this.
Source: WTTC.

Economic impact of tourism, 1990–2000

The contribution of tourism grew from 1.83 per cent of GDP in 1990 to 2.80 per cent in 2000 (Table 15.5). This, however, was still below the worldwide average of 3.75 per cent in 1990 and 3.98 per cent in 2000. Similarly, industry employment was 2.28 per cent of total employment in 1990 rising to 2.78 per cent in 2000, compared with worldwide averages of 2.51 per cent and 2.84 per cent in 1990 and 2000 respectively. In real terms, the contribution declined in 1991, 1993 and 2000, with employment declining in 1991, 1992 and 2000. While the employment contribution lagged the worldwide average, it was not as far behind as the GDP contribution, indicating lower productivity and a higher employment multiplier for tourism in South Africa compared with other countries.

Tourism's economic contribution indicates an industry growing in national importance. Tourism's total impact on the economy had grown to almost 7 per cent by the end of the decade, compared with a worldwide average of 10.7 per cent. South Africa's strong tourism fundamentals suggest that the contribution of the industry should be ahead of the worldwide average. As this had not happened by 2000 there was still room for significant growth.

Tourism institutions and the policy environment

In 1990 there was a very small tourism department, with one functionary, within the National Department of Administration. Thereafter there was briefly a stand-alone Department of Tourism headed by Dr Badra Ranchod. By 1993, when the directorate was transferred to the Department of Trade and Industry, it had grown in size to a handful of people. In 1994 Tourism was amalgamated with Environment Affairs, under Dr Dawie De Villiers, then briefly under Pallo Jordan after the National Party pulled out of the Government of National Unity in 1996 and then under Valli Moosa, who was still at the helm of the Department in 2000. At this stage the Tourism Department had a deputy director, two chief directors, five directors and a further 18 or so staff below them. This represented at least a massive swing of interest towards tourism at the national government level.

In 1990 SATOUR, the statutory national body responsible for promoting tourism, had long-serving white staff at senior level, but was constrained by low budgets and the difficulties of marketing South Africa overseas. There were limited regional SATOUR offices in major cities, no 'provincial' tourism bodies and limited, predominantly private sector, publicity associations marketing local destinations for tourists. The two main tourism associations for the private sector were FEDHASA, the Federated Hospitality Association of South Africa, and SATSA, the South African Tourism Services Association.

In May 1992 the government issued a White Paper on tourism, but it contained little new for the industry, although its very existence did suggest that the government was taking a greater interest in the industry. However, the African National Congress (ANC) also started to take an interest in tourism in 1992, but it was only in 1993 that the National Tourism Forum, led by Peter Mokaba, was created; it brought together the private sector and interested ANC players, mainly in an information sharing and strategy development forum. Unfortunately it came to an end amid accusations of fraudulent use of funds.

When the interim constitution in 1994 delegated powers to the provinces to undertake tourism activities in terms of schedule 6, SATOUR closed its regional offices and transferred the assets to the provinces. This led to each of the nine new provinces of South Africa setting up its own tourism marketing and development bodies.

Concurrently a national process commenced with a workshop in September 1994 resulting in the setting up of the National Tourism Task Team (NTTT), which included the government, the private sector and some union and community representatives. This body orchestrated numerous national and provincial workshops on tourism in 1995 and early 1996, resulting in a new tourism Green Paper in September 1995, which was followed by a detailed White Paper on tourism in 1996. This White Paper became the country's official tourism policy. It stated:

> Our vision is to develop the tourism sector as a national priority in a sustainable and acceptable manner, so that it will contribute significantly to the improvement of the quality of life of every South African. As a lead sector within the national economic strategy, a globally competitive tourism industry will be a major force in the reconstruction and development efforts of the government.[23]

The White Paper articulated nine guiding principles, many of which were in line with the government's political and social aims, rather than concentrating on the economic aspects of tourism. These were:

1 responsible tourism;
2 private sector driven;
3 government provides the enabling framework;
4 effective community involvement to form the basis of tourism;

23 *The Development and Promotion of Tourism in South Africa,* White Paper, Department of Environmental Affairs and Tourism, 1996, section 4.1.

5 tourism development underpinned by sustainable environmental practices;
6 tourism development dependent on the establishment of cooperation and close partnerships among key stakeholders;
7 tourism development to focus on the empowerment of previously neglected communities and women in particular;
8 tourism development to take place in the context of close cooperation with other states in Southern Africa;
9 tourism development to support the economic, social and environmental goals of government.

Throughout 1995 and early 1996, after a series of sometimes tense workshops, the private sector established the Tourism Business Council of South Africa (TBCSA) in February 1996, under which many of the estimated 30 or so associations representing different subsectors of the industry and other key players joined together to address key issues with the government.

In November 1996 the Tourism Amendment Act restructured SATOUR, renamed it SA Tourism, in line with the White Paper, and endowed it with a board of high-powered private sector individuals (not necessarily from the tourism sector). Its budget was increased and peaked in 1997, at R100 million, before dropping to R67 million in 1998. The government produced the 'tourism in GEAR' strategy in 1998 (GEAR being the government's growth, employment and redistribution framework). GEAR set growth targets in terms of arrivals, receipts, jobs and ownership of tourism ventures by previously disadvantaged people. Unfortunately, the poorer overall tourism performance from 1998 to 2000 led to all of these targets being missed.

Also in 1998, the general business community, spurred on by a national labour summit in which the private sector committed itself to partnering government in creating jobs, started the National Business Initiative (NBI) (funded from corporate donations of 2 per cent of after-tax earnings, or 0.15 per cent of market capitalisation), which chose tourism as one of its three key areas to support. The NBI agreed it would provide R50 million for tourism marketing, R10–R20 million into each of tourism training and tourism small and medium enterprise development annually. At the same time the tourism private sector also committed itself to implementing a voluntary tourism levy to swell SA Tourism's marketing funds. Although this was achieved only in 2000, it was well supported and generated R22 million in its first year.

In 1999 Valli Moosa brought together all interested parties in the Tourism Action Plan, a R180 million project based on cooperation between the public and private sector. SA Tourism's biggest budget yet was announced, with R95 million from government, R50 million from the NBI, R25 million from industry voluntary levies and R10 million from SAA. The main thrust of the Action Plan was international marketing and substantial research to underpin the marketing strategy. This action plan provided an unprecedented opportunity for the international tourism marketing of South Africa to reach international benchmark standards.

Conclusion

In 1990 tourism was a Cinderella sector in South Africa, attracting little government or private sector interest, with few institutions, limited funding and scarce data. There was only one international hotel brand operating: the Southern Sun operated Holiday Inns. There were no international convention centres, no mega-casinos, no Sun City Lost Palace and Valley of Waves and no World Heritage Sites. There were few bed and breakfasts or guest-houses. The V&A Waterfront in South Africa had opened just the previous year.

The first few years of the decade were difficult for tourism. A worldwide recession and the first Gulf War dampened international tourism, and this was exacerbated by the uncertainty and violence in South Africa. Overseas arrivals saw little growth until 1994. After the Boipatong massacre in June 1992, reports of foreign tour cancellations were widespread, and more were reported after the breakdown of CODESA negotiations, the Bisho massacre and the Chris Hani assassination. The outlook seemed bleak for the industry. Nevertheless, a few foreign hotel groups saw a future and representatives of seven international brands visited South Africa during 1991.[24]

The middle years of the decade were characterised by euphoria within the industry and by a massive growth in tourism within and to South Africa. By 1995 nearly every major international hotel chain was vying to secure management agreements in South Africa.[25] In 1996 *The Economist* stated that year would 'be a year of prosperity and peace'[26] and South Africa appeared to be well placed for a boom in tourism. Europe was coming out of recession, the world was largely peaceful and South Africa was flavour of the year. Booming tourism numbers were driving the extensive development of hotels and other tourism plant, the casino dispensation was heralding many new leisure and

24 *Tourism Talk*, Kessel Feinstein Consulting, 1993.

25 *Tourism Talk*, Kessel Feinstein Consulting, 1996.

26 *Ibid.*

recreation complexes, and cities strove to develop convention centres. This optimism led to the country bidding for the 2004 Olympics in 1997 and the 2006 Soccer World Cup in 1998.

Such optimism was premature and in the last years of the decade the growth of overseas and African arrivals tailed off significantly, while over-development resulted in low occupancies and a poor performance. Yet the institutional situation was improving, budgets for tourism were expanding and concrete plans were on the table for stimulating and transforming the industry.

In spite of the decline at the end of the decade, significant growth had taken place. The number of international airlines flying into the country had trebled, five new international hotel brands were operating in the country, two major international convention centres were operating in Durban and Sandton, a third was being built and 31 legal casinos were operating in South Africa. To support these developments, tourist accommodation had expanded very significantly. In addition, four World Heritage Sites had been proclaimed – Sterkfontein, Robben Island, the Natal Drakensberg and the Greater St Lucia Wetlands.

Tourism, however, was influenced not only by endogenous developments. Exogenous ones in the form of the international financial crisis in Asia in 1998 and the war in Iraq also affected tourism in the 1990s. Nevertheless, in 2000, South Africa was well positioned to benefit from the future growth of tourism, although crime was beginning to cloud the horizon and depress foreign tourism levels as potential holiday tourists feared for their safety in South Africa.

16

The public sector: state incapacity in the 1990s – a critical evaluation of government performance

Elsabé Loots

Introduction

The early 1990s ushered in a decade of hope. The release of Nelson Mandela, the unbanning of the African National Congress (ANC) and the promise of free and fair democratic elections created expectations of a flourishing economy that would provide job and income-earning opportunities for all and ensure more equal access to services.

The widespread prospects of a better life were based on the status quo before 1994, when the majority of the population did not share equally in the benefits of economic growth and the public provision of services. This is evident in the following brief synopsis of the broader socio-economic circumstances prevailing at the beginning of the 1990s.[1] The deterioration of the long-term economic growth performance had contributed to a decline in real per capita income. The 1990 level of R21,710 was the same as in 1973. The decline in labour absorption capacity – as low as 1 per cent in 1992 – was reflected in the increase in the unemployment rate – from 14.4 per cent in the second half of the 1980s to an average level of 24.6 per cent over 1990–94. The decline in per capita income and the subsequent increase in unemployment, in association with socio-political factors, contributed to the high levels of poverty prevailing in the early 1990s. Estimates show that approximately 18 million people, or 46 per cent of the population, lived below the poverty line in the early 1990s. The poverty figures were as high as 70 per cent for a rural province such as Limpopo and a staggering

1 See A. E. Loots, *Ontwikkelingsbeleid vir post-Apartheid Suid-Afrika*, unpublished thesis, Rand Afrikaans University, 1996, for a detailed analysis of the stance of development in South Africa during the early 1990s.

92 per cent in the former Transkei homeland. This resulted in a highly unequal society, with an average Gini coefficient of 0.65.

Access to services in the early 1990s was also extremely uneven. Estimates show that approximately 25 per cent of the population did not have access to clean drinking water and that more than 50 per cent lacked access to decent sanitation services. Access to services was worse in rural areas, especially in the former homelands. In 1992 there were only 5 hospital beds for every 1,000 people; the figure fell to only 2.4 beds per 1,000 in Mpumalanga. The overall availability of health services was appalling, with some rural clinics serving as many as 30,000 people. The housing shortage was estimated to be between 1.2 million and 3.4 million units. Only 42 per cent of the population had access to electricity, and there was only one mainline telephone per 100 of the black population. Access to, and the quality of, education, especially in the rural areas and former homelands, was also appalling. Although the pupil–teacher ratio nationally averaged 32–1, the figure was estimated to be as high as 45–1 in the former homelands.

These figures are indicative of the impact that poor economic growth performance since the mid-1970s – induced by sanctions and disinvestment campaigns, the increased political violence and instability, and, in general, a discriminatory political system – had had on the broader South African society. The questions raised in this chapter are what policies were put in place by the ANC government to address these (and other) issues, and how successful the government had been in its endeavours by the end of the 1990s.

Role of the state: some concepts and broad guidelines

When one refers to the role of the state and government performance, it is important to understand what exactly is meant by these concepts. The World Bank defines the *state*, in its broader sense, as 'a set of institutions that possess the means of legitimate coercion, exercised over a defined territory and its population, referred to as a society'.[2] The state executes policy making through the medium of an organised *government*. When the government is less well organised, *government failure* occurs, which Dollery defines as 'the inability of public agencies to achieve their intended aims'.[3]

2 World Bank, *World Development Report 1997: The State in a Changing World*, Oxford University Press, 1997, p. 20.

3 B. Dollery, 'The decline of the South African economy: review note', *South African Journal of Economics*, 71(1) (2003), 77–95, at p. 90.

The role of the state in economic policy making has been the focus in economic literature ever since the publication of Adam Smith's *Wealth of Nations* (1776). Within more recent theoretical debate, the proper role of the state varies from what pertains in the so-called *slim state,* with less state intervention in the economy and a free market approach within the neo-classical paradigm, to the more supportive and active role envisaged by the new growth theories or endogenous growth models. In general, the acceptance of a role for the state is supported by the experience of market failure and unequal development in some sections of the global economy. This role has, parallel with the new growth debate since the late 1980s, been enhanced by the human rights movement and the declarations on the implementation of social and economic rights that received wide international recognition in the 1980s and 1990s.[4]

The *World Development Report 1997* is explicit about the fact that an effective state 'is vital for the provision of the goods and services ... that allow markets to flourish and people to lead healthier, happier lives'.[5] It also emphasises the fact that since the late 1980s and early 1990s the state's influence has shifted – from the sheer size of the state and the scope of its interventions to its effectiveness in meeting people's needs. A government has, according to the *Report,* five fundamental tasks:[6] establishing a foundation of law; maintaining a non-distortionary policy environment, including macro-economic stability; investing in basic social services; developing the infrastructure; and protecting the environment. For the purposes of this chapter, the analysis of state capacity in the 1990s will focus primarily on the formation of policy and service delivery.

Dollery,[7] referring to the research done by Michael O'Dowd in 1978, specifies three so-called types of government failure, namely *inherent impossibilities* (where government attempts to do the impossible, such as enforcing apartheid); *political failures* (where what is attempted is possible in theory, but due to political constraints is impossible in practice); and *bureaucratic failure* (in cases where government has the intention of implementing a policy, but the administrative capacity to implement it in accordance with its stated policies is fundamentally lacking). These concepts are used here to analyse the government's performance in the 1990s.

4 E. Loots, 'The fiscal implications of social and economic justice: an overview of the changing theoretical framework', in A. J. Van der Walt (ed.), *Theories of Social and Economic Justice,* Sun Press, 2005, p. 168.

5 World Bank, *World Development Report 1997,* p. 1.

6 *Ibid.,* p. 4.

7 Dollery, 'The decline of the South African economy', p. 90.

Policy and strategy framework in the 1990s

The broader development and strategy framework of economic policy before the 1990s occupied a very low priority in the political and economic agenda of the government of the day. Despite the fact that the government initiated several development initiatives in the 1980s such as the Regional Development Programme, the National Strategy for Community Development, the Population Development Programme, the adoption of a positive urbanisation programme and the funding of several development institutions, no comprehensive growth and development policy or strategy existed.[8] The result was that overlapping and duplication occurred on a large scale. The disadvantaged section of the population regarded these initiatives with suspicion and considered them a consequence of apartheid policy.

From the early 1990s various policy documents appeared, each with the aim of providing policy proposals and strategic guidelines on how a future growth and development framework should be structured. In contrast to the scattered focus of the 1980s, the 1990s were flooded with comprehensive growth and development programmes and related strategies. The most prominent include the normative economic model (NEM) in 1993, the report from the Macroeconomic Research Group (MERG), also in 1993, the *Reconstruction and Development Programme* (RDP) of 1994, and eventually the growth, employment and redistribution (GEAR) strategy of 1996. The most important of these were the RDP and the GEAR strategy, but the NEM and MERG report had a substantial influence on the later ones.

The NEM[9] initiative came from the Central Economic Advisory Service, the South African Reserve Bank, the Development Bank of Southern Africa, the Industrial Development Corporation and various government departments. It provided a five-year macro-economic growth framework, predominantly aimed at addressing the differences between the National Party and the ANC alliance on growth- and development-related issues. It was predominantly a supply-side-driven macro-economic model that suggested structural changes for the market-driven First World economy while simultaneously assuming a trickle-down effect to address the needs of the Third World economy. Policies such as privatisation, deregulation and increased competition

8 A. E. Loots, 'The evolution of development policy in South Africa: lessons from the past and the way forward', *South African Journal of Economic History*, 12(1,2) (1997), 26–53, at p. 51.

9 *Normative Economic Model (NEM): The Key Issues in the Normative Economic Model*, Government Printer, 1993.

were put forward to promote higher investment, growth and employment. The model also referred to the necessity of labour-generating growth to alleviate poverty and redress the socio-economic disadvantages of the past. In principle the NEM was a supply-side model, based on neo-classical principles, in which structural imbalances would be addressed by a market-driven process with limited government intervention. Some of the prominent institutional architects of the NEM were later involved in designing the GEAR strategy.

In the same year that the NEM was published, the Macroeconomic Research Group (which included, among others, a comprehensive array of neo-Marxist researchers such as Alec Erwin, Maria Ramos, Trevor Manuel, Tito Mboweni and Jay Naidoo) published *Making Democracy Work: A Framework for Macroeconomic Policy in South Africa*. The aim of this comprehensive report to the members of the Democratic Movement of South Africa was 'to secure a rapid improvement in the quality of life of the poorest, most oppressed and disadvantaged people of South Africa'.[10] All possible critical issues relating to the functioning of the economy and the redressing of disadvantages were identified and policy options on the social, institutional and economic fronts were researched to provide a coherent set of policies. A developmental state was suggested, in which government expenditure had to increase to redress the disadvantages of the past. The MERG report was based on demand-side principles and an envisaged high level of government intervention, which reflected its leftist economic development ideology. According to Spier, 'the ideological bias of the report … constitutes its major weakness'.[11] Despite the criticisms, the research and findings of the report formed the basis for the RDP.

The final RDP, published in April 1994, was the result of a wide consultation process and the culmination of five separate earlier drafts by the ANC.[12] It was initially used as an ANC election manifesto, but thereafter received wide recognition and was subsequently accepted as an official policy document by the Government of National Unity. The RDP was defined as 'an integrated, coherent socio-economic policy framework'.[13] The Programme was based on six basic principles: an

10 Macroeconomic Research Group (MERG), *Making Democracy Work: A Framework for Macroeconomic Policy in South Africa*, Centre for Development Studies, 1993, p. 2.

11 A. Spier, *Poverty, Employment and Wealth Distribution*, Human Sciences Research Council, 1994, p. 32.

12 B. Munslow and P. FitzGerald, 'The Reconstruction and Development Programme', in P. FitzGerald, A. McLennan and B. M. Munslow, *Managing Sustainable Development in South Africa*, Oxford University Press, 1995, p. 41.

13 African National Congress (ANC), *The Reconstruction and Development Programme: A Policy Framework*, Umanyano Publications, 1994, p. 1.

integrated and sustainable programme; a people-driven process; a programme that aimed to provide peace and security for all; a focus on nation building; linking reconstruction and development; and deepening democracy. All aspects that were identified as deficiencies in the broader development process were addressed within five key themes: meeting basic needs; developing human resources; building the economy; democratising the state and society; and implementation. These themes dealt with wide-ranging issues, from housing backlogs to the expansion of welfare provision, water and sanitation for all, access to basic health care, education, transport, land reform, and environmental security.

In essence, the RDP provided a development vision for the country. The intention was to ensure a successful transition from separate development towards a more sustainable development path. The meeting of basic needs and subsequent improvement in the levels of human development were seen as a significant departure from the economic growth-first debate of earlier policy frameworks. It was a social democratic vision of the state providing a safety net for the poor while promoting major structural adjustment towards a high-wage, high-productivity economy.[14] For the first time in South African history a comprehensive, sustainable development programme – a plan that contained political, economic, social and environmental dimensions – was put on the table. In practice and within the socio-political circumstances prevailing in 1994, the RDP was too broad, too wide ranging, in that it tried to be all things to all people. It contained a so-called wish list that sought to address all existing backlogs in the development of the country without suggesting a framework for how to achieve this. Despite the fact that it was followed by a White Paper on reconstruction and development in September 1994, which was supposedly aimed at providing strategies for its implementation, it was never followed by a final implementation strategy. Aspects such as the devolution of power were suggested in the White Paper but, in contrast to the RDP base document, which focused on socio-economic development to ensure sustainable development, the White Paper emphasised macro-economic strategies to ensure sustainable growth and development.[15] This deviation in focus highlighted the fact that even the architects of both documents were unclear about how critical development issues should be tackled.

14 J. Seekings and N. Nattrass, *Class, Race and Inequality in South Africa*, University of KwaZulu-Natal Press, 2006, p. 346.
15 Loots, *Ontwikkelingsbeleid vir post-Apartheid Suid-Afrika*, p. 164.

Various reasons have been cited for the fundamental failure of the RDP.[16] An overarching limitation relates to the affordability of the programme, with estimates ranging from R40 billion to an astounding R700 billion, at 1994 prices. Furthermore, it was complicated by the institutional uncertainties created with the establishment of the RDP Office under Jay Naidoo, the Minister without Portfolio. This ministry, located within the President's office, had the responsibility for all RDP projects and the allocation of funding. In practice, however, a cabinet committee approved projects and the Department of Finance administered the funds. In the first year of its existence, of the R2.5 billion allocated, only R1.1 billion was actually transferred to the relevant line departments, of which a substantial percentage was not spent.[17] This trend persisted in the following fiscal year.[18] The continuous underspending on RDP projects eventually led to the RDP suffering from a lack of credibility, and in March 1996 President Mandela announced the closure of the RDP Office. This decision was seen as a serious setback for the process of socio-economic uplift and general service provision. Ideological struggles within the ANC and bureaucratic incompetence contributed to the RDP's failure, but essentially the RDP failed because it assumed state capacity instead of building capacity. The trade-off between meeting the increasing needs of the disadvantaged part of the population and reassuring domestic and foreign investors on the economic front became a difficult, almost impossible balancing act. During the early part of 1996 it became evident, according to Bruggemans, that the country was faced with external pressures and a need to gain credibility by committing itself to sound macro-economic policies.[19]

Against this background the government announced the GEAR strategy in June 1996. In contrast to the broad development focus of the RDP, the GEAR strategy represented a macro-economic policy framework with a long-term vision of creating a competitive, fast-growing economy that would generate employment, redistribute income, provide for the availability of services to all and ensure a secure environment.[20] The core elements stated were comprehensive and included an extensive

16 See J. M. Luiz, 'South African state capacity and post-apartheid reconstruction', *International Journal of Social Economics*, 29(8) (2002), 594–614, for a detailed analysis.

17 *Ibid.*, p. 595.

18 See B. Dollery and J. Snowball, 'Government failure and state incapacity: the South African public sector in the 1990s', *South African Journal of Economic History*, 18(1,2) (2003), 310–331, at p. 323.

19 C. Bruggemans, *Change of Pace: South Africa's Economic Revival*, Wits University Press, 2003, p. 57.

20 *Growth, Employment and Redistribution: A Macroeconomic Policy*, Department of Finance, 1996.

list: fiscal reform; monetary and exchange rate reform; trade, industrial and small-enterprise policies; social and sectoral policies; public investment and asset restructuring; employment, wages and training; a social agreement; and, finally, policy coordination. Despite this detailed list of macro-economic reforms, GEAR in principle was concerned with macro-economic issues such as lowering inflation, attracting more foreign direct investment, stimulating exports, creating employment and ensuring fiscal discipline, while retaining broad social objectives. It represented a paradigm shift for the new regime by effectively sidelining the RDP in favour of an outward market-driven and supply-side framework, which, like the NEM, fell within the neo-classical paradigm.

An assessment of GEAR is complicated by some macro-economic successes and failures. Successes included a decline in fiscal deficits, a decrease in the inflation rate and some progress in trade liberalisation. In most other areas GEAR failed, especially those relating to economic growth, investment, export growth and formal job growth. Labour market reforms and privatisation were not implemented. Clearly, mistakes were also made with the sequencing of reforms; for instance, preference was given to exchange control regulation rather than privatisation.[21] Other policy mistakes included a defensive monetary stance, which contributed to a high interest rate environment, inflexible labour market policies and the very limited delivery of quality public services. The lack of coordination between fiscal, monetary and labour market policies also contributed to the decline in employment. The employment situation was further aggravated by the inability of government to create jobs through public works projects. Departments such as the then Department of Welfare and the Department of Public Works were also criticised for their inability to spend funds allocated for poverty-relief and job-creation programmes.[22] In the final analysis, GEAR failed for reasons ranging from state incapacity to wrong policy choices. Another reason for failure relates to the fact that its narrow focus on macro-economic fundamentals had, according to Luiz, confused means and ends.[23]

The economic and broader development policy framework in the 1990s underwent dramatic changes over the decade. The policy stance evolved from being socialistic in nature to one that advocated more market-friendly strategies. In 1990 Nelson Mandela supported nationalisation. Four years later the idea had been discarded and more market-friendly and outwardly orientated policies adopted in response to the reaction

21 Bruggemans, *Change of Pace*, pp. 4–5.

22 Seekings and Nattrass, *Class, Race and Inequality in South Africa*, p. 350.

23 Luiz, 'South African state capacity and post-apartheid reconstruction', p. 598.

of the international business community and the realisation that the country now formed part of a globalised world economy. By the end of the decade the idea was firmly established that the capacity of the state – in both policy formation and policy implementation – determined the effectiveness of both economic and broader socio-economic policies.

State capacity/incapacity?

The evaluation of the state's capacity in the 1990s can be broken down into two distinct periods, namely the neo-apartheid phase (1990–94) and the post-apartheid phase (1994–2000). The neo-apartheid phase was a period in which the government realised that the discriminatory policies of the past had caused huge socio-economic imbalances. A shift in socio-economic policy was evident, but it was still done under the banner of National Party policy and was not generally acceptable to the broader population. The post-apartheid phase was characterised not only by the first democratic elections, in 1994, but also by the adoption of the RDP, followed by the GEAR strategy, and subsequent government attempts to implement these policies.

On the macro-economic policy front the negative economic growth performance of the neo-apartheid phase (–0.6 per cent) was turned around to a positive, but still low, average real growth rate of 2.9 per cent during the post-apartheid phase. Despite this turnaround in economic growth, most of the macro-economic objectives set by GEAR for the period 1996–2000 were not met.[24] The exceptions were the lower-than-targeted inflation rate, the current account deficit and the fiscal discipline that achieved budget deficit reduction. The targets not met included those relating to export growth, real private and public investment growth, private wage growth and formal job growth. The failure to meet these objectives was the result of a combination of over-optimistic assumptions, unintended consequences of some policy choices, mistaken policies and the inability to control general free market actions. Notwithstanding the benefits of fiscal discipline, coupled with a redirection of expenditure to address the socio-economic imbalances of the past, the growth performance after 1994 was totally inadequate to address the crucial issues of both employment generation and wealth creation (Table 16.1). The number of unemployed increased from 1.9 million in 1990 to an estimated (albeit conservative) 4.8 million in 2000 – an increase of 153 per cent over the decade! The result was

24 See Bruggemans, *Change of Pace*, pp. 62–71, for a detailed analysis.

Table 16.1 *An overview of government's performance in the 1990s*

Indicator	*1990*	*1994*	*2000*
Real economic growth	–0.3%	3.2%	3.5%
Real GDP per capita (at constant 2000 prices)	R21,710	R20,214	R21,104
Unemployment: number	1,912,471	3,052,164	4,805,744
Unemployment rate (strict definition)	15.9%	22.8%	30.6%

Sources: South African Reserve Bank, *Quarterly Bulletin*, various issues, and Labour Force Survey, Statistics South Africa.

a decline in real per capita income, from R21,710 in 1990 to a low of R19,996 in 1993, before it improved marginally, to R21,104, in 2000, the level already reached in 1970![25]

The crucial linkage between GEAR and the RDP was through government expenditure, where the objective of the former aimed at reaching some of the goals and promises set out in the latter. As a first step it was recognised that if government were serious about addressing the existing development dilemmas, this should be reflected in the prioritisation of the various budgetary expenditure components. The ratios of various expenditure items between 1990 and 2000 are shown in Table 16.2. Between the neo- and post-apartheid phases, a larger portion of the budget was allocated to education, health and social security and welfare services. By contrast, housing, transport and communication infrastructure, and other economic services received a smaller portion of government expenditure. Despite these trade-offs, the total consolidated government expenditure more than doubled on average and in nominal terms between the two periods. The single largest expenditure component was education, where expenditure increased from 17.7 per cent of total expenditure in 1990 to a record high of 22 per cent in 1997, before tapering off to 20.3 per cent in 2000. While health expenditure was the third largest expenditure component in the early 1990s, it had dropped to fourth position in the latter part of the 1990s. The 9.6 per cent health expenditure ratio in the latter period was only marginally higher than the 9.4 per cent of the neo-apartheid phase. The most significant increase in expenditure over the decade was in the social security and welfare expenditure, which on average increased from 7.6 per cent to 10.7 per cent between the two periods. Between 1990 and 2000 it almost doubled! The drop in expenditure ratios was most

25 South African Reserve Bank, *Quarterly Bulletin*, various issues (available at www.resbank.co.za, accessed 15 February 2007).

Table 16.2 *Consolidated general government expenditure ratios, 1990–2000*

Expenditure item (as % of total expenditure)	*Neo-apartheid phase*	*Post-apartheid phase*
Education	19.5	20.6
Health	9.4	9.6
Social security and welfare	7.6	10.7
Housing and community services	4.1	3.2
Transport and communication	5.5	5.1
Other economic services	2.9	2.5
Total expenditure (R billion)	106.9	243.7

Source: South African Reserve Bank, *Quarterly Bulletin*, various issues.

prominent in housing and communication services, where expenditure halved between 1990 and 2000. These expenditure shifts indicate that the government had clearly prioritised education, health and welfare, with housing, transport, communication and other economic services (including infrastructural expenditure on electricity and water) taking the back seat.

A decisive and expected textbook relationship associated with increased expenditure is the assumption that it will be allocated and used effectively in addressing the developmental needs of the country. In cases where expenditure declines in importance, it is generally accepted that the expenditure component is either becoming less important or that sufficient progress has been made. The question to be answered is whether the redirection of expenditure had a positive effect on service delivery: in other words, to what extent was it effective in addressing the socio-economic backlogs that existed?[26]

Education

Concerning access to and improvement in education, mixed results were obtained. At the beginning of the 1990s the educational system was still very politicised and suffered from the impact of burned classrooms and disrupted school years during the period of unrest in the 1980s. Furthermore, the governing system was still fragmented between the Ministry of Education, responsible for white education,

26 The following analysis relies on data and information obtained from: Loots, *Ontwikkelingsbeleid vir post-Apartheid Suid-Afrika*; and *Race Relations Survey*, South African Institute of Race Relations (SAIRR), 1991/92, 1992/93, 2000/01, 2001/02 and 2002/03.

and the Department of Education and Training, responsible for the rest. In 1990 it was estimated that a classroom backlog of 6,358 existed. This had increased more than 10 times, to a staggering 67,199, by 2000. The pupil–teacher ratio, estimated to be 32–1 in the early 1990s (those of the independent homelands were as high as 48–1), increased marginally, to 33–1 in 2000, probably as a result of more children attending school. On a more positive note, the percentage of under-qualified teachers showed a 39 per cent improvement between 1994 and 2000, although, in 2000, 22 per cent of all teachers were still under-qualified.

The results of the senior certificate examinations also serve as an indication of the quality of education. In 1990, a total of 360,452 candidates enrolled for the exam, and there was a 53 per cent pass rate, of which a mere 17 per cent obtained a university entrance pass. The pass rate improved to 58 per cent in 1994, before slipping to a low of 47 per cent in 1997, when the various departments started to write the same exams. The pass rate improved to 58 per cent in 2000, when 489,941 pupils enrolled, but only a disappointing 14 per cent obtained a university pass. In 1990, a total of 374,919 students were enrolled at universities and technikons, a figure that had only marginally improved, to 380,168, in 2000. A definitive shift is evident in the racial breakdown of those gaining degrees, diplomas and certificates awarded by universities and technikons. In 1991, 64.0 per cent of degrees, diplomas and certificates were awarded to whites and a mere 23.7 per cent to Africans; in 2000, 51.3 per cent were awarded to Africans, in comparison with 36.4 per cent to whites. Notwithstanding these improvements, the majority of African tertiary-level students (82 per cent) in 2000 were still enrolled in human sciences, in comparison with 66 per cent of their white counterparts.

The higher investment in education contributed to only a marginal improvement in the adult literacy rate over the decade – from 82.2 per cent to 85.3 per cent. Despite the fact that more people have access to education, the quality is still poor and the number of illiterate adults remains a serious concern.

Health

A healthy population leading productive and long lives can support economic growth and development. The health of the population is a function of a multitude of factors, such as the level and incidence of poverty, the health expenditure of government, access to health services and the quality of health service provision, to mention just a few. In almost all of these categories the government had a poor track record in both the neo- and post-apartheid periods. The governments in both periods were faced not only with the expansion of health services to all population groups, but also with the HIV/AIDS pandemic, which exploded during the decade. The fact that the health system in the 1980s and early 1990s was extremely fragmented (spread between 10 homelands, four provinces and a national department) complicated reporting and therefore the general reliability of data comparisons over time. A number of summary statistics are, however, worth mentioning:

- The under-five mortality rate increased from 73 per 1,000 live births in 1990 to 79 in 2000, an increase of 8 per cent. This increase is in contrast with substantial declines experienced in comparable countries such as Mexico (–22 per cent), Turkey (–36 per cent) and Malaysia (–48 per cent). Coupled with this increase, the infant mortality rates in 2000 were higher among Africans and in rural provinces such as the Eastern Cape, KwaZulu-Natal, Mpumalanga and the Northern Cape, where health facilities were poor or nonexistent.
- The communicable infection and death rates increased in almost all categories. In some cases (such as malaria) this could be ascribed to under-reporting in the early 1990s; in the case of tuberculosis, the HIV/AIDS infection rate was a factor. In 1990, a total of 64,865 tuberculosis cases were recorded (a third in association with HIV). By 2000, there were 275,846 cases, a more than four-fold increase.
- The most pronounced deterioration in the quality of health in the 1990s was associated with the spread of the HIV/AIDS pandemic during the decade. In 1990, only 318 cases of HIV/AIDS were reported, in comparison with an estimated 3.7–5.5 million cases in 2000, affecting between 9 and 13 per cent of the population. In 2000 almost 25 per cent of all women attending antenatal clinics were classified as HIV infected. Despite the explosion in infection rates, only 74 per cent of all urban clinics and a mere 40 per cent of rural clinics had HIV testing facilities. The situation was further exacerbated by the fact that the Department of Health was dragging its feet in the accreditation of hospitals and the subsequent rolling out of anti-retroviral drugs.
- HIV/AIDS is one of the largest contributing factors to the decline in life expectancy, to below 50 years by 2000, from 63 years in 1991.
- The provision of health services is also closely associated with the availability of medical personnel and hospital beds. The number of registered doctors increased from 23,130 in 1990 to 29,788 in 2000. Of the registered 29,788 doctors in 2000, only 35 per cent catered for the 35 million people who used public sector health care facilities. The availability of hospital beds was also a serious concern: in 2000 only 2.87 public hospital beds per 1,000 of the population were available. As a result of the fragmentation of the public health system in the early 1990s, no reliable figure exists for the earlier period.

- Notwithstanding the shift in health policy in the late 1990s from curative tertiary medicine towards preventive primary health care, many clinics lacked supplies and staff, with the result that hospitals were still relied upon for basic health care.
- The country's overall health system performance was rated 175 out of 191 member states in the World Health Organization's *World Health Report 2000.* This appalling health status was the most pronounced example of government failure and state incapacity in the 1990s.

Social security and welfare

Over the 1990s expenditure on social security and welfare almost doubled as portion of total expenditure. This increase should be seen against the background of estimates indicating that, in 1991, 16.3 million people or 45 per cent of the population were living below the accepted minimum standard of living. However, the welfare system was still skewed in favour of the minority white section of the population. In 1990 the ratio of white to African old age pensions was 1.6–1. Exact figures on the number of people benefiting from the grant system in the early 1990s are not available. Taking into account the high incidence of poverty as well as the unfairness of the apartheid grant system, the welfare challenges faced by the government were immense. The new Department of Social Development expanded the categories in the grant system (by for instance including a child support grant), which resulted in an increase in the number of beneficiaries. At the end of 2000 some 3.4 million people benefited from the 10 categories of grants, at an average monthly per capita payment of R462. Despite this increase in the number of beneficiaries, the Department was plagued with problems, ranging from underspending (due to a lack a managerial capacity) to fraudulent claims by so-called 'ghost' pensioners. As a result, despite the increase in budget allocation and the expansion of the social security net, the incidence of poverty at the end of the 1990s had not changed. This was yet another example of government failure.

Basic services

The onset of the 1990s was characterised by the existence of huge basic service disparities between racial groups as well as between urban and rural areas. Access to basic services such as housing, clean drinking water and sanitation, energy, transport and communication is vital for human development. The absence of these basic services was detrimental not only to individuals but also to sustainable development. A few examples of the state of basic service provision in the early 1990s can be mentioned: the housing shortage was estimated to be between 1.2 million and 3.4 million units; the Development Bank of Southern Africa estimated that about 7 million people were living in informal settlements; only 42 per cent of households had access to electricity, implying that 23 million people, 86 per cent of all schools and 4,000 clinics were without electricity; 48 per cent of people in rural areas had to walk long distances to work, while 53 per cent of people used bus or taxi transport to work, some of whom spent more than 16 hours per day away from home; 5 per cent of the country's roads were in a poor condition; the telephone–person ratio was 1–100 among Africans, in contrast to a ratio of 100–60 for white people; 12–15 million people did not have access to fresh drinking water and 21 million lacked access to sanitation facilities; in certain rural areas such as in the Transkei and KwaZulu-Natal only 25 per cent of inhabitants had access to clean drinking water.

Mixed results were obtained during the decade in relation to housing conditions and general service provision. Despite the fact that close to 1 million low-cost houses were built between 1994 and 2000, the housing shortage was still estimated to be between 3 and 4 million units, on a par with the upper end of the 1990 estimate; by the end of the century 12 per cent of the population still lived in informal settlements and 11 per cent in traditional dwellings. The provision of electricity had improved to such an extent that 66 per cent of households had access to electricity at the end of the decade. On the transport front, wide disparities still existed. A large number of taxis were illegal and/or unroadworthy. The fact that 33 per cent of all roads and a staggering 50 per cent of rural roads were classified as being in a poor condition is also indicative of the fact that budget cuts had damaged the infrastructure. On the communications side, there were improvements. Despite the fact that, by 2000, some 5 million people had access to fixed telephone lines, 80 per cent of African households still did not have telephones in their dwellings. Internet access and cell phone usage had improved, but both were expensive in comparison with other developing countries. After 1994 the Department of Water Affairs and Forestry provided water to an additional 6.5 million people. Notwithstanding this increase, by 2000 the number of people without fresh drinking water still remained unacceptably high, at 7.5 million. It is also disturbing that 10 per cent of rural people still had to travel one kilometre or more to reach water. The provision of sanitation could not keep up with demand and an estimated 21 million people were still without sanitation facilities at the end of the decade.

On both the macro-economic stability and service delivery fronts mixed results were obtained, with the failures probably outweighing the successes. The reasons for failure in both cases ranged from external shocks and incorrect policy reactions and choices to a general lack of capacity and inability to deliver services.

Conclusion

This chapter has highlighted the fact that government has a fundamental role in facilitating economic growth and development. Apart from the establishment of a foundation of law and order, it also needs to protect the currency, guarantee property rights, maintain a non-distortionary macro-economic policy environment and invest in social services.

From the 1990s various policy initiatives appeared on the South African scene, of which the RDP and GEAR were the most prominent. The subsequent government responses regarding implementation provided mixed results. Fiscal and monetary policy provided a favourable macro-economic background but unfortunately did not spill over into service delivery. On the socio-economic front, a clear expenditure re-prioritisation took place, but also with mixed results in implementation. Most policies were predominantly of the First World type, adopted to address Third World development challenges, a situation that was exacerbated when government bodies proved unable to implement them and spend the money allocated to them.

In conclusion, the principal reason for the inability to address socio-economic backlogs and service delivery can be attributed to bureaucratic failure; but perhaps the greatest failure was the failure to invest in the infrastructure that was the key to successful economic growth – a failure that was compounded by failure to allow the private sector to take on this task.

17

External trade

Stuart Jones

Introduction

South Africa's external trade in the 1990s was not transformed in ways comparable to what happened in the political sphere; but the direction of trade was affected by the ending of embargoes, by the new communist-dominated government's identification with Third World causes and the Non-Aligned Movement, by the new global environment that emerged in the wake of the collapse of the Soviet Union and by trade reform in South Africa. In the 1990s, Third World countries could no longer play the West against the Soviet bloc and had to adjust to the triumph of market capitalism. In South Africa the former hard-line Stalinists who dominated the African National Congress (ANC) began to discard the Marxist rhetoric of yesteryear and, at least when addressing German or Swiss bankers, to proclaim their faith in market forces and the virtues of privatisation. In external trade, there was concerted pressure to make the country less Eurocentric by encouraging business with their non-aligned allies and especially with countries whose rulers had financed the ANC in exile. As a result, the base of South Africa's trade broadened and the importance of Europe declined. Some caution, however, is needed in interpreting the statistics, because some of the trade with Afro-Asian countries that was routed via third parties before 1994 now came direct and was not new trade.

Globalisation, hyped by the media as a new phenomenon of the 1990s, was identified with the expansion of market capitalism that occurred after the collapse of the Soviet Union. In reality globalisation has been underway ever since the voyages of discovery in the fifteenth century. It led to a truly international economy emerging in the nineteenth century and to the impact of America upon world prices in the last quarter of that century. Western countries, led by Britain, experienced trade-led growth in the second half of the nineteenth century. South Africa by contrast experienced the reverse. The growth of external trade was a consequence of the growth initiated by the mineral discoveries and, in recent decades, by industrialisation.

Ironically, in the heyday of gold mining, South Africa never experienced trade-led growth, but in the 1990s, both before and after the 1994 election, the country did so. This achievement, however, was less the consequence of booming export markets than of a depressed domestic economy, in which real per capita GDP had been declining for two decades. Also, before 1994, the pressure of financial sanctions forced the country to maintain large balance of trade surpluses in order to service international debts. These were primarily achieved by a combination of exchange controls, import permits and currency depreciation. After 1994, when financial sanctions ended, the economy was able to revert to its earlier pattern of deficits on the current account, balanced by inflows on the capital account. What was unusual in the 1990s was the experience of both import-led and export-led growth. This occurred because external trade responded more rapidly to signals coming from the international economy than did the depressed domestic economy.

This trade-led growth of the 1990s owed little to so-called globalisation. Indeed, the post-war rapid and sustained expansion of world trade came to an end in 1973, with the first of the Arab oil price rises. Thereafter, the international economy had a bumpier ride, which saw the triumph of market capitalism, a global trading boom in the 1990s, the Asian crisis of 1997, the stagnation of the Japanese economy and the collapse of the stock market boom in 2000. In this harsher business environment at the end of the twentieth century, the rapid growth of international trade came to an abrupt halt. From growing at the rate of 7 per cent a year in the 1990s, the growth of global trade fell to 2 per cent in 2000 and thence to stagnation in 2001.[1] Moreover, despite the protests against globalisation at meetings of the World Trade Organization and the International Monetary Fund, the world was becoming less, not more globalised. In the 1990s countries with a total population of 2 billion became less globalised, with the ratio of their trade to GDP decreasing.

The flow of foreign direct investment followed a similar pattern. From 1994 to 1997 emerging economies received $655 billion in foreign direct investment. In the next three years this fell to $19 billion, and in 2001 there was a net outflow of $30 billion from the 29 biggest emerging economies. Because South Africa is considered an emerging economy by its government and the donor lobby, this had serious implications for

1 'Special report on globalisation', *The Economist*, 2 February 2002.

the economy, which relied upon foreign investment to stimulate growth and which, in the later 1990s, was increasingly relying on markets north of the Limpopo – markets that in turn were increasingly dependent upon foreign aid and investment. At the same time the economy's return to its pre-sanctions pattern of running balance of trade deficits, balanced by inflows of foreign direct investment, made the economy of the late 1990s increasingly vulnerable to developments taking place in the global arena.

The extent of external trade

In absolute terms at current prices, South Africa's external trade experienced massive growth in the last decade of the century. It almost quadrupled, from R105,341.7 million in 1990 to R395,772.8 million in 2000. Much of this growth came from the increase in prices resulting from the depreciation of the rand. Yet external trade was increasing its weighting in the economy, rising from 42.6 per cent of GDP in 1990 to 58.4 per cent in 2000. Almost all this increase occurred after 1994, when the ANC government replaced the former National Party government. This would suggest that sanctions were holding back the growth of external trade in the sanctions era. On the other hand, external trade was increasing its weighting in the economy before 1994, while the growth in the second half of the decade coincided with the global boom associated with the new economy.

Moreover, after the communist-dominated ANC government came to power, the depreciation of the rand accelerated, thereby increasing the cost of all imports and raising the value of all exports denominated in foreign currencies. For example, in the six years 1988–94, the rand depreciated by 33.3 per cent against the dollar and 21.7 per cent against the pound, whereas in the six years 1994–2000 this decline accelerated to 53.4 per cent against the dollar and 49.9 per cent against the pound. Before 1994, the rand had been depreciating against the dollar at the rate of 6.6 per cent a year and against the pound at the rate of 4.2 per cent. After 1994, the rate of annual decline shot up to 12 per cent against the dollar and 10.7 per cent against the pound. This decline in the value of the rand helps to explain why imports were growing faster than exports throughout the 1990s. Importers of producer goods had to pay the higher rand prices, but exporters, faced with more competitive markets than the cosy South African one, were being pushed to hold down their prices. Nevertheless, in the first four years of the decade, when the rand was depreciating against the dollar by 8.3 per cent a year and against the pound by 3.4 per cent, foreign trade was growing by

Table 17.1 *External trade (R millions) of South Africa in the 1990s*

Year	*Imports*	*Exports*	*Total trade*
Value (R millions)			
1990	44,195.2	61,146.5	105,341.7
1991	48,277.4	64,522.2	112,799.6
1992	58,987.5	68,235.0	120,804.1
1993	52,569.1	79,481.1	138,468.6
1994	76,257.5	88,811.7	165,069.2
1995	98,513.1	101,503.4	200,016.5
1996	112,931.3	114,589.8	227,521.5
1997	127,024.0	130,460.5	257,484.5
1998	143,142.6	143,701.3	286,843.9
1999	146,076.2	163,966.5	310,042.7
2000	186,280.7	209,492.1	395,772.8
Growth rates (%)			
Current prices			
1990–94	14.6	9.8	11.9
1994–2000	16.1	15.4	15.7
1990–2000	15.5	13.0	14.2
Constant prices			
1990–94	7.0	2.2	4.3
1994–2000	5.7	6.1	5.9
1990–2000	6.2	4.5	5.3
Proportion GDP			
1990	17.9	24.7	42.6
1994	19.8	23.1	42.9
2000	27.5	30.9	58.4

Sources: South African Reserve Bank, *Quarterly Bulletin*, various issues; Commissioner for South African Revenue Service, *Monthly Abstract of Trade Statistics*, various issues. Figures for 1990 provided by the Department of Customs and Excise.

11.9 per cent a year. In the next six years, when the rate of the currency's decline almost doubled, external trade grew at an annual rate of 15.7 per cent, so that, both before and after the 1994 election, external trade was growing faster than the rand was depreciating. In the decade of 'globalisation', the country's external trade increased its weighting in the economy by 37.1 per cent, with most of the increase occurring after 1994. The new government, dominated by communist-trained former exiles, was in no position to follow the example of Cuba and Mozambique and defy the international economy. The timing of the change in government was such that political and economic realities outweighed ideological preferences.

In constant prices, when the impact of inflation is removed from the figures, the growth of external trade was still impressive. In current prices, both before and after 1994, imports grew at a faster rate than exports, but in constant prices exports went ahead of imports in the period 1994–2000, with an annual growth rate of 6.1 per cent (Table 17.1). In the earlier period, 1990–94, imports had been growing at more than three times the rate of exports. Over the decade, total trade, in constant prices, grew by 67.3 per cent. Unfortunately, this success in foreign trade did not lead to comparable growth in GDP. The benefits of South Africa's only experience of trade-led growth were squandered through populist policies in the areas of: affirmative action, black economic empowerment, labour legislation, education and company ownership. These policies frightened foreign investors and increased the level of inefficiency throughout the economy.

The geographical distribution of South African external trade

By continent

The geographical range of South African trade widened considerably in the 1990s, boosted by the ending of sanctions and trade embargoes. The continental distribution of trade, given in Table 17.2, reflects only the trade that had specific origins and destinations. In 1990 this ruled out much of the trade with Africa north of the Limpopo, as well as that going to prominent critics of South Africa in Europe and Asia. Petroleum imports, bought on the spot market in Rotterdam, appeared in trade with Europe, whereas after 1994 huge increases in imports are shown from Saudi Arabia, Iran and the Gulf states. The effect of these distortions is to exaggerate the growth of trade with Asia and to minimise that with Europe.

The outstanding change in trading patterns was the decline of trade with Europe. This fell from 55.8 per cent of the total of specified trade in 1990 to 49.0 per cent in 1994 and 42.2 per cent in 2000. While this reflected the growth of trade with Africa and Asia, it was also influenced by the depression in the domestic economy, which reduced the demand for producer goods. The depression in the Japanese economy held back only marginally the growth of trade with Asia, because it was counterbalanced by vigorous growth of trade with China, India, Indonesia, Iran and the Arab states. Trade with Europe had been nicely balanced in 1990, with exports exceeding imports by a moderate amount. This situation had changed by 1994 as a result of the loss of export markets, which, in that year, in real terms, were only three-quarters of the level of 1990. By 2000 exports had overtaken their 1990 level in constant prices,

Table 17.2 *Global distribution of the external trade of South Africa, 1990, 1994 and 2000*

	Imports (R millions)	*Exports (R millions)*	*Total trade (R millions)*	*% of allocated trade*
1990				
Africa	789.8	4,010.0	4,799.8	6.0
Europe	21,631.6	22,921.4	44,553.0	55.8
America	6,422.5	3,341.5	9,764.0	12.2
Asia	8,988.7	10,899.8	19,888.5	24.9
Oceania	430.6	349.4	780.0	1.0
Total	41,195.2	61,146.5	102,341.7	
1994				
Africa	2,353.0	8,631.2	10,894.2	8.5
Europe	37,472.1	26,680.6	64,152.7	49.0
America	11,452.2	7,063.8	18,516.0	14.4
Asia	18,432.0	14,500.5	32,932.5	25.6
Oceania	1,180.0	792.9	1,972.9	1.5
Total	75,521.1	89,621.6	165,142.7	
2000				
Africa	5,316.9	28,209.2	33,526.1	9.8
Europe	80,709.2	62,987.1	143,696.3	42.2
America	28,163.2	22,296.4	50,459.6	14.8
Asia	66,846.3	37,369.6	104,215.9	30.6
Oceania	4,988.3	3,590.5	8,578.8	2.5
Total	186,476.5	210,512.5	396,989.0	

Sources: Figures provided by the Department of Customs and Excise for 1990; and *Monthly Abstract of Trade Statistics*, various issues, Commissioner for South African Revenue Service, 1994 and 2000.

but they had not been able make up for those losses in the first four years of the decade. ANC-backed sanctions campaigns consequently contributed to a balance of trade deficit with Europe that had climbed to R17,722.1 million by 2000. With Asia, too, a favourable balance of trade in 1990 was converted into a deficit by 1994 that had widened to R29,255.8 million by the year 2000. Only with Africa did South Africa maintain a balance of trade surplus, but that continent, with its low purchasing power, was in no position to make up for the deteriorating balance of trade with Europe and Asia.

Southern Africa was particularly weak. Not only was South Africa's largest African trading partner collapsing, but the country's linkage to the Southern Africa Development Community (SADC) was, according to Strydom, 'a contradiction in terms, because South Africa's rising intra-industry trade pattern confirms a growing similarity with its major trading partners, which in turn means a growing dissimilarity with the economies of the SADC countries', and dissimilarities 'discourage economic co-operation in a world characterised by intra-industry trade'.[2]

Figures of total trade in constant prices show that growth rates were higher with all continents in the second period, driven mainly by the global boom that characterised these years. In terms of the growth of trade, Oceania was the star performer, boasting a double-digit rate of growth in both periods, even higher than that of trade with Africa. African trade appears to have been held back by the decline in the growth rate of imports in the second period, when the economy of Zimbabwe was collapsing. The growth of trade with Asia was also impressive in the second period, boosted, as mentioned above, by the ending of sanctions and the development of normal business relations with Arab and Iranian petroleum exporters and with China, India and Indonesia. Concern for human rights and support for sanctions, which had characterised ANC policy in exile, did not apply to Arab dictatorships, to the architects of the Tiananmen Square massacre in China, or to those responsible for attempted genocide in Indonesia when Suharto seized power. Indeed, this paymaster of the ANC in exile was awarded South Africa's highest honour by Nelson Mandela. In other words, selective morality was removed from the sphere of trade policy and practice and the market was allowed to determine the course of events.

Arguably, the ending of sanctions should have had the most dramatic impact upon trade with Africa north of the Limpopo, yet, as indicated above, in real terms trade with Africa grew only 1 percentage point faster after 1994 than before 1994. Because trade to the countries north of the Limpopo no longer needed to be concealed, some of the new trade with Africa may not have been new at all and it is possible that the rate of growth of trade with the continent was slower after 1994 than it was before 1994, notwithstanding the rapid growth of exports to a handful of African countries.

South Africa's external trade in the year 2000 was much more balanced than in 1990. In 2000 no one continent was responsible for over half of external trade, in the way that Europe was in 1990. Moreover, throughout the decade, in current prices, trade with Oceania and Africa was expanding at over 10 per cent a year (Table 17.3). After 1994 it was growing rapidly with every continent, but it remains debatable how much of this growth was the result of the ending of sanctions and how much a response to the global boom of these years. In 2000, total trade was lower than in 1999, before the world stock market crash.

2 P. D. F. Strydom, *Economic Growth in Open Economies*, research paper from the Department of Economics, edited by Elsabe Loots and Eric Scheling, Rand Afrikaans Universiteit, September 2000, p. 9.

Table 17.3 *Annual growth (%) of external trade by region, in current and constant prices, 1990–2000*

	1990–94		*1994–2000*	
	Current prices	*Constant prices*	*Current prices*	*Constant prices*
Imports				
Africa	31.4	17.7	14.6	5.6
Europe	14.7	2.7	13.6	4.8
Americas	15.6	3.5	16.2	7.4
Asia	19.7	7.2	24.0	14.3
Oceania	28.7	15.2	27.2	17.3
Exports				
Africa	16.8	8.5	21.8	12.3
Europe	3.9	–7.0	15.4	6.4
Americas	20.6	–8.0	21.1	11.7
Asia	7.4	–3.8	17.1	8.0
Oceania	22.7	9.9	28.6	18.6
Total trade				
Africa	23.0	10.1	20.4	11.1
Europe	9.5	–1.9	9.5	5.5
Americas	17.3	5.1	18.2	9.0
Asia	13.4	1.6	21.1	11.7
Oceania	26.1	12.9	27.8	17.8

Sources: Figures provided by the Department of Customs and Excise for 1990; and *Monthly Abstract of Trade Statistics*, various issues, Commissioner for South African Revenue Service, 1994 and 2000.

Imports by country

The four main sources of imports in 2000 were the same four that had been the main suppliers in 1990, namely Germany, the USA, the UK and Japan (Table 17.4). These four countries had headed the list of suppliers to South Africa for many decades. However, changes did take place within the top four. The decline of the UK as a major source of imports continued, with that country dropping from second place in 1990 to 1994 to third place in 2000. Germany remained the leading supplier, yet imports from that country were growing only at the same rate as those from the UK. From the USA they were growing much faster, as the 'new economy' shifted the balance in favour of imports from there.

Below the top four suppliers there were massive changes as a result of the new opportunities for trade opening up with Asian and African countries. European countries represented seven of the top 10 suppliers in 1990 and seven in 1994, but only four in 2000. Yet in the top 20,

Table 17.4 *Twenty-five largest suppliers (R millions) of imports to South Africa, 1990, 1994 and 2000*

1990		*1994*		*2000*	
Germany	8,687.1	Germany	12,017.9	Germany	24,839.1
UK	5,191.9	UK	8,250.8	USA	21,930.3
USA	5,048.8	USA	7,793.5	UK	15,987.6
Japan	4,341.1	Japan	7,164.8	Japan	14,815.6
Italy	1,940.4	Italy	2,723.2	Saudi Arabia	14,055.9
Taiwan	1,475.1	France	2,403.2	Iran	8,096.4
France	1,435.7	Taiwan	2,403.2	France	7,791.9
Switzerland	1,191.0	Netherlands	1,752.2	China	6,928.1
Belgium	1,051.2	Switzerland	1,750.2	Italy	6,221.1
Netherlands	931.7	Belgium	1,609.8	Australia	4,601.4
Hong Kong	733.2	Hong Kong	1,321.7	Switzerland	4,441.2
Canada	435.9	China	1,283.6	Taiwan	4,220.6
Brazil	419.7	Canada	1,010.0	Netherlands	3,569.8
Australia	396.1	Australia	981.3	South Korea	3,522.6
Spain	318.3	South Korea	978.6	Sweden	2,899.4
Austria	289.9	Zimbabwe	932.2	Belgium	2,881.4
Israel	259.9	Singapore	917.2	Finland	2,560.7
Argentina	196.9	Sweden	753.0	Ireland	2,353.3
Chile	184.5	Brazil	693.6	Spain	2,069.7
Ireland	118.5	Malaysia	688.3	Malaysia	2,066.9
Turkey	102.2	Finland	596.6	Brazil	2,027.0
Sweden	100.2	Austria	595.5	Hong Kong	1,929.5
Portugal	86.4	Israel	584.1	India	1,759.3
Denmark	79.4	Argentina	579.5	Canada	1,736.8
New Zealand	33.1	Thailand	556.4	Austria	1,519.1

Sources: Figures provided by the Department of Customs and Excise for 1990; and *Monthly Abstract of Trade Statistics*, various issues, Commissioner for South African Revenue Service, 1994 and 2000.

Europe provided 10 in 1990, 8 in 1994 and 11 in 2000. After sanctions ended, previous supporters such as Finland, Sweden and Ireland revealed themselves as major suppliers to the South African market. The sanctions-supporting Netherlands, too, which had fallen behind by 1990, recovered and Spain, growing rapidly, appeared among the top suppliers. It is difficult to estimate how much of this growth was the result of the ending of sanctions and embargoes and how much was the result of 'globalisation' and the 'new economy'. Finland's position clearly owed much to the success of Nokia, while the boom in the information technology and electronics industries benefited the Far East and the USA.

It is noticeable, too, that some of the most vociferous advocates of sanctions jumped the gun, so to speak, and pushed trade with South Africa in the years before 1994. This applied to Sweden, Finland, France, the Netherlands, Canada and Australia. Because figures for 1990 are not available for the Asian critics of South Africa, it is not possible to determine whether their trade with South Africa took off before 1994, but it seems unlikely, as the recorded figures for 1994 reveal little direct trade with China, India and the Persian Gulf countries. No doubt Hong Kong was supplying goods from China. This would explain the drop in trade with that country after 1994, when imports also declined from Taiwan. South Korea, however, recovered rapidly from the Asian crisis of 1997–98 and imports from that country rose, in constant prices at 12.8 per cent a year, not far behind China's 20.4 per cent and India's 18.4 per cent.

Growth rates in the period 1990–94 were dominated by long-standing trading partners: European countries, the USA, Australia and Canada, Argentina and Brazil, Israel and the leading East and South East Asian traders, Japan, Hong Kong and Taiwan. The geographical composition was traditional, even if some of the growth rates were extraordinary, such as the 118.8 per cent growth rate of imports from Finland.

Yet the most dramatic changes in the pattern of imports occurred in trade with the Persian Gulf countries and with Saudi Arabia. By 2000 Saudi Arabia had become the fifth most important supplier of goods to South Africa, almost equalling Japan, with a growth rate of 155.2 per cent a year for the period 1994–2000. Iran followed in sixth place, with an equally impressive growth rate of 135.1 per cent. Neither had appeared in the list of the top 25 suppliers in 1994. Very rapid growth rates can be obtained from small bases. Whether they can be sustained is another matter. Nevertheless, in the second half of the decade, growth rates took a marked upward movement, while the composition reflected major changes. Table 17.5 provides the details.

In the second half of the decade many of the traditional suppliers featured at the bottom of the growth rate table. None of the top five was a major supplier of goods to South Africa before 1994, save India very much earlier, in the colonial period. Three of the traditional suppliers experienced absolute declines in their exports to South African, namely Hong Kong, Canada and Taiwan, while those of the UK, Belgium and Japan grew slowly. France and Spain, however, were the traditional traders which maintained a high growth rate in their exports to South Africa, matched by those of Finland and Sweden. The appearance of China and India among the leading suppliers suggests that the trade with other Asian countries may be hit by the lower labour costs of these two giants of Asia in the future.

To place these growth rates in perspective, though, one needs to look at Table 17.4, which lists the leading suppliers in 1990, 1994 and 2000. In this regard the rapid growth in imports from the USA is perhaps the most impressive, because it occurred off a high base. Australia also maintained a high growth rate in its exports to South Africa. Indeed, by

Table 17.5 *Growth rates of imports of leading suppliers into South Africa in order of growth, 1990–2000*

1990–94 [a]		*1994–2000*	
Finland	118.8	Saudi Arabia	155.2
Sweden	54.6	Iran	135.1
Argentina	22.3	Ireland	22.1
Australia	17.2	China	20.6
Canada	15.2	India	18.4
Israel	14.3	Australia	17.8
Austria	11.8	Spain	16.7
Netherlands	9.4	Finland	16.1
Hong Kong	8.2	Sweden	14.0
France	7.3	South Korea	12.8
Brazil	5.9	France	10.0
Japan	5.8	Malaysia	9.4
Taiwan	5.5	Brazil	8.9
UK	4.8	Netherlands	8.4
USA	4.1	USA	8.2
Belgium	3.9	Switzerland	6.4
Switzerland	2.8	Italy	4.5
Italy	1.6	Japan	2.8
Germany	1.3	UK	1.7
		Belgium	0.4
		Taiwan	–0.1
		Canada	–0.3
		Hong Kong	–3.0

[a] Growth rates are only given for countries with recorded figures in 1990.
Sources: Figures provided by the Department of Customs and Excise for 1990; and *Monthly Abstract of Trade Statistics*, various issues, Commissioner for South African Revenue Service, 1994 and 2000.

2000 Australia had established itself among the top 10 suppliers, helped no doubt by the large number of emigrants from South Africa who had settled there.

Exports by country

The four countries that provided South Africa with most of its imports were generally the four largest export markets, if one excludes Switzerland, which was the recipient of gold sales until 1994 (Table 17.6). Thereafter, the UK was the recipient of most of the gold, which was listed as an ordinary commodity from 1996. The Netherlands had overtaken Germany by 1990 as an export destination. The pattern of exports was traditional, with European countries dominating the list of the top 25 export markets, followed by the established markets in Japan,

Table 17.6 *South Africa's 25 largest export markets, 1990, 1994 and 2000*

1990		*1994*		*2000*	
Switzerland	5,474.2	Switzerland	5,708.2	USA	16,751.8
UK	4,931.0	UK	5,401.6	UK	15,919.2
Japan	3,889.4	USA	3,948.0	Germany	13,217.7
Netherlands	3,304.0	Japan	3,799.4	Japan	9,418.3
Germany	2,982.0	Germany	3,352.9	Netherlands	7,028.3
USA	2,432.2	Belgium	2,380.7	Belgium	6,723.1
Taiwan	1,824.7	Zimbabwe	2,216.3	Italy	5,825.1
Belgium	1,526.5	Netherlands	190.0	Mozambique	5,074.3
Italy	1,526.2	Taiwan	1,683.4	Zimbabwe	4,793.1
Hong Kong	1,104.2	Italy	1,604.8	Zambia	4,492.6
Spain	841.4	South Korea	1,601.3	South Korea	4,132.3
France	813.4	Malawi	1,434.6	Taiwan	3,732.8
Turkey	596.6	Hong Kong	1,374.1	France	3,682.1
Norway	469.1	Mozambique	1275.3	Spain	3447.9
Australia	270.0	Spain	1,071.8	Australia	3,339.7
Portugal	293.7	Zambia	1,047.1	India	2,584.4
Canada	207.2	Israel	977.5	China	2,330.4
Chile	203.1	France	895.5	Hong Kong	2,270.1
Ireland	198.7	Brazil	739.3	Switzerland	2,205.8
Greece	177.5	Australia	606.4	Mauritius	2,052.0
Austria	133.7	China	584.5	Malawi	1,638.0
Argentina	47.5	Canada	444.1	Kenya	1,527.2
Columbia	46.1	India	443.4	Canada	1,528.8
Venezuela	41.4	Singapore	407.2	Singapore	1,511.4
		Thailand	297.4	Brazil	1,402.9

Sources: Figures provided by the Department of Customs and Excise for 1990; and *Monthly Abstract of Trade Statistics*, various issues, Commissioner for South African Revenue Service, 1994 and 2000.

the USA, Taiwan and Hong Kong. In 2000 this situation had changed considerably, as the former African markets re-established themselves and new ones emerged in India and China.

Table 17.6 provides the details of the largest 25 export markets in 1990, 1994 and 2000. Six of the top 10 in both 1990 and 1994 were European, but only five in 2000. In 1990 three of the top 10 were in Asia – Japan, Taiwan and Hong Kong – none in Africa. Four years later Hong Kong had dropped out and been replaced by Zimbabwe, while six years later still two more African countries, Mozambique and Zambia, had entered the list of top 10 export markets, replacing Switzerland and Taiwan. This represented a return to the pattern of the early 1960s and was inherently conservative, drawing attention to the strength and resilience of real underlying economic forces.

It was in the second tier (countries ranked 11–20) that the changes were most conspicuous. The six European markets had fallen to three

Table 17.7 *Growth rates (% in constant prices) of the largest export markets in order of growth, 1990–94 and 1994–2000*

1990–94 [a]		*1994–2000*	
Brazil	37.0	India	23.4
Australia	13.9	Australia	22.3
Canada	12.6	Zambia	17.3
USA	5.0	USA	17.1
Belgium	4.0	France	16.5
Spain	–1.0	Mozambique	15.8
Hong Kong	–1.7	China	15.8
Germany	–4.2	Germany	15.6
Israel	–4.5	Mauritius	14.8
France	–4.7	Singapore	14.5
UK	–4.8	Netherlands	14.4
Italy	–5.8	Italy	14.1
Switzerland	–6.0	Canada	13.0
Japan	–7.5	Spain	11.8
Taiwan	–8.8	UK	10.2
Netherlands	–19.0	Belgium	9.4
		South Korea	7.7
		Japan	7.0
		Kenya	5.6
		Taiwan	5.1

[a] Figures for countries in Africa and Asia are not all available for 1990.
Sources: Figures provided by the Department of Customs and Excise for 1990; and *Monthly Abstract of Trade Statistics*, various issues, Commissioner for South African Revenue Service, 1994 and 2000.

in 1994, three African countries appeared – Malawi, Mozambique and Zambia – and South Korea was revealed as a major trading partner. Six years later South Korea, a country that had been desperately poor 40 years earlier – poorer than most of Southern and East Africa – had overtaken Taiwan. By the end of the century, India, China and Mauritius had entered the second tier, but Malawi and Brazil, beset by massive economic problems at home, had fallen out. At the bottom tier of the 25, the appearance of Kenya as an important market shows how the network of economic contacts that had followed the railway lines into Central and East Africa was reasserting itself. Economic realities were more important than political posturing with clapped-out dictators in Cuba, Libya and Indonesia in determining the flows of South African exports in the 1990s.

The growth rates of exports to individual countries in the 1990s (Table 17.7) are perhaps more revealing than the bald figures. In the first four years of the decade, when sanctions were supposedly in force, some of the loudest and most vigorous advocates of sanctions were expanding their imports from South Africa at high rates. This applies to Canada, the USA and Australia – sharp critics of their South African competitor for markets in coal, wine and other natural resource products. While these countries may have been, so to speak, jumping the gun, it is arguable that it was the result of the expansion of traditional trading connections in preparation for the resumption of normal commercial relations. The large number of countries that experienced absolute declines in their imports from South Africa may have owed something to the sanctions campaigns, but in the first years of the decade the boom associated with the 'new economy' had not yet begun, while Japan's recession had already started. Nevertheless, on balance, the figures suggest that the political campaigns against South Africa were beginning to hurt. Declines were experienced in exports to three of the top four markets and in 10 of the top 13 markets for which comparisons can be made, despite the massive depreciation of the rand.

After the 1994 election, exports accelerated, with rapid growth in all the major markets as the depreciation of the rand also accelerated, at twice the level of the pre-1994 years. Real growth of over 10 per cent a year in exports to 15 of the top 25 export markets – including the USA, the UK, Germany, the Netherlands and Italy – gives us an idea of the strength of the boom that was providing South Africa with its first taste of export-led growth.

Even recession-hit Japan managed to increase its imports from South Africa by 7 per cent a year. Other South East Asian countries were less successful. The financial crisis that hit the region in 1997 may have affected their trade with South Africa. The growth of exports to South Korea overtook those to Japan, while those to Taiwan grew and those to Hong Kong remained stable. Exports to all of them were significantly higher than in the first four years of the decade.

Economic difficulties at home depressed the growth of exports to Zimbabwe, Brazil and Malawi, but the decline of sales to Switzerland was the result of gold sales switching back to London. Non-gold sales probably increased. The Indian market was the star performer, with an annual real growth of 23.4 per cent in its imports from South Africa. Exports to India mushroomed from R443.4 million in 1994 to R2,584.4 million in 2000. For exports to China, growth was more moderate and some of that was at the expense of Hong Kong. None of the oil exporters was a significant importer.

Exports to Africa need to be seen in an international context. In the year 2000, 21 markets in Africa took almost R26.9 billion of goods from South Africa, compared with R2.0 billion in 1994. Eight of them took over R1 billion worth of goods and three – Mozambique, Zimbabwe and Zambia – took over R4 billion worth of goods in 2000 (Table 17.8).

Table 17.8 *Largest export markets in Africa, 1994 and 2000, in constant prices*[a]

	1994 (R millions)	*2000 (R millions)*	*Growth rate (%)*
Mozambique	91.9	5,074.3	80.5
Zimbabwe	1,020.9	4,793.1	19.1
Zambia	104.2	4,492.6	72.3
Mauritius	14.8	2,052.0	109.3
Malawi	185.1	1,638.0	32.3
Kenya	28.1	1,527.2	79.1
Tanzania	15.9	1,384.7	93.7
Angola	16.9	1,373.1	93.4
Zaire	353.6	872.9	7.0
Nigeria	21.2	713.0	65.3
Ghana	22.6	676.1	62.1
Morocco	3.3	336.5	98.9
Madagascar	3.7	307.4	92.2
Mali	5.8	269.7	74.5
Ivory coast	85.6	258.4	10.6
Seychelles	4.8	227.8	90.3
Cameroon	7.4	179.7	56.6
Congo	31.3	178.2	22.9
Gabon	0.4	140.9	144.5
Egypt	12.4	138.0	37.5
Benin	9.3	117.4	40.4

[a] These are the recorded growth rates, which exaggerate the extent of the growth in exports, because of the inaccuracy of the 1994 figures, when exports to countries north of the Limpopo were routed via third parties. They do, nevertheless, provide an indication of the growth taking place.
Source: Monthly Abstract of Trade Statistics, various issues, Commissioner for South African Revenue Service.

The fact that Mozambique was a larger market than Zimbabwe is an indication of the damage already done to that country's economy by its President, Robert Mugabe.

The eight largest markets for exports in Africa were all neighbouring countries linked to South Africa by road, rail and shipping services, Nigeria was relatively unimportant, taking not much more than a third of the value of the goods sent to Mauritius. The market in Angola was growing very rapidly, as the civil war ground to a halt and normal commercial contact could be resumed without troubling about Portuguese mercantilism. Conversely, the descent from anarchy into open warfare in the Congo–Zaire brought the growth of exports to that country to a halt.

It was, however, the markets in the former British colonies that were showing the most growth, helped by the English language, common law and familiar ways of doing things. It draws our attention yet again to the enduring strength of the economic legacy of the empire. Developments in the African markets at the end of the twentieth century make it possible to adopt a favourable view of prospects for the future.

Yet the most important development was not the reopening of markets in Asia and Africa: it was the annual 17.3 per cent growth in exports to the USA, now the country's major market. Growth to France, another major market, was not far behind and Australia almost grew its imports as fast as did India. In 2000, the Australian market was more important than that of India or China, just as it had been in 1994. The pattern displayed in 2000 not only suggests a return to normal trading conditions and the triumph of economic imperatives over political posturing: it also provides evidence of the strength of long-term relations and an echo of the pattern of the 1920s, when Australia, India, Canada and neighbouring African states were major trading partners.

The content of trade

Commodities imported

Producer goods have long dominated the pattern of imports into South Africa and the decade of the 1990s was no exception. The top six categories of imports in 1990 were the same as the top six in 1994 and 2000, and they were all producer goods. Indeed, in 1990 the top 12 commodities according to the South African Department of Customs and Excise's classification were all producer goods. In 2000, 15 of the top 16 commodities were producer goods (Table 17.9). The odd one out was precious stones and metals, which reflected the flow of diamonds into the country from Botswana and Namibia. The movement of goods into South Africa accordingly reflected the progress of industrialisation and modernisation taking place.

This was the classic pattern experienced by all developing countries. Vigorous growth at home sucked in increasing quantities of producer goods, which inevitably put pressure on the balance of payments, before the effects of the expansion revealed itself in either reduced imports of consumer goods or an increase in exports. Periodic balance of payments crises have been a characteristic of Australian and South American economic development. In South East Asia and East Asia strict import controls and massive state support for, or control of, exports attempted to curb the dangers of too rapid economic growth. South Africa, by contrast, was blessed with gold, which for a century cushioned the country against severe balance of payments crises.

Tariff reform began to affect the pattern of imports. Import surcharges were abolished and there was a sustained reduction in nominal

Table 17.9 *Top 25 commodities imported into South Africa, 1990 and 2000*

1990		*2000*	
Commodity	*R millions*	*Commodity*	*R millions*
Boilers and machinery	9,552.5	Boilers and machinery	28,881.3
Vehicles and parts	5,187.5	Mineral fuels	26,615.0
Electrical machinery and appliances	3,659.9	Electrical machinery and appliances	23,638.0
Precision instruments	1,679.3	Vehicles and parts	10,334.2
Organic chemicals	1,636.5	Precision instruments	6,456.7
Plastics	1,302.6	Precious stones and precious metals	5,613.5
Articles of iron and steel	807.5	Plastics	5,114.3
Miscellaneous chemicals	747.2	Aircraft and parts	4,705.6
Inorganic chemicals	742.5	Organic chemicals	4,370.0
Man-made fibres	594.3	Pharmaceutical goods	4,287.8
Rubber goods	589.9	Inorganic chemicals	3,797.5
Pharmaceutical goods	556.1	Miscellaneous chemicals	3,111.4
Precious stone and precious metals	469.4	Paper and paperboard	2,436.4
Iron and steel	463.7	Rubber goods	2,291.8
Cereals	462.8	Articles of iron and steel	1,988.5
Aircraft and parts	449.4	Iron and steel	1,703.7
Man-made filaments	391.0	Ceramic products	1,552.1
Dyes and paints	349.9	Footwear	1,406.3
Tools and cutlery	341.1	Dyes and paints	1,361.7
Animal and vegetable fats	324.5	Toys and sports goods	1,292.3
Books and magazines	322.7	Man-made filaments	1,264.6
Ceramic products	299.6	Animal and vegetable fats	1,111.0
Mineral fuels	228.6	Tools and cutlery	1,087.6
Toys and sports goods	213.6	Books and magazines	995.9
		Furniture etc.	993.6

Sources: Figures provided by the Department of Customs and Excise for 1990; and *Monthly Abstract of Trade Statistics*, various issues, Commissioner for South African Revenue Service, 2000.

tariffs. Exceptions were made for motor vehicles and components and for clothing and textiles, 'thereby placing a limit on the extent to which firms can be efficient'.[3] In practice, there were no comparable changes in the effective rate of protection from the beginning of the 1990s to the end of the decade.[4] In agriculture, quantitative restrictions were replaced by *ad valorem* duties, but an agreement with the European Union that led to a considerable increase in imports came into effect only in 2000.

3 Rashad Cassim, 'The pace, nature and impact of trade policy on South Africa in the 1990s', *South African Journal of Economic History*, 18(1,2) (2003), 76–95, at p. 82.

4 *Ibid.*, p. 87.

Table 17.10 *Average annual rates of growth of the 25 largest commodities imported into South Africa, in constant prices, 1990–94 and 1994–2000*

1990–94		*1994–2000*	
Commodity	*% growth rate*	*Commodity*	*% growth rate*
Precious metals and stones	26.1	Inorganic chemicals	18.3
Animal and vegetable fats	19.3	Toys and sports goods	16.6
Footwear	19.1	Aircraft and parts	15.7
Aircraft and parts	16.0	Ceramic products	14.9
Electrical machinery and appliances	10.8	Pharmaceutical products	14.3
Pharmaceutical products	10.1	Mineral fuels	12.6
Toys and sports goods	6.9	Electrical machinery and appliances	10.0
Boilers and machinery	6.6	Footwear	9.6
Inorganic chemicals	6.3	Precious metals and stones	7.5
Miscellaneous chemicals	6.1	Plastics	6.8
Cereals	5.8	Cereals	6.3
Vehicles and parts	5.3	Miscellaneous chemicals	6.1
Dyes and paints	5.0	Rubber products	5.9
Iron and steel	4.8	Man-made filaments	5.9
Precision instruments	4.2	Precision instruments	5.1
Books and magazines	3.5	Tools and cutlery	4.9
Rubber products	3.3	Dyes and paints	4.8
Paper and paperboard	2.3	Iron and steel	3.9
Plastics	2.2	Articles of iron and steel	3.4
Organic chemicals	1.5	Paper and paperboard	1.1
Tools and cutlery	–0.2	Organic chemicals	0.7
Boilers and machinery	–0.7	Boilers and machinery	0.3
Man-made filaments	–1.4	Man-made fibres	–3.6
Ceramics	–1.7	Animal and vegetable fats	–5.8
Man-made fibres	–4.4	Vehicle and parts	–6.5

Sources: Figures provided by the Department of Customs and Excise for 1990; and *Monthly Abstract of Trade Statistics*, various issues, Commissioner for South African Revenue Service, 1994 and 2000.

As Tables 17.9 and 17.10 indicate, the importation of producer goods continued to grow in constant prices, in some cases very rapidly. This applied especially to electrical machinery, both before and after 1994, and mineral fuels and inorganic chemicals after 1994, as manufacturers re-equipped in response to the challenge of increased competition.

In absolute terms the economy was growing slowly, but in per capita terms it continued to decline throughout the decade. With shrinking real per capita incomes, the economic environment was not conducive to dynamic expansion and the pattern of imports reflected this. Vehicles and parts decreased their imports after 1994 and boilers and general machinery, the largest category of imports throughout the decade, managed only a very small increase.

Some consumer goods expanded rapidly. This applied to pharmaceuticals, the imports of which grew at a rate of over 10 per cent throughout the decade, reflecting the increasing importance of patented drugs in modern living. Toys and sports goods and footwear also increased their penetration of the South Africa market, bringing hardship to the boot and shoe industry and to much of the textile industry. Books and magazines, which had always been among the top 25 commodities imported, were missing from the list in 2000, not because of a boom in publishing and printing in South Africa, but because of the escalating cost of books and magazines in relation to incomes. Finally, it should be noted that harvests were good in the 1990s and that cereals, which had appeared as the sixteenth largest import in 1990, did not appear in the top 25 in 1994 and 2000.

The period 1994–2000 witnessed considerable changes in the pattern of imports with the ending of import controls and accession to the World Trade Organization. This enabled consumer goods and vehicles to be imported freely, providing there was a market for them in South Africa. Animal and vegetable fats, which had been among those heading the growth list in the first four years of the decade, had slipped into negative territory in the second period, along with vehicles and parts. It is noticeable, too, that the cost of importing aircraft was becoming a steadily increasing burden, as was the cost of medicines, petroleum products and electrical machinery and appliances, all of which were growing at more than 10 per cent a year in real terms.

Producer goods continued to dominate the list by value, but not always by growth rates. Notable were chemical imports. Inorganic chemicals headed the growth figures, with an annual rate of 18.3 per cent, while miscellaneous chemicals were expanding their imports by 6.1 per cent a year. Yet three of the top five, in terms of growth, were consumer goods, namely: toys and sports goods, ceramic products and pharmaceutical products. Cosmetics and perfumes did not make the top 25 but were growing at a rate of 15.5 per cent a year. While this was a response to the more liberal trading conditions of the later 1990s, it also reflected the difficulties experienced by the manufacturing sectors as a result of declining real incomes and the growing government interference, with its First World labour legislation, its aggressive affirmative action policies and its haste to bring about rapid black economic empowerment, all of which occurred at the expense of efficiency. The growth rates of imports into South Africa in the later 1990s suggest that these policies were beginning to take their toll.

Commodities exported

Gold was not considered a commodity in 1990, but if it is placed in that category it easily heads the list of commodity exports for that year, with a value of R18,994 million. Precious metals and precious stones came second – boosted by the growing platinum output – iron and steel third, coal (mineral fuels) fourth, ores fifth, copper goods sixth and edible fruits and nuts seventh. All achieved exports of more than R1 billion. The top six, moreover, were all the products of mines, emphasising how dependent the balance of payments was on the country's mineral base. Exports of machinery, at R973.2 million in 1990, represented a new development, but it was the only one in the top 10 exports. From the point of view of value, the main developments in the 1980s were the growth of coal exports and iron and steel exports. The Department of Customs and Excise valued coal exports in 1990 at R3,751.4 million; 10 years later, in 2001, the Department of Mineral Affairs had revised this figure to R4,026.9 million. Sanctions campaigns had not seriously damaged essential mineral exports from South Africa before 1990.

In the second tier of exports in 1990, only three of the commodities were mineral products. Two were manufactured products, namely inorganic chemicals, which had benefited from the expansion of Sasol, and motor vehicles and parts. The remaining five were the products of the land. In the third tier, seven of the 10 were manufactured products and there were no mineral products. All in all, the pattern of exports at the beginning of the decade was that of a resource-based economy heavily dependent upon the products of its mines and fields.

In the first four years of the 1990s, only the category precious metals, which included platinum, increased its exports in real terms. Exports of gold, iron and steel, coal and copper goods all declined. Manufactured products fared better. Exports of vehicles and parts, machinery and inorganic chemicals all rose substantially and by 1994 were among the top 10 commodities exported. In the last years of the old regime, major changes were taking place in the pattern of exports as South Africa established itself as an important exporter of inorganic chemicals, machinery and vehicles.

At the end of the decade, when sanctions had been replaced by aid, some traditional exports had recovered and the newer manufactured ones had further strengthened their position. Coal exports had more than doubled, exports of electrical machinery had trebled, those of vehicles and parts had quadrupled and aluminium exports had increased sevenfold. Six of the top 10 export commodities were manufactured goods, of which three were engineering products, one a chemical product and two processed metals.

In the second tier, agricultural and forestry products performed better than they had done four years earlier, led by beverages, wood pulp, fruit and nuts and sugar confectionary. Aircraft and parts appeared in the second tier because of re-exports. The bottom tier of exports was made up primarily of raw materials together with miscellaneous chemicals and fertilisers. The former category was a new entry. Indeed, by 2000, total chemical exports amounted to R8,857.4 million, ahead of ores and aluminium.

Exports in the later 1990s benefited from a depreciating rand and a boom in foreign direct investment in developing countries.[5] It helped South Africa achieve export-led growth, despite the anti-export bias in the economy.[6] The single most important change was undoubtedly the rise in platinum output, which in 2000 overtook gold. In the nineteenth century South Africa had the good fortune to possess diamonds and gold. A century later, when the volume and value of the gold output was dropping, platinum came to the rescue and, as a century earlier, the economic good fortune was accompanied by political change. Meanwhile, the foreign trade proportion of GDP increased so that the South African economy was becoming more dependent upon the international economy.

Tables 17.11 and 17.12 provide details on the rate of growth of exports before and after the ending of sanctions. In the first period, when the economy was struggling, 10 of the country's leading exports experienced negative growth rates, including the most important commodities exported, such as iron and steel, coal, articles of iron and steel, copper goods and wool. Countering their decline, and heading the list, was the rapid growth of alcoholic drink exports and aircraft and their parts. The former was a traditional commodity that was finding markets in Africa, while the latter was growing from a small base and included re-exports. The next one on the list, inorganic chemicals, represented the new science-based industries, while fish and crustaceans were a traditional export. Rubber products and motor vehicles were the voices of modernisation, cereals and wood products those of the past. In other words, the growth pattern of the early 1990s, in very difficult circumstances, displayed the strength of traditional export products combined with elements of the new, which together suggest the economy was in transition.

The picture fits the 1940 description given by the League of Nations that classified South Africa as a semi-industrialised country better than

5 'Survey of world trade', *The Economist*, 3 October 1998, p. 13.
6 Cassim, 'The pace, nature and impact of trade policy', p. 86.

Table 17.11 *Top 30 commodities exported from South Africa, 1990 and 2000*

1990		*2000*	
Commodity	*Value (R millions)*	*Commodity*	*Value (R millions)*
Gold[a]	18,994.0	Gold[a]	25,055.0
Precious metals and stones	5,760.9	Precious metal and stones minus gold	16,988.9
Iron and steel	5,295.2	Iron and steel	18,743.1
Mineral fuels	3,751.4	Mineral fuels	18,585.3
Ores	2,762.0	Vehicles and parts	11,870.8
Copper goods	1,190.0	Machinery	11,819.2
Edible fruits and nuts	1,031.6	Ores	7,586.6
Machinery	973.2	Aluminium	6,329.6
Wool	944.8	Electrical machinery	4,515.7
Articles of iron and steel	883.4	Inorganic chemicals	4,473.4
Pulp	840.2	Edible fruit and nuts	3,981.3
Nickel	807.2	Pulp	3,428.8
Inorganic chemicals	806.4	Furniture	2,983.0
Sugar confectionary	772.8	Paper and paperboard	2,874.9
Lime, cement, etc.	743.7	Articles of iron and steel	2,738.4
Paper and paperboard	716.3	Organic chemicals	2,636.4
Cereals	675.6	Beverages	2,611.6
Vehicles and parts	668.4	Wood products	2,269.7
Aluminium	558.7	Aircraft and parts	2,148.2
Processed fruits and nuts	471.1	Plastics	2,036.6
Raw hides	392.5	Sugar confectionary	2,024.6
Electrical machinery	389.5	Fish and crustaceans	1,765.3
Organic chemicals	333.8	Miscellaneous chemicals	1,747.6
Plastics	321.3	Raw hides	1,548.3
Wood products	318.6	Copper goods	1,371.8
Railway goods	304.5	Rubber goods	1,345.1
Fish and crustaceans	270.3	Wool	1,102.7
Miscellaneous chemicals	190.9	Lime, cement, etc.	1,030.7
Fertiliser	147.8	Railway goods	955.0
Furniture	139.9	Fertilisers	915.1

[a] Gold was classified as a commodity in 1996.
Sources: Figures provided by the Department of Customs and Excise for 1990; and *Monthly Abstract of Trade Statistics*, various issues, Commissioner for South African Revenue Service, 2000.

the ANC view that classified South Africa as a developing state and placed it with its undeveloped African neighbours. The changes in the export growth rates after 1994 confirm this view of the economy. The seven most rapidly growing exports were representatives of the newer industries, namely: aluminium, motor vehicles and parts, aircraft and parts, rubber products, electrical machinery, general machinery and organic chemicals. Coal exports rebounded with the opening of

Table 17.12 *Average annual rates of growth of leading exports, in constant prices, 1990–94 and 1994–2000*

1990–94		*1994–2000*	
Commodity	*Growth rate (%)*	*Commodity*	*Growth rate (%)*
Beverages	33.7	Aluminium	38.5
Aircraft and parts	31.0	Vehicles and parts	26.9
Inorganic chemicals	18.9	Aircraft and parts	22.6
Fish and crustaceans	18.0	Rubber products	22.5
Rubber products	16.9	Electrical machinery	20.7
Vehicles and parts	13.9	General machinery	20.6
Cereals	11.7	Organic chemicals	20.4
Wood products	11.6	Mineral fuels	20.7
General machinery	11.2	Sugar confectionary	15.0
Electrical machinery	10.4	Furniture	14.9
Fertilisers	7.1	Ores	13.4
Plastics	6.9	Miscellaneous chemicals	13.0
Railway goods	5.1	Plastics	11.5
Edible fruits and nuts	4.9	Fertilisers	10.9
Furniture	3.8	Articles of iron and steel	10.7
Raw hides	3.6	Wood products	10.4
Precious metal and stones	3.4	Beverages	8.8
Paper and paperboard	2.3	Pulp	8.1
Processed fruit and nuts	2.2	Paper and paperboard	6.4
Organic chemicals	0.7	Iron and steel	6.0
Pulp	0.2	Raw hides	5.1
Gold	–0.3	Fish and crustaceans	4.9
Iron and steel	–0.4	Edible fruits and nuts	3.9
Mineral fuels	–4.5	Precious metals and stones minus gold	3.7
Articles of iron and steel	–9.7	Processed fruits and nuts	2.7
Aluminium	–10.7	Inorganic chemicals	1.5
Copper goods	–12.0	Railway goods	0.2
Wool	–12.6	Lime, cement, etc.	–0.8
Lime, cement, etc.	–12.9	Wool	–3.9
Ores	–15.5	Gold	–4.6
Sugar confectionary	–18.2	Copper goods	–4.8
		Cereals	–6.4

Sources: Figures provided by the Department of Customs and Excise for 1990; and *Monthly Abstract of Trade Statistics*, various issues, Commissioner for South African Revenue Service, 1994 and 2000.

former closed markets; but this was achieved only at the cost of both a rapidly depreciating rand and a fall in the price of coal. Sixteen export commodities achieved double-digit export growth during these six years and, had 1999 been the bench year, growth rates would have been even higher. Exports fell in the year 2000.

Some of the commodities that had for long been the backbone of the economy were in decline. Most obvious was the fall of 4.6 per cent a year in the value of gold exports. Copper and wool also fared badly, and inorganic chemicals, which had been one of the leaders in the first years of the decade, barely grew in the later years. Perhaps most surprising is the relatively slow growth in the export of precious metals, once gold is subtracted from them, for, as detailed in Chapter 4, on mining, the platinum group metals overtook gold in the value of output in the year 2000.

The African market north of the Limpopo was relatively small, because of low per capita incomes, but it did have a considerable impact upon South Africa. Transport equipment and consumer goods of all kinds moved north in increasing quantities after 1994. This applied particularly to foodstuffs, beverages and furniture, all of which could be readily obtained in South Africa and easily shipped north by road or rail. The very nature of the road and railway network of Southern and East Africa not only favour a possible future union, but give a decided advantage to South African producers over competitors in Europe, America and Asia. Driven mainly by market forces, developments in exports at the end of the century made it possible to adopt an optimistic view of the prospects for the future.

Conclusion

Free trade is always better than protection and the reduction in the latter benefited South Africa in the last decade of the twentieth century. Free trade increases competition, and so limits the power of domestic monopolies and spurs local companies to greater efficiency. Free trade, moreover, enables the law of comparative advantage to come into operation, which benefits everyone. In a survey of world trade in 1998 *The Economist* spelled out clearly and simply how Ricardo's theory worked to the benefit of everyone.[7]

Sadly, this lesson has not been fully learned in South Africa, where television programmes are full of advertisements urging South Africans to buy local products and revert to the harmful autarkic policies of the past. Nor is the theory of comparative advantage widely understood. It is often confused with absolute advantage. In this way, for example, South Africa's absolute advantage in the export market for luxury vehicles is trumpeted loudly, despite the falling rate of growth in value added,

7 *The Economist*, 3 October 1998, pp. 4–5.

while the country's comparative advantage in beneficiating minerals is downplayed. Comparative advantage would support the shift of labour out of the gold mines and into platinum mining, in which the country possesses both absolute and comparative advantage.

The last decade of the century was marked by an increase in market forces and the power of private enterprise. This was revealed in the widening range of manufactured commodities exported and the very rapid growth of a handful of consumer goods imported. Producer goods continued to dominate the flow of imports with an increasing number of items, such as computers, fulfilling a dual role as both producer good and consumer good. It was also revealed in the widening geographical range of the country's trade and the return to some of the earlier patterns that were developed as a result of membership of the British empire and the country's geographical position in Africa. Exports to Australia, India and Canada fell into this category, along with those to much of Southern, Central and East Africa. Above all, the 1990s witnessed the ascendancy of the USA as the country's major supplier.

The shift in the direction of trade away from Europe reflected the more rapid growth of markets elsewhere, as well as the emergence of new suppliers in the form of India, China and the Gulf oil producers. This new geographical arrangement, however, brought with it other challenges. Trade with Asia and Africa was much less balanced than that with Europe. Asia provided far more imports than it took as exports. On the one hand, advanced technological products came in from Japan and South Korea; on the other, the products of cheap labour came from China and India, and petroleum products from the Gulf. South African manufacturers had difficulty exporting manufactured goods to India and China, while the market in the Gulf states was small.

As a result of these changes, South Africa reverted to the traditional pattern of the pre-sanctions era, running a deficit on the current account of the balance of payments, which was met by an inflow of funds on the capital account. In the past, these capital flows had been mainly in the form of direct investment by companies, or the purchase of government or public corporation bonds. In the 1990s the deficit was met by inflows of 'hot money' in response to high interest rates or the attractions of the Johannesburg Stock Exchange. The trading patterns of the later 1990s accordingly depended upon the inflow of short-term funds that could flow out as quickly as they flowed in. And this, it should be noted, took place in a far more volatile global environment.

Both before and after the 1994 election, private enterprise took the lead in driving the growth of the country's external trade. Individual entrepreneurs and large corporations responded to the signals coming out of the international economy. In the 1990s, when General Agreement on Tariffs and Trade and the World Trade Organization were the driving force behind the reduction in tariffs, world trade was growing much faster than world GDP. South Africa responded to this challenge in a myriad of ways and, despite the deteriorating investment climate and the growing political interference in all aspect of business, the country was carried along on a wave of trade-led growth, the like of which had never previously been experienced.

18

The balance of payments

Philip Mohr

Introduction

The most important development in South Africa in the 1990s was the adoption of a new constitutional dispensation. This affected every aspect of life in South Africa, including the economy in general and the balance of payments in particular. The democratisation in the political sphere was accompanied by the reintegration of the South African economy into the international economy. The experience was often traumatic, as the world economy itself had undergone radical changes since South Africa was isolated from certain parts of it in the 1970s and particularly in the late 1980s. The gradual normalisation of South Africa's international economic and financial relations in the 1990s undoubtedly had significant benefits, but it also exposed the country to a degree of volatility, especially in the international financial markets, which posed new challenges to decision makers in both the public sector and the private sector.

During the period leading up to the elections in April 1994, concern was expressed in economic and financial circles about the direction a new government would take. This concern was based on the policy stance of the African National Congress (ANC) and the contents of its election manifesto, the *Reconstruction and Development Programme* (RDP), which, although a significant departure from the party's earlier avowedly socialist policy stance, still contained strong socialistic and populist overtones and anti-market sentiments. One of the main concerns was the strong influence of the Congress of South African Trade Unions (Cosatu) and the South African Communist Party (SACP), the two alliance partners of the ANC.

During the first two years after the 1994 elections there was still no certainty as to the course the new policy makers would take, but in due course the government liberalised South Africa's international trade and finance to a greater degree than any post-war government. This 'move to the market' was evident in many domestic economic policies as well. Much of the liberalisation was, of course, virtually forced upon sometimes reluctant policy makers by the prevailing international economic orthodoxy, but few would have anticipated that an ANC government would, by the turn of the century, be applying more conservative, conventional, market-related policies than any of its predecessors.

The course of the South African economy and its balance of payments in the 1990s can broadly be divided into two distinct sub-periods: the uncertain period of transformation from 1990 to the middle of 1994; and the period after the ANC assumed power (albeit initially as the main partner in a Government of National Unity). Although some of the previous restrictions on South Africa's international trade and finance were gradually removed after President De Klerk's speech on 2 February 1990, which paved the way for the political transition, South Africa was still subject to a severe balance of payments constraint during the early 1990s. Between January 1990 and June 1994 there was a steady net outflow of capital not related to reserves of almost R27 billion, partly as a result of repayments of foreign debt emanating from the 1985 debt standstill arrangement.[1]

As during the second half of the 1980s, the authorities thus had to manage the economy in such a way that surpluses on the current account would be sufficient to cover the country's foreign debt commitments and other capital outflows. An important element of this strategy was to contain domestic spending, so as to keep imports in check. The result was low, often negative economic growth. Real GDP fell by 0.3 per cent in 1990, 1.0 per cent in 1991 and 2.1 per cent in 1992, before increasing by 1.2 per cent in 1993. As a result, real GDP per capita was more than 10 per cent lower in 1993 than in 1989.

From the middle of 1994, once it became evident that South Africa's political transition would proceed relatively smoothly, the net outflow of capital changed to a net inflow, thus allowing the country once again to record deficits on the current account of the balance of payments. Some of the brakes on domestic spending could be released and higher economic growth could be achieved. From July 1994 to December 1999 a total net inflow of capital not related to reserves of more than

1 During the period from 1985 to the second quarter of 1994, the total net outflow amounted to about R52 billion. Unless specified otherwise, all data in this chapter were obtained from publications of the South African Reserve Bank, including *Annual Economic Reports*, *Quarterly Bulletins* and especially the supplement to the *Quarterly Bulletin* of June 2001, titled *South Africa's Balance of Payments 1946–2000.*

R84 billion was recorded. As will be discussed below, the ride was far from smooth, but the net inflow did mean that current account deficits could be sustained and positive (albeit moderate) real GDP growth was achieved from 1994 to 1999. In 1999 real GDP per capita was 3.4 per cent higher than in 1993.

From this brief overview it should be clear that South Africa's economic fortunes in the 1990s were again, as in previous decades, closely related to its economic and financial links with the rest of the world, as reflected in the country's balance of payments. These links are discussed in greater detail in the rest of the chapter. The next section summarises some of the important policy measures taken during the 1990s to liberalise South Africa's international trade and financial relations. This is followed by a brief overview of the South African balance of payments. The main elements of the balance of payments are discussed in sections on the current account, the financial account, unrecorded transactions and the official reserves account. The chapter is rounded off with some concluding remarks.

Liberalisation of South Africa's international trade and financial relations

As mentioned above, significant steps were taken in the 1990s to liberalise South Africa's international trade and financial relations. Trade liberalisation consists of the relaxation of quantitative restrictions on international trade, the reduction of tariffs, devaluation or depreciation of the international value of the currency and direct export promotion measures.[2] Various steps in this direction had already been taken during the 1980s,[3] particularly the dismantling of import quotas, but the most significant changes were introduced in the 1990s. Certain of these steps are summarised in Table 18.1.

The South African trade regime at the start of the 1990s has been described as one 'characterised by numerous quantitative restrictions, a multitude of tariff lines, wide dispersion, and various forms of protection.... The overall result was a complex, highly discretionary regime with a significant anti-export bias.'[4] By the end of the decade, the tariff

2 See T. Bell, 'Trade policy', in J. Michie and V. Padayachee (eds), *The Political Economy of South Africa's Transition*, Dryden Press, 1997, pp. 71–90, at p. 71.

3 *Ibid.*, pp. 71–74.

4 J. D. Lewis, 'Policies to promote growth and employment in South Africa', Informal Discussion Papers on Aspects of the Economy of South Africa No. 16, World Bank, July 2001, p. 42.

Table 18.1 *Some policy measures pertaining to the current account of the balance of payments, 1990–99*

Date	*Measure*
14 March 1990	Reduction in surcharges on imports by about one-third
April 1990	Introduction of the General Export Incentive Scheme (GEIS), a significant set of export subsidies
15 April 1994	South Africa signs the Marrakesh Agreement, following the Uruguay round of multilateral trade negotiations, thus agreeing to liberalise international trade by lowering import tariffs and eliminating non-tariff barriers to trade
June 1994	Abolition of surcharges on imports of capital and intermediate goods
August 1994	South Africa becomes the eleventh member of the Southern African Development Community (SADC)
1 January 1995	New tariff policy comes into force, providing, *inter alia,* for a gradual reduction of *ad valorem* duties by an average of one-third over five years and for the replacement of all remaining quantitative import restrictions and formula duties by *ad valorem* duties
1 April 1995	GEIS revised as part of the process of phasing it out by 31 December 1997
1 October 1995	Abolition of remaining import surcharges (on luxury goods and white goods)
11 July 1997	Final repeal of all GEIS concessions (ahead of schedule)
15 August 1997	Export Marketing and Investment Assistance (EMIA) scheme introduced after abolition of GEIS
December 1997 onwards	Gold production marketed increasingly by the Rand Refinery and the different mining houses (instead of by the South African Reserve Bank)

structure had been rationalised significantly and tariff levels had been reduced in terms of South Africa's offer to the General Agreement on Tariffs and Trade (GATT) during the Uruguay round (see Table 18.2). As a result, South African agriculture and manufacturing were operating in a much less protected environment in 1999 than a decade earlier. The move to trade liberalisation was a conscious effort to switch from import substitution to export-oriented industrialisation. As will be shown below, South African manufacturing exports performed quite well in the 1990s.

The liberalisation of South Africa's international financial relations during the 1990s, in particular after 1995, was at least as significant as,

Table 18.2 *Changes in South African import tariffs, 1990–99*

	1990	*1999*
Number of tariff lines	12,500	7,743
Number of different rates (bands)	200	47
Minimum rate (%)	0	0
Maximum rate (%)	1,389	55
Unweighted mean rate (%)	27.5	7.1

Source: J. D. Lewis, 'Policies to promote growth and employment in South Africa', Informal Discussion Papers on Aspects of the Economy of South Africa No. 16, World Bank, July 2001, p. 43.

if not more than, the liberalisation of the country's international trade. Some of the most important policy changes pertaining to the financial account of the balance of payments are summarised in Table 18.3. The financial rand, which constituted exchange control in respect of non-residents, had been abolished on February 1983 but was reinstated in the wake of the country's foreign debt crisis. The eventual abolition of the financial rand and the re-establishment of a unitary exchange rate on 13 March 1995, which implied the full liberalisation of exchange controls on non-resident investors, was a momentous step which signalled a renewed confidence in South Africa's international economic position. This step was taken after South Africa's remaining foreign debt commitments (emanating from the foreign debt standstill of 1985) had been finalised. This important element of the country's balance of payments constraint had been removed and it was no longer deemed necessary to protect the balance of payments and the currency. The financial rand mechanism also had the disadvantage that the financial account and the foreign exchange reserves could not benefit from any net capital inflows. On the other hand, the abolition of the financial rand meant that the balance of payments, and the financial account in particular, potentially had a much greater impact on the structure and direction of economic policy, especially when financial account crises were experienced.[5]

5 The financial rand mechanism operated as a 'closed pool'. Each capital inflow through the financial rand had to be matched by an equivalent capital outflow, with the financial rand exchange rate adjusting to equalise the desired levels of inflows and outflows. The system thus protected the country's foreign reserves from the pressures of disinvestment but at the same time insulated the reserves from the potential benefits of capital inflows.

Table 18.3 *Some domestic and international policy measures and other steps pertaining to the financial account of the South African balance of payments, 1991–98*

Date/period	*Policy measures/steps*
First half of 1991	Gradual lifting of some financial (and other) sanctions
10 July 1991	USA decides to remove all sanctions imposed in terms of the Comprehensive Anti-Apartheid Act
Second half of 1991	South Africa launches first public foreign loan issues since debt crisis of 1985
First half of 1992	Government, Development Bank, Eskom, IDC and Telkom all borrow abroad
Late September 1993	Final rescheduling of $5 billion of international bank debt on which South Africa had declared a moratorium in September 1985 – to be repaid from 1 January 1994 to 15 August 2001
October 1994	South Africa obtains credit rating from three international rating agencies: Moody's, Standard and Poor's, Nippon Investor Services
7 December 1994	Global government bond issue of $750 million
13 March 1995	Abolition of financial rand system; unitary exchange rate re-established, abolishing exchange control on non-resident investors
16 May 1995	¥30 billion Samurai bond issue
13 July 1995	Start of gradual relaxation of exchange control applicable to residents; insurance companies, pension funds and unit trusts allowed to undertake foreign investments through swap arrangements with foreign investors
Third quarter 1995	Significant foreign borrowing by public corporations such as the IDC ($80 million) and Transnet ($200 million)
23 January 1996	Extension of the asset swap dispensation
14 June 1996	Further package of exchange control liberalisation measures announced, including increase in limit applicable to the procurement of foreign assets by way of asset swaps, authorisation of direct investments abroad by institutional investors up to 3 per cent of the net inflow of funds to these institutions in 1995 and upward adjustments in exchange control limits
12 March 1997	Wide range of further exchange control liberalisation measures announced, including abolition of most remaining controls on current account transactions, increase of annual travel allowances to R80,000 per adult and R25,000 per child, permission to corporates to invest up to R30 million per new investment abroad (up to R50 million in SADC countries) and further extension of scope for asset swops by institutional investors
May 1997	Sale of 30 per cent share in Telkom to a consortium of non-resident companies, yielding R5.6 billion ($1.26 billion)
1 July 1997	Private individuals who are taxpayers in good standing with the tax authorities permitted to invest up to R200,000 abroad, or to maintain foreign currency deposits to the same amount with authorised foreign exchange dealers
November 1997	Reserve Bank terminates its involvement in the foreign currency forward market for transactions with a maturity over 12 months
11 March 1998	Further package of exchange control liberalisation measures announced, including permission for institutional investors (insurance companies, pension funds and unit trusts) to invest 15 per cent of their assets abroad, further extension of asset swap arrangements and raising of foreign investment allowance in respect of individuals to R400,000

South African balance of payments: an overview

The balance of payments consists of five sub-accounts: the current account, the capital transfer account, the financial account, unrecorded transactions and the official reserves account.[6] The annual data for the South African balance of payments during the 1990s are summarised in Table 18.4. The top half of the table contains the data pertaining to the individual components of the balance of payments and the bottom half shows the most important balances and sub-balances in the overall account. In the discussion below, the focus is on the most important items and balances, particularly those pertaining to the current and financial accounts. As is clear from Table 18.4, the capital transfer account is insignificant and is therefore not discussed.

Current account

As indicated in Table 18.4, significant current account surpluses were recorded from 1990 to 1993. However, once net inflows of foreign capital resumed, current account deficits could be afforded again and substantial deficits were recorded from 1995 onwards. The various sub-balances of the current account behaved in traditional fashion: trade surpluses were recorded throughout the 1990s but these were sometimes more than offset by the traditional deficits on the service and income accounts. Note, in particular, the declining trend in the services deficit and the rising income deficit.

Not surprisingly, in view of the liberalisation of South Africa's international trade and the weak performance of the domestic economy, the South African economy tended to become more open in the 1990s, as illustrated in Table 18.5.

Trade account

South Africa's trade balance in the 1990s was characterised by further declines in the contribution of net gold exports, strong growth in non-gold merchandise exports and an increasing import penetration ratio.

South Africa's gold production peaked at 1,002 tons in 1970 and declined fairly consistently during the 1970s and 1980s. During some periods, however, the decline in the physical production was neutralised by rapid increases in the dollar price of gold or significant

6 For a full explanation of the various accounts, see S. S. Walters, 'A note on the revision of the balance of payments accounting framework', South African Reserve Bank, *Quarterly Bulletin*, 212 (June 1999), 54–57; and P. Mohr, *Economic Indicators* (3rd edition), University of South Africa Press, 2005, pp. 127–137.

Table 18.4 *South African balance of payments, 1990–99 (R millions)*

Item/balance	*1990*	*1991*	*1992*	*1993*	*1994*	*1995*	*1996*	*1997*	*1998*	*1999*
Item										
Merchandise exports	44,740	46,147	50,446	58,428	69,866	86,580	103,906	118,012	135,214	150,604
Net gold exports	18,177	19,587	19,391	22,449	23,670	22,538	26,300	25,818	25,907	24,279
Service receipts	8,800	8,804	9,561	10,701	13,306	16,751	21,589	24,587	29,068	31,000
Income receipts	1,701	2,414	2,649	2,286	3,455	4,128	4,663	6,011	7,193	9,424
Merchandise imports (–)	44,706	47,466	51,976	60,512	77,675	99,425	118,658	133,061	150,705	149,540
Payments for services (–)	9,670	10,554	12,427	15,407	18,072	21,667	24,681	27,657	30,927	34,492
Income payments (–)	12,743	11,273	11,050	10,986	12,054	14,554	18,041	20,808	24,524	29,011
Current transfers (net receipts +)	–828	–1,418	–1,042	–2,092	–2,160	–2,340	–3,206	–3,328	–4,093	–5,662
Capital transfers (net receipts +)	–147	–99	–120	–188	–236	–145	–203	–892	–309	–260
Direct investment (net)	–274	111	–5,514	–941	–3,040	–4,557	–970	6,756	–6,673	–2,730
Portfolio investment (net)	16	666	4,950	2,417	10,008	9,020	9,576	30,580	20,375	52,346
Other investment (net)	–1,243	–3,320	–927	–7,145	–2,609	15,318	4,788	–10,287	3,662	–27,266
Unrecorded transactions	–271	538	–3,377	–7,923	–1,572	–3,061	–10,166	–4,870	–8,143	7,173
Balance										
Trade balance	18,211	18,268	17,861	20,365	15,861	9,693	11,548	10,769	10,416	25,343
Services balance	–870	–1,750	–2,866	–4,706	–4,766	–4,916	–3,092	–3,070	–1,859	–3,492
Income balance	–11,042	–8,859	–8,401	–8,700	–8,599	–10,426	–13,378	–14,797	–17,331	–19,587
Balance on current account	5,471	6,241	5,552	4,867	336	–7,989	–8,128	–10,426	–12,867	–3,398
Balance on financial account	–1,501	–2,543	–1,491	–5,669	4,359	19,781	13,394	27,049	17,300	22,350
Change in net gold and other foreign reserves owing to balance of payments transactions	3,552	4,137	564	–8,913	2,887	8,586	–5,103	10,861	–4,019	25,865
Change in gross gold and other foreign reserves	359	2,645	1,698	123	2,818	3,595	–1,864	19,208	6,677	26,943

Source: South African Reserve Bank, *South Africa's Balance of Payments 1946–2000*, supplement to the South African Reserve Bank *Quarterly Bulletin*, June 2001.

Table 18.5 *Openness of the South African economy, 1990–99*

Year	*(a) Exports of goods and services as % of GDP*	*(b) Imports of goods and services as % of GDE*	*(c) Average of (a) and (b)*	*(d) Import penetration ratio*
1990	24.7	19.8	22.3	n.a.
1991	22.4	18.4	20.4	12.8
1992	21.3	18.0	19.7	13.4
1993	21.5	18.5	20.0	14.2
1994	22.2	20.3	21.3	16.0
1995	23.0	22.3	22.7	18.3
1996	24.5	23.5	24.0	19.6
1997	24.6	23.8	24.2	20.2
1998	25.7	24.7	25.2	20.3
1999	25.4	23.5	24.5	18.6

Notes: GDP = gross domestic product; GDE = gross domestic expenditure; import penetration ratio = ratio of imported goods at constant prices to real GDE (as percentage).
Source of basic data: South African Reserve Bank, *Quarterly Bulletin* (various issues).

depreciations in the value of the rand against the US dollar, thus maintaining or even increasing the contribution of the gold mining sector in rand terms. In the 1990s, however, both the physical gold production and the dollar price of gold declined substantially and, despite sometimes sharp depreciations of the rand against the dollar, the contribution of net gold exports to the total value of visible exports fell by more than a half, as indicated in Table 18.6. In 1985 the contribution was still as high as 43.6 per cent but by the end of the 1990s platinum group metals had almost surpassed gold as South Africa's primary export commodity in value terms.

The generally weak gold price during the 1990s can be ascribed to factors such as increased production in countries such as the USA, Canada, Australia and Brazil, significant Soviet gold sales, a considerable increase in forward sales by producers, the negative impact of low inflation and positive real interest rates on speculative demand, official sales by various central banks, negative market sentiment regarding gold, exacerbated by the strength of the dollar and booming international equity markets, concern about the future role of gold as a reserve asset in the European Monetary Union and a weak demand for gold in Asian countries. The continued decline in the volume of gold production, on the other hand, can be ascribed to the weak price, a reduction in the quality of ore milled, the closure of some mines, poor labour productivity and technical difficulties owing to seismic incidents.

Table 18.6 *Net gold exports, gold production and gold price, 1990–99*

Year	*Net gold exports as % of total visible exports*	*Gold production (tons)*	*Average gold price (R per fine ounce)*	*Average gold price ($ per fine ounce)*
1990	28.9	605	992	384
1991	29.8	601	1,000	362
1992	27.8	613	980	344
1993	27.8	619	1,177	360
1994	25.3	580	1,363	384
1995	20.7	523	1,393	384
1996	20.2	498	1,664	388
1997	18.0	490	1,523	331
1998	16.1	464	1,622	294
1999	13.9	457	1,703	179

Sources of basic data: South African Reserve Bank, *Quarterly Bulletin* (various issues); Department of Minerals and Energy, *South Africa's Mineral Industry* (various issues).

An early indication of the lacklustre performance of the gold price during the decade was provided by reaction of the gold market to the oil price increase following Iraq's invasion of Kuwait on 2 August 1990 and the subsequent Gulf War. The price of a barrel of Brent crude oil rose from an average of $17 in July to $26 in August and peaked at $40.90 on 28 September 1990, before falling to $23.36 in January 1991 and $18.52 in June 1991. As during the oil shocks of 1973/74 and 1978/79, the gold price (and the prices of other international commodities) also rose but the increase was neither as strong nor as sustained as during the earlier episodes. The average gold price increased from $362 per fine ounce in July 1990 to $395 in August but fell back to $381 in October and continued falling subsequently. The positive impact of the Iraqi invasion and the subsequent Gulf War was thus minimal and short-lived. This can probably be ascribed to a lack of the fundamental uncertainty which had existed during the previous oil shocks – observers expected the USA to intervene and also expected the war to be over fairly quickly. The availability of alternative safe havens for investors, such as the US dollar and sterling, probably also had an effect.

Another reason why the share of gold in the value of South Africa's visible exports declined was the rapid increase in the value of non-gold merchandise exports (see Table 18.7, p. 395). These exports had performed quite well during the latter half of the 1980s and this momentum was maintained during much of the 1990s. The performance of non-gold merchandise exports was undoubtedly one of the most positive developments in the South African economy during the decade. Among the reasons for this performance were:

- the generally strong world economy;
- the concomitant growth in world trade, fostered by the international trend towards import liberalisation;
- the relatively weak, sometimes quite depressed, domestic economy, which resulted in often high levels of excess production capacity;
- a changed attitude of South African manufacturers to exports – whereas manufacturers had traditionally tended to focus on exports only during downswings in the domestic business cycle, the realisation dawned during the 1980s and 1990s that growth (and indeed survival) depended on the ability to compete in international markets and to exploit all available opportunities to export (this was particularly evident during the domestic upswing which commenced in June 1993);
- the opening up of new, non-traditional markets as sanctions and trade embargoes were lifted and South Africa rejoined the international economic community;
- rapid growth in some of these new markets (compared with the growth in the economies of South Africa's traditional trading partners);
- the decline in the nominal (sometimes even real) effective exchange rate of the rand;
- significant assistance to exporters under the General Export Incentive Scheme (GEIS) – which was probably important initially, although the strong export performance was maintained even after the GEIS was amended and eventually scrapped in 1997;
- the development of new manufacturing enterprises specifically for the export market as the awareness of the importance of exports and the opportunities they present increased (examples included Columbus Stainless Steel and Alusaf's aluminium smelter).

Furthermore, during the second half of the 1990s the growth in exports was further enhanced by the Motor Industry Development Scheme, growing labour productivity in manufacturing and improved access to foreign markets through inward and outward foreign direct investment, as well as licensing and cooperation agreements.

This strong export performance was achieved and maintained despite the existence of trade sanctions in the 1980s and early 1990s, the lowering of trade barriers during the 1980s and 1990s, the abolition of the GEIS in 1997 and the often sluggish demand for South Africa's traditional commodity exports (particularly relative to other commodities such as rubber, coffee, soya beans, copper and cotton).

During the early 1990s merchandise imports remained at a fairly high level, despite the depressed state of the domestic economy. The reasons advanced for this fairly unusual state of affairs include:

- large imports of capital equipment, for example in the mining industry, in reaction to the increasingly volatile and problematic labour market situation;[7]
- the periodic substitution of locally produced goods by imported goods in reaction to a decline in the relative prices of imported goods (measured as the ratio of import prices to the gross domestic expenditure deflator);[8]
- the execution of previously postponed aircraft purchases by South African Airways;
- the increased importance of non-traditional manufactured exports, which required more intermediate imports than traditional exports;
- periodic increases in agricultural imports as a result of serious drought conditions in certain regions;
- periodic pre-emptive buying in anticipation of a depreciation of the rand against the major currencies.

With the recovery in domestic demand from 1994 onwards, merchandise imports (particularly capital goods) rose sharply. The marginal propensity to import was high and the import penetration ratio rose considerably (see Table 18.5). This was partly in response to the trade liberalisation (particularly the lowering of import tariffs) discussed above. Increased international competition also compelled many domestic industries to replace their technologically dated production equipment with more advanced machinery and equipment. Towards the end of the decade import volumes declined significantly in response to the decline in domestic demand, in particular the sharply lower fixed investment spending by the public corporations and private sector.

As indicated in Table 18.7, the South African terms of trade (the ratio of export prices to import prices) deteriorated in seven of the 10 years from 1990 to 1999. Over the decade as a whole, the terms of trade (including gold) fell by 4.5 per cent.[9] The country thus had to export about 4.5 per cent more goods and services (in volume terms) in 1999 to be able to buy the same volume of imports as in 1990, implying that South Africans had become poorer by that percentage (*ceteris paribus*).

7 *Annual Economic Report*, South African Reserve Bank, 1990, p. 28.

8 *Annual Economic Report*, South African Reserve Bank, 1992, p. 24.

9 The terms of trade excluding gold fell by only 0.7 per cent, which further illustrates the impact of the declining gold price on the South African economy during the decade.

Table 18.7 *Annual changes in volume of exports, volume of imports and terms of trade, 1990–99*

Year	*% change in volume of exports (excluding gold)*	*% change in volume of imports*	*% change in terms of trade (including gold)*
1990	3.9	–5.4	–2.0
1991	–2.3	–0.1	–1.5
1992	2.3	4.9	–1.2
1993	6.7	8.2	0.7
1994	8.4	16.0	3.2
1995	15.2	17.0	–1.5
1996	12.3	8.7	1.4
1997	5.5	5.4	–1.2
1998	4.2	1.1	–0.9
1999	2.8	–7.4	–2.4

Source of basic data: South African Reserve Bank, *South Africa's Balance of Payments 1946–2000,* supplement to the South African Reserve Bank *Quarterly Bulletin,* June 2001.

Services account

Deficits were recorded on the services account in each of the years under consideration. South Africa's services account has always been in deficit but there was a marked improvement during the decade, both in absolute terms and as a percentage of GDP. After the political transition the deficit tended to increase, mainly as a result of the increased freight and insurance payments accompanying the increase in imports and increased spending by South Africans travelling abroad. In due course, however, there was a sharp increase in the spending by foreign travellers in South Africa, resulting in a significantly positive tourist (travel) balance.

Income account

Table 18.4 shows that the deficit on the income account (the income balance) was much more significant than the services deficit. Although this had always been the case, there were some noteworthy developments on the income account during the 1990s. Initially there was a continued improvement in income payments as a result of the repayment of foreign debt, which significantly reduced the interest payments to foreign creditors. The lower profitability of the gold mining industry also resulted in lower dividend payments to foreign shareholders. In 1993, however, the monetary authorities borrowed R7.4 billion to boost the country's flagging foreign reserves and the interest payments on these loans increased the deficit on the income account. Once South Africa rejoined the international financial community, the deficit widened significantly as a result of large-scale foreign borrowing and investment by foreigners in South African equities and bonds, which raised interest and dividend payments. Increased profitability of South African companies further increased the dividends paid to foreign shareholders. Towards the end of the decade, however, income receipts also increased quite strongly, as a result of the relaxation of exchange controls, which allowed institutional and private investors to build up foreign assets. Nevertheless, the increase in interest and dividend payments outstripped the increased receipts, with the result that the deficit on the income account continued to increase.

Financial account

As during the 1980s, there were some dramatic developments in the financial account of the South African balance of payments during the 1990s. The first few years basically constituted a continuance of the position during the second half of the 1980s. Ostracised by the international financial community and committed to repay large amounts of foreign debt, South Africa experienced substantial deficits on the financial account, which forced the authorities to manage the economy in such a way that the surpluses on the current account would be sufficient to cover the country's foreign debt commitments. However, after February 1990 there was some improvement in foreign political and economic perceptions regarding South Africa, which resulted in an increased availability of trade finance from abroad to South African firms, while forward cover rates also became more favourable.

During the second half of 1991 South Africa launched its first public loan issues (albeit small) since the debt crisis and in the first half of 1992 the government, Eskom, the Development Bank of Southern Africa, Telkom and the Industrial Development Corporation all borrowed abroad. Capital transactions with the rest of the world were starting to normalise, with short-term capital movements being governed mainly by economic considerations such as trends in foreign trade, expected exchange rate movements and the cost of forward cover. However, political uncertainty and renewed domestic unrest periodically had a negative impact on the financial account, for example towards the end of the second quarter of 1992, when the political negotiations broke down temporarily, and in 1993, when a particularly large net capital outflow was recorded. There was a sharp improvement during the first quarter of 1994, despite continued unrest and political uncertainty during the transition to a new political dispensation. In April 1994, during the run-up to the elections, there was a renewed capital outflow but, once it became clear that the transition was to proceed relatively peacefully, matters improved considerably and a significant financial account surplus was recorded for the full year. This occurred after the country had experienced a total net capital outflow of about R52 billion during the nine and a half years from 1985 to June 1994. Subsequently, annual financial account surpluses became the norm but the country also became much more vulnerable to the volatility of international capital flows. Put differently: the country gained first-hand experience of the risks involved in relying on foreign capital, particularly confidence-sensitive portfolio capital, to supplement domestic saving in the pursuit of higher economic growth. Although the annual figures in Table 18.4 show large financial account surpluses from 1995 to 1999, the shorter-term experience was often more traumatic. The flows to and from the Johannesburg Stock Exchange became volatile and also very sensitive to developments in other emerging-market countries (e.g. in South East Asia, Latin America and Russia) and other African countries (e.g. the Democratic Republic of the Congo and Zimbabwe).

The decision to allow South African financial institutions, firms and individuals to invest abroad added yet another dimension to developments on the financial account. For the first time South Africans could respond legitimately to increased domestic political and economic uncertainty by investing abroad and in the wake of the relaxation of exchange control many of them indeed did so.

Direct investment

Direct investment occurs when investors individually or collectively acquire at least 10 per cent of the voting rights in an enterprise in another country. In addition to the initial transaction, all subsequent transactions between the parties are also classified as direct investment. Net direct investment is the result of changes in foreign liabilities (where an increase in liabilities indicates an inflow of capital) and in foreign assets (where an increase in assets indicates an outflow of capital). As indicated in Table 18.4, net direct investment was mostly negative during the 1990s. The only exceptions were in 1991 (when the amount was relatively small) and in 1997 (when the sale of a 30 per cent stake in Telkom in May of that year yielded R5.6 billion, the equivalent of US$1.26 billion). In particular, foreign direct investment by South African companies increased significantly after the relaxation of exchange control measures allowed companies to finance investments in foreign countries through offshore borrowings and foreign share placements.

Portfolio investment

Portfolio investment includes transactions in financial instruments, such as equity and debt securities, money market debt instruments and financial derivatives, not classified as direct investment. Portfolio investors are primarily concerned about the possible returns on their investment and the likelihood of capital gains.

Portfolio investment became very significant in the 1990s. Prior to that, both the portfolio investment by foreigners in South Africa and net portfolio investment had been relatively small, but in the 1990s foreigners invested a total net amount of R235 billion in South Africa. At the same time, however, portfolio investment by South Africans overseas also increased substantially, particularly after the relaxation of exchange controls on residents. The total net amount during the 1990s was R95 billion, of which R91 billion was invested from 1996 to 1999. Total net portfolio investment (that is, net inward investment by foreigners minus net outward investment by residents) thus amounted to about R140 billion during the decade.

Although net inflows were recorded in each year from 1990 to 1999, the ride was far from smooth. The domestic economy became increasingly vulnerable to the volatile behaviour of the international financial markets, particularly to changes in investor sentiment regarding the country, the continent and emerging market economies in general. The data in Table 18.4 do not fully reflect the volatility of portfolio investment. For example, there were net outflows of portfolio capital in six of the quarters and large variations often occurred from quarter to quarter.

During the early 1990s, loan repayments and political uncertainty gave rise to large capital outflows. At the end of 1992 the overall balance of payments position again became a serious constraint on the execution of economic policy and in 1993 the authorities had to borrow R7.4 billion in the form of reserve-related loans to boost the country's flagging foreign reserves. However, once the political transformation had been achieved and South Africa became re-established as a borrower in the international capital markets there was a marked improvement in the confidence of non-resident investors. This was boosted by the inclusion of the Johannesburg Stock Exchange (as it was then called) in the International Finance Corporation's Emerging Market Index and during the second half of 1994 net portfolio investment amounted to more than R6.5 billion. After the abolition of the dual exchange rate in March 1995 net purchases of securities by non-residents on the Johannesburg Stock Exchange picked up sharply and were reflected in the balance of payments.[10]

During the second half of 1995 the rand appreciated against the major currencies in nominal and real terms and there was a growing

10 Recall that such activity previously affected only the financial rand rate.

belief that the currency was overvalued. There were also concerns about the impact of the possible early removal of exchange controls on residents and about the possibility that sound macro-economic management could be compromised with the appointment of an ANC politician, Trevor Manuel, as Minister of Finance. In addition, there were rumours about Nelson Mandela's health as well as fears that the apparent growing political consensus that had developed since 1994 might disintegrate. These factors combined to give rise to a depreciation of the rand. The nominal effective exchange rate of the rand declined by almost 20 per cent from January 1996 to July 1996, with the depreciation against the US dollar being of the same magnitude. The volatility in the foreign exchange market and negative sentiment towards South African assets resulted in a significant decline in the inflow of portfolio capital, although the inflow remained positive. In this regard it is important to note *that the change in portfolio flows appears to have been a consequence rather than an underlying cause of the rand's instability in 1996*. An examination of daily data shows that portfolio outflows followed rather than led to sharp depreciations in the currency during this period. Moreover, outflows were largely the result of net bond sales, with net purchases of equity generally remaining positive.[11]

Towards the middle of 1996, the National Party left the Government of National Unity and the government adopted the growth, employment and redistribution (GEAR) strategy.[12] At about that time the international credit rating agencies confirmed South Africa's relatively favourable credit ratings. The international value of the rand stabilised and portfolio inflows gained renewed momentum.

The next significant event was the first relaxation of exchange controls on residents. When the Minister of Finance announced the first major package of exchange control reforms in respect of residents in the March 1997 budget, it was feared that this would give rise to a massive capital outflow as soon as the liberalisation came into effect on 1 July. An informal survey of fund managers put the amount at about R3.75 billion in the first month.[13] However, according to the South African Reserve Bank (SARB) the actual amount transferred by private individuals in July was just R144 million. A number of reasons have been advanced for this rather surprising outcome.[14] First, there

11 Centre for Research into Economics and Finance in Southern Africa, *Quarterly Review*, January 1998, p. 10.

12 *Growth, Employment and Redistribution: A Macroeconomic Strategy*, Department of Finance, June 1996.

13 Centre for Research into Economics and Finance in Southern Africa, *Quarterly Review*, July 1997, p. 26.

14 *Ibid.*, pp. 26–28.

had been significant capital flight from South Africa since the early 1980s, possibly indicating that those individuals who feared adverse political developments had already moved large amounts of capital overseas. Second, there was no reason to believe that the authorities would reverse the relaxation of exchange controls. There was thus no need to rush to invest abroad. Decisions to invest abroad could be based on normal portfolio considerations, such as the level of domestic yields compared with yields on possible foreign investments, determined by factors such as the current and expected levels of domestic interest rates compared with those elsewhere and expectations about the movements in exchange rates. At the time, domestic interest rates were relatively high and it was also expected that the currency would remain relatively stable. The country's foreign exchange reserves had more than doubled during the first half of 1997, boosted by the partial privatisation of Telkom, and the SARB emphasised that it was confident that it would be able to meet any demands for foreign currency resulting from the exchange control relaxation. Third, there were various domestic financial instruments available to individuals who wished to diversify their portfolios, for example shares in South African companies that had substantial foreign earnings (the 'rand hedge' stocks) and instruments based on the asset swap mechanism that had been introduced two years earlier. During the first two years, South African pension funds, life insurers and managed funds had used this mechanism to invest a total of R27.7 billion abroad. Further possible reasons for the relatively small initial capital outflows included a lack of funds available to South African households for foreign investment and the government's decision that only individuals in good standing with the tax authorities would be allowed to open foreign accounts. In due course, however, circumstances changed and in subsequent years individuals invested greater amounts abroad, particularly in anticipation of or in the wake of significant, sometimes dramatic, depreciations of the rand against the major currencies.

The next significant event was the Asian crisis that began in mid-1997 with the collapse of the property boom in Thailand and quickly spread to Indonesia, Malaysia and the Philippines. The second phase of the contagion began in September 1997 when share prices started to fall in Hong Kong. In late October the Hong Kong stock market crashed, precipitating a crash in the major world equity markets.

The Asian crisis initially had no significant adverse impact on South Africa. On the contrary, record net portfolio inflows of more than R13,300 million were experienced in the third quarter of 1997. South Africa escaped adverse re-rating by international investors during this period. The reasons included the fact that South Africa had already experienced its own exchange rate adjustment in 1996, the country's flexible exchange rate regime (in contrast to the fixed or pegged exchange rates in the Asian countries), the sound banking system and the limited impact of the Asian depreciations on the South African economy.[15]

The second phase of contagion, however, did affect South Africa. Share prices on the Johannesburg Stock Exchange fell dramatically and there were large outflows from the bond market, resulting in a net portfolio outflow during the fourth quarter of 1997. Large net portfolio inflows were again recorded during the first half of 1998 but a sharp drop in capital flows to emerging market economies in the wake of further Asian contagion and problems in Russia and elsewhere resulted in fairly large net outflows during the second half of 1998. In 1999, however, there were again large and fairly steady net inflows of portfolio capital, despite the continued acquisition of foreign assets by South African investors.

Other investment

Other investment includes all financial transactions which are not classified as direct investment, portfolio investment or as part of South Africa's reserve position. Examples include trade credits, loans, currency and deposits. Until 1997, trade credit was a relatively significant source of external finance, due to the restricted access to other forms of borrowing, but after the normalisation of South Africa's external financial relations the relative role of trade credits reverted to the levels recorded prior to the 1985 foreign debt crisis.[16]

As indicated in Table 18.4, annual net other investment was negative until 1994. In the wake of the relatively favourable credit ratings obtained from Moody's, Standard and Poor and Nippon Investor Services the government launched a global bond issue of R2.7 billion ($750 million) in December 1994, followed by the first-ever Samurai bond issue, of R1.3 billion, in May 1995. After October 1994 the private sector (companies such as Liberty Life, Barlow Rand and Samancor) also started borrowing abroad. In 1995 the banking sector followed and the foreign liabilities of the South African banking sector increased by a massive R10,685 million in that year (spurred by generous forward cover provided by the SARB). Although the situation was volatile, after 1995 the banking sector was a net borrower in most quarters and years during the rest of the decade. The public corporations, which had been consistent

15 See *Quarterly Review*, Centre for Research into Economics and Finance in Southern Africa, October 1997, pp. 27–36.

16 *Quarterly Review*, Centre for Research into Economics and Finance in Southern Africa, January 1998, p. 7.

net repayers of foreign loans until 1994, also started borrowing abroad again in 1995 but subsequently repaid debt in 1996, 1997 and 1999, after the SARB stopped providing forward cover to them. This contributed to the negative annual net other investment recorded in 1997 and 1999.

Although the situation as far as foreign borrowing is concerned became fairly normal from the end of 1994, South Africa also experienced the impact of financial crises elsewhere in a highly integrated international financial system. For example, although the global bond issue of December 1994 was very successful, the bond did not perform well in the secondary market, due to the Mexican financial crisis, which began in the same month, continued into 1995 and affected all emerging economies.

Unrecorded transactions

In principle, the net sum of all credit and debit entries in the balance of payments should equal the change in the country's net gold and other foreign reserves. In practice, however, there are differences in coverage, timing and valuation, as well as errors and omissions in compiling the individual component series. All these are lumped together as unrecorded transactions to ensure that the balance of payments actually balances.

As shown in Table 18.4, unrecorded transactions were negative (indicating a capital outflow) in all but two of the years from 1990 to 1999. These negative amounts can be ascribed to various influences, for instance capital flight (especially prior to the relaxation of exchange controls on residents) and trade-related outflows via 'leads and lags' in foreign payments and receipts. The latter are related to actual and expected exchange rate changes. For example, when the rand is expected to depreciate against the major currencies, importers purchase and pay for the goods as quickly as possible, while exporters and other earners of foreign exchange delay their sales or the collection of their proceeds as long as possible. This was particularly evident in 1996, when the expectation of a depreciation, the depreciation itself and the subsequent exchange rate volatility gave rise to huge trade-related outflows via 'leads and lags' in foreign payments and receipts. The result was a huge amount of unrecorded transactions, which almost neutralised the positive balance on the financial account.

This chain of events was repeated during the first half of 1998, when the rand again depreciated significantly against the major currencies (in the wake of the Asian crisis). However, the subsequent appreciation of the rand during the second half of 1998, followed by relatively stable exchange rates during 1999, reversed the process and unrecorded transactions were significantly positive in the last half of 1998 and the first and fourth quarters of 1999.

Official reserves account: gold and other foreign reserves

The country's net gold and other foreign reserves increased in seven of the 10 years from 1990 to 1999. In the remaining three years (1993, 1996 and 1998) the SARB borrowed large amounts to prevent similar declines in the gross reserve position. In fact, on an annual basis the country's gross gold and other foreign reserves declined only once during the 1990s, namely in the wake of the traumatic events of 1996.

Overall, the country's gross foreign reserve position improved substantially towards the end of the 1990s. In 1990 the reserves were on average only sufficient to cover 5.6 weeks of imports of goods and services. This figure dropped to 5.4 weeks in 1994 and 5.3 weeks in 1996 but subsequently increased to reach 13.1 weeks in 1999. The SARB's overall reserve position was, however, much less impressive, due to the Bank's huge 'net open foreign currency position' (NOFP), which often made the headlines during the latter part of the 1990s. When the SARB intervenes in the foreign exchange market to support the international value of the rand by selling spot US dollars, its foreign exchange reserves are, of course, reduced. But when the SARB tries to achieve the same effect by selling dollars in the forward market the impact on its reserves are not immediately obvious, since it has to supply the dollars only at a later date. The actual position is reflected in the NOFP, which is equal to the Bank's oversold (or overbought) forward position in foreign currency less its net holdings of spot international reserves. At the end of 1994 it amounted to an oversold amount of $25,202 million. This declined to $13,966 at the end of 1995 but increased again to $22,167 million at the end of 1996 as a result of the SARB's efforts to limit and manage the deprecation during that year. The NOFP was subsequently reduced to $16,297 million at the end of 1997 but again rose sharply in 1998 when the SARB tried to protect the rand in the wake of the Asian crisis. At the end of 1999 it was again down to $13,041 million, partly due to the declared intention of Tito Mboweni, who succeeded Dr Chris Stals as Governor of the SARB on 8 August 1999, to eradicate the oversold NOFP as soon as possible.

Conclusion

The 1990s can be termed the Stals era, since macro-economic policy during the decade was dominated by Stals, who served as Governor of the SARB from 8 August 1989 to 7 August 1999. As emphasised above, this period can be divided into two distinct periods: the uncertain and often turbulent period leading up to the 1994 elections and the post-election period. During the former there were substantial net outflows of capital, and economic growth was constrained as a result of efforts to engineer current account surpluses to compensate, in part at least, for the deficits on the financial account. After the elections, international capital movements were reversed, the current account moved into deficit and the resulting overall balance of payments position improved. There was thus increased scope for economic growth but at the same time South Africa became vulnerable to the 'normal' vagaries of the international capital markets.

Foreign exchange crises were experienced from time to time and Stals was prepared to intervene in the foreign exchange markets and to raise interest rates in an attempt to stabilise the international value of the currency. Nevertheless, the US dollar appreciated against the rand from an average level of $1.00 = R2.5562 during January 1990 to $1.00 = R6.1295 during August 1999, when Tito Mboweni took over as Governor of the Reserve Bank. Moreover, Mboweni inherited a NOFP of more than $16 billion, which he immediately set out to reduce, adding that he would refrain from purposely defending the international value of the rand.

Part III

Policy

19

Fiscal policy

Estian Calitz and Krige Siebrits

Introduction

The story of fiscal policy in South Africa during the 1990s is one of a marked turnaround. In the early 1990s South Africa seemed to be heading for serious fiscal problems. However, by the end of a decade that was marked by a global review of the economic role of governments, a sweeping political transition, several adverse shocks to the South African economy and its reintegration into a globalising world economy, the public finances were on a much sounder footing. This chapter sketches the contextual factors, shifting mindsets and most important policy changes that contributed to this improvement. The next section highlights some contextual issues. Against this background, the chapter goes on to outline salient trends in fiscal policy during the 1990s. Following Musgrave, the discussion distinguishes among developments in the pursuit of macro-economic stability, efficiency in the allocation of resources (including economic growth) and fairness in the distribution of income and wealth.[1]

The context

A proper understanding and assessment of fiscal policy in South Africa during the 1990s require cognisance of the impact of various contextual factors. On the international front, the review of the role of government in market economies that had begun in the 1970s continued into the 1990s, as did international integration of economic activity in the

1 See R. A. Musgrave, *The Theory of Public Finance*, McGraw Hill, 1959.

form of regionalisation and globalisation. The reconsideration of the role of government focused on halting or reversing the expansion of the public sector that had occurred in most industrial and developing countries after the Second World War.[2] 'Best practice' in fiscal policy entailed many countries adopting the package of policies known as the Washington consensus, the main fiscal elements of which are low budget deficits, strengthening of public revenue and expenditure planning and management, the restructuring of public expenditure to increase the allocations for social spending and infrastructure, tax reform to broaden the tax base and reduce marginal rates, and the restructuring of institutions and enterprises in the public sector (which may include privatisation).[3]

Globalisation and regionalisation boosted international capital flows, but these flows were volatile and several wide-ranging financial crises occurred during the 1990s. Such volatility further raised the premium on adopting the guidelines of the Washington consensus, as this came to be regarded as a requirement for attracting foreign investment as well as partial protection against the contagion effects of financial crises. Other aspects of economic globalisation and/or regionalisation (including World Trade Organization agreements to reduce import tariffs, tax harmonisation within regional groupings, and the impact of the increased international mobility of tax bases on policy choices related to tax rates and tax bases) further reduced individual countries' degrees of freedom with respect to fiscal policy making.[4]

Three domestic aspects of the context within which fiscal policy had to be crafted during the 1990s are particularly important. The first is that the 1990s were preceded by two decades of progressively worsening macro-economic performance, in which two key issues were declining real economic growth (which contributed to a sharp decline in the job creation capacity of the formal sectors of the economy) and accelerating inflation.[5] Second, the public sector's claim on resources also had increased sharply during the decades leading up to the 1990s. Public sector resource mobilisation, for example, rose from an average of 24.6 per

2 See V. Tanzi and L. Schuknecht, 'Reforming government: an overview of recent experience', *European Journal of Political Economy*, 13 (1997), 395–417.

3 See J. Williamson, 'What Washington means by policy reform', in J. Williamson, *Latin American Adjustment: How Much Has Happened?*, Institute for International Economics, 1990, pp. 5–20.

4 For more detailed discussions of these issues, see E. Calitz, 'Fiscal implications of the economic globalisation of South Africa', *South African Journal of Economics*, 68(4) (2000), 564–606.

5 See P. J. Mohr, 'An overview of the South African economy in the 1990s', *South African Journal of Economic History*, 18(1,2) (2003), 18–19.

cent in the 1960s to an average of 35.7 per cent in the 1980s.[6] Third, the 1990s also were marked by South Africa's transition to democracy. The new government faced the dilemma of reconciling the imperative of fiscal discipline (necessitated by the macro-economic situation and the prevailing views of 'best fiscal practice') with the growing demand for government expenditure resulting from political democratisation.

Salient features of fiscal policy

This section highlights and briefly discusses the salient features of fiscal policy in South Africa during the 1990s. The discussion is preceded by a brief overview of key elements of the 1996 constitution, which demarcates the fiscal policy framework in several ways.

Selected features of South Africa's 1996 constitution

The South African constitution (Act 108 of 1996) and ensuing legislation embody provisions that both enable and constrain the interventionist role of government in a mixed economy. From a fiscal policy perspective, it is particularly notable that the constitution confers rights in respect of various social services and benefits, including adequate housing, health care, food and water, social security and education. This raises the question of whether or not the independent judiciary could intervene in the prioritisation process underlying national budgeting by forcing the government to provide such services and benefits. In a number of cases, the Constitutional Court refrained from granting individual claims and rather took the view that the government should adopt a comprehensive plan that provides in a reasonable manner for the progressive realisation of the rights set out in the constitution.[7] It was also recognised that such a plan should be within the available resources of the state. This approach has enabled the maintenance of a balance between the imperative of fiscal stability and the realisation of these constitutional rights.

Among the options to 'protect' the government against the open-endedness of the fiscal demands resulting from constitutional social rights are constitutional limits to the budget (e.g. an expenditure cap or

6 See P. A. Black, E. Calitz, T. J. Steenekamp, *et al.*, *Public Economics* (3rd edition), Oxford University Press, 2005, p. 9.

7 See for example: *Soobramoney* v. *Minister of Health, KwaZulu-Natal* 1998 (1) SA 765 (CC); *Government of the Republic of South Africa* v. *Grootboom* 2001 (1) SA 46 (CC); and *Minister of Health* v. *Treatment Action Campaign No. 2* 2002 (5) SA 721 (CC).

a balanced-budget provision). Such formal fiscal rules are absent from the South African constitution. As will become apparent in this chapter, this has not created problems for fiscal policy in post-apartheid South Africa, because the government has succeeded in significantly expanding the provision of social services while simultaneously establishing a track record of fiscal prudence.[8]

The constitution also governs the structure of the government and the relationships among its different tiers. The constitutional dispensation provides for three tiers of government: the national government, nine provincial governments and, following extensive rationalisation in 1996, 284 municipalities. From a fiscal point of view, a major issue is that the 'own revenue' sources of the provinces are wholly inadequate to cover their expenditures. A system of revenue sharing between the national and provincial tiers of government applies, which accounts for the financing of about 85 per cent of provincial expenditure.[9] So far this mismatch between expenditure responsibilities and revenue powers has not threatened macro-economic stability. This may be attributed to stringent adjustment conditions in the few cases where the National Treasury was asked to assist provinces experiencing financial difficulties, as well as to the limited borrowing powers of provinces. They can borrow to finance only capital expenditure and no national government guarantees are available.

Stabilisation

Fiscal policy in South Africa continued to reflect aspects of Keynesian thinking well into the 1980s, and anti-cyclical effects fortuitously were achieved from time to time even thereafter. There are nonetheless indications that the South African government abandoned active anti-cyclical stabilisation policy towards the end of the 1970s.[10] The Keynesian framework gave way to a longer-term approach that emphasised structural aspects of fiscal policy. These included the maintenance of fiscal discipline and the pursuit of price stability, both of which came to be seen as prerequisites for improving the longer-term

8 See F. K. Siebrits and E. Calitz, 'Should South Africa adopt numerical fiscal rules?', *South African Journal of Economics*, 72(4) (2004), 759–783.

9 See B. Khumalo, H. Amusa and N. Madabula, 'Assessing provincial own revenues in South Africa's intergovernmental fiscal relations system', in J. Josie, B. Khumalo and T. Ajam (eds), *Review of Transfers in the Intergovernmental Fiscal Relations System in South Africa*, Halfway House, 2006, p. 153.

10 See E. Calitz, 'The limits to public expenditure', in G. Howe and P. le Roux (eds), *Transforming the Economy: Policy Options for South Africa*, Indicator Project SA (University of Natal) and Institute for Social Development (University of the Western Cape), 1992, p. 78.

growth potential of the South African economy.[11] The implied thinking was that the best contribution that the fiscal authority could make to macro-economic stability was to stabilise its own finances. One of the outcomes of the movement away from expenditure fine-tuning was the adoption of medium-term expenditure planning in 1998. The focus on fiscal discipline and other structural aspects of fiscal policy continued throughout the 1990s, and was associated closely with the stabilisation or even the reduction of the public sector's claim on resources, including the total pool of savings. In June 1996, for example, the government announced its macro-economic strategy on growth, employment and redistribution (GEAR), which included fiscal goals such as a step-wise reduction in the budget deficit to 3 per cent of GDP, maintenance of the total tax burden at 25 per cent of GDP, the reduction of general government consumption expenditure as a percentage of GDP and the gradual elimination of general government dissaving.

The adoption of GEAR, with its strong emphasis on fiscal discipline, followed the marked deterioration in the fiscal situation from 1990 to 1993. During this period, a long cyclical downswing depressed tax revenues, at a time when several extraordinary transfer payments and the expansion of social services raised government expenditure.[12] National government revenue and grants dropped from 25.1 per cent of GDP in 1989/90 to 21.7 per cent in 1992/93, while total expenditure and net lending increased from 26.5 per cent of GDP to 28.9 per cent, raising the budget deficit from 1.4 per cent of GDP to 7.2 per cent. The resulting sharp increase in central government debt (from 35.3 per cent of GDP in 1990 to a peak of 50.4 per cent in 1996) gave rise to a debate about whether or not a debt trap was looming.[13] Supported by higher economic growth (which stimulated tax receipts and exerted downward pressure on ratios of which GDP is the denominator) and improved tax collection, the strategy of fiscal discipline paid dividends in the form of a significantly improved fiscal position. From 1993/94 to 1999/00, national government revenue and grants increased from 21.7 per cent to 23.7 per cent, while the expenditure–GDP ratio dropped from 28.9 per cent to 25.8 per cent. The budget deficit accordingly fell to 2.1 per cent of GDP in 1999/2000, and concern about a possible debt trap abated as

11 See E. Calitz, 'An assessment of fiscal policy in South Africa and the 1999/2000 Budget', *Absa Economic Spotlight*, 25 (1999), 24.

12 For more details about these transfer payments, see F. K. Siebrits, 'Government spending in an international perspective', in I. Abedian and M. Biggs (eds), *Economic Globalization and Fiscal Policy*, Oxford University Press, 1998, p. 329.

13 See, for example, E. J. van der Merwe, *Is South Africa in a Debt Trap?*, Occasional Paper 6, South African Reserve Bank, 1993.

central government debt decreased from 50.4 per cent at the end of 1996 to 44.4 per cent at the end of 2000.[14]

The government also made considerable progress towards eliminating dissaving: the excess of general government current expenditure over general government current income dropped from 7.3 per cent of GDP in 1992 to 2.1 per cent (the same level as in 1990) by the end of the decade. Furthermore, the long-term expansion of the public sector in South Africa, referred to above, ended, with the extent of public sector resource use and public sector resource mobilisation decreasing significantly as percentages of GDP from 1990 to 1999.[15] The fact that the curtailment of the growth of government occurred after the country's constitutional change is remarkable given the prediction of theories of public sector growth that the share of government spending in the economy is likely to increase following the extension of the suffrage to lower-income groups in societies with unequal income distributions.[16]

International evidence suggests that the details of fiscal adjustment matter for its sustainability and impact on economic growth. More specifically, the most durable and growth-promoting fiscal adjustments are those based on a combination of expenditure restructuring towards more productive uses and revenue gains based on broadening tax bases and improving tax administration.[17] South Africa's fiscal adjustment during the 1990s largely followed these guidelines.[18] The adjustment combined a modest increase in the total tax burden (through base broadening rather than rate increases) with cutbacks in government spending on subsidies, salaries and wages, interest payments and gross fixed capital formation. Expenditure cutbacks provided the initial impetus to the deficit reduction effort, which was soon to be strengthened by administrative and base-broadening tax reforms. This sequencing of the adjustment effort enabled the fiscal authorities to avoid tax rate increases

14 The fiscal stance nonetheless was expansionary throughout the 1990s, because the budget remained in deficit and government dissaving continued.

15 See Black *et al.*, *Public Economics*, p. 9.

16 See, for example, A. H. Meltzer and S. F. Richard, 'A rational theory of the size of government', *Journal of Political Economy*, 89(5) (1981), 914–927.

17 See S. Gupta, B. Clements, E. Baldacci and C. Mulas-Granados, 'Fiscal policy, expenditure composition, and growth in low-income countries', in S. Gupta, B. Clements and G. Inchauste (eds), *Helping Countries Develop: The Role of Fiscal Policy*, International Monetary Fund, 2004, pp. 23–47; and S. Gupta, B. Clements, E. Baldacci and C. Mulas-Granados, 'Persistence of fiscal adjustments and expenditure composition in low-income countries', in S. Gupta, B. Clements and G. Inchauste (eds), *Helping Countries Develop: The Role of Fiscal Policy*, International Monetary Fund, 2004, pp. 48–66.

18 See M. Horton, 'Role of fiscal policy in stabilization and poverty alleviation', in M. Nowak and L. A. Ricci (eds), *Post-apartheid South Africa: The First Ten Years*, International Monetary Fund, 2006, pp. 79–112.

that could fuel demands for higher wages and reduce the international competitiveness of firms. Arguably the most unfortunate aspect of South Africa's fiscal adjustment during the 1990s was the reduction in gross fixed capital investment – an issue to which we return below.

Economic growth and efficiency in the allocation of resources

During the 1990s the South African government's approach to encouraging economic growth increasingly shifted from efforts aimed at stimulating aggregate demand to supply-side measures. Key supply-side measures to underpin economic growth and investor confidence included the adoption of a credible and consistent fiscal stance, the gradual dismantling of exchange controls and the opening up of the economy to international competition by reducing tariffs. The fiscal authorities also continued to build the country's stock of human capital by investing heavily in education and health care. Over the decade general government expenditure on education ranged from 5.9 per cent of GDP to 7.3 per cent and that on health care from 3.0 per cent to 3.5 per cent – levels well above those in most other developing countries.[19]

On the debit side, persistent (albeit decreasing) general government dissaving reduced the pool of investable funds. Moreover, the general government's own contribution to gross capital formation decreased from an already low 3.9 per cent of GDP in 1990 to 2.6 per cent in 1999, despite repeated statements in policy documents that the government intended to boost its capital spending.[20] The reality that the low levels of government investment were contributing to the deterioration of parts of the infrastructure was a further disincentive to private sector investment. For example, the 1998 Medium-Term Expenditure Framework (MTEF) review of infrastructure investment in South Africa reported that the inadequate maintenance of the existing infrastructure was weakening the country's asset base, especially in the roads, the rolling stock of the railways and in water-supply capacity.[21] Moreover, there are strong indications that inefficiency curtailed the potential growth-promoting impact of some of the largest and most important categories of government spending, including public order and safety, education and health (see below).

Government intervention in the allocation of funds in the private sector can cause inefficiency if it distorts the preferences of individuals

19 See Black *et al.*, *Public Economics*, p. 93.

20 See, for example, *Growth, Employment and Redistribution: A Macroeconomic Strategy* Department of Finance, 1996, pp. 2, 15–16.

21 *Ibid.*, pp. 48–49.

or companies. A number of steps were taken during the 1990s to reduce or eliminate this kind of distortion, the intention being to increase allocative efficiency. The thrust of tax reform broadly was in line with the international trend towards broadening tax bases and reducing marginal rates.[22] The authorities broadened the tax base by eliminating various special tax preference schemes that benefited only particular industries or narrow sectoral interests, including the tax subsidies for training, welfare, health and the General Export Incentive Scheme (GEIS) and the interest rate subsidies for agriculture and housing. The overhaul of tax collection and administration indirectly broadened the tax base by improving taxpayer compliance. In 1997 the Inland Revenue and Customs and Excise branches of the then Department of Finance were restructured into an autonomous revenue collection agency, the South African Revenue Service (SARS). Internal reorganisation and the improvement of information systems and processes enabled SARS to maintain a sound ratio between revenue yields and collection costs and to consistently exceed its revenue targets.[23] This achievement contributed significantly to the reduction in the budget deficit discussed above.

The objective of reducing income tax rates met with mixed success. The authorities reduced the rate of income tax on companies from 50 per cent at the beginning of the 1990s to 30 per cent in 1999, but introduced a secondary tax on distributed company profits (STC) in 1993. The STC rate rose from its initial level of 15 per cent to 25 per cent in 1994 and then fell to 12.5 per cent in 1996. The top marginal rate of personal income tax decreased from 45 per cent to 43 per cent in 1991, but reverted to 45 per cent in 1995. This reflected the reality that the authorities sometimes had to subjugate efficiency considerations to revenue needs during the deficit reduction process. The budgets for 1998/99 and 1999/2000, however, provided significant personal income tax relief by reducing the number of income tax brackets and by adjusting their ranges.

Notable changes to the indirect taxes included the phasing down of tariffs under an offer to the World Trade Organization in 1993 and the replacement of the general sales tax (GST) by a broad-based value-added tax (VAT) on 30 September 1991. South Africa committed itself to replacing all quotas on agricultural and industrial products with

22 See T. J. Steenekamp and J. A. Döckel, 'Taxation and tax reform in LDCs: lessons for South Africa', *Development Southern Africa*, 10(3) (1993), 320.

23 In the four fiscal years from 1996/97 to 1999/00, for example, total revenue collections exceeded the budgeted amounts by some R20.5 billion. The Department of Finance ascribed about 43 per cent of this revenue overrun to efficiency improvements in SARS. See *Budget Review 2000*, Department of Finance, 2000, p. 72.

tariffs, simplifying and rationalising the then highly complex system of industrial tariffs and reducing tariffs in a phased manner over periods of five to eight years. The tariff reform programme reduced the number of tariff lines from 12,500 in 1990 to 7,743 in 1999, and the unweighted mean tariff rate fell from 27.5 per cent to 7.1 per cent.[24] The lowering of import tariffs was a significant step towards eliminating the inefficiencies associated with highly protective trade regimes, but in the 1990s its ameliorating effect on the anti-export bias in the economy was countered by the simultaneous withdrawal of the GEIS.[25]

Described by Steenekamp and Döckel as a 'textbook example of an efficient commodity tax system',[26] VAT eliminated the distorting effects of tax cascading that characterised the GST, and in all likelihood reduced tax evasion. The efficiency of the tax was enhanced by a relatively simple rate structure: a standard rate, and a zero rate applicable to selected basic foodstuffs. It also proved to be a major source of income for the South African government, yielding about 25 per cent of total national government revenue in the late 1990s.

The effectiveness of expenditure control is a key aspect of technical efficiency in government. It is therefore significant that the extent of overspending (expressed as a percentage of budgeted expenditure) generally was lower from 1994 onwards than during the previous 11 years.[27] The introduction of medium-term expenditure planning in 1998 and the reinstatement of the contingency reserve used in 1991 and 1992 contributed to this positive development. Medium-term expenditure planning made fiscal policy making more transparent, and there are strong indications that it improved expenditure prioritisation and efficiency in expenditure planning. Another major initiative to enhance the effectiveness of government spending was the Public Finance Management Act of 1999. The Act emphasised regular financial reporting by government departments and agencies, sound internal expenditure controls, independent audit and supervision of spending control systems, improved accounting standards and training of financial managers, and greater emphasis on outputs and performance.

The 1996 constitution charges provincial and local authorities with responsibility for providing various crucial services, including education, health care, welfare payments, housing, electricity, water and

24 See R. Cassim, 'The pace, nature and impact of trade policy in South Africa in the 1990s', *South African Journal of Economic History*, 18(1–2) (2003), 85.

25 *Ibid.*, pp. 86–87.

26 See Steenekamp and Döckel, 'Taxation and tax reform in LDCs', p. 326.

27 See E. Calitz, 'An assessment of fiscal policy in South Africa', unpublished paper delivered at an International Atlantic Economic Society Session of the Allied Social Science Associations' annual meeting, Boston, USA, 8 January 2000, p. 22.

sewerage systems. The lack of managerial and delivery capacity in many of these authorities meant that this decentralisation of spending powers initially failed to yield the efficiency gains highlighted in the literature on fiscal federalism.[28] The provinces' very limited scope for raising their own revenue, and the constraints that household poverty, the culture of non-payment for services and poor credit ratings placed on the revenue-raising capacity of many local authorities, exacerbated the problem. By the end of the 1990s the situation had improved in some respects – the provinces as a group recorded a surplus of R3 billion in 1999/2000 as against a deficit of R5.5 billion in 1998/99 and most large and medium-sized municipalities had made progress in restructuring their finances and improving the delivery of services,[29] but significant efficiency gains remained elusive.

More generally, there was considerable evidence of technical inefficiency in government expenditure during the 1990s. In 1998 the Presidential Review Commission reported that government departments tended to be much stronger on policy formulation than on delivery.[30] The Commission's report and many reports of the Auditor General highlighted weaknesses in the systems of financial and human resource management in the public sector. Because inefficiency extended to the provision of education and health, the country's heavy investments in such social services yielded poor returns.[31] South Africa's relatively low ranking in *World Competitiveness Yearbooks* also partly reflected aspects of government performance, including perceptions of political interference in the public service and ineffectiveness in the implementation of government decisions, a lack of confidence in the fairness of the judicial system and the inability of the police force to protect persons and property – South Africa had the highest incidence of murders, violent crimes and armed robberies per 100,000 inhabitants among all the countries surveyed.[32]

28 See, for example, Black *et al.*, *Public Economics*, ch. 17.

29 See E. Calitz and F. K. Siebrits, 'After the pain, the gain? An assessment of the 2001/02 budget', *Absa Economic Perspective*, special edition (April 2001), p. 3.

30 See *Developing a Culture of Good Governance*, Presidential Commission on the Reform and Transformation of the Public Service in South Africa, 1998, p. 16.

31 Inefficiency in the use of inputs was reflected in low pass rates in matriculation examinations, the poor performance of South African learners in external assessments (e.g. the standardised tests used in Unesco's Education for All Project), poor graduation and pass rates in the tertiary education sector, and the reality that the health profile of the South African population lagged that of several countries with significantly lower levels of per capita income.

32 In 1998, for example, South Africa ranked forty-second out of 46 countries. See Institute for Management Development, *World Competitiveness Yearbook 1998*, IMD International, 1998, pp. 280–285, 394–398.

Asset management is another important aspect of government efficiency that received increasing attention in the second half of the 1990s. In this respect privatisation of state assets was slow to get going, largely because of the strong opposition from organised labour. Between March 1997 and July 1999, six SABC radio stations, Sun Air and Connex Travel were sold *in toto,* as well as significant stakes in Telkom (30 per cent), the Airports Company (25 per cent) and South African Airways (20 per cent). The proceeds from these transactions amounted to R8.6 billion, of which R3.3 billion was used to reduce the public debt.[33] The decision not to use once-off privatisation income to finance recurrent expenditure strengthened confidence in the soundness of fiscal policy.

Redistribution and poverty alleviation

Distributional considerations were becoming more important in the early 1990s. Significant reprioritisation of expenditure aimed at reducing inter-racial benefit gaps pre-dated the political change in 1994, as per capita social expenditure on Africans increased from 12 per cent of the white level in 1975 to 69 per cent in 1993, with the major portion of the increase occurring between 1990 and 1993.[34] Nonetheless, there can be no doubt that the priorities of the South African government shifted further to distributional and poverty issues, especially after Trevor Manuel became Minister of Finance in 1996. The authorities attempted to pursue the objectives of redistribution and poverty alleviation in a sustainable manner by combining fiscal discipline, as reflected in the step-wise reduction of the budget deficit mentioned above, with major changes in the distribution of public benefits and the incidence of financing costs. Fiscal policy also affected the distribution of income and wealth by means of various regulatory reforms.

Changes in the distribution of public benefits were achieved by effecting shifts in the composition of government expenditure, by improving the targeting of spending programmes and by directly or indirectly privatising the provision of some public and merit goods. The most important development was the marked increase in the share of social spending in total government outlays. Between 1990 and 2000, outlays on social services increased by 17.4 per cent, from 38.6 per cent of total general government spending (12.9 per cent of GDP) to 45.3 per cent (14.2 per cent of GDP). This was made possible largely by expenditure reprioritisation, notably reductions in defence expenditure, the interest

33 See *Budget Review 2000,* p. 107.

34 See S. van der Berg, 'Trends in racial fiscal incidence in South Africa', *South African Journal of Economics,* 69(2) (2001), 257.

bill and outlays on economic services. Reprioritisation within functions, which increased the importance of the primary education and primary health care components of social spending *vis-à-vis* tertiary education and curative health services strengthened the redistributive impact of these shifts. This development encouraged the increased private financing of both schools and institutions of higher education and private hospitals.

A fiscal incidence study initiated in 1999 by the then Department of Finance considered the redistributive impact of some 60 per cent of consolidated government expenditure (education, health, social grants, water provision and housing) during the period 1993–97 and confirmed that a significant shift had taken place in social spending patterns, from the more affluent to the poorer members of South African society.[35] The share of measured expenditure benefiting the poorest quintile of households increased from 27.4 per cent to 30.7 per cent, while that of the richest quintile dropped from 12.7 per cent to 8.7 per cent. From 1993 to 1997 per capita social service expenditure on the poor may have increased by as much as 34 per cent. By contrast, outlays on the richest quintile probably decreased by more than 20 per cent in per capita terms. The study also found that the improved targeting of resources and programmes significantly increased the redistributive impact of social spending. A follow-up study commissioned in 2004 attempted to determine shifts in the incidence of government spending on education, health, welfare and housing from 1995 to 2000. It confirmed the powerful redistributive impact of social spending, finding that the proportion of government spending that went to the poorest 40 per cent of households increased from 53.6 per cent in 1995 to 59.3 per cent in 2000.[36] The earlier study also confirmed the progressive character of the South African tax system. It investigated the incidence of personal income tax, value-added tax, specific excise duties and the fuel levy and found that the lowest decile of income earners paid 11 per cent of their incomes on these four taxes, whereas members of the richest decile paid approximately 30 per cent.[37]

The nature and coverage of social grants are particularly important issues in South Africa in view of the high incidence of income poverty. The primary purpose of the social grants system, namely to assist vulnerable groups who do not form part of the labour force (primarily the aged, the disabled and dependent children), did not change during the 1990s. The scope and impact of the system nonetheless increased

35 See *Budget Review 2000*, pp. 145–146.

36 See *Budget Review 2005*, National Treasury, 2005, pp. 4–5, 122.

37 See *Budget Review 2000*, pp. 103–104.

markedly as a result of two reforms: the deracialisation of benefit structures (which had already been achieved by 1993) and the introduction of a new means-tested child support grant in 1998.

Changes in the tax system during the 1990s had significant consequences for the distribution of income:

- The overall fairness of the tax system was increased by the improvement in collection that resulted from the overhaul of the tax administration, by the broadening of the tax base (including the introduction of the capital gains tax in 2000), by the removal of gender discrimination and by the zero-rating of basic foodstuffs to mitigate the impact of the value-added tax.
- The personal income tax burden increased markedly during the 1990s, with receipts from this tax increasing by 29 per cent, from 33.7 per cent of national government revenue (8.1 per cent of GDP) in fiscal year 1991 to 43.5 per cent (10.4 per cent of GDP) in fiscal year 2000. For most of the decade, the authorities relied on *ad hoc* adjustments to the income tax structure that only partially countered the effects of bracket creep on the tax burden of lower- and middle-income taxpayers. In the budgets for 1998/99 and 1999/2000 the changes to personal income tax were structured to provide most relief to lower- and middle-income taxpayers, in large part neutralising the impact of bracket creep. Yet over the decade as a whole, the relative impact of personal income tax on lower- and middle-income earners increased significantly. Consider, for example, the positions of three hypothetical married taxpayers, each with two children, earning the equivalents of R40,000, R120,000 and R400,000 (in 2000 prices) in 1992 and 2000. Taking into account rebates only, the average tax rates of such taxpayers increased from 6.7 per cent to 10.7 per cent, from 23.9 per cent to 30.3 per cent and from 37.1 per cent to 40.6 per cent respectively. The average tax rate of the taxpayer earning R40,000 therefore increased from 18 per cent of that of the taxpayer earning R400,000 in 1992 to 26 per cent in 2000; the equivalent increase for the taxpayer earning R120,000 was from 64 per cent to 75 per cent.[38]
- User charges and levies proliferated during the 1990s.[39] *Ceteris paribus*, the introduction of a user charge or a levy raises government revenue and creates scope for the reallocation of fiscal resources. In

38 See E. Calitz and F. K. Siebrits, 'Changes in the role of government in the SA economy', *Absa Economic Perspective* (second quarter 2002), 21.

39 User charges include hospital fees, road tolls and other direct payments for benefits received. Levies are taxes dedicated to specific activities benefiting the members of specific groups, for example, the fuel levy for the Road Accident Fund and television licences for the South African Broadcasting Corporation.

many cases, their introduction facilitated efforts to increase the redistributive thrust of fiscal policy by raising the financing burden on the more affluent sectors of South African society, while at the same time freeing resources for transfer to poorer individuals and households.

The redistribution effort was complemented by various regulatory measures, including: a land reform programme involving tenure reform and the redistribution and restitution of land; labour legislation, notably the Basic Conditions of Employment Act of 1997 and the Employment Equity Act of 1998; and a wide-ranging black economic empowerment programme, one element of which was a framework for granting previously disadvantaged groups preferential access to government procurement contracts.

Critics generally argue that the deficit reduction focus of fiscal policy in the 1990s (especially during the GEAR era) was inappropriate in view of South Africa's pressing unemployment, poverty and inequality.[40] A comprehensive assessment of this argument falls outside the scope of this chapter; suffice it to say that the critics underestimate the negative influence that the continuation (and possible worsening) of the imbalances of the early 1990s could have had on the sustainability and credibility of fiscal policy. Furthermore, the capacity constraints that came to the fore towards the end of the 1990s would probably have severely blunted the impact of a more extensive attack on unemployment and poverty driven by public spending.

Conclusion

The 1990s was a period of sweeping fiscal reform in South Africa. Salient elements of the restructuring of the public finances were: fiscal consolidation aimed at reducing the public debt burden and ending the secular increase in the public sector's claim on resources; wide-ranging tax reform; and a concerted effort to increase the redistributive thrust of the fiscal system. The reform effort was not an unqualified success – most notably, it failed to materially improve the capacity of the public sector to deliver key services effectively – but nonetheless it proved to be sustainable in macro-economic terms and effective at mobilising resources for redistributive spending programmes.

40 See J. C. Streak, 'The Gear legacy: did Gear fail or move South Africa forward in development?', *Development Southern Africa*, 21(2) (2004), 279–282.

20

Monetary policy

Roger Gidlow

Introduction

During the 1990s the South African Reserve Bank sought to bring about monetary stability in the economy, and more particularly establish a suitably low rate of inflation, against a background of radically different conditions before and after April 1994. This date signalled a huge shift in the political dispensation of the country and its economic relations with the outside world. In this chapter an assessment is made of the success achieved in lowering the inflation rate. In addition, reference is made to the monetary policy regime employed by the Reserve Bank for the purpose of attaining greater price stability, and in particular the role of money supply guidelines is explained. Thereafter, the main instruments of monetary policy employed by the Bank in the 1990s are adumbrated, with reference to the emphasis upon market-oriented monetary policies. In this latter regard the suitability of the continued reliance on exchange controls during the period is debated.

Goal of achieving stability in prices

For some time, particularly during the mid-1980s, the Reserve Bank had to sacrifice its obligations to try to achieve a suitably low rate of inflation, because of the need to counteract external financial sanctions. However, by the end of the 1980s the Reserve Bank had concluded that it should seek to restore a more stable monetary environment, as well as balanced economic growth, even though the external environment remained exceedingly difficult. It was argued by the Bank that those people who opposed such policies were expecting the Bank to ignore the mandate conferred upon it by the South African Reserve Bank Act 90 of 1989.

It was perceived that a suitably low rate of inflation would exist once inflation ceased to exert a marked influence on the micro-economic decisions of businesses and individuals. This did not by itself spell out just how low the rate of inflation should be, but a basic guideline laid down by the Bank was that a rate that was clearly out of line with the average rates of inflation in other countries could not be reconciled with the objective of price stability, since South Africa was a country with extensive trade relations with the outside world. The objective, therefore, at least initially, was to lower the rate so as to bring it more in line with the average rate of inflation of the country's major trading partners.[1]

The Bank also believed that monetary policy alone could not defeat the inflation problem: a wide array of measures needed to be employed. It was asserted that, at the very least, there should be coordination between fiscal and monetary policies, and that some stability on the balance of payments front was required, a condition which proved to be somewhat elusive in the 1990s (see Chapter 18) as external pressures bore down on the economy. In addition, responsible wage and salary adjustments were necessary.[2]

In the 1990s there was a strong contention in certain quarters that the Reserve Bank's determination to fight inflation by bringing down the growth in the money supply was the sole factor responsible for the prevalence of high interest rates. This was, however, a false assertion, since at certain times the Bank added heavily to the supply of funds. For instance, it facilitated an increase in the total M3 money supply of R50 billion from the end of 1993 to the end of June 1995, partly through intervention in the foreign exchange market to buy dollars and sell rands. The Bank thereby ran the risk of watching inflation move back upwards, and was criticised for such policies by the International Monetary Fund.[3]

Indeed, there was much criticism of the Reserve Bank's basic monetary approach, the allegation being that tight monetary policies kept economic growth at unduly low levels, particularly in the early 1990s.[4] Critics asserted that the Bank kept interest rates too high, which led to reduced levels of investment. In other words, the hurdle rate which companies had to exceed in order to undertake profitable investments became too high, and this depressed economic growth. There was some opportunity cost associated with tight monetary policies in the

1 Chris Stals, 'The end of 1989 – the end of a decade', address at the annual gala of the French Chamber of Commerce and Industries of Southern Africa, 1 December 1999, p. 6.

2 Chris Stals, 'Monetary policy as an anti-inflationary tool', address at investment conference of Frankel, Kruger, Vinderine, Johannesburg, 20 February 1990, p. 3.

3 Chris Stals, 'Interest rates in South Africa', address in Cape Town, 1 November 1995, p. 9.

4 D. J. J. Botha, 'The South African Reserve Bank and the rate of interest', *South African Journal of Economics*, 65(4) (1997), 532–567.

short term but, it was hoped, longer-term gains. Quite apart from this, the growth environment for South Africa in the early 1990s was grim, partly because of trade and financial sanctions and relatively low international commodity prices. Nevertheless, against the background of criticism of monetary policy, the question arises as to what factors prompted the Reserve Bank to place so much emphasis upon pursuing monetary stability. In this regard, one important influence on the Bank was its view of the relationship between inflation and unemployment.

Relationship between inflation and unemployment

In the 1950s and 1960s the monetary policies of many central banks were shaped by the belief that a trade-off existed between economic growth and inflation. At that time it was asserted that higher economic growth could be achieved at the expense of higher inflation. This relationship became known as the Phillips curve, which in the case of the UK showed that a century-long relationship had existed between wage inflation and unemployment. As the rate of unemployment rose, the rate of inflation as measured by wage inflation fell. On the basis of this experience, stretching over such a long period, it was concluded in many quarters that the Phillips curve represented a trade-off of choices facing any government, in which the benefits of lower inflation had to be balanced against their costs in terms of higher unemployment. A trade-off existed between output and inflation.

With the passage of time, however, the Phillips curve came to be increasingly questioned. From the late 1960s onwards, the curve began to shift in character as unemployment and inflation started to move up together in many industrial countries, including the UK. While it was still accepted that a short-run trade-off existed between output and inflation, it came to be increasingly accepted that, in the medium to long term, rising rates of inflation would be associated with unchanged or lower rates of economic growth. In other words, it came to be routinely asserted that if the money supply increases as a result of expansionary monetary policies, prices will not rise immediately and consequently, in the short term, output can increase along with employment. In the long run, however, prices will fully adjust upwards to the rise in the money supply, and the stimulus to output and employment will disappear.

In the 1990s the Reserve Bank adhered to the view that actions on the monetary policy front could affect only the rate of inflation and not the level of output, and therefore it conducted its monetary policies with a view to bringing down inflation. This preference, moreover, was reinforced by the appreciation that inflation had meaningful social and economic costs attached to it, even though these costs were difficult to quantify. It was believed that monetary policy should not be geared to short-term anti-cyclical objectives, but rather to medium-term objectives relating to financial stability. Consequently, during the period of sharp economic slow-down at the beginning of the 1990s, the Bank did not wish to attempt to stimulate the economy through relaxations in monetary policies. Instead, it hoped that the economy would be boosted by external factors such as rising commodity prices, or an internal boost from rising autonomous investments.[5] Unfortunately, such stimuli did not come to pass.

The emphasis upon an anti-inflationary strategy in turn led the Bank to prefer the maintenance of interest rates that were positive in real terms. Such a policy helped to curb the growth in the money supply, while serving as an acknowledgement of the relative scarcity of savings in the South African economy, especially during the first few years of the 1990s, when international financial sanctions were still in place. Indeed, during this latter period, South African monetary policies were conducted in a siege-type environment, in the sense that the economy was buffeted by a breakdown in normal economic relations with the rest of the world. Monetary policies were applied in an abnormal environment as long as financial sanctions against the country were in force. This environment changed after April 1994, when sanctions were lifted, but the politically motivated sanctions in force previously began to be replaced by market sanctions, with runs on the rand in 1996 and 1998 partly prompted by foreign disapproval of internal economic and political developments.

Progress in reducing inflation

Despite the obstacles, progress in this area was forthcoming. In 1989 consumer prices rose on average by 14.7 per cent and in the following three years (to 1992) virtually no progress was recorded in bringing down inflation, the consumer price index averaging 13.9 per cent in the last year. This was partly attributable to rising international oil prices in the wake of the invasion of Kuwait by Iraq in August 1990, as well as the persistence of expectations of high inflation. Thereafter, however, progress became more visible, even though the rand depreciated sharply in both 1996 and 1998. By 1999 the rate of inflation as measured by consumer prices had fallen to 5.2 per cent. The counter-inflationary monetary policy of the Bank had been assisted by: improved fiscal discipline; the liberalisation of foreign trade, with growing competition

5 Chris Stals, 'Economic prospects and monetary policy', address to the South African Chamber of Business, Johannesburg, 20 June 1991, p. 7.

in the domestic goods markets; and some moderation of the growth in nominal wages.

It could easily be argued that the crusade mounted against inflation by the Bank was over-zealous, since there was strong evidence that the negative effects of inflation on economic growth surfaced only after inflation rose above 10 per cent.[6] However, the attempt by the authorities to drive the inflation rate down to a level roughly in line with that of its trading partners could be justified on the grounds that such an outcome would lead to greater stability in the external value of the rand, which in turn could encourage foreign investment.

Nature of the monetary policy framework

In the previous section it was emphasised that the main objective of monetary policy in the 1990s was to bring down the rate of inflation. The Reserve Bank regarded this as the most important contribution it could make to economic growth in the longer term. In order to achieve that objective, however, the Bank for most of the 1990s adhered to an intermediate guideline for growth in the money supply, since the latter had a distinct bearing on the ultimate objective of price stability. Appropriate guidelines for growth in the monetary aggregates were perceived to be the route for success on the inflation front. Such money supply growth was directly influenced by the various monetary policy instruments at the disposal of the Reserve Bank.

The rationale of targeting money supply

Money supply targeting, which in time came to be referred to as guidelines for the money supply, was based on the belief that the cure for inflation was a monetary one. If the rate of growth of the money supply was controlled effectively over time, the same would apply to inflation. The setting of published targets for the growth in the money supply could also be supported on the grounds that it could spread awareness among the public of the link between the money supply and prices. Published targets may have furnished some guidance to the business community, consumers and labour groups concerning the probable monetary policy actions and future policy stance of the authorities. Advance notification of the intended stance of monetary policy would facilitate appropriate adjustments in wage and salary claims, as well

6 Robert J. Barro, *Bank of England Quarterly Bulletin*, 35(2) (May 1995), 166–176.

as the inventory and fixed investment plans of businesses. Guidelines for the money supply would also be useful in curbing the enthusiasm of governments for spending public funds, because the central bank would emphasise to politicians that public spending in excess of certain levels would entail exceeding the money supply guidelines if such spending were financed by resort to bank credit. Such considerations furnished the justification for the adoption of money supply targeting policies in South Africa for most of the 1990s.

In South Africa the broad monetary aggregate M3 was identified as the most suitable for money supply targeting by the Reserve Bank. From the fourth quarter of 1989 to the fourth quarter of 1990 the target rate of growth of M3 was set at 11–15 per cent. In the subsequent three years this was steadily reduced to 6–9 per cent. Thereafter, the target rate was stable at 6–10 per cent, until monetary targeting was abandoned early in 1998. The actual rate of growth in the money supply, however, proved to be somewhat disappointing. From the fourth quarter of 1989 to the fourth quarter of 1990 the M3 measure grew by 12 per cent, and then fell to 5.6 per cent in the period from the fourth quarter of 1993 to the fourth quarter of 1994. Thereafter, however, the growth rate accelerated to 15.2 per cent in the year to the fourth quarter of 1997, in line with mounting difficulties experienced in conducting a monetary targeting regime.

The Reserve Bank did not apply a rigid money supply targeting policy. The guidelines for the growth in the M3 money supply were not something which it sought to attain at all costs in all circumstances. The Bank adhered to the view that some discretion in monetary policies was justified under the targeting regime, and reaching the guidelines could be relegated in importance in the light of mutations in the monetary data, such as bank credit extension, interest and exchange rates and foreign reserves, as well as in government finances.[7]

Some critics of the Reserve Bank's approach recommended that a more restricted definition of the money supply than M3 should be used. Some favoured the employment of M0, which includes only bank notes and coins in circulation outside the Reserve Bank, plus deposits held by banks with the Reserve Bank. This definition, however, was not very useful in South Africa, because local residents did not make extensive use of bank notes and coin in payments transactions. In addition, changes in notes and coins in circulation could be misleading as an indicator of inflationary pressures.[8] An interest rate target was not

7 Chris Stals, 'Monetary policy and inflation', address to the *Financial Mail* Investment Conference in Johannesburg, 1 November 1990, p. 10.

8 Chris Stals, 'Money supply guidelines for 1996', pp. 6–7 (www2.resbank.co.za/internet/Publication.nsf/WCEV/8466C104B71DC2C142256B2F003B8993/?opendocument).

specifically used by the Reserve Bank as part of its monetary targeting policies. Nevertheless, the Bank believed that nominal interest rates should at all times remain above the rate of inflation, and during the entire 1990s this was normally the case.

Difficulties in operating monetary targeting

One important problem, as indicated above, associated with money supply targeting was the choice of an appropriate measure. The identification of a permanently suitable measure of the money supply to use in this respect was a daunting task. In central banking circles Goodhart's law explicitly recognises this problem. This law refers to the notion that any particular targeted money supply indicator becomes distorted over time, and accordingly loses its validity, so that the central bank can no longer employ the indicator as a money supply target. Goodhart's law created growing problems for the Reserve Bank. Even though exchange controls remained in force, albeit in a less pronounced form, the increasing financial integration of South Africa with the rest of the world during the 1990s complicated the application of monetary policies and was an important reason for abandoning the policy of using guidelines for the growth in the money supply early in 1998. The almost explosive increase in the volume of transactions in the South African financial markets introduced a new unstable element in the velocity of money and led to a more unpredictable relationship between changes in the money supply and domestic price movements. This changing relationship arose in part from the greater inflows and outflows of foreign capital, which exerted a stronger effect on the rand exchange rate than previously, which in turn affected the inflation rate. From 1995 onwards the growth in the money supply accelerated, while the rate of inflation decelerated, the exact opposite of what money supply targeting would suggest.

These various developments helped to convince the authorities in 1998 that they should abandon money supply targeting policies. However, even before this date the Reserve Bank had been slowly applying a more pragmatic approach and was taking a broader view of movements in a whole range of financial indicators to guide it in making decisions on monetary policy.

Resort to discretionary monetary policies

The difficulties experienced in applying money supply targets led to some countries in the 1990s to begin to apply discretionary monetary policies without laying down any specific objectives for the growth in the money supply. In effect this involved using a set of indicators rather than one indicator such as the money supply to guide monetary policies. This approach was adopted in South Africa in 1998.

The basic objective behind this policy remained one of curbing inflation, and more particularly trying to bring inflation in line with the average rate of inflation in the economies of South Africa's major international trading partners and competitor countries. The policy could be criticised on the grounds that it was not particularly transparent, and any central bank adopting such a policy faced a credibility problem with the financial markets. Economic agents could not easily discern the exact aims of monetary policies. Moreover, they would find it difficult to predict the reactions of the Reserve Bank to different forms of economic disturbance under such a monetary policy framework.

Nevertheless, in support of such a policy approach, it should be noted that the global trend in the 1990s had moved in this direction. Some central banks, such as those in the USA and Japan, were making use of composite indicators rather than one specific indicator to guide monetary policies. It was, moreover, an approach which had already been employed to some extent in South Africa under the money supply targeting regime, as indicated above. Under that dispensation the Reserve Bank exercised some discretionary judgement, in the sense that it sought to attain an optimal combination of growth in the money supply, bank credit extension, interest rates and exchange rates at any given time.

The adoption of discretionary policies by the Bank, however, proved to be short lived, because in February 2000 it introduced a new monetary policy framework, in the form of an inflation targeting policy. In 1998 the Bank had rejected the resort to an inflation targeting approach, partly because it was unsure of its merits should it become necessary to introduce a formal inflation target that was way out of line with the rate prevailing in the rest of the world. By the late 1990s this had changed and countries targeting inflation had rates of little more than 3 per cent. The Reserve Bank was also unsure about the extent of support it would receive for such a policy in the wider community. However, as the rate of inflation in South Africa receded in the late 1990s, inflation targeting policies became more attractive. The introduction of discretionary monetary policies in 1998 was therefore regarded by the Reserve Bank as transitional as it moved from money supply targeting to the eventual introduction of an inflation targeting policy.[9]

9 Stals, 'Monetary policy challenges in South Africa', p. 8.

Instruments of monetary policy employed

In South Africa, as indicated above, the control of inflation was the ultimate objective of monetary policy in the 1990s, while the broadly defined monetary aggregate M3 was the intermediate target employed for most of the period, although other variables such as bank credit extension and the exchange rate were also monitored. In order to reach its target for the money supply, the Reserve Bank sought to influence short-term interest rates through the use of monetary policy instruments, the most important in this regard being the accommodation instrument (refinancing policy). Accommodation had conventionally referred to credit offered to banks at the so-called discount window of the central bank. Over the years, the Reserve Bank had made extensive changes to the procedures that it employed for extending accommodation to banks that were short of cash. This continued in the 1990s and was illustrated by a shift in policy in May 1993 when the rediscounting of various assets held by banks with the Reserve Bank was discontinued; instead, accommodation by the Bank was provided by overnight loans alone. This system conferred several benefits. The credit risk to which the Reserve Bank had been exposed when it discounted assets was eliminated, because assets were no longer purchased outright. Moreover, by abandoning the system of rediscounting assets, the administrative burden of the Reserve Bank was lightened. In addition, banks receiving cash from overnight loans had to hold cash reserves and liquid assets against increases in their short-term liabilities. In this way the Bank's accommodation policy could have a more immediate effect on short-term interest rates.

The most significant mutation in the accommodation area, however, came in March 1998, with the introduction of a so-called repo tender system. This was an alternative system of accommodating shortfalls in banking liquidity at the borrowing window of the Reserve Bank, by means of repurchase agreements relating to various securities which were tendered by the banks to the Reserve Bank on a daily, or intra-day, basis for purposes of acquiring liquidity. Under this system the repo (repurchase) rates could change on a daily or intra-day basis in line with the results of the daily or intra-day repo tenders, with this repo rate exerting a major influence on the interest rates of banks, including overdraft and mortgage rates. In effect, under this repo system fluctuations in the repo rates were expected to lead to a more flexible structure of interest rates than that which prevailed under the previous Bank rate system.

Although this system helped to depoliticise the process of changing interest rates on the part of the Reserve Bank, it would be wrong to conclude that the new arrangements meant that market forces played a much more influential role in determining short-term interest rates. Under the new dispensation, the Reserve Bank controlled both the demand for cash reserves by banks via its manipulation of the money supply shortage, as well as the supply of funds at the tenders.[10] Nevertheless, the new control techniques for interest rates meant that the Bank could more easily increase short-term rates if the rand came under pressure, a facility which was valuable considering the vulnerability of the currency in 1998.

The Reserve Bank did not view mutations in its accommodation rates as its sole instrument of monetary policy. Its accommodation instrument was supplemented by the use of other monetary policy instruments. Changes in cash reserve requirements imposed on banks could on occasion be employed, as well as open market operations. During the 1990s the latter did not solely incorporate the buying and selling of government bonds by the Reserve Bank with the aim of influencing banking liquidity. On occasion they included repurchase agreements under which tenders were invited from the banks for the sale of certain assets to the Bank for temporary periods before they were bought back. The Bank could also undertake repurchase agreements by selling assets to banks for repurchase at a later date. Foreign exchange swaps with banks were also occasionally executed on the initiative of the Reserve Bank to drain excess liquidity from the banking system.

Besides the repo system, other innovations in the field of monetary policy instruments unfolded in the 1990s. Tax and loan accounts held by the government with commercial banks were introduced in 1993 as a means of influencing banking liquidity and, in March 1998, the Reserve Bank began to issue its own debentures for sale to banks, with a similar aim in mind. Meanwhile, exchange controls were still in force in the 1990s, although steadily diminishing in importance.

Market-oriented monetary policies

The Reserve Bank placed an emphasis upon the use of market-oriented policy measures as a means of achieving its monetary policy aims. It did this by encouraging market participants to take particular actions as regards their lending and borrowing behaviour as a result of price and interest rate incentives or disincentives brought about in the financial markets. More particularly these incentives or disincentives in the 1990s

10 Andre Schoombie, 'The Stals era of monetary policy in South Africa', in Stuart Jones and Jon Inggs (eds), *The South African Economy in the 1990s*, special issue of *South African Journal of Economic History*, 18(1,2) (September 2003), 31–49, at p. 47.

arose out of technical intervention by the Reserve Bank in the various financial markets, which involved the buying and selling of specified financial claims such as government stock and other securities as well as foreign exchange, in order to influence prices and therefore interest rates and exchange rates. Naturally, such operations by the Bank required the existence of well developed financial markets, something which the Bank promoted throughout the 1990s.

The continued use of exchange controls, however, as a means of supporting the rand was totally inconsistent with a market-oriented approach to monetary policy. Exchange controls were progressively eased, starting in March 1995 with the scrapping of controls on non-residents. Exchange controls on residents remained in force. How quickly the remaining exchange controls should be abolished was a very sensitive issue. Some countries had successfully maintained full convertibility on the capital account of the balance of payments after suddenly scrapping exchange controls. Such a bold approach in South Africa in the 1990s might have been received enthusiastically by foreign investors, especially if it had been accompanied by the wholesale scrapping of the apparatus of exchange controls. This would have convinced investors that exchange controls would not be reintroduced.

The abolition of the controls in one fell swoop could have diminished the flight of capital from the country in the wake of a fall in the rand and a rise in domestic interest rates. It could also have precipitated inflows of new foreign capital, as well as encouraged the return of flight capital, which had left the country in previous years. It did not happen, however. The gradualist approach to the elimination of exchange controls chosen by the South African authorities in the 1990s ran the risk of dampening inflows of foreign capital, as foreign investors would have anticipated further liberalisation of exchange controls and a future weakening of the rand. In other words, some foreigners might have postponed investing because of fears that an exchange rate risk still existed.

In the event, the Reserve Bank decided to phase out exchange control on a piecemeal basis. It was argued that this reduced the risk of widespread economic disruption, which could have stemmed from weakness in the exchange rate and higher interest rates if the controls had been suddenly abolished and large-scale net capital outflows materialised. The Bank wanted to dismantle the exchange controls gradually, depending to some extent on developments in the balance of payments.

The desire on the part of the Bank to start removing exchange controls after April 1994 was perfectly understandable, as they were becoming increasingly redundant as an instrument for protecting the rand. The sharp rise in movements of foreign capital in the second half of the 1990s, and the associated large increases in daily turnover on the foreign exchange market, rendered exchange controls less and less relevant in the new political era. The administration of exchange controls was a constant headache for the Bank, with the difficulties in effectively administering them multiplying as the economy became more open.[11] Exchange controls could also be challenged on the grounds that they infringed on human rights, which were a key aspect of the new constitution.

Conclusion

During the 1990s the pursuit of a more stable monetary environment in South Africa became the keystone of monetary policies, against a background of radically different conditions before and after April 1994. Monetary policies before April 1994 were conducted in a siege-type environment. There was some ongoing criticism of this basic monetary approach on the grounds that tight monetary policies kept economic growth at unduly low levels; but the Reserve Bank argued that actions on the monetary policy front could affect only inflation and not the level of output. It therefore adhered to a policy of fighting inflation, which had social and economic benefits attached to it.

In order to achieve this objective, the monetary policy framework incorporated low-profile, flexible targeting of the money supply, with the M3 monetary aggregate identified as the most suitable for such targeting. However, this M3 variable became distorted over time and accordingly lost some of its validity as an accurate measure of future inflation. A changing relationship emerged between the growth of M3 and domestic inflation trends. Such difficulties led to the discarding of money supply targeting and its replacement by discretionary monetary policies in 1998. These were a stepping stone to the adoption of inflation targeting policies in February 2000, which became more attractive as the rate of inflation declined.

As regards monetary policy instruments in use in the 1990s, the most important was the accommodation policy, with the most significant mutation in this area occurring in March 1998 with the introduction of the so-called repo tender system. However, the accommodation instrument was supplemented by other instruments, such as changes in cash reserve requirements, the use of tax and loan accounts, and the retention of exchange controls.

11 Roger Gidlow, 'The collapse in the rand in 2001 and the effectiveness of exchange controls', *South African Journal of Economic History*, 20(2) (September 2005), 1–18.

The Reserve Bank relied heavily on market-oriented policy measures as a means of achieving its monetary policy goals, but the continued existence of exchange controls did not dovetail with this approach, which partly explains why progressive relaxations in the controls occurred after 1994. The remaining exchange controls were becoming increasingly redundant, but the opportunity to abolish them was ignored and they still remained in December 2000.

21

Trade policy

Stuart Jones

Introduction

Trade policy reform had begun before the 1994 election, but progress was slow and only moderate progress had been made before the political situation was transformed by the institution of a black government. Then, contrary to what many had expected, trade reform began to move in the direction of the 'Washington consensus'. This exposed many of the inefficiencies that existed in what was a highly protected economy.

Trade reform was not a gradual process throughout the 1990s. In fact, almost all the important changes took place in two years, 1994–96, when Trevor Manuel was the Minister of Trade. Under the leadership of his successor, Alec Erwin, the former ideologue of the South African Communist Party, trade reform stalled. It would seem, then, that reform owed much to the influence of individual members of the government, which suggests, in contradiction to communist doctrine, that individuals can exert a major influence on the course of events.

It is arguable, too, that the trade reforms of the mid-1990s were not only long overdue, but that they were in tune with the needs of the time. They represented a revival of the old mercantilist conundrum of when do infant industries, that need protection, cease to be infant industries? Further, how could long-standing protection be justified in an international economy no longer dominated by the struggle between capitalism and communism? Throughout the international economy, the old protectionist forces were giving way to the new life breathed into the case for global free trade, with the greater efficiency of market forces

This chapter draws heavily on an article by Rashaid Cassim, 'The pace, nature and impact of trade policy in South Africa in the 1990s', *South African Journal of Economic History*, 18(1,2) (September 2003), 76–95.

set against bureaucratic decision making and the bureaucratic allocation of resources. All Africa was caught up in the movement to liberalise hidebound state economics that was sweeping across the globe: but the more developed economies responded the most rapidly and, for a few years, in the middle of the decade, South Africa appeared to be taking the lead. Trade reform, therefore, in South Africa seemed to be following a pattern not dissimilar to that of England in the seventeenth century, when the key legislative props of mercantilist trade policy were introduced within four years, because the protectionist policies of that mercantilist era appealed to powerful vested interests; the key legislation of 1660 and 1663 was reinforced in later years and in the nineteenth century the celebrated budgets of Peel in 1842, 1845 and 1846 reflected voice of the increasingly powerful manufacturing interests, which were able to overcome the opposition of the vested interests of farmers and landowners. In 1990s South Africa, by contrast, powerful vested interests were opposed to the reforms, the benefits of which were not immediately apparent and, by the end of the decade, backsliding had begun.

Trade policy was influenced by both the private sector and the public sector. In the private sector, the more modern industries, mining, the financial services (especially the export-oriented section of the financial services) and the export-oriented section of agriculture were all in favour of freer trade and a greater role for the market in determining policy; opposed to them were the industries that had grown up behind high tariff barriers and outright prohibitions. These included the textile, clothing and boot and shoe industries, which could not compete with East and South East Asia, grain-growing agriculture, which could not compete with the more efficient producers in America and Australia, the cosseted automotive industry and sections of the fuel industry. Within the government, the Department of Trade held sway with Manuel in charge of it. Outside South Africa, friendly governments, as well as the International Monetary Fund (IMF) and the World Trade Organization (WTO), were urging the case for reform.

Trade reform in the 1990s meant the lowering, or removal, of politically induced barriers to trade. These might be outright prohibitions, high tariffs or foreign currency rationing. Often, at the heart of the matter in South Africa was the difference between the effective rates of protection and the nominal ones, which were so important to the automotive industry. Changes in import penetration could also reflect the progress of trade liberalisation. Subsidies affected efficient resource allocation.

At the same time, what was happening in South Africa's leading trading partners influenced trade policy. These might be currency fluctuations or an acceleration or declaration in a partner's rate of growth. In the 1990s the European economy was growing slowly, and that of the USA was supposedly being transformed into a new economy by consumer electronics and the internet. China was also beginning its period of rapidly growing demand for the raw materials of industrialisation. Closer to home there was South Africa's commitment to regional trading agreements, which expanded from the original agreement with the BSL countries (Botswana, Swaziland, Lesotho) in 1990 to one incorporating all of Southern Africa by 2000.

The chronology of trade reform

South Africa's economy had progressed from tariff-induced import substitution in the 1950s and 1960s to the introduction of export subsidies in the 1970s and 1980s to counter the anti-export bias of import protection. Trade reform focused on imports, with the replacement of quantitative restrictions by tariffs. In the 1980s, a time of sanctions and a need for a balance of trade surplus, there was little room for important reforms, though there were attempts to improve the conditions for exporters by means of custom duty drawbacks and duty exemptions. The high levels of anti-export bias in practice negated the efforts to boost exports. South Africa's economy in 1990 remained heavily protected and dependent upon the export of primary producers, stimulated by sustained currency depreciation.

Trade reform had not made any significant progress by 1990, when the General Export Incentive Scheme was introduced. The slight increase in manufactured exports in the early 1990s was the result of export subsidies and not the result of any moves towards freer trade. Giving firms incentives to export is not evidence of trade liberalisation but had the political advantage of not threatening the existing protection given to weak industries and weak firms.

In the 1990s, before the end of white rule, the government began negotiations with the WTO. This involved a sustained reduction in nominal tariffs and a sharp reduction in import surcharges. Those on luxury goods were reduced from 60 per cent to 10 per cent and those on intermediate and capital goods from 10 per cent to 0. Serious negotiations with the WTO began only in 1993 and led to South Africa joining the General Agreement on Tariffs and Trade (GATT) in 1994. The main aim was to simplify and lower the tariffs in an exceedingly complicated system, which had over 100 different tariff categories. For manufactured goods these were to be reduced to the rates of 0.5 per cent, 10 per cent, 15 per cent, 20 per cent and 30 per cent. Discretionary charges were to be prohibited. The reductions were to take place over 10 years, to allow highly protected sectors such as clothing and motor vehicles and

Table 21.1 *Tariff reductions under the WTO*

	1994	*1995*	*1996*	*1997*	*1998*	*1999*	*2000*
Textiles	30.1	33.8	31.8	24.9	23.4	21.9	20.3
Clothing (excluding footwear)	73.7	73.6	68.2	54.6	50.5	46.4	42.4
Leather and leather products	14.9	14.8	14.1	16.5	15.7	14.8	14.8
Footwear	37.5	41.6	39.1	36.8	34.2	29.1	29.1
Wood and wood products	13.9	3.6	3.4	3.5	3.3	3.1	3.1
Paper and paper products	9.6	9.3	9.1	8.8	8.7	8.5	7.9
Printing and publishing	8.1	1.3	1.2	1.1	1.0	1.0	1.0
Petroleum and petroleum products	1.6	–	–	–	–	–	–
Industrial chemicals	9.3	7.5	7.5	1.7	1.7	1.6	1.6
Other chemical products	9.0	3.8	3.7	2.7	2.6	2.5	2.5
Rubber products	30.5	14.5	14.1	15.8	15.4	14.9	14.6
Plastic products	19.8	14.7	13.7	13.2	12.6	12.0	12.0
Glass and glass products	11.8	9.5	9	8.3	7.9	7.6	7.6
Non-metallic mineral products	10.6	8.7	8.1	8.4	8	7.7	7.7
Basic iron and steel products	7.6	4.4	4.2	4.2	4.1	3.9	3.9
Non-ferrous metal products	2.3	2.3	2.3	2.3	2.2	2.0	2.0
Metal products (excluding machinery)	13.1	8.2	7.8	7.8	7.6	7.4	7.4
Non-electrical machinery	6.5	1.4	1.3	1.4	1.3	1.3	1.3
Electrical machinery	11.0	6.1	6.0	5.8	5.8	5.7	5.7
Radio, television and communication apparatus	12.1	5.1	3.7	2.4	2.3	2.3	2.3
Professional equipment etc.	7.2	0.2	0.2	0.3	0.3	0.3	0.3
Motor vehicles, parts and accessories	55.4	33.5	31.7	29.3	27.9	26.1	24.8
Other transport equipment	1.4	0.4	0.4	0.3	0.3	0.2	0.2
Furniture	28.1	21.4	20.8	20.2	19.6	18.9	18.9
Other manufacturing	2.9	1.0	1.0	5.2	5.1	5.0	4.9
Mining	2.7	0.6	0.6	0.5	0.4	0.4	0.4
Total	11.7	7.2	6.8	6.1	5.8	5.5	5.3

Source: Industrial Development Corporation, Sandton, Johannesburg, 1994.

accessories to adjust to the new dispensation (see Table 21.1). By 2000 the average nominal tariff had declined by over half, from 11.7 per cent to 5.3 per cent, with the phased reductions continuing long after the drive to reform the system had ground to a halt.

In agriculture, quantitative restrictions gave way to tariffs and a reduction in the number of *ad valorem* duties: but this process of replacing outright prohibitions with tariffs had begun in 1992 and was virtually complete by 1994. As with manufacturing, a few highly protected commodities remained, namely sugar, dairy products, beef and veal, mutton and wheat. Eleven commodities were allowed a 20 per cent tariff.

Yet, at the end of the decade, there remained a large number of different tariff levels in different sectors of the economy. These ranged from 0.3 per cent for professional equipment to 42.4 per cent for clothing, 29.1 per cent for footwear and 24.8 per cent for motor vehicles and accessories. As with the USA and the European Union, economic simplification gave way before political lobbying. These moves to simplify the situation were further qualified by bilateral and regional trade agreements with European Union and the Southern African Development Community. The former came into effect in January 2000 and the latter, signed in 1996, was not ratified by a majority of its members until the end of the decade. Neither, therefore, exerted a significant impact upon the economy or policy in the 1990s.

Aspects of trade reform

Subsidies

Trade reform was more successful in abolishing subsidies than it was in simplifying the tariff structure, which continued with a wide variety of tariffs together with significant tariff peaks. At the beginning of the decade, in April 1990, the General Export Incentive Scheme replaced the less effective export incentives of the 1980s. Based on value added and local content, it offered considerable inducement to export, but conflicted with the GATT. As a result, when South Africa signed the GATT in 1994, the incentives introduced in 1990 had to be phased out over three years, beginning in April 1995.

Most of the trade-distorting subsidies were phased out in the 1990s. Their removal coincided with the WTO replacing the GATT. There were, however, two exceptions, sectors that remained heavily subsidised and able to maintain a high degree of protection, namely clothing and textiles, and motor vehicles and components. Neither was in the forefront of technological progress: the former had spearheaded mass production in consumer goods towards the end of the eighteenth century and the latter transport goods a century later. Not only were both significant employers of labour in an economy with a very high level of unemployment, but both were widely considered to be a means by which underdeveloped economies could climb aboard the growth escalator. Removing their protection would have required a very bold political initiative. This was not forthcoming.

The clothing and textile sector was the outstanding beneficiary of the Duty Credit Certificate Scheme introduced in 1993. Manufacturers could obtain duty credit certificates on qualifying exports, which could be offset against the duty on imports that were used in the manufacturing process. Credits could be claimed for up to 35 per cent of the value of exports for clothing and 8–12 per cent for yarn. These credit certificates could be used only for offsetting the duty on goods imported that were similar to those exported. This increased the competitiveness of exporters by allowing them to obtain their inputs at close to international price levels, without reducing the high level of protection that the sector enjoyed. It did not encourage inefficient firms selling to the domestic market to become more efficient.

Removing the protection given to the motor vehicle industry proved to be an even more difficult task, because some of the major manufacturers had their bases in the African National Congress's heartland in the Eastern Cape. The Motor Industry Development Programme, which was introduced in 1995, provided a system of incentives based on selective reductions in import duty and substantial subsidies to investment and export in return for a protected domestic market. The new system was more efficient than the old one, phase VI of the Local Content Programme (see Chapter 6), because it measured local content by value and not by weight.

Tariffs were reduced significantly. On fully built-up vehicles, tariffs were reduced from an effective 115 per cent in 1990 to 65 per cent in 1995, 61 per cent in 1996 and 40 per cent in 2002. Over 1995–2002, the duty on completely knocked-down kits was reduced to 49 per cent. Taking a leaf out of Australia's book, the Programme also aimed to reduce the number of locally produced models from 39 in 1995 to 15 by 2003. Duty-free incentives were introduced that benefited the sale of high-volume models, such as the Toyota Corolla and Volkswagen Golf, at the expense of low-volume ones. This was over-optimistic. New manufacturers from Korea moved into South Africa by making arrangements for assembling their vehicles with existing manufacturers and the number of models was not significantly reduced. Companies that had disinvested in the 1980s also returned and by the end of the decade the South African consumer could once again buy a wide range of imported vehicles. Protection remained formidable, with foreign-owned German, American and Japanese firms able to import motor vehicles at internationally competitive prices and then sell them in the South African market at the international price plus 40 per cent, the level of the tariff. It is, therefore, debatable whether the Motor Industry Development Programme may be considered as a liberal measure and, indeed, whether it represented a serious attempt at reform. South African consumers with incomes considerably smaller than those in America and Europe ended up paying considerably more for their vehicles. Nor is it clear that the higher costs were outweighed in the long run by benefits derived from the country having a local motor vehicle industry.

Nominal and effective tariffs

Nominal tariffs were liberalised in accordance with the country's commitment to the WTO. Unweighted average tariffs fell over the decade from 28 per cent to 10 per cent, a reduction of 64 per cent, and the average manufacturing tariff from 30 per cent to 16 per cent. Moreover, applied import-weighted tariffs decreased from an average of 12 per cent in 1994 to 7 per cent in 2000, with those on manufacturers being reduced from 12 per cent to 8 per cent and those on agricultural products from 10 per cent to 1.5 per cent. This reduction in nominal tariffs was not accompanied by a significant simplification of the system. A large number of different tariff lines remained, in a system that was noted for its complexity and opaqueness – a bureaucrat's delight, but an exporter's nightmare. It is clear from Table 21.2 that reform had virtually come to a halt in 1996.

The anti-export bias in the economy continued after 1993. This is measured by the degree by which trade policy makes production for the domestic market more profitable than production for the export market. Indeed, as Table 21.3 indicates, the anti-export bias got worse after 1993 with the removal of the existing export incentives and, in 2000, textiles and clothing, motor vehicles and components, leather goods, tyres and some food-processing sectors were still experiencing relatively high levels of anti-export bias. By contrast, low levels of anti-export bias existed in industries such as sugar, fertilisers, cement, office machinery and treated metals. The continuance of high levels of anti-export bias was the result of the waning of the reform movement; the deterioration after 1993 was the price paid to join the WTO.

South Africa was less diligent in complying with its commitment to simplify its tariff structure and reduce the number of bands to six. In

Table 21.2 *Summary of tariff changes, 1990–99*

	All rates, 1990	*All rates, 1996*	*All rates, 1999*	*Positive rates, 1999*
Number of tariff lines	12,500	8,250	7,743	2,463
Number of different rates (bands)	200	49	47	45
Minimum rate (%)	0	0	0	1
Maximum rate (%)	1,389	61	55	55
Unweighted mean rate (%)	27.5	9.5	7.1	16.5
Standard deviation (%)	–	–	10.0	8.6
Coefficient of variation (%)	159.8	134.0	140.3	52.2

Note: Positive rates include only non-zero tariff lines; all rates include positive rates, zero and not available entries.

Source: J. Lewis, 'Policies to promote growth and employment in South Africa', Informal Discussion Paper No. 16, World Bank, July 2001.

Table 21.3 *Anti-export bias, 1993 and 1996*

	1993		*1996*	
	Without export incentives	*With export incentives*	*Without export incentives*	*With export incentives*
Total economy	1.63	1.19	1.49	1.32
Manufacturing	1.98	1.27	1.69	1.45

Note: A value of 1 implies export neutrality; values above 1 indicate anti-export bias.
Source: G. Kuhn and R. Jansen, 'The effective protection rate and anti-export bias', IDC Research Paper Series, Technical Series TS I, 1997.

2000 there were still close to 50 bands and 7,000 tariff lines. This tardiness limited the gains from joining the WTO and aided the continuation of protection. Motor vehicles and components, clothing and textiles, processed foods, rubber products and tobacco products still benefited from tariff peaks in 2000.

The effective rate of protection

Effective rates of protection measure the difference between the value added based on input and output tariffs and the value based on free trade prices. The protective effect of a tariff is measured by the proportionate change in the value added of the protected commodity that occurs as a result of the tariffs imposed on the good and its inputs. No changes in the rate of effective protection comparable to that for nominal tariffs occurred in the decade and the effective rate of protection remained high. This can be seen in Table 21.4, with five sectors receiving effective rates of more than 50 per cent. Motor vehicles, for instance, enjoyed the benefit of an effective rate of 81.0 per cent and clothing of 50.7 per cent. Effective rates remained high because in many sectors input tariffs had declined faster than output tariffs.

The economic effects of trade reform

The benefits to the economy of the reforms in the 1990s are difficult to quantify, as many of the changes in the economy may be attributed to the return to normal working of the market with the ending of financial sanctions and trade embargoes. On the other hand, the elimination of subsidies and the lowering of tariffs, together with the continued

Table 21.4 *Effective rates and nominal rates (%) of protection compared*

Sector	*Effective rate*	*Nominal rate*
Carpets	78.6	28.9
Handbags	70.2	30.0
Motor vehicles	81.0	36.2
Motor vehicle parts	64.8	32.7
Footwear	55.8	28.1
Wearing apparel	50.7	29.2
Furniture	38.7	19.3
Soap	35.3	18.9
Tyres	35.1	19
Knitting mills	35.0	21.3
Textile articles	36.5	21.8
Animal feeds	34.0	9.0
Other paper	31.0	15.7
Wire and cable	33.3	14.2
Other food	20.8	13.6
Lighting equipment	23.3	12.4
Confectionery	21.1	13.7
Fruit	17.8	11.4
Other rubber	20.4	11.8
Textiles	17.7	10.9
Plastic	19.3	13.0
Other textiles	17.9	11.9
Containers of paper	15.7	10.2
Paper	11.0	7.2
Glass	11.1	8.9
Beverages and tobacco	12.8	9.7
Other non-metallic	10.3	6.0
Household appliances	8.7	6.7
Primary plastics	8.3	4.8
Oils	6.9	4.9
Structural ceramics	9.2	6.2
Fabricated metal	7.6	5.4
Non-structural ceramics	6.3	5.0
General hardware	7.8	6.3
Structural metal	5.9	4.9
Iron and steel	5.0	3.4
Paints	3.6	4.1
Electricity apparatus	5.1	4.6
Wood	3.6	3.1
Other manufacturing	4.4	4.8
Electric motors	3.4	4.5
Non-ferrous metals	3.1	2.5
Accumulators	2.5	4.1
Radio and television	2.2	2.7
Leather	1.5	6.9
Jewellery	1.9	0.9
Gears	1.2	1.8

Source: R. Cassim, D. Onyango and D. E. van Seventer, 'The state of trade policy in South Africa', Trade and Industrial Policy Strategies, March 2002.

depreciation of the rand and better fiscal discipline at home, pushed the economy in the direction of greater export orientation. This in turn induced some sectoral shifts in the economy.[1]

The evidence for the greater export orientation may be seen in the growing contribution of exports to GDP, which rose from 19.6 per cent in 1991 to 26.3 per cent in 2000, an increase of 34 per cent. Growth, moreover, was greater before 1995 than after, which suggests that it was the normal working of the market rather than government policy that was driving the growth in exports. Accession to the WTO in 1995 did not lead to a significant growth in exports, while the increase in 1994 and 1995 should be attributed to a recovery of confidence in the market once the change of government had settled down without the feared civil war.

The shift towards greater export orientation may perhaps be more accurately described as a shift to greater exposure to international trade, for imports were rising faster than exports. They increased by 45 per cent between 1990 and 1999. Increased dependence upon international trade represented a return to the pattern of an earlier era. However, upon closer scrutiny, we see that the export of primary products declined by 1.5 per cent, while those of manufactured goods increased by 11.2 per cent and services by 9.9 per cent. Again, this may be attributed to the normal working of the market, as South Africa assumed a role *vis-à-vis* Africa north of the Limpopo similar to that of the South East Tigers to South Africa. It cannot be attributed to government policies. South Africa did, however, benefit from the improved fiscal and monetary policies of these years, as they created a more favourable economic background for trade expansion.

These sectoral shifts in the economy may also be seen in the simultaneous increase in import penetration and in the export–output ratios. Import penetration ratios measure the growth of imports relative to domestic consumption; export–output ratios measure the total output of firms that is exported. Table 21.5 provides the details of the extent of these changes. Import penetration was increasing at a slightly faster rate than the export–output ratios, though from different starting bases. Transport equipment other than motor vehicles and 'other mining' experienced the most rapid growth in export–output ratios, with exports taking over half of output. Its export–output ratio was growing almost as fast as its import penetration ratio. The vigorous growth in both ratios

1 There are important measurement issues to consider in calculating effective rates of protection, particularly if tariff rates differ significantly for products within the same sector, as well as the effect of any duty-free credits and other incentives. These calculations are indicative at best, therefore.

Table 21.5 *Average annual percentage change in import penetration and export–output ratios, 1991–2000 (selected sectors)*

Imported penetration	%	*Export versus output*	%
Other transport equipment	79	Other transport equipment	62
Scientific equipment	84	Scientific equipment	48
TV and comms equipment	65	Base non-ferrous metals	58
Machinery	59	Other mining	75
Other mining	70	Base iron and steel	50
Basic chemicals	48	Basic chemicals	40
Motor vehicles and parts	30	Furniture	27
Leather prods	28	Coal mining	38
Electric machinery	30	Machinery	26
Rubber products	24	Leather products	30
Footwear	20	TV and comms equipment	18
Textiles	23	Petrol refinery	21
Base non-ferrous metals	20	Paper and products	21
Glass and products	19	Rubber products	13
Other chemicals	20	Textiles	16
Metal products	16	Agriculture	15
Printing	18	Electric machinery	11
Non-metallic minerals	11	Glass and products	12
Base iron and steel	11	Metal products	11
Paper and products	12	Motor vehicles and parts	10
Furniture	8	Food	9
Petrol ref	9	Beverages	7
Wood and products	9	Clothing	8
Clothing	9	Non-metallic minerals	7
Food	8	Wood and products	7
Plastic products	7	Plastic products	4
Agriculture	6		
Beverages	4		

Note: 'Import penetration' refers to average annual growth in import penetration ratios based on 1995 constant rand prices. 'Export versus output' refers to average annual growth in exports as a percentage of output based on 1995 constant rand prices. The import penetration ratio is defined as the ratio of imports and the sum of total output and imports less exports.
Source: Tips South African Standardised Industry Data Base, 2003.

provides evidence of shifts in the domestic economy and its response to a more favourable international background. Once again, though, it is not clear that this may be placed to the credit of trade policy. A final point, emphasised by Cassim, is that trade reform (in his words 'trade liberalisation') had little effect upon the level of employment. In other words, it was not responsible for the high level of unemployment, particularly in manufacturing, which was shedding labour in the 1990s at the rate of 1.5 per cent a year. If policy was responsible for this, it was the government's labour policy, not its trade policy.

Conclusion

Significant trade reform proved to be more difficult in practice than in theory. Implementing mercantilist protectionism policies has always been easier than removing them, as the vested interests that are behind their introduction grow stronger with the passage of time and are usually able to block reform. In the twenty-first century this may be seen in the agricultural policies of the developed economies and in the industrial policies of developing and underdeveloped economies. The British move into free trade in the 1840s, when a parliament dominated by landowners voted to sacrifice the interests of agriculture, stands out as one of the turning points in the economic history of the world and, in the UK at least, the intellectual attractions of free trade remained dominant for almost a century. The USA, by contrast, came late to the idea of free trade, moving in that direction only after the Second World War and enshrining some of its features in the Washington consensus. In the 1990s the times were propitious for the reform of South Africa's traditional mercantilist policies. The collapse of Soviet communism paved the way for market-driven global economic growth and for the conversion of the South African communist-dominated government to the value of the market in guiding and bringing about economic growth.

In the new post-sanctions, post-embargo era, trade reform was an obvious area in which to embark upon a policy of reform. The vested interests and lobbies that had benefited from protection were both discredited and powerless, which is why it was possible to remove the protection given to agriculture. The farmers had been among the strongest supporters of the previous government. A similar argument could be applied to manufacturers, though with less accuracy, which is why the removal of tariffs on manufactured goods was less far reaching than that on agricultural products.

The key decisions affecting trade reform occurred within a space of two years, 1994–96. Thereafter, the impetus to reform weakened and vested interests, particularly in the motor vehicle industry and in clothing and textiles, were able to reassert their influence over policy. The ending of any effective government by Mandela in 1996 consequently coincided with the end of effective reform involving major new decisions. The implementation of decisions already taken of course continued and this did lead to further tariff reductions, but South Africa's moves towards a more liberal framework for economic development had stalled. The government had bowed to the demands of GATT, but neither Thabo Mbeki (who had become the effective head of government) nor Erwin, the new minister responsible for trade policy, was particularly drawn to establishing a liberal framework in which the market determined investment and production. Their hearts were not in it, so the reform movement flagged and tariff policy remained full of contradictions.

Nevertheless, important changes had occurred in the 1990s, some of which had been initiated before 1994. Subsidies were abolished and tariffs were lowered across a wide range of industries, but too many exceptions were made that permitted the continuance of high nominal tariffs and tariff peaks. In addition, the effective rate of protection remained very much higher in certain key industries, state control remained dominant in the electricity supply industry and controlled prices remained in the petroleum industry. By the end of the decade some changes in the structure of the economy had probably occurred in addition to a reduction in the anti-export bias that had persisted for so long.

How far changes in policy affected the rate of growth of the economy is less clear. The relatively low level of global commodity prices in the 1990s, together with the decline in employment in both agriculture and mining, led to a contraction in domestic demand that exerted a negative impact upon economic growth. It is less likely that trade policy had a significant effect upon economic growth. It is true that external trade increased its contribution to GDP in the 1990s, but this was a response to the ending of embargoes, particularly with Asian countries, such as China, India, Indonesia and the countries surrounding the Persian Gulf. Trade policy in the 1990s may not have been as damaging to the economy as it was before 1990, but it was at best neutral. Indeed, as a consequence of the failure to build on the reforms of 1994–96 and the continuance of high effective tariffs, high tariff peaks and exceptions for favoured sectors, tariff policy may have continued to have a negative effect upon the economy throughout the decade. Trade policy cannot be considered one of the decade's achievements.

22

Agricultural and land policy

Nick Vink and Ruth Hall

Introduction

Agriculture in South Africa is, in some important respects, unusual and exceptional. It is highly 'dualistic', in the sense that it comprises, in the former 'white' rural areas, a capital-intensive commercial farming sector engaged in large-scale production and strongly linked to global markets and, in the former 'black' homelands, an impoverished sector dominated by low-input, labour-intensive forms of production. In 1990 about 60,000 white commercial farmers owned or operated farms on 86 million hectares, while approximately 1.3 million black small-scale farmers worked the remaining 14 million hectares of the country's agricultural land.[1]

Agriculture plays a significant role in the national economy. By 2000, despite contributing only about 3 per cent of GDP, it accounted for over 8 per cent of foreign exchange earnings and about 11 per cent of formal employment.[2] However, when forward and backward linkages into manufacturing are considered, agriculture's GDP contribution amounted to some 13 per cent.[3] As well as its economic role, agriculture has environmental, social and cultural roles and exhibits both positive and negative externalities.

1 *Abstract of Agricultural Statistics,* National Department of Agriculture, 2006. The estimate of small-scale farmers in former homelands is from 1991. As of 2006, this remained the most recent available official estimate and featured in official publications.
2 N. Vink and J. Kirsten, 'Agriculture in the national economy', in Lieb Niewoudt and Jan Groenewald (eds), *The Challenge of Change: Agriculture, Land and the South African Economy,* University of Natal Press, 2003, pp. 3–20. These employment data refer to 1996, the latest available at the time of writing.
3 *Ibid.,* p. 11.

With the advent of democracy in 1994, the agenda of the African National Congress (ANC) was to transform agriculture: to improve efficiency and competitiveness in the commercial sector and to implement land reforms in order to alleviate poverty and promote broad-based rural development.[4] There were clear political as well as economic reasons to do so. This process was to be pursued through parallel policy processes and separate institutions – the Departments of Agriculture and of Land Affairs. These two departments were initially answerable to different ministers – with Agriculture under a National Party (NP) minister, and Land Affairs under an ANC minister – but in 1996 were brought within the ambit of one ANC-led ministry, headed by Derek Hanekom until 1999 and thereafter (to 2006) by Thoko Didiza.

During the 1990s, the commercial agricultural sector experienced growth but at the same time continued its sectoral decline. A number of key policy interventions accelerated existing long-term trends towards mechanisation and job shedding. A rapid process of deregulation brought an end to decades of state support, and trade liberalisation opened up new opportunities but also increased competition for market access. Labour regulation and tenure rights for farm workers imposed new obligations on commercial farmers. The end of apartheid made possible a break from the isolationist past and increased integration into the world economy, with a rapid rise in both imports and exports.

Quite distinct from the trajectory of change in the commercial sector is the sector of smallholder producers. The 'traditional' agricultural sector is located in the former 'homelands', the creations also known as 'native reserves' or 'Bantustans', as designated in the Native Land Act 27 of 1913 and the Natives Trust and Land Act 18 of 1936. These areas were 'dumping grounds' for 'surplus people' forcibly removed from urban centres and rural 'black spots' – at least 3.5 million people were relocated between 1960 and 1983.[5] In effect, the homelands were functionally linked to the economy of industrialising 'white' South Africa, contributing to white capital accumulation by providing labour for white-owned farms, mines and factories, and subsidising wages through agricultural production to support extended families remaining in these 'reserves'.

The underdevelopment of agriculture in these areas was the product of legal and policy manipulation that created overcrowded conditions and weak infrastructure. Nevertheless, many people depended on smallholder agriculture for their livelihoods – often alongside other economic activities. The 'traditional' sector cannot be

4 *Reconstruction and Development Programme*, ANC, 1994.

5 Surplus People Project, *The Surplus People*, Ravan Press, 1983.

accurately described as 'subsistence', but produced less than 5 per cent of the marketed output in the early 1990s and relied largely on informal trading and local markets. Change in the traditional sector has been more limited than in the commercial sector and problems of inadequate farmer support have been aggravated by agricultural policy changes.

This chapter explores the progress made towards equitable and sustainable development in the agricultural sector in the decade of the 1990s and the impact that policy had on employment, inequality and growth in the sector. The chapter has three main sections. The first depicts the situation in 1990, the National Party's policy strategy during the period of negotiations and the challenge faced by the new incoming government in 1994. The following one describes the policy measures taken to transform agriculture and redistribute land from 1994 to 2000. The third main section describes the outcomes of these policies and the current conjuncture in both the commercial and traditional sectors. The conclusion comments on policy-induced changes in the roles that agriculture plays and discusses the political considerations that have shaped agricultural and land policy.

The challenge of agrarian change

The dualistic agrarian structure is characterised by a racially skewed distribution of land and by a highly uneven income distribution – both between white and black farmers, and between farmers and farm workers. The key challenge for agricultural and land policy in 1994 was to overcome this dualism and build a unitary agricultural sector that could play a positive economic, environmental, social and cultural role in the life of a changing South Africa.

Of the total South African population of about 45 million, the rural population accounted for 19 million, or 42 per cent, in 2001.[6] Though the rural population was growing, it had declined as a proportion of the total population; increased rural–urban migration after the removal of influx controls meant that, by the end of the 1990s, more than half

6 MacIntosh, Xaba and Associates, *Land Issues Scoping Study: Communal Land Tenure Areas*, report prepared for the Department for International Development (DFID), Southern Africa, November 2003, p. 2. Although strictly speaking this refers to the 'non-urban' population, that is, to those who do not live in formally proclaimed towns, the non-urban population contains a significant proportion of people (8 million by one estimate) who live in urban-like circumstances outside proclaimed towns. See C. Cross, S. Bekker, N. Mlambo, K. Kleinbooi, L. Saayman, H. Pretorius, T. Mngadi and T. Mbhele, *An Unstable Balance: Migration, Small Farming, Infrastructure, and Livelihoods in the Coastal Provinces*, unpublished report, Development Bank of Southern Africa, 1999.

the population lived in urban areas, even though rural out-migration appeared to have slowed towards the end of the decade in response to urban unemployment. An estimated 16 million people – more than one in three of all South Africans – lived in the communal areas, both in agricultural areas and in denser settlements where agriculture featured only marginally as a source of livelihood.[7] Data from the late 1990s underscore the importance of addressing rural poverty: according to the government's Inquiry into Poverty and Inequality in 1998, 71 per cent of the rural population were poor and, while more than half the South African population lived in urban areas, 72 per cent of the poor were in rural areas.[8]

The commercial farming sector's origins reflect the political nature of agricultural policy making in South Africa. The sector is substantially the creation of successive governments, which systematically built the institutional and economic environment from which white farmers could commercialise – through direct subsidisation but also through protection from competition and a ready supply of cheap black labour. The biases of agricultural policy before 1990 were not only racial, however. The wealth accumulated in the sector shored up the agricultural establishment's commitment to the large-scale commercial farming model it had created, and justified its aversion to smallholder agriculture on the grounds of national food security.

However, the inherited agricultural sector was both economically and socially dysfunctional. Skewed resource allocation subsidised the creation of pockets of prosperity in a context of immense rural poverty – including, notably, among farm workers in the commercial farming areas. Even so, by the end of the 1990s agriculture was a key industry in the rural areas, providing 39 per cent of rural incomes, and must therefore feature centrally in efforts to address the massive challenge of rural poverty.[9]

State support to agriculture included state-run marketing control boards, price regulation, subsidised inputs, soft loans, a highly protectionist trade regime and tax write-offs. An elaborate infrastructure of state support to commercial agriculture until the early 1980s served political ends and produced a sector that was in many senses inefficient:

7 MacIntosh, Xaba and Associates, *Land Issues Scoping Study*, p. 3.

8 Julian May, *Poverty and Inequality in South Africa*, report prepared for the Office of the Executive Deputy President and the Inter-Ministerial Committee for Poverty and Inequality, 1998.

9 Department of Labour, *Determination of Employment Conditions in South African Agriculture*, Government Gazette No. 22648, Regulation Gazette No. 7159, Vol. 435, 13 September 2001.

> Agricultural and economic policies encouraged commercial farmers to increase farm size and to substitute labour with capital. Single-channel fixed price marketing schemes and the cross-subsidisation of agricultural product prices and transport costs caused a distortion of price relationships, which resulted in the incorrect allocation of agricultural resources.[10]

The existence of a highly capitalised commercial agricultural sector in South Africa is an anomaly. Its ongoing inability to achieve a more equal distribution of income formed the basis for the political and economic exigency of transformation and land reform. It was recognised that the repeal in 1991 of apartheid-era land laws was entirely insufficient to bring about changes in the ownership of land or to address the legacy of dispossession. The new government would need to embark on a process to fundamentally transform landholding patterns, to transfer resources to the poor and to deracialise agriculture. Developed as part of the *Reconstruction and Development Programme*, land reform was conceived as a targeted transfer of resources from the state to the poor – one of a number of policies (including housing grants and social welfare payments) that would contribute to poverty eradication. Land reform recognised that agricultural land in South Africa cannot be considered merely a commodity within a commercial production system; instead, it forms a basis for livelihoods, security and identity.

While continuity was the dominant motif in the growth of agricultural output, the 1990s saw major changes in agricultural policy and, to an even greater extent, in land policy. The question of land ownership is, of course, fundamentally political, not least because the existing pattern of access to and ownership of land is widely considered to be unjust and illegitimate – the result of centuries of conquest and coercion. There was, then, from the early 1990s, a tension between a political direction that required a radical restructuring of economic and property relations in agriculture, and the need to retain some stability in the face of a rapidly changing agricultural economy and increased international competition.[11]

Policy for change

A battery of legislative and policy changes affected agriculture in the period. The agricultural, land reform and related policies adopted after 1990 are discussed below, and some key achievements and shortcomings are noted.

10 *White Paper on Agriculture*, National Department of Agriculture, 1995.
11 *Ibid.*

Agricultural policy

Agricultural policy in the 1990s was characterised by the liberalisation of agricultural trade, the deregulation of marketing, institutional restructuring and the decline of state funding for agriculture. The principles guiding policy, as outlined in the 1995 White Paper on agriculture, were to pursue comparative advantages and become more labour intensive, to improve household food security and to support resource-poor farmers. The state's role was to be limited to correcting 'market imperfections and socially unacceptable effects'.[12]

The agricultural trade regime changed as a result of the 1994 Agreement on Agriculture, part of the Marrakesh Agreement that established the World Trade Organization (WTO). As a result of the Agreement, the tariff equivalent of border protections was calculated and bound rates were agreed. Subsequently, South Africa's trade policies also changed, with the result that tariffs were substantially reduced and export subsidies (under the General Export Incentive Scheme – GEIS) were eliminated, although this was balanced by the introduction of tariff rate quota (TRQ) regimes for several products[13] and a system of (largely now ended) variable import tariffs.

Major changes to marketing were introduced through the Marketing of Agricultural Products Act 47 of 1996, which deregulated marketing, abolished commodity control boards and statutory import and export monopolies, and established the National Agricultural Marketing Council (NAMC), charged with overseeing more limited state support.[14] Pan-territorial and pan-seasonal pricing was abolished, as were price supports and a host of other market interventions.[15]

One of the main features of agricultural policy in the 1990s was the extent of institutional restructuring that took place, as institutions associated with apartheid era 'development' were brought into line with new priorities, as the public sector was reorganised in line with new provincial boundaries and as new policies required a new institutional apparatus.[16] In addition to extensive changes in marketing institutions, rural financial institutions were also restructured. The most important initiatives in this regard were the closing of the Agricultural Credit Board (ACB), the repositioning of the Land and Agricultural Bank,

12 *Ibid.*, p. 12.

13 Note that most of these TRQ rates were set at 20 per cent of the World Trade Organization's bound rates, and in general appear not to have acted as a major constraint on imports of these products.

14 Vink and Kirsten, 'Agriculture in the national economy', p. 4.

15 *Ibid.*, p. 28.

16 *Ibid.*, p. 5.

and the restructuring of agricultural development corporations and banks that had been established in the former homeland areas. Other institutions were partially or wholly privatised, while certain services, including research and extension services, were reoriented to focus more on the needs of small farmers.

Direct state funding of institutions servicing agriculture contracted through the 1990s, partly as a result of institutional restructuring. Funding of departments of agriculture dropped by 55 per cent, to R2.5 billion, between 1988 and 2001.[17] State funds for agricultural research also declined sharply, by 45 per cent in the 10 years to 2001.[18]

Improving access for new entrants to the sector was pursued through the Broadening Access to Agriculture Thrust (BATAT), a framework for the policy positions of the National Department of Agriculture (NDA) on agricultural transformation from the mid-1990s to the late 1990s, but little came of this as the NDA did not develop a clear role for itself in supporting the broader land reform effort until after 2000.

From the late 1990s, key discussions on the future of agriculture took place in the Presidential Working Group on Agriculture, which comprised the Presidency, the NDA and the two major farmers' associations: AgriSA,[19] historically the representative of white commercial farmers, and the National African Farmers' Union (NAFU), the representative of black emerging farmers. This culminated in 2001 in the production of the Strategic Plan for South African Agriculture, which set out a joint vision for a transformed sector.[20]

Land reform policy

In parallel with the above changes in agricultural policy, initiatives to transfer land ownership and to strengthen tenure rights were launched under the rubric of land reform – first by the National Party and then from 1994 by the ANC-led Government of National Unity.

In 1991, the Nationalist government introduced a White Paper on land reform that envisaged a dual process of redistribution through subsidised land purchases and restitution of land.[21] The Advisory Commission on Land Allocation (ACLA) was set up to oversee limited restoration of certain categories of state land to dispossessed communities. Alongside this circumscribed process of restitution, the Provision

17 *Ibid.*, p. 6.
18 *Ibid.*, pp. 6–7.
19 AgriSA was previously known as the South African Agricultural Union (SAAU).
20 *Strategic Sector Plan for Agriculture*, National Department of Agriculture, 2001.
21 *White Paper on Land Reform*, Department of Land Affairs, 1991, p. 1.

of Certain Land for Settlement Act 126 of 1993 aimed to broaden access to land by enabling black entrepreneurs to purchase state or private land, while retaining state powers of regulation over land use, including the prohibition of subdivision. These subsidised land purchases would enable black people to buy farms at market price – but they would need to do so in groups. The state would provide a subsidy of 80 per cent of market price (up to a maximum of R7,500 per household); the community would need to contribute 5 per cent in cash and repay a 15 per cent loan over five years at an 8 per cent interest rate.[22] Despite high levels of indebtedness among commercial farmers, the state and its parastatal Land and Agricultural Bank did not foreclose on bad debt, which would have greatly increased the availability of land for redistribution, as it preferred instead to bail out the most extreme cases through the Agricultural Credit Board.

The ANC rejected this limited programme of reform and engaged in its own process of policy development, which similarly embraced a market-based approach to reform. The *Reconstruction and Development Programme* embraced land reform in 1994 as 'the central and driving force of a programme of rural development', which, according to ANC goals, was to transfer 30 per cent of agricultural land to black South Africans in the first five years.[23] This framework for land reform differed from the pre-emptive reforms of the National Party in several important respects, including:

- the inclusion of a programme of tenure reform aimed in particular at farm workers and others living on commercial farms, and residents of communal areas;
- legislative confirmation of the right to restitution of private as well as public land, with all those unfairly dispossessed since 1913 being eligible;
- land purchase subsidies under redistribution would be set at a higher level and there would be no requirement that applicants contribute their own capital or loans.

The land reform's three components were further specified in the White Paper on South African land policy.[24] A land redistribution programme was created to broaden access to land among the country's black majority, in order to alleviate poverty and stimulate development. A land restitution programme was adopted to restore land or provide

22 'State strategy on land reform', unpublished document, National Land Committee, November 1993, p. 4.

23 *White Paper on Reconstruction and Development*, Office of the President, 1994.

24 *White Paper on South African Land Policy*, Department of Land Affairs, 1997.

alternative compensation to those dispossessed as a result of racially discriminatory laws and practices since the introduction of the Native Land Act 27 of 1913. Alongside these two initiatives to transfer land, a tenure reform programme was designed to secure the rights of people living under insecure arrangements on land owned by others, including the state and private landowners, by upgrading their rights or providing them with alternative land or settlement opportunities.[25]

A peculiarity of South Africa's land reform is that it has been market based, in the sense that land is bought from those landowners willing to sell – an approach advocated by the World Bank and generally described as the 'willing buyer – willing seller' principle. Though in general there is sufficient land for sale, this approach precludes planned interventions to make land available in areas of high demand or where historical claims have been made to particular land in terms of the restitution programme. The new constitution includes both protection for property rights and an injunction to the state to pursue land reform, empowering it to expropriate property for this purpose, subject to the payment of 'just and equitable' compensation.[26] Though the government chose not to invoke expropriation in the 1990s, it later amended the Restitution of Land Rights Act in 2003 to empower the minister to expropriate property for restitution and other land reform purposes without a court order.[27]

The main thrust of land reform in the 1990s was land redistribution, a programme in which applicants could obtain state grants with which to purchase land. Initially, this was via a one-off means-tested 'settlement/land acquisition grant' (SLAG), available only to poor households and set at R16,000. Because the market price of land was in most areas high compared with the grants available from the state, large numbers of people were forced to combine resources and form 'communal property associations'[28] to purchase land jointly and engage in collective production. What information is available on land use practices, including through official 'quality of life' surveys, indicates that little

25 R. Hall, P. Jacobs and E. Lahiff, *Final Report*, Programme for Land and Agrarian Studies, Evaluating Land and Agrarian Reform in South Africa No. 10, University of the Western Cape, 2003, p. 1.

26 Constitution of the Republic of South Africa Act 108 of 1996, Government Printers, 1996.

27 Restitution of Land Rights Amendment Act 48 of 2003.

28 Communal property associations (CPAs) are juristic persons through which people can hold and manage property jointly; CPAs have a written constitution and there are certain democratic checks and balances. CPAs were created by the Department of Land Affairs specifically for use in the land reform context, as an alternative to existing legal entities like trusts or closed corporations, which were deemed unsuited to the needs of large groups of rural people.

agricultural activity ensued in most projects and livelihood benefits were few.[29] This was at least in part due to the absence of post-transfer support to beneficiaries, either for production and for the newly formed institutions charged with managing the land, which has restricted the beneficial impact of land reform. In response to the acknowledged limitations of the SLAG programme, by the end of the 1990s the policy was being revised. Upon her appointment in 1999, the new minister (Didiza) imposed a moratorium on all further projects, while her departments and their advisers developed a revised integrated programme – the Land Redistribution for Agricultural Development (LRAD) programme – with a sliding scale of grants between R20,000 and R100,000 per individual, depending on the level of the applicants' own contributions towards the project in the form of 'sweat equity', own capital, assets and loans. LRAD grants were available to all black South Africans, not only to the poor.[30] Ostensibly, LRAD provided for a range of commercial and 'food safety net' projects but in practice favoured commercial uses of land by individuals or small groups. Organised agriculture, including AgriSA, supported this new direction of policy and committed itself to playing a role in mentoring new black farmers and, through its commodity sector organisations, assisting with access to inputs and markets.

The budget for all aspects of land reform remained at about 0.2 per cent of the national budget throughout the 1990s.[31] Most of the budget for 'restitution' was spent on cash compensation rather than land acquisition, and this allocation had grown by 1999 to R164 million, while the budget for 'land reform' to fund redistribution and tenure reform stood at R276 million in the same year.[32] Although the allocations were low compared with the amount required to meet targets, the budget was regularly underspent right up to the end of the 1900s.

Farm workers and their families have historically lived on commercial farms under insecure conditions, without any rights to the homes they inhabit, to land or to other resources they use. As part of the land reform programme, two laws were enacted to protect their tenure rights: the Extension of Security of Tenure Act 62 of 1997 (ESTA) and

29 J. May and B. Roberts, *Monitoring and Evaluating the Quality of Life of Land Reform Beneficiaries 1998/99*, summary report prepared for the Department of Land Affairs, 19 June 2000.

30 *Land Redistribution for Agricultural Development: A Sub-programme of the Redistribution Programme*, Ministry of Agriculture and Land Affairs, 2001.

31 *Estimates of National Expenditure 2000–2001*, National Treasury, 2000.

32 *Ibid.*

the Land Reform (Labour Tenants) Act 3 of 1996 (LTA). They prohibit arbitrary eviction – any eviction must be mandated by the courts – and provide for farm dwellers to get long-term secure rights, including becoming owners of land. Labour tenants, those people who have access to land for their own production in return for their labour, are clustered in KwaZulu-Natal and Mpumalanga and are able, through the provisions of the LTA, to apply to become the owners of the land they already use, with the state paying market prices to the current owners.

Land reform in the communal areas remained in the planning stages. It was only at the end of the decade that the new minister mooted the transfer of land to 'tribes' or to 'traditional communities', as the state's response to the chaotic state of land administration and insecure tenure in the former homelands. A Land Rights Bill, in the drafting stages from the mid-1990s, proposed that legislation extend statutory provision to land users in communal areas by recognising their *de facto* rights to land. As in Botswana, local land boards would adjudicate land disputes and clarify the nature and content of rights. By the end of 1999, however, this bill had been shelved, and new processes were initiated to confirm the rights of traditional authorities (chiefs), where they existed, to administer and allocate land rights.[33] This policy of transferring private title to communal land to poor and often internally divided communities, under systems of undemocratic governance, remains highly controversial. Critics highlight its inadequacy to secure women's rights to land, the need for democratic measures to define and protect the tenure rights of community members, and the withdrawal of the state from land administration.

Progress with transferring land ownership in the commercial farming areas was exceedingly slow during the 1990s, despite some improvements at the end of the decade, in the transfer of land through redistribution and the settling of restitution claims. A total of 1 million hectares of land had been transferred through all aspects of land reform by the end of 1999. This amounts to less than 1 per cent of commercial agricultural land, of which 263,868 hectares were transferred through restitution and 752,027 hectares through redistribution and tenure

33 In terms of the Traditional Leadership Framework Governance Act 41 of 2003, tribal authorities are to be partially democratised over a set period. This is to involve the inclusion of elected representatives and women, and the resulting institutions are to be called 'traditional councils'. Where such councils exist, they will administer land rights and will have the power to alienate land. Where no tribal authorities currently exist, communities will be allowed to elect representative structures to manage their land rights.

reform.[34] A new target was set, to transfer 30 per cent of commercial farmland by 2015. Thus far, however, land reform has failed to make inroads into the structural problem of dualism, poverty and inequality.

Water, environment, social security and labour

Agriculture has also been changed through the indirect impact of policies relating to the realisation of the socio-economic rights enshrined in the Bill of Rights (1996). These affected the use of water, the environment, social security and labour.

A new water policy was developed to favour smallholder farmers and to remove the subsidies available to commercial farmers, which had distorted water prices. The Water Act 36 of 1998 introduced integrated catchment management, terminated subsidies and the riparian principle and redefined water as a public resource.[35]

New environmental policies pursued soil conservation and the protection of biodiversity.[36] The National Environmental Management Act 107 of 1998 provided a framework for integrated and cooperative environmental governance. New steps were taken to improve veld management and to combat invasive alien plants through the Working for Water programme. Despite a more progressive environmental policy framework, South Africa has been one of the fastest adopters of genetically modified organisms (GMOs), providing a testing ground for biotechnology multinationals in the production of, among others, maize, cotton, sugar cane, sorghum and potatoes, yet, for most of the 1990s, agricultural and land policies were pursued in the absence of a wider rural development policy.

Over the decade there was substantial growth of social assistance in the form of direct transfer payments by the state to citizens, in the form of monthly social grants – including child support grants, disability grants, old age pensions and related grants.[37]

The new labour laws, though, did affect agriculture. In 1994 agricultural workers had no legislated labour rights, but by the end of the decade they were protected by labour laws applicable to all sectors, and the Minister of Labour had announced his intention to regulate agricultural wages by imposing a minimum wage in the sector.

34 Commission on the Restitution of Land Rights, 'Honouring the promise of our constitution: strategic plan 2003/04 to 2005/06', unpublished document, Department of Land Affairs, February 2003 (internal electronic data supplied by the Department of Land Affairs Monitoring and Evaluation Directorate).

35 Vink and Kirsten, 'Agriculture in the national economy', p. 4.

36 J. Kirsten and N. Vink, 'National report: South Africa', in *Roles of Agriculture Project International Conference,* Agricultural and Development Economics Division (ESA), Food and Agriculture Organization of the United Nations, 2003, p. 7.

37 *Ibid.*, p. 8.

The changing terrain

Radical shifts in agricultural and related policies over the 1990s resulted in a sector that received little support from the state, a state of affairs that had different effects on commercial agriculture, the former homeland areas and on those living in denser settlements. Before 1994, South African agriculture counted among the world's most protected agricultural sectors. By 2000, the level of support to producers was among the lowest in the world.[38]

The policies described above affected the structure of commercial agriculture: the mode of production (labour and capital intensity), the location and composition of production, farm size, and export orientation. These changes are discussed in Chapter 3. The impact on the rural economy in general, and on new entrants to agriculture in particular, are discussed in this chapter. These policies have resulted in both positive and negative externalities, which have been unevenly distributed across the commercial and traditional sectors.

The commercial sector

Policy effects on the rural economy

The new policy environment for commercial farmers affected rural areas in three ways. First, there were increased opportunities for small and medium-size businesses in processing and distributing maize and maize products. This increased activity provided a stimulus to rural economies. Second, there was a marked increase in agro-tourism throughout the country. Third, small-scale farmers gained, in theory at least, better access to the market, as the cooperatives that had previously acted as agents under single-channel schemes would take delivery only in bulk.

The abolition of pan-territorial and pan-seasonal pricing also had interesting consequences for the rural finance sector. Under the control schemes, the control boards appointed agents, mostly farmer cooperatives, to carry out the physical functions of receipt of the crop, payment, storage and onward consignment to the processors. These input supply cooperatives therefore became effectively regional monopolies, which enabled them to become preferred suppliers of seasonal credit to farmers. They generally used the Land Bank as their preferred source of funds. With deregulation, however, the commercial banks were able to expand their share of this market.

38 Vink and Kirsten, 'Agriculture in the national economy', p. 18.

A final consequence of the abolition of pan-territorial and pan-seasonal pricing was the advent of a wide range of strategies (increased part-time farming, contract farming, strategic selling throughout the season, price hedging, etc.) and institutions (the agricultural futures market, or SAFEX, grain trading firms, brokerage firms, etc.) that enabled farmers to participate in the market with greater certainty. These institutional changes generally served to lower the transaction costs of market participation.

The effects of deregulation on the livestock subsector have received relatively little attention, partly because of the heterogeneity of the sector and partly because of the lack of reliable data, especially on the consumption of red meat. The 1990s saw an increase in the proportion of red meat sold in the informal sector directly into poor urban and peri-urban communities. While it is known that this trade made up a substantial proportion of total sales of red meat, its exact magnitude has not been estimated. Similarly, there remained an active market in pig and poultry by-products. Deregulation also resulted in a rapid increase in the number of smaller abattoirs in rural areas. This proliferation of slaughtering facilities across the country created challenges for health inspectors in local municipalities to ensure that minimum hygiene conditions were maintained.

The 1990s also saw a rapid increase in the cash loans business as the banking sector was deregulated and commercial banks failed to move into the low-income market. While most cash loans were supplied in urban areas, anecdotal evidence shows that many borrowers used the funds in small businesses, including the distribution and retailing of fresh produce (vegetables, meat, fruit) in poor urban and peri-urban areas. There was also an increase in the volume of business conducted through the micro-lending industry in rural areas and there is evidence that some of these funds were invested in businesses engaged in the small-scale processing, distribution and retailing of fresh produce.

Policy effects on new entrants to agriculture

The composite effect of policy changes in agriculture in the 1990s meant that new entrants faced a difficult economic environment in a sector characterised by increased competition and high potential profits but also increased risk, as many of the support systems created for white farmers were dismantled. By the late 1990s there was 'an almost total absence of small farmer support services in the country'.[39] Land reform involved 'parachuting' black, often capital poor, people into

39 Kirsten and Vink, 'National report: South Africa', p. 14.

the commercial farming sector. Throughout the 1990s, there was no strategy to promote subdivision so as to make available smaller parcels of land that could suit the needs of the would-be beneficiaries of land reform. Instead, 'commercial farming units [were] usually offered for sale in their entirety, and subdivision [was] rare due to the high transaction costs involved'.[40] This resulted in two parallel trends: the creation of pockets of 'traditional'-type farming in the commercial areas (e.g. in restitution and larger redistribution projects); and the substitution of white commercial farmers with black commercial farmers, who often started farming with onerous debt burdens. Budgetary provision for agricultural support for new farmers was not forthcoming in the 1990s, and official reviews acknowledged a chronic lack of 'post-settlement support', either for the beneficiaries of land reform or for smallholders in the former homelands.

Policy prospects

In addition to these observed effects of policy changes on the structure of agriculture there were a number of other expected consequences. Because the tariff structure afforded greater protection to value-added products, farmers generally sold their products into oligopolistic markets and bought their inputs from oligopsonistic suppliers, and this adversely affected their terms of trade. Commercial farmers countered these effects by increasing multifactor productivity. However, continued improvements in productivity depended on the development of new technologies, which were partly dependent on state funding. The main effects of the decline in direct government spending on agriculture at the national level were evident in the decline in state spending on agricultural research and technology transfer systems. While this decline was a real concern, there is no evidence that private sector spending changed. To the extent that private sector investment substituted for state spending, or even increased beyond that level, there would be little cause for concern. Nevertheless, farmers' ability to remain competitive depends on their ability to increase multifactor productivity.

Finally, an increasing proportion of consumption spending during the 1990s was on the redistribution of access to health, education and social welfare spending (human capital investment) and not on agricultural products. The agricultural sector will benefit in the long run

40 Hall *et al.*, *Final Report*, p. 8. The Subdivision of Agricultural Land Act 70 of 1970 was originally intended to prevent the fragmentation of agricultural holdings into 'uneconomic' units – a concept now largely discredited. Although a law repealing it was passed in 1998, at the time of writing this was yet to be signed into law by the President and so the restrictions remain in effect – though the minister can waive them.

from this shift, as it will lead first to increased consumption of starchy staples, then, as incomes rise, to increased protein consumption and finally to increased consumption of horticultural products.

The 'traditional' sector

Throughout the 1990s about 70 per cent of households in the former homelands had some access to land – but most remained restricted to small plots of one hectare or less. Those with no access to arable land were more likely to be chronically poor.[41] Despite the small-scale nature of production, agriculture in this 'traditional' sector contributed up to a quarter of the nutritional needs of unemployed households.[42] Here, agricultural production was both for direct consumption and for cash income – though only a small proportion of production was marketed. As a result, much of the value of agricultural production in the homelands remained 'invisible' and did not feature in agricultural data.

Livelihoods

The fundamental problem that persisted in the 'traditional' sector was that 'low returns to agriculture have made it difficult to generate the sort of revenue that would permit access to finance, and without access to finance, investment in the items that might increase returns is difficult'.[43] As a result, the 'traditional' sector in the homelands, and also in some land reform projects, was where 'the poor engage in multiple livelihoods primarily as a coping mechanism against poverty, and are not generally able to reinvest scarce cash resources in agriculture'.[44] Similarly, with the exception of commercially oriented land reform projects, land reform beneficiaries' land use tended to 'follow the practice of people in communal areas'.[45] As a result, land reform led to the creation of pockets of 'traditional' types of land use in commercial farming areas, as poor people, having acquired land, engaged in agricultural production while seeking to minimise risk and to find in addition non-agricultural sources of income.

Land and environment

The legacy of planning which reconfigured land use zones – separating residential, arable and grazing land – continued to hamper producers

41 MacIntosh, Xaba and Associates, *Land Issues Scoping Study*, p. 23.
42 *Ibid.*, p. 22.
43 *Ibid.*, p. 26.
44 *Ibid.*, p. 24.
45 Hall *et al.*, *Final Report*, p. 21.

in the former homelands. Spillover from settlements intensified rural overcrowding and the shortage of both arable and grazing land. Here, agriculture had negative environmental externalities, though these were often exaggerated and misunderstood. Farming in both the commercial and 'traditional' sectors can be environmentally hazardous; however, the focus on soil erosion in the homelands (a result of overcrowding, compounded by insecure tenure) deflected attention from the much larger scale of environmental spillover effects from the commercial sector.

In quantitative terms, little is known about the changing nature of agricultural production in the former homelands in the 1990s. This is significant in itself, reflecting the low level of investment in monitoring the traditional sector. However, certain broad trends can be observed.

Trends in crop production

In some regions, a discernible trend was an intensification in crop production in response to new market opportunities.[46] Out-grower schemes, particularly prevalent in the sugar and timber industries, provided new opportunities for farmers in the former homelands, as they enabled farmers in communal areas to have access to markets as well as to a source of inputs and extension services, while providing large corporations with a ready supply of raw inputs for processing industries. This shift towards cash crops offered opportunities for accumulation and commercialisation but may have compromised the production of food crops – with significantly different implications for women and men.[47] It also may have displaced livestock production as grazing lands were used for the production of cash crops.

Poor people in the communal areas generally use land productively and resourcefully, but are subject to considerable constraints. Central challenges still faced by those involved with agriculture in the homelands in the 1990s were market access, insecure land tenure and the demise of farmer support institutions.

Market access and market failures

A lack of access to markets, due partly to poor transport networks but also to an inability to generate surpluses, imposed limits on the commercialisation of 'traditional' agriculture.[48] This had a spatial

46 M. Andrew, A. Ainslie and C. Shackleton, *Land Use and Livelihoods*, Evaluating Land and Agrarian Reform in South Africa No. 8, Programme for Land and Agrarian Studies, University of the Western Cape, 2003, p. 7.

47 D. Mayson, *Joint Ventures*, Evaluating Land and Agrarian Reform in South Africa No. 7, Programme for Land and Agrarian Studies, University of the Western Cape, 2003; MacIntosh, Xaba and Associates, *Land Issues Scoping Study*.

48 MacIntosh, Xaba and Associates, *Land Issues Scoping Study*, p. 26.

dimension: proximity to commercial farming areas and regions with a market infrastructure was a factor. In general, though, producers in the homelands had limited access to downstream industries and received low prices for agricultural produce, particularly livestock, in local markets. Market failure was also prominent in the information and credit markets. Poor people had limited access to credit.[49]

Further enduring constraints to improved production and productivity in the 'traditional' sector included: a shortage of capital to purchase inputs; a shortage of labour, given the high opportunity costs and out-migration of the economically active population; difficulties in obtaining agricultural inputs and tractor services; a lack of fences, resulting in livestock damage to crops, as well as the loss of crops to theft; and a shortage of draught oxen.[50]

Insecure land tenure

The lack of clarity on the status of land rights fuelled uncertainty and conflict over land, which both presented an obstacle to investments in production by users and precluded external investment, infrastructure development and service provision that would support economic development in these regions. The problem was compounded by the breakdown of land administration – historically the domain of native commissioners and magistrates, and later the homeland agricultural bureaucracies – which completely collapsed in the 1990s. Many smallholder farmers continued to live and produce under the jurisdiction of 'tribal authorities', the creation of the Black Administration Act 38 of 1927 and the Bantu Authorities Act 68 of 1951, that occupied the vacuum left by the state and played a major role in allocating land to – and extracting dues from – residents.

Lack of farmer support

The closure of parastatal development corporations in the former homelands (or in some cases their conversion into commercial entities) led to unemployment and reduced support for the 'traditional' sector.[51] The Strauss Commission of Inquiry into rural financial services (1995–96) had judged that the corporations were a considerable drain on public finances. Even so, their closure led to a gap in the provision of services such as input supplies, extension and advice, credit, ploughing services

49 Kirsten and Vink, 'National report: South Africa', p. 2.

50 Andrew *et al.*, *Land Use and Livelihoods*; MacIntosh, Xaba and Associates, *Land Issues Scoping Study*.

51 Kirsten and Vink, 'National report: South Africa', p. 29.

and irrigation infrastructure to small-scale farmers.[52] Services that were down-scaled or withdrawn entirely included agricultural extension and the compulsory livestock dipping programme.[53] While commercial farmers were able to switch to private service providers, the traditional sector had little or no access to such private services and remained reliant on dwindling public services; the traditional sector fell victim to both market failures and policy failures.[54] In this context, livestock production continued to play a role of central importance, not least as a store of wealth.[55]

Policy prospects

'Traditional' agriculture continued to play a crucial role in the livelihoods of many of the poorest South Africans through the 1990s. Its importance was underscored by the trend observed at the end of the decade, of increased rural-to-rural migration as well as a less marked trend of reverse migration, in which labour migrants returned from urban centres in response to job losses and HIV/AIDS, among other factors.[56] In some respects, the volume and value of agricultural production in the traditional sector increased at the same time that the distribution of production and incomes across regions and across households became more uneven.[57] The very limited improvement in conditions in the traditional sector reflects the apparent absence of any state strategy to intervene decisively.

Conclusion

Rapid policy changes in the 1990s led to efficiency gains in commercial agriculture and to increased success in pursuing global market share. These changes were not accompanied by a restructuring of the dualistic agrarian structure through substantial land reform or comprehensive support to farmers in the former homelands. Land reform did not advance sufficiently to make inroads into rural poverty but cannot be expected, by itself, to have absorbed the social fallout from deregulation and liberalisation. While the commercial sector

52 *Ibid.*, p. 14.

53 Andrew *et al.*, *Land Use and Livelihoods*, p. 11.

54 Kirsten and Vink, 'National report: South Africa', p. 22.

55 Palmer and Ainslie, 2002, cited in Andrew *et al.*, *Land Use and Livelihoods*, p. 10.

56 Cross *et al.*, *An Unstable Balance*; C. Cross, 'Why does South Africa need a spatial policy? Population migration, infrastructure and development', *Journal of Contemporary African Studies*, 19(1) (January 2001), 111–128.

57 Andrew *et al.*, *Land Use and Livelihoods*.

underwent dramatic shocks and adjustments, the 'traditional' farming sector in the former homelands continued to suffer neglect and did not inherit the state resources previously reserved for white farmers, although some better-positioned smallholders were able to reap benefits from new market opportunities.

Both agricultural and land policies attempted to transform the agricultural sector, but were influenced by different imperatives. Agricultural policy was guided by the need to end the cosy corporatist relations between the state and organised agriculture, to roll back the extensive public support for an inefficient and highly protected sector, to improve productivity, profitability and competitiveness and to maintain a stable commercial sector. Land reform policy was guided by the need to transform the commercial sector and to introduce new entrants to agriculture, as well as to make available land and related support services for non-agricultural use in rural areas. There are dissonances and tensions between these imperatives. In particular, the dismantling of state support to agriculture – precisely at the time when new entrants needed this to compete with long-established producers – compromised the land reform policies aimed at supporting the growth of a smallholder sector.

The major change in the agricultural sector during the 1990s was the massive growth in agricultural exports alongside robust growth in domestic demand for agricultural goods. Despite receiving diminished support from the state, the sector made impressive strides in productivity and profitability. Diversification of goods and markets bodes well for the future resilience of commercial agriculture. There have been winners and losers from the restructuring process. This has reinforced the divide between the commercial and traditional sectors and reduced the contribution of agriculture to the incomes of the poor. While the sector remained 'healthy' in its own terms, its potential to form the basis for broad-based participation and growth in the rural economy was largely untapped.

While further transformation of the commercial farming sector is needed, this should recognise the many important roles played by agriculture. Transformation needs to be conceptualised as the nexus of multiple positive roles. In particular, in the context of rural poverty and the central importance of agriculture to the rural economy, further policy development needs to focus on the social role of agriculture and to support *socially efficient* uses of state resources and of natural resources in the countryside. There is a need for a vision for a rural economy in which agriculture on a variety of scales plays an important part but in which non-farm economic activities become more salient.

Land reform, if vigorously pursued, can broaden participation in and alter the structure of production in agriculture. To achieve this, policy changes are needed: a clear strategy to respond to the land needs of the poor, promoting subdivision of land; and the provision of farmer support for commercial and non-commercial land users. By the end of the 1990s, the political temperature around land reform in South Africa was on the rise, and this later led to the emergence of the Landless People's Movement (LPM), formed in 2001, which threatened illegal land occupations to pursue their demands that land reform be speeded up. Critical challenges now include budgets for land acquisition, more proactive means of responding to the land needs of the poor and the integration of those institutions that play a role in the programme.

The need for the macro-economic reform of the economy, as well as factors outside the control of the state like international pressure for trade liberalisation and deregulation, were the main determinants of government policy. These considerations continued to influence agricultural and land policy after 2000, though the period of most dramatic change had passed. Agriculture in South Africa in the 1990s consisted, arguably, of two worlds following different trajectories in response to the changes in policy and in the institutional environment. The state's policies and, increasingly, the functioning of markets perpetuated and in some respects strengthened the dualism in agriculture. The transformation agenda for agriculture was therefore only very partially realised. Growth was achieved in the agricultural economy alongside the persistent problems of poverty and inequality in the rural areas. The significance of agriculture in the national economy diminished, but it remained the mainstay of the rural economy and central to prospects for equitable rural development.

23

Mineral and energy policy

Stuart Jones

Introduction

Mining policy is important in South Africa because, ever since the discovery of diamonds towards the end of the third quarter of the nineteenth century, mining developments have been the engine of economic growth. There were two approaches to mining policy in the 1990s, that of the government and that of the industry. The former is the one that usually comes to mind when thinking of policy in South Africa, particularly in the 1990s, when there was so much talk about change and transformation. In response to all this talk there emerged a more vigorous reaction by the Chamber of Mines, which in practice represented all the significant components of the mining industry in South Africa. Both bodies experienced fairly considerable change in the decade. The government's views poured out of the mouths of politicians and were then faithfully echoed by the bureaucrats in the Department of Minerals and Energy. In this respect there was little difference between the pre- and post-1994 periods. The Chamber of Mines, by contrast, underwent more far-reaching changes as it transformed itself from being a body that provided comprehensive services to its member mines and mining houses into a body that focused almost entirely on public relations – a lobby group that aimed to get its views across to the public and the government and in this way influence the formation of policy.

The governmental approach to policy

While the Department of Minerals and Energy did not change in its response to government policy, that policy underwent significant change, even before the impact of a communist-dominated government. The security of property rights began to be questioned and the value of mining rights re-examined. Both the pre-1994 and the post-1994 governments were late converts to the virtues of a market-driven economy. The National Party began moving in that direction in the 1970s; the government under the African National Congress (ANC) did so almost immediately after taking office. But neither was a wholehearted convert to the new political philosophy. The former had welcomed a leading role for the state, but had never considered a state takeover of the entire economy along communist lines. Traditional mining policy, operating in a global market before 1994, reflected this reality.

In the 1990 *Report of the Department of Minerals and Energy* the goal of that Department's Mining Engineers' Branch was said to be 'to promote safe and efficient exploitation of minerals', and that of the Minerals Bureau Branch 'to advise on the promotion of the optimum utilisation of mineral resources'. In similar vein, the goal of the Mineral Laws Administration and Management Services Branch was 'to regulate prospecting for and exploitation of minerals and to render a management service' and that of Geological Survey Branch 'to promote safe and efficient exploitation of Minerals'. Even more explicitly, the second part of the 1990 *Report*, the Government Mining Engineers' report, stated: 'It is the Branch's policy to encourage minerals exploitation development thus stimulating private enterprise in order to strengthen the economy of the Republic of South Africa'. Policy along these lines could have easily fit into the goals of mining policy in Australia or Canada. They were 'econo-centric', reflecting the views of mainstream economics and the fact that mining needed to be profitable and well managed. Implied was the fact that mining companies needed to command large amounts of capital, to have long time horizons and to ensure efficient management. Government policy before 1994, therefore, was built around helping the market to do its job. Benefits to the whole economy would come from the direct taxation of the mines and the linkages that accompanied the growth of the mining industry.

This traditional economic approach changed after 1994, when a host of non-economic considerations representing the views of ANC politicians were tacked on to policy. There was no serious talk of nationalising the mines as Zambia had done – that was an obvious route to ruin – but mining rights were no longer as secure as they had been and mining seemed to be looked upon as a milch cow to finance the dreams of populist politicians. Departmental policy reflected the changing political environment amidst a welter of special committees and special reports. In 2001 the *Integrated Implementation Programme* was published. In the section headed 'Strategic planning process', a re-positioning and restructuring programme was launched to consolidate:

> Standardisation of business processes, especially the incorporation of overall government priorities, such as Rural Development, Gender-based Development, Human Resource Development, HIV-AIDS, Small Scale Mining and Black Economic Empowerment.

This approach to mining reflected the ANC government's love of talk and paper policies that were not likely to be implemented, without killing the goose that laid the golden eggs. The fact that mines needed to provide both a market-related income and a return on and of capital from what was, after all, a diminishing asset was ignored. So too was the need for efficient management and the ability to compete in international markets. A rush into affirmative action was just as likely to lead to inefficiencies in the mining industry as it so obviously did in government departments and government-controlled enterprises such as the electricity supply industry. At a time when closing down gold mines was the market's response to rising costs and a falling gold price, government mining policy moved in the direction of raising the costs of mining operations. The Department of Minerals and Energy provided a good example. Between 1994 and 2000, staff numbers rose by 28 per cent, with the number of blacks increasing by 789 per cent, that of coloureds by 433 per cent and that of Indians by 1,200 per cent. The number of whites employed fell by 32 per cent. The year 2000 ended with the publication of the Minerals Development Bill, which sought 'to place the country's wealth under the custodianship of the state'. It was this Bill that introduced the idea of revoking existing mining rights and making companies reapply for them, and this was a factor in the failure of South Africa to benefit from the worldwide investment boom in mining that occurred in the following decade. Property rights were no longer as secure as in the past.

The element of unreality that suffused the Department may be seen in the manner in which it supervised the provision of electricity. It pompously announced:

> The Department of Mineral and Energy Affairs continues to reform the Electricity Supply Industry and Electricity Distribution in order to maximise potential for adequate, reliable, and low cost electricity.

Its positive achievements were then enumerated. These were: a strategy to develop a world-class jewellery industry, a mine environment management award system, a campaign against blood diamonds, an HIV/AIDS project in Mpumalanga, a strategy for a national electrification programme, completing a consultation process for a strategy for renewable energy and a liquid fuels charter that required existing businesses to hand over 25 per cent of their equity to previously disadvantaged persons, which in practice meant blacks, more often than not affiliated to the ANC. The section on mineral development continued the move into social activism as an essential component of mining policy. Heading the list of activities was mining industry promotion, the purpose of which was not to develop new mines but to maximise job creation through investment forums. Beneficiation focused yet again on another committee to promote a jewellery industry which would have to compete with existing industries in Belgium, Israel and India.

Cyclical volatility and further depletion of the mining industry led to yet another 'social plan to reduce job losses' and a 'coordinated rural development programme' was built around sustainable job creation. State assistance was being given to loss-making gold mines. This was not a new development in South Africa, but when the ERPM mine was closed down an affirmative action company, Enderbrooke Investments (Pty) Ltd, took over and operated the mine with 2,500 employees, 2,000 fewer than were employed by the old ERPM mine. Small-scale mining projects were to be promoted with the Investment in Africa Mining Indaba, held in Cape Town in February 2001. Arguably the best way to promote investment in mining in South Africa would have been to guarantee property rights, to provide an efficient infrastructure and to maintain a fair taxation system; but African politicians preferred to talk about it and to appoint committees that produced reports that would lead to further discussion and in turn further reports.

The crowning achievement of the Department in 2000 was the publication of the new Mineral Development Bill in December 2000. Of the nine items enumerated in the draft, only one was concerned with economic growth; two emphasised the state's rights to ownership of the country's mineral resources and the enforcement of these rights, and six focused upon social and environmental matters. The third item stated that it was policy to promote equitable access to the country's mineral resources to all the people and the fourth that the state should expand the opportunities for historically disadvantaged people to enter the mining industry. The fifth item stated that the aim of policy was to promote the social and economic welfare of all South Africans, the sixth referred to providing security of tenure in respect of prospecting and mining operations, and the ninth one stated that it was the government's policy to ensure that the holders of mining rights contributed to the socio-economic development of the areas in which they were operating. Mineral resources were also to be developed in an orderly and ecologically sustainable manner. Government policy as enunciated by the Department of Minerals and Energy in 2000 had moved a long way from its 1990 goal of promoting 'the safe and efficient exploitation of minerals' and advising on the 'optimum utilisation of mineral resources'.

The industry approach to policy

The Chamber of Mines maintained close relations with government policy makers and was able to influence policy making to some extent. In 1990 its own bureaucratic structure was not very different from that of the Department of Minerals and Energy. It was, for example, top heavy with committees. Offsetting this were its obligations to the private sector, which financed it, even though the private sector involved was a cartel, whose membership included other cartels (mining houses). The Chamber was divided into five sections, dealing with corporate services, recruitment services, external affairs, health care services and operations. The first of these involved the Chamber in many of the management functions of individual mines, while the second involved close relations with the government of the day, as a result of the Employment Bureau of Africa's monopoly of mine recruitment.[1] Health care services involved the operation of a hospital and convalescent home; operations, the hands-on management of the Chamber of Mines Research Organisation, the Rand Refinery, the Rand Mutual Assurance Company, the Nuclear Fuels Corporation (which marketed uranium) and a number of safety and technical services. It was in the External Affairs Division that the Chamber was most closely involved with the government and policy making.

The External Affairs Division covered industrial relations, legal services, public affairs and communications, education and economic and statistical services. Two of the sections, legal services and public relations, brought the Chamber into the arena of policy making, and in 1990, when the government was committed to market-friendly policies, this gave the Chamber considerable influence. This changed after 1994, when the government represented a tripartite alliance between the ANC, the South African Communist Party and the Congress of South African Trade Unions.

In 1990 the legal services section had an important part to play because of concern over the impending imposition of new taxes, such the value-added tax (VAT) and coal levies, the perennial question of customs duties on essential equipment for the mines, and ring-fencing. The Chamber argued that ring-fencing discouraged investment in South Africa. Of particular concern in 1990 was the future of mineral rights, which of course was still a matter of concern in 2000.

1 The Employment Bureau of Africa (TEBA) was the new name for the Witwatersrand Native Labour Association. All black mine workers were recruited by TEBA.

In 1990, the new Deposit Taking Intermediaries Bill was threatening the ability of the mining houses to control funds raised by associated companies. Since 1965 mining houses had not been regarded as operating banking businesses. On the question of housing, the Chamber supported the repeal of the Group Areas Act, which had prevented the building of permanent houses for black employees in white areas.

External relations also included the thorny area of industrial relations, in which a major agreement was signed in May 1990. This was an accord between the South African Employers Consultative Committee (Saccola), the National Council of Trade Unions (Nactu) and the Congress of South African Trade Unions (Cosatu). It was the result of two and a half years of discussions that had begun when P. W. Botha was still the country's President. It was an agreement to modify the 1956 Labour Relations Act on the recommendation of the National Manpower Commission, which led to a Conciliation Board being set up in August 1990. The Board established a working party with five tasks: to agree on a definition of racial discrimination, to issue a declaration of intent to remove racial discrimination, to agree on a programme of action on how to remove racial discrimination, to agree on a charter or manifesto of race discrimination and to establish a mechanism for dealing with discriminatory practices. It brought an end to legally enforced racial discrimination at the workplace. A skills crisis as well as a political crisis lay behind this breakthrough in labour relations that was to overshadow policy makers throughout the decade. The 1990 *Annual Report* of the Chamber of Mines put it bluntly:

> South Africa is in a manpower crisis largely due to the failure of the country's education system to produce school leavers with the necessary academic background and work skills to meet the country's manpower requirements.

(Little had changed in this regard by the time of writing – evidence that the problem was deep rooted.) Nevertheless, in the last years of the 'old South Africa' significant steps were taken to bring an end to discrimination in the mining labour force and in introducing what might be termed normalcy into industrial relations.

Finally in 1990, the External Affairs Division of the Chamber included a public affairs and communications section, which maintained representatives in London, Bonn, Washington and Brussels to present a positive view of investment in South Africa and to counter the ban on new investment in the country and sanctions on the export of coal and Krugerrands. The Chamber was successful, aided of course by the installation of the new De Klerk government in South Africa, when the European Economic Community lifted its ban on investments in South

Africa in December 1990. In practice, though, it is hard to believe that the bans on investment in South African mines had had much effect at a time when exchange control had locked capital in the country and been the driving force that converted all the major mining houses into unwieldy conglomerates. Their problem had been a lack of opportunity to invest in mining outside South Africa, not a lack of capital inside the country. On the question of investment and exports, the policies of the government and the Chamber were in full agreement.

By the end of the decade the role of the Chamber was much diminished. Major corporations had moved their headquarters to London to free themselves from the constraints of exchange control and what was perceived as a more hostile political environment in South Africa. The traditional mining houses were unbundled and control of mining operations was given to individual mines. In the process, the Chamber was itself transformed into a more focused vehicle for public relations.

The changes occurred in 1996, at a time when its membership included five mining finance houses, 29 gold mines, 17 coal mines and 18 other mines, from traditional diamond mines to copper and platinum mines. Two major decisions were taken:

- to refocus the Chamber as the principal advocate of major policy decisions endorsed by mining employers;
- to end the Chamber's direct involvement and financial subsidisation of industry services.

These decisions were implemented in July, when the non-core activities of the Chamber were consolidated into the Chamber of Mines Services (Pty) Ltd and were to be run as independent businesses. Included were the Rand Mines Hospital, the Rand Refinery, the Nuclear Fuels Corporation, the Rand Mutual Assurance Company and the recruitment body, TEBA. The 'new Chamber' quickly developed close relations with the government. After Marcel Golding had been replaced by Duma Nkosi as Chairman of Parliament's Portfolio Committee on Mineral and Energy Affairs in February 1997, Committee members were routinely fêted and the gravy train took off. Beginning in 1997, Nkosi led delegations of parliamentarians to Elandsrand Gold Mine and the Rand Refinery. A few months later they were being taken on a study tour of India and Europe. These attempts to educate Members of Parliament did not prevent the Chamber from criticising the new labour policy that was emerging. The Basic Conditions of Employment Bill was described as 'prescriptive of best conditions of employment',[2] which the Chamber argued should be left to collective bargaining. The government's policy

2 See *Annual Report*, Chamber of Mines, 1996–97.

on unskilled and semi-skilled migrants was also criticised. Taxation policy was also an issue, with the Chamber once again attacking ring-fencing and arguing for taxation only on profits.

By the end of the decade the Chamber of Mines was not only transformed but was also less influential than it had been before 1994. Policy decisions were discussed at length by committees of Parliament; but the feeling remained that key decisions were being taken by ANC committees rather than by Parliament. The proportional representation system of government in practice reduced the power of individual Members of Parliament and hence the institution of Parliament itself and increased that of the party's hierarchy. As a lobbyist for the private sector, the Chamber needed to get its message through to the party's top people, but learning how to do this took time and the Chamber was only just beginning to adapt to the realities of the new political dispensation by the end of the decade.

Conclusion

Policy on the mining industry after 1994 was dominated by the government's social policies and the growing problem of rising unemployment. The labour laws pushed through Parliament by Tito Mboweni as the minister responsible for labour affairs was the result. They were not drawn up with the mining industry in mind, but they probably had more effect upon mining than did any other piece of legislation. And they were not alone. They were followed by all the social policies of the government, which were enshrined in Mineral Development Bill of 2000. Mining policy was in danger of becoming a wish list for things that were desirable rather than a means to efficient production. It led Eskom to purchase some of its coal from small enterprises owned by the previously disadvantaged, who were unable to maintain quality control. This contributed to the supply-side failure of electricity a few years later. This less economic approach to mining coincided with a threat to property rights in the form of the revocation of mineral rights. These ominous developments, moreover, took place at a time when the cost of mining gold was rising faster than the number of employees. Between 1989 and 1999 working costs per kilogram of gold rose by 111.3 per cent, but the kilograms of gold per employee by only 92.3 per cent. Global commodity prices were not particularly favourable to large-scale investment in mining projects in the 1990s, despite the rapid growth underway in China. In these circumstances, government policy was at best neutral, at worst harmful. The response of the private sector was relatively low key. The major mining houses hastened to transfer their bases to London, leaving the Chamber of Mines to transform itself into a public relations body that sought to bring the government's attention to some of the more harmful consequences of its policies, while at the same emphasising the Chamber's commitment to improving basic education, the health and the safety of its members' workforce and to caring for the environment. The last mentioned was a response to the increasing number of overseas shareholders.

The new Chamber of Mines that emerged in 1997 remained a vigorous spokesperson for the mining industry, yet the impression remains its influence had diminished *pari passu* with the decline in the numbers employed by the gold mining industry that had originally brought it into existence. After 2000 the gold mining industry was still very important; but it was no longer the country's engine of growth and the industry's influence over policy reflected the change in its relative standing in the economy. Conversely, policy had little impact upon the fortunes of the gold mining industry outside the sphere of labour costs, with the main determinant being geology and the gold price.

24

Environmental policy

Anthony B. Lumby

Introduction

By the last decade of the twentieth century, the debate surrounding the urgent need to implement sustainable development in both developed and developing economies was of particular relevance to South Africa. Given the racial and class divisions that characterised all facets of South Africa's development, the economy contained some elements to be found in more developed economies as well as elements more characteristic of less developed economies.[1] Furthermore, South Africa had not been exempted from the global trend in environmental degradation: that is, a long phase of environmental decay that had become particularly grave during the last 50 years of the century.[2]

As the history of environmental degradation in South Africa is well documented elsewhere,[3] our attention here is limited to highlighting the major areas of concern in 'building the foundation for sustainable development in South Africa'.[4] This is followed by a discussion of the development of the concept of sustainable development and the debate

1 J. Nattrass, *The South African Economy: Its Growth and Change* (2nd edition), Oxford University Press, 1989, pp. 143–148.

2 J. M. Erskine, 'Ecology and development', *Development Southern Africa*, 2(1) (1985), pp. 70–73.

3 See, for example, R. F. Fuggle and M. A. Rabie (eds), *Environmental Concerns in South Africa*, Juta, 1983; W. Beinart (ed.), Special issue on the politics of conservation in South Africa, *Journal of Southern African Studies*, 15(2) (1989); and R. A. Preston-Whyte and G. Howe (eds), *Rotating the Cube: Environmental Strategies for the 1990s*, Indicator Press, 1990.

4 G. Noble, *Building the Foundation for Sustainable Development in South Africa*, Department of Environmental Affairs, 1991. The Noble report was commissioned by the Department of Environmental Affairs for submission to the United Nations Conference on Environment and Development (the so-called 'Earth Summit') held in Rio de Janeiro in June 1992.

over the use of economic instruments versus direct regulation for guiding policy implementation. Thereafter, the focus is placed on the role of the state in environmental issues and the shaping of environmental policy during the 1990s.

Environmental issues in South Africa: an overview

It is well known that South Africa is richly endowed with a wide variety of mineral resources, and that the export of raw, semi-processed and processed minerals played a crucial role in South Africa's economic growth during the twentieth century. During the 1990s, South Africa had the largest known deposits of gold, chromium, manganese, vanadium and the platinum group metals, as well as rich supplies of coal, diamonds, zinc, asbestos, iron ore, lead and uranium. It has been calculated that, directly and indirectly, mining contributed some 15 per cent to South Africa's GDP and that approximately 40 per cent of its total exports came from mining.[5] It is also well known that mining (and therefore a significant portion of South Africa's growth) was dependent upon the exploitation of non-renewable resources. Furthermore, on the basis of the mining technology that existed in 1990, it was estimated that the gold mining industry had a future life expectancy of no more than 30 years.[6] Ultimately, therefore, a transition to a renewable resource base was needed. Meanwhile, deep-level mining of low-grade ore resulted in the gold mining industry being one of the largest consumers of water and electricity in the country.[7] In the case of coal, South Africa's coal deposits were estimated at 116 million tons in 1982, of which 58 million tons were regarded as extractable. While these reserves were considered sufficient to meet South Africa's domestic and export needs for another 100 years, approximately 50 per cent of local coal consumption was used for electricity generation and as such constituted a major source of environmental pollution.[8]

Indeed, the major environmental problems associated with mining appear to have received little attention until recent years. The uncontrolled use of water by the mining industry led to the depletion of ground-water supplies and to the drying up of wetland systems,

5 Nattrass, *The South African Economy*, pp. 145–146.

6 *Towards Sustainable Development in South Africa*, Environmental Monitoring Group, 1991, p. 12.

7 Noble, *Building the Foundation for Sustainable Development*, pp. 45, 76.

8 A. A. Eberhard and A. T. Williams, *Renewable Energy Resources and Technology Development in South Africa*, Elan Press, 1988, p. 10.

while mining also contributed significantly to the pollution of both surface- and ground-water resources.[9] The mining industry was also a major source of air pollution, such as arsenic from gold-bearing ore in Mpumalanga Province and sulphur fumes from the country's coal-mines. Furthermore, by the early 1990s it was estimated that the mining industry was responsible for no less than 80 per cent of all industrial waste generated in South Africa.[10]

Rural land use constitutes another major area of environmental concern. Although the agricultural sector in South Africa is characterised by a remarkable degree of diversity, it is customary to identify three broad subsectors: 'white' commercial agriculture; the semi-subsistent agriculture in the former African 'homelands'; and commercial forestry. White commercial farming is generally believed to be efficient and productive. Indeed, Noble has pointed out, with considerable pride, that 'the wide variety of climate conditions – from subtropical through Mediterranean to semi-desert – permits farmers to grow virtually every known crop and rear and graze cattle (for beef and dairy products), sheep (for wool and mutton) and goats (for mohair and meat)'.[11] However, less than 12 per cent of South Africa's arable land is suitable for dry-land crop production, with the result that white commercial farming is inefficient in terms of energy and water use, and has had to be maintained by a system of financial support from the state.[12] In general terms, the result has been environmental degradation through widespread soil erosion, over-grazing and, as a legacy of the 'green revolution' of the 1970s, the over-use of artificial fertilisers, pesticides and herbicides.[13]

It is in South African agriculture, perhaps more than any other facet of the country's economy and society, that the unequal access to natural resources is to be found. 'From the mid-seventeenth century onwards', wrote Mamphela Ramphele,[14] 'black farmers and pastoralists were gradually dispossessed of most of their land through armed conquest, spurious treaties and economic pressure'. This pattern was formalised in the Land Acts of 1913 and 1936, which restricted black land ownership to 13 per cent of the total land mass. Thereafter, the cornerstone of

9 J. Ridl, 'Of mines and men', in R. A. Preston-Whyte and G. Howe (eds), *Rotating the Cube: Environmental Strategies for the 1990s*, Indicator Press, 1990, pp. 78–79.

10 *Hazardous Waste in South Africa*, Council for Scientific and Industrial Research, 1992, p. 15.

11 Noble, *Building the Foundation for Sustainable Development*, p. 73.

12 *Towards Sustainable Development*, pp. 14–15.

13 M. Laing, 'Jekyll-and-Hyde herbicides', in R. A. Preston-Whyte and G. Howe (eds), *Rotating the Cube: Environmental Strategies for the 1990s*, Indicator Press, 1990, pp. 41–44.

14 M. Ramphele, 'New day rising', in M. Ramphele and C. McDowell (eds), *Restoring the Land*, Panos, 1991, p. 3.

the National Party government's apartheid policy from 1948 onwards was the African 'homelands' system, buttressed by massive forced removals.[15] Demographic pressure on limited natural resources in the former 'homelands' wreaked environmental disaster through deforestation, soil erosion and desertification.[16]

Rural environmental degradation also had an effect on the urban environment. With the former 'homelands' unable to support their swollen populations, the repeal of influx regulations and pass laws in 1986 opened the floodgates of black urbanisation. The resultant overcrowding in urban townships led to the mushrooming of squatter settlements in most metropolitan centres, accompanied by inevitable environmental decay.[17]

Within the commercial forestry sector, which is largely under the control of the state and a few large private enterprises, 'The history of the indigenous forests is ... a tragic story of mismanagement, wastage and over-exploitation'.[18] Rapid population growth, especially in the overcrowded former 'homelands', forced inhabitants to over-exploit forest resources for firewood, hut poles, food and fodder. The result was yet further deforestation, increased water run-off and soil erosion.[19] Elsewhere, large-scale afforestation with alien species (especially eucalyptus and pine) was undertaken without due regard for their wider environmental impacts.[20]

Industry, too, contributed its share to environmental degradation. The growth of secondary industry was an outstanding feature of the development of the South African economy during the twentieth century, especially after the adoption of a policy of tariff protection in 1925. Indeed, after 1965, the manufacturing sector's contribution to South Africa's GDP was greater than the combined contributions of the mining and agricultural sectors.[21] By the 1990s, the three largest subsectors within the manufacturing sector, in order of size, were: metals, metal products, machinery and equipment; petroleum products,

15 *Ibid.*, pp. 3–4.

16 Erskine, 'Ecology and development', pp. 72–73; and F. Wilson, 'A land out of balance', in M. Ramphele and C. McDowell (eds), *Restoring the Land*, Panos, 1991, pp. 31–36.

17 The Urban Foundation estimated that, between 1985 and 2010, 9 million blacks (or an average of 360,000 per annum) moved into the urban areas.

18 Noble, *Building the Foundation for Sustainable Development*, p. 109.

19 *Towards Sustainable Development*, pp. 14–15.

20 H. A. Witt, Trees, *Forests and Plantations: An Economic, Social and Environmental Study of Tree-Growing in Natal, 1860–1960*, unpublished PhD thesis, University of Natal, 1998, pp. 363–369.

21 A. B. Lumby, 'Industrial history in South Africa: an exploratory survey', *South African Journal of Economic History*, 10(1) (March 1995), pp. 3–4.

chemicals, rubber and plastics; and food, beverages and tobacco. A study by the Council for Scientific and Industrial Research (CSIR) submitted the first two of these subsectors to input–output analysis in order to assess their direct and indirect usage of non-renewable resources and their pollution effects.[22] This study revealed not only that these industrial subsectors were heavily dependent on non-renewable resources, but also that they were major sources of environmental pollution (after mining and electricity generation).

It is evident from the foregoing description that some of South Africa's most serious environmental problems arose from the established pattern of energy use. Given the limited supplies of water as a source of energy, approximately 84 per cent of South Africa's energy needs were met by coal, half of which was used to generate electricity.[23] Although most of South Africa's power stations were fitted with electrostatic precipitators to remove dust and ash particulates, they were not all equipped with flue-gas scrubbers to remove sulphur and nitrogen oxides, which, when combined with water vapour, contribute to 'acid rain'.[24] Furthermore, the concentration of South Africa's coal reserves and electricity generation in Mpumalanga Province, combined with meteorological conditions and topographical features in the region, made this area one of the worst air pollution regions in the world.[25] To make matters worse, 'half of South Africa's agriculturally productive land and commercial forests and a quarter of its surface water runoff are in this region giving rise to considerable concern about the environmental and economic impact of acid rain'.[26]

Although the foregoing sketch does not exhaust the list of issues relating to environmental degradation in South Africa – other factors include inadequate conservation of marine resources and excessive marine pollution, coastal mismanagement and low levels of community health[27] – it is abundantly clear that South Africa faced a daunting task in the implementation of sustainable development. Nevertheless, sustainable development has been accepted as the fundamental objective

22 See Noble, *Building the Foundation for Sustainable Development*, pp. 64–66.

23 B. Huntley, R. Siegfried and C. Sunter, *South African Environments into the 21st Century*, Human and Rousseau, 1989, p. 64.

24 *Ibid.*, pp. 64–68.

25 P. D. Tyson, F. W. Kruger and C. W. Louw, *Atmospheric Pollution and Its Implications in the Eastern Transvaal Highveld*, National Scientific Programmes Unit, Council for Scientific and Industrial Research, 1988.

26 *Towards Sustainable Development*, p. 33.

27 See, for example, Noble, *Building the Foundation for Sustainable Development*, pp. 50–57, 145–154, 158–162.

of environmental policy, and it is recognised that 'any significant movement towards the goal of sustainable development will require major intervention by the state'.[28] It has to be said, however, that over the years South Africa has developed a plethora of laws and international agreements relating to the environment. Therefore, there appears to be a paradox: despite the state's role in enacting a relatively sophisticated body of environmental legislation, there remains an urgent need for the state to intervene in order to promote a shift towards sustainable development. The following section provides an overview of the development of the concept of sustainable development.

The development of sustainable development

It appears that the term 'sustainable development' was first fashioned in the *World Conservation Strategy* unveiled in 1980,[29] although this strategy received its most popular exposition in the well known Brundtland report of 1987.[30] The rather narrow ecological interpretation of sustainable development adopted in the *World Conservation Strategy* was rejected by the Brundtland report in favour of a deceptively simple definition: 'Sustainable development is development which meets the needs of the present, without compromising the ability of future generations to meet their own needs.'[31] This is usually taken to mean that the natural capital stock – that is, the total stock of all environmental resources – should not diminish over time, and that the achievement of this objective may necessitate some trade-off with economic growth.[32]

It is not always clear, however, whether this strategy means the preservation of the existing natural capital stock or the optimum stock level, an issue of particular relevance for many developing countries where existing stocks are significantly below the optimum.[33] In similar

28 *Towards Sustainable Development*, p. 13.

29 The *World Conservation Strategy*, International Union for the Conservation of Nature and Natural Resources, 1980, defined sustainable development as 'the maintenance of essential ecological processes and genetic diversity, and the sustainable utilisation of species and ecosystems'.

30 World Commission on Environment and Development, *Our Common Future*, Oxford University Press, 1987.

31 *Ibid.*, p. 8.

32 See, for example, M. Redclift, *Sustainable Development: Exploring the Contradictions*, Methuen, 1987; and R. K. Turner (ed.), *Sustainable Environmental Management*, Westview Press, 1988.

33 David Pearce, Anil Markandya and Edward B. Barbier, *Blueprint for a Green Economy*, Earthscan, 1989, pp. 6–7.

vein, it is not clear whether maintenance of the natural capital stock means either a constant physical stock or a constant economic value of the stock.[34] A constant physical stock may be applicable to renewable resources, but is obviously inapplicable to non-renewable resources (unless there is zero utilisation of these resources or one can be sure of the development of backstop technology). On the other hand, maintaining a constant economic value of the stock would depend upon market forces and provide little meaningful information on physical supply. Another area of debate concerns the notion of discounting: while the private discount rate is generally rejected as harmful to the interests of future generations, there is no unanimity over accepting a (lower) social discount rate.[35] Furthermore, advocates of sustainable development have tended to issue lists of desirable priorities – such as enhanced productivity, stability, equitability and sustainability – without explaining how conflicts between these priorities are to be resolved.[36]

Notwithstanding these difficulties, Barbier's research provides eloquent testimony to the relevance of sustainable development for both developed and developing countries.[37] The historical emphasis on 'resource-intensive, growth-oriented development ... in the handful of "successfully" industrialised advanced economies' is not only inimical to inter-generational and intra-generational equity, argued Barbier, but it is also unsustainable in the long run:

> If advanced economies seek to increase economic growth in this manner without adequately analysing the trade-offs in terms of long-term sustainability then problems of high unemployment, resource scarcity, environmental degradation and misallocation of capital resources will get worse.[38]

In the case of developing economies, with their characteristic dependency on exports of natural resources, the adoption of sustainable development is seen as imperative.[39] While it is acknowledged that

34 D. Hall and J. Hall, 'Concepts and measures of natural resource scarcity', *Journal of Environmental Economics and Management*, 11 (1984), pp. 363–369.

35 See Pearce, Markandya and Barbier, *Blueprint for a Green Economy*.

36 See C. Tisdell, 'Economics, ecology, sustainable agricultural systems and development', *Development Southern Africa*, 2(4) (1985), p. 517.

37 E. B. Barbier, *New Approaches to Environmental and Resource Economics*, Springer, 1987.

38 E. B. Barbier, *Economics, Natural Resource Scarcity and Development*, Earthscan, 1989, pp. 189–190.

39 See Barbier, *New Approaches*, pp. 194–195, tables 8.2 and 8.3. In 21 low-income economies and 21 lower-middle income economies, primary exports constituted between 50 and 100 per cent of total exports in the mid-1980s. The situation in most of these countries was (and still is) complicated by their heavy dependency on export earnings to finance their growing external debts.

demographic pressure, unequal access to resources and poverty have led inexorably to the over-exploitation of natural resources, Barbier warned that there is the danger that, in the absence of sustainable development, 'the successful transformation from a resource-dependent to a fully developed economy may not be complete before the resource base and its essential environmental functions are irreversibly degraded and depleted'.[40]

'Command and control' versus economic instruments

Much of the scholarly work on environmental economics has focused on the issue of limited natural resources and the implications of this for economic growth. However, the more recent literature has argued that the critical environmental problem has been the pollution associated with waste disposal.[41] In fact, these two major categories of environmental problem – excessive natural resource depletion and excessive waste generation – are not independent. Through the physical law of the conservation of mass, materials extracted from the environment must be returned there in approximately equal mass. Thus the rate of natural resource usage has crucial implications for the rate of production of waste and, where these are not in assimilable amounts or forms, for pollution.

Nevertheless, the latter-day concentration on pollution is fully justified. Ecologists have illuminated the complexity and diversity of natural ecosystems and humanity's dependence upon them. In addition, they have drawn attention to the urgent need to curb pollution because of the existence of undetermined 'threshold effects', beyond which ecosystems can experience dramatic and perhaps even irreversible decline.[42] Furthermore, while the damage costs of pollution may be extremely difficult to measure, the revealed trend is unambiguously serious. According to admittedly incomplete estimates, the deterioration in environmental quality accounts for a loss of up to 5 per cent in potential GNP for the developed economies, while the figure for less developed economies may be as high as 10 per cent.[43] Thus there are compelling economic reasons – as well as related ecological, ethical and aesthetic ones – why pollution should be controlled.

40 *Ibid.*, p. 193.

41 M. L. Cropper and W. E. Oates, 'Environmental economics: a survey', *Journal of Economic Literature*, 30(2) (June 1992), pp. 675–740.

42 Barbier, *Economics, Natural Resource Scarcity and Development*, pp. 39–55.

43 D. Hay (ed.), *Itala Environmental Policy Workshop*, Institute of Natural Resources, 1992, pp. 14–15.

While there is general agreement on the need to curb pollution, the current debate between (and among) environmental economists and environmental policy makers concerns the type of controls to be employed: direct regulation or market-related instruments? Throughout the history of pollution control, direct regulation (commonly referred to as 'command and control') has been the dominant approach and, as shown below, South Africa was no exception to this trend. Nevertheless, the development of alternative market-related measures has been greeted with a growing chorus of approval from the ranks of interested economists. Broadly speaking, the pricing techniques advocated by economists fall into two groups: either taxes are imposed, or subsidies given, to curb pollution; or permits allowing predetermined levels of pollution are issued and then traded among interested parties.[44]

Role of the state in environmental management in South Africa

Even in a free market system, the state has a role to play, such as the enforcement of individual property rights and the laws of contract. In the case of environmental matters, the state's role may be extended to 'remedy' market failures by the imposition of taxes/subsidies, marketable emission permits and environmental standards. If, however, the free market approach to environmental problems is rejected in favour of sustainable development, then substantially increased state intervention will be required in order to promote both inter-generational and intra-generational equity. In South Africa's case, environmental issues have been (directly or indirectly) the subject of a wide variety of legislative measures: some 60 parliamentary Acts and several hundred provincial ordinances and local by-laws, as well as some 30 international agreements.[45] Indeed, the Environmental Monitoring Group, a body that has been severely critical of environmental conditions in South Africa, readily acknowledged that South Africa had 'a relatively sophisticated body of environmental law.'[46] How, then, does one account for the prevalence of widespread environmental decay?

At the legislative level, the explanation lies in at least three factors: the nature of South African law; the historical fragmentation of environmental legislation; and the inadequate enforcement of this legislation.

44 T. Tietenberg, *Environmental Economics and Policy*, Prentice Hall, 1994, pp. 219–223.

45 J. Glazewski, A. Dodson and H. Smith, 'Tightening up the law', in M. Ramphele and C. McDowell (eds), *Restoring the Land*, Panos, 1991, pp. 140–143.

46 *Towards Sustainable Development*, p. 75.

South Africa's legal system is based on Roman Dutch law, which is not well suited to the resolution of environmental problems: Roman Dutch common law is generally regarded as strong on private law but weak on public law (which is the legal arena for the most pressing environmental issues).[47] The emphasis in private law on the protection of individual rights means that it is only where those rights coincide with an environmental concern that their enforcement will serve the cause of environmental conservation.[48] Thus the common law solution to South Africa's environmental problems has been an inadequate one, and reliance has had to be placed on statutory regulation.

As noted above, there has been no shortage of statutory provisions dealing with environmental issues in South Africa, but those provisions were scattered throughout many pieces of legislation, administered by several government departments. For example, prior to 1998, pollution control was governed by no less than 30 Acts administered by nine government departments and all of the provincial administrations.[49] This thoroughly inefficient, not to say ineffective, means of legislative control is perhaps partly explained by the fact that it was not until the 1970s that the government began to recognise the importance of environmental issues,[50] but perhaps it should also be borne in mind that governments are not the 'purposive, integrated actors' that economists and environmentalists expect them to be.[51]

Whatever the reason, the Department of Environmental Affairs was not solely, or even primarily, responsible for environmental matters. Unfortunately, this highly unsatisfactory situation was perpetuated in the much-vaunted Environmental Conservation Act 73 of 1989. In terms of section 2(a) of this Act, the Minister of Environmental Affairs could act only with the consent of all other government departments whose interests might be affected. Given the conflict of interests between and within many government departments (for example, the Department of Minerals and Energy was responsible for promoting mining interests and regulating mining pollution; similarly, the Department of Agriculture was responsible for promoting agricultural production and

47 M. A. Rabie, 'Legal remedies for environmental protection', *Comparative and International Law Journal of Southern Africa*, 5(3) (1972), p. 280.

48 M. A. Rabie and C. Eckhart, '*Locus standi*: the administration's shield and the environmentalist's shackle', *Comparative and International Law Journal of Southern Africa*, 9(2) (1976), pp. 158–160; and W. Bray, '*Locus standi* in environmental law', *Comparative and International Law Journal of Southern Africa*, 22(1) (1989), pp. 37–38.

49 Noble, *Building the Foundation for Sustainable Development*, pp. 187–191.

50 *White Paper on a National Policy Regarding Environmental Conservation*, Department of Water Affairs, Forestry and Environmental Conservation, 1980, pp. 5–6.

51 J. S. Dryzek, *Rational Ecology: Environment and Political Economy*, Blackwell, 1987, p. 84.

monitoring the use of artificial fertilisers, pesticides and herbicides), the arbitrary legislative decomposition of environmental problems resulted in 'problem displacement' rather than 'problem solution'.

Another stumbling block was the content of some of this legislation. It is often said that the language of law is the language of rights, but in South Africa's case this did not always extend to the right to know. For example, sections 1 and 2 of the Atmospheric Pollution Act 45 of 1965 stipulated that information relating to air pollution was a 'confidential matter' between the industries concerned and the Department of Health. Elsewhere, section 17 of the Hazardous Substances Act 15 of 1973 made disclosure of information a criminal offence. While it is true that the Environmental Conservation Act of 1989 improved the situation by making it possible to request reasons for decisions reached in terms of the Act, only those persons 'whose interests are affected' were entitled to do so. In addition to the difficulty of establishing *locus standi*, it is arguable that this provision conflicted with section 32 of the Act, which encouraged the involvement of non-governmental organisations.

A more general, though no less serious, criticism of the content of South Africa's environmental legislation relates to ambiguity and the extent to which issues were left to the relevant minister's discretion. The laws governing environmental matters can be only as effective as their substantive content, and the latter has not been a strong feature of environmental legislation in South Africa. To cite one of many examples, section 2(b) of the Sea Fishery Act 12 of 1988 states that the purpose of the Act is 'the promotion, protection and sustained utilisation of the sea, its living resources and derivatives thereof', a statement that has no real meaning in law. Similarly, section 2(1)(b) of the Environmental Conservation Act of 1989 stipulated that the minister 'may determine the general policy' relating to environmental matters, but in view of the fact that successive ministers failed to 'determine the general policy', the Act had no purpose or effect.[52]

Another explanation for the apparent paradox lies in the failure to enforce environmental legislation. The problem of inadequate enforcement is widely cited in the literature, and is accompanied by the usual recommendations for greater funds for policing and increased fines.[53]

52 P. D. Glavovic, 'Some thoughts of an environmental lawyer on the implications of the Environmental Conservation Act of 1989: a case of missed opportunities', *South African Law Journal*, 107 (1990), pp. 108–109. See also R. Lyster, 'The protection of environmental rights', *South African Law Journal*, 109 (1992), p. 518.

53 See, for example, *Towards Sustainable Development*, pp. 74–75; and Noble, *Building the Foundation for Sustainable Development*, p. 194.

However, unless enforcement and penalties are applied reasonably consistently both within and between countries, yet further 'problem displacement' may result. Thus, to cite a US example, 'a large segment of California's furniture industry, faced with tougher emissions standards, fled to Mexico, where pollution laws are not enforced'.[54] In South Africa's case, even the limited enforcement of environmental standards (along with the incentives for industrial decentralisation) resulted in 'problem displacement' to some of the former 'homelands', and even beyond South Africa's borders.[55] The latter highlights a particularly thorny problem: the effective enforcement of the multitude of international agreements on the environment. Given the well known difficulties relating to the enforcement of international law, Dryzek drew the pessimistic conclusion that 'transboundary pollution and general abuse of the ecosphere constitute perhaps the most intractable class of ecological problems'.[56]

All of the foregoing problems received detailed consideration in the President's Council's *Report on a National Environmental Management System*, published in October 1991. The report called for a declaration of environmental policy along the lines of sustainable development and recommended that the Minister of Environmental Affairs should not have to consult other departments before environmental legislation could be enacted or enforced. It also recommended the increased involvement of non-governmental organisations, as well as freer access to environmental information. Furthermore, the report recognised the urgent need to rationalise the myriad legislative provisions, and suggested that the statutory revisions should make 'integrated environmental management' legally enforceable. However, it also recommended that the streamlined legislation still be administered by several government departments, which would undermine the authority and independence of the Ministry of Environmental Affairs. Furthermore, whereas numerous calls were made for the entrenchment of environmental rights in the constitution, the report equivocated on this issue.[57] In the event, the implementation of the recommendations of the President's Council report was overtaken by negotiations for a new constitution for South Africa and the run-up to the 1994 election.

The African National Congress (ANC) government, elected in 1994, strongly favoured a policy of 'sustainable growth' – that is, economic

54 D. Moberg, 'Environment and markets', *Dissent*, 38:4 (September 1991), at p. 515.

55 F. Kruger, 'The Ciskei: dumping ground of the Eastern Cape', in M. Ramphele and C. McDowell (eds), *Restoring the Land*, Panos, 1991.

56 Dryzek, *Rational Ecology*, p. 178.

57 *Report of the Three Committees of the President's Council on a National Environmental Management System*, 1991, pp. 268–280.

growth that makes 'rational use of our natural resources'.[58] Furthermore, section 23 of South Africa's new constitution, adopted in 1996, makes specific reference to the state's commitment to the protection of the environment.[59] In line with this commitment, the South African government ratified the United Nations Framework Convention on Climate Change in 1997. Thereafter, attention was focused on the need to revise both the Water Act 54 of 1956 and the Environmental Conservation Act 73 of 1989.

National Water Act 36 of 1998

One of the earliest pieces of South African legislation on water use – the Irrigation and Conservation of Waters Act 8 of 1912 – was concerned with the regulation of irrigation water for agricultural purposes. This Act reflected both English legal principles and the domination of the economy by the agricultural sector, so that the rights of riparian owners were entrenched. However, the growth of industrial development in South Africa during the 1930s and 1940s gave rise to conflicts, exacerbated by the government's policy of prioritising water use for farming. As a result, the Water Act 54 of 1956 was enacted in order to provide for a more equitable distribution of water between agricultural and industrial users. However, the interests of the broader South African population – especially the rural poor – were largely ignored. At this stage, there did not appear to be an urgent need to provide for water demand management. In the absence of reliable data on the availability of water resources, the thrust of the government's approach was towards regulating water supply rather than water demand. With the availability of more accurate information on over-allocation – especially after the severe drought of 1966 and the subsequent Commission of Inquiry into Water Matters (1970) – it was increasingly recognised that it was necessary for the government to shift the focus of attention to water demand management. Nevertheless, it took over 20 years of relative inaction, during which the water crisis worsened, and the election of the ANC government in 1994 to bring about a recasting of national legislation, in the form of the National Water Act 36 of 1998.

58 *Reconstruction and Development Programme,* African National Congress, 1994, pp. 10–11, 38–40.

59 Section 23 states: 'Everyone has the right (a) to an environment that is not harmful to their health or well-being; (b) to have their environment protected through reasonable legislative and other measures designed to (i) prevent pollution and ecological degradation; (ii) promote conservation; and (iii) secure sustainable development and use of resources'.

The 1998 Act contains a succinct overview of the premises upon which the government's approach to water resource management is grounded. Six aspects are emphasised:

- water is a scarce and unevenly distributed national resource which occurs in many different forms, although all are part of a unitary, inter-dependent cycle;
- although water is a natural resource that belongs to all people, the discriminatory laws and practices of the past have prevented equal access to, and use of, water resources;
- the government has a responsibility to ensure the equitable allocation of water for beneficial use;
- the aim of water resource management is the sustainable use of water for the benefit of all users;
- the protection of the quality of water resources is necessary to ensure sustainability of the nation's water resources in the interests of all water users;
- there is a need for the integrated management of all aspects of water resources and, where appropriate, the delegation of management functions to a regional or catchment level so as to enable everyone to participate.

The new National Water Act describes an integrated water resource management (IWRM) philosophy. IWRM is simultaneously a process and an implementation strategy to achieve equitable access to, and sustainable use of, water resources by all stakeholders at catchment, regional, national and international levels. The implication that flows from this strategy is that, at its most basic level, IWRM will be grounded in a catchment-basis approach. Accordingly, the National Water Act provides for the formal and widespread establishment of statutory, directed catchment management (CM) processes. In summary, then, the framework for IWRM in South Africa will evolve in a three-tiered framework comprising: a national water resources strategy (NWRS); a statutory framework for catchment management (CM); and CM processes/strategies/plans in specific catchment areas.

The Water Act gave the Minister of Water Affairs and Forestry, with the concurrence of the Minister of Finance, the authority to establish a pricing strategy for any water use. The pricing strategy 'may contain a strategy for setting water use charges for funding water resource management, including the related costs of water conservation' (section 56). This suggests that there will be an important role for water demand management strategies other than legislative – that is, a role for the wider use of economic instruments in water demand management.

National Environmental Management Act 107 of 1998

Within this context, the Minister of Environmental Affairs and Tourism embarked upon a series of consultations in the formulation of a national environmental policy. A green paper – *An Environmental Policy for South Africa* – was issued in October 1996, and the draft National Environmental Management Bill, published in July 1998, became law as Act 107 of 1998.[60]

A careful reading of the Act evokes reactions of both jubilation and concern. On the positive side, section 1 defines sustainable development along the lines of the Brundtland report's definition, which contains a strong commitment to the principles of intra-generational and inter-generational equity (although the problems associated with this definition, mentioned earlier in this chapter, have not been addressed). Section 2(4)(b)–(g) clearly acknowledges the need for inclusivity, so that the 'interests, needs and values of all interested and affected parties' are taken into account; while section 2(4)(k) provides a commitment to 'transparency' by way of open access to the information needed for informed participation and decision making. Perhaps most importantly, section 2(4)(l) provides a forthright statement on the need to avoid potential conflicts of interests through the centralisation of environmental policy control in the hands of the Minister of Environmental Affairs. Of course, these policy recommendations will remain mere wishes on paper until appropriate action is taken. And it is precisely this area – the lack of a clear vision as to how sustainable development is to be translated into practice – that constitutes the Act's greatest weakness.

Section 2(4)(a) provides a long list of factors to be taken into consideration to produce sustainable development. These include: the maintenance of ecosystems and biological diversity; the 'responsible' use of both renewable and non-renewable natural resources; the avoidance or minimisation of both waste and pollution; and, given the paucity of our current knowledge of the complexity of the environment, the need to operate on the precautionary principle. While this section in effect summarises many of the key environmental concerns associated with sustainable development, it ignores the well known problems that are encountered when attempts are made to give effect to these recommendations. For example, what is meant by the 'responsible' use of non-renewable resources? Are they to be extracted at the optimal rate calculated in terms of the widely accepted Hotelling model? This

60 The National Environmental Management Act 107 of 1998 came into effect on 29 January 1999. It has subsequently been amended on five occasions.

would imply acceptance of the neo-classical paradigm, which is widely rejected by proponents of sustainable development. The latter would prefer extraction rates to be calibrated according to the development and availability of 'backstop technology' (although they fail to explain how this should be implemented).

Similarly, the statement relating to the need to avoid or minimise pollution does not stipulate whether it refers to 'fund' pollutants (for which it is believed that the environment has some absorptive capacity) or 'stock' pollutants (for which it is estimated that the environment has extremely limited absorptive capacity). It is generally understood that 'stock' pollutants need to be phased out and ultimately banned, while 'fund' pollutants need to be regulated according to emission standards set in terms of public health norms. Nevertheless, even if the reference is to 'fund' pollutants, how do we avoid the 'threshold effects' to which E. P. Odum has directed our attention? Ecologists such as Odum have pointed out that, although the environment may have some absorptive capacity for 'fund' pollutants, we do not know the 'tolerance thresholds' for different types of 'fund' pollutants. Furthermore, if the 'tolerance threshold' is exceeded and the ecosystem(s) collapse, we do not know whether the damage is reversible. In this context, the bland statement that pollution should be avoided or minimised is less than helpful.

Sections 3–6 of the Act established a National Environmental Advisory Forum, whose purpose is to 'inform the Minister of the views of stakeholders', while sections 7–10 established the Committee for Environmental Co-ordination, whose function was to 'promote the integration and co-ordination of environmental functions by the relevant organs of state, and in particular to promote … the objectives of environmental implementation plans and environmental management plans'. Following this, section 11(1)–(2) stipulates that every government department and every province 'must prepare an environmental implementation plan … and an environmental management plan … within one year of the promulgation of this Act and at least every four years thereafter', but little is provided in the way of guidelines as to what would constitute acceptable plans. Furthermore, apart from an unfortunately vague reference to the need to promote 'integrated environmental management' (sections 23, 24), the Act's stipulations relating to 'Compliance, Enforcement and Protection' (sections 28–34) seriously underestimate the major problem of estimating the damage cost of environmental degradation.

Finally, there remains the problem of enforcement. We have seen that the lack of enforcement was a serious problem with earlier environmental legislation, and it is arguable whether the current Act comes to grips this thorny problem.

Conclusion

It remains to be seen whether the South African government's policy on sustainable development is actually carried into practice. It has to be said, however, that the thrust of the Environmental Management Act of 1998 ignores many of the practical problems associated with any attempts to make sustainable use of environmental resources, and falls short of the paradigm shift needed to give substance to its stated commitment to the principles of sustainable development. In the final analysis, it may be argued that until and unless there is a proper appreciation of the role of the state in attempts to achieve sustainable development, existing and proposed environmental legislation in South Africa will fail to achieve this laudable objective.

25

Black economic empowerment

Philip Black, Rachel Jafta and Rulof Burger

Introduction

Black economic empowerment (BEE) has been around for many years, albeit in different guises. Even before the formal establishment of a democratic state in 1994, the public sector and private corporations had started to act affirmatively by appointing black persons to senior management positions – partly to prepare or 'gear up' for the then widely expected political transformation.[1] After 1994, affirmative action was applied extensively at all levels in the public sector, including government departments, as well as Eskom, Transnet and other state-owned enterprises. The first democratic government then provided a formal framework by entrenching basic economic rights in the new constitution and launching its *Reconstruction and Development Programme* (RDP) in 1994. Several new parliamentary Acts – pertaining to small-business development, preferential procurement and competition policy – carried provisions aimed at promoting businesses owned or controlled by black persons, on a preferential basis. Similarly, the Employment Equity Act 55 of 1998 in effect enforced affirmative action programmes that favoured the appointment of black persons, women and the disabled. On the ownership front, too, government took the initiative through its National Empowerment Fund Act 105 of 1998, which gave it the legal power to hold equity in state-owned enterprises on behalf of disadvantaged black persons.

The above process gained momentum when the Broad-Based Black Economic Empowerment (BEE) Act 53 of 2003 was signed into force – a direct consequence of a major report prepared by the Black Economic

1 P. A. Black, 'Affirmative action: rational response to a changing environment?', *South African Journal of Economics*, 61(4) (1993), 330–334.

Empowerment Commission in 2001. The overall objective of the Commission and the Act was a further development of the government's erstwhile 'growth, employment and redistribution' (GEAR) strategy, namely to provide 'a framework for economic growth with black participation as a fundamental pillar'.[2] Due partly to popular criticisms of the elitist nature of earlier *de facto* empowerment initiatives, the Commission opted for a broadly based strategy that would spread ownership and managerial appointments among black persons as widely as possible. This was to be achieved through the normal fiscal processes, the various parliamentary Acts referred to above and, more directly, via the BEE Act, by involving black workers at all levels as well as pension funds in new ownership deals with some of the major listed and non-listed private companies.

Before looking at progress made in the 1990s, it seems apt to say a few words about the basic *rationale* underpinning BEE in South Africa. This is done briefly in the next section. In a subsequent section we look at some of the early BEE measures aimed at achieving employment equity in the labour market, and also consider the more recent 'balanced scorecard' approach adopted by the Department of Trade and Industry. There then follows an empirical analysis of the effect of BEE legislation on discrimination in the labour market, broadly defined. We could not consider the impact of changes in specific occupational categories (e.g. management) or in ownership patterns, due to the short time horizon involved.

Why BEE?

The fundamental and most obvious rationale for BEE lies in the legally based system of racial discrimination put into practice under apartheid and, before that, in the socially exclusive policies adopted by preceding governments and the old colonial powers.[3] Theoretically, a similar rationale can be found in Robert Nozick's[4] famous entitlement theory, which also served, albeit implicitly, as a basis for the general approach followed and recommendations made by the Truth and Reconciliation Commission (TRC). According to Nozick, a distribution of wealth is 'just' if it is derived from a prior just distribution by just means. If this process were violated, as was evidently the case in South Africa under apartheid, there is a *prima facie* case for 'rectification', or for giving back to those individuals and communities the wealth unjustly taken away from them.

2 *Report of the Black Economic Empowerment Commission*, Skotaville Press, 2001, p. 9.

3 S. J. Terreblanche, *A History of Inequality in South Africa, 1652–2002*, University of Natal Press, 2002.

4 R. Nozick, *Anarchy, State and Utopia*, Basic Books, 1974.

But Nozick[5] himself was prudent in setting the conditions for successful rectification, and raised the critical question of how far one should go back in time to 'wipe clean the historical slate of injustice'. This is evidently a difficult and sensitive question when viewed historically from a South African perspective. The TRC decided on a cut-off date of 1 March 1960, partly, one suspects, because the human resettlement policies of the National government had reached some momentum at that stage, and partly to facilitate the extensive and intricate analyses required to quantify both the damage itself and the distributional pattern that would have emerged in the absence of the violation.

The BEE policies did, however, go well beyond the activities of the TRC and, it seems, were justified on the basis of a much longer span of South African history. The racial composition of skilled labour and of land and capital ownership has never come close to reflecting that of the total South African population, not only because of historical injustices but also because of a failure (adequately) to recognise and entrench basic human rights in past constitutions. Here one could invoke the notion of a 'social contract', as in Kant's 'original contract' and John Rawls' theory of justice.[6] Rawls' basic conclusion – that people in the 'original position' would agree to a constitution and set of policies aimed at enhancing the interests of the least advantaged – does seem to be relevant to the South African government's attempts (in the latter part of the 1990s and subsequently) to redistribute wealth via the fiscal process and through its empowerment initiatives.

James Buchanan,[7] perhaps the pre-eminent neo-contractarian of his day, also uses a Rawlsian principle when setting guidelines for the evaluation of policy at the constitutional level. Using Wicksell's principle of 'unanimity and voluntary consent', he imagines a situation in which all members of society are involved in evaluating and comparing alternative constitutional rules under conditions of uncertainty, that is, when no one can be sure how these rules would affect them personally. Stripped of their own life experiences, so to speak, individuals will thus reveal what the French philosopher Kolm[8] calls their 'fundamental' preferences, which, in addition to their private ones, include the preferences they hold in respect of the community of which they are a part.

The latter proposition is similar to the notion of a social welfare function *à la* Bergson, according to which the community – in addition to the individual – is assumed to reveal its relative preferences for different

5 *Ibid.*, p. 67.

6 J. Rawls, *A Theory of Justice*, Harvard University Press, 1971.

7 J. M. Buchanan (ed.), *The Collected Works of James M. Buchanan*, Liberty Fund, 1999.

8 S. C. Kolm, *Justice and Equity*, MIT Press, 1997.

distributions of wealth. Thus it may prefer a distribution different from the prevailing one, even if the policies required to achieve the former may entail some sacrifice in the form of a lower level of real output. BEE may also be justified in terms of some of the 'resource-based' and 'desert-based' principles of justice advocated by Dworkin, Lamont and others (e.g. Sen, Riley).[9] They argue for an (assumed) initial equal distribution of natural resources, and for appropriate compensation for people adversely affected by circumstances beyond their control. But such a hypothetical equal distribution may or may not lead to equal outcomes (or to a so-called 'patterned' outcome), insofar as the benefits derived from an initial (and fair) endowment depend, *inter alia,* on individual preferences for work as opposed to leisure. Unequal distributional outcomes may thus result from voluntary choices and/or productivity differences unrelated to discrimination – a point we return to in the section below presenting our empirical analysis.

In a similar vein, Bowles and Gintis[10] argue the case for 'efficiency-enhancing' redistributions, under the terms of which people who are disadvantaged – for whatever reason – are given an opportunity to become owners of productive assets. Such a redistribution will ensure 'equal freedom and dignity' and, depending on how these assets are utilised, may even enhance efficiency. Although this argument is both tenuous and unlikely to apply universally, it does seem to lie at the root of the attempts by the South African government to bring about a major restructuring of ownership in favour of black persons.

Evolution of the BEE institutional framework: an incentive perspective

That a newly elected democratic government would implement measures to redress the racial inequality resulting from the apartheid system and its antecedents was never in doubt. These intentions were made clear in policy documents from the African National Congress (ANC) and

9 R. Dworkin, 'What is equality? Part 1: equality of resources', *Philosophy and Public Affairs,* 10(3), 185–246; R. Dworkin, 'What is equality? Part 2: equality of welfare', *Philosophy and Public Affairs,* 10(4), 283–345; J. Lamont, 'The concept of desert in distributive justice', *Philosophical Quarterly,* 44(174) (1994), 45–64; J. Lamont, 'Problems for effort-based distribution principles', *Journal of Applied Philosophy,* 12 (1995), 215–229; A. Sen, 'Inequality of what?', in A. Sen (ed.), *Choice, Welfare and Measurement,* Cambridge University Press, 1982; J. Riley, 'Justice under capitalism', in J. W. Chapman (ed.), *Markets and Justice,* New York University Press, 1989.

10 S. Bowles and H. Gintis, 'Efficient redistribution: new rules for markets, states, and communities', *Politics and Society,* 24(4) (1997), 307–342.

presentations by leading ANC/alliance spokespersons. What format these measures would take, however, was not as clear. In this section of the chapter we trace the evolution of the institutional framework aimed at facilitating the 'corrective' (BEE) measures. Central to this account is a focus on the incentives (positive and negative) employed to induce the South African private sector to conform to the exigencies of the government's redress programme.

Early measures

The new constitution of South Africa, adopted in 1996, enshrines the principle of equality, except in instances where it is necessary for the government to take measures to redress the inequalities resulting from the system of apartheid. Not long after the 1994 election, two processes aimed at altering the situation in the South African labour market commenced, namely the work of the Labour Market Commission[11] and the policy-making process to introduce employment equity in the workplace started by the 1996 Green Paper *Employment and Occupational Equity*.

The Labour Market Commission

A report of the Presidential Commission investigating labour market policy, entitled *Restructuring the South African Labour Market*, was published in June 1996. The Commission was established under an Act of Parliament in 1995. Its terms of reference included, *inter alia*, the proposal of mechanisms to redress discrimination in the labour market. In particular, the Commission considered 'a policy framework for Affirmative Action in employment with due regard [to] the objectives of employment creation, fair remuneration, productivity enhancement and macroeconomic stability'.[12] The report defined *employment equity* as a broad term intended to describe the labour market as both *non-discriminatory* and *socially equitable*. Along the same lines of thinking, equal opportunity meant 'non-discrimination'. The report, however, maintained that social equity in the labour market requires that extra-market factors that perpetuate unequal opportunities be taken into account.[13]

11 Labour Market Commission, *Restructuring the South African Labour Market. Report of the Presidential Commission to Investigate Labour Market Policy*, Government Printer, 1996.

12 *Ibid.*, p. xiv.

13 *Ibid.*, pp. 138–139.

Green Paper on employment equity
The Green Paper on employment equity[14] proposed that employer organisations embark on an organisational audit, develop equity plans and fulfil certain obligations towards stakeholders in this process.

The organisational audit was to be conducted in cooperation with employees in order to garner information on employment, pay and benefits in major occupational categories by race, gender and disability (e.g. programmes and policies on human resource development, including levels of expenditure, certification, and the race, gender and disability status of trainees) as well as organisation of work in terms of the skills and responsibilities required by different positions, and hours worked. It was further to cover: information on transport, housing and caring arrangements and preferences of employees, by race and gender, including options for hours worked; languages used and language competence; physical facilities for disabled people and women; procedures for hiring, training, promotion, retrenchment and transfers; and grievance and internal appeals procedures.

All employers were expected to draw up employment equity plans, but only certain categories of employers (to be decided by cabinet) were to file equity plans with the Department of Labour. Other employers might have their plans inspected by the Department of Labour following requests by representatives of 'important stakeholders'.

Employment equity plans were to include:

- a profile of employees by race, gender and disability, with problem areas such as under-representation of designated groups, remuneration disparities and so on clearly identified;
- measures to restructure procedures for hiring, training, promotion, retrenchment and transfers, aimed at preventing discrimination, identifying and minimising aspects of work and training that hindered people from historically disadvantaged groups, accelerating recruitment, training and promotion in order to achieve a more equitable representation of designated groups, and developing an organisational culture that welcomed diversity;
- goals and timetables for implementation;
- details on the roles of representatives of employees or, where relevant, other stakeholders in the formulation of the plans.

Employers were to consult with employees and possibly other important stakeholders on employment equity measures, including the

14 This Green Paper formed the basis for the affirmative action legislation contained in the Employment Equity Act of 1998.

audit and plan. All employer organisations were to provide key data on employment on a regular basis, as defined by the Department of Labour. Employers were to undertake procedures to end discriminatory decision making about employees and to ensure equal pay and benefits for equal work. All employers were to review grievance systems to ensure their effectiveness in handling discriminatory behaviour or harassment. Employers in some categories would have to submit employment equity plans for approval by the Minister of Labour. Other employers would have to submit plans if requested by employees or other stakeholders, or in order to get subsidies or tendering rights. Once approved, employers were legally obliged to carry out the plans and to report on their implementation. Large and strategically placed or persistently unrepresentative employers would be asked to implement employment equity processes more rigorously and report on them in greater detail. Incentives to comply with these requirements included access to subsidies, such as training grants and tenders for government or parastatal contracts. Sanctions included appearance before the Commission for Conciliation, Mediation and Arbitration and thereafter the Labour Court. The Department of Labour intended to formulate further sanctions for non-compliance, such as the imposition of fines.

Later measures

In the late 1990s, the perception still existed that BEE in the private sector was nothing more than window dressing as opposed to a strategic imperative for doing business in South Africa. In 1997 a University of Cape Town survey on affirmative action, for example, concluded that transformation in the private sector was cosmetic. It was found that 96 per cent of top management positions were still held by whites.[15]

Following a long period of discussions and consultations after the introduction of the Green Paper on employment equity, the Employment Equity Act 55 of 1998 was promulgated and came into effect on 9 August 1999.[16] This Act applied to all employers, workers and prospective employees, but not to members of the National Defence Force, the National Intelligence Agency and the South African Secret Service. It formalised the obligations of employers and made provision for the Minister of Labour to set and review the limits for fines to be imposed on non-compliant companies. Labour inspectors were to visit designated firms to ensure compliance with employment equity

15 *Cape Times*, 21 March 1997.

16 See www.constitutionalcourt.org.za.

provisions.[17] The Act also provided for the establishment of the Commission for Employment Equity, to advise the Minister of Labour on the various codes and regulations required for the implementation of the Act. This Commission would analyse the employment equity reports submitted by designated employers and disseminate the results.

Skills development

Towards the end of the 1990s, the government introduced the Skills Development Strategy (SDS), aimed at improving the skills of the South African labour force. Although the strategy was meant to improve the skills of all people, it prioritised the skills development of black people, women and people with disabilities. To this end, the Skills Development Act of 1998, which came into effect on 10 September 1999, allowed for the creation of learnership programmes. The SDS set particular targets for the beneficiaries of these programmes, namely 84 per cent of their participants should be black, 54 per cent women, and 4 per cent people with disabilities.[18] This was followed by the Skills Development Levies Act (1999), which obliged all employers to give attention to the training and education of employees and to contribute 1 per cent of their payroll to the relevant sectoral education and training authority.

Although diverse pieces of legislation and private sector initiatives attempted to redress aspects of past discrimination, the belief persisted that it was too fragmented and not sufficiently targeted. Cyril Ramaphosa, chairman of the BEE Commission, articulated this view as follows:

> Precisely because the economic disempowerment of black South Africans was so far-reaching in its effect and so broad in the areas in which it was effected, it was necessary, as we entered the era of democracy, that our efforts at black economic empowerment be similarly broad and far-reaching.[19]

17 After implementation of the legislation, the Department of Labour adopted a 'name and shame' approach, in that it published the names of non-compliant companies in the print and broadcast media. See 'Minister to tighten the noose on EEA violators in 2007', Department of Labour press release, 20 November 2006. Available at www.labour.gov.za/media-desk/media-statements/2006/minister-to-tighten-the-noose-on-eea-violators-in-2007 (accessed 5 March 2007).

18 *Annual Report 1999–2001*, Commission for Employment Equity, 2001, p. 7.

19 C. Ramaphosa, 'Black empowerment: myths and realities', in F. Sicre (ed.), *South Africa at 10*, Human and Rousseau, 2004, pp. 72–84, at p. 74.

Empirical analysis of the impact of BEE legislation on labour market outcomes

An evaluation of the BEE legislation necessarily requires analysing the actual effects that these policies had on the South African economy. Ideally, one would like to study all the aspects of BEE legislation, including the effects of the changing composition of company ownership. Given the lack of data that can be used for such purposes, we restrict ourselves to an analysis of the effects of affirmative action legislation on the labour market.

The Employment Equity Act of 1998 targeted women, blacks (i.e. members of the African, coloured and Indian population groups) and the disabled, and set itself the goal of promoting 'equal opportunity and fair treatment in employment through the elimination of unfair discrimination'. The most salient institutional aspects of this Act were discussed above, but it still remains to be shown whether these policies had the intended consequences. Given the scope of this book, we are interested in the effect that the implementation of these policies – as well as the anticipation of the implementation of these policies – had in the 1990s. To this end, we attempt empirically to assess the trends in racial and gender discrimination in labour market outcomes. This section starts by briefly describing a few post-apartheid labour market trends, before explaining the methodology used in our empirical analysis. This is followed by a discussion of our results.

Post-apartheid labour market trends

Using household survey datasets collected by Statistics South Africa since 1995, it is possible to track important labour market trends, particularly with respect to racial and gender differences. Table 25.1 reports the unemployment rates for the (broadly defined) labour force, by race and gender, for 1995 and 2000. Clearly, there were large racial and gender disparities in the probability of finding work in South Africa. For all the years after 1994, black women had the highest unemployment rate, followed by black men, white women and white men.

The years between 1995 and 2000[20] were characterised by an increase in the unemployment rate, mainly driven by a very rapid increase in

20 The September 2000 Labour Force Survey appears to have suffered from an over-capturing of informal-economy workers, which would imply that the increase in unemployment between 1995 and 2000 is understated. The actual increases in the unemployment rates of black men and black women would have been substantially higher, whereas the unemployment rates of white men and women would not have been greatly affected.

Table 25.1 *Unemployment rate (%) (broad definition), by race and gender, 1995 and 2000*

	1995	*2000*	*Growth (%)*
All workers	31	34	3.3
By race and gender			
Black males	27	32	4.8
Black females	44	44	−0.3
White males	4	5	1.6
White females	9	11	2.3

Source: Own calculation from the 1995 October Household Survey and the September 2000 Labour Force Survey (Statistics South Africa, various years).

Table 25.2 *Average monthly earnings (R, 2000 prices), by race and gender, 1995 and 2000*

	1995	*2000*	*Growth (%)*
All workers	2,919	3,160	8.3
By race and gender			
Black males	2,176	2,219	2.0
Black females	2,076	2,212	6.6
White males	7,650	8,207	7.3
White females	4,054	4,760	17.4

Source: Own calculation from the 1995 October Household Survey and the September 2000 Labour Force Survey (Statistics South Africa, various years).

the labour force participation rate.[21] Although the full period was associated with an increasing unemployment rate for all gender and race groups, the bulk of this burden fell on those who already faced high unemployment, black men.

Table 25.2 shows that there also existed a substantial earnings gap between black and white formal-sector employees for both genders, and between white men and women. This was in contrast to the relatively small gender earnings gap observed for blacks. Between 1995 and 2000, the average South African experienced an 8.3 per cent increase in real earnings, or an average annual increase of 1.5 per cent. This increase was the largest for white women, followed by white men, black women and black men. Between 1995 and 2000, white women were the only group that increased their earnings faster than white men.

21 Both trends started to subside only after 2002.

Table 25.3 *Share of workers (%) in skilled occupations, by race and gender, 1995 and 2000*

	1995	*2000*	*Growth (%)*
All workers	21	19	–1.8
By race and gender			
Black males	12	11	–1.1
Black females	19	12	–6.7
White males	45	51	5.6
White females	36	47	11.8

Source: Own calculation from the 1995 October Household Survey and the September 2000 Labour Force Survey (Statistics South Africa, various years).

Table 25.3 reveals the share of the formal-sector employees who were working in skilled occupations, here defined to be legislators, senior officials and managers; professionals; and technicians and associate professionals. White men had a much larger share working in skilled occupations in 1995 than black men or black women, and this 'occupational gap' remained largely unchanged between 1995 and 2000. Only white women managed to increase their share of skilled workers at a faster rate.

Data and methodology

Measuring discrimination

It was reported in Table 25.2 that the average white worker earned substantially more than his/her black counterpart, but this in itself is not evidence of racial discrimination. White workers on average had higher levels of educational attainment and were more likely to live in urban areas, and both of these characteristics are generally associated with higher labour market earnings. Although differences in these characteristics can themselves be the product of pre-labour market discrimination or affected by anticipated labour market discrimination, our interest lies primarily in the extent of discrimination that occurred after participants entered the labour market.

When analysing the racial earnings gap we had to control for differences in the average set of personal characteristics, so that we could determine the difference between what a white and black worker *with the same productive characteristics* could expect to earn in the South African labour market. Once we knew this, it was possible to decompose the total observed racial wage gap into two components: one which was the result of the difference in average skill levels, and one which remained after controlling for this difference. If productivity differences can be completely controlled for, it follows that the latter component was the result of racial discrimination. The same argument also holds when considering gender discrimination.

Blinder[22] and Oaxaca[23] developed a decomposition technique that allows us to identify the share of the average wage gap which is attributable to differences in observable productive characteristics. Under the fairly common assumption that the log of wages is a linear function of a set of individual characteristics, x_i, the wage earnings function can be estimated with equation 1:

$$\ln w = \beta_0 + \sum_{i=1}^{k} \beta_i x_i + \varepsilon \tag{1}$$

where w denotes wages, the β_i series captures the effect of a change in the x_i series on the log of wages, and ε is an error term. In matrix notation:

$$\ln w = X\beta + \varepsilon \tag{1a}$$

where X includes a constant. If we now average this equation over two groups, say blacks and whites, we obtain the following expression for the average wage gap:

$$\overline{\ln w_W} - \overline{\ln w_B} = \overline{X}_W \beta_W - \overline{X}_B \beta_B \tag{2}$$

where $\overline{\ln w_i}$ is the average log of wages for group i, $\overline{X}_i$ is the vector containing the productive characteristics evaluated at the average for group i, β_i is the vector of coefficients representing the market's valuation of the characteristics in $\overline{X}_i$ for group i, and subscripts W and B refer to the white and black population groups. If the two β_i vectors differ, then this implies that the market rewards the same characteristics differently if possessed by members of different population groups. Equation 2 can be rewritten as:

$$\overline{\ln w_W} - \overline{\ln w_B} = (\overline{X}_W - \overline{X}_B)\beta^* + \overline{X}_W(\beta_W - \beta^*) + \overline{X}_B(\beta^* - \beta_B) \tag{3}$$

where β^* is the vector of coefficients that would prevail in the absence of discrimination.

22 A. S. Blinder, 'Wage discrimination: reduced form and structural estimates', *Journal of Human Resources*, 8(4) (1973), 436–455.

23 R. Oaxaca, 'Male–female wage differentials in urban labor markets', *International Economic Review* 14(3) (1973), 693–709.

The wage gap can now be seen to consist of three components: the difference in the average level of productive characteristics between whites and blacks, $(\bar{X}_W - \bar{X}_B)\beta^*$, the difference between what white workers were receiving and what they would have been receiving in a non-discriminating labour market, $\bar{X}_W(\beta_W - \beta^*)$, and the difference between what blacks would have been paid in the absence of discrimination and what they were actually being paid, $\bar{X}_B(\beta^* - \beta_B)$. The last two terms reflect white advantage and black disadvantage respectively, and discrimination collectively.

In practice, determining the extent of discrimination is somewhat more complicated. First, it is not clear what the wage structure would look like in the absence of discrimination. In the international literature it is often assumed that white workers are paid their marginal productivity, and that the wage gap is thus solely due to black disadvantage. This implies that the white wage structure would prevail in a non-discriminating labour market, so that $\beta^* = \beta_W$. In South Africa, where the advantaged group is also a minority, it is unlikely that firms could afford to equate the earnings of all workers at white levels and still remain competitive. According to the theoretical model by Neumark,[24] β^* can be obtained from a regression on the pooled sample of the two groups. This may well be a more realistic assumption in the South African context, and also offers the additional advantage of producing the smallest standard errors for the estimated components.

A second difficulty with measuring discrimination is that there are certain personal characteristics – like motivation or the quality of education – that are almost certainly important in determining wages but that cannot be easily observed and hence do not appear in our data-sets. If we cannot control for these factors in our regression, then it is untrue that the share of the wage gap that remains after controlling for productive characteristics necessarily represents discrimination. For this reason we need to be cautious, whenever we suspect the omission of potentially important unobservable characteristics, in drawing inferences about the level of discrimination from the unexplained component of the wage gap. If both the distribution of unobservable skills and the relationship between these skills and earnings remained fairly stable over the period under consideration (as is likely to have been the case), however, then we should be able to interpret changes in the unexplained component as being derived mainly from changes in discrimination.

24 D. Neumark, 'Employers' discriminatory behaviour and the estimation of wage discrimination', *Journal of Human Resources*, 23(3) (1988), 279–295.

Data issues

The empirical analysis uses data from the household surveys conducted by Statistics South Africa (StatsSA) after 1995. From 1995 to 1999 the data were collected in the form of the annual October Household Surveys (OHS), which were replaced in March 2000 by the bi-annual Labour Force Surveys (LFS).

The questionnaires used in the OHS were frequently changed in order to improve the quality of the data obtained, but this complicates comparability across surveys. The surveys have been much more consistent since the switch to the LFS. One of the main concerns regarding data inconsistencies is the improved capturing of low-income employment (particularly between October 1999 and March of 2000), which resulted in an artificial decrease in the average wage levels in the economy. As demonstrated by Burger and Yu,[25] this issue can be resolved by omitting informal-economy workers, the self-employed and those earning more than R200,000 per month (in 2000 prices). In tracing the effect of affirmative action policies, our interest lies primarily with formal-sector employees, so that these omissions do not severely curtail our analysis. The earnings threshold of R200,000 results in dropping 0.02 per cent of the sample.

A second concern in analysing the data is what appears to be a fairly high degree of survey-specific sampling error. The added variability of survey estimates makes it somewhat more difficult to identify time trends accurately, and for this reason we present trends graphically below, by plotting three-year moving averages. Even with these adjustments, there remain some data inconsistencies.

Our regression analysis controlled for the following variables: education (linearly and squared), experience (linearly and squared), whether the person was the household head or not, whether the person was married or not, the number of children in the household, union membership, province of residence, hours worked on average and years of tenure. When analysing gender discrimination, the household headship variable was omitted, since it was likely to be partly endogenous and result in an overestimation of the explained component of the earnings gap.

Empirical results

Using the Oaxaca–Blinder decomposition, as described above, it is now possible to investigate the trend in the part of the wage gap that

25 R. P. Burger and D. Yu, 'Wage trends in post-apartheid South Africa: constructing an earnings series for South Africa from household survey data', *Labour Market Frontiers*, 8 (2006), 1–8.

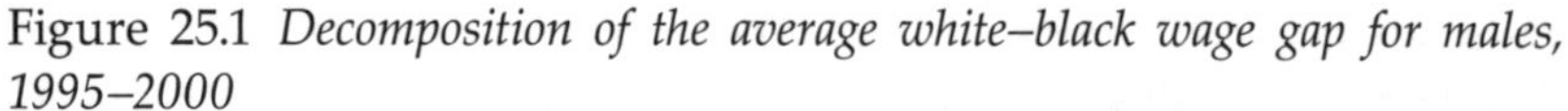

Figure 25.1 *Decomposition of the average white–black wage gap for males, 1995–2000*

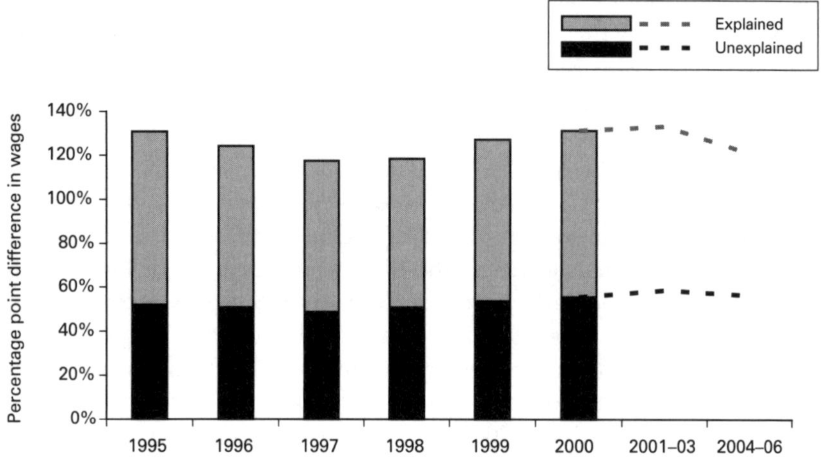

Source: Own calculations from October Household and September rounds of Labour Force Surveys (Statistics South Africa, various years).

remains unexplained after controlling for average differences in productive characteristics. Figure 25.1 displays the percentage difference in the average earnings received by black and white men (the racial wage gap), as well as the parts attributable to differences in the average set of productive characteristics (denoted on the graph as 'Explained') and that which remains unexplained.[26] The wage gap is clearly very high, and did not change much between 1995 and 2000. A detailed decomposition, using the technique suggested by Yun,[27] shows that the declining wage gap was largely driven by a narrowing of the education differential between white and black male workers. Even with these improvements, the wage gap was still very large in 2006, and *there was little evidence to suggest that racial discrimination had diminished considerably as a result of affirmative action policies.* The detailed decomposition also shows that the large unexplained component was mostly the result of the much higher rewards earned by whites for each additional year of education attained. This suggests that a large part of the wage gap,

26 Note that the proportional wage gap calculated when using log wages – as is the case in Figure 25.1 – is only approximately equal to the exact wage gap, and could therefore be different from that suggested by the figures in Table 25.2.

27 M. Yun, 'A simple solution to the identification problem in detailed wage decompositions', *Economic Inquiry*, 43(4) (2005), 766–772.

Figure 25.2 *Decomposition of the average white–black wage gap for females, 1995–2000*

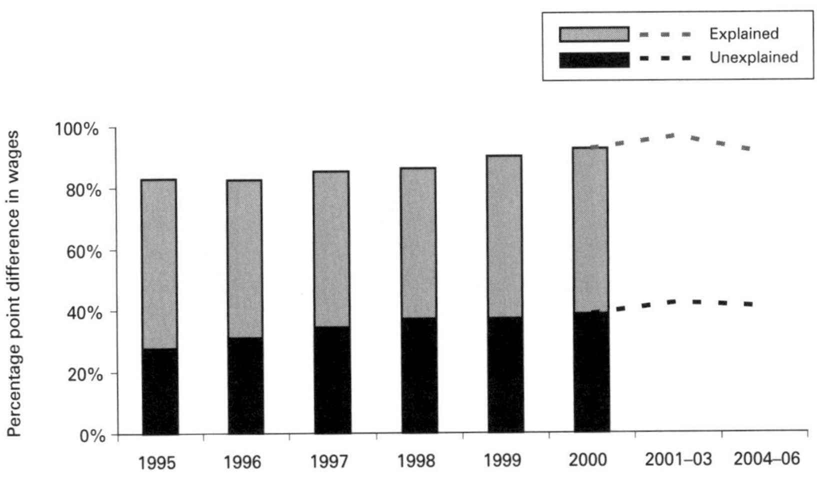

Source: Own calculations from October Household and September rounds of Labour Force Surveys (Statistics South Africa, various years).

which is unexplained by differences in observable productive characteristics, represented perceived differences in the quality of education received by blacks and whites – a perception for which there is some empirical evidence.[28]

The racial wage gap was slightly smaller for women than for men: the unexplained and explained components were both around 20 per cent lower on average than for men (Figure 25.2). This wage gap did not decline over time: it was even larger in 2000 than in 1994. The explained component was relatively stable over time, but decreased slightly in the last few years, mainly as a result of a narrowing education gap. The unexplained component, on the other hand, which contains the effect of discrimination, increased over the period. Figure 25.2 shows that white women experienced a more rapid increase in their wages over the period than any other subgroup. White women and black women both suffered from wage discrimination in comparison with white men; but although white women were at a smaller disadvantage than their black counterparts in 1995, they managed to gain more in the subsequent

28 S. Van der Berg, 'How effective are poor schools? Poverty and educational outcomes in South Africa', paper delivered at SACMEQ International Invitational Research Conference, Paris, September 2005.

Figure 25.3 *Decomposition of the average male–female wage gap for blacks, 1995–2000*

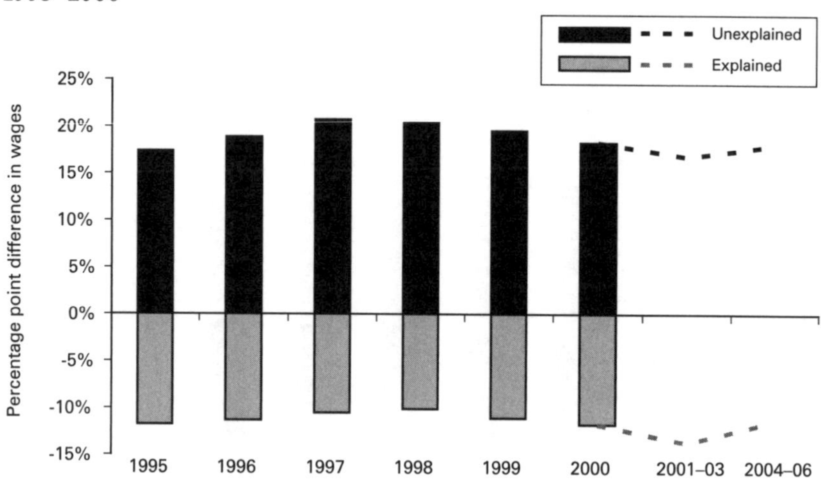

Source: Own calculations from October Household and September rounds of Labour Force Surveys (Statistics South Africa, various years).

period. Figure 25.3 demonstrates that the earnings acceleration experienced by white women was accompanied by a large increase in the proportion of women employed in skilled occupations. The largest contributor to the unexplained component was once again the differential returns to education between blacks and whites.

Turning to the issue of gender discrimination, the small gender gap of around 6 per cent for the black population reveals no clear trend over time. This gap was slightly larger for the coloured than for the African population group, 9 per cent as opposed to 6 per cent, and considerably larger for Indians (30 per cent), but no time trends can be identified for any of these subgroups. Moreover, the wage differential in favour of males existed despite an explained component in favour of women. This corresponds to the results obtained by Shepherd,[29] who offers a more comprehensive analysis of the gender gap in the post-1994 period. Among formal-sector employees, women had higher levels of educational attainment, on average, and this accounts for the bulk of the negative explained component. The reason why black women in the

29 D. Shepherd, 'Gender discrimination in the South African labour market: the impact of employment equity legislation', unpublished manuscript, University of Stellenbosch, 2007.

Figure 25.4 *Decomposition of the average male–female wage gap for whites, 1995–2000*

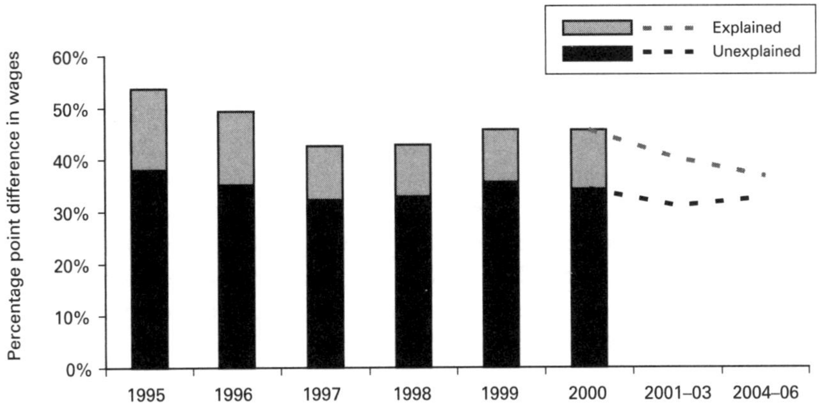

Source: Own calculations from October Household and September rounds of Labour Force Surveys (Statistics South Africa, various years).

formal sector had more education than their male counterparts (whereas that was not true for the population as a whole) is mainly because of the high degree of discrimination they faced when looking for work. Black women had a higher hurdle to cross before finding work, making those who had work a more select group.

Finally, Figure 25.4 shows the gender gap and its components for whites between 1995 and 2000. This decreased substantially. The small explained components demonstrate that the gender gap was not the result of a large difference in productive characteristics between men and women, but was rather the result of either a large gap in unobservable skills or gender discrimination. Relative to other subgroups, white women did well in terms of increasing their earnings and their representation among the skilled. The wage gap was still fairly high in 2000 and a large part of this may have been the result of gender discrimination, *but white women appear to have benefited more than any other subgroup from the newly enacted affirmative action policies.*

The racial and gender earnings gaps are both large in South Africa, with the former being larger than the latter. There have been some improvements in narrowing the racial wage gap among men, as a result of a decrease in the difference in average years of educational attainment between white and black workers. There is little reason to believe that racial discrimination among men decreased. Affirmative action policies were not successful in reducing the racial discrimination experienced by blacks when attempting to find work,[30] while their effect on the wage distribution was limited to a small narrowing of the unexplained component. Although black women managed to narrow the wage gap when compared with white men, white women did even better. The unexplained component of the racial wage gap (for both men and women) was largely the result of differential returns to education, including, possibly, differences in the perceived quality of education. If the objective of government policy is to improve income equality among the races, an improvement in the quantity and quality of education received by the average black labour force participant needs to feature prominently in the solution. Gender discrimination did not decrease for black women but it declined substantially for white women.

Conclusion

A brief historical inquiry into the reasons for BEE indicated that the fundamental rationale for it lay in the legally based policies of racial discrimination under apartheid. The activities of the Truth and Reconciliation Commission were a first step towards rectification and had much in common with Robert Nozick's entitlement theory. From a constitutional perspective, much common ground can also be found in respect of Rawls' theory of justice, Buchanan's contractarian approach and the 'resource based' notions of justice propounded by Dworkin, Lamont and Bowles and Gintis.

During the late 1990s the BEE Commission and the subsequent BEE Act provided a comprehensive framework for BEE. Its three main components were: increased black ownership and control of assets and businesses; human resource development; and a host of indirect measures, including preferential procurement and black business development. While it is probably too early to judge the success or otherwise of these initiatives, it does appear that their impact has been limited to a small number of relatively privileged black individuals – rather than the underprivileged and disadvantaged majority.

The impact of BEE legislation on racial and gender discrimination in the South African labour market also appears to have been limited during the 1990s. The household survey data from Statistics South Africa for the period 1995–2000 show that the racial wage gap remained

30 R. P. Burger and R. Jafta, *Returns to Race: Racial Discrimination in the South African Labour Market*, Stellenbosch Economic Working Paper 04/06, Stellenbosch University, 2006.

fairly stable over this period, despite the implementation of affirmative action policies in the mid- and late 1990s. Such policies would of course take time to affect labour market outcomes. For women, however, the racial wage gap increased slightly, because white women benefited more than black women from affirmative action. As far as the gender wage gap is concerned, the wage gap for whites decreased significantly, while that for blacks remained the same.

The BEE legislation had virtually no impact on the wage gap in the 1990s. The general message that emerges seems to be that BEE initiatives would have a better chance of success if they were accompanied by a larger investment in human capital and an improvement in the quality of education for black persons.

As mentioned above, we could not consider the impact of BEE-induced changes in specific occupational categories, especially senior and middle-level managers, simply because the time horizon is too short to conduct time-series analyses of the productive contributions made by them. And yet the widespread replacement of highly qualified and experienced managers by less qualified and inexperienced officials during the 1990s and beyond may well have made a significant contribution to power disruptions and the lack of investment in electricity supply, water, sewerage, roads and harbours. There is clearly a need for further work based on decomposing the labour market (as well as the capital market) and estimating BEE-induced changes in productivity among different occupations generally, and management in particular.

26

Competition policy

Stuart Jones

Introduction

In the 1990s, in the field of competition, the main issue at stake in South Africa was what role competition policy should play in an advanced market economy. A secondary issue was whether or not South African policy should differ from policies adopted by other countries. No simple answer was forthcoming because three different disciplines with very different approaches to the problem are involved, namely: economics, politics and law.

Economic liberals argue that markets are better than governments at curbing monopoly power, with the assumption that the best policy is one that allows the market to do its job, rather than government intervention. Economic interventionists, ranging from establishment mercantilists of the French and Latin American types to old-fashioned Marxists, argue that vigorous efforts on the part of the state are required to spur competition and curb excessive market power. Their competition policy is consequently directed at monopolies and the alleged abuse of their position. Excessive market power is a woolly concept that opens the way for politicians to intervene, especially those on the left of the political spectrum.

Lawyers, by contrast, focus on narrower topics, such as the definition of monopoly. Is it, for example, determined by a firm's share of the market or the size of its capital base or even the magnitude of its turnover? The

Professor W. D. Reekie was unable to contribute a chapter on competition policy, but kindly gave permission for extensive use to be made of the two editions of his monograph *Monopoly and Competition Policy in South Africa* (1st edition 1996, 2nd edition 2000), Free Market Foundation.

South African experience in the 1990s provides evidence of all these different strands of thought trying to influence the government.

Nor does overseas experience provide clear guidance on this matter. Hong Kong, like the nineteenth-century USA before the Civil War, gave free rein to the market. South Korea and Singapore adopted the dirigiste route. They sought to manage the market in order to achieve economic growth. In developed economies, too, politicians have pushed through some extraordinary laws and made contradictory decisions about mergers and acquisitions. In the USA, the 1936 Robinson–Patman Act, pushed through by President Franklin D. Roosevelt, is such an example. It made it unlawful for a manufacturer to grant discounts to a wholesaler or to sell directly to retailers.[1] It was unenforceable and today stands out as an egregious example of weak and opportunistic politicians responding to determined lobbyists. Anti-trust legislation in the USA goes back to Theodore Roosevelt's attack on Standard Oil in 1911, when size *per se* was judged to be against public interest. Thirty-four years later Alcoa was condemned for the same reason. In the UK the Labour government of Clement Attlee passed the Monopolies and Restrictive Practices Act in 1948, described by Professor G. C. Allen, a member of the Monopolies Commission, as consisting of a string of platitudes, which the Commission found valueless.[2] Competition policy was being formulated within a framework of attacking bigness *per se* and not on focusing on whether size brought benefits to the consumer or was in the public interest.

At the heart of the problem was the failure of almost all the parties involved, economists included, to understand the real nature of competition. This was eloquently stated by Duncan Reekie in the first edition of *Monopoly and Competition Policy*:

> It is over forty years since Schumpeter (1950) emphasised that the competition 'which counts' is not traditional price competition but rather the continuous and universal search for substitutes, for replacing the less desirable by the more. The substitution begins with consumers seeking to distribute their incomes to their optimal benefit, and proceeds through to producers striving to replace less sought-after products by more sought-after ones and by substituting better ways of producing for less effective ways. The essence of this competition is consumer choice and the response to changing consumer preferences by competing firms.[3]

1 W. Duncan Reekie, *Monopoly and Competition Policy in South Africa*, Monograph 24, Free Market Foundation, 1996, p. 59.

2 *Ibid.*, p. 9.

3 *Ibid.*, p. 39.

The situation in South Africa

In 1990 in South Africa the rationale for competition policy was public interest, which should have been the interest of the consumer. In practice, though, the market for goods was inextricably mixed with the market for capital and the market for votes. This presented an opportunity for lobbying by pressure groups, which were more effective than consumers. This explains 'why the seemingly innocuous phrase *public interest* has been so damaging in UK and South African competition policy history'.[4] This damage, moreover, took place despite the fact that economic theory is 'hard pressed definitively to predict negative behavioural effects from structural conditions' such as size, integration and the diversification of industry.[5] Public interest can mean different things to different people. As a result, it sometimes allows politicians and lawyers to interpret the law in a way diametrically opposite to that of the law makers. If, therefore, the law, as Henry Ford suggested, is an ass, it is because politicians have made it so.

This confusion was enshrined in the legislation that governed competition policy in South Africa throughout the 1990s. This happened because, after 1948, South Africa had a severely restricted market economy. In practice there was often little difference between politicians tarred with the brush of National Socialism and those deeply dyed with Marxist socialism. In both cases politicians think they know how to manage the economy better than the market. Implicit in a dirigiste or semi-dirigiste system is the idea that market capitalism needs to be controlled or to be forced to operate within politically prescribed boundaries; but by the late 1970s new thinking in industrial economics was challenging the previously dominant view that monopolies and large firms were always inherently harmful to the consumer. The Maintenance and Promotion of Competition Act 96 of 1979 reflected some of these changing views, despite the concentration of control that characterised the Johannesburg Stock Exchange, in which four mining financial houses controlled the gold mines, one company the diamond market and another the beer market, alongside state corporations dominating transport, telephony and electricity production. The new Act accordingly down-played the importance of structure and set up a Competition Board to examine the three main aspects of business: monopoly situations, acquisitions and restrictive practices.

The definitions of these three aspects of business, incorporated in the Act, were drawn in very general terms, which allowed much room for

4 *Ibid.*, p. 13.

5 *Ibid.*

lobbying by vested interests and publicity-seeking politicians. Globalisation was not yet the fashion, but in 1979 South Africa set out to follow the lead of both the USA and the UK in converting competition policy into a circus, dependent upon the contradictory views of bureaucrats and politicians sitting on boards and commissions, for, as Professor Reekie so aptly observed, 'the rigorous use of economics was as rare in the UK after 1948 as in the US after 1890'.[6]

A monopoly was defined in the 1979 Act as:

> a situation where any person, or two or more persons with a substantial economic connection, control in the Republic or any part thereof, wholly or to a large extent, the class of business in which he or they are engaged in respect of any commodity.

And the definition of acquisition was also broad:

> the acquisition by the holder of a controlling interest in any business or undertaking involved in the production, manufacture, supply or distribution of any commodity, of such an interest –
> (a) in any other business or undertaking so involved; or
> (b) in any asset which is or may be utilised for or in connection with the production, manufacture, supply or distribution of any such commodity, provided such acquisition has or is likely to have the effect of restricting competition directly or indirectly.

The definition of an acquisition was precise, though, in that it referred to restricting competition, as did the definition of restrictive practice. A restrictive practice was said to be:[7]

> (a) any agreement, arrangement or understanding, whether legally enforceable or not, between two or more persons; or
> (b) any business practice or method of trading, including any method of fixing prices, whether by the supplier of any commodity or otherwise; or
> (c) any act or omission on the part of any person, whether acting independently or in concert with any other person; or
> (d) any situation arising out of the activities of any person or class or group of persons which restricts competition directly or indirectly by having or being likely to have the effect of
> (i) restricting the production or distribution of any commodity; or
> (ii) limiting the facilities available for the production or distribution of any commodity; or
> (iii) enhancing or maintaining the price of or any other consideration for any commodity; or
> (iv) preventing the production or distribution of any commodity by the most efficient and economical means; or

6 *Ibid.*, p. 10.
7 *Ibid.*, p. 48.

(v) preventing or retarding the development or introduction of technical improvements or the expansion of existing markets or the opening up of new markets; or
(vi) preventing or restricting the entry of new producers or distributors into any branch of trade or industry; or
(vii) preventing or retarding the adjustment of any profession or branch of trade or industry to changing circumstances.

The new thinking in industrial economics was not influential for long. The first annual report of the Competition Board referred to the preservation of the free market system and healthy competition; but the following year the Board began to 'tilt its interpretation of the definition of monopoly to a structural rather than a behavioural one' and to consumer welfare was added that woolly concept 'public interest'.[8] By the middle of the 1980s a strict structural approach was being questioned and the Board's second chairman, Dr Naude, acknowledged the counter-revolution that had taken place in US policy towards monopolies and ascribed it to the increased influence of economic analysis.

As a result of these developments, by the time the last decade of the century arrived, competition policy in South Africa embraced both the old structuralist approach that condemned size *per se* and aspects of newer thinking derived from the work of Yale Brozen at Chicago and Harold Demsetz at the University of California, Los Angeles. Not surprisingly, the Competition Board did not always apply consistent criteria in its decisions and recommendations.

A few contentious issues, though, continued to attract attention and spark debate. Among these were the questions of parallel and uniform prices, the favouring of associated firms, predation, restrictive practices and price discrimination.

Parallel and uniform prices

Uniform pricing should be accepted if it is a function of market competition that benefits the consumer. Parallel pricing occurs when two or more sellers set their prices at about the same level and change up or down by the same amount at about the same time. Areas where this was of concern to the Competition Board in the 1990s included cement prices, bank interest rates and cell phone rates, but generally:

> changes in demand conditions in the market, or in the costs of all or a significant number of sellers, will result in prompt change in the market price at which the total supply and total demand are balanced in the new condition. The fact that sellers' prices change at or about the same

8 *Ibid.*, p. 48.

> time and by the same amount in these circumstances would be evidence of a highly competitive situation. Moreover, with the further condition that entry of new sellers into such markets is easy, there would be no reason to expect the rate of profit to deviate for long from the minimum necessary to attract investible funds, given the risks involved. We call this rate of profit the competitive or normal rate of profit ... there can be no long-run tendency for profit rates to remain above the competitive level.[9]

Moreover, according to George Stigler, even collusive parallel pricing will not persist. Cheating takes place, as cartel members try to increase their share of sales. The experience of the Opec cartel suggests this is an accurate assessment of cartel behaviour. 'Uniform parallel prices simply represent convergence on the competitive norms.'[10] If, however, government protection is given to cartels, their behaviour changes and consumers suffer. In South Africa this was strikingly clear in the price of medicines and petrol. The prices of both were the result of outmoded distribution channels, which prevented Clicks from employing dispensing chemists and Pick n Pay from cutting petrol prices.

Favouring associated firms, and predation

The favouring of associated firms was another area for controversy. It was believed that large conglomerate firms selectively favoured associate companies. Economic theory questions the validity of this belief. Judge Bork in his analysis of the US experience argues that 'it is impossible for a firm actually to sell to itself for less than it sells to outside firms because the real cost of any transfer includes the return that could have been made on a sale to an outsider'.[11] Despite the apparent opportunity for this sort of behaviour on the part of South African conglomerates such as Anglo American, the debate over competition policy did not focus on this particular issue.

Nor was predation an issue that troubled either the media or economists in South Africa, despite the earlier example of SA Breweries' destruction of Louis Luyt's Luyt Lager.

Restrictive practices and price discrimination

Restrictive practices and price discrimination were not the object of specific legislation as they had been in both the USA and the UK. Uniform pricing was favoured by the South African government,

9 *Ibid.*, pp. 52–53.
10 *Ibid.*, p. 56.
11 *Ibid.*

even though it might be anti-competitive and not in the interest of the consumer. 'Uniform pricing provisions should be recognised for what they are: anti-competitive policies designed to protect a diminishing segment of the increasingly price-sensitive retail marketplace.'[12] Competition policy should encourage price flexibility. Sadly, in South Africa, policy was often the result of the opposite view, with support for a single exit price. This was perhaps most glaring in the National Drug Policy, but motorists came face to face with it every time they filled up their cars with petrol.

Though not the object of specific legislation, price discrimination could be considered a form of restrictive practice if it was against public interest. In such cases section (l)(b) of the 1979 Act gave the minister the power to ban it, but, as Professor Reekie points out, the seven criteria laid down by the Act to determine whether a pricing practice is restrictive all yield a negative response. In theory, price discrimination expands or maintains output.[13] It is uniform pricing which discriminates and works against the interests of the consumer.

Throughout the 1990s competition policy remained a mix of the old and the new. On the one hand, the failure of Soviet Union and its model of economic development gave a tremendous boost to market forces throughout the world. These influenced both the National Party government of De Klerk and the African National Congress (ANC)–Communist government after 1994. Both had begun as anti-free market parties and both were yielding to economic imperatives; but this took time. It was difficult for dirigiste and economically illiterate politicians to accept that markets (and not they) should decide competition policy. Inertia and confusion in the ruling party consequently led to the old 1979 Act and the annual reports of the Competition Board determining policy until 1999, when the new Competition Act of 1998 came into operation.

The Competition Act of 1998 and the new competition policy

The Competition Act of 1998 was the result of many discussions over a number of years between various interested parties motivated by political or economic ideas. With an interventionist government in power political lobbyists of both left-of-centre and nationalist persuasion had a field day, despite the government's distancing itself from the Marxist policies enunciated by Nelson Mandela in 1990. The government was

12 *Ibid.*, p. 60, citing E. R. Bendt, *Uniform Pharmaceutical Pricing*, 1994.

13 *Ibid.*, p. 67.

under considerable pressure from the international community to avoid the mistakes of Samora Machel in Mozambique and Kenneth Kaunda in Zambia. Yet the government's conversion to the virtues of the market did not always ring true, a state of affairs not helped by the policy enunciated by its allies in the Congress of South African Trade Unions and the Communist Party and by its own, not so young, Youth League. In such a situation it is not surprising the Act proved to be a great disappointment and was not an improvement on the 1979 Act it replaced. The official purpose of the Act was to promote and maintain competition, for which six policy objectives of a very general nature were given. Four of these do not fall within the scope of competition policy but rather represent a wish list of desirable economic policies. Only the first two really focus on competition policy; and taken together the six are often contradictory. They are as follows:[14]

(a) to promote efficiency, adaptability and development of the economy;
(b) to provide consumers with competitive prices and product choices;
(c) to promote employment and advance the social and economic welfare of South Africans;
(d) to expand opportunities for South African participation in world markets while at the same time recognising the role of foreign competition in the Republic;
(e) to ensure that small and medium-sized enterprises have an equitable opportunity to participate in the economy; and
(f) to promote a greater spread of ownership, in particular to increase the ownership stakes of historically disadvantaged persons.

The first two of these are superfluous as they fall within the ambit of promoting and maintaining competition, while (c) and (d) could result in outcomes contrary to those aimed at in (a) and (b). The fifth objective 'is perfectly compatible with the promotion and maintenance of competition and with the objectives (a) and (b) provided that such enterprises produce what consumers want, do so efficiently, and that there are no artificially imposed entry barriers preventing them or others from doing so'.[15] The word 'equitable', though, is open to many interpretations and could lead to conflict with objectives (a) and (b). The sixth objective does not belong in competition policy. By expanding the scope of competition policy, with (c), (d), (e) and (f) the Act probably made a consistent and workable competition policy impossible. Indeed, according to Reekie, by favouring specified activities and groups, the

14 W. Duncan Reekie, *Monopoly and Competition Policy* (2nd edition), Free Market Foundation, 2000, p. 43.
15 *Ibid.*, p. 44.

Act was likely to encourage rent seeking, to discourage productive and allocative efficiency and to encourage the misallocation of resources.[16]

The Act prohibited both horizontal and vertical restrictive practices, save where the parties could prove pro-competitive efficiencies as a result of greater technological efficiency. A horizontal agreement was prohibited if:

i. it has the effect of substantially preventing or lessening competition in a market, or
ii. it involves any of the following:
    a) directly or indirectly fixing a purchase or selling price or any other trading condition,
    b) dividing markets by allocating customers, suppliers, territories, or specific types of goods, or
    c) collusive tendering.

> The prohibition in ii(a) may be questioned if the monopoly price resulting from the agreement is below the competitive price as a result of the cost curve moving down sufficiently to make this possible. All the prohibitions in ii(b) are prohibited with the support of most economists. GJ Sigler is the outstanding exception, arguing that firms in horizontal agreements are likely to cheat, leading to competitive prices, particularly where there is a high ratio of fixed to total costs. Prohibitions of such agreements are unnecessary where only a very small share of the total market is involved. Cartel agreements may lead to lower transaction costs, when there are peculiarities on the demand side of the market as in the diamond industry.

Vertical agreements were prohibited if they substantially lessened competition. Exceptions were allowed, save for resale price maintenance, even though well known economists such as O. E. Williamson have argued strongly that retail price maintenance is a device for minimising transaction costs, while Bork has shown that it is impossible for a firm to sell to itself for less than it sells to outside firms.[17]

Dominant firms also come within the jurisdiction of the 1998 Act. A firm is dominant if:

i it has at least 45 per cent of its market; or
ii it has 35 per cent of its market, but under 45 per cent, and cannot show that it does not have market power; or
iii it has under 35 per cent of its market as well as market power.

These percentages, moreover, may refer to sales or assets and the competition authorities must stipulate in advance how these percentages relate to a particular industry. The use of the word 'industry' in the Act here

16 *Ibid.*, p. 45.
17 *Ibid.*, p. 48.

opens the way for much confusion in interpretation. Economists can define an industry from a technological or market point of view using the concepts of cross-elasticity of supply or cross-elasticity of demand. Lawyers might use a different definition. Reekie has aptly observed:[18]

> Given the position of adversarial advocacy necessarily adopted by opposing lawyers at competition authority hearings, it becomes ever more important that economists determine the appropriate emphasis to be laid on either the supply or demand side of the market, and in turn the appropriate level of aggregation.

Underlying the debate before the Act was passed and implicit within it was the assumption that monopolies are necessarily harmful to the public good, a state of affairs that may apply to a state-controlled entity such as Telkom but that does not seem to apply to a non-state-controlled entity such as South African Breweries. While the theory underlying this model of monopoly behaviour has been disputed by both Reekie and Leach, there are still economists who argue that dominance leads to abuse, so it is understandable that politicians should be confused in this matter and that the Act might reflect their confusion. It explains, too, why the Act raised the possibility of breaking up a monopoly, an idea borrowed from the US experience of 'trust busting', even though the US anti-trust legislation had not been effectively used in the USA since the First World War and the equivalent provision was unlikely to be used in South Africa. In fact, in the 1990s the market was leading the way in unbundling, thereby reducing the legislation-induced concentration of the pre-1994 era.

Price discrimination is also prohibited by the 1998 Act. Economic theory generally considers price discrimination as a measure that leads to greater efficiency. Its prohibition seems to have crept into the Act as a result of the somewhat ill-informed popularity of Roosevelt's New Deal in the 1930s. In particular, it borrowed its ideas from the 1936 Robinson–Patman Act and the two main groups lobbying for it in the USA in the mid-1930s – small retailers in foodstuffs and pharmaceutical products – were the same two groups lobbying for it in South Africa in the later 1990s. Back in 1933 Joan Robinson showed that price discrimination was likely to benefit poorer buyers. As the 1998 Act expressly stated that one of its aims was to help the previously disadvantaged section of the population, 'It was perverse to prohibit a practice that can be both pro-competitive and redistributive in effect'.[19]

18 *Ibid.*, p. 51.
19 *Ibid.*, p. 54.

Exemptions from prohibitions

Apart from the confusion in interpretations of the 1998 Act's prohibition of purportedly anti-competitive practices, a number of exemptions were written into the Act that either were, strictly speaking, irrelevant or opened the way to welfare-reducing rent-seeking behaviour. These exemptions applied to both vertical and horizontal agreements and to price discrimination. Exemption to the prohibition of a vertical or horizontal agreement may be made if the agreement contributes to the following:

- i maintenance or promotion of exports;
- ii promotion of the ability of small business controlled or owned by historically disadvantaged persons to become competitive;
- iii change in productive capacity necessary to stop decline in an industry; or
- iv the economic stability of any industry (so designated by the authorities).

The first two fall within the scope of economic and political policy, respectively. Points iii and iv are 'quaint and again irrelevant to competition policy',[20] for arresting the impact of industrial decline or instability fall within the scope of social and economic policy.

Exemptions to the prohibition of price discrimination also open the way to non-economic interpretations of the Act. Exemptions are set out in the Act in relation to a firm practising price discrimination that in its practice:

- a makes only reasonable allowance for differences in cost or likely cost of manufacture, distribution, sale, promotion or delivery resulting from the differing places to which, methods by which, or quantities in which, goods or services are supplied to different purchasers;
- b is constituted by doing acts in good faith to meet a price or benefit offered by a competitor; or
- c is in response to the actual or imminent deterioration of perishable goods; changing conditions affecting the market for goods and services concerned, including:
  - i any action in the response to the actual or imminent deterioration of perishable goods;
  - ii any action in response to the obsolescence of seasonal goods;
  - iii a sale pursuant to a liquidation or sequestration procedure; or
  - iv a sale in good faith in discontinuance of business in the goods or services concerned.[21]

Because both the legal definition of price discrimination and the technical definition involve examining cost–price ratios and not price alone, identical prices can be discriminatory, which is why exemption (a) was put into the Act. Costs are not a precise measure, which provokes further

20 *Ibid.*, p. 58
21 *Ibid.*, pp. 58–59.

disputes, while it is surely reasonable for a manufacturer attempting to increase share of the market to offer larger discounts to channels with the greater growth potential. Such legislation gets through Parliaments but is not enforceable.

Mergers and competition

In terms of the 1998 Act a merger occurs when one or more persons acquire direct or indirect control of significant interests of the business of competitors. Control, as exemplified by Anglo American, includes the ability to command a majority of the share votes without necessarily owning a majority of the shares.[22] The intention to merge must be stated to the authorities, which then have the power to permit or prohibit the merger according to whether it is likely to prevent or lessen competition. Bureaucrats are given the power to take into consideration any factor that is relevant to competition. Eight of them are listed in the Act:[23]

- i the actual and potential level of impact of competition in the market;
- ii the ease of entry into the market, including tariff and regulatory barriers;
- iii the level, trends of concentration, and history of collusion, in the market;
- iv the degree of countervailing power in the market;
- v the likelihood that the acquisition would result in the merged firm having market power;
- vi the dynamic characteristics of the market, including growth, innovation, and product differentiation;
- vii whether the business, or part of the business, of a party to the merger or proposed merger has failed or is likely to fail; and
- viii whether the merger will result in the removal of an effective competitor.

By these all factors, 'in addition to the difficulties of assessing current dominance, the authorities will have added to their brief the very difficult (if not impossible) task of assessing how the competitive situation could evolve in the future'.[24] Competition policy in this form has become an interventionist policy for politicians and lobbyists.

This authority to intervene also permits the authorities to act when the 'public interest' is involved. This 'public interest' phrase requires them to consider the effect of the merger upon:

22 The Oppenheimers owned around 8 per cent of Anglo American but were able to control the company. This had enabled them in turn to take control of De Beers by using Anglo American's resources. De Beers then acquired a large holding in Anglo American. This process was replicated with other subsidiaries.

23 Reekie, *Monopoly and Competition Policy* (2nd edition), pp. 62–62.

24 *Ibid.*, p. 63.

i a particular industrial sector or region;
ii employment;
iii the ability of small business, or firms controlled or owned by historically disadvantaged persons to become competitive; and
iv the ability of national industries to compete in international markets.

Apart from the scope for error and the subjectivity of judgement, the socio-economic objectives of the Act incorporated all the grandstanding policies of the ANC–Communist government: redistribution, labour interests and black economic empowerment. Such goals, whether appropriate or not, do not belong in competition policy. Indeed:

> overall welfare is greatest when society's resources are allocated in the economy so that consumers are able to satisfy their wants as far as technological and physical constraints permit. In this way the wealth of a nation is maximised. Competition policies aim should be to help to bring this about.[25]

Conclusion

South African competition policy was contradictory and ineffective in the 1990s, just as it had been in the preceding decades. The views of economists, lawyers and politicians differed widely. In theory, in a market economy, competition policy would not be necessary, but South Africa was not a market economy. It was a managed market economy in which lobbyists with loud voices were able to influence the government. National Socialist–populist politicians and Marxist socialist politicians were united in supporting government intervention against monopolies, which were presumed to be harmful. Bigness *per se* was bad, with almost all the parties involved failing to understand the true nature of competition, despite the fact that Schumpeter had explained that it involved research and the quest for substitutes to replace the less desirable by the more desirable. In such a situation it is not surprising that competition policy not only contained contradiction, but was unenforceable.

This confusion applied to both the 1979 Act and the 1998 Act and, as the 1998 Act was even more muddled than the 1979 one, competition policy in the 1990s developed into opposition to large private corporations (but not the mismanaged state corporation), coloured over with a wish list of what the ANC–Communist alliance considered to be desirable social objectives. What G. C. Allen had said about the 1948 British Monopolies and Restrictive Practices Act could with equal justice be

25 *Ibid.*, p. 64.

said about the South African 1998 Competition Act. An intellectual regression had taken place. Whereas the views of economists began to be heard and reflected in the 1979 Act, in the 'new' South Africa, by 1997–98, economic analysis was conspicuously absent. As a result, the needs of the consumer tended to be given short shrift and equality of opportunity yielded place to equality of outcome. In the process the consumer was the loser. Adam Smith's dictum that consumption is the sole end and purpose of all production was either forgotten or ignored, not in favour of producers, as in the age of mercantilism, but in favour of a host of non-economic considerations thought up by populist politicians. In the 1990s there was no real competition policy in South Africa, and when consumers did benefit it was not as a result of government competition policy, but as a result of South Africa becoming a member of the World Trade Organization and the ending of import prohibitions, together with some tariff reductions. This suggests that competition policy was not only ineffectual: it was unnecessary.

27

Labour policy

Frans Barker

Introduction

Changes in labour policy were the harbinger of the political changes that took place in South Africa during the 1990s. Many say that changes in labour policy were in fact the instigator of changes in the political landscape, because forces were thereby unleashed that made political change inevitable. It all started more than a decade earlier, in fact as far back as 1977, when the government of the day appointed a commission of inquiry (the Wiehahn Commission) to investigate and report on all existing labour laws. Discrimination was endemic throughout the labour legislation, as was the case with much of the country's legislation. One of the first recommendations of the Wiehahn Commission was that the statutory prohibition on black workers to form or join trade unions should be scrapped, and that black workers should enjoy full freedom of association. These and other recommendations were, in the main, accepted and implemented by the government of the day, thereby opening the way for the removal of statutory discrimination in the world of work, and probably eventually in society as a whole.

During the course of the 1980s these changes resulted in the development of a strong union movement, which was not only a force to be reckoned with in the workplace but also with regard to national issues. Key sections of organised business very soon realised the importance of building cooperative relations with the union movement.

The need for cooperation between employers and unions became very evident in 1988, when the then Department of Labour made some

The views expressed in this chapter are personal and do not necessarily represent those of any organisation with which Dr Barker is associated.

very unpopular amendments to the Labour Relations Act (LRA) of 1956. These amendments were forced through in spite of strong opposition from the principal body that advised the Minister of Labour on labour policy, the National Manpower Commission (NMC). The labour union federations that were not represented on the NMC, namely the Congress of South African Trade Unions (Cosatu) and the National Council of Trade Unions (Nactu), also strongly opposed these amendments. The employer federation of the time, the South African Employers Consultative Committee on Labour Affairs (Saccola), and the two union federations thereafter started to cooperate with each other to address the crisis caused by these amendments to the LRA.

Climate of cooperation

The release of Nelson Mandela in 1990 greatly stimulated this climate of cooperation between business and labour regarding various national issues. The political developments were probably an important stimulus for organised business and labour to redouble their efforts to find consensus on the very controversial labour law amendments, which had the potential to undo all the progress made during the 1980s to build greater cooperation in the labour field.

It was therefore not unexpected that organised business and labour in 1990 set the scene for what later turned out to be a sustained period of high-level interaction, characterised by an unprecedented search for consensus between the most important stakeholders in the labour field. In May 1990 the representatives of business and labour signed the so-called SCN (Saccola–Cosatu–Nactu) Accord. The agreement related to proposals for interim changes to the LRA to address the most important criticisms of the Act, pending a comprehensive review of it, which the parties agreed should be undertaken by the NMC.[1]

The SCN parties thereafter engaged with government. The government was a very reluctant participant in these discussions, but eventually the SCN parties and the then Minister of Labour, Eli Louw, signed the so-called Laboria minute in September 1990. In terms of this minute, the government agreed to proceed with amendments to the LRA as proposed in the SCN Accord. The government also agreed to restructure the NMC, which would essentially be a tripartite body representing government, organised business and organised labour, rather than individuals in their personal capacity being appointed from

1 *Commemorative Issue 1979–1995*, National Manpower Commission, 1995, pp. 2–3.

the various constituencies. Cosatu and Nactu agreed to join the restructured NMC. Furthermore, the government also agreed to channel all other issues affecting labour legislation through a restructured NMC.

One of the first tasks undertaken in 1990 in terms of this newly found cooperative relationship between the parties was to consider labour legislation for farm and domestic workers. The NMC was not yet restructured, but Cosatu and Nactu were informally involved in these projects and in the redrafting of the LRA. The government's renewed commitment to the views of the NMC eventually culminated in the passing of labour legislation in 1993 which extended the protection of basic labour laws to farm and domestic workers.

However, the structural problem of the NMC remained, and the government appeared to be not fully committed to restructuring it. All parties involved with the NMC in 1991 decided unanimously to force the hand of government by suspending the activities of the NMC until it had been restructured. This happened only when Leon Wessels took office as Minister of Labour, and the restructured NMC held its first meeting in February 1993. The vision of employers and unions seemed to have been achieved, which was that all stakeholders, including the government, would be fully committed to cooperation and the search for consensus on labour legislation and labour policy.

The restructured NMC introduced new principles in the process of making labour policy.[2] Principles such as transparency, mandating, negotiation and consensus seeking formed the basis of a legitimate, broadly accepted and participative policy-making system. These principles were also to form the basis of the National Economic Development and Labour Council (Nedlac), which was formed in 1995 as the successor body to both the NMC and another, more informal body that had been created to consider economic policy, the National Economic Forum (NEF).

Original expectations for Nedlac

As detailed in Chapter 28, Nedlac was launched in February 1995 in terms of the National Economic Development and Labour Council Act 35 of 1994, which was one of the first pieces of legislation to be passed by the new government. It was a multipartite body, with the principal participants being business, labour and the government. However, during the deliberations on its establishment, the government indicated that it wanted to prevent a narrow corporatist arrangement and to involve the so-called community and development constituency. Deciding whom

2 *Ibid.*, pp. 3–4.

to appoint to represent the community presented quite a challenge. These needed to be organisations that represented a significant community interest on a national basis, that should have a direct interest in reconstruction and development, that should be constituted democratically and that should be able to get mandates. Only three of the 60 organisations that applied for membership were accepted, representing women, youth and civic interests. These organisations were primarily represented in the Development Chamber of Nedlac.[3]

Labour and to some extent business felt that the NMC, an advisory body, was too often ignored by government. They wanted a stronger role for its successor. Parties were encouraged by the consensus-seeking role regarding economic policy of the National Economic Forum and attempted to build this informal negotiating role into the legislation in terms of which Nedlac was formed. A further frustration experienced with regard to the predecessors of Nedlac was that the previous government sometimes submitted legislation (in particular labour legislation) to Parliament without consulting these bodies. They were sidetracked and the parties wanted to prevent this happening in Nedlac.

The parties envisaged the following role for Nedlac:

- Nedlac should be a body whose objective was to achieve social consensus on all socio-economic issues. It should not simply be an advisory body to government. The Nedlac Act, in section 5(1)(b), attempted to address this by providing for Nedlac to 'seek to reach consensus and conclude agreements on matters pertaining to social and economic policy'.
- Nedlac should be a type of clearing house for all policy initiatives. This was to some extent accommodated in legislation, in that the Nedlac Act, section 5(1)(c,d), provided for all labour legislation to be submitted to Nedlac before being submitted to Parliament, and for it to consider all significant changes to social and economic policy before it was implemented or introduced into Parliament.

Clearly, the first role in particular was overambitious. Even though social consensus is important, consensus will not be possible on all issues under all circumstances. Not only has the government the responsibility to govern, but not all interest groups are represented on Nedlac (the unemployed and consumers being the most obvious examples). This increasingly became a source of tension between the stakeholders.

At the time of the creation of Nedlac, business was also trying to become more organised, and the first step in this direction was the

3 See F. S. Barker, *The South African Labour Market* (5th edition), Van Schaik, 2007, p. 259.

formation of Business South Africa (BSA) in 1994. It was a confederation of the most important business organisations in South Africa, but excluded important black business organisations such as the National African Federation of Chambers of Commerce (Nafcoc) and the Black Business Council (BBC). Black and white business interests (as represented by BBC and BSA respectively) were merged only with the formation of Business Unity South Africa (BUSA) in October 2003.

New Labour Relations Act

One of the first tasks of Nedlac was to redraft the LRA. The negotiations took up most of 1995, and culminated in agreement among all stakeholders on most of the major issues, and on the implementation of the new Labour Relations Act (Act 66 of 1995) in 1996. The Act contained several major innovations:

- provisions to codify and extend the protection afforded to employees against unfair dismissal;
- the establishment of the Commission for Conciliation, Mediation and Arbitration (CCMA) as a means of expediting dispute resolution and making it more efficient and cost-effective;
- far-reaching provisions on industrial action, including protection against dismissal for striking employees and the right to embark on protest action to promote socio-economic interests, including the protection of employees against dismissal for absence from work while participating in such protest action;
- provisions conferring on representative trade unions certain organisational rights, including the right to information;
- the establishment of workplace forums designed to promote joint problem solving and participation on certain subjects.

At the same time, there was much more emphasis on the promotion of sectoral bargaining, through bargaining councils, even though the principle of such councils was carried over from the previous LRA.

Unfair dismissals

The original intention of the new LRA with regard to unfair dismissals was to ensure that employers followed fair procedure when dismissing for misconduct or incapacity and that they should dismiss someone only for a fair reason. Disputes about dismissals were excluded from the ambit of the right to strike and had to be referred to arbitration. Furthermore, the new LRA also introduced various measures to discourage retrenchments, for example by ensuring proper consultation between employers and representatives of workers on the intention to retrench.

CCMA

The CCMA was formed in November 1996 to deal with mediation and arbitration, in particular with regard to unfair dismissals. Initially, the CCMA achieved a very high settlement rate (about 80 per cent) but this later declined significantly. The CCMA experienced an unexpectedly large case load and suffered from under-funding. The strong emphasis on fair procedure in some cases resulted in procedural requirements that were inappropriate, for instance in the case of small business.

Strikes and protest action

The provisions on strikes in the old LRA proved to be seriously defective, primarily because it would not pass constitutional muster, because of the lack of protection against dismissal for employees embarking on a 'legal' strike. There were also technical and complicated pre-strike procedures to be followed, which the new LRA attempted to address. Strikes were decriminalised, which resulted in strikes being protected if certain basic procedures were followed, and unprotected if not. The right to strike in some disputes was replaced by arbitration, in particular in disputes over unfair dismissal.

The new LRA also for the first time acknowledged the right of employees to embark on industrial action to promote or defend their socio-economic interests, and provided protection against dismissal for participation in such socio-economic protest action. This was in line with fundamental rights of workers outlined by the International Labour Organization (ILO). Certain limitations were introduced to protect the economic interests of the country; for example, the issue in dispute needed to be referred to Nedlac for its consideration before employees could embark on such action.

Initially, it seemed as if the government's new labour policies were successful in reducing industrial action in South Africa. The number of work days lost through strikes declined from about 2,700,000 in 1990 to 650,000 in 1997. Some of the reasons for the optimism were the success rate in settling disputes at the CCMA, the smooth settlement of disputes in bargaining councils, and an apparent growing maturity in collective bargaining by the relevant parties. However, the optimism about improved labour relations and reduced industrial action was short lived. In 1998 and 1999 the number of work days lost through strikes and the number of workers involved in strikes increased back to the 1990 levels and in some cases even exceeded those levels.[4]

4 Barker, *The South African Labour Market* (5th edition), p. 103.

Workplace forums

The new LRA made provision for workplace forums, which were intended to establish a basis for cooperative workplace relations between workers and management. Productivity improvements had to be achieved, by making workers part of the decision-making process. However, Cosatu was reluctant to move towards a more cooperative form of engagement with employers. Its members had a preference for the use of power-based forms of interaction.[5] Klerck refers to the concern in union circles that workplace forums could undermine the militant unionism that had been quite successful in South Africa.[6] Because of the extensive requirements regarding consultation, joint decision making and disclosure of information, employers were also not enthusiastic about workplace forums. They were concerned that the forums could inhibit and delay decision making, which might negatively affect productivity. It is consequently not surprising that relatively few workplace forums were established. Instead, there is evidence of a trend towards 'lean production', based on the casualisation of work and attempts to bypass unions rather than involve them in restructuring initiatives.

Cracks in the consensus

It was not long after the new LRA had been implemented with the support of all the parties that the first cracks in the consensus-seeking approach, which had characterised the period up to 1995, started to appear. The Presidential Commission to Investigate Labour Market Policy reported in 1996. The Commission consisted of individuals drawn from the major constituencies. It was charged with the task of developing the labour market policies necessary to meet the employment-related objectives of the government's *Reconstruction and Development Programme* (RDP). The Commission made recommendations on a wide range of issues, but also started to question some of the principles of labour market policies. For instance, it was concerned about the impact of rapidly increasing labour costs on employment. It therefore proposed a national Accord for Employment and Growth, involving the social partners – business, labour and government. It was also proposed that the minister should require explanation of wage

5 K. Van Holdt, 'The world of work and the economy', *South African Labour Bulletin*, 19(2) (1995), 23–30, at p. 24.

6 G. Klerck, 'Mapping the terrain of participation: workplace forums and shopfloor industrial relations', *South African Journal of Labour Relations*, 24(1) (autumn/winter 2000), 4–27, at p. 12.

settlements that varied considerably from the terms of the Accord. The Commission argued that employment considerations should be the major factor for the minister in deciding to extend bargaining council agreements, rather than the representativeness of the parties, and that there should be special schedules for small business.[7]

Growth, employment and redistribution (GEAR) strategy

A major blow to consensus seeking was the unilateral implementation of the government's growth, employment and redistribution (GEAR) strategy. The government made it clear that GEAR was not negotiable, and the policy was roundly rejected by Cosatu and the South African Communist Party. GEAR emphasised higher economic growth and significant job creation as the key challenges of economic policy. With regard to labour policy in particular, GEAR referred to structured labour market flexibility within the collective bargaining system, enhanced human resource development and a social agreement to facilitate wage and price moderation.

Employment growth would come from three sources:

- one-third of the increase in jobs would result from economic growth;
- special government programmes would provide a quarter of the new jobs;
- some 30 per cent of the increased employment would flow from institutional reforms in the labour market, employment-enhancing policy shifts and private sector wage moderation (regarding the last, the policy emphasised that wages and salaries should not increase more rapidly than productivity and envisaged real wage growth in the private sector averaging no more than 0.8 per cent per annum).

According to the GEAR strategy, flexibility in the labour market required the market's regulation in a manner that would allow for flexible collective bargaining structures, variable application of employment standards and so-called 'voice regulation', that is, allowing employees (and their unions) and employers (and their associations) to set their own minimum labour standards through bargaining. These objectives were not achieved.

Wage moderation

GEAR postulated achieving a social agreement to facilitate wage and price moderation in order to ensure that wage increases did not exceed

7 *Restructuring the South African Labour Market*, Presidential Commission to Investigate Labour Market Policy, 1996, p. 59.

average productivity growth. There were a number of references to the importance of wage moderation, with the point being made that the country should guard against an upsurge in nominal wage demands, as these would erode the benefits of exchange rate depreciation.

During the 1990s, nominal wages increased at a much higher rate than productivity, resulting in relatively sharp increases in unit labour cost.[8] The improvement in labour productivity, moreover, was partly achieved through firms shedding labour, as there was a continuous decline in employment throughout the decade. The economy experienced a sharp increase in capital intensity, which enabled employers to reduce their workforce and maintain production. The wage moderation objectives of GEAR were consequently not achieved at a time when South Africa's most important trading partners were able to keep their unit labour costs under control.[9]

Employer-provided entitlements to cover contingency risks were also relatively high in South Africa compared with those in other countries at the same level of development. Neither the state nor rural kinship support systems played a major role, because of the legacies of apartheid.[10]

Bargaining council agreements

Regarding flexible collective bargaining structures, the GEAR policy stated that bargaining council agreements should be extended to non-parties only if the prevention of job losses could be ensured, and it recommended that the minister's discretion in this regard should be broadened to allow the minister to take into account 'labour market considerations'. The labour market considerations referred to included greater sensitivity in wage determination to capital intensity, skills, regional circumstances, a firm's size and the need to foster training opportunities for new entrants to the labour market.

However, the bargaining council system was not changed; if anything it was made more onerous. Even today, the LRA law requires the minister to extend bargaining council agreements to all employers falling under the scope of the bargaining council if requested to do so by the trade union representing the majority of the employees in the particular sector and the employers' organisation employing the majority of employees in that sector. The major consequence of the extension is that wages and conditions of employment are standardised throughout the

8 F. S. Barker, *The South African Labour Market* (4th edition), Van Schaik, 2003, p. 137.

9 *Ibid.*, p. 178.

10 G. Standing, J. Sender and J. Weeks, *Restructuring the Labour Market: The South African Challenge*, International Labour Organization, 1996, p. 214.

industry.[11] The extension of the agreement prevents employer parties (usually the larger and more profitable firms) from being undercut by non-party employers. Another advantage for the larger, more profitable employers was that the wage rate agreed to in the council was likely to be lower than what they might have had to pay under a decentralised system. At the same time, the wages were higher than what the smaller, more labour-intensive and less profitable firms (often not members of the council) paid. Wage levels agreed in bargaining councils did have a significant impact on smaller firms.[12]

If the labour costs of all employers increase in tandem, the possibility of all enterprises passing on the increased cost to the consumer is much greater. This form of indirect price fixing is in the interests of both the employer and union parties to the council. Not only is competition on the basis of wages eliminated, but the incentive for employers in the council to resist wage demands is reduced. Some economists have maintained that the bilateral monopoly created by bargaining councils amounts to tacit collusion between employer and union to control both the labour and product markets and consequently suppress competition. In such circumstances both product prices and wages will be increased, to the disadvantage of the consumer, the non-participative employer and the unemployed worker.[13]

Bargaining councils also make the link between wages and productivity much more tenuous. Wages and productivity cannot be effectively linked at industry level. Productivity bargaining can really only take place at enterprise or workplace level, whereas wage levels and wage increases are regulated at industry level.

The lack of discretion on the minister's part to take economic considerations, and particularly job-creation objectives, into account when deciding to extend agreements was criticised on three fronts: the GEAR policy,[14] the authors of the ILO review of South Africa[15] and the government's Presidential Commission.[16] This type of meso-centralised wage-bargaining system does not perform well in terms of employment, economic growth and price stability. In the ILO country review it was pointed out that either highly centralised or highly decentralised

11 F. S. Barker, 'On South African labour policies', *South African Journal of Economics*, 67(1) (1999), 1–33.

12 Boccara and Moll as quoted by N. Nattrass, *Growth, Employment and Economic Policy in South Africa: A Critical Review*, Centre for Development and Enterprise, 1998.

13 See sources quoted by Barker, 'On South African labour policies', pp. 286–288.

14 *Growth, Employment and Redistribution: A Macro-economic Strategy*, Department of Finance, 1996, p. 21.

15 Standing *et al.*, *Restructuring the Labour Market*, pp. 194–195.

16 *Restructuring the South African Labour Market*, Presidential Commission, p. 59.

bargaining systems perform much better than intermediary systems such as bargaining councils. The review questioned whether this system of sectionalism is appropriate for South Africa.[17]

The opening up of South African borders to international competition in the 1990s had a significant impact on industries covered by bargaining councils. Many of them suddenly faced competitive forces that did not previously exist and the pressure on employers to reduce costs and increase productivity greatly increased. Tariff reform outpaced labour market reform, with negative consequences for employment creation and unemployment.

Conclusions about GEAR

Research undertaken by this author and also commissioned by the Centre for Development and Enterprise (CDE) indicates that there was a fundamental inconsistency between the policies pursued by the Minister of Labour and the vision embedded in GEAR.[18] Actual labour market policies fitted broadly into a high-wage, high-productivity (and consequently low-employment) growth strategy. As such, they contradicted the GEAR goals of labour-intensive growth and rapidly expanding job opportunities for the poor, the vast majority of whom are unskilled and need low-skill, low-productivity jobs. As far as labour legislation is concerned, therefore, the GEAR policies were not implemented. Neither was the policy of wage moderation achieved.

Basic Conditions of Employment Act

The government published policy proposals for a new Basic Conditions of Employment Act (BCEA) in 1996. These proposals elicited strong opposition from both employers and unions, but for completely opposite reasons. The employers were of the view that the proposals would significantly increase the indirect cost of labour, whereas the unions were of the opinion that the proposals did not go far enough with regard to certain issues, such as the introduction of a 40-hour working week. The negotiations around the BCEA became long and protracted. By the end of 1996 they had broken down, with much animosity on both sides. This was followed in 1997 by stay-away action and attempts by employers to interdict such action.[19]

17 Standing *et al.*, *Restructuring the Labour Market*, p. 16.

18 Barker, 'On South African labour policies'; and *Policy-Making in a New Democracy: South Africa's Challenges for the 21st Century*, Centre for Development and Enterprise, 1999.

19 *Ten Years of Social Dialogue and the Nedlac Experience: Discussion Document, 1995–2005*, National Economic Development and Labour Council, 2005, p. 21.

The BCEA signified a shift away from the determination of prevailing employment conditions through collective bargaining, in favour of an increased role for legislation and ministerial decree, unless the bargaining took place in a bargaining council. Collective bargaining between a union and an employer was afforded a relatively minor role.[20] This was the opposite of the well documented trend towards decentralised bargaining found in most other countries. The BCEA also contained certain 'core rights' that could not be varied under any circumstances, for instance a maximum working week of 45 ordinary hours.

This approach contrasted with the new LRA, which was implemented less than a year before the BCEA and which had as one of its primary aims the promotion and facilitation of collective bargaining. Even the government's Presidential Commission and the authors of the ILO country review proposed so-called 'voice regulation'.[21] Apart from within the bureaucracy of a bargaining council, there was practically no scope for an individual employer and a representative union to regulate minimum standards.

Another method of introducing some flexibility was the making of 'sectoral determinations' for a particular sector and area, although some might argue that such determinations were more likely to introduce more onerous or additional provisions than greater flexibility. This was partly because the BCEA allowed the Minister of Labour more discretion in relation to the powers of the Employment Conditions Commission than was the case with the former Wage Board and because the scope of sectoral determinations was much wider than that of wage determinations under the previous Act. However, these fears regarding sectoral determinations in the main turned out to be unfounded.

Cost of labour

Apart from these considerations, the BCEA increased the direct and indirect costs of labour.[22] Besides provisions such as longer annual, maternity and family responsibility leave, and an expanded definition of remuneration that increased the indirect cost of labour, two other provisions probably increased labour costs significantly.

First, the Act reduced hours of work. It had the effect of reducing South Africa's working year to 2,132 hours, 23 working days (184 hours)

20 Barker, *The South African Labour Market* (5th edition), p. 138.

21 *Restructuring the South African Labour Market*, Presidential Commission, p. 3; Standing *et al.*, *Restructuring the Labour Market*, p. 10.

22 F. S. Barker, 'Best conditions in the Basic Conditions of Employment Act', *Contemporary Labour Law*, 7(5) (1997), 41–50; Barker, 'On South African labour policies', pp. 152–155.

shorter than that of the country's peers.[23] A legislated reduction in hours worked in most instances increases the unit cost of labour and production costs in general because of the impact on fixed production costs. The fixed cost of production, that is, the capital costs and the fixed cost of labour (e.g. leave pay, social security, office space, protective clothing, recruitment costs, costs associated with education and training, etc.) do not change in proportion to hours of work. If employees work fewer hours, the fixed costs associated with their employment are spread over fewer hours, and so the hourly fixed costs increase. As far as variable labour cost is concerned, if workers are paid on a weekly or monthly basis (which is the norm in most industries), and the weekly or monthly rates remain unchanged, reduced hours would increase the hourly cost of labour. The take-home pay of employees may remain constant, but because reduced hours increase production costs and thus inflation, while employment also declines, the real disposable income of households will generally decline.[24] Also, because of the effect of the increased labour cost on price levels, international competitiveness and the substitution of labour by capital, most researchers have found that reduced hours are likely to have a *negative* effect on employment creation, rather than any positive effect often claimed by special interest groups.[25]

The second significant increase in labour cost caused by the new BCEA was the 12 per cent increase in overtime premium. This premium was higher than in comparable countries and also kicked in at an earlier level (i.e. at 45 hours rather than the 48 hours in most comparable countries). This resulted in the total overtime premium in South Africa amounting to up to two and half times that of an employee working the same hours in a comparable upper-middle-income country.[26]

Labour policy as contained in this Act generally moved in the opposite direction to that of the government's macro-economic policy of the day, GEAR. It did not meet the needs of economic liberalisation and the declining indirect cost of labour, which was transforming workplaces around the world.

23 *Questions and Answers on Basic Conditions of Employment*, Business South Africa, 1997.

24 See survey of 11 studies by the Commission of the European Communities as quoted by F. S. Barker, *The Implications of a Reduced Working Week*, unpublished report, Johannesburg, 1995, pp. 56–57.

25 See discussion by Barker, 'Best conditions in the Basic Conditions of Employment Act'.

26 *Questions and Answers*, Business South Africa.

Disillusionment with Nedlac

The unilateral implementation of GEAR undermined the role of Nedlac, because it was never referred to that body. Similarly, Nedlac considered the BCEA for many months, but was unable to achieve any substantial consensus. It was therefore not surprising that the government in general seemed to become increasingly disillusioned with Nedlac. By the end of 1997, Labour Department Director-General Sipho Pityana warned that Nedlac's role in policy formulation would have to be reviewed, as adversarial stances by its members were slowing government attempts to implement socio-economic reforms.[27] Even though the parties tried to improve relations and return to the consensus-seeking mode of operation that had characterised the early 1990s, they were not very successful. The 1998 Presidential Job Summit became a general turning point in perceptions of Nedlac[28] and 'in the post-summit phase widespread disenchantment set in about the efficacy of the Nedlac process'.[29]

Nedlac was also affected by the emergence of other, non-statutory institutions for consultation and discussion, such as the bipartite Millennium Labour Council (MLC) and various presidential working groups. The MLC was formed as a bilateral structure between business and labour. Its objective was to develop a shared analysis of the crisis of unemployment and poverty in the country and to pursue potential solutions with government and Nedlac.[30] It comprised 12 members each from business and from trade union constituencies. The trade unions were generally represented by the leadership of the three main trade union federations in the country, namely Cosatu, Fedusa and Nactu. The business representation was more *ad hoc* and consisted of a number of individuals, as well as the chief executives of certain business associations. More fundamentally, the business representatives on the MLC were not elected or appointed by any business organisation. The business representatives on the MLC not only functioned without a mandate from business, but also without the implicit support of a large part of business. By contrast, the union representatives on the MLC and union negotiators in Nedlac were the same people. This enabled the labour representatives to play the MLC business representatives off against the Nedlac business negotiators.

27 *Ten Years of Social Dialogue*, National Economic Development and Labour Council, p. 21.

28 *Ibid.*, p. 24.

29 Parsons, as quoted *ibid.*

30 Barker, *The South African Labour Market* (4th edition), p. 313.

Broad consensus on workplace transformation

In spite of disillusionment with the role of Nedlac, it was able to achieve substantial consensus on important policies relating to workplace transformation. The most important of these was the Employment Equity Act of 1998. The main elements of this Act were:[31]

- the prohibition of direct or indirect unfair discrimination by any employer on any arbitrary ground, among which were race, gender, age and sexual orientation (excluded from the definition of unfair discrimination were affirmative action measures and preferential treatment on the basis of the inherent requirements of the job; applicants for employment were also protected by this part of the Act);
- affirmative action measures, which applied to so-called designated employers (and excluded small employers);
- a reduction in so-called disproportionate income differentials.

The Act required designated employers to prepare plans to achieve progress towards employment equity and to submit these plans to the Department of Labour for assessment. In this sense, the approach was to encourage workplace transformation through partial self-regulation by employer and employee parties. The Act specifically excluded the imposition of a quota system. However, the employer was required to set numerical goals for achieving equitable representation of suitably qualified persons from so-called designated groups (black persons, women and disabled persons) and a timetable for achieving the goals. The Director-General of the Department of Labour could review an employment equity plan to determine if an employer was complying with the Act. Factors that the Director-General (or for that matter any other person or body applying this Act) was to take into account included:

- whether suitably qualified persons from designated groups were 'equitably represented' within each occupational category and level, as determined by
  - the profile of the national and regional economically active population (i.e. demographics)
  - the pool of suitably qualified persons from designated groups from which the employer could appoint or promote persons
  - the economic and financial circumstances of the employer and of the particular sector in which the employer operated
  - present and planned vacancies and labour turnover of the employer;

31 Barker, *The South African Labour Market* (5th edition), p. 245.

- progress made by other employers in the same sector and operating under similar conditions;
- reasonable efforts made by the employer to achieve employment equity;
- the extent to which the employer had eliminated employment barriers that adversely affected persons from designated groups.

The most important argument in favour of the affirmative action provisions in the Act, and the reason why business in general supported it, was that the dismantling of discrimination could not take place instantly, simply by getting rid of discriminatory legislation.[32] After many years of such legislation, the people who were discriminated against would still be far behind in terms of ownership of the wealth of the country and the filling of skilled occupations. Furthermore, theory teaches that if discrimination is caused by market imperfections (such as employers of their own accord discriminating against black persons), it will not be eliminated unless there is intervention by government.[33]

However, the Act was also criticised on a number of grounds. It was said to be re-racialising South African society, by categorising racial groups that should receive preferential treatment, rather than individuals who had been discriminated against. Furthermore, the Act denied employers the opportunity to apply merit in appointing or promoting persons; indeed, the best person for the job might not be appointed or promoted where a person from a designated group who was only 'suitably qualified' was given preference. Jefferies, for instance, objected to the Act on three grounds[34]:

- It mandated state intervention in the private domain and this exceeded the proper role of government in a liberal democracy.
- Such intervention on a racial basis was counter to the constitution, which permits, rather than requires, race discrimination in the form of affirmative action.
- It failed to address the country's key problem – the poverty attendant on widespread unemployment – and instead adopted an approach likely to provide a disincentive to job creation.

Most observers recognise that legislative mechanisms alone will not be sufficient to achieve employment equity in South Africa. Special programmes of affirmative action and black advancement are required

32 Barker, *The South African Labour Market* (5th edition), p. 250.

33 See discussion in Barker, *The South African Labour Market* (5th edition), pp. 205–206.

34 A. Jefferies, *The Employment Equity Bill of 1997: A Briefing to Business*, South African Institute of Race Relations, 1998, p. 9.

and these should include: literacy training, quality education, accelerated training, mentorship, targeted recruitment practices and various other programmes. These should be aimed at ensuring that the composition of the labour force, and especially of skilled occupations, is more fully representative of South Africa's population, without reducing standards and efficiency.

Because these programmes assisted only those persons already in employment, special attention needed to be given to reducing the high level of unemployment; but policies to implement affirmative action and those to increase economic growth were likely to be contradictory in the short term. Despite this, the approach of the Employment Equity Act was probably the best possible 'fit' that could be achieved between these divergent objectives.

The labour market flexibility debate

In spite of basic agreement on the important measures to be taken to transform the workplace, the core differences between business and labour about whether the new labour legislation in South Africa would help or hinder the country in achieving its growth and employment objectives became increasingly apparent. The debate on so-called 'labour market flexibility' intensified. However, this was probably something of a misnomer, because although the concept of labour market flexibility encompasses a wide range of aspects, the parties tended to focus narrowly on legislative provisions that might inhibit 'flexibility'.

In fact, one of the core ways of ensuring flexibility is to encourage voice regulation, by allowing more scope for parties to arrange their own affairs through collective bargaining, especially at the enterprise or operational level. In this regard, labour policies in most instances moved towards increased prescription and centralisation – in the opposite direction to that envisaged in GEAR. In such cases it is not always the legislation as such that has the effect of increasing the cost of labour and reducing flexibility, but the effect of increased centralisation and strong unionism.

Increased centralisation as a result of bargaining council agreements being extended to non-parties went against the international trend towards greater decentralisation of workplace bargaining and, in some countries, even individual contracts of employment.[35] Greater

35 S. Hayter, G. Reinecke and R. Torres, *Studies on the Social Dimensions of Globalization: South Africa*, International Labour Organization, 2001, p. 85.

centralisation results in less flexibility being incorporated into collective agreements and less provision being made for the circumstances of individual enterprises or workplaces. The link between productivity bargaining and wage bargaining was also compromised in a bargaining council system. This further reduced flexibility.

Apart from the cost of labour, there were other labour market flexibility issues. One such concerned the increase in job security brought about by the changes in the LRA. Obviously, this was an important social advance. However, job security is far from cost free.[36] Not only do legal and other processes incur high costs, but job security regulations are likely to make employers reluctant to engage new workers on indefinite contracts. In addition, employers may substitute labour with capital or utilise subcontractors, casual and temporary workers, thereby increasing rather than reducing job insecurity. On the other hand, greater job security may encourage employers to ensure better job matching and to invest more in training to promote productivity. Workers may also become less resistant to technological change and more amenable to operational changes.[37]

Firm conclusions about the flexibility of South Africa's labour laws and labour environment are difficult. Studies on labour market flexibility have divergent conclusions with regard to whether the South African labour market is more or less flexible than that of other countries.[38] In comparing the South African unfair dismissal regime with data from the Organisation for Economic Co-operation and Development (OECD), Van Niekerk[39] concluded that South African laws were not significantly less flexible than those applicable in most OECD countries, with regard to severance pay, notice periods, probation periods, fairness criteria, reinstatement procedures and temporary employment. However, this is not to deny the existence of significant problems with the implementation of dismissal law in South Africa, particularly in relation to dispute resolution structures and procedures. Inappropriate procedures might have been the biggest cause of perceptions of labour market inflexibility.

Research findings present divergent outcomes, depending on whether the research was based on the perceptions of employers, on a

36 P. A. K. Le Roux, 'South African unfair dismissal law: time for a reassessment?', *Contemporary Labour Law*, 3(12) (1994), 117–123; Barker, *The South African Labour Market* (5th edition), p. 129.

37 See discussion in Barker, *The South African Labour Market* (5th edition), p. 129.

38 *Ibid.*, pp. 139–141.

39 A. Van Niekerk, *Regulating Flexibility and Small Business: Revisiting The LRA and BCEA – A Response to Halton Cheadle's Draft Concept Paper*, DPRU Working Paper No. 07/119, Development Policy Research Unit, University of Cape Town, 2007.

comparison of complex legislative regimes, or whether a range of other factors was taken into account. Four factors have commonly played a role in this regard:

1 There will always be one or more countries that have one or more provisions in labour legislation that are similar to or even more onerous than the legislation in South Africa. However, it is the cumulative effect of all labour and labour-related policies (against the background of issues such as the management of HIV/AIDS, the risk profile of the country and crime) that needs to be considered. It is practically impossible to do such an analysis.
2 It is not always the level of regulation that is important, but the change in that level. For instance, for South Africa to have come from a system of relatively little regulation of dismissal to the regulatory system found in some European countries caused a shock to the system for a number of years and contributed to perceptions among employers of labour market inflexibility.
3 South Africa experienced a sharp increase in the level of unionisation, and has one of the highest levels of union density. In addition, bargaining councils gave unions further power. Not only did this probably increase the general level of labour costs, but it also ensured a higher level of compliance with labour laws than in other developing countries with similar levels of regulation.
4 The quality of human resources is important. Labour productivity is lower in a country with a legacy of poor education and training, as is the case in South Africa; together with the historic discrimination this aggravated the skills shortages. Compliance with labour legislation is less onerous where labour productivity is relatively high.

End of the decade: the end of cooperative relations?

The decade under review ended on a quite different note than that on which it started. Even though there was much talk about a social compact, and the parties recommitted themselves to ensuring that Nedlac remained the pre-eminent institution of social dialogue in the country, the facts pointed to a rather different picture.

First, Nedlac faced substantial competition and encroachment upon its functions by other bodies, some non-statutory, such as the MLC and the presidential working groups, and others statutory, such as the various commissions and boards appointed to deal with specific labour laws. Second, Nedlac was increasingly being regarded by many stakeholder parties as ineffective. This resulted in efforts to sideline

Nedlac. Furthermore, the senior leadership figures among the various stakeholders were less active in the negotiating processes than they had been earlier in the decade. This lengthened the negotiating process and further frustrated the government, anxious to implement its new policies as soon as possible.[40]

The increasing tension between the parties was perhaps best reflected in the proposed amendments to labour legislation that were tabled by the Minister of Labour in Nedlac in July 2000. Nedlac established a negotiating team to deal with the proposals, but the parties were unable to reach agreement.[41] By the end of the decade Cosatu had tabled an application to embark on protracted protest action. Its general secretary was threatening 'blood on the floor' if government went ahead with the proposed amendments. Even though some level of compromise was eventually reached between representatives of business and the labour federations, business in general was not satisfied with the labour law amendments. There seemed to be little prospect of the parties again achieving the high levels of cooperation and consensus seeking that had characterised the first half of the decade and involved senior figures in both labour and business.

Conclusion

At the beginning of the decade, the leadership of both organised business and labour were enthusiastically working at finding consensus, and in most cases were able to achieve compromises that both could live with. The relationship between business and labour during this time was particularly constructive, assisted by their joint opposition to the policies of the government of the day.

This constructive relationship gradually became more strained, particularly after the election of the new government in 1994, as the parties attempted to convince the government to introduce policies that best suited their own interests. The government obviously had its own agenda, which in some cases suited business and in others the unions. With regard to labour policy, however, some important aspects of the GEAR strategy remained on paper only: it was never implemented. It is notable that in spite of these disagreements with regard to micro-economic labour policies, organised business and labour were in substantial agreement on the need for transformation at the

40 Barker, *The South African Labour Market* (5th edition), p. 261.

41 *Ten Years of Social Dialogue*, National Economic Development and Labour Council, p. 28.

workplace and on the instruments required to achieve such transformation. However, the structures created to enhance the cooperative relationship between the various stakeholders, in particular Nedlac, were increasingly being seen by various stakeholders as inefficient and incapable of delivering on original expectations. This undermined regular, constructive engagement between the senior leadership of business, labour and government.

In 1990 there was a realisation that consensus was a critical ingredient of successful and credible policies, while consensus takes time and cannot be rushed. It also required all parties to be prepared to compromise. Their willingness to do this had weakened by 2000. Furthermore, South Africa needed policies based on an objective, continuous reassessment of successful international policies to address the critical problems of unemployment and inequalities, but a coalition government of the African National Congress, the Communist Party and a powerful union movement made it difficult to implement such policies. Labour policy consequently remained filled with contradictions and unreal expectations.

28

Role of social dialogue in policy making in South Africa

Raymond Parsons

Introduction

'History', it is often said, 'is lived forward but is written in retrospect. We know the end before the beginning and we can never wholly recapture what it was to know the beginning only.' This analysis therefore seeks to convey the political and economic setting in which the origins of South African social dialogue and the National Economic Development and Labour Council (Nedlac) can be detected. Ideas tend to take root when the soil has been fertilised by social and economic trends – and in South Africa's case, by political developments as well. This helps to explain both the emergence of 'institutionalised social dialogue' in the country and also the extent to which that had its roots in workplace issues.

An encompassing working definition of social dialogue was given by the International Labour Organization (ILO) in 1996 as:

> All types of negotiation, consultation or simply exchange of information between, or among, representatives of governments, employers and workers, on issues of common interest relating to economic and social policy. It can exist as a tripartite process, with the government as an official party to the dialogue or it may consist of bipartite relations only between labour and management (or trade unions and employer associations), with or without indirect government involvement. Consultation can be informal or institutionalised, and often it is a combination of the two. It can take place at national, regional or at enterprise level. It can be inter-professional, sectoral, or a combination of all of these.

My thanks go to Friede Dowie, Peter Duminy, Corinna Gardner, Bobby Godsell, Gavin Keeton and Herbert Mkhize for valuable comments on earlier drafts. They also helped to recapture that elusive element in looking back – 'how it seemed at the time'. Responsibility for the views expressed nonetheless remains mine.

To assess and understand Nedlac's role in the 1990s it is first necessary to acknowledge some key developments that led up to its creation. The year 1990 was a crucial year, in which the future President Nelson Mandela was released from prison, unleashing the various political and social forces which ultimately culminated in a negotiated full democracy in 1994. To that extent at least, the advent of representative democracy and the development of institutionalised social dialogue must be said to have converged in South Africa.

Genesis of Nedlac

Although (as detailed below) Nedlac arose from a merger of the National Economic Forum (NEF) and the National Manpower Commission (NMC) the genesis of 'tripartism' in South Africa can be traced back to the labour relations arena which developed in the wake of the watershed report of the Wiehahn Commission.[1] The acceptance of most of the recommendations of the Wiehahn Commission by the National Party government of the day was significant, because it paved the way for legitimising black and multiracial trade unions, and their subsequent recognition by commerce and industry. It was a major step forward at the time to normalise labour relations in South Africa.

We should not, at this remove, underestimate the significant impact which the Wiehahn report made on the political and socio-economic circumstances then prevailing. The recommendations of the Wiehahn Commission – appointed in 1977 – produced a veritable watershed in labour relations in South Africa. The report was unique in its consequences. It constituted the first crack in the wall of apartheid. After Wiehahn, nothing would ever be the same again – no other official inquiry has had as incisive an effect on the South African economy as the Wiehahn report had. An independent study found that more than 80 per cent of the recommendations were adopted by the government.[2]

In this process, the power relations within the South African economy started to shift from a highly paternalistic framework – which essentially had government deciding what was best for the country, and commerce and industry bosses deciding what was best for their workers – towards a more inclusive and consensual framework of decision making. This shift pre-dated, but would in many respects be synchronised with, South Africa's gradual movement towards

1 *Report of the Commission of Inquiry into Labour Legislation*, RP47, 1979.

2 J. Botha, 'N. E. Wiehahn (1929–2006), obituary', *South African Journal of Economics*, 74(2) (June 2006), 359–361.

a democracy that would place value on, and give full recognition to, human rights. Business sought to reach out to emerging new stakeholders on the labour and political fronts.

It might therefore be argued that, in spite of the mounting exogenous pressure on the industrial relations system by 1990, the foundations of trust were slowly being laid between the different constituencies. Unfortunately, much of this trust developed between individual personalities involved in the industrial relations process – rather than at an institutional level – so that then, as now, the consensus-building exercise was subject to the vagaries of leadership moving into different spheres of activity.

Negotiations between business and labour continued, resulting in an historic agreement being reached in 1990, which was subsequently endorsed by the cabinet – and which was signed by the then Minister of Manpower. Apart from providing the foundations for a new Labour Relations Act, the important 'Laboria minute' – as the agreement came to be known – also made provision for the formation of an appropriate forum to discuss the impact of labour relations on the economy. However, the trade unions interpreted this provision more widely, arguing that such a forum should discuss, and even negotiate, all micro- and macro-economic policy issues.

Although many business people were in any case strongly convinced that political change *was* essential, as the negotiations over a new political dispensation developed – and it became clearer that the African National Congress (ANC) and its allies would assume the dominant role in any future government – so concern grew within business over the extent of the ideological 'divide', the kind of economic policies that might be adopted, and its own ability to influence future policy makers. There was clearly a growing need to move away from a dominant culture of 'adversarialism' in the socio-economic arena towards one of consultation and dialogue – and perhaps even one of forging agreements.

The National Economic Forum and the background to Nedlac, 1992–95

Against this backdrop, both organised business and organised labour began to see advantages in a negotiating forum for constructive engagement. The then Consultative Business Movement (CBM)[3] also played an important role in facilitating this process. As a result, a series of meetings between labour and business occurred and agreement was

3 A business grouping specifically dedicated to promoting socio-economic change.

reached about a forum to discuss economic issues. The next step was to get a hesitant government on board in the early 1990s.

Ongoing trade union opposition at the time to the introduction of value-added tax on a wide range of 'basic' foodstuffs, which were previously exempt from general sales tax, and the firm opposing stance adopted by the then Finance Minister, Barend du Plessis, contributed to the reluctance on the part of government to join the forum process. However, when du Plessis resigned in April 1992 and was replaced as Minister of Finance by Derek Keys (who came from the business community), this obstacle to government's participation was removed. Following a 'summit' meeting between Keys and a joint business–labour delegation, the cabinet agreed to the formation of the NEF. The founding documents were soon drafted and the NEF was established administratively. Keys referred at the time to the 'golden triangle' of government, labour and business.

Several participants believed that the NEF's strength at the time was its *informality*. The creation of the NEF in 1992 was the result of a needs-driven voluntary process mainly initiated in its early stages by labour and business, reflecting a political will to make it work and deliver. It was not a statutory body, yet bound its key players to important agreements. The role of informal discussions, the combination of constituency mobilisation (sometimes in the form of strikes) and tough bargaining at the NEF created the platform on which the future social dialogue framework would be built.

Most obvious of all, but no less significant for that, the mere process of establishing or improving cross-cultural human relationships must have done something – and perhaps did quite a bit – to facilitate the formation of 'social capital' at a crucial stage. If so, a large part of its genesis lay in workplace changes. It was necessary to rebuild the trust which the apartheid system had seriously damaged. The transitional NEF was a good apprenticeship for the more formalised Nedlac that still lay ahead. There was also significant personal 'chemistry' among the key participants, which, in a sense, carried through to the eventual establishment of Nedlac.

At roughly the same time as the NEF was established, the NMC was restructured, with commissioners being selected on the basis of representativeness, rather than expertise – as had previously been the case. While the focus of attention of the NMC continued to be on the labour market and the labour relations system, it also became an embryonic tripartite negotiating structure, along similar lines to the NEF.

Another source of renewed cooperation and trust building lay in addressing the endemic political violence which characterised the early 1990s and which threatened to derail the political negotiations. Apart from the start of engagement around workplace challenges, critical developments were also unfolding on a broader political level which began to involve other formations such as organised labour and business in the National Peace Accord. The negotiated National Peace Accord was an important mechanism, as it helped to keep political violence to manageable proportions, and it involved more or less the same 'actors' as were participating in the NEF. They were all linked, to a greater or lesser extent, to the tough and tumultuous political process then underway.

The process leading up to the creation of Nedlac was nonetheless characterised by robust and intensive negotiations. However, there was a real commitment to make Nedlac work – which spurred a group of constituency leaders to want a social dialogue structure which would help to address South Africa's serious socio-economic challenges. These included the challenge of transforming the economy from one which was inward-looking, uncompetitive, excessively protected and somewhat isolated from the world economy into one which would be open, competitive and growing. South Africa had a very open economy as measured as a percentage of GDP.

In view of the fact that both the NEF and the NMC had effectively developed along tripartite lines, representing the same constituencies, it was logical for any new structure to incorporate the two bodies. Discussions in the latter half of 1994 centred on how this could best be done. Nedlac was then established as a statutory body with its structure, operational powers and characteristics being prescribed in the Nedlac Act 35 of 1994. The Nedlac Act was one of the first pieces of legislation passed by the new government. In summary, therefore, it could be said that the four main stepping stones to the creation of Nedlac were the Wiehahn report, the NMC, the Laboria minute and finally the NEF.

Nedlac

The structure of Nedlac

Nedlac was launched on 18 February 1995. High expectations and enthusiasm in many quarters surrounded the launch of this institution. It was intended to inaugurate a new era of inclusive decision making and consensus seeking in the economic and social arenas. The legislation creating Nedlac spelt out its task formally to pursue the goals of growth, equity and participation. As the legislation indicated, Nedlac had a broad scope of activity, covering all aspects of social and economic policy and decision making.

Nedlac drew heavily on the experience of its predecessors – the NEF and the NMC. It also modelled itself to a large extent on successful institutions of social dialogue in other parts of the world, such as the Netherlands and Ireland, but with adaptations to take account of the development challenges of South Africa.[4] It was also hoped that the formalised process of information sharing at the national level would enable participants to strengthen commitment and build trust. This collective knowledge could become a valuable asset in decision making and in finding workable compromises.

Compromise, of course, did not mean the surrender of one side to the others. All parties had to make some contribution. Up to a point, the agreement might represent a genuine accord which had developed out of conflict or controversy. Beyond that point, the contribution made by each side to Nedlac would depend, on the whole, upon the respective strengths of the parties and the skill of their negotiators at any given time. It is granted that there could be compromises which were weak or difficult to defend. Often social dialogue outcomes could result in policies that secured agreement rather than ones that achieved a given set of objectives efficiently. This was partly why some critics disliked Nedlac 'compromises'.

Nedlac was a distinctive institution in several ways. It was the most representative policy body South Africa had ever had, since it included government, labour, business and the 'community'.[5] The community constituency, however, was not, for certain specific reasons, represented at all levels in Nedlac. The line between *social* dialogue and *civil* dialogue was blurred. Nedlac was an agreement-making body of broadly equal partners and not merely an advisory body. It was, at the time, only one of two Nedlac-type structures internationally with negotiating powers. Nedlac also required mandated representatives, which meant that constituencies were held accountable for the consequences within their sphere of influence. South Africa therefore developed its own 'hybrid' system of social dialogue through Nedlac – the 'golden triangle' having now become a 'quadrilateral' or 'quadrangle'.

What was social dialogue expected to do? Institutionalised social dialogue was to be mobilised to help undo the damaging legacy of apartheid and address the challenges of growth, job creation and poverty. Pitched at its highest, it was intended to provide the

4 We must also recognise that there are successful national economies that do not depend on 'institutionalised social dialogue' in the form we are currently discussing – in itself a valuable source of comparative analysis.

5 The 'community' constituency widened participation in social dialogue and to a large extent reflected the constituency with the then biggest stake in the new government's *Reconstruction and Development Programme*. It broadly included women's, rural, youth, civic and similar organisations. For some years it was a difficult group from which to derive mandates.

socio-economic dimension of the reconciliation and nation building to which President Mandela was strongly committed. Each of the main participants in Nedlac – such as the ANC government, business and labour – had its reasons for engaging in the Nedlac process. From their various perspectives they all hoped that, in one way or another, Nedlac would help to keep the country 'governable', and to maximise their own influence in the process.

How Nedlac operated

At its inception in 1995, Nedlac's objectives were broadly defined as being:

- to promote economic growth, participation in economic decision making and social equity;
- to seek a policy to reach consensus and to conclude agreements on social and economic policy;
- to consider all proposed labour legislation relating to labour market policy before it was introduced into Parliament;
- to consider all significant changes to social and economic policy before it was implemented or introduced into Parliament;
- to promote the formulation of coordinated policy on social and economic matters.

Although Nedlac was regarded at the time as an agreement-making body rather than an advisory one, it was recognised by all participants that the Nedlac process was *not* supposed to be a substitute for Parliament. While agreements could be reached between the social partners, such agreements were not intended to be binding on the country's elected representatives and could not result in changes in legislation without parliamentary approval.

The fact that the parties that were likely to be most affected by such legislation had reached agreement on it was expected to significantly reduce the likelihood that there would be parliamentary opposition to its promulgation – given the then political power balance in South Africa and the formal alliance between the ANC, the Congress of South African Trade Unions (Cosatu) and the South African Communist Party (SACP). Nonetheless, problems did soon develop in the relationship between Nedlac and Parliament – the perception that there were 'two parliaments' – and these had not been completely resolved by 2000.

The 'engine rooms' of Nedlac were the four chambers in which representatives of the different social partners discussed issues related to the specific portfolio of each chamber, and attempted to reach agreements, which were then sent to the Executive Council for ratification. The community constituency, however, was represented only in the

Development Chamber and not in the Labour Market, Finance and Monetary Policy, and Trade and Industry Chambers. Nedlac's decision making was supported by a Management Committee and an Executive Council, which were both constituency driven.

A perspective on some of Nedlac's achievements[6]

During its first five years Nedlac's main focus was on negotiating the introduction of the government's new labour market policy and legislation (discussed in Chapter 27). While the Labour Market Chamber therefore enjoyed a high profile in the early years, the Trade and Industry Chamber also began to do important work around trade negotiations, preliminary discussions on the formulation of an industrial strategy, and competition law reform. Labour issues predominated.

Soon after the 1994 elections the Labour Minister, Tito Mboweni, launched a complete overhaul of the South African labour market, which would have to be referred to Nedlac in due course. This reform was set out in the Department of Labour's five-year plan and started with the review of the Labour Relations Act (LRA) and the appointment of the Presidential Commission on the Labour Market. However, the far-reaching changes to both the LRA and the Basic Conditions of Employment Act (BCEA) were prematurely rushed into the Nedlac process – the LRA even before the Presidential Commission had been appointed, and the BCEA before the Commission had reported.

The first important issue addressed by Nedlac in 1995 was therefore the new LRA. It proved to be a stern test of the fledgling organisation and of 'quadrilateralism'. Pressure to reach agreement was heightened by the Minister of Labour setting short deadlines for the completion of negotiations. Less than three months were provided for the respective parties to reach consensus, which in the circumstances was rather inadequate. Labour market changes, after all, lay at the crucial intersection of economic, social and political policies and were bound to be a heavily contested terrain, requiring careful strategic planning and an integrated approach.

An authoritative historical perspective on the way the new labour legislation was handled then – and the problems it created – has been

6 The developments and trends in the work of Nedlac 1995–2000 are mainly captured in the detailed annual reports which the organisation is required by law to submit to Parliament each year. Although they tend to put a favourable gloss on Nedlac's activities, they are nonetheless a reliable overview of the institution's work programme. The 10-year review of Nedlac has also been helpful in recalling events: *Ten Years of Social Dialogue and the Nedlac Experience: Discussion Document, 1995–2005*, National Economic Development and Labour Council, 2005.

given by a prominent labour lawyer involved in the process at the time. As a leading labour expert who was one of the main architects of the legislation, it is worth quoting him at length:

> There are two aspects of this history that need to be stressed: –
>
> First, the policy underlying the LRA was never properly considered by the Presidential Commission, either on its own terms or as part of the labour law reform process as a whole. The reform of the LRA and the BCEA accordingly operated without a thorough labour market evaluation – either in respect of their particular subject matter or in respect of the linkages to other aspects of the labour market, such as skills development and social security.
>
> Secondly, the phased nature of the negotiations prevented the presentation and negotiation of a single and coherent package of reforms. To some extent this can be attributed to high expectation of a broad social accord at the time and that the Government's introduction of meaningful reforms quickly would prove its commitment to protecting workers in any social accord. There had been a positive history of social dialogue and there was a real expectation of a broader social accord to stabilise and drive the post-apartheid economy. Negotiations between the social partners and government had preceded the start of the new democracy. The Nedlac Act with its ambitious agenda for social dialogue was one of the first new order laws to fill the post 1994 statute book and it specifically contemplated 'consensus' and 'agreements' on 'social and economic policy'.
>
> The accord never happened. Accordingly the different aspects of the labour law reform process, albeit always tripartite in composition, were separately introduced and negotiated. Many of the recommendations of the Presidential Commission never saw the light of day. And those that were introduced (such as the amendment to give the Minister of Labour the discretion whether or not to extend sectoral collective agreements) were withdrawn in response to the fierce opposition from organised labour. The effect therefore was that the labour law reform process degenerated into piecemeal negotiations.[7]

This was to have serious unintended socio-economic consequences.

From the broader perspective, the experience with the LRA was thus an inauspicious and stressful start to Nedlac's operations. It was Nedlac's 'baptism of fire'. It tended to reinforce the view of those sceptics who felt that the close ties between the ANC and Cosatu would ultimately result in business being coopted into 'agreements' which were not in its best interests. Labour, on the other hand, believed that the government's proposed five-year labour law reform programme was no more than rectifying unacceptable historical imbalances in collective bargaining and that the time had arrived for a strong boost to labour rights.

7 Halton Cheadle, 'Regulated flexibility and small business – revisiting the LRA and the BCEA', concept document circulated as part of the ASGISA process, 2006, pp. 5–6 (released for publication).

It was argued by business that the approach adopted by the LRA and related legislation would – through 'over-regulation' – introduce rigidities into the labour market at a time when several important markets in South Africa were being liberalised, not least through the trade reform policies then being implemented. If taken too far, business claimed, certain changes to labour law in a developing economy like South Africa would thereby serve only to exacerbate the already severe unemployment problem.

Another important strategic 'gap' in the early days of Nedlac's operations was the fact that attempts were being made to reach agreement on the issues in the absence of an overall framework for economic policy making. Similar tensions accompanied other elements of the Ministry of Labour's five-year labour programme – such as the BCEA – even after the release of the growth, employment and redistribution (GEAR) strategy in 1996, which referred to 'a more flexible labour market'.[8]

Initial attempts by the South African Foundation (SAF, an organisation representing big business at the time), and subsequent attempts by Cosatu, to fill this 'gap' early in 1996 by making public their broad economic policy proposals served only to harden attitudes and to emphasise the ideological gulf that still existed between business and labour on a number of critical issues. However, because of this experience, participants in the Nedlac process began to emphasise the need for government to assume a leadership role in this regard.[9] The result was eventually the publication of the GEAR strategy by government in mid-1996, which set out its broad economic vision for the South African economy in the period leading up to the new millennium.

Initially, the government indicated that the basic policy issues in the GEAR strategy were *not* negotiable, even within Nedlac. This was partly because implementation of the strategy was deemed to be urgent, partly because some elements like interest rates, taxes and fiscal deficits were not practically negotiable in *any* modern economy, and partly perhaps because the government surmised (correctly) that organised labour would strongly oppose GEAR.

This economic direction was indeed rejected by organised labour, who felt their positions threatened by several of the policy choices made in the GEAR, and which they considered were too market friendly. They began to use their influence within the ANC alliance to reopen

8 *Growth, Employment and Redistribution: A Macro-economic Strategy,* Department of Finance, 1996.

9 The RDP (1994) did not, for various reasons, fill this gap, although it dominated public debate up until 1996.

negotiations on the strategy.[10] The fact that certain cabinet ministers were known to be ambivalent about the GEAR strategy provided organised labour with additional leverage. Comments made by certain senior government representatives at Cosatu meetings at the time suggested that the trade unions had some success in generating equivocal official attitudes to GEAR. It also frustrated the work of the Public Finance and Monetary Policy Chamber in Nedlac for several years. This chamber became the lightning conductor for opposition to GEAR.

Nedlac continued to be involved in trade negotiations. South Africa's 41-strong delegation to the World Trade Organization (WTO) ministerial conference in Seattle in 1999 reflected a substantial social dialogue component, with 11 Nedlac participants included in the delegation. The preparations for the meeting by South Africa were structured to facilitate social dialogue involvement in the discussions of strategy and tactics prior to the negotiations.

Another major event in Nedlac's first phase was the Presidential Jobs Summit in October 1998. Although the path to the Jobs Summit was strewn with delays and controversies, the actual process yielded some 40 programmes and projects for employment creation. While not all the projects were of equal magnitude, they succeeded to the extent that: (a) the problem of unemployment was tackled as a multidimensional phenomenon; and (b) there was acknowledgement that the cooperation of all key stakeholders was required. The Jobs Summit was unlucky in its timing, being held in the midst of the Asian financial crisis, while domestic interest rates were rising sharply. It would have completely failed had it not sidelined the underlying ideological differences over macro-economic policy.

The Jobs Summit in 1998 in many ways represented a key event for Nedlac, but it also marked a negative turning point in perceptions about the organisation. After the summit, widespread disenchantment set in about the efficacy of the Nedlac process. Indeed, the seeds of this disillusionment had already been sown with the earlier deadlocked negotiations around the BCEA in 1997. The government in particular was starting to believe that Nedlac might be obstructing, rather than facilitating, its policy outcomes. This may also partly have been the result of the sheer exhaustion after the Jobs Summit negotiations, which led to serious doubts among the participants as to whether the process was worthwhile. Questions were raised about Nedlac's failure to provide a 'shared economic vision' and its apparent inability to monitor the proper implementation of policies. Ironically, this tension arose among

10 Organised labour had thrown its weight behind the RDP but the document did not embody an economic strategy.

some stakeholders partly *because* the government was seen to be adhering to its basic GEAR strategies. All the constituencies expressed their strong frustrations and – as the decade came to a close – there was an apparent loss of confidence in the Nedlac process. Some critics even suggested that perhaps after five years Nedlac was no longer necessary and should be abolished. The efficacy of institutionalised social dialogue was already being seriously challenged.

Overall evaluation of the role of Nedlac

Any assessment of Nedlac's role in the second half of the 1990s would, in part at least, be bound to reflect one's overall perspective on the South African economy, politics and society at that time.[11] Nedlac and social dialogue over this period undoubtedly attracted critics; and to give the most strident of those their day in court, the most sweeping of all possible questions should be posed: Would South Africa have been better off without Nedlac?

While much more empirical analysis is clearly needed to evaluate Nedlac's interventions in specific policy matters, the interim and overall qualitative answer must be 'no'. Without the conflict-management potential of a structure like Nedlac, the transition to successful democracy would have been even more difficult. Indeed, it could be argued that the recurring spectacle of labour and capital sitting down together to discuss policy under the auspices of Nedlac was reassuring to investors. Economies are vulnerable during transition phases. There are difficult perceptions to handle, in what are often periods of acute uncertainty. We must accept that to move from a 'closed' regime to an 'open' one, a country usually has to go through a transitional period that may require its leaders to spend huge amounts of political capital with no guarantee of success. Nedlac helped make a success of the transitional phase.[12]

Overall, it is evident from an analysis of the Nedlac experience in this period that there were certain quite fundamental issues on which the Nedlac constituencies were far apart and where substantial dialogue and negotiation would still be needed to forge greater consensus. However, there were policy areas, as the series of agreements and reports outlined earlier confirm, where there was a high degree of commonality of interests and views and where consensus was worth achieving.

11 Some political analysts, on the other hand, seem to offer an assessment of South Africa's political development since 1994 without any reference to Nedlac at all. See, for example, Tom Lodge, *South African Politics since 1994*, David Philip, 1999.

12 See also Ian Bremmer, *The J Curve: A New Way to Understand Why Nations Rise and Fall*, Simon and Schuster, 2006, reviewed in *The Economist*, 2 September 2006, p. 75.

Did social dialogue make a quantifiable difference to South Africa's economic performance over this period? It is extremely difficult to link a specific institutional set-up to a particular set of economic results. It is not possible to establish a *direct* correlation between extensive peak-level social dialogue and higher economic growth rates, or a rising human development index. All that can safely be said of South Africa is that the average economic growth rate rose from nearly 0 in the early 1990s to about 2.5 per cent in the six-year period post-1994.

To the extent that certain processes, such as Nedlac, promoted social stability and reduced perceived country risk, they must have made a positive contribution. South Africa's international credit ratings did slowly begin to improve in these early years. These were developments over a period which has been historically designated as one of 'consensual stability',[13] underpinned by processes and policies intended to build confidence over time and to which Nedlac could claim to have contributed. Yet, as Nedlac reached the cusp of a new millennium, a critical evaluation began to identify a number of challenges. These included: the limits of 'consensus' or 'compromise' in South Africa; the boundaries of inclusion and the coordination of processes; limited effectiveness in achieving real change – the 'vision thing'; the relationship between social dialogue and representative democracy/parliament; the gap between national representation and provincial/local action; problems of monitoring and follow-up; and the role of overlapping consultative mechanisms like the presidential working groups and the Millennium Labour Council (MLC). Five years of Nedlac's operations were nevertheless not a long time for a society in fundamental transition. It would need more years, and further empirical research, to provide some answers in the context of institutions, transaction costs, and economic performance as to the contribution of institutionalised social dialogue to public policy choices in South Africa.

Conclusion

In summary, the early history of Nedlac and social dialogue in South Africa presents, as one would expect, a mixed record. Like the new democracy, social dialogue was still young and fragile and exhibited its identifiable quota of organisational and other weaknesses. While Nedlac undoubtedly influenced official policy in several key areas,

13 Frederick van Zyl Slabbert, *The Other Side of History*, Jonathan Ball, 2006, pp. 142–143, gives several reasons for the development and maintenance of 'consensual stability' in South Africa since 1994.

the priorities of the elected government, no less than party politics, remained determining factors, especially for an administration coming under increasing pressure by 2000 to 'deliver'. Lack of effective delivery was beginning to become the perceived Achilles' heel of the fledging democracy. South Africa remained in a phase of democratic trial with the verdict of history on Nedlac still undecided.

Yet the reasons that prompted the creation of Nedlac inevitably led to *excessive expectations* as to what social dialogue could achieve in South Africa in the short term. Given the bitter legacy of apartheid, it was unrealistic to expect significant levels of trust to be established more or less overnight. Social dialogue, as important as it was as a mechanism to manage change, could in a mere five years do little to repair decades of mistrust and suspicion. Criticisms that Nedlac was failing to achieve its goals were based on unrealistic hopes, or wishful thinking, about how South Africa could best respond to the challenges of transformation and globalisation. As imperfect and frustrating as social dialogue structures often seemed to be, there nonetheless remained the question of what the alternatives would be in the absence of such processes.

It needs to be emphasised again that social dialogue in South Africa was a not full-blown or mature 'social partnership', as understood in countries such as the Netherlands or Ireland. By 2000 social dialogue in South Africa had not yet been translated into the more concrete solidarity that 'partnership' implies. There were times in the early years of Nedlac's existence when social dialogue assumed high prominence in policy processes and other times when it played a more 'behind the scenes' role.[14] All stakeholders in Nedlac were on a steep learning curve in the first five years of its existence.

Although social dialogue in South Africa had undoubtedly been *widened* in the early years of Nedlac, the extent to which it had been *deepened* remained an open question. While the jury was still out on the ultimate success or failure of Nedlac, its influential forerunner, the NEF, remained a significant contributor to social dialogue and an indispensable institutional bridge between the 'old' and 'new' regimes in South Africa.

14 *Annual Report*, Nedlac, 2000, p. 49.

Part IV

Conclusion

29

Conclusion

Stuart Jones

The decade of transformation in South Africa was not good for the economy. In fact it was a decade of disappointment, in which both internal and external forces were working against the economy. The internal forces damaging the economy were the neglect of the infrastructure, unbridled affirmative action, most noticeable in Eskom, declining standards in both schools and universities, deteriorating conditions in the state hospitals (hospital beds were even stolen from Johannesburg General Hospital) and the steady increase in crime. In such a situation it comes as no surprise that life expectancy was falling and infant mortality rising. South Africa was becoming a Third World state.

In the economic sphere this was revealed in rising unemployment, falling per capita GDP and the lack of direct investment in manufacturing. The primary sector, upon which South Africa had for so long depended, was suffering from worldwide low prices, both for agricultural products and for minerals. The traditional engine of growth was so overwhelmed by both the falling price and the falling output of gold that not even the rise in the platinum price at the end of the decade could make up for the catastrophic decline of the gold mining industry. Gold output fell from 602,999 kg in 1990 to 427,981 kg in 2000 and employment in the industry from 473,685 to 200,000, a decline of 58 per cent. Unemployment was not helped by the policies of the African National Congress (ANC)–Communist government. The new labour laws added to costs and made it difficult to retrench labour, with the result that employers throughout South Africa sought to replace labour with capital, in a country experiencing a population explosion and high unemployment! Tito Mboweni, as the Labour Minister, responsible for the new labour legislation, must be held accountable for this extraordinary state of affairs.

Labour legislation was not alone in causing a rise in unemployment. The threat to property rights was also a factor. It discouraged investment in both agriculture and mining. With regard to the former, security of land ownership was being questioned; in the latter, mining rights were being repossessed by the state. Both discouraged enterprise in the sectors that provided the bulk of the country's foreign exchange earnings.

This was allowed to happen because of the propaganda put out about transformation in the secondary sector. Manufacturing was expected to lead South Africa out of poverty in the way that it had done in South Korea and Taiwan, but instead of looking at how these two countries had achieved their remarkable success, the ANC–Communist government chose the old failing African route: state ownership, state control and everywhere an abandonment of colonial standards. The educational policies introduced by Kadar Asmal were the exact opposite of what the country needed, which was a well educated elite, able to compete and speak on equal terms with Europe and Asia, and not the mass production of low-standard degrees and high-school diplomas. Asmal's policies made it well nigh impossible for South Africa to compete internationally in high-tech industries at a time when low-tech industries were exposed to the full weight of competition from China and India, where labour was both very much cheaper and more skilled. It was not reasonable to think that South Africa could experience an export-led boom in the way that Italy had done half a century earlier, or South Korea 20 years earlier. It simply was not possible in the 1990s. The failure of Marxism in the Soviet Union and the conversion of China to a form of capitalism had permanently altered the balance of economic power in the world. India, following somewhat half-heartedly on the heels of China, further reinforced the changes taking place in the international economic order.

There was no export-led boom in South Africa in the 1990s, because there had been no investment boom in agriculture, mining or manufacturing. There had been no investment boom in manufacturing because there was little prospect of being able to compete with the Asian countries in low-tech industries. This was seen after South Africa joined the World Trade Organization, when the country's boot and shoe and textile industries began to shrink rapidly, before the impact of cheap imports. This collapse of low-level industries occurred without any counterbalancing boom in the export of high-tech manufactured goods. As a result, South Africa, as a developing country, found itself with a shrinking secondary sector – the opposite of what was supposed to happen. With two and half billion East and South Asian people being brought into the global economy, the opportunities for export-led growth in manufacturing were very limited.

The prospects for high-tech exports were also almost nonexistent, given the state of the country's schools and the formidable standards prevailing in the secondary schools of Japan, South Korea and Taiwan. Export-led growth driven by manufacturing was a mirage of the media and politicians.

In services, a vibrant internationally oriented financial sector did not come into being in the 1990s, despite the existence of a well established banking and insurance base. Threats from a communist-dominated government and trade unions, together with exchange controls, made even steps in that direction impossible. By 2000 some of the foreign banks that had entered the country after 1994 were leaving and the currency was crashing on the international markets. The earlier communist destruction of virtually all the capitalist institutions in Mozambique had frightened foreign capitalists and discouraged investment in South Africa. In Zimbabwe, Robert Mugabe's regime seemed to be repeating the process. This situation discouraged the development of even a regional financial centre in South Africa. Other parts of the tertiary sector, with the one exception of tourism, offered few prospects for growth in the 1990s. Retailing and wholesaling reflected the depressed conditions in the economy, with falling per capita sales, while transport, dominated by the government, remained poor, with a lack of investment in roads, ports, railways and airways. High telephone charges retarded the growth of the internet.

As for the government departments, they were a by-word in inefficiency, with services deteriorating at local, provincial and national levels. There was no serious attempt to root out corruption in the provincial and local governments and corruption appeared to have got worse. Many parts of the sector acted more as wealth destroyers than as wealth creators in the 1990s. The 'Bantu-isation' of South Africa was well underway by the end of the decade.

Tourism was the exception. It was the one area where South Africa may have had comparative advantage, as a mysterious and fascinating country, with beautiful beaches and exciting game parks, all with First World standards of hospitality. As a result, once the election was over there was a burst of hotel building and significant growth in international tourism occurred, though towards the end of the decade this was tapering off. There was a limit to how far tourism could be an engine of growth. South Africa was not Spain, a country that had been propelled into growth by its tourist industry. Spain was adjacent to a wealthy region with a population more than seven or eight times that of itself. South Africa was situated next to very poor countries. Its prospects for tourism lay in the markets of Europe, Asia and America, where competition was great.

Tourism in the 1990s did not offer a golden route to national prosperity. This lay in mining and the beneficiation of minerals. The platinum boom at the end of the decade pointed in the right direction. Aluminium refining also expanded; but there was not sufficient investment in mining developments to transform the structure of the economy. The question, therefore, that remained unanswered at the end of the decade was: how was the country going to pay for its imports in the long run? Significant direct investment had *not* taken place and the country was increasingly relying on portfolio investment and the sale of existing assets. The first of these was a fair-weather strategy; the second was clearly not sustainable. No solution to the balance of payments problem had been found by 2000. In the new world order of the Washington consensus, South Africa was becoming less and less competitive, with a diminishing share of world trade and global GDP, and, unlike China, had made no attempt to restrict population growth, which lay at the heart of the unemployment problem. A peaceful political revolution had been achieved; but the economy was in a poorer shape in 2000 than it was in 1990, and the financial situation remained precarious as the country's relative position in the global economy continued to decline.

Subject index

People index